The Edinburgh Companion to the Prose Poem

Edinburgh Companions to Literature and the Humanities

Published

The Edinburgh Companion to Virginia Woolf and the Arts
Edited by Maggie Humm

The Edinburgh Companion to Twentieth-Century Literatures in English
Edited by Brian McHale and Randall Stevenson

A Historical Companion to Postcolonial Literatures in English
Edited by David Johnson and Prem Poddar

A Historical Companion to Postcolonial Literatures – Continental Europe and its Empires
Edited by Prem Poddar, Rajeev Patke and Lars Jensen

The Edinburgh Companion to Twentieth-Century British and American War Literature
Edited by Adam Piette and Mark Rowlinson

The Edinburgh Companion to Shakespeare and the Arts
Edited by Mark Thornton Burnett, Adrian Streete and Ramona Wray

The Edinburgh Companion to Samuel Beckett and the Arts
Edited by S. E. Gontarski

The Edinburgh Companion to the Bible and the Arts
Edited by Stephen Prickett

The Edinburgh Companion to Modern Jewish Fiction
Edited by David Brauner and Axel Stähler

The Edinburgh Companion to Critical Theory
Edited by Stuart Sim

The Edinburgh Companion to the Critical Medical Humanities
Edited by Anne Whitehead, Angela Woods, Sarah Atkinson, Jane Macnaughton and Jennifer Richards

The Edinburgh Companion to Nineteenth-Century American Letters and Letter-Writing
Edited by Celeste-Marie Bernier, Judie Newman and Matthew Pethers

The Edinburgh Companion to T. S. Eliot and the Arts
Edited by Frances Dickey and John D. Morgenstern

The Edinburgh Companion to Children's Literature
Edited by Clémentine Beauvais and Maria Nikolajeva

The Edinburgh Companion to Atlantic Literary Studies
Edited by Leslie Eckel and Clare Elliott

The Edinburgh Companion to the First World War and the Arts
Edited by Ann-Marie Einhaus and Katherine Isobel Baxter

The Edinburgh Companion to Fin de Siècle Literature, Culture and the Arts
Edited by Josephine M. Guy

The Edinburgh Companion to Animal Studies
Edited by Lynn Turner, Undine Sellbach and Ron Broglio

The Edinburgh Companion to Contemporary Narrative Theories
Edited by Zara Dinnen and Robyn Warhol

The Edinburgh Companion to Anthony Trollope
Edited by Frederik Van Dam, David Skilton and Ortwin Graef

The Edinburgh Companion to the Short Story in English
Edited by Paul Delaney and Adrian Hunter

The Edinburgh Companion to the Postcolonial Middle East
Edited by Anna Ball and Karim Mattar

The Edinburgh Companion to Ezra Pound and the Arts
Edited by Roxana Preda

The Edinburgh Companion to Elizabeth Bishop
Edited by Jonathan Ellis

The Edinburgh Companion to Gothic and the Arts
Edited by David Punter

The Edinburgh Companion to Literature and Music
Edited by Delia da Sousa Correa

The Edinburgh Companion to D. H. Lawrence and the Arts
Catherine Brown and Susan Reid

The Edinburgh Companion to the Prose Poem
Mary Ann Caws and Michel Delville

https://edinburghuniversitypress.com/series/ecl

The Edinburgh Companion to the Prose Poem

Edited by Mary Ann Caws
and Michel Delville

EDINBURGH
University Press

Edinburgh University Press is one of the leading university presses in the UK. We publish academic books and journals in our selected subject areas across the humanities and social sciences, combining cutting-edge scholarship with high editorial and production values to produce academic works of lasting importance. For more information visit our website: edinburghuniversitypress.com

© editorial matter and organization Mary Ann Caws and
  Michel Delville, 2021, 2025
© the chapters their several authors, 2021, 2025

Edinburgh University Press Ltd
13 Infirmary Street, Edinburgh, EH1 1LT

First published in hardback by Edinburgh University Press 2021

Typeset in 10/12 Adobe Sabon by
IDSUK (DataConnection) Ltd

A CIP record for this book is available from the British Library

ISBN 978 1 4744 6274 7 (hardback)
ISBN 978 1 3995 4854 0 (paperback)
ISBN 978 1 4744 6275 4 (webready PDF)
ISBN 978 1 4744 6276 1 (epub)

The right of Mary Ann Caws and Michel Delville to be identified as the editor of this work has been asserted in accordance with the Copyright, Designs and Patents Act 1988, and the Copyright and Related Rights Regulations 2003 (SI No. 2498).

Contents

List of Illustrations	vii
Notes on Contributors	viii
Preface	xiii
Rosemary Lloyd	
Introduction	1
Mary Ann Caws and Michel Delville	

Part I: Origins and Beginnings

1. The Birth of the Prose Poem in Nineteenth-Century France Joseph Acquisto	11
2. Impressionism and the Prose Poem: Rimbaud's Artful Authenticity Aimée Israel-Pelletier	23
3. Novalis' *Hymnen an die Nacht* and the Prose Poem *avant la lettre* Jonathan Monroe	35

4. Thyrsus & Palimpsest: De Quincey's influence on Baudelaire's
    Le Spleen de Paris
    Nikki Santilli
	50

5. A Dangerous Hybridity: The Prose Poem at the *fin de siècle* Margueritte S. Murphy	67

Part II: Visual Mediations

6. Cubism and the Prose Poem Mary Ann Caws	91
7. The Modern French Prose Poem and Visual Art Emma Wagstaff	103
8. The Homeless Heart: Abstraction and the Prose Poem Richard Deming	121

Part III: Genres and Discourses

9. The Prose Poem, Flash Fiction, Lyrical Essays and Other Microgenres   137
   Michel Delville

10. The Prose Poem and the Antinovel: Unsettling Form in Nathalie Sarraute's *Tropismes*   150
    Jane Monson

11. Bishop, Lowell, and the Confessional Prose Poem   168
    Lizzy LeRud

12. Trans-verse: Prose Poetry, Translation and Border Crossing in Baudelaire and Emerson   181
    Adam R. Rosenthal

Part IV: Issues and Contexts

13. An Interruption of Boundaries: On Gender and the Prose Poem   197
    Alyson Miller

14. Pastoral and Ecocritical Voices in Modern Prose Poetry   213
    Lynn Domina

15. Grzegorz Wróblewski's *Kopenhaga* and the Process of Inscription   230
    Piotr Gwiazda

16. The Chinese Prose Poem: Generic Metaphor and the Multiple Origins of *sanwenshi*   247
    Nick Admussen

17. The *sanbunshi* (Prose Poem) in Japan   262
    Scott Mehl

18. The Arabic Prose Poem in Iraq   281
    Sinan Antoon

19. After Poet's Prose: Postgeneric Writing in the Ongoing Crisis of Verse   295
    Stephen Fredman

20. Prose in Prose in Contemporary French Poetic Practice: Appropriation, Repurposing and Pornography   310
    Jeff Barda

Index   328

List of Illustrations

Figures

Figure 15.1	The cover of *Kopenhaga*. Photo by Wojciech Wilczyk	243
Figure 20.1	Christophe Hanna, from "Le mauvais vitrier"	317
Figure 20.2	Jacques-Henri Michot, from *ABC de la barbarie*	322

Plates

Plate 1   Juan Gris (José Victoriano González-Pérez, 1887–1927. Spanish, active in France), *Still Life Before an Open Window, Place Ravignan*, 1915. Oil on canvas, $4^{5}/_{8}$ × 35 inches (115.9 × 88.9 cm). Image courtesy of Philadelphia Museum of Art: The Louise and Walter Arensberg Collection, 1950-134-95.

Plate 2   Juan Gris, *Still Life with Poem by Pierre Reverdy*, 1915. Image courtesy of Norton Simon Art Foundation.

Plate 3   Juan Gris, *Still Life with Open Window*, 1921. Image courtesy of Archivio fotografico, Museo Reina Sofia.

Plate 4   Juan Gris, *Le Canigou*, 1921. Oil on canvas, 25½ × 39½ inches (64.77 × 100.33 cm). Collection Albright-Knox Art Gallery, Buffalo, New York; Room of Contemporary Art Fund, 1947 (RCA1947:5). Image courtesy of Albright-Knox Art Gallery.

Notes on Contributors

Joseph Acquisto is Professor of French at the University of Vermont. He specializes in nineteenth- and twentieth-century poetry and the novel, with particular emphasis on the relations among literature, music, and philosophy. His books include *Poetry's Knowing Ignorance* (2020), *Proust, Music, and Meaning* (2017), *The Fall Out of Redemption: Writing and Thinking Beyond Salvation in Baudelaire, Cioran, Fondane, Agamben, and Nancy* (2015), and *French Symbolist Poetry and the Idea of Music* (2006).

Nick Admussen is an associate professor of Chinese literature at Cornell University. He is the author of the scholarly monograph *Recite and Refuse: Contemporary Chinese Prose Poetry* (University of Hawaii Press, 2016), the translator of Ya Shi's poetry collection *Floral Mutter* (Zephyr, 2019), and the author of two collections of original prose poetry, *Movie Plots* (Epiphany Editions, 2011) and *Stand Back, Don't Fear the Change* (New Michigan Press, 2018).

Sinan Antoon is the internationally acclaimed, multi-award-winning author of several collection of poems in English and Arabic and four novels which have been translated into many languages. His co-translation of *Unfortunately, It Was Paradise*, a selection of Mahmoud Darwish's poems, was nominated for the PEN Prize for translation in 2004. He teaches modern and modern Arabic literature and contemporary Arab culture and politics at NYU's Gallatin School.

Jeff Barda is a lecturer in French cultural studies at the University of Manchester. He is the author of *Experimentation and the Lyric in Contemporary French Poetry* (Palgrave, 2019) and the co-editor with Daniel Finch-Race of *Textures: Processus et événements dans la création poétique moderne et contemporaine* (Peter Lang, 2015). His solo publications include several articles that bring French poetic practice into contact with sound, performance, digital practice and law. He is currently co-editing with Philippe Charron a special volume on Pierre Alféri (forthcoming with Classiques Garnier) and working on his second monograph.

Mary Ann Caws is Distinguished Professor Emerita of Comparative Literature, English, and French at the Graduate School of the City University of New York. She is an *Officier* of the *Palmes académiques* and a *Chevalier dans l'ordre des Arts et des Lettres*, holds a Doctor of Humane Letters from Union College, and is the recipient of Guggenheim, Rockefeller, and Getty fellowships, a fellow of the American Academy of Arts and Sciences, and the past president of the Modern Language and Literature Association and of the American Comparative Literature Association. She is the author of: *The Eye in the Text*; *The Surrealist Look: an Erotics of Encounter*; *The Modern Art Cookbook*; *Blaise Pascal: Miracles and Reason*; and *Creative Gatherings: Meeting Places of Modernism*. She is also a translator of Mallarmé, Char, des Forêts, Reverdy, Breton, and Desnos, and the editor of *HarperCollins World Literature*, *The Yale Anthology of Twentieth Century French Poetry*, *The Surrealist Painters and Poets*, and *Milk Bowl of Feathers: Essential Surrealist Writings*.

Michel Delville teaches literature and comparative literature at the University of Liège, where he directs the Interdisciplinary Center for Applied Poetics. He is the author or editor of some thirty books pertaining to contemporary poetics and intermedial studies, including *The American Prose Poem* (University Press of Florida, 1998), *Frank Zappa, Captain Beefheart and the Secret History of Maximalism* (with Andrew Norris; Salt, 2005), *Food, Poetry, and the Aesthetics of Consumption: Eating the Avant-Garde* (Routledge, 2009), *Crossroads Poetics: Text, Image, Music, Film & Beyond* (Litteraria Pragensia, 2013), ~~Undoing~~ *Art* (with Mary Ann Caws; Quodlibet, 2017) and *The Politics and Aesthetics of Hunger and Disgust* (with Andrew Norris; Routledge, 2018). His books of prose poetry include *Le troisième corps* (Le Fram, 2005), which was translated into English by Gian Lombardo as *Third Body* (Quale Press, 2009) and *Anything & Everything* (Quale Press, 2016).

Richard Deming, Director of Creative Writing in the Department of English at Yale University, is a poet, art critic, and theorist whose work explores the intersections of poetry, philosophy, and visual culture. His first collection of poems, *Let's Not Call It Consequence* (Shearsman, 2008), received the 2009 Norma Farber Award from the Poetry Society of America. His most recent book of poems, *Day for Night*, appeared in 2016. He is also the author of *Listening on All Sides: Toward an Emersonian Ethics of Reading* (Stanford University Press, 2008); *Art of the Ordinary: The Everyday Domain of Art, Film, Literature, and Philosophy* (Cornell University Press, 2018); and *Touch of Evil* (Bloomsbury/British Film Institute, 2020).

Lynn Domina is the author of several books, including two collections of poetry, *Corporal Works* and *Framed in Silence*. Her scholarly work includes books on the Harlem Renaissance, Leslie Marmon Silko's *Ceremony*, and Lorraine Hansberry's *A Raisin in the Sun*. She has also published articles on Elizabeth Keckley, N. Scott Momaday, ecocriticism, and other topics. She serves as Head of the English Department at Northern Michigan University.

Stephen Fredman, originally from California, is Emeritus Professor of English at the University of Notre Dame, Indiana, where he taught from 1980 to 2017. He is the author of four monographs: *Poet's Prose: The Crisis in American Verse* (1983, 1990); *The Grounding of American Poetry: Charles Olson and the Emersonian Tradition* (1993); *A Menorah for Athena: Charles Reznikoff and the Jewish Dilemmas* of *Objectivist Poetry* (2001); and *Contextual Practice: Assemblage and the Erotic in Postwar Poetry and Art* (2010). He has edited four volumes: *A Concise Companion to Twentieth-Century American Poetry* (2005); *Form, Power, and Person in Robert Creeley's Life and Work*, with Steve McCaffery (2010); *How Long Is the Present: Selected Talk Poems of David Antin* (2014); and a critical edition of Robert Creeley's *Presences: A Text for Marisol* (2018). His most recent book, *American Poetry as Transactional Art*, appeared in June 2020 in the Modern and Contemporary Poetics Series of the University of Alabama Press. His article "A Poetry of All Poetries: Robert Duncan at 100" was posted on the Poetry Foundation website on February 7, 2019.

Piotr Gwiazda has translated Grzegorz Wróblewski's *Kopenhaga* (2013) and *Zero Visibility* (2017). He is also the author of two critical studies, *US Poetry in the Age of Empire, 1979–2012* (2014) and *James Merrill and W.H. Auden: Homosexuality and Poetic Influence* (2007), and three books of poetry: *Aspects of Strangers* (2015), *Messages* (2012), and *Gagarin Street* (2005). His essays and reviews have appeared in many journals, including *American Poetry Review*, *Asymptote*, *Chicago Review*, *Contemporary Literature*, *Jacket2*, *Journal of European Studies*, *Modernism/Modernity*, *PN Review*, and the *TLS*. He is a professor of English at the University of Pittsburgh, USA.

Aimée Israel-Pelletier is Professor of French at the University of Texas at Arlington. Her most recent book, *On the Mediterranean and the Nile: The Jews of Egypt* (Indiana, 2018), examines the work of Francophone and Anglophone writers in the context of expulsion and immigration. She is also the author of *Rimbaud's Impressionist Poetics. Vision and Visuality* (Wales, 2012) and *Flaubert's Straight and Suspect Saints: The Unity of Trois Contes* (Purdue, 1991), as well as of articles on French film. She is currently working on narratives of heterodoxy and coexistence in the works of Levantine and North African Francophone writers.

Lizzy LeRud is a Marion L. Brittain Postdoctoral Fellow at Georgia Institute of Technology, where her research and teaching focus on American poetry and the politics of literary genres. LeRud was the National Endowment for the Humanities Post-Doctoral Fellow in Poetics at the Bill and Carol Fox Center for Humanistic Inquiry at Emory University, and she has taught at Emory, the University of Oregon, and Willamette University. She is completing a book-length study on the history of the poetry–prose dichotomy, provisionally titled *Against Prose*.

Rosemary Lloyd earned her PhD from Cambridge University before teaching on the faculty there and at Indiana University, Bloomington. Her research focuses on nineteenth- and twentieth-century French literature and the visual arts, with a particular interest in Baudelaire and Mallarmé. In retirement she devotes much of her time to birding.

Scott Mehl is Assistant Professor of Japanese at Colgate University, where he teaches Japanese language, literature, and culture. He has published articles on modern Japanese poetry (in *Japan Review*, *Japanese Language and Literature*, and *Southeast Review of Asian Studies*) and on topics in comparative literature (in *Japanese Studies*,

Comparative Literature Studies, and *Studia Metrica et Poetica*). His translations of Japanese poetry and criticism have appeared in print and online (in *Japan Forum*, *Monumenta Nipponica*, and *The Politics and Literature Debate in Postwar Japanese Criticism*). He is currently writing a book on form and translation in modern Japanese poetics.

Alyson Miller is a senior lecturer in Writing and Literature at Deakin University, Melbourne. Her critical scholarship and creative work, which focuses on literary scandal, the relationship between literature and extremity, and prose poetry, has appeared in both national and international publications, including two critical monographs, *Haunted by Words: Scandalous Texts*, and *The Unfinished Atomic Bomb: Shadows and Reflections*, and three books of prose poetry: *Dream Animals*, *Pika-Don*, and *Strange Creatures*.

Jonathan Monroe's most recent book is *Framing Roberto Bolaño: Poetry, Fiction, Literary History, Politics* (Cambridge University Press, 2019). Author of *A Poverty of Objects: The Prose Poem and the Politics of Genre* and *Demosthenes' Legacy* (prose poems and short fiction), and editor of *Roberto Bolaño in Context* (under contract, Cambridge University Press), *Writing and Revising the Disciplines*, *Local Knowledges, Local Practices: Writing in the Disciplines at Cornell*, and two special journal issues, *Poetry, Community, Movement* and *Avant-Garde Poetries after the Wall*, he is Professor of Comparative Literature at Cornell University.

Jane Monson is a poet based in Cambridge, UK. She works as a mentor for disabled students at the University of Cambridge and was Associate Lecturer in Creative Writing at Anglia Ruskin University. She edited the first anthology of contemporary British prose poetry, *This Line Is Not for Turning* (Cinnamon Press, 2011), praised by Pascale Petit as "necessary and ground-breaking," and has two collections of prose poetry with Cinnamon Press, *Speaking Without Tongues* (2010) and *The Shared Surface* (2013). Her PhD, *Crossed Tongues: The Crisis of Speech in the Prose Poetry of Francis Ponge* (Cardiff University, 2008), focused on modernism and the French prose poem, and she edited *British Prose Poetry: The Poems Without Lines* (Palgrave Macmillan, 2018), the first collection of essays on the British prose poem.

Margueritte S. Murphy is author of *Material Figures: Political Economy, Commercial Culture, and the Aesthetic Sensibility of Charles Baudelaire* (2012) and *A Tradition of Subversion: The Prose Poem in English from Wilde to Ashbery* (1992), and co-editor with Samir Dayal of *Global Babel: Questions of Discourse and Communication in a Time of Globalization* (2007). She has published widely on nineteenth- and twentieth-century poetry and fiction, on literature and economics, and on community-based learning. She is currently an independent scholar and serves on the board of a regional puppet theatre.

Adam R. Rosenthal is Assistant Professor of French and International Studies at Texas A&M University. He received his PhD in Comparative Literature in 2014 from Emory University. His work focuses on deconstruction, romantic poetry, and posthumanism. He is the co-editor of *Oxford Literary Review* 40.2, "Deconstruction and the Survival of Love," and editor of *Poetics Today* 42.1, "Derrida's Classroom," forthcoming in 2021. He has published articles in *SubStance*, *MLN*, *Studies in Romanticism*, and *Nineteenth-Century French Studies*, and is completing a manuscript on the gift in poetry.

Nikki Santilli is an independent scholar and early-jazz dancer/teacher. Her most recent research examined the relationship between prose poetry and the spirit of jazz. Beyond traditional research and publications, she has also danced to work composed and read by poets Jaime Robles and Vahni Capildeo. Santilli is the author of *Such Rare Citings*, an account of the prose poem in the UK spanning Blake to Beckett.

Emma Wagstaff is Senior Lecturer in French at the University of Birmingham, UK. She is the author of *Provisionality and the Poem: Transition in the Work of André du Bouchet, Philippe Jaccottet and Bernard Noël* (Rodopi, 2006), *Writing Art: French Literary Responses to the Work of Alberto Giacometti* (Peter Lang, 2011), and *André du Bouchet: Poetic Forms of Attention* (Brill, 2020), and has co-edited volumes on contemporary French poetic practice.

Preface

Rosemary Lloyd

Paris, 1968. In my memory a time not just of political revolution, but also, and for me more vitally, of an upheaval in my thinking about genres. Our tutor in the "Cours de civilisation française pour les étrangers" sets before us two passages which she insists are "des poèmes en prose," one by Baudelaire, one by Ponge. My initial reaction is revolt: how can these two passages, set out like short stories (very short short stories) without apparent rhyme and rhythm, possibly be poetry? Poetry is surely all about the beauty of predictable sound patterns balancing and enhancing beautiful images. Then I start reading, and I notice, to my amazement, that there is rhythm, that there are rhymes, that these pieces, for reasons I can't yet explain (still can't satisfactorily explain), are not short stories but something else, a mixed form that clearly offers a potential I hadn't yet seen. Irony, sarcasm, humour, even the transformation of the banal experience of rain, things I hadn't before associated with poetry, all seem possible in this new form. I rush back to my attic room in Neuilly and try it for myself, with results that I hurl into the wastepaper bin in fury.

I reread the passages from class. Baudelaire's is "Chacun sa chimère," chimères being for me the stone statues on Notre Dame, beautiful in their grotesque rejection of the classical beauty of statues, powerful in their suggestion of both wit and evil. In Baudelaire's poem, the heavy rhythm of feet tramping across the great dusty plain, the alliterations that suggest a constantly repeating scenery, the unexpected image of the men bent over under the weight of their own personal chimeras leap out at me from a passage whose lack of the expected structure had initially made me reject the idea that poetry might be present in it. The sentence structure repeats and echoes the sound and feel of the great claws crushing the unsuspecting person carrying their individual chimera. One sentence in particular seized my attention:

> Tous ces visages fatigués et sérieux ne témoignaient d'aucun désespoir; sous la coupole splénétique du ciel, les pieds plongés dans la poussière d'un sol aussi désolé que ce ciel, ils cheminaient avec la physionomie résignée de ceux qui sont condamnés à espérer toujours.

> [None of these weary, serious faces revealed the slightest trace of despair. Under the splenetic vault of the sky, feet deep in the dust of a soil as desolate as that sky, they pursued their way with the resigned physiognomies of those condemned to hope forever.] (Baudelaire 1975: 283)

The word games (*sol, désolé*), the repeating sound patterns (*pieds, plongés, poussière*), the inescapable rhythms (*résignée, condamnés, espérer*) and the overturning of Dante's line ordering all who enter Hell to abandon hope (Baudelaire's people are "condamnés à espérer toujours"—so much worse) all shook my previously-held conviction that I knew what poetry was.

Although its subject matter was immediately familiar, the prose poem by Francis Ponge, "Pluie," was more problematic. The first sentence seemed banal to the point of pedestrianism: "La pluie, dans la cour où je la regarde tomber, descend à des allures très diverses" (Ponge 2006: 31–2). But then I began to notice word games even more playful and revealing than Baudelaire's. The rain forms a *rideau* or *réseau*, the deadpan narrator's voice informs us, releasing the word for water from nouns that would normally be resistant to that element. The precipitation is wittily described as sempiternal, the rain drops are transformed into wheat, peas, marbles, candy. The letter "i" in *brise, rejaillit, aiguillettes, brillantes* reflects the bouncing droplets, and the complicated mechanism Ponge invokes to describe the rainfall becomes at the same time a metaphor for the prose poem itself, "une horlogerie dont le ressort est la pesanteur d'une masse donnée de vapeur en précipitation" or "un concert sans monotonie, non sans délicatesse." And both the expression "glou-glou des gouttières" and the pun in "Il a plu" insist that poetry can be funny without losing the charisma I associated with it.

Over the half century that has, unbelievably, passed since that first encounter, I have spent many hours delighting in, grappling with, and revolting against prose poetry (what, after all, is the use of revolt that is not periodically rekindled?). Teaching it has enabled me to see again and again that same rejection followed by gradual and sometimes only partial acceptance. In the essays that follow, readers will be able to explore prose poetry not just in many of its guises, but also across languages and countries and through time. They reveal the extent to which prose poetry, to quote Ponge, offers us an "amphibiguïté" that is consistently "salubre" (Ponge 2006: 33).

Works Cited

Baudelaire, Charles (1975), *Œuvres complètes*, Vol. 1 (Paris: Gallimard).
Ponge, Francis (2006), *Le Parti pris des choses* (Paris: Gallimard), pp. 31–2.

Introduction

Mary Ann Caws and Michel Delville

As Barbara Johnson has observed, there is no dearth of theories and speculations about the birth and emergence of the prose poem: "the list of revised and amended genealogies extends indefinitely: from the *Livre du promeneur* to *Télémaque*, from Chateaubriand to the Bible, one keeps finding the 'origins' of prose poems further upstream in the muddy waters of literary history" (Johnson 1979: 19). One might add to the list the names of James Macpherson, William Blake, Friedrich Schlegel, Novalis, Samuel Taylor Coleridge, Ralph Waldo Emerson and Aloysius Bertrand, among countless other putative precursors. That said, most, including Johnson herself, consider Charles Baudelaire's *Paris Spleen* (begun in 1855 and first published in full in 1869) as the first instance of a cultivated and motivated endeavor to create "the miracle of a poetic prose, musical though rhythmless and rhymeless, flexible yet rugged enough to identify with the lyrical impulses of the soul, the ebbs and flows of revery, the pangs of conscience" (Baudelaire 1989: 25). As Joseph Acquisto argues in the opening essay of this book, Baudelaire's project was linked at least as much to "a set of aesthetic, social, and political transformations in mid nineteenth-century France" (Caws and Delville XXX) as to considerations of poetic form and language. In a similar vein, the chapters that follow do not take the prose poem as an aesthetic object carrying meaning and values within itself without attending to the practical circumstances of the genre's production and reception (in Baudelaire's case, the social transformations brought about by the new urban environment and the "devaluation of the poet in the age of high capitalism" [Caws and Delville XXX]). All in all, we have tried to acknowledge the dizzying, multifarious volatility of a genre which, since Baudelaire's times, has spread in directions as diverse as Gertrude Stein's Cubist vignettes in *Tender Buttons*, Francis Ponge's object poems, Julio Cortázar's hybrid "prosems," and the postgeneric experiments of Claudia Rankine's award-winning *Citizen*. Baudelaire's generic *enfant terrible* now seems to have generated so many trends, modes and schools that any attempt at a final definition and classification of the genre would be self-defeating.

Michael Benedikt's *The Prose Poem: An International Anthology* (1976) represents the first significant attempt in the English-speaking world to provide an extensive selection of prose poems arranged by languages covered and ranging from the mid-nineteenth century to the 1970s. Benedikt's 621-page volume includes such diverse writers as Stéphane Mallarmé, Ivan Turgenev, Velemir Khlebnikov, Pablo Neruda, Günter Eich, Julio Cortázar, and Attila József, some of whom arguably never thought of themselves as practitioners of the prose poem. Published almost half a century after Benedikt's anthology, Jeremy Noel-Tod's 2018 *Penguin Book of the Prose Poem* gathers nearly three hundred prose poems and retraces the history of the genre from the mid-nineteenth century to such contemporary writers as Anne Carson, Peter Gizzi, Vahni Capildeo and Rod Mengham. That more than 80 percent of the poets included in Noel-Tod's anthology are anglophone writers (some of them relatively unknown and included at the expense of, say, Czesław Milosz or Julio Cortázar) may be perceived by some as an Anglocentric limitation. Others may regard it as a rightful tribute to the recent success story of the genre in the English-speaking world, and in the United States in particular, where it is no longer regarded as a mere curiosity for Francophiles.

The sheer diversity of writers and "schools" represented in Benedikt's and Noel-Tod's anthologies calls for a reconsideration of the prose poem, one which is grounded in an attempt to historicize and problematize the genre not only from an international but also from a transdiscursive, transgeneric and transmedial perspective. The present collection of essays offers students and scholars a historically and culturally informed introduction to the genre's main practitioners and trends since Baudelaire. It takes stock of the most recent scholarship on the genre and focuses on its multiple and changing trends and definitions, reaching into the literary as well as the social, cultural, historical and political contexts and movements out of which they emerged. Each essay was written by an authority in the field and is be designed to be introductory while addressing some of the most pressing questions about the permutations of modernism and postmodernism and examining the most pivotal debates and controversies surrounding modern and contemporary poetry and poetics. On a scholarly level, *The Edinburgh Companion to the Prose Poem* builds on the discoveries and insights offered by such foundational comparative studies as Jonathan Monroe's *A Poverty of Objects: The Prose Poem and the Politics of Genre* (1987) and Steven Monte's *Invisible Fences: Prose Poetry as a Genre in French and American Literature* (2000), as well as on the editors' own efforts to understand and contextualize a genre that arguably began as a revolt against dominant poetic forms, French and otherwise (Mary Ann Caws and Hermine Riffaterre (eds), *The Prose Poem in France: Theory and Practice*, 1983; Michel Delville, *The American Prose Poem: Poetic Form and the Boundaries of Genre*, 1998), an "anti-genre" which often exists by virtue of its relationship with other literary or extraliterary forms and which can therefore only be apprehended through "negative differentiation" (Monte 2000: 240). In addressing these issues, this Companion covers a whole range of disciplines and contexts while raising the thorny question of how non-poetic genres such as journalistic prose, the essay or the novel—or even non-literary forms of artistic expression—have influenced or interacted with the development of prose poetry since its historically sanctioned inception in the mid-nineteenth century.

The four major sections and the general structure of this book largely follow this process, which takes us from British and German Romanticism to the Decadents, before venturing into modernist territory (e.g. Gertrude Stein, Max Jacob, Pierre Reverdy) and examining contemporary figures such as Miroslav Holub, Julio Cortázar and Claudia Rankine, and on to recent experiments in postgeneric and "uncreative writing." While not claiming to be exhaustive (an ambition which would be doomed to failure by virtue of the sheer diversity and proliferation of prose poetry over the last two centuries), the volume also covers much geographical, cultural and ideological ground while acknowledging the centrality of the French and American influences which have determined the history of the genre as it has been theorized and practiced in the English-speaking world.

The chapters gathered in Part I investigate the specific historical and cultural circumstances of the birth of the prose poem in the nineteenth century, focusing more specifically on the foundational figures of Baudelaire, Rimbaud and Mallarmé. In France, the popularity of the prose poem was in direct proportion to its capacity to break through the metrical and rhythmic constraints of the alexandrine. Outside the French-speaking world, we could argue that the genre's subversive potential lies in its capacity not only to enact a continuation and re-evaluation of familiar French Symbolist and Surrealist paradigms, but also to respond to, pastiche or subvert genres other than traditional, versified poetry, genres which, like fiction or the essay, are considered the private domain of prose literature. Joseph Acquisto's opening chapter considers the origins of the prose poem in the work of French maverick Aloysius Bertrand's *Gaspard de la Nuit* (published posthumously in 1842) before turning to Baudelaire's genre-founding *Paris Spleen*, which he considers not only in terms of formal aesthetics but also as an attempt to respond to the changing social and political geographies of his time, especially as regards the goals and functions of poetry in the modern urban environment. Embodied by the figure of the *flâneur*, such ambition was nourished by Baudelaire's fascination with the complex, meandering architectures of the modern city which provided inspiration for the very stylistic and thematic textures of his prose poems. "The notion of such an obsessive ideal," he writes of this new amphibian invention, "has its origins above all in our experience of the life of the great cities, the confluence and interactions of the countless relationships between them" (Baudelaire 1989: 26), at a time when Paris was being modernized and refashioned by Georges-Eugène Hausmann. Such changes prompted the poet to write about the new landscape of boulevards and avenues gradually taking the place of dark and narrow medieval streets while "valorizing the city as a properly 'poetic' setting along with the humble objects to be found there and the full range of social classes one may encounter" (Caws and Delville XXX).

Acquisto's chapter concludes with a consideration of the prose poetry of Mallarmé and Arthur Rimbaud, who were profoundly influenced by Baudelaire's aesthetics but develop the prose poem in divergent ways, laying the groundwork for significant further innovations by later poets. Considering the Baudelairian legacy, and pausing importantly with Zola's critical appraisal of the state of contemporary poetry, Aimée Israel-Pelletier likewise turns to the new imaginative possibilities inaugurated by Rimbaud's *Les Illuminations*. In her discussion of Rimbaud's impressionist poetics, the prose poem emerges as a form especially apt to convey the loosening of sense and the loss of stable centers of meaning which characterize the artist's experience of the new and the modern. Rimbaud's prose poems advance a critique of the language and logic of prose based on an understanding of the "illumination" as a revolutionary moment of resistance to the (formal and political) harmonies and certainties of rhyme and meter. In doing so, they challenge what Jonathan Monroe has called elsewhere "the uncomplicated linear narrative of history-as-progress" (Monroe 1987: 153). Here, however, Monroe proposes a different history of the development of prose poem as genre, considering German Romanticism (and Novalis in particular) as an early framework from which to consider the struggle between the "present" environment of prose and the "past" ages of poetry, a struggle set against the background of Schlegel's and Novalis's respective notions of "universal poetry" (*Universalpoesie*) and "universal history" (*Universalgeschichte*).

Straddling the Romantic and the Victorian periods, as well as French and British literary histories, Nikki Santilli's contribution discusses De Quincey's influence on Baudelaire, who was translating the former's autobiographical *Confessions of an*

English Opium-Eater during the time he was composing his *Paris Spleen*. Focusing on Baudelaire's interpretation of the *Confessions* as a succession of discrete prose pieces, Santilli reads the prose poem through the lens of De Quincey's idea of the palimpsest, a notion which subordinates linear succession to a proto-modernist aesthetics of simultaneity whose dynamics will be further explored in Part II.

The last chapter of Part I takes us to the end of the nineteenth century. In it, Margueritte Murphy explores the paradoxes of this prose poem and other forms of "poetic prose" for the *fin de siècle*: of a genre associated with decadence that is at the forefront of innovation and radical speech. She argues, *contra* Eliot's dismissal of the form as yet another manifestation of the stylistic ornamentalism and technical "charlatanism" of the Decadents (Eliot 1917: 158), that the *fin de siècle* for the prose poem effectively began as early as in the 1860s and 1870s, with young emerging writers such as Mallarmé, Judith Gautier, Catulle Mendès, and J.-K. Huysmans. As Murphy suggests, considering the works under scrutiny as well as the Wilde trials of 1895, it is precisely the rivalry between Decadence and Symbolism which created the necessary condition for the birth of a modernist aesthetic of the prose poem, one which calls for reassessment and takes us beyond the polarities between the decorative and the subversive, the decadent and the revolutionary.

The second section of *The Edinburgh Companion to the Prose Poem* turns to the importance of visual models in the history of prose poetry, a tendency which is already apparent in Bertrand's above-mentioned pioneering *Gaspard de la Nuit*, whose indebtedness to seventeenth-century printmaking is already made clear in its subtitle: "fantasies in the manner of Rembrandt and Callot." In the opening chapters of the section, Emma Wagstaff and Mary Ann Caws show that the visual arts are central not only to the early developments of the prose poem but also to the works of modernist and post-1945 writers who played a part in expanding the methodological and epistemological ambit of the genre. Caws' chapter addresses the thorny issue of interpreting Cubist writings and visual works, as well as the even thornier issue of the origin of the Cubist prose poem. It shows that the influence of Cubism proved crucial in the development of a modernist aesthetic and ethos of the prose poem, as the examples of Jacob, Stein, Reverdy and others suggest. A collection of literary "Cubist" still lifes, Gertrude Stein's *Tender Buttons* (1914) is also emblematic of the preoccupation with objects which characterizes the work of a number of other major representatives of the modern and contemporary prose poem, such as Max Jacob and, later, Francis Ponge and Robert Bly. In her close readings of Jacob, Reverdy and Juan Gris, Caws addresses the complex and intricate sense of perspectival and interdisciplinary inbetweenness which characterizes the prose poem form. Wagstaff's essay traces the genealogy of the post-ekphrastic prose poem from Stein, Reverdy, Jacob, Ponge and René Char to the American Objectivists and on to recent examples of intermedial poetic practice such as those of Alessandro De Francesco and Anne Portugal. It argues that the modernist prose poem conceived as a self-reflexive aesthetic object is often used as a means of investigating and questioning the goals and methods of poetic language while turning increasingly to the poetic function and possibilities of everyday language. The Cubist and post-Cubist experiments discussed by Caws and Wagstaff point to the (post) modernist obsession with simultaneism, dislocation, juxtaposition and—perhaps even more importantly—abstraction, a subject discussed by Richard Deming in connection with John Ashbery's *Three Poems*, which Deming positions in the legacy of William

Carlos Williams' 1923 *Spring & All*. Deming's notion of "abstraction" in prose poetry refers to a kind of writing which is guided by word, phrase, and thought rather than by story or representation. In the last analysis, Deming concludes, the prose poem is a self-reflexive genre which capitalizes on generic and discursive unsettledness and "enact[s] the restless conversation with itself, the ongoing conversation between literary history and poetic maker, between text and reader" (Caws and Delville XXX).

In distinct but related ways, the chapters contained in the third part of this book approach the history of the modern and contemporary prose poem in light of the complexities and complications generated by the genre's interdiscursive and intergeneric negotiations with prose genres, some of which (e.g. the novel, the fairy tale, the newspaper article, the short narrative, the philosophical fragment . . .) are already analyzed in different contexts in Part I and Part II. Delville and Monson concentrate on the prose poem's affinities with narrative genre and modes (the short short and the novel, respectively), returning us to the definition of the prose poem provided by Des Esseintes (the protagonist of Huysmans' *Against the Grain*) as a kind of "condensed novel," "containing in its small compass, like an extract of meat, so to say, the essence of the novel, while suppressing its long, tedious analytical passages and superfluous descriptions" (Huysmans 2009: 162). By defining the genre as a concentrated and supreme avatar of the novel ("Then the words chosen would be so unpermutable as to substitute for all the others; the adjective, placed in such an ingenious and so definitive a way that it could not be legally divested of its position, would open such perspectives that the reader could dream for weeks on end about its meaning, at the same time fixed and multiple, could take note of the present, reconstruct the past; could guess the future of the characters' souls, revealed by the light of that unique epithet" [162]), Des Esseintes also prefigures Roland Barthes' notion of the "novelistic," which considers the novel less as a genre per se than as a modal category which, once transposed onto the poetic medium, turns the concentrated brevity and semantic ambiguity of poetic language into a means of revisiting and problematizing the creation of plot and character.

Monson's contribution examines the influence of the novel on prose poetry, specifically during the radical changes and experiments in French and British literature during the early-to-mid-twentieth century. Using Nathalie Sarraute as a key channel for these fundamental shifts away from the traditional novel's objective treatment of plot, time, space and character, Monson explores how she arrived at the prose poem and simultaneously foreshadowed the French Nouveau Roman, known more broadly as the antinovel, through her first book, *Tropisms* (1939). Delville's chapter considers to what extent the metapoetic foregrounding of discourse and writing-as-process which characterizes many prose poems of the "fabulist" variety is linked with an understanding of poetic language as a deviant use of the language of rational logic and of a number of specific conventions underlying short fictional genres. In the first part of his contribution Delville examines other forms of prose poetics hybrids reclaiming and questioning the language of logic and the syllogistic movement of essayistic or scientific writing, a tendency which has characterized the development of the prose poem from Poe's *Eureka* to Rosmarie Waldrop's Wittgensteinian *Lawn of Excluded Middle* (1993). Lizzy LeRud's chapter on the confessional prose poem takes another major interdiscursive paradigm of the genre. It describes how the dominantly self-reflexive style of the genre can coexist with the poetics of immediacy often associated with the confessional mode in twentieth-century poetry. Dwelling on Robert Lowell's and Elisabeth Bishop's prose memoirs, LeRud sustains the argument that prose-poetic forms of autobiography promote a confessional mode that blends self-present, transparent lyricism and impersonal, opaque realism, thereby expanding the methodological ambit of a dialogical genre resisting the neat dichotomies promoted by traditional taxonomic generic classifications. Part III closes with Adam R. Rosenthal's proposal to theorize the generic quandary of the prose poem by extending its inherent transgenericity to the notion of translation, a word which Rosenthal uses to describe an analogon of prose-poetry composition, not only of cross-linguistic transference, but of any process of cross-pollination such as that which can be found to be at work not only in Baudelaire's *Petits poèmes en prose* but also in Ralph Waldo Emerson's little-known 1839 "prose sonnet," "Woods."

In his foundational study of the prose poem, *A Poverty of Objects* (1987), Jonathan Monroe argues that the prose poem operates as "a critical, self-critical, utopian genre, a genre that tests the limits of genre" and "aspires to be poetic/literary language's own coming to self-consciousness, the place where poet and reader alike become critically aware of the writer's language." With this question of the inherently deviant and self-referential nature of the genre as a prelude, Monroe draws upon Bakhtin's theories on the novel and proceeds to emphasize the prose poem's "heteroglossia": its refusal to develop itself along the line of the poet's personal voice and its willingness to accommodate a multiplicity of voices representing "various speech types in conflict with one another." Examples of such "heteroglossic" possibilities for the genre include Baudelaire's "dialogues between men and women and rich and poor," "the intersection of religious, economic, scientific, pagan, political, historical, and other modes of discourse" in Rimbaud's *Illuminations*, Jacob's "condensed Cubist parodies of the popular novel," the "rhetoric of objects" at work in Ponge's *proèmes*, and Stein's "intermingling of the languages of method, conversation, domestic life, dinner parties, sex, violence, and detective stories."

By allowing different linguistic and social registers to combine and compete within a single poetic space, the prose poem, Monroe speculates, rejects poetry's "dream of itself as a pure other set apart in sublime isolation" and is therefore in a position to focus on "unresolved contradictions and problems of everyday life, the world of prose in which we live and breathe." It enacts a symbolic confrontation of ideological conflicts which every historical period necessarily maintains, sometimes in contradiction to its own self-proclaimed homogeneity. Ultimately, the prose poem—far from fusing its hybrid poetics into a single, unified whole—becomes a writing practice that integrates a network of public and personal voices into a complex poetic idiom that allows each of them to be heard.

The last nine chapters of this volume reflect the mosaic-like richness and polyphonic diversity of the contemporary prose poem. Rather than attempting a chronological or typological survey of the genre's numerous heteroglossic exemplars over the last two centuries, Part IV discusses a number of key issues, contexts and theories which have continued to haunt the history of the prose poem from its official inception to the present day. These issues are successively approached through the prism of gender theory and identity politics (Alyson Miller on the permutations of genre, gender and race), ecocriticism (Lynn Domina on the prose poem and nature writing), the challenges of translating hybrid genres and transnational literary influences (Piotr Gwiazda on Grzegorz Wróblewski's *Kopenhaga*), non-Western models of prose poetry (Sinan Antoon, Scott Steele and Nick Admussen on the little-known histories of the Arabic, Japanese and Chinese prose poem, respectively), postgeneric prose (Stephen Fredman on recent genre-benders by the likes of Theresa Hak Kyung Cha, Kathy Acker, D. J. Waldie and Laura Mullen), and the relevance of "uncreative" writing to current developments in experimental prose poetry (Jeff Barda on the reappropriation and poetic repurposing of the "prose of the world" in recent French experimental poetry). These essays expand the major issues and contexts framed in the earlier sections of this volume. In doing so, they individually and collectively contribute to establishing the ground for a historically and theoretically informed discussion of how the prose poem problematizes the linearity and coherence we have been taught to expect from most histories of modern and contemporary poetry. We hope that the reader finds in this intersecting diversity of angles and methods a creative and intellectual challenge to rethink the prose poem's multifaceted history and, more generally, an incentive to explore those axiomatic forces that shape literary tradition, as well as the world outside the text.

Works Cited

Baudelaire, Charles (1989), *The Poems in Prose*, ed. and trans. Francis Scarfe, London: Anvil.
Benedikt, Michael (1976), *The Prose Poem: An International Anthology*, New York: Dell.
Caws, Mary Ann, and Hermine Riffaterre (eds) (1983), *The Prose Poem in France: Theory and Practice*, New York: Columbia University Press.
Delville, Michel (1998), *The American Prose Poem: Poetic Form and the Boundaries of Genre*, Gainesville: University Press of Florida.
Eliot, T. S. (1917), "The Borderline of Prose," *The New Statesman*, No. 9 (19 May), pp. 157–9.
Huysmans, J.-K. (2009), *Against the Grain*, trans. Margaret Mauldon, Oxford: Oxford University Press.
Johnson, Barbara (1979), *Défigurations du langage poétique*, Paris: Flammarion.
Monroe, Jonathan (1987), *A Poverty of Objects: The Prose Poem and the Politics of Genre*, Ithaca: Cornell University Press.
Monte, Stephen (2000), *Invisible Fences: Prose Poetry as a Genre in French and American Literature*, Lincoln: University of Nebraska Press.

Part I

Origins and Beginnings

1

THE BIRTH OF THE PROSE POEM IN NINETEENTH-CENTURY FRANCE

Joseph Acquisto

UNDERSTANDING THE ORIGINS OF THE PROSE POEM in France is entirely bound up with understanding its reception history. It is Charles Baudelaire, the author of a highly influential posthumously published set of prose poems entitled *Le Spleen de Paris* (1869), who is most often associated with the birth of the genre in France. This view has not gone unquestioned, however, and to assign such a prominent place to Baudelaire is in some sense to consider literary history from the point of view of the way literature developed since the time of Baudelaire rather than to consider the way he was himself influenced by what came before. What does emerge in Baudelaire's collection of prose poems is that the genre is one which, from the start, is obviously related to formal concerns but is also inextricably linked to a set of aesthetic, social, and political transformations in mid-nineteenth-century France which call into question the nature and role of art in the modern urban environment. In what follows I will consider Baudelaire along with two important poets in the generation following his, Arthur Rimbaud and Stéphane Mallarmé. While all three poets maintain a privileged status for art, at the same time they craft their poems in an age of unquestioned social transformation and against the background of an anxiety about the devaluation of the poet in the age of high capitalism. Such a threat has the potential both to forge an ironic attitude toward the prose poem as the debased art form that their era requires or demands and to allow the prose poem to become a vehicle for the transformation of poetic language in search of ever newer imaginative possibilities.[1]

It is important to recognize at the outset that the prose poem as a genre has always been marked by its heterogeneity, both from author to author and among the prose poems of a single author. The modern prose poem is marked by its brevity, and this is something that distinguishes it from novel or epic-length works of the eighteenth century which were called *poèmes en prose*.[2] It is also to be distinguished from what is called *la prose poétique*, a kind of prose whose melodic or rhythmic or other typically "lyric" qualities suggest an attention to the formal qualities of the words such as that developed by Jean-Jacques Rousseau in the eighteenth century or François-René de Chateaubriand in the early nineteenth. In the modern prose poem, brevity often goes hand in hand with an intensity of expression which for some is also one of the markers of this genre which otherwise resists, owing to its heterogeneity and hybrid character, most attempts to provide a blanket characterization.

The term *poème en prose* itself is not precisely coextensive with the development of the genre. As Christian Leroy has noted:

> The expression 'prose poem' comes into general usage only after 1880, which obviously raises the problem of the value of Baudelaire's *Petits poèmes en prose*. On the other hand, we note the appearance, starting in the 1860s, of *petits poèmes* called by that name and designating short lyric pieces in strophes. (Leroy 2001: 143)[3]

This is not to say that Baudelaire did not himself use the expression *poème en prose*, but Leroy's remark about the use of the term as a common indicator of genre coming a half-generation after Baudelaire serves as a helpful reminder against hastily imposing categories back in time. This is where we should be mindful of the way the history of the prose poem is inseparable from its reception history. For Leroy, it is only in the 1950s that a canonical characterization of the modern prose poem emerges, due in no small measure to Suzanne Bernard's extensive study entitled *Le Poème en prose: De Baudelaire jusqu'à nos jours* (*The Prose Poem: From Baudelaire to Our Own Day*) (1959), whose very title places Baudelaire at the origin of the genre. Leroy claims that what would eventually become part of the canonical genre was gradually worked out in literature from the mid-nineteenth to the mid-twentieth century. He identifies the now-canonical characteristics of the genre as follows: "short text, self-enclosed, and aiming to create emotions by a strategy of poetic effect proportional to the density of the statement. Still, these ideas are of varying pertinence" (Bernard 1959: 170).

In the decades leading up to Baudelaire's experiments with the prose poem, there is a concern not only with the development of "poetic" prose but also a move toward the formation of a new aesthetics *of* prose, as opposed to introducing flowery vocabulary or poetic syntax into prose. LeRoy Breunig, in an essay that seeks to answer the question of why France in particular was the place that saw the birth of the prose poem in this period, identifies "the very tyranny of French verse," the rigid constraints that classical French prosody imposes on its poets (Breunig 1983: 30). The prose poem emerges, along with freer approaches to verse forms, as a reaction against such constraint, at the same time as poetry, in verse and prose alike, will also invite readers to rethink what constitutes objects of poetic value. Here again, Baudelaire plays an important role, in his poetry in both verse and prose, in valorizing the city as a properly "poetic" setting along with the humble objects to be found there and the full range of social classes one may encounter.

The most important precursor to Baudelaire's prose poems is a volume of texts by Aloysius Bertrand, *Gaspard de la Nuit*, published posthumously in 1842 to an indifferent reception at first. Bertrand's texts mark a departure from prior typical practice in a way that Suzanne Bernard characterized as follows: "no longer any pompous phraseology, no more pseudo-Hellenism or made-to-order exoticism, but a particular picturesque quality, very personal, and served by a heightened technique of the prose sentence" (Bernard 1960: 51). Bertrand's prose poems are marked by several key features of Romantic texts, including a taste for the fantastic and the grotesque, even as they combine potentially contradictory tones. For Bernard, their "union of lucidity and vertigo, of realism and poetry, of fright and bantering gives to these fantastical works of Gaspard an absolutely original tone" (Bernard 1960: 56). In that sense, they look back in time by one generation thematically as they set the stage in terms of form for the emergence of the modern prose poem which, most would agree, takes its form in Baudelaire.

Those who seek Baudelaire's own characterization of his project in the prose poems can find it in a short letter to his publisher Arsène Houssaye that is often published as a preface to *Le Spleen de Paris*. He describes the work as one where "tout . . . est à la fois tête et queue, alternativement et réciproquement" (1: 275) ["everything . . . is both tail and head, alternative and reciprocally" (in Baudelaire 1997: 129). In full ironic mode, Baudelaire claims that one can break off reading where one wishes and that each part can live independently of the whole. If one begins with this letter as a basis for establishing the aesthetics of the prose poem, it is tempting to see the genre in opposition to verse poetry rather than as complementary to it, since presumably Baudelaire's insistence on the fact that the collection can be torn apart and read in any order is a reaction to the trial and condemnation of his verse collection *Les Fleurs du Mal* (*The Flowers of Evil*); he had argued that the collection must be considered in its entirety and not condemned on account of individual poems taken out of context. His defense was not successful, and several poems were condemned and literally ripped out of extant copies of the collection. In this context, the prose poems would be a new and degraded form that has no unity to violate and that the public could manipulate as it saw fit.

It is in this preface that Baudelaire indicates that *Gaspard de la Nuit* had been his source of inspiration in that it had led him to attempt to "tenter quelque chose d'analogue, et d'appliquer à la description de la vie moderne, ou plutôt d'*une* vie moderne et plus abstraite, le procédé qu'il avait appliqué à la peinture de la vie ancienne, si étrangement pittoresque" (Baudelaire 1975–6: 275) ["try something similar, and to apply to the description of modern life, or rather of *one* modern and more abstract life, the procedure he had applied to the depiction of ancient life, so strangely picturesque" (Baudelaire 1997: 129)]. The ironic tone of the beginning gives way to this famous description of Baudelaire's ambitions for the prose poem: "Qui est celui de nous qui n'a pas, dans ses jours d'ambition, rêvé le miracle d'une prose poétique, musicale sans rythme et sans rime, assez souple et assez heurtée pour s'adapter aux mouvements lyriques de l'âme, aux ondulations de la rêverie, aux soubresauts de la conscience?" (Baudelaire 1975–6: 275–6) ["Which of us has not, in his ambitious days, dreamed of the miracle of a poetic prose, musical without rhythm and without rhyme, supple enough and choppy enough to fit the soul's lyrical movements, the undulations of reverie, the jolts of consciousness?" (Baudelaire 1997: 129)]. Baudelaire thus announces a double agenda for the prose poem: it will serve as an appropriate vehicle for the poetry of modern urban life while still retaining the musicality more typically associated with verse poetry than with prose.

There is reason, however, to be skeptical of Baudelaire's claim here that lyrical prose is what is best suited for the depiction of modern urban reality, given that Baudelaire makes reference in this letter to Houssaye's own prose poem "La chanson du Vitrier" (1857), a lyrical evocation of an impoverished glazier with an insistent, lyrical refrain "Oh, vitrier!" punctuating its paragraphs.[4] One of Baudelaire's most often-studied prose poems, "Le Mauvais vitrier," in which the narrator enacts impulsive sadistic cruelty on a glazier, presents itself as a rather biting satire of the pathos and lyricism of Houssaye's prose poem. Instead of empathizing with the glazier's plight, he chases him away, after having made him climb to the narrator's top-floor apartment, and grabs a flower pot as he sees him back on the sidewalk:

[Q]uand l'homme reparut au débouché de la porte, je laissai tomber perpendiculairement mon engin de guerre sur le rebord postérieur de ses crochets; et le choc le renversant, il acheva de briser sous son dos toute sa pauvre fortune ambulatoire qui rendit le bruit éclatant d'un palais de cristal crevé par la foudre.

Et, ivre de ma folie, je lui criai furieusement: 'La vie en beau! la vie en beau!' (Baudelaire 1975–6: 287)

[[W]hen the man reappeared at the door entrance, I let my engine of war drop down perpendicularly on the back edge of his pack. The shock knocked him over, and he ended by breaking his entire poor itinerant fortune under his back which produced the brilliant sound of a crystal palace smashed by lightning.

And, drunk with my madness, I shouted at him furiously, 'Make life beautiful! Make life beautiful!'] (Baudelaire 1997: 15)

In light of such portrayals of biting irony that enact scenes of traumatic shock in settings of urban poverty, we may well want to be cautious about quoting Baudelaire's letter to Houssaye as a straightforward description of his ideal of the prose poem.[5] In fact, considering the letter in light of the textual interplay between Houssaye's poem and Baudelaire's even gives the lie to Baudelaire's initial claim that each text could be read on its own terms and without an organic relation to other texts in the collection. The potential for an ironic reading of the letter that is so often published as a preface to the work is only revealed by reading it in dialogue with "Le Mauvais vitrier," which itself establishes itself in an ironic relation to Houssaye's own text.

So we see that, while Baudelaire's letter-preface presents one potential story that could be told about the nature and objectives of the modern prose poem, it is not uncomplicated by the questions of irony that enter into any consideration of Baudelaire's works. And we should also take into account, when considering the rise of the prose poem, that situating its origins with Baudelaire is also the result, as I have indicated above, of the canonization of the genre in the mid-twentieth century, largely through Suzanne Bernard's influential study.[6] Christian Leroy has offered a critique of this reception history, claiming that "this collection could not constitute—in the first degree, at least—the prototype of the French prose poem. At most, it could be considered at first as its totalization, translating more of an ending point than a beginning" (Bernard 1959: 146). Seeing Baudelaire's collection as a culmination helps to account for the diversity of the forms that it contains. The poems vary considerably in length and in tone, from the short dialogue form of the first poem "L'Etranger" ("—Eh! Qu'aimes-tu donc, extraordinaire étranger? —J'aime les nuages . . . les nuages qui passent . . . là-bas . . . là-bas . . . les merveilleux nuages!" (Baudelaire 1975–6: 277) ["So! Then what do you love, you extraordinary stranger?"] love clouds . . . drifting clouds . . . There . . . over there . . . marvelous clouds!" (Baudelaire 1997: 1)] to the rhapsodic hymn-like nature of poems such as "Le Thyrse," to the energetic injunctions of "Enivrez-vous" ("Get High") ("Il faut toujours être ivre. Tout est là: c'est l'unique question" (Baudelaire 1975–6: 337) ["You must always be high. Everything depends on it" (Baudelaire 1997: 89)], to longer narratives such as "Le gâteau," which recounts a train ride the narrator takes, during which he watches two children engage in a vicious fight over a piece of bread which they call cake, destroying the bread in the process. The collection also includes lyrical poems such as "L'Invitation au voyage," which can be seen as a counterpart to the poem in verse of the same name,[7] and bitingly ironic narratives such as "Assommons les pauvres!" ("Let's Beat Up the Poor"), in which the narrator beats a pauper to a pulp with a tree branch, after which the pauper does the same to him, prompting the narrator to declare him his equal and give him alms, asking him to spread the word about the lesson he has just learned.

So in an important sense, to use Baudelaire's prose poems as a way to define the genre is to beg the question of that definition, on account of the considerable variety one finds there. Baudelaire's place as the inventor of the modern prose poem could thus be complicated by an alternative view that sees him as the one who culminates certain tendencies in lyric prose that existed before him but who also introduces irony and parody as an essential element in his prose poetry. In that sense, his project in the prose poems would not be so different from what it was in the verse poems, where he both sums up a lyric tradition and infuses it with an unrelenting irony that complicates any attempt to provide a simple or one-sided reading of the poems. And indeed, while the chronology of the publication of *Les Fleurs du Mal* in 1857 (and its second edition in 1861) and *Le Spleen de Paris* in 1869 might encourage readers to think that Baudelaire transitioned neatly from writing poetry in verse to writing poetry in prose, there is a significant overlap of years in which he was actively pursuing both.

So while Baudelaire uses the term *poème en prose*, mainly in his correspondence, to describe these works, it is something of a simplification to say that he invented the genre, since that would ignore the precedents in earlier literature, including use of the term itself as a generic marker. It also fails to account for the fact that it was not until a generation later that the term began to be used to describe a consistent genre. Leroy proposes that, rather than seeing Baudelaire as an inventor, we see him as responding to a series of crises in lyric verse in a process that is related to disenchantment:

> With Baudelaire, the lyric poem in prose is confronted with a crisis: crisis of material—does prose truly permit one to compose a poem?—; aesthetic crisis—the lyric poem shows its incapacity to express beauty while privileging the grotesque—; crisis of genre—what does a poem look like from now on? The three aspects of this crisis relate to what we could call a process of disenchantment: lyricism in prose experiences its limits and reveals its ambiguities. Of course, that does not mean that it is going to disappear, but rather that the object of prose poems will be to stage this disenchantment: if there is still a beauty in prose, it is essentially "dark" and depressive. (Leroy 2001: 154–5)

This disenchantment at the level of form and aesthetic crisis goes hand in hand, in Baudelaire, with social disenchantment in a society where Baudelaire keenly sensed the degradation of the poet and his reduction to a merchant selling his wares on the market like any other commodity. If there is a poetic beauty to be captured in the city, modern Paris is also a fundamentally alienating place where interpersonal relations are often cruel and where sights of widows, the elderly, the poor, and the disenfranchised inspire pity. Baudelaire's prose poems are a site of contestation, and ironic undoing, of visions of social harmony and progress, and he often stages brutal cruelty. Sometimes the figure of the poet is explicitly represented in the poems, as in "Perte d'auréole" ("Loss of Halo"), a poem in dialogue form where the poet meets a friend in "un mauvais lieu" (Baudelaire 1975–6: 352) ["a house of ill fame" (Baudelaire 1997: 113)] and explains that his halo had fallen into the mud at the edge of the city street and he had not had the courage to pick it up, preferring to leave it where it is: "Ensuite je pense avec joie que quelque mauvais poète la ramassera et s'en coiffera impudemment. Faire un heureux, quelle jouissance! Et surtout un heureux qui me fera rire!" (Baudelaire 1975–6: 352) ["And I'm glad to think that some bad poet will pick it up and insolently stick it on his head. Make someone happy, what a delight! And especially a happy someone I can laugh at!" (Baudelaire 1997: 113)]. The poet establishes himself here in contrast to those naïve enough to retain the older, romantic model of the poet as invested with a sacred mission, not realizing that that role has ended up in the gutter and can only be taken up once again to be ridiculed or dismissed as naïve. Prose here seems to be an appropriate vehicle for the disenchantment of the poetic vocation in the face of modern urban capitalist alienation, and the prose in this poem is indistinguishable from narrative, retaining none of that magical, rhythmic prose that Baudelaire had evoked in the letter to Houssaye.

In Baudelaire's wake, several major poets who were significantly influenced by him also adopted the prose poem in the latter half of the nineteenth century. In his short but brilliant career as a poet, Arthur Rimbaud composed prose poems between 1873 and 1875 that were collected in a volume entitled *Illuminations* in 1886. As LeRoy Breunig has claimed, if Baudelaire wrote prose poems as an experiment, Rimbaud wrote them as a "revolt . . . against the yoke of French prosody" (Breunig 1983: 3). While Baudelaire "never rejected the constraints of French prosody," for Rimbaud "the prose poem became a necessity, a kind of Copernican step, the only form of expression that remained after the rejection of the conformities imposed by the meter and rhyme of the French poetic language" (Breunig 1983: 3–4). For Suzanne Bernard, the interplay between destruction and creation is an important constitutive aspect of the prose poem: from the destruction stemming from anarchy and revolt springs a new form committed to experimentation, a tool for destruction that results in new creative potentials unleashed by that very destruction:

> Assuredly the prose poem contains an anarchic and destructive principle, since it is born of a revolt against the laws of metrics and prosody . . . The prose poem wants to go beyond language, and it makes use of language; it wants to break form, and it creates forms; it wants to escape literature, and there it is having become a catalogued literary genre. It is this internal contradiction, this essential antinomy that gives it its character of an Icarian art, tending toward an impossible overcoming of itself, toward a negation of its own conditions of existence—and by that very thing, no doubt, representative in its way of the efforts of all French poetry since the nineteenth century. (Bernard 1959: 13)

Rimbaud's poetics pushes these destructive forces into new territory, intensifying Baudelaire's stylistic experimentation and, like Baudelaire, including heterogeneous forms among his prose poems which include unadorned prose writing, free verse, of which Rimbaud was one of the first practitioners in French (see, for instance, "Marine"), and what is referred to as *verset*, longer, irregular verse lines patterned loosely after biblical verse form (as in "Après le deluge" ["After the Flood"] which opens the collection). Likewise, the content of the poems varies, from the slightly troubling lyrical description of "Ville" ("De ma fenêtre, je vois des spectres nouveaux roulant à travers l'épaisse et éternelle fumée de charbon,—notre ombre des bois, notre nuit d'été!—des Erinntes nouvelles, devant mon cottage qui est ma trie et tout mon Coeur puisque tout ici ressemble à ceci" (Rimbaud 2005: 326) ["From my window, I see new ghosts rolling through thick, everlasting coal smoke, our shadow in the woods, our summer night!—new Furies in front of my cottage which is my country and my heart since everything here resembles it" (Rimbaud 2005: 327)[8]]) to evocations of the speaker's memories (see "Vagabond," for instance), to the oracular or prophetic tone of "Génie":

> O ses souffles, ses têtes, ses courses; la terrible célérité de la perfection des forms et de l'action.
> O fécondité de l'esprit et immensité de l'univers! (Rimbaud 2005: 352)

> [His breathing, his heads, his racings; the terrifying swiftness of form and action when they are perfect.
> Fertility of the mind and vastness of the world!] (Rimbaud 2005: 353)

And, again like Baudelaire's prose poem collection, Rimbaud's could be said, following Bernard, to be "anarchic" or "chaotic" in structure (Bernard 1959: 177), with each poem holding its own place in the collection without an implication of organic unity with the others, along with an often feverish and intense use of language. This poetic language refuses closure or straightforward interpretation in favor of the verbal energy that emerges from the poet who saw himself as a *voyant*, a seer, and refuses stability in favor of dynamic movement in rhythms and images of the texts. In terms of Rimbaud's poetics there is continuity between his poems in verse and prose; both push the poetic image to a new degree of intensity and proto-surreal imagination. This poetry is the result of a paradoxical, intentional process of undoing. As Rimbaud famously put it in a letter to Paul Demeny of 15 May 1871, commonly referred to as "La Lettre du voyant" ("The Letter of the Seer"):

> Le Poète se fait *voyant* par un long, immense et raisonné *dérèglement* de *tous les sens*. Toutes les formes d'amour, de souffrance, de folie; il cherche lui-même, il épuise en lui tous les poisons, pour n'en garder que leurs quintessences. Ineffable torture où il a besoin de toute la foi, de toute la force surhumaine, où il devient entre tous les grand malade, le grand criminel, le grand maudit,—et le suprême Savant!—Car il arrive à l'*inconnu*! (Rimbaud 2005: 376)

> [The Poet makes himself a *seer* by a long, gigantic and rational *derangement* of *all the senses*. All forms of love, suffering, and madness. He searches himself. He exhausts all poisons in himself and keeps only their quintessences. Unspeakable torture where he needs all his faith, all his superhuman strength, where he becomes among all men the great patient, the great criminal, the one accursed—and the supreme Scholar!—Because he reaches the *unknown*!] (Rimbaud 2005: 377)

The poem thus becomes in a certain sense the written record of the poet's experience, and at the same time the vehicle by which the reader, in reading and making meaning from the occasional apparent chaos of the poems, also participates in that undoing and refashioning of the self through extreme experience and its verbal traces.[9] In the intensity and unusual character of Rimbaud's imagery, we can see a precursor of surrealism, as in "Bottom," for instance:

> La réalité étant trop épineuse pour mon grand caractère,—je me trouvai néanmoins chez ma dame, en gros oiseau gris bleu s'essorant vers les moulures du plafond et traînant l'aile dans les ombres de la soirée. [. . .] Tout se fit ombre et aquarium ardent. (Rimbaud 2005: 348)

> [Reality being too prickly for my lofty character,—I became at my lady's a big-blue-gray bird flying up near the moldings of the ceiling and dragging my wings after me in the shadows of the evening. [. . .] Everything grew dark like a burning aquarium.] (Rimbaud 2005: 349, translation modified)

Poetry, on this view, both reflects and participates in the unknown, as the poet seeks to give expression to the as-yet unfathomable; and yet poems such as "Bottom" are steeped at the same time in the literary tradition, from the title taken from the character's name in Shakespeare's *A Midsummer Night's Dream* to more subtle echoes such as Victor Hugo's claim, in his novel *Les Travailleurs de la mer* (The Toilers of the Sea", that "le rêve est l'aquarium de la nuit" ["dream is the aquarium of the night"].[10] Rimbaud both evokes and negates Hugo's dark aquarium for those who notice the reference, evoking or inscribing a precursor poet in ways that make us note the uncanniness of some of Hugo's imagery and see how Rimbaud both participates in and overturns the poetics of the recent past by evoking this bit of poetic prose. In Rimbaud's prose poems, the search for new forms participates as an integral part of his larger poetic project of finding new ways of seeing and experiencing; his "chaos of unreality," as Hugo Friedrich put it, "spelled salvation from the confines of reality" (Friedrich 1974: 40).

In this same period, Stéphane Mallarmé also pursued prose poetry alongside his poems in verse. While very different in style and approach from Rimbaud, they share a desire to reimagine and push the boundaries of possibility of poetic language in both verse and prose, and there is thus an important continuity rather than a rupture between their verse poems and prose poems. Mallarmé's earliest poems, in verse and prose alike, show the strong influence of Baudelaire's language, style, and themes. But, as Bernard notes, even in these earliest poems "est déjà entrée en lutte contre la facilité, l'effusion, le cliché; il conçoit le travail poétique comme un exercice tout de rigueur et de concentration" (Bernard 1959: 263). From there he goes on to evolve a fiercely original and famously difficult style, pushing the boundaries of meaning via innovative lexical and syntactic developments, an evolution visible in the styles of his earlier and later prose poetry and marked by abstraction, concentration, and syntactical innovation.[11] While not an innovator like Rimbaud in terms of experimenting with versification, by the end of his life Mallarmé had published the highly experimental poem "Un coup de dés" (1897) with its lines of prose stretching across a two-page format and written in a variety of fonts and sizes that invite a complex and variable reading of the various "levels" of the poem, whose format vaguely suggests that of a musical score. Throughout the last years of his life, he had worked on a performative literary project called *Le Livre*, which comes down to us only in fragmentary notes left behind at his death, but which suggests that his later work is concerned with the way poetry can either transform the page or leave it behind entirely as poetry may become a quasi-ceremonial performance event. The prose poems are thus, as they were with Rimbaud, part of a larger poetic project developed simultaneously in verse and prose poems as well as more experimental forms.

While he wrote what would be considered prose poems, it is important to note that he himself published them under the more ambiguous collective title "Anecdotes ou poèmes" as a section of prose writings entitled *Divagations* (1897) that also included essays and articles. Mallarmé's poetry, in verse and prose alike, is highly and carefully crafted and the poet relentlessly reworked many of his texts. His prose poems are only ten in number; some of them served, as did some of his verse poems, as laboratories for the development of his mature style. In the period 1870–5, his syntax gradually takes on the sophistication which became a hallmark of his style, a development that is notable in his letters and articles and particularly in prose poems which exist in earlier and later versions. This is the case, for instance, for "Un spectacle interrompu," which was substantially reworked for its 1875 publication from a version first written several years before. Along with stylistic developments, the later prose poems also feature subject matter that is enigmatic and increasingly concerned with absence and nothingness, with many of the poems serving as allegories of sorts of the poetic process itself. This turn to self-reflexivity in the poetry is characteristic of Mallarmé's later work in both verse and prose, and is evident, for instance, in "Le Nénuphar blanc" ("The White Waterlily"), which was the first prose poem Mallarmé published after a hiatus in the genre between 1875 and 1885, and which was followed by poems such as "La Gloire" ("Glory") and "La déclaration foraine" ("The Fairground Declaration") in the following years. "Le Nénuphar blanc" traces the story of an idealized absence, a speaker who, rather than meeting up with a woman he had made a journey to see, returns instead with an imaginary flower culled from a dream. It concludes with this evocation of the speaker's experience:

> Si, attirée par un sentiment d'insolite, elle a paru, la Méditative ou la Hautaine, la Farouche, la Gaie, tant pis pour cette indicible mine que j'ignore à jamais! car j'accomplis selon les règles la manœuvre: me dégageai, virai et je contournais déjà une ondulation du ruisseau, emportant comme un noble neuf de cygne, tel que n'en jaillira le vol, mon imaginaire trophée, qui ne se gonfle d'autre chose sinon de la vacance exquise de soi qu'aime, l'été, à poursuivre, dans les allées de son parc, toute dame, arrêtée parfois et longtemps, comme au bord d'une source à franchir ou de quelque pièce d'eau. (Mallarmé 2002–3: 101)

> [If, attracted by the feeling of something different, she appeared—the Meditative or Haughty one, the Shy or Forward one—too bad for the ineffable face I will always not know! For I accomplished the maneuver according to the rules: I extracted myself, turned around, and followed the curve of the river, carrying with me like a noble swan's egg, from which flight will never arise, my imaginary trophy, which will never fill with anything but the exquisite vacancy of itself, that every woman, in summertime, on the pathways of her park, likes to pursue, arrested perhaps for a long time by some water, or by some stagnant pool.] (Mallarmé 2007: 36)

In "La Déclaration foraine," the poetic subject recounts a journey to a fairground with a female companion, in a style that contrasts with the rustic landscape through which he is traveling. The first sentence invites us into a textual labyrinth of sound and silence floating between the painting of the scene and the poet's interior world:

Le Silence! Il est certain qu'à mon côté, ainsi que songes, étendue dans un bercement de promenade sous les roues assoupissant l'interjection de fleurs toute femme, et j'en sais une qui voit clair ici, m'exempte de l'effort à proférer un vocable: la complimenter haut de quelque interrogatrice toilette, offre de soi presque à l'homme en faveur de qui s'achève l'après-midi, ne pouvant à l'encontre de tout ce rapprochement fortuit, que suggérer la distance sur ses traits aboutie à une fossette de spirituel sourire. (Mallarmé 2002–3: 93)

[Silence! It is certain that beside me, as in a dream, stretched out to the rocking of the coach under whose wheels dies an interjection of flowers, any woman, and I know one who can see through this, would exempt me from proffering a single vocable: to compliment her aloud on her inquiring outfit, almost an offer of self to the man whose favor the afternoon draws to a close, would only imply compared to all this fortuitous closeness, a certain distance from her features ending in a dimple that turns into a witty smile.] (Mallarmé 2007: 27)

The reader is drawn into decoding the action of the scene, which involves the poetic subject witnessing a spectacle inside a fair tent which is presented in the prose poem under the guise of Mallarmé's own sonnet "La chevelure vol d'une flamme. . ." ("The hair the theft of fire. . ."), an enigmatic verse poem that stages a woman tossing her hair, a gesture by which she "casts rubies on doubt's dark night" (Mallarmé 2007: 30) ["semer de rubis le doute qu'elle écorche" (Mallarmé 2002–3: 96)]. What is staged in the poem is thus poetry itself, as its relation to the external world is both posited and called into question by the appearance of this "vivante allégorie" (Mallarmé 2002–3: 97) ["living allegory" (Mallarmé 2007: 30)].

To examine the rise of the prose poem in later nineteenth-century France is thus to engage with the history of poetry and poetics more broadly in this period, since, increasingly, the development of the genre is inextricably linked to new developments in poets' understandings of their role, which they articulated not only in prose poetry but also in the verse poetry which all the poets I have considered here continued to write along with their prose poems, and also in their letters and essays. Prose poetry thus represents for these poets a unique opportunity to work on language, to reinvent it in such a way that it is capable of revealing something hitherto unknown about itself or about the world and our way of seeing or conceiving it; acts of creative destruction can yield new kinds of creation. Baudelaire establishes points of both continuity and rupture with the lyric tradition in verse within his prose poems, in a collection of heterogeneous texts that invite us to reimagine modern poetic subjectivity in a sometimes violent urban environment and to carve a new place for irony in the poetic encounter. Rimbaud seeks to push language to its limits in order to craft new ways of seeing and new intensities of experience that the reader is drawn to share with the poet through the experience of reading the poet-seer's text. And Mallarmé often stages poetry itself within the prose poem, reorienting poetic subjectivity in a complex web of relations between poetry and the world from which it springs. Working at the limits of language while all the time maintaining a relationship, even if only of opposition, to the poetic world that comes before implies the risk of failure. The perceived failure of the poetic experiment is what may perhaps have driven Rimbaud to abandon poetry, but there is at the same time victory in terms of the productive ways in which prose poetry forces us to reconsider what poetry has meant, and what it can continue to mean in the face of the breakdown not only of traditional poetic forms and meters but also of the coherence of the world in which modern subjects understand themselves to dwell. If, in its beginnings, the prose poem was what one critic has called a "(non-) genre . . . paradoxical . . . dependent on a nearly nonexistent reception" (Vincent-Munnia 2003: 565), the prose poem goes on to become an important space of negotiation of subjectivity in and through language given form, in a play of similarities and differences, of continuities and ruptures with what has come before.

Notes

1. The rate at which the prose poem went from a seldom-discussed genre in the time before Baudelaire to a central element in developments in poetry in the later nineteenth century may be gauged, for instance, by this remark in Joris-Karl Huysmans' 1884 novel *À Rebours* [*Against the Grain*]: "En un mot, le poème en prose représentait, pour [le protagoniste] Des Esseintes, le suc concret, l'osmazome de la littérature, l'huile essentielle de l'art" (Huysmans 1978: 222) ["In a word, the prose poem represented, for [the protagonist] Des Esseintes, the concrete sap, the osamazome of literature, the essential oil of art"].
2. These trace their lineage back to the seventeenth century in works such as Fénelon's *Télémaque*. See Bernard 1959: 15. For a series of essays on the French prose poem from 1750 to 1850, see Vincent-Munnia et al. 2003.
3. Unless otherwise noted, all translations are my own.
4. The poem can be found in Baudelaire 1975–6: 1,309–11.
5. For studies of the intersection of the formal and political implications of irony in Baudelaire's prose poems, see Stephens 1999 and Scott 2005.
6. For more on this canonization, see Leroy 2001: 155–60.
7. For a now-canonical deconstructionist reading of these pairs of verse and prose poems, see Johnson 1979.
8. All translated passages from Rimbaud are from Fowlie's bilingual edition revised by Whidden (Rimbaud 2005).
9. As Bernard puts it: "Thus we can say that from Rimbaud date at once a new poetic *attitude*, implying a metaphysical revolt against our fixed and rationalized universe, and a new poetic language, the instrument of that revolt" (Bernard 1959: 211).
10. André Guyaux notes the echo in his edition of Rimbaud's *Œuvres complètes* (Rimbaud 2009: 977 n. 2).
11. For more on this, see Bernard 1959: 295–9.

Works Cited

Baudelaire, Charles (1975–6), *Œuvres complètes*, Vol. 1, ed. C. Pichois, Paris: Gallimard.
Baudelaire, Charles (1997), *The Parisian Prowler*, trans. E. K. Kaplan, Athens: The University of Georgia Press.
Bernard, Suzanne (1959), *Le poème en prose de Baudelaire jusqu'à nos jours*, Paris: Nizet.

Breunig, LeRoy (1983), "Why France?," in M. A. Caws, and H. Riffaterre (eds), *The Prose Poem in France: Theory and Practice*, New York: Columbia University Press, pp. 3–20.
Friedrich, Hugo (1974), *The Structure of Modern Poetry*, Evanston: Northwestern University Press.
Huysmans, Joris-Karl (1978), *À Rebours*, Paris: Flammarion.
Johnson, Barbara (1979), *Défigurations du langage poétique*, Paris: Flammarion.
Leroy, Christian (2001), *La poésie en prose française du XVIIe siècle à nos jours*, Paris: Champion.
Mallarmé, Stéphane (2002–3), *Œuvres complètes* (2002–3), Vol. 2, ed. B. Marchal, Paris: Gallimard.
Mallarmé, Stéphane (2007), *Divagations*, trans. B. Johnson, Cambridge, MA: Belknap.
Rimbaud, Arthur (2005), *Complete Works, Selected Letters: A Bilingual Edition*, trans. Wallace Fowlie, updated and revised by S. Whidden, Chicago: University of Chicago Press.
Rimbaud, Arthur (2009), *Œuvres complètes*, ed. André Guyaux, Paris: Gallimard.
Scott, Maria (2005), *Baudelaire's* Spleen de Paris: *Shifting Perspectives*, London: Routledge.
Stephens, Sonya (1999), *Baudelaire's Prose Poems*, Oxford: Oxford University Press.
Vincent-Munnia, Nathalie (2003), "Conclusion: Le poème en prose comme genre?," in Natalie Vincent-Munnia, Simone Bernard-Griffiths and Robert Pickering, *Aux origines du poème en prose français*, Paris: Honoré Champion, pp. 557–71.
Vincent-Munnia, Nathalie, Simone Bernard-Griffiths and Robert Pickering (2003), *Aux origines du poème en prose français*, Paris: Honoré Champion.

2

Impressionism and the Prose Poem: Rimbaud's Artful Authenticity

Aimée Israel-Pelletier

The *Salon* of 1866 was a watershed moment in discussions of modernist art. By focusing the attention of visitors and critics on what was absent from the *Salon*, as opposed to what was on display there, *Salon* critics helped articulate the principles of this new art. Zola wrote in his review of that *Salon* that the Jury had deliberately excluded modern artists:

> C'est dire que le jury n'a pas voulu des toiles fortes et vivantes, des études faites en pleine vie et en pleine réalité . . . De haut en bas, de long en large, vous pouvez regarder: pas un tableau qui choque, pas un tableau qui attire. On a débarbouillé l'art, on l'a peigné avec soin; c'est un brave bourgeois en pantoufles et en chemise blanche . . . Cette année, le jury a eu des besoins de propreté encore plus vifs. Il a trouvé que l'année dernière le balai de l'idéal avait oublié quelques brins de paille sur le parquet. (Zola 1991: 99–101)

> [It is clear the Jury has rejected forceful and lively paintings, paintings that are full of life and breathe in the air of reality . . . From top to bottom, left to right, you can see for yourself: not one shocking painting, not one painting that draws your attention. Art has been cleaned up, washed and groomed with a fine tooth comb; it is stiff like a good old *bourgeois* in slippers and a white shirt . . . This year, the Jury had even greater needs for cleanliness. Its broom went after the few straws of idealism it had forgotten to pick up the year before.][1]

Art, Zola felt, had to reflect modern life or else be relegated to the sidelines in the safe spaces reserved for elites and bores. The new artists, the Impressionists *avant la lettre*, saw themselves first and foremost as avant-garde revolutionaries battling against conventional aesthetics which promoted the finished effect, the tableau, and rules of perspective. In contrast, modernists sought to loosen rigid forms and break up smooth surfaces as a way of evoking the liveliness, multiplicity and edginess of modern life. Impressionists exhibited an acute distaste for old forms. To signal their radical aesthetics, they produced works that were unmistakably not of the old *look*. Zola, a poet himself before his ambitions turned to the novel, saw modern artists in a unique position as the shapers of the new aesthetics. But he could not imagine poets responding in kind. Baudelaire could. He had already written "Tableaux parisiens" (1861), published the "Peintre de la vie moderne" (1863) and composed the prose poems that made up the *Petits poèmes en prose* (1862–9). Mallarmé, also, was able to imagine a new kind of poetry that responded to contemporary reality. Mallarmé was the author of eleven prose poems published in the *Parnasse Contemporain* in 1866.

It is notable, I think, that neither Zola nor Rimbaud were satisfied with what Baudelaire and Mallarmé had produced in their efforts to *renew* and turn poetry around. It is clear that Baudelaire was not radical enough for Rimbaud. He famously accused him in the *voyant* letters of being too timid in matters of formal innovation and criticized him for staying in a "milieu trop artiste," of being too much an artist (Rimbaud 2009: 348).[2] A decade after the 1866 review, Zola's position was unchanged. He expressed dismay at what he believed to be the sad state of poetry. In the 1870s, in a series of articles written in *Le Messager de l'Europe*, *Le Voltaire* and *Le Figaro*, Zola addressed the state of contemporary poetry. The essays were later collected and published under the title *Les Poètes contemporains* (Zola 1909: 408). In these essays, Zola expressed the dismal state of poetry in even more disparaging words than he had done in the *Salon* reviews. In this, he was reflecting the opinion of many at the time who believed that since 1848 poetry had declined and become irrelevant. Flaubert fantasized about a "prose poétique" ["poetic prose"] that would replace poetry. Zola claimed that if poetry was failing so miserably it was because it was no longer able to address the new sensibility being nurtured by the bustling contemporary landscape. Poetry simply looked and felt antiquated. He was convinced that the future of poetry was bleak because the new generation of poets were not interested in the subject of modern life, "le terrain de l'époque" ["the contemporary landscape"] (PC, 408). They were overly concerned with form at the expense of subject matter, as he put it. In their attentiveness to form they had killed poetry. Zola goes a step further. He suggests that poetry may itself be inherently unsuitable for the representation of modern life: "D'ailleurs, si la prose a une souplesse qui lui permet de devenir l'outil par excellence de nos civilisations modernes, la poésie est d'essence stationnaire" ["It is a fact that prose is supple, this makes it an ideal form of expression for our modern societies, whereas poetry is essentially a stationary form"] (PC, 405). Literary, personal and social revolutions needed open, experimental and prodigious forms; poetry, as Zola saw it being written, simply could not embody and transmit this voracious, erotic and positivistic élan (PC, 410). Zola faults principally Gautier for taking poetry down the wrong path. Gautier, Zola writes, was the first to work form like a goldsmith, producing still and frozen poetry (PC, 408), and Mallarmé, Mendès and Leconte de Lisle weakened poetry further by introducing peculiar theories:

> Avec des théories si étranges, le mouvement que les Parnassiens voulaient déterminer, était à l'avance frappé de mort. Ce ne pouvait être là qu'une fleur artificielle qui se fanerait vite, parce qu'elle ne poussait pas dans le terrain de l'époque. (PC, 408)

> [With such strange theories, the Parnassian movement was struck dead before it could even develop. It is like an artificial flower destined to wilt away for failing to take root in the soil of its epoch, a poetry out of step with the times.]

In Zola's sharply worded opinion, the Parnassians were "out of their minds." He writes about Mallarmé: "C'est chez lui que toute la folie de la forme a éclaté. Poursuivi d'une préoccupation constante dans le rythme et l'arrangement des mots, il a fini par perdre conscience de la langue écrite" ["In his work, form falls into madness. Constantly preoccupied with the rhythm and arrangement of words, he has lost touch with written language"] (PC, 409). And again: "L'esthétique de M. Mallarmé est de donner la sensation des idées avec des sons et des images. Ce n'est là, en somme, que la théorie des Parnassiens, mais poussée jusqu'à ce point où une cervelle se fêle" ["Mr. Mallarmé's aesthetics is to give the sensation of ideas by means of sound and images. To put it bluntly, this is nothing more than the theory of the Parnassians pushed to the brink of madness"] (PC, 409). The first spoiler of poetry according to Zola was Baudelaire, whom he accused of introducing a "dark palette" to poetry. This darkness suggested a penchant for self-degradation, pessimism and horror. These features, Zola was certain of it, were exercising a nefarious influence on younger poets like Verlaine, "a victim of Baudelaire" (PC, 409). Zola admired Verlaine's lighter and brighter palette, just the kind of effects Zola was recommending for poetry to help it save itself from itself.

The prose poem was not an obscure genre when Rimbaud was writing the poems of the *Illuminations*. The *Illuminations* were, however, the most radical experiments in poetic prose of their time. They ushered in a distinctly different *look* and *feel* for poetic experience. The *Illuminations*, more than anything Baudelaire or Mallarmé had written, took Parisian literary circles by storm because they had radically altered the look of poetry beyond effacing line breaks, edge rhymes and meter, as had been done previously. In a more dramatic way, the *Illuminations* produced unexpected effects of spontaneity, strikingness and flatness, the very hallmarks of Impressionist aesthetics. As with Impressionist art, the prose poems of the *Illuminations* looked radically different and required that they be addressed differently. Zola was right when he suggested that, to accomplish the needed revolution in poetry, "il suffit qu'un poète de génie invente la nouvelle langue poétique. L'obstacle est la forme à trouver" ["one needs a poetic genius to invent a new poetic language. But the difficulty lies in finding the form it would take"] (PC, 412). His concluding remarks in the same essay bring sharply into focus Rimbaud's project in the *Illuminations*:

> C'est pourquoi j'imagine que le grand poète de demain devra commencer par faire table rase de toutes les esthétiques qui courent les rues à cette heure. Je crois qu'il sera profondément moderne, qu'il apportera la note naturaliste dans toute son intensité. Il exprimera notre monde, grâce à une langue nouvelle qu'il créera. (PC, 413)

> [This is why I believe that the great poet of tomorrow will have to begin from scratch by wiping out all the aesthetic movements fashionable today. I believe he will be deeply modern, that he will strike the Naturalist note in all its intensity. He will express our world, thanks to a new language which he will create.]

Les Poètes contemporains stresses the need for formal innovations and calls for a poetry to rival the accomplishments of Impressionist art. Rimbaud accomplished many of the directives of *Les Poètes contemporains*: he had dismantled Romantic and Parnassian poetics, parodied the weaknesses indicated by Zola and proposed a new, more radical form of poetic expression: an aesthetics in the spirit of the *voyant* letters and "Ce qu'on dit au poète à propos de fleurs" ("What Is Said to the Poet Concerning Flowers").[3]

When Impressionists sought to defend their work, they appealed to the importance of authenticity, the "direct treatment of the thing" (Pound, cited in Perloff 1981: 45). Similarly, the idea that poetic verse is prone to inflate the importance of message contributed to their view that, in contrast to verse, prose poetry was the best way to represent the self and the world. Nineteenth-century epistemology hinged on the awareness that knowledge of the world was subject to point of view and that point of view was not stable. It was also understood that external phenomena depend upon the method of observation of the perceiving subject. There were no independent objective criteria for judging reality. To understand the real, one relied on individual experience. This is the paradigm that informs Impressionism. It was an article of faith of the new art forms that representations of modernity were necessarily uncertain and provisional because the poet's and the painter's consciousness and perceptions of the world were such. Accordingly, Impressionists defined their aims in terms that highlighted instability, changeability, the fractured and provisional nature of what they took to be characteristic of modern life. This is what Rimbaud means by *poésie objective*, a poetry of external phenomena that implicates the poet's way of seeing. The provisional then becomes a metaphor for modernity and the signature of Impressionist poetics. Jules Laforgue explains:

> Même en ne restant que quinze minutes devant un paysage, l'oeuvre ne sera jamais l'équivalent de la réalité fugitive, mais le compte-rendu d'une certaine sensibilité optique sans identique à un moment qui ne se reproduira plus identique chez cet individu . . . L'objet et le sujet sont donc irrémédiablement mouvants, insaisissables et insaisissants. (Laforgue 1988: 172)

> [Even by staying only fifteen minutes in front of a landscape, the work will never be the equivalent of fleeting reality, but rather the account of a certain unique optical sensitivity taking place at a particular moment that will no longer be identical in this individual . . . The object and the subject are therefore irremediably shifting, elusive and unaffecting.]

The self, nature and the social environment are elusive and always subject to change. "Je est un autre" ["I is another"]. Change makes it difficult to fall back on the past for models and ready-made formulas: "libre aux *nouveaux*! d'exécrer les ancêtres: on est chez soi et l'on a le temps" ["The *young* are free to disregard their ancestors. We are at home and time is on our side"] (italics in text; Rimbaud, 343). What made Impressionism revolutionary was that it formalized a way to imagine the world and the self as most alive and most authentic at moments of change. It was the understanding, implicit in its forms, that all meanings are provisional and that the provisional was desirable. Rimbaud finds in the prose poem a vessel where Impressionist aesthetics can work as a stimulant to his creative production and to his reader's speculative and interpretive faculties. Just as Impressionist art threw away classical training with its emphasis on "correct" drawing and its valuation of historical topics and mythology as appropriate subject matter for art, so too the prose poem and Rimbaud's experiments in the *Illuminations* left in the dust line verse, rhyme schemes, strict meter, and other constraints.

After they broke the rules, the challenge for the Impressionists was to create an identifiable look, a new look to replace the old. The new look had to express the freedom recently gained. Rimbaud's *Illuminations* is such a work. We can attest to the fact that Impressionist painters shared a certain *look*, such as the lighter palette, the looser brushstrokes, stunning effects, a predilection for effects of light and a resistance to absorptive effects. We can also speak about their general aims and procedures. What brings the Impressionists together is a set of values regarding the representation of modern life by means of formal qualities that embody those values. The Impressionists were fascinated by the new, that is, by new social formations, new social freedoms, new technologies, the increasing accessibility of popular leisure, entertainment and travel. And even when they did not buy into it, like Degas, they did make it the subject matter of their work. Or, as in Manet, they problematized the modern by quoting the past alongside it. Around modernity then they created a set of expectations that put faith in the new and held it above other values like tradition, conventions and the art forms of the past. Impressionism took it as a given that artistic practice had to change to respond to this changing material reality. Women, men, and institutions could be seen trying to figure out what it meant to live in a time of expanding opportunities and shifting relationships. The Impressionists could also agree that artistic expression needed to be truthful. And they understood that truth in representation was a matter of subjective vision, temperament and point of view. All this can be observed in the *Illuminations*.

Quite apart from its privileging of modernity as subject matter, literary Impressionism is a writing practice and a relationship to language. For these writers, words hang loosely, their referent always approximate. The belief that language had authority to fix meaning appears to be unsustainable in the face of rapid social change. And the valorization of point of view over epistemological certainty and stable centers of consciousness further undermines the view of language as fixed and reliable. But this looseness between words and their referents presents the Impressionist poet with opportunities to use language to explore consciousness and the world. The authority once attributed to language is delegitimized. Language becomes the object of the poet's *will*. But also, and significantly, a *will* that is tested and tried by language. Any power the poet might have had in the past to fix meaning, draw relationships and shape affect is now less secure.

By the time he is writing the *Illuminations*, Rimbaud seems to have come to terms with the fact that while he can still turn language on and off, as in "je suis maître du silence" (Rimbaud 2009: 177) ["I am the master of silence"], he can also engage spectacularly with it. The looseness inherent in language and perception have become opportunities for extroverted play. The fragment is an Impressionist trope and the prose poem its playground, so to speak, one that Rimbaud exploits relentlessly in the *Illuminations*. Fragmentation, incompletion, the disembodied eye and mobility are the structural underpinnings of his representational practice. Freed from the rules of versification, language and the self are opened up to fresh evocations of the world, perceptions, sensations, feelings, and affect. The management of that freedom is at the heart of individual styles. It explains in part how it is that painters as different as Monet and Degas, Renoir and Manet could be grouped together as Impressionists and still remain distinctly different from one another. We can say the same for Rimbaud, Mallarmé, Verlaine and Proust, who, in different ways, and in some cases not all, can indeed be said to have produced Impressionist works.

It is precisely because of its experimental nature and because it was the site of heated debates that contemporary discourse on Impressionism is important to consider in an attempt to grasp what it was and how it applies to the prose poem in its different iterations. When we study the lexicon used in the contemporary press, we find that it was not the painters themselves who established the parameters of the discourse on Impressionism. Rather, it was the reviewers and the public, both those favorably disposed and those who were not. Impressionist art responded to that discourse and sought to advance itself in reaction to it. Impressionism was a discourse as well as a practice. The discourse helped frame the way the art was perceived, how it would be recognized and how it might be put into practice. I have singled out key topoi useful in discussing Rimbaud's Impressionism. These follow on Michael Fried's discussion of Impressionism, which I have adapted to the literary text (Fried 1996). Impressionist paintings and texts can be said to display the following in various degrees: (1) the effect of incompletion or of the *ébauche*; (2) a new *look* to represent the new reality, "strikingness"; (3) the appearance of flatness, in the figurative sense; (4) the representation of movement. Other effects, like the representation of effects of light, air and atmosphere, follow from these.

The *ébauche*—the Provisional and Spontaneous

The *ébauche*, or the sketch-like appearance of Impressionist paintings, was one of the most scandalous and "bizarre" aspects of Impressionism to supporters of the art establishment, for whom a painting's "polished" and "finished" look was a mark of its "quality." They saw the *ébauche* as an impertinence and as a slap in the face to traditional aesthetic values. The words critics used to qualify these features of Impressionism, and most particularly the *ébauche*, suggest a loosening of rigor, ineptitude and moral laxity. Critics used expressions like "non-distingué," "inachevé et superficiel," "le lâché," "mode lâché," "esquisses lâchées," "rognures d'atelier" (Lecomte-Hilmy 1993: 34–5) ["undistiguished," "unfinished and superficial," "slovenly," "stylistic looseness," "wild sketches," "studio scraps"]. We would agree today, as did contemporaries, that the *ébauche*'s effect of informality was in fact what was most original in Impressionism. The *ébauche* is best understood by comparison with the tableau. In contrast to the effect of closure desired in the tableau, it manifests incompletion, as well as spontaneity, improvisation and expressiveness. As the ultimate and complete work, the *ébauche* suggests a disinclination to fix and bring closure, thus stressing the experimental nature of Impressionism.

Applied to writing, the *ébauche* translates into verbal and visual jottings loosely connected to each other. The fragments, bits and pieces of sense, are offered to the reader for possible interpretation. Rimbaud's "Jeunesse" ("Youth"), for example, is composed of scenes from a past the poet seems to not have processed but that he has grouped under these subtitles: Dimanche ("Sunday"), Sonnet, Vingt ans ("Twenty Years Old"); any coherence we find is based on what our interpretive appetite brings to the table and how we interpret the seemingly random descriptions. The poet's halting and harried consciousness comes up with more things than it can possibly compose and organize. We are invited to take what is necessary, to stake out our position with respect to the overwhelming given. Were it not for the titles, it would be difficult to imagine what we might say about them or think. The *ébauche* served Rimbaud as a way to express more authentically than he had in previous works both his enthusiasm for modern life and his cynicism and uncertainty. This should not surprise us. Modernity raised issues that could best be handled in a form that allowed for ambivalences, uncertainties and the shattering experience of the new. In the last two years of his poetic career, starting around mid-1873, in the *Illuminations*, we see a poet who neither fully embraces nor adamantly distances himself from the myths of modernity. The *ébauche* is a metaphor for open, unresolved, multiple and unstable states of affairs and states of mind. It is a metaphor for undecidability and uncertainty.

A Striking New *Look*

The novelist and art critic Edmond Duranty writes in 1876: "Nous voilà loin des anciennes habitudes, je veux dire des habitudes d'il y a quarante ans, où le bitume ruisselait à flots" ["We are far from old habits, I mean habits from forty years ago, where asphalt flowed freely"]; instead, the new painting, he continues, " à pour but de frapper les yeux des foules par des images saillantes, textuelles, aisément reconnaissables en leur vérité denuées d'artifices, et de nous donner exactement les sensations de ce que nous voyons dans la rue" (Durenty 1946: 22) ["strikes our eyes, quite literally, with images easily identifiable as plain truths devoid of artifice. The new painting reproduces in us the exact sensations we have when we see the same scenes in the street"]. The *Illuminations* is made up of striking poems that relate the experience of the poet as he encounters a reality so utterly disorienting that the best way to represent it would be to produce forceful phrases and images able to match his highly turned-on attention. In these poems, Rimbaud puts a premium on excess and the disruption of expectations. He creates unpredictable juxtapositions, as in "La cascade sonne derrière les huttes d'opéra-comique" ["Waterfalls ring out behind the opéra-comique booths"] (Rimbaud, 308). He multiplies strange associations, as in "on joue aux cartes au fond de l'étang" ["They are playing cards at the bottom of the lake"] (Rimbaud, 311). He stages provocative and enigmatic *mises en relief* (direct phrases that call on the reader to engage in the interpretive process), as in "trouvez Hortense" ["find Hortense"] (Rimbaud, 314) and "j'ai seul la clef de cette parade sauvage" ["I alone have the key to this crazy circus"] (Rimbaud, 294). He puts together images that demand our attention by their coloration, their mobility, their ongoing emergence, as in most poems in the *Illuminations*, like "Métropolitain" ("Metropolitan") and "Promontoire" ("Promontory"), for example. He describes scenes containing a richness of detail, as in "Fleurs" ("Flowers"): "Des pièces d'or jaune semés sur l'agate, des piliers d'acajou supportant un dôme d'émeraudes, des bouquets de satin blanc et de fines verges de rubis entourent la rose d'eau" ["Gold coins sown on agate, mahogany pillars holding up an emerald dome, bouquets of white satin and delicate stalks of rubies surround the water-rose"] (Rimbaud, 306). Excess and dislocation are the hallmark of the *Illuminations*, and they have a direct bearing on how we process, or are unable to process, the meaning of the poems. The stunning effects of the poems disrupt (interrupt, distract and confuse) the way we process information. And because the poems do that, the reader's attention is arrested on their surface a bit longer than in conventional texts. What we are left with as readers, helped to a great extent by the titles of individual poems, is the striking effect that is not easily (if at all) assimilable. Strikingness, to use Michael Fried's term, is a *mise en relief* that extends beyond the local effect to the poem as a whole. "Après le déluge" ("After the Flood"), "Fleurs" ("Flowers"), "Barbare" ("Barbarian"), "Soir historique" ("Historic Evening"), like countless other poems, are striking because they provide in excess and with intensity details that will not be assimilated, that "resist absorption." The visually stunning effect is a dominant trait of Impressionism and the quality that the Impressionist painters, starting with Manet, most deliberately aimed for. It is a trope that implicates others, like the *ébauche*, flatness, movement and instantaneity. Its aim is to seize immediately the beholder's attention and deny it the absorptive convention of a more reassuring art. Alongside the *ébauche*, its signatory strikingness blocks meaning and denies closure. What would previously have been considered unacceptable excess becomes an artistically valid mode of intensity. By courting unintelligibility, keeping attention on the surface of the work and multiplying and intensifying the sense of dislocation we experience as readers, Rimbaud ensures that interpretation will circulate and not settle.

Flatness: This *Is* All There Is

Contemporary and present-day critics of Impressionism have called attention to the effect of flatness in Impressionist works. With Manet, a period begins when the value of visual depth and three-dimensionality in painting is put into question and progressively undermined. In literature, dimensionality translates into modes, figures and registers. So, although we can speak of a literal flattening, as in a leveling of difference and evenness of tone and register, I find it more useful to use flatness figuratively. Technically, flattening in the poems is eventuated by the *ébauche*, by an act of incompletion that problematizes meaning. It is also brought about by the effects of strikingness. Flatness is the resistance to and the denial of depth. This resistance to depth is fundamental to the *Illuminations*. These poems privilege the experiences of the senses and of the real made manifest in the poem's visual density and, by extension, its semantic thinness. Flatness, like stunning images, detains the reader on the surface. Dazzled and dazed by visual effects and uncertainties, the reader is not inclined or able to seek out a coherent and stable meaning.

I submit the poem "Ouvriers" ("Workers") as an example that lends itself to a discussion of flattening as a formal matter rather than a thematic one. In many respects, the poem presents a straightforward depiction of a working-class couple, a man and a woman, on their day off. They are taking a walk in the outskirts of the city. The man is dissatisfied with his life and his companion, Henrika, is content. As readers we sort of grasp the setting and the feelings both of these characters are experiencing. But there are details that problematize this coherence and make the picture hang rather oddly and loosely. The first paragraph beginning with "O cette chaude matinée de février" (Rimbaud, 189) ["Oh! that warm February morning"] and the part that begins approximately with "O l'autre monde" ["Oh! that other world"] to the end of the poem are juxtaposed to the description of the promenade with Henrika in the *banlieue* (suburban area). The lyrical and the prosaic stand side by side. Several questions jump to mind when we read this. Do we know the difference between Sud, or South (with a capital letter) and sud, or south (with a small letter)? What do we understand as being the "*chère image*" ["*beloved image*"]? Is it Henrika? Is it a memory back in the man's, the poet's, childhood? And what about the warm weather in the month of February? Where are we? Is the answer to be found in some geographical location or is it a metaphorical evocation of a place somewhere beyond everything we know here on earth? As I said, the poem works; we have a general idea and a general effect of what is taking place and how the poet feels and what he wants—in any case, we know what he does not want. Yet, there are these questions and they are prominently exposed. I think we would be right to suspect that these questions are not appropriate, relevant and useful. The Impressionist poet would ask us to see in them signs of uncertainty and ambivalence, a state of mind inherently associated with the experience of living in modern times. Flatness would be this resistance to the possibility of meaning, that is, of depth. Flatness is both a fact of modern life and an inability to cut through complications. To experience flatness, as the poet does and as we are asked to, is to be stuck on the surface of a consciousness barely able to see where it might be made whole. Henrika invites the poet to look at "de très petits poissons" ["teeny-tiny fish"], that is, to read this promenade as a nice outing. He resists and turns his attention elsewhere. He turns perhaps to "la ville, avec sa fumée et ses bruits de métiers" ["the city, with its smoke and factory noises"] or to "l'autre monde, l'habitation bénie par le ciel et les ombrages!" ["that other world, that dwelling blessed by heaven and by shade"] Is this the countryside? Even in his dream of an elsewhere, the city and the countryside, work and leisure, stand side by side. They are unable to be integrated into a coherent whole. The lead character in this prose poem tells his story in an odd and mystifying patchwork of prosaic and lyrical expression that does not add up. This we might well take as an Impressionist effect, and as a distinctly modern state of affairs.

Moving, Morphing, Light and Air . . .

The art historian Meyer Schapiro wrote that the paintings of the Impressionists, especially in the 1860s and 1870s, "possess, for the most part, an imagery of the environment as a field of freedom of movement and an object of sensory delight in everyday life" (Schapiro 1997: 19). One of the most beautiful poems in the *Illuminations* is "Ornières" ("Ruts"). It exemplifies Impressionist aesthetics in that it evokes a scene of popular entertainment using tropes of strikingness, flatness, instantaneousness and speed. Its flatness does not derive from a view of the popular as uninspiring and uninspired, as is the case in "Ouvriers." It arises from the poet's visual *parcours* which compels us to stay focused on a brilliant surface that is boldly delineated and suggestive. "Ornières" creates the same sort of cut-out effect we see in Manet's *La Musique aux Tuileries* (1862) or *La Plage à Boulogne* (1868). The poem suggests movement, speed and instantaneousness and not the plodding effort of a carriage. Like "Ouvriers," "Ornières" takes place in the *zone* between city and country, a recurrent topos in Impressionism. The poet identifies the scene as "une pastorale suburbaine" (Rimbaud, 161), a place not far from the city because populated by the "élément démocratique" ["democratic element"]. Made up of men and children, it is a scene of popular leisure. The poet is describing something like a circus or a merry-go-round. These were usually located just outside the city. Unlike "Ouvriers," the poet lavishes attention on a scene freshly stumbled upon. This world, the poet tells us, is even more astonishingly magical than any the poet could have imagined. He stays on it and, as if in one prolonged breath and glance, takes the measure of what unfolds in front of his eyes. As in "Les Ponts" ("Bridges"), the scene fills his eyes and his senses. Unlike "Les Ponts," however, it does not end suddenly in a blinding flash, "Un rayon blanc, tombant du haut du ciel, anéantit cette comédie" ["A white ray coming down from the sky obliterates this comedy"]; rather, it runs out of breath, as it were, with the last words, "bleues et noires" ["blue and black"]. Movement and speed are evoked thematically. They are also captured by the rhythm and flow of rich alliterations and the repetition of entire words like "et" ["and"] and "enfant" ["child"]. Yet, apart from the first sentence, there is no absorptive pull. Instead, we and the poet are struck by the brilliance of the surface. Popular entertainment, leisure and the simple pleasures of everyday life outdoors are captivating and somewhat edgy, uncertain. In "Ornières," the dash that introduces the concluding and disquieting line, "Même des cercueils sous leur dais de nuit dressant les panaches d'ébène" ["Even coffins under dark canopy with ebony colored plumes"], introduces a note of darkness and doom not befitting this wild celebratory pastoral. This line, a *mise en relief* of sorts, is an emblematic representation of the unfinished and the problematization of coherence.

Rimbaud's taste for effects of mystery and mystification is paradoxically another sign of this resistance to depth. These *mises en relief* are a literary device for flattening meaning by denying accessibility. At the end of "Après le déluge" ("After the Flood") we are told: "la Reine, la Sorcière qui allume sa braise dans le pot de terre, ne voudra jamais nous raconter ce qu'elle sait, et que nous ignorons" ["The Queen, the Witch lighting her coal in the earthen pot, will never tell us what she knows and what we do not know"] (Rimbaud, 290); in "Conte" ("A Tale"), he writes: "La musique savante manque à notre désir" ["The most subtle music falls short of our desire"] (Rimbaud, 293); in "Parade' ("Circus"), "J'ai seul la clef de cette parade sauvage" ["I alone hold the key to this wild circus"] (Rimbaud, 294); in "H," he exhorts us to find Hortense without providing as much as a hint about who it is and thus motivating all sorts of interpretations. These are only a few of the many other instances of Rimbaud's predilection for the secret, for blocking access to meaning. Unintelligibility is a provocation and a metaphor for the poet's own uncertainty. These questions are meant to remain unanswered. They incite a recognition of what it means to be modern. To be modern is to not have answers to the mysteries, uncertainties and contradictions of modern life. In the stunning images of "Enfance," the poet wraps his childhood in an air of mystery. Something like a hushed tone reigns as he shows the reader around the property and the spaces of his childhood and then tells us, in part II, what we have suspected all along, namely, that behind the walls and doors of these enclosures of this childhood there is actually "nothing" to see. We are told that "Les palissades sont si hautes qu'on ne voit que les cimes bruissantes. D'ailleurs il n'y a rien à voir là-dedans" ["The fences are so high that you can only see the tops of trees rustling in the wind. Anyway, there is nothing to see in there"] (Rimbaud, 291). Behind the dazzling surface of the words of the poem and behind the mysteries entertained by the poet for our curious attention, there is nothing to see. A prose poem like Rimbaud's can be striking and yet flat. Like Impressionist art it calls attention to itself and in the same beat signals that what you see is indeed all you get. Meaning is not in the forms. Rather it is suggested in the effects these forms have on sentient subjects. The very activity of reading is unstable and volatile. By offering interpretations in surplus, Rimbaud and the Impressionists dramatize the fact that, for some of us, fixed structures are repressive; they hold back, enclose, reduce possibilities, limit mobility, hamper freedom and reinforce the status quo. Impressionist literature, as does Rimbaud's poetry, subverts rigid linear thinking—and here I am thinking of works like Flaubert's *L'Education sentimentale* (*Sentimental Education*) and Proust's *A la recherche du temps perdu* (*In Search of Lost Time*), for example. It defies Cartesian logic and substitutes instead the looser forms of visual discourse. Rimbaud's *Illuminations* is Impressionist in part because it embraces modernity in all its uncertainties and because it shows little interest and seeks no consolation in the prospect of recuperating fixed and stable centers of coherence.

Banville, in his *Petit traité de poésie française* (*Handbook of French Poetry*) (1872), understood that it was important to begin "par faire table rase de tout ce qu'on a appris, et se présenter avec l'esprit semblable à une page blanche" ["by emptying one's mind of all that has been learned and be like a blank page"] (Banville 1881: 1).[4] But he did not turn his back on verse. In fact he tightened the grip on classical rules and categorically rejected prose poetry, as he writes: "Car il est impossible d'imaginer une prose, si parfaite qu'elle soit, à laquelle on ne puisse, avec un effort surhumain, rien ajouter ou rien retrancher" ["No matter how perfect a text in prose is, it is not impossible to imagine that, with the necessary effort, it can be improved upon"] (Banville, 6). Banville misses the point. Rimbaud would have known the *Petit traité*. His use of the prose poem in the *Illuminations* can be taken in part as an act of defiance in a rebellious defacement of the past and the conventions of poetry for which Banville stood. And, unlike Baudelaire, he invents a striking new *look*, the *ébauche* as finished work, privileges surface and flatness over depth, and dislocates and multiplies point of view, using series or ensembles—the "Villes" ("Cities") poems, for example—as ways to amplify and reflect differing perspectives. In this way, Rimbaud constructs a form and a style around principles of openness, circulation and a leveling of distinctions. Also, by turning contemplation outwards and into the world instead of reflectively on the form itself, as we detect in Baudelaire, the prose poem can be said with Rimbaud to exemplify the ideal form of the modern. By doing all this, Rimbaud's prose poem shows us, more forcefully than does Baudelaire's, that the prose poem is not an empty vessel whose function is to negate lyricism. It stands for something. It forges a new—call it subversive—way of writing about the world that is unencumbered by established rules of how one looks at things, writes and reads. In Rimbaud's hand, the prose poem is a radical form and a new-informed way of writing and of thinking about the self and the world.

Notes

1. All translations are my own.
2. Further page references to this work are placed in parentheses in the text and abbreviated Rimbaud, plus page number.
3. I argued Rimbaud's relationship to Impressionism more fully in my book *Rimbaud's Visual Poetics*.
4. Further page references to this work are placed in parentheses in the text and abbreviated Banville, plus page number.

Works Cited

Banville, Thédore de (1881), *Petit traité de poésie française*, Paris: Bibliothèque de l'Echo de la Sorbonne.

Duranty, Edmond (1946), *La Nouvelle Peinture. Avant propos et notes par Marcel Guérin*, Paris: Librairie Floury.

Fried, Michael (1996), Manet's *Modernism or The Face of Painting in the 1860s*, Chicago and London: The University of Chicago Press.

Israel-Pelletier, Aimée (2012), *Rimbaud's Visual Poetics. Vision and Visuality*, Cardiff: University of Wales Press.
Laforgue, Jules (1988), "L'Impressionnisme. Mélanges posthumes," in *Jules Laforgue. Textes de critique d'art. Réunis par Mireille Dottin*, Lille: Presses Universitaire de Lille.
Lecomte-Hilmy, Anne (1993), *La Formation du vocabulaire de la peinture impressionniste*, Toronto: Canadian Scholar's Press.
Perloff, Marjorie (1981), *The Poetics of Indeterminacy. Rimbaud to Cage*, Princeton: Princeton University Press.
Rimbaud, Arthur (2009), *Œuvres complètes*, édition établie par André Guyaux, Paris: Éditions Gallimard, 2009.
Schapiro, Meyer (1997), *Impressionism. Reflections and Perceptions*, New York: George Braziller.
Zola, Emile (1906), "Les Poètes contemporains," in *Œuvres complètes Illustrées de Emile Zola. Œuvre critique*, Tome Premier, Paris: Charpentier.
Zola, Emile (1991), *Écrits sur l'art*, Paris: Editions Gallimard.

3

Novalis' *Hymnen an die Nacht* and the Prose Poem *avant la lettre*

Jonathan Monroe

To speak of a word as *avant la lettre* does not necessarily imply a fixed origin; it does imply a history of usage.[1] Thus, for example, Breton credits Apollinaire with inventing the term *surréalisme*, though he himself would doubtless take credit, as well he should, for making the word current. To make a list, then, as Breton goes on to do, of "surréalistes avant la lettre" is to provide a retrospective patterning of literary history with reference to a term which earlier was, even if known, not familiar, even if "invented," not in common usage. In the case of the prose poem, a genre which should be of much interest to contemporary genre theory not only because of its current wide dissemination but also because it is a genre with a relatively short history, the term *avant la lettre* must have reference to Baudelaire, for it is his collection of *Petits poèmes en prose*, his naming of them as such, that establishes the currency of the prose poem within literature. If Aloysius Bertrand also has a strong claim to being, as Max Jacob called him early in the twentieth century, the true inventor of the modern prose poem, still it must be acknowledged that without Baudelaire, Bertrand's most important reader, the historical value attributed to his *Gaspard de la Nuit* would at the very least be severely diminished. It is not my aim here, however, to consider the emergence of the modern prose poem with Bertrand and Baudelaire in France, where it acquires currency as a literary genre for the first time. Nor do I intend to argue that Novalis' *Hymnen an die Nacht* constitutes the "real" or "true" origin of the prose poem. Rather, I hope to show that, just as Friedrich Schlegel's project of *Universalpoesie* provides a broad horizon within which to situate the conditions and limits of the prose poem's possibilities, so the *Hymnen an die Nacht* provides an early framework within which to consider the emerging conflict between prose and poetry, a conflict that defines one of the prose poem's principal concerns from Bertrand and Baudelaire to the present.

Suzanne Bernard, in her otherwise peerlessly exhaustive study of the French prose poem, does not make mention of *Hymnen an die Nacht* as a precursor of the prose poem, though she does emphasize the importance of literary translation, especially from verse into prose. In particular, the prose translations of folk ballads, as also of Edward Young's *Night Thoughts* and fragments of Macpherson's *Ossian*, are credited with a significant role in the prose poem's emergence (Bernard 1959: 24–47). Young and Macpherson were translated not only into French, but into German as well. A journal entry confirms Novalis' familiarity with Young's *Night Thoughts* at around the time he began working on the *Hymnen an die Nacht*, and he would have had contact with Ossian through Goethe's translations at the end of *Werther*. Yet Novalis' *Hymns*, with their alternation of prose and verse, figure in the history of the prose poem in a qualitatively different way than either of these other works.

Hymnen an die Nacht is one of the first works in which the relation between prose and poetry is not only conceived but presented in antinomial fashion. Prose, the way the world is, and poetry, the way it might, could or should be, are set against each other in terms of two modes of printing—the one *en bloc*, the other *en vers*. In this sense, one would have every right to consider *Hymnen an die Nacht* as a prose poem *avant la lettre*, except for the fact that the modern prose poem as it emerges with Baudelaire has, so to speak, "internalized" the conflict between prose and poetry, prose and verse, into prose alone. What *Hymnen an die Nacht* does is not so much typify the future form of the prose poem, for the most part all prose, as provide a kind of early battleground for its opposing terms in which some of the earliest fragments of prose poems make their appearance only to be "conquered" by fragments of rhymed metrical verse. As the first issue of *Atheneum* introduces the problematic of a fusion of genres, of prose and poetry and of the poetic and the speculative within the framework of *Universalpoesie* as fragment, so the last issue of *Atheneum*, with the publication of *Hymnen an die Nacht*, develops this problematic in explicitly formal terms which anticipate equally strongly the prose poem's characteristic concerns.

The strategy of dividing up and distributing segments of "ordinary" prose (as for example from a newspaper) into lines resembling free verse in order to demonstrate that an act of attention does or does not result which one may call "literary" was described by Barbara Smith as early as 1968 as "only too familiar" (Smith 22). Much less discussed is the effect of reworking free verse into prose, as Novalis did between 1797 and 1800 in the two versions of *Hymnen an die Nacht* which have been left us. Composed roughly fifty years before Whitman's *Leaves of Grass* and seventy years before the free verse poems in Rimbaud's *Illuminations*, the handwritten draft of *Hymnen an die Nacht* attests to Novalis' experimentation with free verse, just as the final draft printed in *Atheneum* reveals his even bolder experimentation with a form resembling the modern prose poem. Both innovations serve, in their respective versions, as the ground on which is figured the rhymed metrical verse of *Hymnen an die Nacht*. With slight alterations and some omissions, each section printed in free verse in the handwritten draft is replaced in that of *Atheneum* by prose, while the rhymed metrical verse remains, again with slight variations, constant from one draft to the next. The effect of the change from free verse to prose is to intensify the figure/ground relationship considerably. This intensification is not only highly appropriate to the poem's thematic concerns generally, but also lends a visible formal dimension to the poem's conflict between the world of prose and the world of poetry, the real world and the ideal world, which would be lacking had the prose passages been left in free verse.

Free verse may be seen as a kind of intermediary form between poetry, understood conventionally as rhymed and/or metrical verse, and prose ("free verse is born of a desire to render classical verse more supple and to bring it closer to the rhythms of prose" [Bernard 1959: 592]). It is a form with which Rimbaud also experimented, but its role in his poetic innovation is clearly subordinate to that of the prose poem. The latter implies a revolutionary break with conventional verse as opposed to the compromise gesture of free verse. If free verse is an attempt to "reason" with the world of prose as well as the world of conventional verse, to mediate as it were diplomatically between them, the prose poem is a genre of provocation; it sets the two worlds into direct contact with each other. Whether this proximity results in harmonic reconciliation or in explosive confrontation may vary considerably from writer to writer and from poem to poem. That *Hymnen an die Nacht* begins in prose and ends in verse, after what may be described as a protracted, if "foreordained" struggle between the two, indicates more than a formal preference on Novalis' part. The distribution of prose and verse among the various sections exemplifies the thematic development of the poem as a whole, and is rigorously integrated into it.[2]

In a short tribute to his friend Novalis, Friedrich Schlegel writes, "Nicht auf der Grenze schwebst du, sondern in deinem Geist haben sich Poesie und Philosophie innig durchdrungen . . ." ["You are not one of those who hovers at the threshold: in your spirit, poetry and philosophy have deeply penetrated one another"] (R.I., 493).[3] As for Schlegel, so also for Novalis, the fusion of poetry and philosophy was a major concern. "*Schlegels Schriften*," says Novalis, "sind lyrische Philosopheme . . . Der lyrische Prosaist wird logische Epigramme schreiben" ["Schlegel's writings are lyrical philosophemes . . . The lyrical prosaist will write logical epigrams"] (B., 462/105). Yet just as Schlegel's fragments seem more appropriately considered as speculative, philosophical discourse, so Novalis' *Hymnen an die Nacht* would seem strangely situated were one to consider them other than as poetic discourse, first and foremost. Indeed, for Novalis, poetry is the key to philosophy, its goal and significance: "Wenn der Philosoph nur alles ordnet, alles stet, so lösste der Dichter alle Bände auf" ["If the philosopher only orders everything and sets everything upright, the poet is the one who would break all bonds"] (L.F., 533/32); further, "Die Poesie ist das echt absolut Reelle. Dies ist der Kern meiner Philosophie. Je poetischer, je wahrer" ["Poetry is the true absolute real. This is the core of my philosophy. The more poetic, the more true"] (T.F., 647/473).

The *allerfreuliche Licht* ["all-joyful light," p. 130], the sun, which opens *Hymnen an die Nacht* is, as Jacques Derrida has observed, one of the most frequent of metaphors, common both to poetic and to speculative/philosophical discourse. It is even possible to claim, as does Derrida, that "the orbit of the sun is the trajectory of metaphor" per se:

> Such metaphorology, when it moves into the area of philosophy, is destined always to find the same—the same *physis*, the same sense (sense of being as presence or, *what comes to the same*, as presence or absence), the same circle, the same fire of light that is manifest or hidden, the same turning of the sun. When we search for metaphor, what could we find *other* than this return of the same? For are we not searching for resemblance? And when we try to determine the dominant metaphor of a group which interests us because of its capacity to gather things together, then what else should we expect but the metaphor of domination augmented by that power of dissimulation which allows it to escape domination in its turn, what else but God or the Sun? (Derrida 1974: 68)

What else, in *Hymnen an die Nacht*, but the sun as a double metaphor?—in the first instance for that dominant framework against which Novalis' poetic discourse situates itself, that Hymn of Hymns to the sun as the metaphor of human reason, Enlightenment philosophy; in the second instance the sun as metaphor for the Son, Christ, whose religion the sun of the Enlightenment threatened to extinguish (a motif treated by Novalis in *Christenheit oder Europa*). "Wer keinen Sinn für Religion hätte," says

Novalis, "musste doch an ihrer Stelle etwas haben, was fur ihn das wäre, was andern die Religion ist" ["Whoever had no taste for religion would have to have something in its place which would be for him what religion is for others"] (P.S., 563/53). *Hymnen an die Nacht* presents a kind of hymn to onto-theology, yet its concern is less explicitly with the *Verschmelzung* [fusion], as for Schlegel, of poetry and philosophy than with that of poetry and religion. The latter is described by Novalis, in his notes to Schlegel's *Ideen*, as *ein umgebendes Meer* ["a surrounding sea"] (R.I., 489). What has been said recently of the early romantic view of the artist in general is especially true for Novalis: "l'artiste n'assure la fonction de médiateur (ou d'éducation) que dans l'unique mesure où, en lui, poésie et philosophie trouvent à se concilier ou a 'fusionner'. Pour autant, donc, qu'il est un homme religieux" (Lacoue-Labarthe and Nancy 193) ["the artist is only able to assure his function of mediator to the precise extent that, in him, poetry and philosophy manage to be reconciled or to 'fuse' with one another. Inasmuch, that is, as he is a religious man"]. While Schlegel typically values most the interpenetration of poet and philosopher, Novalis holds the reunification of poet and priest above all:

> Dichter und Priester waren im Anfang Eins, und nur spätere Zeiten haben sie getrennt. Der ächte Dichter ist aber immer Priester, so wie der ächte Priester immer Dichter geblieben. Und sollte nicht die Zukunft den alten Zustand der Dinge wider herbeiführen?

> [In the beginning, poet and priest were one, and only in later times have they become separated. The true poet, however, is always a priest, just as the true priest has always remained a poet. And shouldn't the future give rise again to the old state of things?] (B., 441/71)

Thus, against the advice of Schleiermacher to entitle the work only *An die Nacht*, Novalis insists on *Hymnen an die Nacht*, the latter title suggesting from the outset the specifically religious/Christian dimension to be developed in the poem, without which it would be entirely other than it is.

Novalis is far from rejecting the Enlightenment metaphor of the sun as it stands for human reason. Man, he says, "ist eine Sonne—seine Sinne sind seine Planeten" ["is a sun—his senses are his planets"] (F.S., 573/130), and light is the "Vehikel der Gemeinschaft—des Weltalls—ist die echte Besonnenheit in der geistigen Sfäre nicht ebenfalls?" ["vehicle of community—of the universe—is the true presence of mind in the intellectual sphere not likewise?"] (T.F., 619/435). Yet Novalis will not stop here, content with the resemblance of man to the sun: "Wie wir, schweben die Sterne in abwechselnder Erteuchtung und Verdunklung" (T.F., 619/436) ["Like us, the stars are suspended in alternating illumination and eclipse"]. *Hymnen an die Nacht* emerges, not so much as a rejection of the visible, of what can be understood in the light of reason, as an attempted balancing of reason and unreason, the visible and the invisible, of life and death, presence and absence. The term "illumination," or "enlightenment," is one which resists the neat separation of kinds of discourse such as poetry, philosophy and religion. In contrast to merely additive knowledge in a fixed ground of knowing, illuminating knowledge helps us see connections among previously disparate domains of knowledge.[4] For the speculative thought of onto-theology and of Christianity, this implies the ongoing process of perceiving an underlying unity among similarities and differences. Thus, Novalis begins by acknowledging the principal source of illumination in the physical world, the sun. Following the title, this beginning comes as a shock. The presence of the sun, which alone opens up the marvelousness of the kingdom of earth even as it reigns over it, is also in this opening paragraph the presence of man. Not mentioned explicitly at this point in the poem is the Son of man, Christ, who is, however, implicitly present. The progress of the poem will be one in which the naming of Christ appears in increasingly specific terms, from the *König der irdischen Natur* and *himmlisches Bild* of the first section, through the *dürren Hügel* of section 3, the *heiligen Grabe* and *Kreuz* of section 4 and the *Sohn der ersten Jungfrau and Mutter* of section 5, to *Jesus, dem Geliebten* among the poem's final verses ["king of earthly nature ... heavenly image ... barren hill ... holy grave ... cross ... Son of the first virgin and Mother ... Jesus, the beloved"]. As during the night the sun is buried in memory only to be followed by its simultaneous presence and absence at dawn when it appears as itself in the morning sky, so the present sun of man is to be replaced by the past and future Son of man, the reign of Christ over men. This progress corresponds to the movement of the poem from its beginnings in prose (secs. 1–3) through the middle sections' alternations of prose and verse (sec. 4–5) to its verse conclusion (sec. 6). Just as the speaker's high praise of the sun creates a shock following the title *Hymnen an die Nacht*, so he surprises the reader a second time by turning "Abwärts ... zu der heiligen, unaussprechlichen, geheimnisvollen Nacht" (131) ["Down ... to the holy, unspeakable. mysterious night"]. The strategy is a highly effective one, creating what may aptly be called a "conceptual need" (Ricoeur 1977: 296). In this case the conceptual need created is for a reunification of day, the absence of which is felt all the more intensely because of the praise lavished upon it, with night, which is praised even more highly. The separation of day from night could be described in terms of the speculative thought of onto-theology as a split between the philosopher's sun and the theologian's Son. The latter is presented here in the beginning not in the absolute presence of his true self, but as night, the absence of philosophy. Mediating between them in order to bring about the desired reconciliation is the poet, the *Sänger* who emerges only in section 5 coincident with Christ's birth. Before this reunification can take place, however, the speaker, and with him the reader, must move through a poetic sequence that presents what Derrida calls, with reference to philosophical metaphor, "a detour in (or in view of) the reappropriation, the second coming, the self-presence of the idea in its own light" (Derrida 1974: 55).

The sun separates because it delineates; its blessing, like that of metaphor, is ambiguous. If it permits us to see similarities, it also allows for the play of difference which in its negative aspect will be perceived as separation. For the thinker or poet of an onto-theological perspective, such as Novalis, this separation is, although painful, only a surface phenomenon. This is why the onset of night makes the day appear in retrospect as "arm und kindisch" ["poor and childish"] (133); beneath the poverty of objects, "der funkelnde, ewigruhende Stein, die sinnige, saugende Pflanze, und das Wilde, brennende, vielgestaltete Tier" ["the sparkling, ever resting stone, the sensible, sucking plants, and the wild, burning. animal of many forms"] (133), and comprehending as well the world of men, "der herrliche Fremdling mit den sinnvollen Augen" ["the magnificent alien with the meaningful eyes"] (131), which is revealed by the light of day, the night seems to provide evidence of a fundamental unity. In the night difference is less perceivable; hence the feeling of the infinite that contrasts so sharply with the day's sense of limits, definitions. In the absence of the sun things draw toward a state of nondifferentiation, that absence of difference which would promise its obverse—the absolute presence of self to self, self to others and self to world. In the night is the welcome chaos of origin and of the return to origin, "deine Wiederkehr—in den Zeiten deiner Entfernung" ["your return—in the days of your distance"] (133), as well as the end of sexual separation in union with the loved one, "zarte Geliebte—liebliche Sonne der Nacht" ["gentle lover—lovely sun of night"] (133). This return to origin in the reunion with the loved one is, however, at the end of the first section, a thing hoped for, a promise rather than an accomplished fact.

Thus, section 2 begins, "Muss immer der Morgen wiederkommen?" ["Does morning always have to come again?"] (133). Morning is here suggestive of the world of work, that "Unselige Geschäftigkeit" ["accursed industry"] in which everything is separated and measured: "Zugemessen ward dem Lichte seine Zeit; aber zeitlos and raumlos ist der Nacht Herrschaft" ["The light has its allotted time: but night rules over time and space"] (133). The world of work is the world of prose, of separation and difference, the way things are rather than the way things might be, of unity and identity; it is the present and the threat that the future will continue as the same. Given this state of affairs, the function of the third section is to give background as to how things got the way they are. Thus the past tense dominates for the first time: "Einst da ich bitte Tränen vergoss" ["Once, when I shed bitter tears"] (135). The personal pain of the speaker at the loss of his loved one is linked, still implicitly, to Christ's death on Calvary, *am dürren Hügel*. Yet this same hill becomes the place of a reversal comparable to the turning away from day to night in the first section. In contrast to the hard definitions of objects in daylight, the hill suddenly appears as a transparent cloud of dust, through which the loved one appears. Yet the promise implied by this vision is still not actualized in the real world: "Es war der erste, einzige Traum" ["it was the first, the only dream"] (135).

Section 4, with its beginning, "Nun weiss Ich, went der letzte Morgen sein wird" ["Now I know when the last morning will be"] (135), provides an answer to the question posed in the second section. Having indicated how the speaker arrived at the painful sense of separation in which he finds himself, as well as the promise of an end to that separation, the poem returns to the present and the possibilities of the future. The pilgrimage to the grave of the loved one, "zum heiligen Grabe, drückend das Kreuz" ["to the holy grave, hugging the cross"] (137), has served as a reminder of the promise of Christ's death. The present of the speaker, however, remains "das Treiben der Welt . . . wo das Licht in ewiger Unruh hauset" ["the bustle of the world . . . where the light lives in eternal unrest"] (137). Allowed a glimpse into "das neue Land" ["the new land"] (137), which will soon be heralded by the first appearance of verse in the poem, the speaker nevertheless cannot for the time being leave the obligations of the everyday world: "Noch wecks Du, muntres Licht den Münden zur Arbeit" ["Once again, bright light, you wake the weary to work"] (137). He performs his job as overseer faithfully:

> Gern will ich die fleissigen Hände rühren, überall umschaun, wo du mich brauchst—rühmen deines glanzes volle Pracht—unverdrossen verfolgen deines künstlichen Werks schönen Zusammenhang—gern betrachten deiner gewaltigen, leuchtenden Uhr sinnvollen Gang—ergründen der Kräfte Ebenmass und die Regeln des Wunderspiels unzähliger Raüme und ihrer Zeiten.

[I'll gladly stir hard-working hands, look round everywhere, where you need me—praise the full magnificence of your brightness—tirelessly pursue the beautiful coherence of your artificial works—gladly observe the ingenious running of your enormous shining clock—investigate the symmetry of forces and the rules of the miracle play of innumerable spaces and of their times.] (137)

Yet though he goes about his task "gladly," with lip-service paid to its "ingenious running," his heart is not in it. He remains true to the dream of the end of the separation of labor and love: "In mir fühl ich deiner Geschäftigkeit Ende—himmlische Freiheit, selige Rückkehr" ["Inside I feel an end to your industry"] (139). The way things are is not the way things have been or must be, as the speaker's recollection of Christ suggests: "Wahrlich ich war, eh du warst" ["Truly I was, before you were"] (139). The promise of Christ is also the promise of the end of the workaday world of prose. Hence, for the first time in the poem, verse appears. Yet as it ends section 4 the status of such a *Rückkehr* to the world of poetry, of rhymed metrical verse, is still uncertain:

> Ich lebe bei Tage,
> Voll Glauben and Mut
> Una sterbe die Nächte
> In heiliger Glut
>
> [I live by day
> Full of courage and faith
> And die at night
> In holy fire] (139)

Like the worker who returns home at the end of a grueling day to drown his sorrows, the speaker dreams of a better day to come which, however, turns out to be all too much like the day he has just spent. He is still in the world of prose, and this first appearance of verse provides only the drunkard's delusion of escape from it.

Naturprosa and *Kunstprosa*

As section 4 provides an answer to section 2, so section 5 returns, like section 3, to the past. At issue here, however, is less the personal situation of the speaker of that earlier section than the collective fate of mankind. It is in this, the longest section of the *Hymns*, that the struggle between the world of prose and the world of poetry-as-verse is carried out most directly. The conflict is not as simple as it may first appear, for the text actually presents two worlds of prose. One of these, to which the reader has been exposed throughout the first four sections, is the workaday world of the present, of what might be called, to use a term familiar to Novalis, *Kunstprosa*; the other, standing at the very origin of the world like an Eden from which we have been expelled, is that of *Naturprosa*. In the world of *Naturprosa*, there is no freedom or language as such: "Über der Menschen weitverbreitete Stämme herrschte vor Zeiten ein eisernes Schicksal mit stummer Gewalt" ["In olden times an iron destiny ruled over the widely scattered tribes of man with silent power"] (141). Yet this world is at least not one of tragic separation, as is the *Kunstprosa* which characterizes the modem period. Life in the age of *Naturprosa* is "ein ewig buntes Fest" ["an eternally bright celebration"] (43). In contrast to the poverty of objects and of the physical world in the modem age, a kind of enchantment and animation reigns over everything: "Flüsse, Bäumen, Blumen and Tiere hatten menschlichen Sinn" ["Rivers, trees, flowers and animals had human sense"] (141). The principal difficulty is that this world never really existed: "Ein Gedanke nur war es, Ein entsetzliches Traumbild" ["it was only an idea, a terrible vision"] (143). And then there is death. That the tale of death's appearance is written in verse may be seen as paradoxical at first, for death, one would think, belongs to the world as it is, the world of prose. Yet this interpretation does not do justice to the dual function of verse as it is used here by Novalis. First of all verse, the division of thought into lines of unequal length, functions here as a disruption of the original *Traumbild*, suggesting difference as well as similarity. Its artifice marks an end to the mythical *Naturprosa* which was only *Ein Gedanke*. Secondly, although death, like the sun, separates, delineating the difference between the animate and the inanimate and thus ushering us into the world of *Kunstprosa* which is our own, it anticipates the Son, Christ, whose death will be an end to death.

Following the three verse stanzas which have introduced the reader to death, but also to the as yet "unenträtselt ... Nacht / Das erste Zeichen einer fernen Macht" ["undeciphered ... Night / The first sign of a distant power"] (143) which will be realized in the triumph of the new sun/Son, Christ, over death, of poetry over prose, the poem brings us back to the world of *Kunstprosa*. As Christ's birth contains within it the seed of his death and his triumph over death, no sooner is the world of *Kunstprosa* born than it begins coming to an end: "Zu ende neigte die alte Welt sich" ["The old world drew to a close"] (145). The old world here is not to be confused with the world of the *Traumbild*, the *Naturprosa* which was never more than a dream. Rather, it is the world of *Kunstprosa*, the end of which was proclaimed by the hour of Christ's birth but which has been waiting ever since to be realized by the second coming. Once again the reader is back in the world of separation, loneliness, the banishment of Christ and, which is the same for Novalis, poetry.

In the first section, even though the world of objects and of plants and animals was presented as separate from that of men, the breathing of the above-quoted "sparkling, ever resting stone" functions as a sign of former animation and nondifferentiation from the living. In section 4, by contrast, the last signs of the impoverished life of objects are extinguished. While in the *Traumbild* there was an eternally bright and colorful celebration but no language as such, in the modem world there is language, but it is inadequate to connect the inner and the outer worlds. In the *Traumbild* it is as if words were characterized by a transparency which allowed unmediated access to the world of objects. In the real world of the modern era which is that of *Kunstprosa*, however, if a never-before-known freedom of language from the world of objects is acquired, it is only at the cost of the loss of language's transparency: "Einsam und leblos stand die Natur ... Wie in Staub and Lüfte zerfiel in dunkle Worte die unermessiliche Blüte des Lebens. Entflohn war ... die Phantasie" ["Nature stood alone and lifeless ... the measureless flower of life fell apart in dark words as in dust and breezes. Imagination ... had fled"] (145).

As Novalis writes elsewhere: "Die Zeit ist nicht mehr, wo der Geist Gottes verständlich war. Der Sinn der Welt ist verloren gegangen. Wir sind beym Buchstaben stehn geblieben" ["The days are gone when the mind of God was knowable. The meaning of the world has been lost. We have remained stuck at the letter"] (*A.*, 594/316). In order to restore the transparency of absolute presence of self, of the world and of God, some mediation is necessary:

> Nichts ist zur wahren Religiosität unentbehrlicher als ein Mittelglied, das uns mit der Gottheit verbindet. Unmittelbar kann der Mensch schlechterdings nicht mit derselben in Verhältniss stehn. In der Wahl dieses Mittelglieds muss der Mensch durchaus frey seyn.
>
> ['Nothing is less dispensable for true religiosity than a middle term that connects us with godhead. Without mediation, man simply cannot measure up to it. In the choice of this middle term, man must be completely free.] (*B.*, 441–2/74)

The selection of a means of mediation must remain free, yet clearly, for Novalis, poetry is the privileged mode of discourse, the linguistic mediation *par excellence*. Poetry is "Darstellung des Gemuths—der innern Welt in ihrer Gesamtheit. Schon ihr Medium, die Worte deuten es an, denn sie sind ja die aüssere Offenbarung jenes innern Kraftreichs" ["Presentation of the spirit—of the inner world in its entirety. Already in its medium, words suggest it, for they are the outer manifestation of that inner realm of power"] (*F.S.*, 650/553). Words are the outer manifestation of the inner person, yet in the age of *Kunstprosa* they cannot be other than inadequate. Thus the sense for poetry "hat viel mit dem Sinn für Mystizism gemein . . . Er stellt das Undarstellbare dar. Er sieht das Unsichtbare, fühlt das Unfühlbare" ["has much in common with the feeling for mysticism. It presents the unpresentable. It sees the invisible, feels the unfeelable"] (*F.S.*, 685/671). Language, Novalis says, ist "für die Philosophie . . . nicht das rechte Medium der Darstellung" ["not the right medium of presentation for philosophy"] (*F.S.*, 573/124). In the world of prose, language in its various modes is ambivalent:

> Selbstentaüsserung ist die Quelle aller Erniedrigung, so wie im Gegentheil der Grund aller ächten Erhebung. Der erste Schritt wird Blick nach Innen, absondernde Beschauung unsers Selbst. Wer hier stehn bleibt, gerät nur halb. Der zweyte Schritt muss wirksamer Blick nach Aussen, selbstthätige, gehaltene Beobachtung der Aussenwelt seyn.
>
> [Self-expression is the source of all degradation, as well as, on the contrary, the ground of all true elevation. The first step is to look inward, isolated contemplation of self. Whoever stops here, arrives only half-way. The second step must be to look effectively outward, spontaneous, prolonged observation of the outer world.] (*B.*, 423/24)

Only with the birth of the Christ-child, according to the narrative logic of Novalis' *Hymns*, will the gap between the outer and the inner worlds, difference and similarity, the visible and the invisible, between absolute signification in absolute unfreedom (*Naturprosa*) and meaningless freedom (*Kunstprosa*), be breached.

Christ emerges in the *Hymns* as the poet-mediator who brings "Unerschöpliche Worte" ["inexhaustible words"] (147), the *Sänger* who offers "Ein tröstlich Zeichen in der Dunkelheit" ["a comforting sign in the darkness"] (147). Just so, like the tune whistled by the little boy in the dark, the Singer's eight lines of verse appear preceded and followed by two longish blocks of prose. The return to prose is necessary because Christ must die in order to be born again. Thus, the speaker says, "In entsetzlicher Angst nahte die Stunde der Geburt der neuen Welt . . . Schwer lag der Druck der alten Welt auf ihm" ["The hour of birth of the new world neared in terrible fear . . . The weight of the old world lay heavily on him"] (147). It is tempting here to understand the word "Druck" not only as in "the weight of the old world," but also as in "the print of the old world," for as we have seen, the birth of the new world has been figured all along in verse. Thus the "hour of birth" of the new world, which is really, for Novalis, the world of Christ, of poetry-as-verse, will be marked by the banishment of prose and the final triumph of rhymed, metrical verse at the end of section 5 and in the final section's coda, "Sehnsucht nach dem Tode" ["Longing for Death"].

The banishment of prose is heralded in the text by the removal of the stone from Christ's (prefiguring the loved one's) "dunkeln Grabe" ["dark grave", p. 149]. Stone, as symbol of the world of objects at its most opaque and inanimate, must be "Gehoben" (p. 149), raised by the death and rebirth, the reanimation of Christ necessary for poetry to reappear. Also a symbol of separation, the stone must be penetrated to get through to the invisible unity of things which Christ embodies in the poem. Christ's resurrection announces the renewal of poetry, when words and things will once again be adequate to each other, "Unerschöpflich" ["inexhaustible"].[5] Once again, however, the time of such a renewal is postponed and the poem returns abruptly, still in the world of prose, to the present:

> Noch weinen deine Lieben Tränen der Freude, Tränen der Rührung und des unendlichen Danks an deinem Grabe . . . Worte sagen, wie vom Baum des Lebens gebrochen; sehen dich eilen mit voller Sehnsucht in des Vaters Arm, bringend die junge Menschheit, und der goldnen Zukunft unversieglichen Becher.
>
> [Still your loves cry tears of joy, tears of emotion and of infinite thanks at your grave . . . say words, as if broken from the tree of life; see you hurry full of longing in the Father's arm, bringing the young human race, and the golden future's inexhaustible cup.] (149)

The "golden future" which echoes the golden age of the past remains like it, *Ein Gedanke*, unrealized in the present. The closest we can get to it in the world of the present is suggested among the closing lines of the final prose passage, where the most regular non-verse rhythms of the poem are located: "und Tausende zogen aus Schmerzen und Qualen, voll Glauben und Sehnsucht und Treue dir nach" ["and thousands drew near you in sorrow and pain, full of longing, loyalty and faith"] (149). These one and a half lines of prose, set off as they are only by dashes from the surrounding text, are easily read as two lines of verse, the first a full, the second an approximate alexandrine. As such they anticipate the new age of poetry-as-verse to come which is yet, for the present of *Schmerzen und Qualen*, more a matter of *Glauben*, *Sehnsucht* and *Treue*, still more dream than reality.

The seven stanzas of rhymed metrical verse which conclude the fifth section, figuring the triumph of poetry over prose and of eternal life over death, also attempt to unify the personal with the collective, similarity with difference. Christ's resurrection, the renewal of language as poetry, is also the resurrection of humanity, which is to be realized as for the first time: "Gehoben ist der Stein— / Die Menscheit ist erstanden" ["The stone is removed—humanity is arisen"] (149). Not only are human beings imaged for the first time in the poem as at one with themselves and at one with their language in the absolute presence of their own voices which Christ, as poet/mediator, has restored to them, but the separation of sexuality is also overcome. Replacing the *Schattenleben* ["Shadow life" (50)] of sexual difference is a new androgyny, a "non-generic unity," in which man and woman are one. Schlegel's comment, "Wenn Christus wiederkommt, wird er Eins sein mit Maria" ["If Christ were to come again, he would be one with Mary"] (Schlegel 221), is echoed in Novalis' *Hymns* by the poem's conclusion. Yet despite the formal triumph of verse over prose and the positing of a non-generic unity which would end all separation, thematically the poem affirms that the world of prose is still with us:

> So manche, die sich glühend
> In bittrer Qual verzehrt
> Und dieser Welt entfliehend
> Nach dir sich hingekehrt . . .
>
> [So some, consumed
> In bitter, burning pain
> Have fled this world
> And turned to you . . .] (151)

Maria, the "you" of the last verse here, is, like rhymed metrical verse itself, like Christ, like religion, a turning away from the present, from the modern world of prose and its separations of labor and love to a world which does not exist: "Gestrost das Leben schreitet / Zum ewgen Leben hin" ["Confident life strides forth / To gain eternal life"] (153). Although the verse conclusion of section 5 speaks of a life where there is "keine Trennung mehr . . . das volle Leben" ["no more separation . . . the full life"] (153), poetry remains unrealized in life. The affirmation of a new world of poetry in verse carries its own reminder that verse is itself a form of separation, of line breaks in contrast to the even distribution and unified appearance on the page of prose.

"Sehnsucht nach dem Tode," the final and only titled section of *Hymnen an die Nacht*, is also the only section in the poem entirely in verse. As such it confirms the triumph of the world of poetry over the world of prose which is one in the poem with the triumph of Christ over death. Having begun in prose with praise of life and of the day, the poem ends in verse with a return to the night of death which the title had initially affirmed. Whether the poem as a whole achieves a truly dialectical resolution of contraries, first and foremost in the formal alternation of prose and verse, remains doubtful, however. Although the poem concludes with praise of the night as the carrier of the seed of the new day, its final note is one of longing, *Sehnsucht*, not of the actualization of poetry in everyday life: "Was sollen wir auf dieser Welt / Mit unsrer Lieb and Treue" ["What's there for us to do on earth / With all our love and faith"] (155). The harmonies of the final section's rhymed metrical verse, sounding somewhat wooden against the background of the more supple and interesting (because less predictable) prose, find no echo in the real world. To the prose complaint of the section preceding, "Einsam und leblos stand die Natur" ["Nature stood alone and lifeless"], the verse of section 6 can only offer confirmation: "O! Einsam steht und tiefbetrübt / Wer heiss und fromm die Vorzeit liebt" ["He who passionately, piously loves / Past ages stands alone and deeply sad"] (155). Its measured rhythms provide no final consolation for the way things are: "In dieser Zeitlichkeit wird nie / Der heisse Durst gestillet" ["The hot thirst never will be stilled / In this life here on earth"] (155). The fullness of absolute presence which Christ's coming had promised turns out still to be its opposite: "Das Herz ist satt—die Welt ist leer" ["The heart is full—the world is empty"] (157). As the *Traumbild* or world of *Naturprosa* presented at the beginning of section 5 never existed, so the promise of the second coming has yet to be fulfilled in reality: "Ein Traum bricht unsre Banden los / Und senkt uns in des Vaters Schoss" ["A dream breaks open all our bonds / And sinks us in the Father's womb"] (157). The hopeful androgyny implied by "süssen Braut / Zu Jesus, dem geliebten" ["to the sweet bride / to Jesus, the beloved"] (157), as also in "des Vaters Schoss" (the Father's lap or womb), is undercut by the final image of sinking in the last line as the dream is swallowed up by reality.

"What is called prose," says Novalis,

ist aus Beschränkung der absoluten Extreme entstanden—Sie ist nur ad interim da und spielt eine subalterne, temporelle Rolle. Es kommt eine Zeit, wo sie nicht mehr ist. Dann ist aus der Beschränkung eine Durchdringung geworden. Ein wahrhaftes Leben ist entstanden, und Prosa and Poesie sind dadurch auf das innigste vereinigt, und in Wechsel gesetzt.

[has arisen out of restriction of the absolute extremes—It is only there ad interim and plays a subordinate, temporal role. A time is coming when it will no longer be. For restriction has turned into penetration. A true life has arisen, and through this prose and poetry are most intimately united and set in alternation.] (L.F., 536/61)

As in Schlegel's *Universalpoesie* not only prose and poetry, the poetic and the speculative, but the three ages of Greek poetry as well, epic, lyric and dramatic, are to be melted together, *verschmolzen*, so also for Novalis, in what he refers to as *Universalgeschichte* ["Universal history" (L.F., 537/54)]. Yet Schlegel's understanding of history and of poetry, as also of how the fusion of genres is to come about, differs from that of Novalis in at least one decisive feature. This feature may be most clearly indicated by two opposing terms which occur frequently in their respective works—for Schlegel, *Universalpoesie* is first and foremost progressive; for Novalis, on the other hand, *Universalgeschichte* will be conceived of as a return. In the last section of the poem, shortly after three stanzas each beginning with the term, "Die Vorzeit" ["past ages"], the speaker sums up this attitude with the line, "Was hält noch unsre Rückkehr auf" ["what holds up our return"] (57). That the conflict between the present world of prose and the past world of poetry is decided for Novalis in favor of poetry-as-verse indicates an aesthetic of return which by and large turns its back to the present as well as to the future. The significance of having, not just metrical verse, but rhymed verse in *Hymnen an die Nacht* lies in this aesthetic of the harmonious return which rhyme, more than any other stylistic device, tends to enforce.

In contrast to Schlegel's *Universalpoesie*, the whole movement of the *Hymns* tends to be retrograde, from light to dark, differentiation to non-differentiation, prose to poetry, from the increasingly secularized world of the present to the religious past. A correspondence between a past and a future golden age is more or less explicit in both writers, but in Novalis the future resolution of contraries tends to be posited as a pure return to the past, with the present losing its significance as the place of struggle on which any resolution must be based. For Schlegel, by contrast, the present plays the more decisive role—it is the novel, not the epic, prose, not poetry (as verse) which provides the basis for *Universalpoesie*. Thus, in *Hymnen an die Nacht*, the old conventional form, verse, emerges victorious over the more contemporary form of prose. The formal struggle which Bertrand, Baudelaire, and Rimbaud each in his turn would decide in favor of prose, the printed medium of the modern age, is anticipated by Novalis briefly, brilliantly. Just as quickly, however, like the speaker turning "Abwärts . . . zu der heiligen, unaussprechlichen, gehimnisvollen Nacht" where the world lies "Fernab" ["far down and away"], Novalis turns away from this struggle to the security of a vanished age, that of the reign of Christianity, and to verse as its representative form. It is because both Christianity and verse come to seem increasingly anachronistic in the post-Enlightenment, post-revolutionary bourgeois world of the nineteenth century that *Hymnen an die Nacht* looks in retrospect like a rearguard attempt to resist the overwhelming "progress" of the modem world. It is in response to this challenge of the modem world and against the background of the hegemony of the novel among literary forms that the prose poem will be born. If, for Novalis, the world of prose is only here *ad interim*, as an ephemeral surface phenomenon, Bertrand, Baudelaire and the prose poets who come after them perceive it as a world that is here to stay. From the nineteenth century on, as Schlegel says, "Soll Poesie und Prosa gemischt, so muss das ganze 'offenbar' prosaisch sein" ["If poetry and prose are to be mixed, the whole must be 'manifestly' prosaic"] (*L.N.*, 114/1024).

As Lacoue-Labarthe and Nancy have pointed out, German Romanticism may be said to offer two fundamentally opposed critical gestures—the first that of Schelling and subsequently of Hegel involving the subject's *Aufhebung* through its own critical self-representation, the other the Schlegelian critique of the very possibility of such a self-recuperation (Lacoue-Labarthe and Nancy 1978: 378–83). Seen in relation to these two dominant orientations, Novalis's work clearly tends toward the former. Where Schlegel's *Athenäum* fragments articulate a prose critique of the notion that any individual subject, discourse, or genre may be undialogically cordoned off from its overdetermining others, the formal figuration of the return of Christ the singer-poet in the rhymed, metrical verse that concludes the *Hymns* gestures toward a wished-for restoration of the monological through the mediation of a single representative, redemptive, unifying, "poetic" voice. While the former exemplified the "first romanticism"'s turn to prose as the site of a necessary critique of the idealist subject and of poetry's subject-centeredness, the final decision of the *Hymns* to privilege poetry-as-verse over poetry-as-prose tends rather to confirm the more widespread popular image of Romanticism as the site not of a rigorous self-critique but of mere self-expression and self-affirmation. Since in fact, as Lacoue-Labarthe and Nancy have also pointed out (Lacoue-Labarthe and Nancy 1978: 37), Schlegel produced relatively little poetry compared to Novalis and to his own production of critical and theoretical texts, it is not altogether surprising that the latter view of Romanticism and of poetry should have gained wider currency. In any case, however regrettable this popular image might be of Romantic poetry—and indeed of poetry in general—as pure "lyricism," and however much writers and critics have fought against it, it has been a formative one not only for the popular imagination but also for those who have made a more serious commitment to reading and writing poetry from the nineteenth century through the surrealists and beyond (Lacoue-Labarthe and Nancy 1978: 287). It is largely with reference to this functional, historically-situated "mythology" or informing ideology of the "poetic" that the prose poem has carried on its dialogical struggle with the verse lyric, from Baudelaire and Rimbaud to the present.

Notes

1. This essay was originally published in the Spring 1983 number of *Studies in Romanticism* and is reproduced here with kind permission of the publisher. The essay subsequently appears as Chapter 2 in Part I ("Two Precursors") of *A Poverty of Objects: The Prose Poem and the Politics of Genre* (Ithaca: Cornell University Press, 1987).
2. Previous studies of the *Hymns* have tended either to overlook the formal strategy of the poem's division into prose and verse entirely or to treat it as arbitrary, merely incidental to theme and imagery, rather than seeing the integrity of these formal combinations to the thematic and imagistic dimensions with which they are so tightly interwoven.
3. The following abbreviations, followed by page and, where applicable, by fragment number, are used in the text to indicate works by Novalis: *Schnfien II—Blüthenstaub* = B.; *Logologische Fragmente* = L.F.; *Anekdoten* = A.; *Teplitzer Fragmente* = T.F.; *Schiften III—Randbemerkungen zu Friedrich Schlegel's "Ideen" (1799)* = R.I.; *Fragmente und Studien 1799–1800* = F.S. References to *Hymnen an die Nacht* are drawn from *Schriften I* and are indicated in the text by page number alone. Translation are mine, unless otherwise indicated.
4. My thanks go to Austin Quigley for this concise differentiation.
5. In a ten-line free verse stanza from the handwritten draft which is omitted in the *Athenäum* version, the absence of Christ is imaged in terms of the absence not only of poetry, but of speech altogether:

> Von ihm will ich reden
> Und liebend verkünden
> So lang ich
> Unter Menschen noch bin.
> Denn ohne ihn
> Was wär unser Geschlecht,
> Wenn sie nicht sprächen von ihm
> Ihrem Stifte, Ihrem Geiste.
> (S., 140)

> [I want to speak of him
> And lovingly proclaim his word
> So long as I'm
> Still here among men.
> For without him
> What would become of our kind,
> If we didn't speak of him
> Of our Author, our Spirit.]

These lines may well have been omitted in part because they speak of the salvation of poetry through the resurrection of Christ in such an unrhymed and prosy fashion, in contrast to the rhymed metrical verses which normally have this function in the poem. For Novalis, of course, Christianity is the sum of all religions: "Es giebt keine Religion die nicht Xstenthum wäre" ["There is no religion which would not be Christianity"] (F.S., 566/82). Without religion, poetry is drowned in the workaday world of prose.

Works Cited

Bernard, Suzanne (1959), *Le Poème en prose de Baudelaire à nos jours*, Paris: Nizet.

Derrida, Jacques (1974), "White Mythology: Metaphor in the text of Philosophy," trans. F. C. T. Moore, in *New Literary History*, Vol. 6, pp. 5–74.

Herrnstein Smith, Barbara (1968), *Poetic Closure*, Chicago: University of Chicago Press.

Lacoue-Labarthe, Philippe, and Jean-Luc Nancy (1978), *L'Absolu littéraire*, Paris: Seuil.

Ricoeur, Paul (1977), *The Rule of Metaphor*, trans. Robert Czemy, Toronto: University of Toronto Press.

Schlegel, Friedrich (1980), *Literarische Notizen 1897–1801*, ed. Hans Eichner, Frankfurt am Main: Ullstein.

4

Thyrsus and Palimpsest: De Quincey's Influence on Baudelaire's *Le Spleen de Paris*

Nikki Santilli

THE *Confessions of an English Opium-Eater* by Thomas De Quincey first appeared in France in anonymously translated fragments in *La Pandore* on 29 and 30 September 1827. These went largely unnoticed until an adaptation, *L'Anglais mangeur d'opium* by Alfred de Musset, appeared in 1828, becoming an immediate, popular success.[1] De Musset's editors suggest that Baudelaire was aware of this translation, but his dislike for de Musset's work prevented him from ever mentioning it.[2] Epistolary evidence shows that Baudelaire considered producing his own translation at the beginning of 1857. In July of that year he wrote to his mother:

> But I have jobs to do which cannot be done in a place without libraries, prints or galleries. First of all I must clear up the question of
> the *Aesthetic Curiosities*,
> the *Nocturnal Poems*,
> and the *Confessions of an English Opium-Eater*.
> The *Nocturnal Poems* are for the *Revue des Deux Mondes*: the *Opium-Eater* is a new translation of a magnificent author who is unknown in Paris. It's for the *Moniteur*. (Baudelaire 1973, I: 411)

"Poèmes nocturnes" was one of the working titles for *Le Spleen de Paris*, which is generally considered to be the first "authorized" collection of prose poems because Baudelaire introduces and discusses the form in his Preface.

The first six prose poems from that collection to appear were published in 1857. Meanwhile, *Un mangeur d'opium* appeared in *Revue contemporaine* on 15 and 31 January 1860 before being collated with articles on wine and hashish to produce the single work, *Les Paradis artificiels opium et haschisch*, in spring of that year. It is clear, therefore, that Baudelaire was developing his prose poems concurrently with his work of translating and editing the *Confessions*.

Charles Baudelaire was a man in very similar circumstances to De Quincey's. Threatened, continually, by creditors and an overbearing mother, he also tended to procrastination, which in turn led to missed deadlines and angry exchanges with his publishers. In the light of these similarities, Baudelaire's rewriting of the *Confessions* (which included parts of the *Suspiria*) also ran along comparable lines to the original compositions. Baudelaire's initial plan to produce a translation of the complete *Confessions* was thwarted mainly by his publisher's restrictions on the space allowed for the work in the *Revue contemporaine*.[3] This problem was soon compounded when Baudelaire became aware of the existence of *Suspiria de Profundis* and decided to include it in his translation. Finally, he resigned himself to a version of the *Confessions* (which included the *Suspiria*) that was part-translation, part-paraphrase/summary and, increasingly, an abridgement. The rendering of foreign works into translated fragments was, at that time, a favored method in France. Indeed, *une traduction* became a concession for original French works in the new and unfamiliar concise-prose format.[4] Baudelaire took this practice one step further. In his Preface to *Le Spleen de Paris*, Baudelaire claimed these were failed attempts to imitate Aloysius Bertrand's prose fragments, *Gaspard de la Nuit* (1842), themselves "translations" of paintings by Rembrandt and Callot.

It is immediately evident that Baudelaire retains most of the *Confessions*, sacrificing more of the *Suspiria*, probably because his aim appeared to be a tidying up of the original.[5] His utilization of the form of the *Suspiria* in the prose poem collection suggests that he regarded the original work as being overstretched in its accommodation of the contextual narrative that frames the visions. The re-edited *Confessions* was to form part of his own *Paradis artificiels*, an investigation into the whole subject of drug-taking, so digressions and footnotes are edited out in order to produce a discussion of the power and effects of opium: the work that De Quincey "intended" to write but ostensibly failed to realize. The result, inevitably, is a tighter construction where discrete biographical context is actually juxtaposed with the dreams. However, such editing also dangerously presupposes a volume of extraneous material and is in itself a statement on the status of De Quincey's texts as reducible and, moreover, requiring reduction. Baudelaire's treatment of the *Confessions* to create the text that it was "meant to be" assumes an inherent flaw in the original text and offers a problematic response in its correction.[6]

Ironically, Baudelaire is led, like De Quincey, into numerous apologies and statements of intention concerning the work as projected and what has been realized on the page. Indeed, the thyrsus image, a dry stick surrounded by flowering tendrils, which De Quincey uses to describe and explain his particular narrative style and which Baudelaire takes for the subject of one of his prose poems, is generally the only accredited influence of De Quincey on Baudelaire's prose poems and may have been included at a later date, and then only as a gibe against his publisher and an apology to his readers for having to omit the arguably organic and indelible digressions.[7] Elsewhere, Baudelaire describes De Quincey as "a dreadfully conversationist and disgressionist author" almost turning his meanderings into a profession (Baudelaire to Auguste Poulet-Malassis, Paris, 16 February 1860, in Baudelaire 1973, 1: 669). In fact, he found these aspects of De Quincey's idiosyncratic prose difficult to edit as severely as he was required. The thyrsus thus becomes a symbol of the crucial factor of abridgment that he finally achieved, and it was subsequently shifted away from De Quincey's extensive poetic prose to serve instead as a model for the relatively intensified prose poem:

> Straight line and arabesque, intention and expression, firmness of will, sinuosity of the word, unity of the aim, variety in the means, an all-powerful and indivisible amalgam of genius, what analyst would have the odious courage to divide and separate you? (Baudelaire 91, 84–5)

We can gain a deeper understanding of how the prose poem restrains the traditionally expansive tendencies of prose by examining Baudelaire's treatment of De Quincey's texts at this time, which undoubtedly helped him develop his "miracle of a form of poetic prose" for *Spleen de Paris*.

In Pursuit of a Starting Point

At the close of the original version of *Confessions of an English Opium-Eater* (1921), Thomas De Quincey pauses to contemplate the pain of birth: "Jeremy Taylor conjectures that it may be as painful to be born as to die: I think it probable: and, during the whole period of diminishing the opium, I had the torments of a man passing out of one mode of existence into another" (De Quincey 1890, III: 448).[8] This coupling of suffering and change introduces a leitmotiv to the *Autobiographical Sketches*, and the first of these, "The Affliction of Childhood," begins, conversely, with an emphasis on endings: "About the close of my sixth year, suddenly the first chapter of my life came to a violent termination . . . "*Life is finished!*" was the secret misgiving of my heart" (De Quincey 1853, I: 1; De Quincey 1890, I: 28).

With the first chapter of his life, and therefore his narrative, violently lost at its very outset, the Beginning is presented as a moment already in transition. In the revised version of the *Confessions*, the narrative opens not with the "confessor" himself but with a discussion of opium and of Samuel Taylor Coleridge. De Quincey claims that, like Coleridge, he took opium as a medical treatment—in his own case, for ailments that were a consequence of his early life. In this way, the childhood incidents that he is led to explain become the object of narration: postponing and replacing the proposed text (a candid description of the opium dreams), now reduced to three brief examples at the end of the work.

In each of the cases above, birth and death are posited as gateways to another "mode of existence." These modes are not subject to linear time but, like Wordsworth's "spots of time," can occur at any point (for example, De Quincey is "reborn" at his recovery). In addition, these states are associated with writing because the moment of transformation signals an apprehension of the end through which the previous condition can be more accurately interpreted. In literary terms, De Quincey claims that the opium dreams represent the moment before the end, the climax in which the current condition is perfected. The ideal nature of this end is one of synthesis: collecting and presenting all elements in an experience of simultaneity.

Yet it is the starting point—so eagerly pursued that it becomes, ironically, the final objective—that eludes De Quincey. He is more defensive than penitent; his priority lies in locating the source of his addiction, which will provide him with an immediate justification for the life he feels obliged to narrate. The subsequent narrative evolves by a movement of continual regression as he attempts to locate the crucial event through analytical retrospection. The actual texts are produced in the pursuit of their own starting point, which is projected as the source of authority that will, *by necessity*, generate the process of cause and effect coinciding with the proposed narrative. In other words, the *Confessions* has become a substitute for the starting point that, if ever found, would have engendered an entirely different work. This proposed goal, or "Absent Work," is continually projected as the next piece. De Quincey's preoccupation with sequence derives, in part, from his reading of Kantian philosophy, which he writes about in *Tait's* magazine ("German Studies and Kant in Particular" in *Tait's*, June 1836). Kant not only argues that causality is rooted in one function of the human understanding (the category of relation), but furthermore, that this idea forms one of the a priori preconditions for any possibility of experience. De Quincey is left with a problem. His defense for the plethora of substitute texts rests on a claim to his powerlessness within an indifferent machinery of events. Necessity is denied him as a source, so his starting point must disappear because there is nowhere and no point at which a system of authority can be introduced that will legitimize and predict the process of narrative. Yet to remove the starting point would leave a series of impressions and associations of ideas where the role formerly assigned to necessity would be appropriated by the imagination. De Quincey approached this more modernist style in "The English Mail Coach" (1849), but was later obliged to provide a note to the reader in order to supplement and explain the resulting elliptical text. In other words, De Quincey's philosophy draws his writing toward a more twentieth-century and prose-poetic style of stand-alone, associative pieces of prose, but this is still too avant-garde for his audience. It was precisely what Baudelaire noticed in his search for a new modern prose.

In 1848, De Quincey published an article entitled "System of the Heavens as Revealed by Lord Rosse's Telescopes." The article is based on Kant's proposal that even if we knew the age of the earth, it would not enable us to determine how much more time it had remaining because we are ignorant of the scale on which such a calculation would be based. De Quincey accuses Kant of dozing: the earth may be a phoenix, both old and young; bound to a series of fluctuating cycles as opposed to linear or human time—in the same way, we may add, as memory. In other words, with his characteristic scrupulousness, De Quincey refutes Kant's own starting point (the assumption of linear time for all things) as an inadequate hypothesis and goes on to deny the subsequent proposals that it logically, if erroneously, engenders. De Quincey redresses the problem of sequence in the *Confessions*, by returning to Kant and the source of knowledge. If ideas are preconditions for the possibility of experience, then a certain form of "nexus" is validated, but De Quincey's audience must be in possession of his ideas before they are able to participate in the experience of the proposed narrative (the dreams). In other words, if apprehension is subjective, communication is rendered virtually impossible unless the reader is drawn into an ontological communion with the narrative self so that reading becomes a shared experience rather than an objective deciphering. An extreme example of this occurs in the revised *Confessions* when the young absconder is returned home:

> If in this world there is one misery having no relief, it is the pressure on the heart from the *Incommunicable* . . . At this moment, sitting in the same room of the Priory with my mother, knowing how reasonable she was–how patient of explanations–how candid–how open to pity—not the less I sank away in a hopelessness that was immeasurable from all effort at explanation. She and I were contemplating the very same act; but she from one centre, I from another. (De Quincey 1853, 5: 114–15; De Quincey 1890, III: 315)

Analogy to the writing process is quite clear here. The passage quoted above appears only in the revised version and reveals De Quincey's concern about the effectiveness of any form of revision when on one level it merely involves juggling with an essentially inadequate language system. His later recourse to "impassioned prose" registers this despair in real terms, because it is an idiom he has been obliged to invent, which takes us a step further from the communion he seeks. Similarly, without a conscious attempt by his readers to adopt the author's mask in an act of temporary self-alienation, De Quincey's text "dies away into a sigh" of unproductive self-pity that ultimately invalidates the legitimacy of its own ambiguous and fragile starting point.

The image of initiation as a retreating power source is repeated in figures of authority: God, father, guardians, Ann and the "immortal druggist" who mythically appears in the narrative to sell the first tincture of opium to the narrator before vanishing completely. In the face of such precarious origins, and by a Cartesian logic, De Quincey is led quite specifically into autobiography. Even if his own self proves to be as elusive as those around him, he is more able to follow its course rather than wander around in the disorientating breeze of a sudden departure.

In the 1821 version of the *Confessions*, De Quincey locates the end of the work with the exit by opium from the narrative stage. "Not the opium-eater, but the opium, is the true hero of the tale; and the legitimate center on which the interest revolves. The object was to display the marvelous agency of opium, whether for pleasure or for pain: if that is done, the action of the piece has closed" (De Quincey 1985: 78). This passage again reveals De Quincey stepping aside from the crucial moment of initiation. In the 1856 version, a preface pre-empts the earlier problem by stating that what was intended as "a crowning grace," twenty to twenty-five dreams and visions, is lost. Yet, his very reluctance to hand over his work to the public, which manifested in missed deadlines and no definitive edition, bears witness to a continuing incomplete attempt to reconcile his fragmented self into a coherent whole. The partial alienation of the projected self means that De Quincey is able to recognize himself in past events but is not under pressure to identify with the character he has produced. The shadings in tone between pedestrian narrative and a set-piece reflects moments of recognition that occur during the otherwise objective perspective on his former self. In other words, an ambiguous and possibly substitutive starting point secures a split self that, in turn finds expression in a divided prose style.

At the opening of the *Suspiria*, De Quincey immediately mentions the *Confessions* (making an end of a beginning) and introduces the present work as a reconcentration of the themes set out in the last. The *Confessions* therefore is a model for the *Suspiria*, which is reflected in the tighter construction of the latter.

On the whole this concentration is effected by omission. There is much less autobiographical material and the structure of the *Suspiria de Profundis* is more episodic, marking the end of continuous narrative and the beginning of a unit-based form of composition, a disjunction that is only fully realized in the "Dream Fugue" section of "The English Mail-Coach." At the same time, the title of the *Suspiria* applies both to the whole work and to its individual sections. Thus, the individual episodes of which this work is composed do not relate to a larger context because that wider, final framework is never adequately established, confirmed, or even seen to exist. Such a structure allows the incorporation of numerous prose pieces and an equal liberty to decant them (into "Autobiographical Sketches," for example).

The episodic form of the *Suspiria* means that separate units can continue to exist regardless of the contextual frames they acquire. This works for De Quincey on several levels: he can use the same material in separate works, always adding layers to an ever-incomplete text so that, secondly, and economically, he is able to maximize his income from minimum material (it being a naïve reading that does not take into account the market value of each piece). Ideologically, it allows De Quincey to view his life as a pattern or musical theme that gains significance by continuing to exist under an unceasing series of variations. A final advantage to De Quincey lies in the fact that the episodic composition allows him to conserve the fragmentary nature of the sections and therefore his own ability to re-evaluate them. In other words, only at the moment of the unforeseen end, his own death, can the set of possibilities be exhausted—one that De Quincey feared because it occurs independently of the artist himself. His somewhat paranoid rewriting demonstrates that his fear centers on the loss of control over the position of interpretation and he engages in a power struggle with the Press, which he projects as the responsible agent of finality.[9] The relationship between De Quincey and the Press, however, is actually one of mutual necessity. As the *Confessions* showed, De Quincey needed to perceive an end in order to begin writing. His years of solitary study and meditation amounted only to procrastination, but once he became a regular contributor to the magazines, his output, however fragmentary at the level of individual articles, became profuse: "The magazines might not wait for De Quincey's truth; but *because* they would not wait, they got it" (Devlin 1983: 13).

De Quincey's double-edged prose is crucial to a developing prose poetry that is rooted in dialectic and paradox. His aesthetic relies heavily on logic as an authority with which to support any form of artistic extension—here most obviously narrative. However, it is clear that this system gives De Quincey trouble with the edges of his texts: for example, no single starting point will, by necessity, generate his convoluted narrative. So while the *Confessions*, and later *Suspira de Profundis* and "The English Mail Coach," seek to present detached moments or visions, these moments are never finally released from his need to authorize all forms of connection between different areas of the text, and between the text and its audience.

Baudelaire's Translation

De Quincey reaches for a new form and leaves traces of it in his work. Baudelaire appears to intuit and excavate this hidden version while preparing to present his new prose. In a letter of 1858, Baudelaire describes the effect of the editing he is forced to make in his translation of the *Confessions*. The result of his part-translation, paraphrase, and commentary is an uneven foreshortening of the characteristically purple prose and produces a new narrative tone, "freer" (in appearance) and jerky (see his letter to Alphonse de Calonne in 1858, where he compares his narrative tone here to the one he employs in *Haschisch*; Baudelaire 1973, 1: 552). That is, he identifies the difference in his own prose by its capacity to be both relaxed and jerky. This description clearly has a bearing on his oft-quoted dedication to *Le Spleen de Paris* where he attributes the innovation of the genre to the suppleness of its prose: "Which of us has never imagined, in his more ambitious moments, the miracle of a poetic prose, musical though rhythmless and rhymeless, flexible yet strong enough to identify with the lyrical impulses of the soul, the ebbs and flows of revery, the pangs of conscience?" (Baudelaire 1991a: 25). The new language of prose poetry is produced in part by his attempts to distill De Quincey's struggling narrative.

However, another factor of the new prose is Baudelaire's role of commentator besides that of translator. Despite several statements concerning his intention to conflate the two texts (narrative and translation), Baudelaire's rejection of De Quincey's narrative "I" makes this goal untenable. Baudelaire's shift from autobiography to biography replaces the split self with a simple third person narrative. Alan Astro reasonably states that Baudelaire's use of "he" for "I" has two opposing effects: it distances him from De Quincey's rhetorical excesses but also allows him to appropriate the language of an author with whom he identifies so closely (Astro 1989: 168–9).

The unification of this original dualism is also reflected in Baudelaire's single, consistently clear prose style, which in turn, replaces De Quincey's alternation between journalistic and impassioned prose. For example, the famous description of the dreams at the end of "Pains of Opium," where image is heaped upon image with the agitation they produce, is rendered more calmly in French:

> Je tombais soudainement chez Isis et Osiris; j'avais fait quelque chose, disait-on, j'avais commis un crime qui faisait frémir l'ibis et le crocodile. (Baudelaire 1975: 485; Baudelaire 1976: 194)

> [I came suddenly upon Isis and Osiris: I had done a deed, they said, which the ibis and the crocodile trembled at.] (De Quincey 1853, 5: 268; De Quincey 1890, III: 442)

Baudelaire translates the "deed" as a "crime," which particularizes the ambiguity and relaxes the pace of the sentence. Language considerations mean that certain effects such as alliteration cannot be imitated: "J'étais baisé par des crocodiles aux baisers cancéreux" for "I was kissed, with cancerous kisses, by crocodiles" (De Quincey 1853 5: 268; De Quincey 1890, III: 443). An additional element in Baudelaire's text is the announcement of De Quincey's death, a shadow that haunted the original work and necessitated a succession of fictional ends. It is ironic that another man's revision, something De Quincey feared more than death, should finally realize it.

Baudelaire's acute observations of the potential in circumscribing De Quincey's text is revealed from the very opening to *Un mangeur d'opium*. Baudelaire eschews the "Notice to the Reader" in favor of a passage taken from the end of the section preceding "The Pleasures of Opium." This passage, now titled "Précautions Oratoires," is, in almost a single sentence, an extended apostrophe to the drug and is defined as a unit by the final echo of its opening phrase: "O just, subtle and mighty opium!" (De Quincey 1853 5: 213)[10] By decontextualizing the piece and placing it at the head of the translation, Baudelaire's first comment on De Quincey's work is an illustration of the autonomous tendencies of the prose (in the *Confessions*, this passage does not even appear as a discrete paragraph). It is significant, therefore, that the detached passage is taken from an impassioned moment inside the general narrative as opposed to any of the dreams that De Quincey himself had composed as separate entities. Baudelaire borrows freely from both works (the *Confessions* and *Suspiria*) in his collation and therefore could easily have opened with one of the composed set-pieces from the *Suspiria*. Instead, Baudelaire places this "first" prose poem *before* the preface, obscuring the starting point with a rhetorical flourish. In effect, De Quincey's apostrophe, set apart in this way, provides a model, in terms of extension and closure, for Baudelaire's new prose compositions in *Le Spleen de Paris*, which often appear to have been themselves lifted from a larger narrative and, in similar prayer-like apostrophes, employ some form of repetition as a framing device. It is noticeable that Stäuble-Lipman Wulf, a scholar of French literature, instantly identifies De Quincey's now displaced text as a "poème en prose." By contrast, it is somewhat surprising that the famous thyrsus image, incorporated throughout the *Confessions*, never appears in direct translation—only by reference and allusion.

In general, attempts to identify points of influence between the two writers can never be conclusive owing to Baudelaire's interests preceding his reading of De Quincey and his subtle use of anything which he *does* take from the *Confessions*. Stäuble-Lipman Wulf claims on the one hand that, having completed the translation, Baudelaire could no longer distinguish his own feelings from De Quincey's, but she nevertheless rejects the notion that the influence can be traced in the prose poems. And yet, several themes and phrases from these texts by De Quincey do find echoes in *Le Spleen de Paris*. For example, the episode in which the school porter drops the absconding pupil's suitcase down the stairs (and which Baudelaire translates in full) clearly contributes to the scenario, anticipation and "sense of the ludicrous" in "The Useless Glazier" where the narrator lures a glazier up to his flat in order to make him negotiate the stairs with his fragile merchandise before actually throwing the panes out of his window. Again, from the *Confessions*, comes De Quincey's narration of his first experiences of opium. The feelings it induces lead him to wander, aimlessly, through London's streets, mingling with the crowd and losing himself in obscure alleys. Later, when the "honeymoon" period is over and his past returns in the shape of nightmares, De Quincey describes being tormented by "the tyranny of the human face" (De Quincey 1853, 5: 266; De Quincey 1890, III: 441). Baudelaire, who generally presents himself in the prose poems as a *flâneur*, wandering through the streets of Paris, mixing with the crowd, includes an alternative piece in his collection. In "One O'Clock in the Morning," the narrator celebrates being alone, at last, in his room: "At last, the tyranny of the human face has gone, and I'll suffer no more except from my own self" (Baudelaire 1991a: 53). Baudelaire resented the artistic power of opium, describing it as "an inexhaustible stock of caresses and betrayals" in "The Twofold Room," which accounts for his using De Quincey's hallucinated imagery in more "pedestrian" circumstances.

Baudelaire's prose poem "Evening Twilight" provides the most telling example of De Quincey's influence on the prose poem. The piece was first written in 1855, that is, before work began on the *Confessions*. In this original version, the narrator contrasts the deranging effect of twilight on his friends with the happiness he discovers at the same time of day, in himself. The poem was published with substantial changes in August 1857, after work on the *Confessions* had begun. The original piece is retained, with minor variations, but is couched in entirely new paragraphs which form a revised beginning and end. It is the final images which are reminiscent of the opening apostrophe to "juste, subtil et puissant opium!" and other passages in *Un mangeur d'opium*: the rise of labyrinthine cities from the darkness of solitude; the power generated by opposing forces; the sun and the night; fascination with the Orient.

The final paragraph does not refer back to the anecdote that makes up the body of the prose poem, to create closure, but rather continues expansively the image of light and dark:

> Or it suggests one of those ballerina's exotic costumes, whose dim transparent gauze hints at the splendours of a brightly coloured skirt, just as the delicious past shows through the darkness of the present; and the shimmering gold and silver stars which spangle it are the will-o'-the-wisps of Fancy, which only start to shine in the deep mourning of the night. ("Evening Twilight," Baudelaire 1991a: 99)

The concept of a past that shines out like a star through the obscuring gauze of the present is clearly influenced by his reading of De Quincey. In fact, the passage follows his paraphrase of the English author:

> de même que les étoiles voilées par la lumière du jour reparaissent avec la nuit, de meme aussi toutes les incriptions gravées sur la mémoire inconsciente reparurent comme par l'effet d'une encre sympathique. (Baudelaire 1975: 481; Baudelaire 1976, 184)

> [just as the stars veiled by the light of day reappear with the night, so too all the inscriptions engraved on the unconscious memory will reappear as if by the effect of invisible ink.][11]

Appropriately, the original context of the passage above is a developing formulation of the palimpsest, which states that no record can be erased by future emendations:

> Of this, at least, I feel assured, that there is no such thing as ultimate forgetting; traces once impressed upon the memory are indestructible; a thousand accidents may and will interpose a veil between our present consciousness and the secret inscriptions on the mind. Accidents of the same sort will also rend away this veil. But alike, whether veiled or unveiled, the inscription remains for ever; just as the stars seem to withdraw before the common light of day, whereas, in fact, we all know that it is the light which is drawn over them as a veil; and that they are waiting to be revealed, whenever the obscuring daylight shall have withdrawn. (De Quincey 1853, 5: 261; De Quincey 1890, III: 437)

Typically, this passage appears near the end in "The Pains of Opium." However, the same concept works vice versa, that is, looking from the present into the future, an idea that De Quincey expounds in similar terms just before "The Pleasures of Opium," in its preface, as it were: "And yet, if a veil interposes between the dim-sightedness of man and his future calamities, the same veil hides from him their alleviations; and a grief which had not been feared, is met by consolations which had not been hoped" (De Quincey 1853, 5: 190; De Quincey 1890, III: 377). De Quincey's imagery shows the act of writing to be, itself, a dance with veils because it obscures and reveals the past in the present. So too, the defamiliarizing form of Baudelaire's prose poems did not transform the elements he found in De Quincey but constituted a new perspective in which to present them: a perspective that, in its disjunction, had its roots in the source material itself. This transformation can best be explored through the twin images of the Thyrsus and the Palimpsest.

Baudelaire's act of translating and editing De Quincey's *Confessions* clearly had a direct bearing on his construction of the "first" prose poems (*Le Spleen de Paris*). This is borne out in the fact that little work was needed on the *Suspiria*. Partly owing to considerations of magazine space, but principally for aesthetic reasons, Baudelaire simply cut out most of the narrative before the Oxford Visions and translated "this melancholic gallery of paintings," the visions, as they stood (although he removed all the footnotes). The sole exception is his rendition of "The Palimpsest." The original piece is an explanation of this ancient form of writing tablet, which received several impressions in succession, each one superseding the last. Ironically, the use of the palimpsest as a literary image had been used by Coleridge seventeen years previously in his Prefatory Note to *The Wanderings of Cain*, which, I have argued elsewhere, is a project that also has a place in the history of the prose poem. In place of, or *overlaying*, De Quincey's exemplum, which conflates Coleridge's image with another from Shelley, Baudelaire substitutes a section in which most of the discursive introduction is cut and another illustration is inserted.[12] In Baudelaire's prose piece:

> Un homme de génie, mélancolique, misanthrope, et voulant se venger de l'injustice de son siècle, jette un jour au feu toutes ses oeuvres encore manuscrites. Et comme on lui reprochait, cet effroyable holocauste fait à la haine, qui, d'ailleurs, était le sacrifice de toutes ces propres espérances, il répondit: 'Qu'importe? Ce qui était important, c'était que ces choses fussent *créés*; elles ont été créés donc, elles *sont*.' (Baudelaire 1975: 506; Baudelaire 1976: 242)
>
> [A man of genius, melancholic, misanthropic and wanting to take revenge on the injustice of his age, one day casts into the fire all his works still in manuscript. And to those who were reproaching him for this horrific holocaust made in hatred, and which was, moreover, the sacrifice of all his own hopes, he replied: 'What does it matter? What was important was that these things were *created*; they were created, therefore they *are*.']

The narrator goes on to apply this indestructibility to thoughts and actions past and future. That is, while this concept of permanence in the palimpsest may allow us a complacency in our retrospections, it makes the prospect fearful, as future actions loom indissolubly before us. In addition, the narrator cites the dream visions as illustrations of the truth that nothing is entirely erased by the human mind. Yet in terms of a collection of prose poems, the palimpsest, as De Quincey describes it, proves to be a pivotal image because it belies the concept of representational succession in favor of experienced simultaneity. De Quincey's insistence that the monkish legend is not displaced by the knightly romance contains direct implications for the following sequence of dream visions. Following the principle of the palimpsest, Baudelaire soon concerned himself with the possibility of a moveable order for his prose poems in *Spleen*.

Curiously, the scene that Baudelaire creates for the palimpsest episode (above) is reminiscent of the fate of the original *Suspiria*, which was lost to the flames of a small (accidental) fire which De Quincey narrates in the preface to the *Confessions* of 1856. Baudelaire's scenario offers recognizable elements of his later prose poems: principally the character of the splenetic author/narrator protagonist and the soliloquy that provides the resolution. In addition, we witness the beginning of a style that uses anecdote and discussion without creating a specific plot. The final sentence of the inserted passage, "The palimpsest of the memory is indestructible," exemplifies this, being more provocative than conclusive.

There is another aspect of the palimpsest image that Baudelaire employs in his prose poems. After referring specifically to various "romances" in his literary illustration of the palimpsest, De Quincey's narrator introduces the Oxford Visions, which are revivified at the moment of delirium. Displacement of the visions (and the textual romances) by subsequent experiences is belied by the truth of the palimpsest. Analogous to either mind or text, the palimpsest counters linearity with co-presence and non-chronological spontaneity. De Quincey employs the palimpsest image to disrupt the sequence of visions that follow, emphasizing the point by describing the visions as choruses concluding the overture of Part One. Similarly, Baudelaire's *Spleen* is a collection of often transient moments experienced in a city. Yet the significance of recording these episodes appears to belong, rather, to the play of their interrelation.

The Palimpsest and the Thyrsus

De Quincey first refers to the thyrsus as a *caduceus* in his Introductory Notice to the *Suspiria*:

> I tell my critic that the whole course of this narrative resembles, and was meant to resemble, a caduceus wreathed about with meandering ornaments, or the shaft of a tree's stem hung round and surmounted with some vagrant parasitical plant. The mere medical subject of the opium answers to the dry withered pole, which shoots all the rings of the flowering plants, and seems to do so by some dexterity of its own; whereas, in fact, the plant and its tendrils have curled round the sullen cylinder by mere luxurience of *theirs*. (De Quincey 1985: 93–4)

De Quincey outwardly rejects brevity and aims at the experience of the arabesque, the context, the flowers of the caduceus. Brevity is forced upon him, however, by Baudelaire in his translation. Despite being employed by De Quincey to defend the expansive nature of his text, the thyrsus image is simultaneously evoked and rejected in the paraphrase that Baudelaire substitutes for this passage: "No doubt I will abridge a lot; De Quincey is essentially digressive; the term '*humourist*' can be applied more appropriately to him than to anyone else; at one point he compares his thought to a thyrsus, a simple stick which takes all its charm and appearance from the foliage which envelops it" (Baudelaire 1976: 104).[13] The image is also displaced from the *Suspiria* to the beginning of the *Confessions* in Baudelaire's version. In his prose poem "Le Thyrse," first published in 1863, Baudelaire applies the symbol to Liszt in what he describes as an intersexual quality to his genius:

> Ne dirait-on pas que toutes ces corolles délicates, tous ces calices, explosions de senteurs et de couleurs, exécutent un mystique fandango autour du bâton hiératique? Et quel est, cependent, le mortel imprudent qui osera décider si les fleurs et les pampres on été faits pour le baton ou si le bâton n'est que le prétexte pour

montrer la beauté des pampres et des fleurs? ... Le bâton, c'est votre volonté, droite, ferme et inébranlable; les fleurs, c'est la promenade de votre fantaisie autour de votre volonté; c'est l'élément féminin exécutant autour du mâle ses prestigieuses pirouettes. (Baudelaire 1918: 106–7)

[Does it not seem that all these delicate corollas, all these calyxes, these explosions of perfume and colour, perform a mystical fandango around the hieratic stick? And yet who is the impudent mortal who would dare decide whether the flowers and the tendrils were made for the stick or whether the stick is merely a pretext to reveal the beauty of the tendrils and flowers? ... The stick is your will-power, straight, firm, and unmovable; the flowers represent your fantasy wandering around your will; they are the feminine element executing around the masculine element its prestigious pirouettes.] (Baudelaire 1991a: 84)

Yet, the writer's context is not simply expendable. Joris-Karl Huysmans, in the guise of his most celebrated protagonist, Des Esseintes, holds up the prose poem as his favorite genre and, in reference to its brevity, "the essential oil of art." For him, the circumscribed form of the genre evolves from the absolute precision involved in the creation of its sentences:

The words chosen for a work of this sort would be so unalterable that they would take the place of all the others; every adjective would be sited with such ingenuity and finality that it could never be legally evicted, and would open up such wide vistas that the reader could muse on its meaning, at once precise and multiple, for weeks on end, and also ascertain the present, reconstruct the past, and divine the future of the characters in the light of this one epithet. (Huysmans 1959: 199)[14]

In other words, the prose poem represents, for Des Esseintes, a telescoping of the novel genre and its brevity is the consequence of eliminating circumstantial details now considered to be superfluous.[15] Compared to the novel, the prose poem is not subversive so much as expurgatory. Huysmans' image implies that the prose poem is the kernel of a larger and rather more amorphous literature from which the prose poem is reduced but to which it may also return. In fact, Huysmans' metaphor of the essential oil is more useful to us than a simple call to concision as some abstract yet recognizable quality. An essence is extracted by distillation or reduction but can be reconstituted through a reversal of the initial process.[16] There is clearly a parallel here between Huysmans' reversible metaphor and the reader/writer dialectic that operates around narrative context in the prose poem. I would like to examine this comparison a little more closely.

De Quincey's influence on Baudelaire is usually referred to only in passing in relation to the image of the thyrsus, which was appropriated as the model for the prose poem genre.[17] However, this is actually the most tenuous link. It was precisely his treatment of what he termed De Quincey's "bizarre" texts that guided Baudelaire into achieving the goal to which De Quincey's autobiographical work increasingly tended. In turn, he developed these extracted prose pieces into the first legitimate collection of prose poetry.

For De Quincey, the context of the dream visions (his childhood experiences and so on) are used to legitimize the artistic vision, to reveal the concordance between the beginning and the end—an objective that is subverted by his own belief in the infinite complexity of causal structures. As a result, the Oxford Visions are overrun by marginal discourse of contextual detail to prove their visionary status. Ultimately the parenthetical method proves unproductive and precludes the possibility of the visions appearing on the page in ideal isolation. De Quincey flounders. Moreover, the self-generative nature of context, in which digression acts on regression, prevents him from emerging from its now labyrinthine possibilities. He habitually gets lost in the contextual intermedium on which he has embarked and which is marked by its own peculiar sublimity.[18]

J. Hillis Miller interprets De Quincey's apparent disorientation inside his contextual maze as the search for God and likens the regressive structure of the narrative to the proliferation of motifs in Baroque art. The Baroque period was a watershed in the history of the labyrinth. What had previously been a religious exercise in perseverance as the would-be pilgrims made their way across a path on the cathedral floor became, in the Baroque period, a battle of wits. The traveler was now expected to apply their own logic in order to solve the design now hidden amongst other similar, but possibly misleading paths (Paolo Santarcangeli, quoted in Faris 1988: 3).[19] Wendy Faris neatly corresponds this double perspective to the diachronic and synchronic experiences of the literary text. On the one hand, someone inside the labyrinth wanders around attempting to construct a pattern at each step (diachronically). On the other, synchronic vision perceives the whole and its inlaid design from above, as it were (Faris 1988: 4).

The two approaches to a labyrinthine text return us to the reversible metaphor (Huysmans' prose poems as essential oil). Michel Charles argues that De Quincey writes digressively in his attempt to provide a full and comprehensive text while the reader, faced with pages of these intertwining threads, sets about retracing their paths to a starting point. This is, in effect, the same way as Edmund Baxter reads it: constantly aware of the continual interplay between the "text-as-written" and "text-as-read" (Baxter 1990: 20).

It is not a surprising coincidence that the image of the caduceus is intimately linked to the prose poem form, becoming emblematic of the genre itself. Baudelaire takes the thyrsus image (and not the more obvious, writerly palimpsest) for his prose poem. Despite representing the guided reader who obediently follows its arabesque, the thyrsus is held up as a model of omission—it is removed from Baudelaire's translation of the *Suspiria* only to reappear as a decontextualized prose piece within a collection of similarly truncated fragments in *Le Spleen de Paris*. The thyrsus is thus "forgotten" only to re-emerge as one image among many within a palimpsest structure of continual appearance and forgetting in the prose poem collection. Context in the *Suspiria* becomes implied in *Spleen de Paris*.

In the transformation of the thyrsus image from one text to the other, Huysmans' metaphor has been successfully reversed: the thyrsus and the palimpsest prove to be opposite sides of the prose poem coin. The readerly connotation in De Quincey's *Suspiria* has become the writerly fragment in *Spleen de Paris* (the thyrsus couched in the palimpsest) and the amorphous nature of narrative context has been reduced in anticipation of a future expansion. "The Palimpsest," a set piece and the symbol of the double-headed text, heads the Oxford Visions, which aspire to greater concision than they achieve; proof that De Quincey could theorize more successfully than he could realize the prose poetic structure.

Baudelaire ends his translation with De Quincey's seminal idea: "Death we can face: but knowing, as some of us do, what is human life, which of us is it that without shuddering could (if consciously we were summoned) face the hour of birth?" (De Quincey 1890, XIII: 359). If death is a sublimation into a desired synthesis, life, with its tenuous causality and proliferating misinterpretations, proves infinitely more fearsome. The prospect of the palimpsest is dizzying in its possibilities. Baudelaire ends his work with a notice on De Quincey's project for the *Suspiria*, which was in fact set in a footnote to "Levana and Our Ladies of Sorrow." According to the note, the *Suspiria*, in its pared form, could be projected into a larger (absent) whole. De Quincey's death, announced by Baudelaire at the end of his translation of the *Confessions*, meant that the plan was fixed in this prospective form, outlined in a footnote. The irony of the process is not lost on his translator, who closes his text musing on the end that De Quincey continuously evoked but inevitably failed to realize in his work. The end of writing, in this case, corresponds literally with the death of the author.

Baudelaire posits De Quincey's death as the reason for the abruptness of the work, suggesting that had he lived long enough, De Quincey could have investigated every avenue that writing opened up before him. Be that as it may, the end of De Quincey's text (as text proper) marks the beginning of Baudelaire's interpretation of the *Confessions* as essentially a series of discrete prose pieces. Baudelaire's translation is piecemeal because the problem of causality is not pursued. The outcome is also a moment of transition, into a new "mode of existence" for both De Quincey and his work—now redefined as seeds of the concept of a prose poetic genre.

Notes

1. De Quincey's name, which he did not use in the British magazines, signing himself only "X.Y.Z.," was not published in these translations. Michèle Stäuble-Lipman Wulf gives a comprehensive account of the history of the *Confessions* in France (Baudelaire 1976: 33–8).
2. See de Musset 1960: 1021. It is known that Baudelaire read a work on hallucinations that contained a long quotation from de Musset's translation, but there is no evidence to prove he was acquainted with the rest of de Musset's rendering.
3. Baudelaire's deals with the *Moniteur* and *Revue Française* having broken down completely. See Baudelaire to Alphonse de Calonne, Paris, 10 November 1858 (Baudelaire 1973, 1: 522): "I assure you that it was no easy thing to fit the description of a very complicated book into a SMALL space and without losing a single nuance."
4. Bernard 1959: 24–5, 35. Translations of works such as Young's *Night Thoughts* into abridged prose were very popular, but also instrumental in liberating poetry from the constraints of verse in the pre-Romantic era. In these translations, narrative and digression were eliminated to produce a heightened unity and intensity not available in the novel or the epic genres.
5. G. T. Clapton claims that the inclusion of details in *Un mangeur d'opium*, which had been corrected in *Selections Grave and Gay*, reveal that Baudelaire did not know of the 1856 revision or, possibly, preferred the shorter version (Clapton, 1931: 13). An original source for the *Suspiria* seems to be virtually impossible to confirm. Stäuble-Lipman Wulf suggests that the American collection may have served for both of the texts, but she adds that *Blackwood's* may also have been consulted for the *Suspiria* (Baudelaire 1976: 43–6).
6. Baxter distinguishes between failure and flaw in De Quincey's texts, a distinction that is helpful in separating the effect of the work (failure can be Romantic or comic) and criticism

of its relation to what Baxter terms an implied "aesthetic absolute" (Baxter 1990: 9–11). Baudelaire's treatment does fall into the second category, but criticism must be qualified by the fact that his preference for a full translation was thwarted through the directives on length issued by his publisher.

7. "The Thyrsus" from *Le Spleen de Paris* is dedicated to Franz Liszt but could equally apply to De Quincey: "The straight line and the arabesque; intention and expression; unyielding will-power and oblique Word; the one and only end and the multiplicity of means; the all-powerful amalgam of genius—what analyst will make as bold to divide and separate you?" ("The Wand" [Le Thyrse], Baudelaire 1991: 145). Cf. Baudelaire 1976: 365. Stäuble-Lipman Wulf includes evidence put forward by M. Zimmermann and R. Kopp for other possible sources for this prose poem.

8. "Jeremy Taylor" is corrected to "Lord Bacon" in the 1856 version for his own collected edition, *Selections Grave & Gay* (De Quincey 1853, 5: 275).

9. Cf Baxter 1990: 22: "[In the *Selections*] De Quincey destroys the historical actuality of the publication of his texts in journal form by repeatedly referring to other works as if they had still to be completed ... The destruction of a given historical actuality (that the work has been once and for all published in a specific form) articulates De Quincey's reaction to the Press: within his work he attempts to subvert the way the Press tends to render his writing permanent and finished."

10. The passage begins, "O just, subtle, and all-conquering opium!" (De Quincey 1853, 5: 212; De Quincey 1890, III: 395). As Lindop and others have pointed out, De Quincey's apostrophe is an echo of Raleigh's conclusion to his *History of the World*, "O eloquent, just and mighty Death!" Baudelaire had to battle with his publisher to use this piece as the opening. He broaches the argument by stating that an author of his renown would not normally participate in such pettinesses as he has had to endure. He goes on, "The same thing this morning! An opening was painfully sought for and prepared. At last I found the beginning which, in its solemnity, resembles the first bars of an orchestra. But *voilà!* you decide that, for an opening, it would be wiser to incorporate an obituary notice," Baudelaire to Alphonse de Calonne, January 5, 1860 (Baudelaire 1973, 1: 651).

11. Translations are mine unless otherwise indicated.

12. Baudelaire's passage is inserted between the case of the drowning woman and the literary palimpsest.

13. Michel Charles points out that *"essentiellement digressif"* is an oxymoron (Charles 1979: 397–400). He makes sense of the image by explaining that, despite the dialectic nature of the caduceus, De Quincey favors the arabesque whereas Baudelaire prefers not to make the choice and to suspend his aestheticism in a kind of hermaphrodite state.

14. Huysmans' own collection of prose poems, *Le Drageoir à épices*, had been published ten years previously in 1874.

15. Baudelaire had expressed a very similar notion in his essay on Poe: "There must not creep into the entire composition a single word which is not intentional, which does not tend, directly or indirectly, to complete the premeditated design" (Baudelaire 1991b: 396). Huysmans' theory is surely influenced by Mallarmé, whose best prose poems Des Esseintes claims as the masterpieces of the genre. Mallarmé (who also translated Poe) was influenced by Poe's commitment to *le mot juste*.

16. Cf. Coleridge's statement in *Biographia Literaria*, "Essence, in its primary signification, means the principle of *individuation*, the inmost principle of the *possibility*, of any thing, *as* that particular thing. It is equivalent to the *idea* of a thing, whenever we use the word idea, with philosophic precision" (Coleridge 1983, 2: 62). Coleridge also speaks of reduction and restoration of a text in his preface to "The Blossoming of the Solitary Date Tree."

17. Cf. Murphy 1992: 50. Also Todorov 1990: 65–6. In his discussion of the fundamental dualism in Baudelaire's prose poems, Todorov retains the thyrsus as symbolic model, but he does not mention the link to De Quincey.
18. Cf. Beer 1985: 337. Beer has suggested that De Quincey believed a center of security and peace lay at the "heart" of any true labyrinth; the nightmare of being inside a labyrinth, therefore, always contained the immediate possibility of turning into an "experience of peace." Moreover, Beer adds, it was "as important to engage with the terms of the labyrinth as to enjoy the peace at its center."
19. See also Miller 1975: 7.

A note on source texts.
Owing to difficulties with Masson's disordered and unsatisfactory edition of De Quincey's collected writings, I have used the author's own *Selections Grave & Gay* as a source text. For the *Suspiria de Profundis*, which does not appear there, I have used the original 1821 edition in *Blackwood's Edinburgh Magazine*. However, I have included page references to Masson. In addition, I have found Michèle Stäuble-Lipman Wulf's parallel edition of Baudelaire's *Un Mangeur d'Opium* and De Quincey's *Confessions* to be invaluable for offering and immediate and precise comparison between the texts. However, I have again supported my own use of this edition with references to Baudelaire's *Œuvres complètes Complètes* and the appropriate source for De Quincey, as above.
De Quincey, Thomas, *Suspiria de Profundis: being a sequel to the Confessions of an English Opium-Eater*, *Blackwood's Edinburgh Magazine* 57 (March 1845), pp. 269–85; (April 1845), pp. 489–502; (June 1845), pp. 739–51; 58 (July 1845), pp. 43–55.

Works Cited

Astro, Alan (1989), "Allegory of Translation in Baudelaire's *Un Mangeur d'Opium*, *Nineteenth-Century French Studies*, 1989–90, vol. 18, pp. 165–71.
Baudelaire, Charles (1918), *Œuvres complètes*, Vol. 3, Paris, Éditions de la Nouvelle revue française, 1918.
Baudelaire, Charles (1973), *Correspondance de Baudelaire*, ed. Claude Pichois, Paris: Éditions Gallimard, Vol. 1, Baudelaire to Madame Aupick, Paris, 9 July 1867.
Baudelaire, Charles (1975), *Œuvres complètes*, ed. Claude Pichois, Paris: Éditions Gallimard.
Baudelaire, Charles (1976), *Un mangeur d'opium*, ed. Michèle Stäuble-Lipman Wulf, Neuchâtel (Suisse): Les Éditions de la Baconnière.
Baudelaire, Charles (1991a), *The Prose Poems and La Fanfarlo*, translated by Rosemary Lloyd, Oxford: Oxford University Press.
Baudelaire, Charles (1991b), "New Notes on Edgar Poe," trans. Louis and Francis Hyslop, in *Edgar Allan Poe: Critical Assessments*, ed. G. Clarke, East Sussex: Helm Information.
Baxter, Edmund (1990), *De Quincey's Art of Autobiography*, Edinburgh: Edinburgh University Press.
Beer, John (1985), "The Englishness of De Quincey's Ideas," in *English and German Romanticism: Cross Currents and Controversies*, ed. James Pipkin, Heidelberg: Carl Winter Universitätsverlag, pp 323–47.
Bernard, Suzanne (1959), *Le poème en prose de Baudelaire jusqu'à nos jours*, Paris: Librairie Nizet.
Charles, Michel (1979), "Digression, régression (Arabesques)," *Poétique*, vol. 40, pp 395–407.
Clapton, G. T. (1931), *Baudelaire et De Quincey*, Paris: Les Belles Lettres.
Coleridge, Samuel Taylor (1983), "Biographia Literaria," ed. James Engell and W. Jackson Bate, in S. T. Coleridge, *Collected Works*, Princeton: Princeton University Press, Vol. 7.

De Quincey, Thomas (1836), "German Studies and Kant in Particular," *Tait's*, June.
De Quincey, Thomas (1853), *Writings Published and Unpublished of Thomas De Quincey, Revised and Arranged by Himself*, Edinburgh: James Hogg & Sons.
De Quincey, Thomas (1890), *The Collected Writings*, ed. David Masson, Edinburgh: A. & C. Black.
De Quincey, Thomas (1985), *Confessions of an English Opium-Eater and Other Writings*, ed. Grevel Lindop, Oxford: Oxford University Press.
Devlin, D. D. (1983), *De Quincey, Wordsworth and the Art of Prose*, London: Macmillan.
de Musset, Alfred (1960), *Œuvres complètes en prose*, Paris: Gallimard.
Faris, Wendy B. (1988), *Labyrinths of Language: Symbolic Landscape and Narrative Design in Modern Fiction*, Baltimore and London: Johns Hopkins University Press.
Huysmans, Joris-Karl (1959), *Against Nature*, trans. Robert Baldick, Harmondsworth: Penguin.
Miller, J. Hillis (1975), *The Disappearance of God: Five Nineteenth-Century Writers*, Oxford: Oxford University Press.
Murphy, Margueritte (1992), *A Tradition of Subversion: The Prose Poem in English from Wilde to Ashbery*, Amherst: University of Massachusetts Press.
Todorov, Tzvetan (1990), *Genres in Discourse*, trans. Catherine Porter, Cambridge: Cambridge University Press.

5

A Dangerous Hybridity:
The Prose Poem at the *Fin de Siècle*

Margueritte S. Murphy

. . . dangereuse comme la poésie en prose (Baudelaire)
    (epigraph to Barbara Johnson's *Défigurations du langage poétique*)

IN 1917, T. S. ELIOT OFFERS THIS retrospective view of the prose poem of the *fin de siècle*:

> [I]n the long-forgotten 'Nineties when sins were still scarlet, there appeared a little book called *Pastels in Prose*. It was mostly, if not altogether, translations from the French—from Ephraim Mikhaël, Judith Gautier, Mallarmé, and many less-remembered names. This book introduced to the English reader the Prose-Poem.
>   It was after the time when Gautier had written the *Symphonie en blanc majeur*, and Whistler had painted symphonies in various colours, and programme music was not unknown. So that several serious critics took alarm at the confusion of the genres, cried out upon an age of decadence and charlatanism. Charlatanism, no doubt, still exists; but decadence is far decayed; and it is now a little late to assume this motherly perturbation. Time has left us many things, but among those it has taken away we may hope to count *A Rebours*, and the *Divagations*, and the writings of miscellaneous prose poets. (Eliot 1917: 157–8)

Eliot's sneer, aimed at the presumed aesthetic failings of the genre, targets a "decadence" that is more passé than immoral, a time of "pastels" when sins were "scarlet." But it is a sneer that hides a moralizing underbelly: Eliot's mentor at Harvard College, Irving Babbitt, undoubtedly one of the "serious critics" he refers to, censured the prose poem, among other hybrid forms, for a neglect of "the firm and fast distinction" characterized as "male," allowing for a "decadence, of what M. Lasserre calls 'an integral corruption of the higher parts of human nature'" (Babbitt 1910: 236–7). The prose poem played a role in Oscar Wilde's trials and can hardly be disentangled from that association and the Decadent movement in the aftermath.

Putting aside for the moment reasons for this knot of Anglophone prejudices and assumptions, we can look back at Eliot's remarks with our own strong sense of how wrong he was in 1917. Stéphane Mallarmé's *Divagations* has only grown in importance for poetry and literary theory, *À Rebours* is still considered the central work of the French decadent movement, and Whistler and Théophile Gautier (Judith's famous father) have hardly lost their places in their respective canons. Eliot also reminds us of other prose poets who were prominent in their time and had a crucial impact on the course of the form in the latter part of the nineteenth century and, for some, into the Modernist period. Over a century after Eliot's retrospective assessment, how might we map the landscape of the prose poem of the late nineteenth century that he so roundly dismisses?

While Charles Baudelaire, in the dedication of *Petits poèmes en prose: Le Spleen de Paris*, cites Aloysius Bertrand's *Gaspard de la Nuit* as inspiration and forerunner, the appearance of Baudelaire's prose poems, beginning in 1861, sparks a proliferation of prose poems in both mainstream newspapers and literary journals. The trajectory of the genre in the wake of Baudelaire's *Petits poèmes en prose* may be described through various lenses. Suzanne Bernard, in her monumental work on the French prose poem, *Le Poème en prose de Baudelaire jusqu'à nos jours*, observes a scission that emerges by 1891: the "artistic" prose poem with a strict form, taking *Gaspard de la Nuit* as model, diverges from the anarchic, more free-form prose poem; the "musical" Symbolist prose poem serves as perhaps an intermediate form (Bernard 1959: 491). This formalist distinction assumes a second, more basic polarity between the decorative and the revolutionary in poetry, a polarity that the prose poem may well dispute. Barbara Johnson's *Défigurations du langage poétique* approaches the prose poem as a deconstructive genre and finds a development from Baudelaire's *Petits poèmes en prose* to late texts by Mallarmé in the deconstructive strategy undertaken. With Baudelaire, she argues, the prose poem not only enacts a dissolution of the poetry/prose duality, but Baudelaire's career as he moves from *Les fleurs du mal* to *Petits poèmes en prose* stages the duality verse/prose chronologically, setting up another deconstructive strategy. That is, Baudelaire's prose poems, as the later works, function to deconstruct figuration in the verse poems, especially the prose poems that recast certain verse poems (see her chapter "La chevelure et son double"), and the prose poems work to put in question the operation of figurative language itself. She finds a further "more complex" breakdown of dualities in Mallarmé's career and writings. He composed prose poems in two separate periods: first from 1862 to 1867, and then again from 1885 until his death in 1898. In the first period, Mallarmé composed and published poems in verse and in prose, maintaining the verse/prose binary that Baudelaire's career staged. But Johnson contends that in the latter period Mallarmé complicates this dichotomy to put in question prose itself—stating "il n'y a pas de prose"—while "Un coup de dés" materially erases the distinction between verse and prose (Johnson 1979: 184–6). Yet he publishes collections that rely on this distinction: *Vers et Prose*, *Album de vers et de prose*. She concludes that in the second period, Mallarmé substitutes the "plus complexe et contradictoire" dichotomy "entre le maintien et l'éclipse, entre l'affirmation et l'infirmation, de la dichotomie entre vers et prose" (Johnson 1979: 187) ["between the maintenance and the eclipse, between the affirmation and the annulment, of the dichotomy between verse and prose"]. In other words, Mallarmé does not abandon difference in poetic language and form, but foregrounds difference as a place of contestation, opening the way to what he names "poëme critique" as both poem of the crisis (*Crise de vers*) and of the critique of poetic language (189).

Richard Terdiman, noting how Johnson's approach demonstrates the prose poem's deconstructive functions within "linguistic *and social* systems" (Terdiman 1985: 269), traces more explicitly a sociopolitical trajectory for the genre. He argues that it disrupts the antinomies and polarization of the dominant discursive structure that privileges prose: "the dialectical force of the prose poem's practice, and the intensity of its engagement with its antagonist, proceed from this turning of prose, of its self-evidence and its solidity, inside out" (270). Terdiman notes the risks of such a strategy—that "by situating itself at the furthest border of a dominant social apparatus while resolutely declining to cross it," the prose poem nearly becomes "inaccessible" and thereby irrelevant (272). Jonathan Monroe, too, highlights the genre's sociopolitical bearings, noting its "self-thematizing figurations of the struggle of literary genres" and frequent thematic treatment of gender and class struggle (Monroe 1987: 21). Monroe describes its relationship with the newspaper as an "apparent democratization" that in practice works quite differently:

> If the prose poem's block print and brevity make it look accessible, like a newspaper article, to those with only minimal literacy and verbal sophistication, the genre's polemical tendencies risked from the very beginning making potential bourgeois readers decidedly uncomfortable, if not openly hostile. (24)

He cites the suppression of Baudelaire's 'Assommons les pauvres!' as an early instance of such hostility. Contemporaries were well aware of the sociopolitical import of the prose poem: in a letter to Mallarmé in 1882, Joris-Karl Huysmans wrote: "the prose poem terrifies the Homais (bourgeois character in Flaubert's *Madame Bovary*) who make up the great majority of the public" (quoted in Lloyd 1999: 90).

Andreas Huyssen, in tracing the emergence of the "metropolitan miniature," likewise points to the relationship between Baudelaire's prose poems and the press of the Second Empire. The strict censorship of critical or oppositional press coverage after the coup of December 2, 1851 prompted the "proliferation of nonpolitical and literary boulevard magazines and papers that created and saturated a depoliticized reading public." Such publications favored genres like "narrative short prose, miniature portraits, celebrity anecdotes, brief dialogues, fictive letters, reflections, society gossip" mostly focused on private life. In this context, Baudelaire's prose poems enacted a "strategy to appropriate and to transform the genres of *la petite presse*" (Huyssen 2015: 33), rendering instead multiple perspectives, multiple layers of consciousness, and the glaring social and economic contradictions of modern urban life. It is, in Huyssen's thesis, an early example of "remediation in reverse." Huyssen derives the term "remediation" from Marshal McLuhan to describe a linear process whereby older media reappear as content in the next, newer media technology. Huyssen finds that this process not only is "multidirectional" but also may operate in moments "when an older medium reasserts itself by critically working through what the new medium does and does not do," the prose poems, in this instance, playing off the *feuilleton* model while exposing the class assumptions and perspectival limitations of its typical content in mass media journalism (8). Huyssen, however, distinguishes the "metropolitan miniature" from prose poems generally, emphasizing its close antithetical relationship with the boulevard press and "realistic" short prose. Clearly this distinction is important, yet the "instability of genre" that Huyssen argues is a product of "remediation in reverse," a new form as "anti-form" (11), characterizes the prose poem as well, even those that hark back to older genres. Emerging at a time when "modernity" was being identified and theorized, the prose poem is not only a counter-discourse to short journalistic forms, but also takes on, updates and indeed "remediates" ancient prose genres like the fable, fairy tale or biblical parable. While such texts may at first glance seem nostalgic, they offer little comfort, making apparent the incapacity of traditional prose genres to do the social sorting and provide the epistemological foundations and moral frameworks that they were imagined to have provided in the past.

Jacques Rancière's concept of an "aesthetic regime" illuminates yet another dimension of the emergence of this form. In *The Politics of Aesthetics*, Rancière argues that the "aesthetic regime" appears around the beginning of the nineteenth century, replacing the "representative regime" of the Classical Age. While the representative regime relied on a "fully hierarchical vision of the community" that supported "the hierarchy of genres according to the dignity of their subject matter" among other features, the aesthetic regime "is based on distinguishing a sensible mode of being specific to artistic products" (Rancière 2004b: 22). Consequently,

> the aesthetic regime of the arts is the regime that strictly identifies art in the singular and frees it from any specific rule, from any hierarchy of the arts, subject matter, and genres. Yet it does so by destroying the mimetic barrier that distinguished ways of doing and making affiliated with art from other ways of doing and making, a barrier that separated its rules from the order of social occupations. The aesthetic regime asserts the absolute singularity of art and, at the same time, destroys any pragmatic criterion for isolating this singularity. (23)

This dynamic is operative in the prose poem: the status of each text as both poetry and prose asserts a singularity (and a contestation, following Johnson and Monroe), yet plays off forms associated with everyday life. The very subversion of hegemonic prose occurs in ways that are singular and without set criteria while shared concepts of what constitutes poetry are in flux.

In sum, the prose poem uses prose in ways that may seem familiar, evidence of its relationship with "other ways of doing and making" in Rancière's terms, yet enacts what is singular, often "difficult," surprising or disconcerting to a bourgeois audience, thereby participating in a "remediation" of prose while disrupting the category of poetic discourse.

Thus the prose poem was hardly Eliot's faded creature of the *fin de siècle*, but a more robust and radical form associated with changes in nineteenth-century discursive apparatuses and reading habits. It also emerges much earlier: Stuart Merrill's collection, *Pastels in Prose*, includes translations of Maurice de Guérin's *Le Centaure* (1833) and Bertrand's *Gaspard de la Nuit* (1842). Further, the *fin de siècle* for the prose poem effectively began in the 1860s. As the genre took off, some of its most prominent practitioners were young poets like Judith Gautier, Mallarmé, and Catulle Mendès—in their twenties, or younger in Gautier's case—just beginning their writing careers. It was in the November 1861 issue of Mendès' recently founded *La Revue fantaisiste* that the first prose poems by Baudelaire were published; twenty prose poems would appear in 1862 in the mainstream *La Presse*. Many of the texts from the 1860s would be collected and republished in later decades, often to greater acclaim and broader circulation than when they first appeared. Mallarmé's prose poems are a key instance of this prolonged arc of influence, as all of his prose poems from the first stage of composition were republished in *Pages* in 1891, five of these early texts were republished in *Vers et Prose* (1893), and finally all of his prose poems, joined by "Conflit" (earlier published among *Variations sur un sujet* in *La Revue Blanche* in 1895), appear in *Divagations* (1896). Judith Gautier's collection, *Le Livre de Jade*, first appearing in 1867, was republished in an expanded and revised edition, with a new "Prelude," in 1902 and again in 1908. New editions of Lautréamont's *Les Chants de Maldoror* (first published in 1868 and 1869) and Arthur Rimbaud's *Illuminations* (composed 1873–5; published first in 1886) also appeared in 1891. As Bernard notes, with Mallarmé's *Pages*, these collections reignited interest in the form for the final decade of the nineteenth century (Bernard 1959: 488–90). Prose poems were among the earliest publications by Huysmans: *Le Drageoir aux épices* (*The Spice Box*) in 1874 and *Croquis parisiens* (*Parisian Sketches*) in 1880. In his most famous work, the 1884 novel, *À Rebours* (*Against the Grain*), the protagonist, Des Esseintes, has compiled an anthology of the prose poem that he leafs through; the list of prose poets proposes a canon for the genre: Baudelaire, Bertrand, Villiers de l'Isle-Adam, Judith Gautier, and above all Mallarmé, whose works, especially "Plainte d'automne" ("Autumn Complaint") and "Frisson d'hiver" ("Winter Shiver"), count among "les chefs-d'oeuvres du poème en prose" ["the masterpieces of the prose poem"] (Huysmans 1884: 743). Merrill's collection of translations includes prose poems by all the poets from Huysmans' list and adds seventeen more, among them Huysmans himself. Des Esseintes' tastes are influential: Merrill translates the two prose poems by Mallarmé that Huysmans' character singles out—"In Autumn" and "In Winter." Judith Gautier, however, is the most represented poet, with fourteen prose poems in the volume; Bertrand comes in a close second with thirteen.

Chinese Poetry as French Prose: Judith Gautier, *Le Livre de Jade*

Taking our cue from Merrill, we turn now to a work that illustrates a significant trend in the prose poem's history: the translation of poetry as prose, anchoring the prose poem firmly in the category of "poetry." This practice was hardly new. As Bernard documents, translation was fundamental to the emergence of the prose poem with the popularity of prose translations of the Old Norse poetry of the *Edda*, of the pseudo-Gaelic Ossian cycle, of the Swiss writer Salomon Gessner's *Idylls* and of the English poet Edward Young's *Night-Thoughts* in the latter part of the eighteenth century (Bernard 1959: 25). Bernard finds a similar trend among the Parnassian poets, Gautier's circle, who, cognizant of translations of songs and poetry in prose form, produced their own pseudo-translations; she offers Charles Cros' *Chanson de la route Arya* (1873) as an example (Bernard 1959: 340–1).

Yet the question of authorship of *Le Livre de Jade* was not a simple one. The title page states "par Judith Walter," a germanization of "Gautier" chosen by her father as pseudonym (Camacho 1939: 32). For individual poems, she indicates another author, or at least inspiration, with the tag "selon" followed by a Chinese name. Hence these texts were initially presented as Chinese or Chinese-inspired poems rendered in prose. Much of the scholarship on *Le Livre de Jade* has focused on the infidelity of her translations. Indeed, she did not claim close translation. When seventeen poems first appeared in *L'Artiste* in 1864 and 1865, she called them "variations sur des thèmes chinois" ["variations on Chinese themes"] (Stocès 2006: 337; Thomas 2018: 78). The scholarly consensus is that they are at best loose translations; some may be fabrications and many are translations of just the first few lines (Yu 2007: 470). Clearly they reflect Gautier's interests and sensibilities to a significant degree. But that hardly diminishes their influence. While a collection of Chinese poetry in translation had appeared in 1862, *Poésies de l'époque des Thang* by the sinologist Léon d'Hervey-Saint-Denys, this more scholarly, "dustier" book did not have the impact of Gautier's; she is generally credited with introducing Chinese poetry to the French reading public (Détrie 1989; Yu 2007: 468). *Le Livre de Jade* was an immediate success among her contemporaries, as Pauline Yu observes:

> To the Parnassian and symbolist colleagues of Théophile Gautier, the exquisite imagery, subdued emotions, esteem for the poetic vocation, and lapidary quality of the Chinese poems as represented by Judith Gautier embodied to a remarkable degree their ideals of a finely wrought and dispassionate aesthetic that both elevated the work of art and salutarily countered an earlier, more declamatory style and the fetters of French meters. (Yu 2007: 474)

And they were important for twentieth-century poets, as Kenneth Rexroth notes:

> There was an important but usually ignored influence. All the Imagists were familiar with Judith Gautier's *Livre de Jade*—that precious minor classic of French letters. From it they got their first intimation of Chinese poetry—a poetry which fulfilled and surpassed the Imagist Manifesto beyond the abilities or dreams of even the best of the Imagists. (quoted by Thomas 2018: 83)

Of course, Judith Gautier could have translated these poems into French verse, so choosing prose reinforces the notion that poetry does not depend upon versification. What alternative definition for poetry does *Le Livre de Jade* intimate? Poetry is central to the cultural life represented in this volume. Gautier devotes a section of the collection to "Les Poëtes," and several pieces in the "Le Vin" ("Wine") section poke fun at inebriated poets. More significant, throughout the collection prose poems depict acts of composition, weaving the creation of poetry into the narrative of daily life. An example is "Pendant que je chantais la nature":

> *Selon Thou-Fou.*
> Assis dans mon pavillon du bord de l'eau, j'ai regardé la beauté du temps; le soleil marchait lentement vers l'occident au travers du ciel limpide.
>
> Les navires se balançaient sur l'eau, plus légers que des oiseaux sur les branches, et le soleil d'automne versait de l'or dans la mer.
>
> J'ai pris mon pinceau, et, penché sur le papier, j'ai tracé des caractères semblables à des cheveux noirs qu'une femme lisse avec la main;
>
> Et, sous le soleil d'or, j'ai chanté la beauté du temps.

Au dernier vers, j'ai relevé la tête; alors j'ai vu que la pluie tombait dans l'eau. (Gautier 1867: 28–9)

[*After Thou-Fou.*
Seated in my pavilion at the water's edge, I beheld the beauty of the moment; the sun moved slowly towards the west through the limpid sky.

Ships swayed on the water, lighter than birds on branches, and the autumn sun poured out its gold on the sea.

I took my brush, and, bent over the paper, I traced characters like the black tresses a woman smooths with her hand;

And, under the golden sun, I sang the beauty of the moment.

At the last verse, I raised again my head; then I saw that rain was falling on the water.][1]

This prose poem narrates a moment when nature inspires poetic composition and uses precise images and analogies to evoke both the scene to be described—ships floating on the water lighter than birds on branches—and the scene of writing—characters like a woman's black hair smoothed by her hand. This analogy, while invoking a register of desire, also makes visible the writing: strokes drawn with black ink on the paper, as much an image in the poem as those of nature, highlighting the materiality of writing (and its difference from French, as the writing is pictographic).

The writing depicted in the poems also produces poetry that is literally material: characters written on a fan in "L'éventail" ("The fan"); the ephemeral inscription of "Pensée écrite sur la gelée blanche" ("Thought written on white frost"); the intention to embroider verse among the flowers on a robe for an absent lover in "Chant des oiseaux, le soir" ("Birdsong, evening"); the embroidered silk a wife offers her husband as he is about to ride to war in "Les adieux" ("Farewells"). While undeniably there is a distancing in the Orientalizing that these prose poems indulge, there is also an intimacy in the detailing of day-to-day life, including those moments that give rise to poetry. As Mary Ann Caws observes regarding Gautier's many works about Asia, "Her writings do not feel simply Orientalizing: they feel authentic in their strangeness" (Caws 2006: 17). There is also oblique political and social commentary in some texts: the first poem of the section "Les Voyageurs" is "L"exilé" ("The exile"), about the sadness of exile; Victor Hugo's exile following the 1851 coup d'état comes to mind.[2] There are poems about the sorrow of separation enforced by war and emphasis on the composition of poetry by women, despite their confined condition in life. As Yu notes, "Her section on war, for example, does not follow Hervey-Saint-Denys's lead; it includes none of Du Fu's famous poems on the depredations of army conscription officers but, rather, presents the sorrows of conflict largely from the perspective of the women left behind" (Yu 2007: 469). Women as poets will be even more prominent in the 1902 edition as Gautier adds several poems by a woman,

"Ly-y-Hane," whom she describes as "cette Sapho chinoise" ("that Chinese Sappho") (Gautier 1902: 41).

Judith's famous father, Théophile, praised this volume, as she remembers in one of her autobiographical works, *Le second rang du collier* (*The Necklace's Second Strand*):

> Il aima beaucoup mon premier livre et me fit l'exquise surprise d'écrire quelques lignes sur lui, à propos du poème en prose de Baudelaire, *les Bienfaits de la lune*: 'Nous ne connaissons d'analogue à ce morceau délicieux que la poésie de Li-Taï-Pé, si bien traduite par Judith Walter, où l'impératrice de la Chine traîne parmi les rayons, sur son escalier de jade, diamanté par la lune, les plis de sa robe de satin blanc . . .' (Gautier 1900: 205–6)
>
> [He liked my first book very much and gave me the exquisite surprise of writing a few lines about it, with respect to Baudelaire's prose poem, *The Gifts of the Moon*: 'We know nothing like this delicious morsel other than the poetry of Li-Taï-Pé, so well translated by Judith Walter, in which the empress of China draws, among the rays, on her jade staircase, sparkling in the moonlight, the folds of her white satin gown . . .']

In fact, her prose poems conjure a mood that is markedly different from that of Baudelaire's: the melancholy of the woman in solitude, confined, separated from her lover, unlike the acrid and irony-laden ennui of "Les Bienfaits de la lune" ("The Gifts of the Moon") addressed to a "maudite chère enfant gâtée" ["dear damned spoiled child"] and mocking the romantic notions of "*lunatiques*" (Baudelaire 1975: 342, italics in the original). While Baudelaire's prose poems were undoubtedly a model, in Gautier's volume the composition of poetry is often an almost routine part of everyday life, a making that appears as embroidery on sleeves, inscriptions on fans, and as a process by which the subject bears life's emotional burdens. It is significantly part of a life that a secluded woman would recognize.

Huysmans: Artists, *Flâneurs*, and Paris *louche*

Baudelaire's project of urban prose poetry is more apparent in the work of other poets. Huysmans' *Le Drageoir aux épices* (1874) and *Croquis parisiens* (1880) are prominent examples. Besides taking up Baudelairean aesthetic concerns such as the correspondence between color and scent and explorations of how and where art is made, and themes like prostitution, inebriation, and flânerie, these prose poems thrive on a discordant and almost parodic relationship with the genres and discourses of the press. Indeed, Huysmans wryly presents them as commodities in the dedication and introductory verse poem fronting his first volume, *Le Drageoir aux épices*. In the dedication the volume is described as a "drageoir fantasque" ["fantastical box"] with "menus bibelots et fanfreluches" ["slight trinkets and baubles"]; according to the verse poem, this "spice box" contains:

> Un choix de bric-à-brac, vieux médaillons sculptés,
> Émaux, pastels pâlis, eau-forte, estampe rousse,
> Idoles aux grands yeux, aux charmes décevants,
> Paysans de Brauwer, buvant, faisant carrousse,

Sont là. Les prenez-vous? A bas prix je les vends.
(Huysmans 1874: n.p.)

[A choice of bric-à-brac, old sculpted medallions,
Enamels, pale pastels, an etching, a reddish print,
Idols with large eyes, and deceptive charms,
Peasants by Brauwer, drinking, carousing,
Are there. Do you take them? I sell them cheap.]

The texts are so many material objects, goods for sale, which, with a satirical modesty, he prices cheap. While mentioning "émaux" recalls Théophile Gautier's acclaimed collection of verse *Émaux et camées* (*Enamels and Cameos*) (1852), Huysmans chooses prose over verse, not only honoring Baudelaire's legacy but also mimicking the prose of a commercial press. Note, too, that the objects he lists are forms of representation available to the public and affordable to the middle class: antique medallions, enamels, pastels, an etching, an engraving. In the prose poems themselves, he elevates the texts' aesthetic stature through reference to great artists and the Louvre, but here he presents his works metaphorically as if they were available for purchase in Parisian shops. Their subject matter supports this characterization of these texts as devalued: these are "croquis de concerts & de bals de barrière" ["sketches of the concerts and balls of the outskirts"], he declares in the first line of the introductory poem, venues on the outskirts of Paris where the poor find entertainment. Likewise in his second volume, *Croquis parisiens*, the title of the collection and subsection titles echo the headings one would find in a newspaper of the time: "Croquis parisiens" ("Parisian Sketches"), "Types de Paris" ("Parisian Types"), "Petits Coins" ("Little Corners")—descriptive of Parisian life.

Section titles also name visual art genres in the tradition of Bertrand: "Paysages" ("Landscapes") and "Natures-mortes" ("Still-lifes"). Titles of individual prose poems refer to visual art forms and styles, particular paintings and painters: "Rococo japonais," "Camaïeu rouge" (a red monochrome painting on porcelain), "La Kermesse de Rubens" (title of a painting), "Adrien Brauwer" and "Cornélius Béga" (seventeenth-century Dutch painters) in *Le Drageoir aux épices*, "Vue des remparts du Nord-Paris" ("View of the Ramparts of North Paris") (suggesting a painting) and "Image d'Épinal" (popular prints) in *Croquis parisiens*. Yet while highly descriptive, these texts are not exercises in ekphrasis, but the art named serves as a point of reference, a means of elevating the scene being described and narrated.[3] "La Kermesse de Rubens," for instance, begins with the narrator on the road coming across a "bal des pêcheurs et des matelottes" ["a ball for fishers and sailors"] in Picardie (Huysmans 1874: 18). "Le Hareng Saur" ("Smoked Herring") in *Drageoir* (which reappears in *Croquis parisiens* under "Natures-mortes") gorgeously describes the fish in sensorial and painterly terms:

Ta robe, ô hareng, c'est la palette des soleils couchants, la patine du vieux cuivre, le ton d'or bruni des cuirs de Cordoue, les teints de santal et de safran des feuillages d'automne! (Huysmans 1874: 49)

[Your dress, oh herring, it is the palette of setting suns, the patina of old copper, the burnished gold tone of Cordoba leather, the sandalwood and saffron tints of autumn leaves!]

But this description which uses painting as a touchstone does not refer to a particular work, as the final paragraph makes evident:

> O miroitant et terne enfumé, quand je contemple ta cotte de mailles, je pense aux tableaux de Rembrandt, je revois ses têtes superbes, ses chairs ensoleillées, ses scintillements de bijoux sur le velours noir, je revois ses jets de lumière dans la nuit, ses traînées de poudre d'or dans l'ombre, ses éclosions de soleils sous les noirs arceaux! (Huysmans 1874: 50)

> [Oh glistening and monotone smoked fish, when I contemplate your coat of mail, I think of Rembrandt's paintings, I see again his superb heads, his sun-lit flesh, how his jewels glitter against black velvet, I see again his streams of light in the night, his trails of gold dust in the shadows, his dawning suns beneath black vaults!]

The beauties of the fish scales call to mind, rather, the most striking instances of Rembrandt's art, especially his handling of light. This attention to the making of art and to the effect of lighting and perspective on representation occurs repeatedly in the two collections; in "Ballade en prose de la chandelle des six" ("Ballad in prose for candles, six a pound"), for instance, illumination by candle, thematized as outmoded, is heralded for its part in paintings by "Rembrandt, Gérald Dow, Shalken" (Huysmans 1880: 74).

Huysmans also calls attention to the workings of literary art, noting the ability of analogy to bring to life memory. The narrator describes such an experience while watching a performance by acrobats at the Folies-Bergère:

> Et voilà que je songe à Anvers maintenant, au grand port où dans un roulement pareil s'entend le 'all right' des marins Anglais qui vont prendre le large. C'est ainsi pourtant que les lieux et les choses les plus disparates se rencontrent dans une analogie qui semble bizarre, au premier chef. L'on évoque dans l'endroit où l'on se trouve les plaisirs de celui où l'on se ne trouve pas. Ça fait tête-bêche, coup double. C'est la courte joie que le présent inspire, déviée à l'instant où elle lasserait et prendrait fin et, renouvelée et prolongée, en une autre qui, vue au travers du souvenir, devient tout à la fois plus réelle et plus douce. (Huysmans 1880: 18)

> [And then suddenly I dream of Antwerp, of the great port where, with a similar rolling sound, the 'all right' of English sailors about to put out to sea is heard. And yet that is how the most disparate places and things are joined through an analogy that seems bizarre at first. You call up from memory in the place where you find yourself the pleasures of the absent place. That creates a head-to-tail situation, a double hit. It is the brief joy that the present inspires, diverted the moment the joy fades and dissipates and, renewed and prolonged, turns into another joy that, seen through memory, becomes at once more real and sweeter.]

The murmur in the audience as the acrobats launch their most difficult feat and the sound of the rolling net in which the female acrobat is flung evoke a memory of English sailors preparing to set sail. This "analogy" renews and prolongs the present sensation of joy, making it "more real and sweeter." Analogy as the bringing into relation of disparate things and moments often drives the revelations of these two collections: fish scales recall the brilliance of the play of light in a Rembrandt; a humble dance of fishers and sailors a Rubens.

In other prose poems, Huysmans focuses squarely on Baudelaire's project articulated in the dedication of the *Petits poèmes en prose* to Arsène Houssaye: "C'est surtout de la fréquentation des villes énormes, c'est du croisement de leurs innombrables rapports que naît cet idéal obsédant" (Baudelaire 1975: 276) ["It is above all from the frequenting of enormous cities, it's from the crossing of their innumerable relations that this obsessive ideal is born"]. Huysmans' narratives of flânerie in Paris, especially in economically and geographically marginal neighborhoods, record the observations, reactions, and meditations of a roaming subject who savors the sordid, relishing the *frisson* of slumming. These texts include "La Rive gauche" ("The Left Bank") in *Le Drageoir aux épices* and "La Bièvre," "Le Cabaret des Peupliers" and "La Rue de la Chine" in *Croquis parisiens*. The *flâneur* also observes "types": the title of an entire section of *Croquis parisiens* that includes portraits of "Le conducteur d'omnibus" ("The bus conductor"), "L'ambulante" ("The streetwalker"), "La Blanchisseuse" ("The washerwoman") and "Le Marchand de marrons" ("The chestnut seller"). The texts concerned with La Bièvre, soon to disappear as part of Baron Haussmann's enormous public works project (the reconstruction of Paris and destruction of the medieval city), combine detailed observations of environmental degradation, the impact of the centuries-old pollution of the river by tanneries, butchers, and dye-makers, with descriptions of the impoverished inhabitants of the neighborhood and an anticipatory nostalgia for this river, soon to be buried, and the way of life it sustains:

Eh oui, la Bièvre n'est qu'un fumier qui bouge! mais elle arrose les derniers peupliers de la ville; oui, elle exhale les fétides relents du croupi et les rudes senteurs des charniers, mais jetez au pied de l'un de ses arbres, un orgue qui crachera en de lents hoquets les mélodies dont son ventre est plein, faites s'élever dans cette vallée de misères, la voix d'une pauvresse qui lamentablement chantera devant l'eau une de ces complaintes ramassées au hasard des concerts, une romance célébrant les petits oiseaux et implorant l'amour et dites si ce gémissement ne vous prend point aux entrailles, si cette voix qui sanglote ne semble pas la clameur désolée d'un faubourg pauvre! (from "La Bièvre," Huysmans 1880: 57–8)

[Ah yes, the Bièvre is nothing but a garbage dump that moves! but it waters the last poplars in the city; yes, it emits the fetid stale smell of putrid water and the harsh stench of the grave, but throw at the foot of one of its trees, an organ that will spit in slow hiccups melodies of which its belly is full, raise up in this valley of tears, the voice of a poor woman who will sing in lamentation by the water one of these plaintive ballads picked up by chance at concerts, a sentimental song extolling the little birds and beseeching love and say that this moaning doesn't grab you in the gut, that this sobbing voice does not seem to be the disconsolate clamour of an impoverished suburb!]

The scene produces its own dirge, again, art from urban blight, compounded by the expectation of imminent extinction, creating a nostalgia for that which is soon to be lost. A title like "Vue des remparts du Nord-Paris" invokes landscape painting; the perspective, however, shifts between a distant view of a plain leading to the city, dotted with smokestacks, chimneys, and their emissions, and close-ups of the inhabitants of the *banlieue*. The narrator describes sardonically "une idylle faubourienne, là, une maternité dont un enfant pompe avec acharnement la gorge sèche" (Huysmans 1880: 68) ["a working-class idyll, there, a maternal tableau in which a baby sucks tenaciously on a dried-up breast"]. Later, the focus is on a beggar with his two underfed dogs, leading to the narrator's summation of the relation between nature and humanity: "Et c'est alors surtout que le charme dolent des banlieues opère; c'est alors surtout que la beauté toute puissante de la nature resplendit, car le site est en parfait accord avec la profonde détresse des familles qui le peuplent" (69) ["And thus the melancholy charm of the outskirts works; thus the all-powerful beauty of nature shines brightly, for the site is in perfect harmony with the profound distress of the families who live there"]. This note of harmony is of course ironic; in a final observation, the narrator compares this scene to the new buildings and parks of the Haussmann project that benefit the wealthy. Both are instances of forcing nature "d'encadrer et de réfléchir"—to frame and reflect our lives, whether they be easy or pitiable (69).

Mallarmé: "Decadence" and Modernity

As noted earlier, Huysmans in *À Rebours* places Mallarmé's prose poems among "les chefs-d'oeuvres du poème en prose" (Huysmans 1884: 743) ["the masterpieces of the prose poem"]. At the time, his works were largely either lauded as exemplars of contemporary poetry by particular literati or ridiculed for their impenetrability. The latter complaint surfaces especially with the publication of "Le Démon de l'Analogie" ("The Demon of Analogy") in 1874: Francis Magnard deemed it "absolument incompréhensible" ["absolutely incomprehensible"] in *Le Figaro* in 1874 (Marchal 1998: 35). Gustave Kahn recalls "cette fameuse Pénultième, dont on parlait il y a dix ou douze ans de la rive gauche à partout: la Pénultième était alors le nec plus ultra de l'incompréhensible, le Chimborazo de l'infranchissable et le casse-tête chinois" (*Symbolistes et Decadents*, p. 138, quoted in Mallarmé 1945: 1557) ["that famous Penultimate, discussed ten or twelve years ago from the left bank to everywhere else: the Penultimate was then the nec plus ultra of the incomprehensible, the Chimborazo of the insurmountable and the Chinese puzzle"]. Already in 1884 Maurice Barrès interpreted this very dichotomy between his followers and the larger public to Mallarmé's disadvantage: "Il écrit pour lui seul, et quelques blasés le savourent" (Marchal 1998: 97) ["He writes for himself alone, and a few blasé followers relish it"]. In the 1890s, Adolphe Retté's attacks on Mallarmé were so fierce as to elicit a letter of protestation from André Gide, signed by Paul Valéry, Marcel Schwob, Paul Fort, and Emile Verhaeren, published in *Mercure de France* in 1897 (417–18). Yet in 1898 Tolstoy wrote in *La Revue blanche*: "Quant à ses écrits en prose, tels que *Divagations*, il est impossible d'y comprendre quoi que ce soit" (458) ["As for his writings in prose, such as the *Divagations*, it is impossible to understand anything there, no matter what"].

Mallarmé is crucial to the *fin-de-siècle* prose poem as one of its most prominent and revolutionary practitioners (and the scholarship on Mallarmé is vast), but also for his reputation as the author of effete, obscure works. Yet it is striking that the prose poems that the young Mallarmé composed in the 1860s are the most explicitly decadent, incorporating motifs that value the past: past models of beauty in "Le Phénomène futur" (like Baudelaire's verse poem "J'aime le souvenir de ces époques nues" ["I love the memory of those naked times"]), the devotion to reading the "derniers auteurs de la décadence latine" ["last authors of the Latin decadence"] in "Plainte d'Automne," the fixation on old things in "Frisson d'hiver"—"N'as-tu pas désiré, ma sœur au regard de jadis, qu'en un de mes poëmes apparussent ces mots 'la grâce des choses fanées'?" ["Didn't you desire, my sister with the look of long ago, that in one of my poems would appear these words, 'the grace of faded things'?"] (Mallarmé 1975: 271–2), even the climax of "Le Démon de l'Analogie" when the narrator flees after seeing the ancient instruments and dead birds at the lute-maker's shop, reminding him of the "sensation proper d'une aile glissant sur les cordes d'un instrument" ["actual sensation of a wing gliding over the strings of an instrument"] that opens the prose poem (272–3). In *À Rebours*, Des Esseintes finds that Mallarmé's prose poems, owing to their syntax and content, represent the essence of French decadence—"de la façon la plus consommée et la plus exquise" (Huysmans 1884: 744) ["in the most consummate and exquisite manner"].

But in "Un Spectacle interrompu" (published 1875), Mallarmé takes on contemporary newspaper discourse, imagining instead an ontology of dream journalism reflecting a poet's perspective:

> Que la civilisation est loin de procurer les jouissances attribuables à cet état! on doit par exemple s'étonner qu'une association entre les rêveurs, y séjournant, n'existe pas, dans toute grande ville, pour subvenir à un journal qui remarque les événements sous le jour propre au rêve. Artifice que la *réalité*, bon à fixer l'intellect moyen entre les mirages d'un fait; mais elle repose par cela même sur quelque universelle entente: voyons donc s'il n'est pas, dans l'idéal, un aspect nécessaire, évident, simple, qui serve de type. Je veux, en vue de moi seul, écrire comme elle frappa mon regard de poëte, telle Anecdote, avant que la divulguent des *reporters* par la foule dressés à assigner à chaque chose son caractère commun. (Mallarmé 1975: 276)

> [How far civilization is from supplying the delights attributable to such a state! for instance, it's astonishing that the dreamers who live in every major city never form an association to support a journal that reports events in the light peculiar to dreams. *Reality* is a mere artifice, good for providing the average intellect with stability amid the mirages of a fact; but for that very reason, it does rest on some universal understanding: let's see, then, whether there is, in the realm of the ideal, some necessary, obvious, simple quality that can serve as a type. I want to write, purely for my own benefit, a certain Anecdote, just as it struck my gaze (a poet's gaze), before it can be divulged by the 'reporters' whom the crowd appoints to assign a common character to each individual thing.] (Blackmore and Blackmore 2006: 95, 97)

Although the project of creating a dream-filtered newspaper remains unrealized, Mallarmé does employ the prose poem to record life in modernity. Two prose poems from his second period of composition describe changes in the experience of everyday life wrought by technology and industrialization, specifically the impact of train travel on the subject's imaginary ("La Gloire") and the impact of the construction of railroads on interaction among people from different classes ("Conflit").[4] For instance, the second paragraph of "La Gloire" (1886) renders the sensation of visual assault by advertisements rapidly passed as the eye focuses on the horizon, en route toward the forest of Fontainebleau, thereby threatening the subject's anticipated experience of nature as "apotheosis":

> Cent affiches s'assimilant l'or incompris des jours, trahison de la lettre, ont fui, comme à tous confins de la ville, mes yeux au ras de l'horizon par un départ sur le rail traînés avant de se recueillir dans l'abstruse fierté que donne une approche de forêt en son temps d'apothéose. (Mallarmé 1975: 288)

> [A hundred posters absorbing the days' misunderstood gold—a betrayal of letters—fled past, as if to every corner of the town, my eyes being drawn to the level of the horizon by a departure on the rails before being drawn into the abstruse pride bestowed by a forest at its time of apotheosis.] (Blackmore and Blackmore 2006: 123)

Much of the rest of the prose poem evokes a state of disillusionment produced by modernity—imagining and anticipating the psychological refuge of the forest, the subject hears it barked out as a mere railroad destination by the conductor, to which he inwardly responds:

> Tais-toi! Ne divulgue pas du fait d'un aboi indifférent l'ombre ici insinuée dans mon esprit, aux portières de wagons battant sous un vent inspiré et égalitaire, les touristes omniprésents vomis. Une quiétude menteuse de riches bois suspend alentour quelque extraordinaire état d'illusion, que me réponds-tu? (Mallarmé 1975: 288)

> [Be quiet! Don't, with any commonplace howl, reveal the shadow that has now been instilled in my mind to the carriage doors banging beneath an inspired and egalitarian wind, when the ever-present tourists have been spewed out. All around, a deceptive tranquillity of opulent woodlands is holding some extraordinary state of illusion poised, what answer can you give me?] (Blackmore and Blackmore 2006: 123)

Is the rich natural environment that he desires an illusion? The prose poem ends with his desire to be "l'intrus royal"—the royal intruder who enjoys solitude and singularity, unlike the crowd of whom he was part, while the retreating train itself seems "chimerical":

> j'attendis, pour l'être, que lent et repris du mouvement ordinaire, se réduisît à ses proportions d'une chimère puérile emportant du monde quelque part, le train qui m'avait là déposé seul. (Mallarmé 1975: 289)

> [I waited, in order to be that very person, until the train that had set me down there alone, once more under the influence of its habitual motion, slowly shrank in scale to the proportions of childish monster carrying various people somewhere.] (Blackmore and Blackmore 2006: 125)

Writing the alternative discourse of dream, he would save language from the "betrayal of letters" that is advertisement. He composes the elusive script of the dreamer and imagines his experience as different from that of his fellow travelers, yet he understands the irony of this assumption and sees through his own delusions of grandeur and superiority. It is especially in the prose poems of Mallarmé that Terdiman finds the risk of irrelevance because of their difficulty, but also the contestatory struggle with dominant discourses. They contributed to the image of the prose poem as an effete form, but they also produced an awareness that poetry and language were in crisis.

Rimbaud's *Illuminations* and the Future of the Nineteenth Century

Returning to the judgments of T. S. Eliot, we find he draws a different conclusion regarding the achievement of Arthur Rimbaud:

> Now, reverting for a moment to the 'Nineties, it must be observed that the prose poetry of this epoch was probably based upon the work of a man much greater than any poet then living—and that is Arthur Rimbaud. Few people in England have heard of the *Illuminations*, and most of them perhaps believe that the title indicates a supposed divine insight, instead of meaning simply 'Picture-book illustrations.' Rimbaud, who I suspect is responsible for everything that is good in Verlaine, wrote his prose poems between 1872 and 1875. They are short prose pieces, as obscure as *Kubla Khan* or *Christabel* and of a similar inspiration. They are amazingly convincing, and their prose is good French prose . . . Beside the prose of Rimbaud, the laboured opacity of Mallarmé fades colourless and dead. (Eliot 1917: 158)

Eliot was close to correct about the timing of Rimbaud's death and the ascent of his fame: Rimbaud died in 1891, the same year as his *Poésies* appeared with a new edition of *Illuminations* as well as *Une Saison en Enfer*, published by Vanier (Bernard 1959: 490). This edition of *Illuminations* reached a much wider public than the 1886 publication, first in Kahn's journal, *La Vogue*, then in a limited run: "Rimbaud a été non seulement le maître, mais le dieu de la seconde génération Symboliste, comme peuvent nous en assurer les témoignages de Paul Fort, de Claudel, de Valéry, la correspondance de Gide" (Bernard 1959: 490) ["Rimbaud was not only the master, but the god of the second generation of Symbolists, as the testimonies of Paul Fort, of Claudel, of Valéry, of Gide's correspondence confirm"]. Of course, the impact of Rimbaud's texts was felt even more widely in the twentieth century—on Ezra Pound, on the French Surrealists and on prose poets in France and internationally to the present day. John Ashbery emphasizes the importance of Rimbaud's aesthetic for twentieth-century avant-garde works in multiple media. Citing Rimbaud's 1871 letter to Georges Izambard, Ashbery reflects that

> absolute modernity was for him the acknowledging of the simultaneity of all of life, the condition that nourishes poetry at every second. The self is obsolete: in Rimbaud's famous formulation, '"I" is someone else' ("*Je est un autre*"). In

the twentieth century, the coexisting, conflicting views of objects that the Cubist painters cultivated, the equalizing deployment of all notes of the scale in serial music, and the unhierarchical progressions of bodies in motion in the ballets of Merce Cunningham are three examples among many of this fertile destabilization. (Ashbery 2011: 16)

That the prose poem plays off other genres is explicit in the titling of many of Rimbaud's *Illuminations*: for fairy tales, we find "Conte" ("Tale") and "Fairy"; "Devotion" is a subversive litany; "Après le deluge" ("After the Flood") rewrites Genesis;[5] "H" is a sort of riddle. Yet as many critics have observed (and the scholarship on Rimbaud is immense), these prose poems destabilize not only particular prose genres, but also subjectivity, the representation of space and time, and representation itself. For instance, in "Fleurs" ("Flowers"), description cedes to a metamorphic process:

D'un gradin d'or,—parmi les cordons de soie, les gazes grises, les velours verts et les disques de cristal qui noircissent comme du bronze au soleil,—je vois la digitale s'ouvrir sur un tapis de filigranes d'argent, d'yeux et de chevelures.

Des pièces d'or jaune semées sur l'agate, des piliers d'acajou supportant un dôme d'émeraudes, des bouquets de satin blanc et de fines verges de rubis entourent la rose d'eau.

Tels qu'un dieu aux énormes yeux bleus et aux formes de neige, la mer et le ciel attirent aux terrasses de marbre la foule des jeunes et fortes roses. (Rimbaud 2009: 306)

[From a tier of gold,—among silk cords, grey gauzes, green velvets and crystal discs that turn black like bronze in the sunlight,—I see the digitalis open on a carpet of silver filigree, of eyes and hair.

Pieces of yellow gold strewn on agate, mahogany columns supporting a dome of emeralds, bouquets of white satin and delicate ruby stems surround the water rose.

Like a god with huge blue eyes and snowy forms, the sea and sky draw to the marble terraces the crowd of young and strong roses.]

Flowers are figuratively composed of sumptuous materials: silk, gauze, velvet and crystal. The note of the hard mineral and bronze, however, is off-key in a list of soft fabric items. Bernard has suggested that, alternatively, this description is that of a theater: the décor is literal, the flowers metaphoric (Bernard 1960: 510). There are two actions described: the subject's viewing is central to the first paragraph, with "je vois" ["I see"] as climax. And the scene is dynamic as the subject views action, the opening of the digitalis. Again the mix is disconcerting: the carpet an amalgam of metal and body, silver filigree along with eyes and hair. The second paragraph continues to list what might be décor or descriptors for flowers: agate, mahogany with golden coins, the emeralds of the domed ceiling, white satin and rubied trim—gowns or flowers surrounding a flower? Besides this indeterminacy of metaphor, the perspective here shifts as the subject notices the dome, presumably no longer looking down from above. Finally in the third paragraph the view is up and down at once, as the blue of the god's eyes figures as a simile for the sea and the sky which again are in motion, drawing to marble terraces a "foule" ["crowd"] of roses. The metaphoric relationships remain indeterminate and in suspension while the scene metamorphoses.

As for the urban prose poem, the collection includes "Ville" ("City"), two texts titled "Villes" ("Cities"), "Métropolitain" ("Metropolitan"), and texts like "Les ponts" ("The Bridges") that destabilize and recreate description of the bridges of London in a narrative of metamorphosis and "Ouvriers" ("Workers") that, like some of Huysmans' *Croquis parisiens*, describes a walk in the *banlieue*, with an impoverished woman as companion. At moments these texts play off a gritty, sardonic Baudelairean model, as in "Ville," a prose poem about London: "Je suis un éphémère et point trop mécontent citoyen d'une métropole crue moderne" ["I am an ephemeral and not at all dissatisfied citizen of a metropolis thought to be modern"] (Rimbaud 2009: 300; Ashbery 2011: 75). But Rimbaud's "Villes" prose poems also present a mash-up of futuristic elements that Rancière has identified:

> a journey through the century, arranged in the space of a vision whose levels are confused and disjointed. In the city of the fragment there are many cities or fragments of 'cities of the century': the industrial metropolis, the New Babylon girded with its suburbs; the Charles Fourier city of the future with its galleries and passageways; the phantasmagoria of World's Fairs and Crystal Palaces; the bandstands and the esplanade of Luna Parks, the city that puts on spectacles of the entire universe, that raises up in its theaters, its festivals, and its stage sets of forests, mountains, waterfalls, deserts, the Orient, the Pole. (Rancière 2004a: 51)

Rancière finds here a "code of the century" (52). Referential description of urban scenes explodes into phantasmagoria, and the "I" of the poems is a baffled seer in "Villes [I]":

> Sur quelques points des passerelles de cuivre, des plate-formes, des escaliers qui contournent les halles et les piliers, j'ai cru pouvoir juger la profondeur de la ville! C'est le prodige dont je n'ai pu me rendre compte: quels sont les niveaux des autres quartiers sur ou sous l'acropole? Pour l'étranger de notre temps la reconnaissance est impossible. (Rimbaud 2009: 303)

> [From several points on the copper footbridges, platforms, staircases that round the covered markets and pillars, I thought I could judge the depth of the city! It is the marvel of it that I could not take in: what are the levels of other neighborhoods above or below the acropolis? For the stranger in our time exploration is impossible.]

In the futuristic city of the nineteenth century, the subject as viewer, tourist or *flâneur* is left utterly disoriented.

Pierre Louÿs' Hoax and "girls of the future society"

To understand the reception of the prose poem in the *fin de siècle*, the work of one more prose poet is worth noting. Pierre Louÿs published his translations from ancient Greek, *Les Chansons de Bilitis* (*The Songs of Bilitis*), as prose poems in 1894, yet these works were not translations, but Louÿs' own compositions. According to Louÿs' preface to the volume, "Vie de Bilitis" ("The Life of Bilitis"), Bilitis lived in the sixth century BCE and learned to compose poetry from Sappho. Her poetry, much of it lesbian erotica, was discovered by a German scholar, Monsieur G. Heim, etched on plaques of amphibolite on the walls of her burial cave along with three epitaphs that ornament her sarcophagus. (Vendula Štáfová notes that this fictitious scholar's name means "secret"—*geheim* in German [Štáfová 2017: 206].) Louÿs creates a visceral description of the tomb with a still fragrant vial of perfume hanging there, and a mirror and the stylus with which she applied eye shadow (Louÿs 1895: 14). Louÿs underscores the origin of these prose poems as ancient Greek poetry when he faux-speculates as to whether Bilitis composed them herself: "Comment une petite bergère de montagnes eût-elle appris à scander ses vers selon les rythmes difficiles de la tradition éolienne?" ["How would a little mountain shepherdess have learned how to scan verses in accordance with the difficult rhythms of the Aeolian tradition?"] (Louÿs 1895: 12) The hoax was so successful that several eminent Hellenists were taken in, including one who claimed to be familiar with all of her work (Shultz 2001: 378). A professor of Greek archaeology at the University of Lille, Gustave Fougère, congratulated Louÿs on having translated the Greek text so successfully (Štáfová 2017: 206).

The hoax was not to last long. Rowland Strong's January 1898 "Paris Letter—Pierre Louÿs's Success as a Decadent Greek—Vandal at the Academy" is revelatory. He praises Louÿs lavishly as a writer and scholar, calling him "certainly the most successful young writer in France" and a "consummate Hellenist." He paints the sensation produced by *Bilitis* in Paris:

> The stalls have been heaped with it, and this in spite of the Christmas and New Year's season, when little is bought as a general rule by the public except livres d'etrennes [*sic*; high-quality books offered as New Year's gifts]. M. Pierre Louÿs is so consummate an artist that he deserves very serious consideration. His productions are not of a kind that would appeal to the mother of a family or could be safely placed in the hands of the jeune fille; but for the serious student of French literature who desires to be in touch with the new movements in art it is indispensable to read them. (Strong 1898: BR34)

Strong goes on to note, citing an accompanying bibliography as his source, translations of *Bilitis* into German, Czech, and Swedish, a translation of six of the prose poems into French verse for *La Revue des Jeunes Filles* (*The Journal for Girls*), a lecture on them delivered in Göttingen, and music inspired by six of the poems by Debussy (here "Charles de Bussy, a young French composer of real genius"). Then he reveals the "secret"—that "Bilitis is none other than M. Pierre Louÿs himself" (Strong 1898: BR 34).

While Strong warns against *Bilitis* as a gift for *jeunes filles*, he nonetheless mentions the verse poems published in a magazine meant for girls without further comment. Louÿs, in the dedication of the volume, seems to intend such an audience: "ce petit livre d'amour antique est dédié respectueusement aux jeunes filles de la societé [*sic*] future" ["this little book of ancient love is dedicated respectfully to the girls of the future society"]. Indeed, *Les Chansons de Bilitis* would come to play a significant role in twentieth-century lesbian literature and circles. As Gretchen Schultz details, the American Natalie Clifford Barney, who knew and explicitly drew inspiration from Louÿs, formed a group of international lesbians in Paris that came to be known as Sappho 1900. While Louÿs' prose poems are now criticized as voyeuristic poetry whose real audience was men, they nonetheless inspired lesbian groups as late as the 1950s in New York:

> Indeed, in 1955, some sixty years after the publication of the *Songs*, Del Martin, Phyllis Lyon, and six other women founded the first lesbian social-political organization in the United States, the Daughters of Bilitis (DOB) . . . For the DOB, *Bilitis* came to signify secrecy, respectability, femininity, and romanticism, an interpretation that can be fathomed only in its midcentury context. (Schultz 2001: 380)

The proliferation of limited or private editions of the work provides further evidence of its underground popularity.

The case of *Bilitis* is illuminating. As (pseudo)-translation of ancient Greek verse, it emphasizes the poetic nature of the prose poem. Yet, as lesbian erotica, it underscores a culturally subversive role. It also claims, according to Louÿs' dedication, a future orientation.

Oscar Wilde: The Prose Poem in Evidence

We return now to events in 1890s England to understand better Eliot's desire in 1917 to put the genre into a box of tidily antiquated decadence. Wilde and Ernest Dowson both published prose poems during this decade. Wilde's *Poems in Prose* (1894) adopt the English Bible as literary model, employing an archaic diction, syntax and pacing in ironic parables. According to Frank Harris, W. B. Yeats, André Gide, and others, Wilde regaled his friends with these stories. But the spoken versions were simpler than the published ones where embellishments such as Hellenic references and trains of prepositional phrases simulate a formulaic primitivism. Dowson, too, in his collection *Decorations in Prose* (1899), draws on ancient literary traditions—of folk- and fairy tales. In both cases, the poets employ archaic and syntactically stilted language in expressions of modern disillusionment.[6] As Rachel Blau DuPlessis observes, Wilde's prose poems

> provide a blandly ironic *détournement* of Christianity: Christ's sacrifice is judged as based in His masochistic desires; His healing skills are busybody meddling and provoke further pain and suffering; the unintended consequences of the most sacred stories derail their apparently noble goals and deturn their sanctified conventionalized morals. (DuPlessis 2014: 31)

But what was more damning for the prose poem in England was the course of Wilde's trials in 1895. As I detail in *A Tradition of Subversion*, Wilde not only faced a legal system that criminalized homosexual acts; he also faced suspicions of the literary and artistic spheres, middle-class norms and the language of journalism that opposed the aestheticism that he perceived as beyond moral judgment. (The classism of the case made against Wilde is especially striking, a harsh questioning of his association with men from lower social classes.) There were three trials: one instigated by Wilde charging libel against the Marquess of Queensberry, Douglas's father, a charge that Wilde's lawyer finally withdrew, a second charging Wilde with indecency ending in a hung jury, and a third ending in a conviction of "gross indecency" with a sentence of two years' hard labor in Reading Gaol. The prose poem was embroiled in this saga through a piece of evidence produced at all three trials: Wilde's letter to Lord Alfred Douglas, that he characterized in court as "a kind of prose poem in answer to a poem Lord Alfred had written to me in verse"[7] (Hyde 1948: 312). In his sentencing, Justice Wills inveighed:

> But suppose such letters are 'prose poems,' suppose that they are things, of which the intellectual and literary value can only be appreciated by persons of high culture, are they thereby any the less poisonous for a young man? Is the language of those letters calculated to calm and keep down the passions which in a young man need no stimulus? (Hyde 1948: 331)

Thereby, the prose poem was judged criminally dangerous.

A more immediate influence on Eliot derives from his Harvard days. Irving Babbitt, a professor close to Eliot, was the author of *The New Laokoon: An Essay on the Confusion of the Arts*, which condemns hybrid forms in highly gendered terms, characterizing the masculine as that which holds to clear "distinctions" as opposed to writing "intended primarily for women and men in their unmasculine moods" (Babbitt 1910: 244). Nonetheless, Eliot wrote at least four prose poems and published one, "Hysteria" (1915), and later translated St. John Perse's long prose poem, *Anabase*, into English. But in 1917 Eliot was ready to draw his own clear "distinctions" ridiculing hybrids of poetry and prose.[8] Eliot distances himself from the moralism of Babbitt, but evidently did not forget the lessons of categorical distinctions.

Conclusion

W. D. Howells, in his introduction to *Pastels in Prose*, invokes the modernity of the form—"a peculiarly modern invention" (Howells 1890: v)—while depicting it as a fragile thing. He notes that they avoid moralizing: "The very life of the form is its aerial delicacy, its soul is that perfume of thought, of emotion, which these masters here have never suffered to become an argument." But in understanding their difference, he reifies the form in a way that implies weakness and impermanence. He finds the title, "Pastels," all too appropriate: "more than once, forgetting that modern invention has found a way of fixing the chalks, I have felt, in going over these little pieces, that the slightest rudeness of touch might shake the bloom, the color, from them" (Howells 1890: viii). A reviewer in the April 13, 1890 *New York Times* adopts Howells' theme, calling the collection "A Dainty Volume" ("Dainty" 1890: 19). One imagines that this sort of characterization fed Eliot's negative assessment twenty-seven years later. As the prose poem circumvents the didactic, its potency may be underestimated by such critics. While Huysmans coyly downplays the value of his own prose poems by naming them "trinkets and baubles," their depictions of marginal populations in both seventeenth-century Holland and nineteenth-century France are nevertheless searing. To categorize the *fin-de-siècle* prose poem as either ornamental or subversive, as decadent or anarchic, represents a false choice. The power of even the most faded or "pastel" productions is due for reassessment.

Notes

1. Translations are mine unless otherwise noted.
2. Indeed, Judith Gautier sent the volume to Hugo in Guernsey, with his name inscribed in Chinese letters meaning "To the triumphant exile who walks with solemnity, saying immortal things" (Knapp 2004: 76).
3. See Joseph Acquisto for a detailed study of how Huysmans as "literary *flâneur*" adopts and parodies contemporary modes of writing in *Drageoir* (Acquisto 2007).
4. See Terdiman's insightful reading of the interaction between the poet and workers in "Conflit" (Terdiman 1985: 323–37).
5. See James Lawler's convincing reading (Lawler 1992: 130 ff).
6. I offer readings of Wilde's and Dowson's prose poems to this effect in *A Tradition of Subversion* (Murphy 1992: 30–43).
7. An interesting connection: Louÿs composed a sonnet in French based on the letter, published in 1893 in the Oxford undergraduate journal, *The Spirit Lamp*, edited at that time by Alfred Douglas (Hyde 1948: 112).
8. Eliot's contemporary target was the prose poems of Richard Aldington, whose flaw, to his mind, was their hybrid nature. As Michel Delville points out, "if Eliot had been the lesser poet, and Aldington one of the most respected and influential men of letters of his time, the history of the contemporary prose poem in English might have taken a totally different turn," although Delville rightly notes another influencing factor: the weakness of British *fin de siècle* prose poems as models (Delville 1998: 6).

Works Cited

"A Dainty Volume" (1890), *The New York Times*, April 13, p. 19.

Acquisto, Joseph (2007), "The Decadent Writer as Collector and Flâneur: On Intertextual Networks and Literary Spaces in Huysmans," *French Forum*, vol. 32, no. 3, Fall, pp. 65–80.

Ashbery, John (2011), Introduction, Arthur Rimbaud, *Illuminations*, New York and London: Norton.

Babbitt, Irving (1910), *The New Laokoon: An Essay in the Confusion of the Arts*, Boston: Houghton Mifflin.

Baudelaire, Charles (1975), *Œuvres complètes*, ed. Claude Pichois, Paris: Gallimard Pléiade.

Bernard, Suzanne (1959), *Le Poème en prose de Baudelaire jusqu'à nos jours*, Paris: Librarie Nizet.

Bernard, Suzanne (1960), Notes, Arthur Rimbaud, *Œuvres*, Paris: Éditions Garnier Frères.

Blackmore, E. H. and A. M. (trans.) (2006), Stéphane Mallarmé, *Collected Poems and Other Verse*, Oxford and New York: Oxford University Press.

Camacho, Mathilde (1939), *Judith Gautier: Sa vie et son œuvre*, Paris: Librairie E. Droz.

Caws, Mary Ann (2006), *Glorious Eccentrics: Modernist Women Painting and Writing*, New York: Palgrave Macmillan.

Delville, Michel (1998), *The American Prose Poem: Poetic Form and the Boundaries of Genre*, Gainesville: University Press of Florida.

Détrie, Muriel (1989), "*Le Livre de Jade* de Judith Gautier: un livre pionnier," *Revue de Littérature Comparée*, July 1, vol. 63, no. 3, pp. 301–24.

DuPlessis, Rachel Blau (2014), "'Virile Thought': Modernist Maleness, Poetic Forms and Practices," in Natalya Lusty and Julian Murphet (eds), *Modernism and Masculinity*, Cambridge: Cambridge University Press, 2014, pp. 19–37.

Eliot, T. S. (1917), "The Borderline of Prose," *The New Statesman*, 19 May, pp. 157–9.

Gautier [Walter], Judith (1867), *Le Livre de Jade*, Paris: Alphonse Lemerre, <http://www.gutenberg.org/ebooks/46828> (last accessed August 2, 2020).

Gautier, Judith (1900), *Le Collier des Jours: Le second Rang du collier*, Paris: Félix Juven.
Gautier, Judith ([1902] 2004), Prélude, *Le Livre de Jade*, Paris: Imprimerie nationale.
Howells, W. D. (1890), Introduction, *Pastels in Prose*, trans. Stuart Merrill, New York: Harper & Brothers.
Huysmans, Joris-Karl (1874), *Le Drageoir à [sic] épices*, Paris: E. Dentu.
Huysmans, Joris-Karl (1880), *Croquis parisiens*, Paris: Henri Vaton.
Huysmans, Joris-Karl ([1884] 2005), *À Rebours* in *Romans I*, ed. Pierre Brunel, Paris: Robert Laffont, pp. 561–762.
Huyssen, Andreas (2015), *Miniature Metropolis: Literature in an Age of Photography and Film*, Cambridge, MA and London: Harvard University Press.
Hyde, H. Montgomery (ed.) (1948), *The Trials of Oscar Wilde*, London: William Hodge.
Johnson, Barbara (1979), *Défigurations du langage poétique: la seconde révolution baudelairienne*, Paris: Flammarion.
Knapp, Bettina L. (2004), *Judith Gautier: Writer, Orientalist, Musicologist, Feminist: A Literary Biography*, Dallas, Lanham, MD: Hamilton Books.
Lawler, James (1992), *Rimbaud's Theatre of the Self*, Cambridge, MA and London: Harvard University Press.
Lloyd, Rosemary (1999), *Mallarmé: The Poet and His Circle*, Ithaca and London: Cornell University Press.
Louÿs, Pierre ([1895] 1898; 4th edn), *Les Chansons de Bilitis*, Traduites du grec par Pierre Louÿs, Paris: Société du Mercure de France.
Mallarmé, Stéphane (1945), *Œuvres complètes*, ed. Henri Mondor and G. Jean-Aubry, Paris: Gallimard Pléiade.
Marchal, Bertrand (ed.) (1998), *Mallarmé: Mémoire de la critique*, Paris: Presses de l'Université de Paris-Sorbonne.
Merrill, Stuart, translator (1890), *Pastels in Prose*, New York: Harper & Brothers.
Monroe, Jonathan (1987), *A Poverty of Objects: The Prose Poem and the Politics of Genre*, Ithaca and London: Cornell University Press.
Murphy, Margueritte S. (1992), *A Tradition of Subversion: The Prose Poem in English from Wilde to Ashbery*, Amherst: The University of Massachusetts Press.
Rancière, Jacques (2004a), *The Flesh of Words: The Politics of Writing*, trans. Charlotte Mandell, Stanford: Stanford University Press.
Rancière, Jacques (2004b), *The Politics of Aesthetics: The Distribution of the Sensible*, trans. Gabriel Rockhill, London and New York: Continuum.
Rimbaud, Arthur (2009), *Œuvres complètes*, ed. André Guyaux, Paris: Gallimard Pléiade.
Shultz, Gretchen (2001), "Daughters of Bilitis: Literary Genealogy and Lesbian Authenticity," *GLQ: A Journal of Lesbian and Gay Studies*, vol. 7, no. 3, pp. 377–89.
Štáfová, Vendula (2017), "'Je est un autre'. Le pastiche et la parodie chez Pierre Louÿs," *Echo des études romanes*, vol. 13, no. 2, pp. 205–13.
Stocès, Ferdinand (2006), "Sur les sources du *Livre de Jade* de Judith Gautier (1845–1917) (Remarques sur l'authenticité des poèmes)," *Revue de Littérature Comparée*, July–September, 319, pp. 335–50.
Strong, Rowland (1898), "Paris Letter—Pierre Louÿs's Success as a Decadent Greek—Vandal at the Academy," *The New York Times*, January 15, p. BR34.
Terdiman, Richard (1985), *Discourse/Counter-Discourse: The Theory and Practice of Symbolic Resistance in Nineteenth-Century France*, Ithaca and London: Cornell University Press.
Thomas, Andrea S. (2018), "Judith Gautier, *Vers Libre*, and the Faux East," *Symposium*, vol. 72, no. 2, pp. 77–88.
Yu, Pauline (2007), "'Your Alabaster in This Porcelain': Judith Gautier's *Le livre de Jade*," *PMLA*, vol. 122, no. 2, pp. 464–82.

Part II

Visual Mediations

6

Cubism and the Prose Poem

Mary Ann Caws

The Cubistic Mode

When we think of Cubism as an art style, we instantly consult several volumes: for the art historical side, Robert Rosenblum's *Cubism and Twentieth-Century Art*, and from the poetic side Guillaume Apollinaire's *The Cubist Painters*. The latter will give us the view from inside, as it were, because we all remember with delight the photos of the Bateau Lavoir, where Picasso hung out, as did Max Jacob, and so we can salute the three of them, as in the celebrated Picasso rendering of the *Three Musicians*, believed to be showing a Harlequin (Picasso), a Pierrot (Apollinaire) and a monk (Max Jacob), as if they were performing a sardana, that Catalan dance.

Apollinaire's preliminary essay in *Méditations Esthétiques: Les Peintres Cubistes* [*Aesthetic Meditations: The Cubist Painters*] of 1913, simply called "On Painting," is of course the starting point, as it reflects on creativity and the lasting if effervescent novelty of truth. It reminds us of his poem "Toujours" ["Always"] as he is always wanting to demonstrate what is new and lasting. This is also, no surprise there, the foundation of surrealism, in the Cubist orientation. It was Reverdy whose journal *Nord–Sud* (named after the metro line running north and south) laid down the techniques of what had come to be known known as Cubism, and subsequently that confrontation of images Reverdy explosively advocated became the founding theory of surrealism's aesthetics.

This new art, claims Apollinaire, will be to painting as music is to literature: pure of subject matter, but, and this is an urgent matter for all that remains to be said, no style will be refused, Cubism will forever consist of multiple perspectives on whatever subject or object is considered. In that fashion, the static is ruled out, since the point of view is changeable. Ah yes, the cubic form of shapes like houses and other human constructions leading Matisse and others, like Louis Vauxcelles, to use the term, then accepted by Apollinaire, as he says, in the Brussels exhibition of 1911—and it bears pointing out that it was also the same poet's use of the term "surrealism" for his play *Les Mamelles de Tiresias* which initiated that appellation. He was a great beginner.

Cubism is, says the poet, a conceptual art "which reaches up to the heights of creation" (Rosenblum 1976: 93). Pantheisms abound in Apollinaire's view of knowledge and of greatness, and it seems worth quoting his first line about Picasso, in all its undeliberate referentiality:

If we knew, all the gods would awaken. (Apollinaire 2004: 25)

His was the voice of Cubism, and yet he often protested against the idea of Cubism as a system, and so shall we. From my point of view, deeply influenced by that of Pierre Reverdy as well as Apollinaire, the entire surrender to formula, any formula, is deeply erroneous. Thus the "Cubist" or "Cubism-oriented" question of such prose poems as will come into this chapter will resemble more a diverse assemblage of fragmentary remarks than a unified clump of harmonious statements.

Let me advocate the joyful simplicity—in the good sense—of Rosenblum's descriptions of the Cubist moment, as the odd appearance of "something strangely unstable and shifting" in an exploration of an "ever more ambiguous and fluctuating world" (Rosenblum 1976: 31). Yet Rosenblum also points out the discovery of Cubism that each style is singular and that any can exist together, independently justified and enabling the pluralism essential to the environment of Cubism. In his introduction to his masterful *The Cubist Poets in Paris: An Anthology*, Leroy Breunig reminds us that Reverdy thought the term "Cubist poetry" absurd, but very much advocated the fixing on the poem as an object as you would on a pin, and sketches out some of the varied elements in the prose poems as we have them: the multiple perspectives, the spaces as solid, transcribed as the empty blanks in a poem, the flat surface of the canvas as the verbs in the present tense, the contradiction between the view of the prose poem as an object and also as an experience, the idea of *simultanism*, and the use of the shapes of letters as elements of significance (Breunig 1995: xxiv–xxv).

Now the poets I want to call upon here are three: Gertrude Stein, Max Jacob, and Pierre Reverdy, who illustrate remarkably different features we consider reflective of the prose poem. These elements in their individuality appear to me as so many elements gathering somehow to make up a poetry of prose, not to be reduced to some overall statement, but rather to remain with their separate angles, a painting in itself for us to deal with, at once an experience and an interesting object, as it deals with us.

Gertrude Stein's Permissions

First, I want to think about the particular American-ness of Gertrude Stein's prose poetry, even as she was in Paris, doing and often ruling over her Cubist Thing. Let us try, first of all, Stein's "A Box":

A BOX

Out of kindness comes redness and out of rudeness comes rapid same question, out of an eye comes research out of selection comes painful cattle. So then the order is that a white way of being round is something suggesting a pin and is it disappointing, it is not, it is so rudimentary to be analysed and see a fine substance strangely, it is so earnest to have a green point not to red but to point again. (Stein 1967: 165)

No strange wording here, but so much deliberate indicating. For this being of a box is about pointedness, and once the disparate elements are assembled it makes its point finely. So the red/rude hints at, points to, the omitted yet sounded "read," and leads to, points to the stated term "round." The pin is pointing to "not to red" or to the unstated but roundly heard "read," and to the further point: "to point again." And the repetitions shout. No pain here, but in that heard and actually stated "painful," and the audible sibilant hissings, "something suggesting," "substance strangely," enhance the fineness of the "pin" and that point it makes so well.

One of the finer points of the prose poem as conceived by and constructed by Gertrude Stein is the humor, the straight-faced humor of the brief scenes. One of my favorites is non-hurriedly but summarily stated: "A Time to Eat." It says what it has to say in a succinct manner, repetitious, to be sure, and strung out, but totally sufficing:

A TIME TO EAT

A pleasant simple habitual and tyrannical and authorised and educated and resumed and articulate separation. This is not tardy. (Stein 1967: 171)

No, in fact, it is just on time, as the title indicates. This particular prose poem entitles itself just as it should: that is in fact, again, just what Stein does, as perhaps her American-ness permits. We might talk, then, about *Permissions*. And, to chime in with another table—important as it is to see how the prose poems of this period can rhyme together—we could call upon Gertrude Stein's "A Table," still in our *Tender Buttons* reference:

A TABLE

A table means does it not my dear it means a whole steadiness. Is it likely that a change. A table means more than a glass even a looking glass is tall. A table means necessary places and a revision a revision of a little thing it means it does mean that there has been a stand, a stand where it did shake. (Stein 1967: 174)

I am thinking of the table in a celebrated poem about and within a painting, in the combined work of Pierre Reverdy and Juan Gris, which will come later, as another sort of still life still very much alive.

Max Jacob's Character

Max Jacob's prose poem "Mauvais caractère," which I translate as "Shady Soul," perfects the shifting viewpoint in a wildly oppositional manner, taking in the being of the world as well as (the) being in the world:

Mauvais caractère

J'aime trop l'univers pour vivre avec un seul être.
Comment m'entendre avec un humain sans l'offenser au nom de tous? Démon, je ne puis m'entendre avec Dieu; ange, avec le démon. Comment m'entendre avec toi si je ne m'entends pas avec moi-même? Où fuir si le ciel et l'enfer me sont aussi fermés que la terre?

[Shady Soul

I am too fond of the universe to live with just one being.
How could I get along with a human and not offend him in the name of everyone? A demon, I can't get along with God; an angel, with the demon. How could I get along with you if I don't get along with myself? Where to escape, if the sky and hell are as closed to me as the earth?] (Caws 2008: 50)[1]

More ambivalent than ambiguous, and also set at an extreme, in fact two of them, depending on which angle we take: celestial or grounded, this prose poem asks a fundamental question in our face and cannot deliver an answer: is not a truly poetic prose an unanswerable excitement of this- and/or thatness?

Max Jacob was, and remains for us, the most tragic of beings—hauled away by the Nazis after he had been to morning Mass at St. Benoit-sur-Loire, having been "converted" even as his Jew self would never change.[2] He was in himself a piece of poetic prose. His genuflections, highly observable and melodramatic, were no less real in their performance. They were "genuine genuflections" as his query about the heaven–hell of the world and the word and the life he so dramatically lived reads as real: where on earth to go and be? The very opposite of a "still life" in a static sense, they are as genuinely their desperate contrasts as the notion of "still" is with the notion of "life." Having defined the prose poem as the oxymoron of a genre, we have also, as theoreticians of the form, our prismatically impossible convergence, here. Where to go, asks this poet? Here, we say.

Sometimes the Jacobian prose poem simply plays out a story: the narrator is humiliated, or some figures appear, even dryads, who disappear, or some keys are lost and then found. "C'est un conte, c'est seulement un conte." ["It's a story, it's just a story."] And, equally on the level of poetic play, some of the prose poems in the *Cornet à dés* operate purely with resonance and puns: in *Equatoriales solitaires* [*Solitary Equatorials*], a fighting man is laid low ["combat, bas!"], windows are born ["les fenêtres, naître!"] and so on, ending with "Un million de souris. . .de sourires" ["A million mice . . . smile"] (Jacob 1967: 54).

More interestingly, he can play on the inside/outside combination, as will Pierre Reverdy so often—see his *"Poème de la lune"* ["Poem of the Moon"]:

Il y a sur la nuit trois champignons qui sont la lune . . . Il y a dans le jardin des fleurs rares . . .

Il y a dans ma chambre obscure une navette lumineuse . . . Il y a dans ma tête une abeille qui parle. (76)

[There are in the night three mushrooms which are the moon . . . There are rare flowers in the garden . . .

There is in my dark room a luminous shuttle bus . . . There is in my head a talking bee.]

Or again, in "Erreurs de la miséricorde"

J'irai plutôt avec lui en prison pour qu'il ne s'échappe pas! Ainsi fût fait! Nous sommes dans une grosse tour. Une nuit, dans mon sommeil, je fis le geste de le retenir, je ne touchai plus qu'un pied blanc qui montait vers le plafond et me voici seul dans la tour. Sur le haut des grosses charrettes de foin les yeux des paysans me regardent à la fenêtre avec miséricorde. (64)

[I will go with him to prison so he can't escape! Done! We are in a large tower. One night, in my sleep, I tried to hold him back, I only touched a white foot rising towards the ceiling and I am alone in the tower. Atop big carts of hay, the eyes of the peasants look at me in the window with pitying eyes.]

What Max Jacob is perhaps most memorably the author of are the prose poems about vision. He can show all the glittering elements of a text without forcing them into any easy convergence: they shine forth as separate selves, illuminating some of the prime examples of the complicated genre. Take first his kaleidoscope, which, when you shake it, gives entirely different pictures:

Kaléidoscope

Tout avait l'air en mosaïque: les animaux marchaient les pattes vers le ciel sauf l'âne dont le ventre blanc portait des mots écrits et qui changeaient. La tour était une jumelle de théâtre; il y avait des tapisseries dorées avec des vaches noires; et la petite princesse en robe noire, on ne savait pas si sa robe avait des soleils verts ou si on la voyait par des trous de haillons. (163)

[Everything seemed a mosaic: the animals walked with their paws skyward except the ass whose white stomach bore some written words which kept changing. The tower was an opera glass; there were gilded tapestries with black cows; and the little princess in a black dress, you couldn't tell if her dress had green suns or if you were seeing it through the holes of rags.]

This is surely a perfect illustration of different perspectives: upside down, changing letters and readings, opera glasses, gold and black colors, cows and asses and a princess, poverty and wealth and majesty.

Here is an inside/outside text, architectural and geographical, earthly and celestial, cloudy and watery:

Mystère du ciel . . .

En revenant du bal, je m'assis à la fenêtre et je contemplai le ciel: il me sembla que les nuages étaient d'immenses têtes de vieillards assis à une table et qu'on leur apportait un oiseau blanc paré de ses plumes. Un grand fleuve traversait le ciel. L'un des vieillards baissait les yeux vers moi, il allait même me parler quand l'enchantement se dissipa, laissant les pures étoiles scintillantes. (203)

[Coming home from the ball, I sat at the window and I contemplated the sky: it seemed to me that the clouds were immense heads of old men seated at a table and that someone was bringing them a white bird decked in his feathers. A great river was crossing the sky. One of the old men lowered his eyes towards me, he was even going to speak to me when the magic spell faded, leaving just the pure stars sparkling.]

The vision is dreamlike and magical; it brings in the world outside the window, and the animal world as well as the natural one, and the dissolution of the fanciful makes sense of both.

A poem that I had not appreciated before will serve as ending for this Max Jacob salute, for it now appears to me to be a perfect poetic statement about contraries (ink and diamonds, sky and river), the poetic self-consciousness (the madheaded star-nibbler), and the upside-down-ness of the thing—very Max Jacob in all his irony and self-ironic reflection!:

Un peu de modernisme en manière de conclusion

Dans la nuit d'encre, la moitié de L'Exposition universelle de 1900, illuminée de diamants, recule de la Seine et se renverse d'un seul bloc parce qu'une tête folle de poète au ciel de l'école mord une étoile de diamants.

[A little modernism as a kind of conclusion

In the night of ink, half of the Exposition universelle of 1900, lit by diamonds, pulls back from the Seine and turns over all at once because a madheaded poet in the sky of the school bites into a star of diamonds.] (228)

Pierre Reverdy's Genius

From my point of view, Pierre Reverdy is the *summum cum laude* of the prose poem. I will attempt to show, briefly as his succinct genius deserves, in a few of his prose poems, how his genius worked, generally with a characteristic oddness.

The Ambivalent Situation

One of the defining characteristics of the prose poem in its Cubist mode is the ambivalent situation of an in-between verse between two others: it could go with one or the other, like this Reverdy so wonderfully titled "Perspective":

    On pense à demain
        Mais où seront-ils
        Morts sans y penser
Quand le mur s'efface
        Le ciel va tomber (Caws 2013: 94)

    [Think of tomorrow
        Where will they be
        The thoughtless dead
When the wall vanishes
        The sky will fall]
        (Caws 2013: 95)

So we read where the dead will be when that wall disappears, but also that when that happens, the sky will collapse. They are both part of the view, and the certainty of the ending has no influence whatever on the betwixtness of the wall: precisely a wall, the perfect element to separate two sides.

Here is the scene, which is itself the situation:

La Lampe

Le vent noir qui tordait les rideaux ne pouvait soulever le papier ni éteindre la lampe. Dans un courant de peur, il semblait que quelqu'un put entrer. Entre la porte ouverte et le volet qui bat—personne! Et pourtant sur la table ébranlée une clarté remue dans cette chambre vide. (Caws and Terry 2015: 274)

[The Lamp

The black wind twisting the curtains couldn't lift the paper or put out the lamp. Fear was sweeping through—it seemed that someone could have come in. Between the open door and the shutter clacking—no one! And on the still shaking table a radiance stirs in the empty room.] (Caws and Terry 2015: 275)

How very Reverdy to start with an inability: that wind, dark as it is, can twist the curtains, whatever color they might be, but can't raise anything or extinguish anything. Too much fright: where or when did someone enter, or are we wrong? Perhaps nothing at all, and yet the table is trembling, where the lamp must still be lit, and the paper (was someone writing on it?) remains . . . The emptiness belies an absence and yet the radiance (the lamp indeed, but perhaps something else) is stirring that space.

A perfect Cubist space, in its almost malevolent mystery. Such a dark wind, such a movement of the curtains, such a clattering of a shutter, such an unclosed door . . . and yet despite that gloom, there is not a threat but a radiance . . . so here there reign at least two perspectives. We are looking at the same table, where the "still life" is quaking. Elsewhere, on that table, another still life is both painted and written, in the Juan Gris–Pierre Reverdy collaboration with which this chapter will conclude, as the Max Jacob prose poem ended the penultimate part.

Who Goes There?

Plus lourd

On attendait que l'homme étendu en travers du chemin se réveillât. La courbe de la nuit s'arrêtait à la chaumière encore éclairée, au bord du pré, devant la forêt qui fermait ses portes. Toute la fraîcheur au-dedans. Les animaux n'étaient là que pour animer le paysage pendant que tout le reste marchait.

    Car tout marchait, sauf les animaux, le paysage et moi, qui étais, avec cette statue, plus immobile que l'autre, là-haut, sur le piédestal des nuages. (Caws 2008: 76)

Heavier

[They waited for the man stretched out across the road to waken. The curve of the night stopped at the thatched cottage which was still lit up, at the edge of the meadow, in front of the forest which was closing its gates. All the freshness inside. The animals were there only to enliven the landscape while all the rest walked.

For everything was walking, except the animals, the landscape, and me, who with that statue, more immobile than the other one, was up there, on the pedestal of clouds.] (Caws 2008: 76; trans. John Ashbery)

Initially, we have only questions. How indefinite is this "they," and who might that be? We will not be told, nor will we know who this man is, and what he is doing there, lying down in the street. Is he asleep in the night's curvaceous being, in this cottage retaining its freshness while outside some animal beings just posed there, to give life to the picture . . .

Where are the walkers going? I, narrating this story, I am not going with them, I am staying, and some statue not dreaming like that man stretched out is up there like me, in the sky?

Some still life, this, and yet we feel how the elements are indeed shifting about, myself and that man, the picture and the dream, and indeed everything is heavy, heavier and less mobile than the dreamer.

And also than myself. This poem is as characteristic of Reverdy as that last poem was of Max Jacob and as Gertrude Stein's tender complications are of her American Parisianness.

Nothing, then, for her, is ever closed off, and we return to Reverdy's perfect openness of the poem "'. . . Is Ajar'":

'. . . S'entre-bâille'

Du triangle des trottoirs de la place partent tous les fils et la faux de l'arc-en-ciel, brisée derrière les nuages.
Au milieu celui qui attend, rouge, ne sachant où se mettre.
Tout le monde regarde et c'est au même endroit que le mur découvre sa blessure.
La main qui ferme le volet s'en va, la tête que coupe le rayon ne tombe pas—et il reste cette illusion qui attirait, même instant, tous les regards vers ce drame qui se jouait, face au couchant, sur la fenêtre. (76)

['. . . Is Ajar'

From the triangle of the sidewalks of the square, wires start, and the scythe of the rainbow, broken behind the clouds.
In the center the one who waits blushes, not knowing where to stand.
Everyone is looking and in that same place the wall reveals its wound.
The hand that closes the shutter disappears, the head cut by the ray doesn't fall—and there remains that illusion which at the same moment drew everyone's eyes toward the drama that was being enacted, opposite the sunset, against the window.] (76)

What an open and opening picture, already from the title, with its origin geometrically squared and its lighting both cutting and clouded, delayed! All attention concentrates on the stage, where uncertainty creates a painful gap, right there. No disaster and no agent visible, while the performance takes place as the light is about to fade, in full view both in and out, natural and set up, for the actor and the audience.

The perspective is initially on the base line, then radiates out and up skyward, before settling on the principal actor touched by the rainbow's color, far from immobile, and gathering all the glances. As if the action were to be lit now from inside, with the shutter closed, the figure illuminated, and now framed against the exterior glow.

It would be interesting to contrast this poetic spectacle of cubistic and ambivalent suggestive shape (where to stand? where to be placed, especially with all eyes upon you?) with such a symbolist spectacle as that of, say, a Mallarmé sonnet such as the early hospital drama before a window, with little ambiguity about the placing, called "Les Fenêtres," where life is fled by the narrator hanging on wherever he can:

> Je fuis et je m'accroche à toutes les croisées
> D'où l'on tourne le dos à la vie . . . (Mallarmé 1982: 10)

> [I flee and cling to all the window frames
> Whence one can turn his back on life . . .] (Mallarmé 1982: 11; trans. Hubert Creekmore)

Cubist prose poetry takes, with delight, a shifting stance, not only about shape and placement, visuality and interpretation, but about the very angles of possible perception. Nothing is to be pinned down, as the prose and the poetry are free to rub up against each other as they choose. This is the drama itself.

The Narrative Issue: Structure and Scenes

Were a prose poem to tell a story, it might verge over into prose narrative as opposed to remaining in its double nature. In both the cases of Max Jacob and Pierre Reverdy, some of the more challenging texts tell a story with a resolution—therefore a closure, whereas the prose poem in Cubist mode depends on ambivalence—or a recap—a repetition thus undoing the binary balance by tipping it toward one sense.

Here is a repetition that rules out the openness that is a necessary part of the Cubist prose poem: "The Poets" begins with an unmoving musician whose severed hands are playing the violin, and who ends the poem playing "avec ses mains qui ne l'écoutent pas" (Caws 2013: 4) ["with his hands that do not listen" (Caws 2013: 5; trans. Ron Padgett)]. Quite as if they were indeed no longer part of him whom they cannot or do not hear. Neither the melody nor the player, albeit the self. This prose poem is indeed about separation, but is resolved in a violence too clear.

Another Reverdian example is "Belle étoile," with a nightmare scene of the narrator's losing his keys amidst others who all have keys, and a sense of lostness, of insults flying from all sides, and then the utter relief: the finding of a door and unlocked gate, as he huddles in a curtained and protective night in which he could sleep: "J'ai pu dormir." A perfect ending, from lostness until a finding, of self and shelter, and a total closing of the story.

Or then, as in the so Picasso-like "Saltimbanques," with a juggler, a thin child dancer, to whom no one would give anything, given his size, because the slightest coin might weigh him down: "Il est si maigre." Such thinness ironically rules out his reward that might save him: it feels like a parable, and thus, nothing remains to say.

And there might be a temporal close-off, the contrary of something pending, as we often feel in a prose poem. Take the twilight poem "Entre Deux Crépuscules" ["Between Two Twilights"], where we hear tranquil steps, a refrain of joy or prayer, and then a delay, so that nothing happens, hearts are reassured, and everything is delayed until tomorrow: "Puisque tout est encore remis au lendemain." We could say here, as in the Max Jacob poem, "This is just a story." *Ceci n'est qu'un conte*, indeed.

As opposed to that, take a seeming repetition which is sufficiently altered to permit the necessary difference–openness:

> Plus Loin que là
> A la petite fenêtre, sous les tuiles, regarde. Et les lignes de mes yeux et les lignes des siens se croisent. J'aurai l'avantage de la hauteur, se dit-elle. Mais en face on pousse les volets et l'attention gênante se fixe. J'ai l'avantage des boutiques à regarder. Mais enfin il faudrait monter ou il vaut mieux descendre et, bras dessus bras dessous, allons ailleurs où plus personne ne regarde. (Caws 2013: 2)

> [Further Away Than There
> At the little window, under the roof tiles, look. And the lines of my eyes and the lines of hers intersect. I'll have the advantage of height, she says to herself. But across the way they push open the shutters and the embarrassing attention is fixed. I have the advantage of the shops for looking. But really, I'd have to go up or it's better if you come down and, arm in arm, let's go somewhere else where no one looks at us.] (Caws 2013: 3; trans. Ron Padgett)

A very strange poem, to be sure. And all the stranger, when the looking repeats three times. We are threatened by the others who watch us, but at least I can have the pretense of just gazing—we just choose to go either way, up or down, and this alternate motion (with its unbalance, since one way is better) preserves the elsewhereness and the absence of obvious performance.

Poems and Paintings

The most impressive of the prose poems seem to jibe perfectly with the Cubist paintings. A few examples come to mind instantly: the way in which Juan Gris and his paintings of windows and their lookouts work as complications of space inside and outside, within both the mind and the world and the word: thus, the poem as object and the way it permits us a view of how it all works together.

Take these paintings of Juan Gris: the window on the Rue Ravignan of 1915 (Plate 1), and then, in the same year, the still life with a poem of Reverdy (Plate 2) (he carefully painted, as if in the writing of the poet, and collaged the cardboard on the canvas), and then a still life at a window (Plate 3), and then the mountain Le Canigou, right behind Collioure, of 1921 (Plate 4). They each, all four, exhibit one of the functions of the prose poem as we might conceive of it and view it: the play of inside and out, the window and the view, the swerve between the apparent and the "real," the object right side up and the upside down, and the various perspectives composing the complexity of the prose poem at its most complicated.

In the various windows, with their door frames, the multiple perspectives work within each other. In his *Still Life with Poem*, as René de Costa's superb article on "Juan Gris and Poetry: From Illustration to Creation" points out, this card table and poem call upon another work, Cézanne's *Card Players*. This insertion of another space and angle works in a fascinatingly same way as the window and the table and the frame. The Cubist prose poem looks out and in and across in much the same way, so that these three canvases reflect on each other and across. And in the still life, that pipe and those cards and the bottle give the sense of living to the frame and table and door.

The Reverdy poem, as painted by Juan Gris imitating Reverdy's handwriting, says this:

> Se tiendrait-elle mieux sous ton bras ou sur la table? Le goulot dépassait d'une poche et l'argent dans ta main, moins longue que la manche. On avait gonflé le tuyau de verre et aspiré l'air. Quand celui qu'on attendait entra, les premiers assistants s'attablèrent. . . . Et la flamme qui luit dans leurs yeux . . . d'où leur vient-elle?

> [Would it hold up better under your arm or on the table? The bottleneck protruded from a pocket and the money in your hand, not as long as the sleeve. Someone had blown into the glass pipe and drawn in the air. When the one they were awaiting came in, the ones who got there first sat at the table . . . . And the flame shining in their eyes . . . where did it come from?]

Reverdy's poem displays the same objects as in so many cafés: the cards, the pipe, the wine bottle swaying on the table top. The poem was never published and feels all the more valuable as a commentary by the poet on the painterly work: "et moi aussi je suis peintre" ["and I too am a painter"], as Apollinaire would have said.

I want to make the point that the Cubist prose poem calls out as well as in, calls across as well as in dialogue, is aware of its own complicated being. This seems an appropriate way to close, as with a play of words and image, and a toast, a commentary on that binary issue of the already interdisciplinary mode of Cubism in prose poetry.

Notes

1. Translations are mine, unless otherwise indicated.
2. See information in Warren 2020.

Works Cited

Apollinaire, Guillaume (2004), *The Cubist Painters*, trans. Peter Read, Berkeley: University of California Breunig, Leroy C. (1995), *The Cubist Poets in Paris: An Anthology*, Lincoln: University of Nebraska Press.
Caws, Mary Ann (ed.) (2008), *The Yale Anthology of Twentieth-Century French Poetry*, New Haven: Yale University Press.
Caws, Mary Ann (ed.) (2013), *Pierre Reverdy*, New York: New York Review Books.
Caws, Mary Ann, and Patricia Terry (eds and trans.) (2015), *Pierre Reverdy: Poems Early to Late, a Bilingual Anthology*, Boston: Black Widow Press.
Costa, René de (1989), "Juan Gris and Poetry: From Illustration to Creation," *Art Bulletin*, vol. 81, no. 4, pp. 674–92.
Jacob, Max (1967), *Le cornet à dés*, Paris: Gallimard.
Mallarmé, Stéphane (1982), *Selected Poetry and Prose*, ed. Mary Ann Caws, New York: New Directions.
Rosenblum, Robert (1976), *Cubism and Twentieth-Century Art*, New York: Abrams, 1976.
Stein, Gertrude (1967), *Look at Me Now and Here I Am: Writings and Lectures 1909–45*, London: Penguin.
Warren, Rosanna. *Max Jacob: A Life in Art and Letters*. New York: Norton, 2020.

7

THE MODERN FRENCH PROSE POEM AND VISUAL ART

Emma Wagstaff

Not only is the development of the prose poem central to modern poetry in French, but poets of the period, from Charles Baudelaire through the Surrealists to Francis Ponge, are also known for a keen interest in visual art, writing in particular on the art of their contemporaries. It would therefore seem natural that poets should devote prose poems to individual works of art or to artists. Baudelaire, however, suggested that the best response to a work of art might be a sonnet or an elegy, thereby privileging verse forms (Baudelaire 1992: 78). Indeed, modern French writers of prose poetry who write about art rarely do so in the form of the prose poem and favor instead the longer-form text: either the essay or pieces of poetic prose.[1]

This essay will examine examples of prose poetry in French since the early twentieth century. Without claiming to encompass all the manifestations of the prose poem in French, it will argue that the prose poem conceived as object, dominant in the first half of the twentieth century, gives way to two distinct tendencies: the prose poem that offers a form for reflection on poetry; and an insistence on the part of poets that poetry should use only everyday language. The distinction could be said to hinge on the extent to which writers deem the poem to be prosaic, a question that preoccupied French poets in the latter part of the century. While an interest in art is not overtly part of that debate, it is striking that those writers who propose that there is no separate poetic language are much less likely to write texts in response to art than are those for whom reflection on poetry and poetic forms part of their creative project.

As Michel Delville writes, "traditional categories associated with the 'poetic'—including metaphorical density, stylistic sophistication and lyric intimacy—have long ceased to be the convenient hallmarks which, at the time of Oscar Wilde and Walter Pater, enabled one to separate the wheat from the chaff by making the difference between 'poetic prose' and the undecorative, utilitarian matter-of-factness of 'prosaic' prose" (Delville 1998: 3–4). The quotidian nature of American poetry has inspired some French writers, adding a further transatlantic connection to the established enthusiasm of writers such as Gertrude Stein for European modernism.

The Cubist Prose Poem?

Gertrude Stein knew artists such as Picasso while living in Paris and traveling in Spain. She also wrote what Delville describes as "an early example of . . . Stein's art of 'impersonal' portraiture" in her text "Picasso," one of the *Three Lives* that adopt the form of a short prose text written in paragraphs (Stein 1909; Delville 1998: 53). The prose poems of *Tender Buttons* (1914) are often as brief as two or three lines, and are statements evoking straightforward subject matter, though their interpretation is far from limpid: the collection is divided into sections called "Objects," "Food," and "Rooms." They offer an early lens through which to view possible connections between prose poetry focused on things and an art movement characterized by paintings and collages that draw attention to their status as objects, while also depicting them through the genre of still life. Stein's texts might be called Cubist in that they appear to suggest still life painting, and the lack of expressive poetic subject could also be compared to the Cubist dismantling of a secure subject position. Stein herself cited the influence of Cézanne (also often seen as precursor to the Cubists) and Flaubert, although literary references are not clearly made in the texts themselves:

> Everything I have done has been influenced by Flaubert and Cézanne, and this gave me a new feeling about composition. Up to that time composition had consisted of a central idea, to which everything else was an accompaniment and separate but which was not an end in itself, and Cézanne conceived the idea that in composition one thing was as important as another thing. (Stein 1973: 15)

Leonard Diepeveen explains that Stein frequently uses the words "why?" and "what?," suggesting causation, and deictic words such as "this" (Diepeveen 2018: 18). The texts have no narrative and little punctuation. He writes: "At its core is an examination of language as a system and of our desires for meaning. Reading *Tender Buttons* is a process of watching meaning fade in and out of presence" (Diepeveen 2018: 19). Titles suggest the texts will be about named things, but this does not often turn out to be the case.

The most significant connection with Cubism might therefore stem from the lack of importance accorded to the content. As John C. Stout argues in *Objects Observed*, his study of the American and French poetry of objects, "since the subject matter or content of the poems is conventional, she can focus entirely on the elaboration of distortionary techniques. The process of writing itself replaces the actual subject matter" (Stout 2018: 23). Both Stein and Cubism draw attention to the form of the work. The poem "Dirt and not copper," from the first section, "Objects," illustrates the way in which Stein frequently opens a text with the promise of a logical statement, only to thwart a search for meaning as the statements continue:

DIRT AND NOT COPPER.
    Dirt and not copper makes a color darker. It makes the shape so heavy and makes no melody harder.
    It makes mercy and relaxation and even a strength to spread a table fuller. There are more places not empty. They see cover.

Many of the poems in the "Objects" section refer to color, either by naming particular colors or by mentioning color as a phenomenon, and, as such, they incite visualization of a scene that appears to be evoked. After the opening sentence of "Dirt and not copper," however, it is no longer possible to link the elements of color, shape, heaviness, melody, mercy, relaxation, strength, table, fuller, places, not empty and cover into a meaningful whole. Aspects of a still life painting emerge (copper, table, places), but the actions suggested do not make conventional sense: dirt and heaviness are not obviously connected to making a melody harder, and the inclusions of mercy and relaxation are in an unclear and uneasy relationship with places at a table. The repeated use of "makes" suggests and then frustrates any attempt to understand a change in state. At the end it is not clear who or what "they" are, or how or why they might "see cover." The prose poems of *Tender Buttons*, while comparable to Cubist art in their privileging of the creative process over narrative or expression, are nevertheless far from ekphrastic evocations of visual phenomena, even in the broad definition of ekphrasis as proposed by Murray Krieger: "any attempted construction of a literary work to make it, as a construct, a total object, the verbal equivalent of a plastic art object" (Krieger 1998: 4).

Pierre Reverdy was an early champion of Cubist artists as well as a writer of prose poetry, and objects feature heavily in his best-known collection, *Les Ardoises du toit* (1918). However, the poems of his earlier collection, *Poèmes en prose* (1915), depict visual scenes, with fewer objects and more frequent use of the first person than in his subsequent work. The link with still life paintings was not yet visible. In "Gardiens" (Guards), for instance, he evokes a complex atmosphere in visual terms:

Au coin de la rue sous le seul bec de gaz, trois ombres attendent. Je passe, et déguisant ma crainte comme ils affichent leur force, j'ai l'air de me rassurer en regardant leurs uniformes.
  Il fait sombre, plus loin, et la nuit est pleine de dangers. (Reverdy 2004: 51)

[At the corner of the street, under a single gaslamp, three shadows are waiting. I pass by and, disguising my fear just as they display their strength, I seem to reassure myself by looking at their uniforms.
  It is dark further on, and the night is full of danger.][2]

Fear and uncertainty are closely linked to darkness, shadows, flickering light and an inability to see clearly, with the uniformed figures suggested only via glimpses. Reverdy thwarts any clarity in perspective because the subject also appears to be viewed momentarily from the outside: "j'ai l'air de." It is hard to discern whether the impression he gives is to the three figures or to himself.

In addition to the many poems that convey a strong visual sense, Reverdy suggests an interest in painting in this collection through references to tropes of the period familiar in works of artists such as Picasso, including "Saltimbanques" ("Acrobats") (Reverdy 2004: 52), and phrases such as the sentence that concludes "Fronts de bataille" ("Battle Fronts"): "Mais celui qui les aurait peints n'était plus là" ["But the one who would have painted them was no longer there"] (Reverdy 2004: 50).

Reverdy wrote about the work of the new Cubist artists in the journal he founded and edited, *Nord–Sud*, and elsewhere. In particular, he published an early piece on Cubism in the first issue of *Nord–Sud* (1917) and another in the journal *Art* in 1919. His important article on Braque called "Une aventure méthodique" ("A Methodical Adventure") appeared in *Note éternelle du présent* (Reverdy 1973: 39–104). In *Nord–Sud* he wrote, of Cubism:

Il s'agit seulement d'une figuration dans l'espace sans l'aide de la perspective; de l'utilisation de la matière sans l'atmosphère qui l'enveloppe, et au total d'une création à l'aide d'objets réformés et conçus par l'esprit, d'une œuvre qui est le résultat d'une émotion au lieu d'en être la répétition; c'est par là que les œuvres qu'apporte cette esthétique nouvelle constituent des réalités en elles-mêmes. Il s'agit de réalité artistique, bien entendu, par opposition à l'œuvre d'art imitative de la réalité. (Reverdy 1975: 145–6)

[What is at stake is simply setting out figures in space without the help of perspective; using material without the atmosphere that surrounds it. Overall, it is about creating a work that is the result of an emotion rather than the repetition of it, with the help of objects remade and conceptualised by the mind. That is how works emanating from this new aesthetic constitute realities in themselves. This is artistic reality, of course, in contrast to a work of art imitating reality.]

Objects are vital to Cubist work as Reverdy sees it, because painting them enables the artist to create a feeling in the artwork rather than attempting to convey or imitate one. Critical discussion of the extent to which Reverdy's poetic writing might be classified as Cubist has had to take into account his own assertion that there was no such thing as Cubist writing: "la poésie cubiste n'existe pas" ["Cubist poetry does not exist"] (Reverdy 1975: 145). Among those who do apply the epithet to his work, Andrew Rothwell cites Jean Rousselot and Jean Cassou, arguing himself that "it does at least seem legitimate to talk of a cubist poetics" (Rothwell 1989: 32–3 (33)). Reverdy asserted the connection in reverse, entitling an essay in *Nord–Sud* "Le cubisme, poésie plastique" ("Cubism, plastic poetry").

Certainly, in the poems of *Les Ardoises du toit*, elements of what might be deemed Cubist work are identifiable. They frequently evoke domestic interiors, quiet and still, calling to mind still lifes. Any single perspective is lacking: things are seen and heard, but by whom, and from where? Despite the domestic setting, space is not fixed or easy to visualize. Viewpoints are disrupted, even threatened. There is no clear first-person subject position to express thoughts or emotions, though the "je" is not absent. For example, the poem "Sortie" ("Exit") opens:

> Le Vestiaire
>   Le Portemanteau
>   La lumière
> Au mur des têtes inclinées
>   Un rayon d'éléctricité
> La voix qui chante

(Reverdy 2004: 185)

[The Cloakroom
        The Coatrack
                The light
Bowed heads on the wall
        A beam of electricity
The voice singing]

(Reverdy/Caws and Terry 1981: 55)

The poem names things and phenomena without a clear subject position, while implying a temporal setting and the potential for an emotional response.

The poems of *Les Ardoises du toit* are not prose poems because they contain line breaks.[3] Nevertheless, clear continuities are visible between them and the prose poems of *L'Étoile peinte*, published in 1921. Those texts take up the allusion to specific moments in time while increasing the narrative element and smoothing over the fragmented evocation of things. For example, the opening poem, "Vieux port" ("Old Port"), reads:

> Un pas de plus vers le lac, sur les quais, devant la porte éclairée de la taverne.
> Le matelot chante contre le mur, la femme chante. Les bateaux se balancent, les navires tirent un peu plus sur la chaîne. Au dedans il y a les paysages profonds dessinés sur la glace; les nuages sont dans la salle et la chaleur du ciel et le bruit de la mer. Toutes les aventures vagues les écartent. L'eau et la nuit sont dehors qui attendant. Bientôt le moment viendra de sortir. Le port s'allonge, le bras se tend vers un autre climat, tous les cadres sont pleins de souvenirs, les rues qui penchant, les toits qui vont dormir.
> Et pourtant tout est toujours prêt à partir. (Reverdy 2004: 307)

> [One more step towards the lake, on the docks, before the tavern's lighted door.
> Against the wall, the sailor sings, the woman sings. The boats sway, the ships pull a little harder on their chains. Inside there are deep landscapes etched in the glass: clouds are in the room, and the heat of the sky and the sea's sound. All the vague adventures set them to one side. Water and night wait beyond. Soon will come the moment to go out. The port lengthens, the arm stretches towards another clime, all the frames are full of memories, the streets sloping, the roofs about to sleep.
> And yet everything always stands upright ready to leave.] (Reverdy/Caws and Terry 1981: 231)

Rather than offering fragments of a scene from different perspectives, the poem proposes hints of a narrative without linking the parts together in relationships of sequence of causation. There is a strong visual sense, combined with unexpected personification that thwarts any ekphrastic impulse, and the suggestion that while a perceiving human subject is not named, s/he is present as a self that sees and remembers. The final line proposes that the scene is provisional without allowing secure temporal anchoring. As such it calls to mind Rimbaud's prose poems in *Illuminations*, which frequently end by suggesting that the scene evoked is about to disappear or be destroyed. "Les Ponts," for example, concludes with the sentence "Un rayon blanc, tombant du haut du ciel, anéantit cette comédie" (Rimbaud 1984: 171) ["A white ray falling from high in the sky destroys this comedy" (Rimbaud/Varèse 1957: 55)]. The visual effects of the poem might suggest comparisons between representative paintings, drawings, or engravings that evoke a scene, but Reverdy ensures that the text subverts the genres of still life and narrative paintings and introduces precarity, or the possibility of its own erasure.

The Prose Poem as Narrative

"Vieux port" suggests a visual moment captured in time as much as an object, despite the references to frames and glass. It stops short of telling a story, but implies that the reader is witnessing an instant that might be part of a longer sequence of events. A writer who takes this further in texts that do respond to visual art is René Char, a former Surrealist who, among writings on other artists, published two short pieces about the art of Alberto Giacometti: a prose poem, "Célébrer Giacometti" ("Celebrate Giacometti"), from the collection *Retour amont*, and a piece of "poésie critique" (critical poetry, or poetic criticism), "Alberto Giacometti," which nevertheless resembles a prose poem in its form. Char's texts therefore constitute an exception to the argument that writers of prose poetry usually adopt a longer form for their texts on art. Robert W. Greene claims that it "would be difficult to identify major points of divergence" between the two texts on Giacometti (Greene 1994: 169).

"Célébrer Giacometti" (Char 1983: 431) presents a visit to the artist's studio "en cette fin d'après-midi d'avril 1964" ["at this end of an afternoon in April 1964"]. Giacometti is not named in the text itself, but presented as an ancient despotic eagle and subsequently as a blacksmith, the fire resulting from his impassioned determination as he forms his works. The poem has been described as resembling a *fait divers* evoking a crime scene in a newspaper: a painting of the artist's model and lover Caroline emerges from a process involving "combien de coups de griffes, de blessures, d'hématomes?" ["how many scratches, injuries, and bruises?"] (Char 1983: 431; Eichbauer 1989: 136). The reason for this violence is that the artist feels the need to destroy his creation in order to advance its progress, so the analogy with the blacksmith begins to fall away. Char writes of "nous autres, ses témoins temporels" ["the rest of us, his temporal witnesses"], continuing the suggestion of a crime, and involving writer and reader together in producing a contemporaneous testimony to what is observed.

Char's other text, "Alberto Giacometti," is not included in a poetry collection, but among a series of writings on his artist friends. Rather than taking the form of art criticism, it sets up a scene, though this time the atmosphere created is one of calm contemplation rather than violent or frenetic activity. There is no artist present; indeed, to start with there appear to be no people at all in the landscape: instead, there is domestic detail including washing that had been left outside on a line overnight, and "les paysans n'avaient pas ouvert leur porte" (Char 1983: 686) ["the peasants had not opened their doors"]. Then "un couple de Giacometti" ["a Giacometti couple"] comes into view. Readers familiar with Giacometti's elongated sculptures will have in mind thin, isolated figures: "Nus ou non. Effilés et transparents" ["Naked or not. Frayed and transparent"]. The scene is cinematic, as if the camera were panning around a village and zooming in on certain images in preparation for the action to begin. It is created, however, using a combination of the imperfect and past historic tenses, implying a narrative rather than straightforward visual picture. The story then becomes one of allusion to suffering, with the couple compared to the windows of burned-out churches, but the atmosphere of damage is leavened by the man's gesture: "l'homme toucha le ventre de la femme qui remercia d'un regard, tendrement" ["the man touched the woman's stomach, and she thanked him with a look, tenderly"]. The final sentence includes the first mention of the artist himself: Giacometti is said to have been asleep inside the house. Brief suggestive narratives of this kind are a feature of post-Surrealist writing, and the text also invites comparisons with micro-fiction, especially where that "presents itself in terms of singularities which evade easy classification, and which by their extremity come to constitute events in their own right, often evoking an aesthetics of the sublime" (Botha 2016). The text is anchored in time at a moment of transition: the night and the coming day are both present: the doors will soon be unlocked, the peasants will soon begin work, it will become hot; the dew marks the end of the night, but will disappear. There is no clear narrative conclusion, but rather an intense impression of significance, or sense of "access to a reality which transcends the work" (Botha 2016). Art is embedded in the text here, but the text itself emphasizes narrative over its own formal coherence: Char's texts do not attempt to take the form of Giacometti's work.

Poems of Objects

Like Reverdy, Francis Ponge writes about art in poetic prose texts rather than in prose poems; like Char and many poets and prose writers of the twentieth century, he responded to the work of Alberto Giacometti, but his texts on Giacometti span several pages. Ponge's essays and poetic prose on art by his contemporaries were collected in *L'Atelier contemporain* (1977a); his subjects range from the Cubists to *art informel* exponent Jean Fautrier. In 1943, for example, he wrote an essay on the *Otages* (Hostages) series of paintings by Fautrier, who created the works in response to the torture and executions carried out by Nazi guards in the grounds of the asylum in which Fautrier was staying, and which he overheard but did not see. Ponge reflects on the extent to which it is possible to write a text about these works, suggesting that "[c]e que Fautrier a exprimé par sa peinture ne peut être exprimé autrement" (Ponge 1977a: 32) ["what Fautrier expressed in his painting cannot be expressed otherwise"]. That does not prevent him from writing the essay; instead it encourages an approach that would not attempt to imitate what Fautrier does, but rather respond to the material forms in the artworks—the colors and the thickness of the paint—by manipulating his textual material. He suggests that the challenge he faces is not exclusive to the difficult subject matter of Fautrier's work, writing: "De toute façon, la bonne peinture sera celle dont, essayant toujours de parler, on ne pourra jamais rien dire de satisfaisant" (Ponge 1977a: 16) ["In any case, good painting is that about which one will never be able to say anything satisfactory, however hard one tries"]. Art as a medium is distinct from writing, such that a textual answer to it will never be "adequate."

In place of the poets creating prose poems as either object or story, Ponge writes poems that could be said to be "of" objects in his best-known collection *Le parti pris des choses* (1942). Here he produces dense evocations of everyday objects that are, if not verbal equivalents of an art object, then at least verbal equivalents of natural or man-made objects. He theorized the process humorously, suggesting that it involved writing from the "objet" [object] by means of the neologism "objeu" (Ponge 1962: 133–65) [objest; "jeu" meaning "game"], and arriving thereby at "objoie" [objoy] (Ponge 1967b: 26–8). This was, nevertheless, a serious exercise, and one that resembles an activity familiar to French schoolchildren of the period: Stout reminds us that during the Third Republic (1870–1940) pupils were required to enumerate the features of an object as daily writing practice in school (Stout 2018: 3).[4]

Generally, Ponge's object poems adopt the short form of one or two pages, though he occasionally wrote longer poetic prose texts on objects, such as the radio play *Le Savon* (1967b) and *Comment une figue de paroles et pourquoi* (1977b). In both long and short formats, he occasionally incorporates musings on what he can say about a thing or an artist, whether he can do justice to it, and the extent to which it is possible to "exhaust" a subject. For instance, he opens his text "Le Galet" ("The Pebble") with the following thought:

> Le galet n'est pas une chose à bien définir.
> Si l'on se contente d'une simple description l'on peut dire d'abord que c'est une forme ou un état de la pierre entre le rocher et le caillou.
> Mais ce propos déjà implique de la pierre une notion qui doit être justifiée.
> Qu'on ne me reproche pas en cette matière de remonter plus loin même que le déluge. (Ponge 1967a: 92)

> [The pebble is not an easy thing to define.
> If one were to be content with a straightforward description one could say first of all that it is a form or a state of stone somewhere between a rock and a small stone. But that statement already implies a notion of stone that needs justification. Please bear with me therefore if I go back further even than the Flood.]

A further important similarity between his writing on art and his object poems is that his apparent focus on the object gives way—rapidly or gradually—to the revelation that Ponge's is a subjective exercise: he writes his way towards, into and around the subject of his text, which, as it is literally objectified, emphasizes that any perspective on it is a subjective one. In the poem "De l'eau" ("On Water"), for example, he writes:

> L'eau m'échappe . . . me file entre les doigts. Et encore! Ce n'est même pas si net (qu'un lézard ou une grenouille): il m'en reste aux mains des traces, des taches, relativement longues à sécher ou qu'il faut essuyer.
>   Elle m'échappe et cependant me marque, sans que j'y puisse grand-chose. (Ponge 1967a: 62–3)

> [Water escapes me. . . runs between my fingers. And more! It is not even that obvious (as a lizard or a frog would be): traces of it stay on my hands, spots, which take a fairly long time to dry or which I have to wipe.
>   It escapes me and yet marks me, without my being able to do much about it.]

The poetic subject acknowledges his embeddedness in the material world (which includes art) that is his subject and object. Viewed from this perspective, his prose poems are not verbal equivalents of objects or art objects, and the prose poem has no particular affinity with visual art. Rather, they reveal a writer exploring his relationship to the world around through a form that appears at first sight to accord the writing subject secondary status in comparison to the realm of things, but in fact builds across his œuvre to a sustained engagement with what it means to write.

Late Twentieth-Century Prose Poetry and Art

In the subsequent generation of poets who began writing after World War II, the three features of Ponge's writing outlined above continue: an interest in visual art, and especially that of modernist contemporaries; poetic writing that includes the prose poem; and overt reflection on poetry's own processes. Jacques Dupin exemplifies those poets of the postwar generation who wrote about art, having produced important works of criticism on artists such as Joan Miró (1961) and, again, Giacometti (1962), alongside his poetic writing. He did not write poems explicitly about artists or artworks. His poetry includes texts in prose form, in volumes such as *L'Embrasure*, of 1969, that reflect on the workings and power of poetry; the prose poem appears for Dupin to be a form that enables self-reflection. For instance, he writes:

> Expérience sans mesure, excédante, inexpiable, la poésie ne comble pas mais au contraire approfondit toujours davantage le manque et le tourment qui la suscitent. Et ce n'est pas pour qu'elle triomphe mais pour qu'elle s'abîme avec lui, avant de consommer un divorce fécond, que le poète marche à sa perte entier, d'un pied sûr. Sa chute, il n'a pas le pouvoir de s'en approprier, aucun droit de le revendiquer et d'en tirer bénéfice. Ce n'est qu'un accident de route, à chaque répétition s'aggravant. Le poète n'est pas un homme moins minuscule, moins indigent et moins absurde que les autres hommes. Mais sa violence, sa faiblesse et son incohérence ont le pouvoir de s'inverser dans l'opération poétique et, par un retournement fondamental, qui le consume sans le grandir, de renouveler le pacte fragile qui maintient l'homme ouvert dans sa division, et rend le monde habitable. (Dupin 1999: 153)

> [As a limitless, excessive, inexpiable experience, poetry does not fulfil, but rather constantly deepens the lack and the torment that incite it. And the poet walks confidently towards his complete loss, not in order that poetry should triumph, but that it should be spoiled with him, before perpetrating a fruitful divorce. He does not have the power to take ownership of his fall, or the right to claim it and benefit from it. Poetry is no more than an accident on the way, worsening with every repetition. The poet is not less diminutive, poor or absurd than other men. But his violence, weakness and incoherence can be reversed through the workings of poetry and, through a fundamental return that consumes the poet without aggrandising him, have the power to renew the fragile pact that keeps man open in his division, and makes the world habitable.]

In insisting on the limits of poetry's power here, Dupin actually works to magnify its importance. By suggesting that the poet is no different from other people yet can be transformed through poetry, he implies that poetry is set apart from other uses of language. In a possible allusion to Hölderlin's phrase "dichterisch wohnet der Mensch" ["people live poetically"], which has been taken up by French poets concerned to investigate the ways in which poetry inhabits the world, Dupin's closing expression, "rend le monde habitable," emphasizes less a wish to make life bearable than a recognition that through poetic language it is possible fully to engage with the surroundings in which one lives. The prose poem does not have privileged status here as object, but affords the opportunity for reflection on poetry that is not obvious in Dupin's verse poems. Where this poetry intersects with his writing on art, it is to reflect on the ways in which the creative process is analogous for poet and for artist, as the artist, too, is in Dupin's view seeking to understand how he or she lives in the material world. In his writing on the sculptor Eduardo Chillida, for example, Dupin insists on the ways in which Chillida handles his materials (Dupin 2009). As Evelyne Lloze argues, Dupin's work results from the resistance of the material world, revealing an awareness that poetry can only approach, but not appropriate it (Lloze 1993: 47). Dupin conceives of some artists and poets as engaged in an analogous endeavor.

A subsequent generation of poets sometimes known as exponents of lyricism, following a reclaiming of the term by the poet and critic Jean-Michel Maulpoix (1989), frequently both adopt the prose poem as form and also pursue an interest in modernist art, writing on artists and collaborating with them to produce artists' books. The poet Béatrice Bonhomme, for instance, takes inspiration from a variety of artistic media including the Fayum portraits on sarcophagi (Bonhomme 2013) and the work of her artist father, Mario Villani, as well as exploring photographs and the idea of photography in her poetry. While she has worked with artists such as Henri Maccheroni (1998) and includes drawings and photographs in her collections, she does not publish art criticism, so the divide between poetic writing and art criticism identified in the work of Reverdy, Ponge and Dupin does not apply. As Clémence O'Connor argues, photographs for Bonhomme encourage reflection on absence, especially when a beloved person has been photographed, underscoring the material existence and subsequent loss of that person (O'Connor 2013: 137). Bonhomme writes in both verse and prose, her prose poems frequently joined together as fragments in a sequence. For example, in the volume presented as a journal, *Photographies*, she writes, of photographs that were never taken:

> Comme un peintre qui travallerait à partir de photos (ce mauvais peintre) j'essaye de cerner ton visage tu es seul assis dans le cloître de cet abbaye à Sainte Trophime ce visage de Raphaël posé sur fond de pierre l'asymétrie de ton visage d'amant brûle au soleil de ton absence à Florence cette fois. (Bonhomme 2004: 61)

> [Just as a painter would work from photos (that bad painter) I try to make out your face you are alone sitting in the cloister of that abbey at Sainte Trophime that Raphael face on a stone background the asymmetry of your face as a lover burns in the sun of your absence in Florence that time.]

Repeated deixis ("ce," "cet," "ce," "cette") reinforces the confusion between presence and absence, the enduring presence of a figure in memory that is nevertheless hard to discern, overlaid with the burning absence of that person in a time and place. Once again, this is far from ekphrastic writing, visual art and photography being used to give both material presence and an unavoidable absence to a real person. Moreover, Bonhomme also obliquely reflects on her own writing process, and the limitations of her poetic prose, despite its syntactical license here: she writes "j'essaye," and implies that the attempt is bound to be unsuccessful.

Prose Poetry and "Littéralité"

A rejection of the kind of contemplative writing practiced by poets such as Bonhomme marks a striking alternative approach in French poetry, one that moves away from the visual arts and takes inspiration instead from American writing. Despite their name, their interest in the materiality of the poem and the apparent connections with Stein's work, the Objectivists cannot be said to write verbal equivalents of objects. They were a disparate grouping linked via the famous *An Objectivists' Anthology* of 1932 edited by Louis Zukofsky and his issue of *Poetry* magazine the previous year, and did not constitute a literary movement. As Mark Scroggins argues, the "tangibility" of their work might suggest an affinity with art movements, but the Objectivist writers themselves would be unlikely to have recognized themselves in that description (Scroggins 2013: 18). More concerned with music than the plastic arts, their primary concern was frequently political, expressed as a left-leaning Materialism. Zukofsky emphasized "the detail, not mirage, of seeing, of thinking with the things as they exist, and of directing them along a line of melody" (Zukofsky 2000: 194; Scroggins 2013: 17). The act of seeing and thinking with things, and then taking them to a creative form, recalls Ponge's poems of objects: it implies that things are not transformed, nor responded to by a writer, but instead that they are given voice. Poets associated with the Objectivist anthology rarely employed the form of the compact prose poem; Zukofsky's "A," its sections composed over the decades following 1928, is a long-form poem with end-stopped lines, for instance.

Recent research has demonstrated the influence of Objectivist poets on French writers, many of whom translated Objectivist works (Lang 2018). Such writers employ a combination of prose poems and writing with end-stopped lines, and resist the attribution of lyricism, a term some refer to pejoratively as *la poésie* (Gleize 1992). Serge Fauchereau edited a special issue of the journal *Les lettres nouvelles* that presented *41 poètes américains d'aujourd'hui* (41 Contemporary American Poets) (December 1970–January 1971).[5] Of all the Objectivists who were important to French poets of the time, frequent reference is made to Charles Reznikoff's *Testimony* (1934). Reznikoff used real documents—nineteenth-century court records—copying them and setting them out as poetry. Abigail Lang stresses the role of this text, which resists generic classification, in helping poets of the 1980s develop the notion of "littéralité," which insists on saying things as they are, using everyday language (Lang 2018: 117; Gleize 1992). *Testimony* would also go on to influence a subsequent strand in French poetry, discussed elsewhere in this volume by Jeff Barda, which reuses fragments of existing legal documents in such a way as to expose or explore networks of influence or absurdity in legal practices.

A prosaic vehicle for everyday language, or non-literary journalistic or technical language, the prose poem is nevertheless able to use the brevity of the form to suggest connections and ideas without making them explicit. The contemporary poet Alessandro De Francesco, who writes in Italian, French and English, sets out texts in two columns in the poem "Espaces habités" ("Inhabited Spaces"), in which he brings acute political and social concerns into contact with medical terminology:

en moyenne 800 demandeurs d'asile
résident au petit château la ville
de bruxelles comptabilise quelque
250 visites par mois de demandeurs
d'asile tout demandeur d'asile
doit demander à sa commune une   sac gestationnel intra-utérin à l'intérieur
attestation d'inscription celle-ci doit   duquel on peut observer un embryon
être renouvelée plusieurs fois si le   unique avec CRL 53 mm CN 1.2 mm
demandeur d'asile est reconnu en tant   RCF présent biométrie 11.5 semaines
que réfugié la commune délivre un
permis de séjour sous la forme d'une
carte électronique pour étranger en
cas de décision négative un ordre de
quitter le térritoire lui est délivré
(De Francesco 2015: 119)

[800 asylum seekers on average live in the petit château in the city of brussels records about 250 visits per month by asylum seekers each asylum seeker must ask their commune for a registration certificate this must be renewed multiple times if the asylum seeker is recognised as a refugee the commune provides a residence permit in the form of a foreigners' electronic card in the case of rejection an order to leave the area is sent to them]

intra-uterine gestational sac inside which one can see a single embryo with FL 53 mm and NT 1.2 mm HR present dated 11.5 weeks

The inhabited spaces of this series of texts are, in the left-hand column, the temporary residences of asylum seekers, whose future depends on whether the authorities deem them to be refugees, and, on the right, the uterus as viewed by medical professionals making use of scanning equipment. De Francesco conveys perspectives on shelter and precarity, contrasting measurement and bureaucracy with the human consequences of having, losing, or failing to gain access to a home. He suggests personal stories within the figures and bluntly presented records, and does so without lyrical expression, metaphor, or dense layering of meaning. Form is still important, as the block forms of the text, without capital letters or punctuation, work to emphasize the contrast between left- and right-hand columns. Form is distinct from metrical constraint, and the poems read as fragments rather than self-contained framed narratives or scenes.

De Francesco's work is concerned with vision—he is also an artist and works with technologies affording access to "augmented reality"—and the texts in this volume, while taking relatively traditional format on the page of a book, also highlight the different ways in which we see, and fail to see, the human beings around us. The political is bound up with the visual without visual art being in any way linked to poetry in this text.

Fifteen years after Fauchereau's bilingual anthology, Emmanuel Hocquard and Claude Royet-Journoud edited *21 + 1 American Poets Today* (1986), which focused on L=A=N=G=U=A=G=E poets, including those for whom the Objectivists had been an influence, as well as work by Zukofsky and George Oppen themselves. In 1989, Hocquard brought together French and American poets to translate and discuss Objectivist texts at the Fondation Royaumont, encounters that led to various publications including a special issue of the review *Java* (1990). Lang argues, citing Hocquard:

Si la souplesse de la syntaxe anglaise et particulièrement de l'usage américain séduisent, c'est que le français est ressenti comme 'essentiellement une langue écrite', figée par 'le bon usage', 'appauvrie', 'une langue aux structures rigides' qu'il est difficile de faire bouger et dans laquelle il n'est pas toujours aisé de se mouvoir. (Hocquard 2001: 29–30; Lang 2018: 116)

[If poets are attracted by the suppleness of English syntax, and particularly by American English, that is because French is experienced as 'essentially a written language', immobilised by 'correct usage', 'impoverished', 'a language with rigid structures', that it is difficult to shift and within which it is not always easy to manœuvre.]

One of the poets invited to Royaumont was Anne Portugal. She, too, suggests that she was attracted less by a focus on ordinary everyday objects in American poetry than by the syntax:

C'est-à-dire le dérouler d'une phrase sur la longueur et comment on peut l'alléger, et comment elle peut être à la fois fantaisie et comment, en même temps, elle se pose sans cesse des questions sur son système de production. (Portugal 2010b: 195)

[That is to say the way a sentence unwinds along its length and how it can be lightened, and how it can both be imaginative and, at the same time, ask questions about its own system of production.]

Even in the comment cited here, Portugal demonstrates her argument by building up clauses in a structure that unfolds rather than offering concision and balance: "et comment [. . .] et comment [. . .] et comment, en même temps." Her poetic texts frequently adopt a colloquial tone that is far from the metrical precision of French verse. In *définitif bob*, for instance, the protagonist bob, who seems to be a video game character, appears periodically as a kind of refrain in lines such as the following: "mais bob il peut comme ça officiel résister aux pressions dans les courbes" ["but that's how bob can officially resist the pressure of linebreaks"] (Portugal 2002: 47; Portugal/Moxley 2010a: 47). "Il peut comme ça officiel" is highly informal and departs from standard French formulations.

American poetry offered a freedom from form itself, so while everyday language was important politically to the Objectivists and the French writers who read and translated them, it is not simply the prosaic nature of prose that inspires French poets. By admiring the looser syntax of American English, they reveal an interest in the inventiveness of language outside the style afforded by meter and rhythm. Even a writer of "littéralité" such as Nathalie Quintane, who is known for phrasing that appears as mechanical, or "plat" ["flat"], as possible, uses the unfolding of a sentence to creative effect, often producing deadpan humor or irony. For instance, in the opening of one section of *Chaussure* she writes:

Lacer des chaussures est une chose que je peux faire yeux fermés (ou dans une pièce obscure).
Je peux très bien lacer mes chaussures en ne pensant à rien d'autre.
Cependant, si, dès le réveil, un air de musique m'a poursuivie (j'ai continué à le chanter 'intérieurement' quelles que soient mes activités), j'aurais bien plus de difficultés à lacer mes chaussures sans poursuivre ma chanson, ou, sans, à la fois, poursuivre ma chanson et déplorer qu'elle me poursuive. (Quintane 1997: 67)

[Tying my shoes is something I can do eyes shut (or in a dark room).
I can tie my shoes just fine while thinking of nothing else.
Still, if, since waking up, I can't shake a piece of music (I go on singing it 'internally' whatever I'm doing), I'll have considerable trouble tying my shoes without continuing my little song, or, without, all at once, continuing my song and cursing it for haunting me.] (Quintane/Card 2016: 29)

Those writers who reject overt examination of poetry's power and limitations (and who not do not engage in print with the visual arts) still explore poetry's processes in their own verbal creations. The prose poem in their hands is not an object, or an intense narrative, or a means of reflecting on creativity, but it does still offer a vehicle for stretching the French language beyond its habitual word order, classification of register, and stylistic expectations of the lyric.

Twenty-First Century Intermedial Practice

In the twenty-first century, poetic writing continues to engage with the arts, but increasingly branches out from plastic art to a range of forms and media without insisting on the specificities of form. Sabine Macher, for example, produces performances including dance, and Jean-Michel Espitallier performs as a drummer as well as a writer. Pierre Alferi, meanwhile, works from and with classic Hollywood cinema in "cinepoems" where sequences are juxtaposed with texts and a soundtrack composed by his collaborator Rodolphe Burger (2004). Among poets born in the 1980s, Jérôme Game also cites film as a significant inspiration. For example, the following is typical of his volume *Flip-Book*:

À Los Angeles j'ai vu comment Ben Gazzara sort en *tux* à huit heures le matin le point aveugle après la nuit, s'encadre dans la porte. Les putes sont au repos. Les danseuses se rhabillent à six dans une voiture souple en cuir noir à la conduite souple. Une baleine démarre à l'embrayage souple, un grand chapeau garée devant la boîte de l'autre côté du Strip démarre doucement. (Game 2007)

[In Los Angeles I saw how Ben Gazzara goes out in a tux at eight in the morning blind spot after the night, appears framed in the doorway. The whores are off work. The dancers are putting their clothes back on six of them in a smooth car with black leather that drives smoothly. A whale starts up smooth geared, a land yacht parked in front of the club on the other side of the Strip starts up softly.] (Game/Beck 2016: 73)

It is a highly visual account, introduced by the words "j'ai vu," that takes its inspiration from the cinematic rather than the plastic arts, and does not attempt to present the poetic text as an object drawing attention to its own processes. Game has worked with performers, musicians, and filmmakers, and describes the importance to him of those encounters in an interview:

Examining the ways in which a filmmaker with whom I collaborate on a videopoem builds her frame, how she edits a narrative, how she synchs noises and music for a soundtrack, etc., all of that will help me formulate issues pending in the text I'm writing. As a poet, I seek to expose my writing reflexes to other syntaxes, other grammars, other setups, other economic ecosystems too, other technological line-ups. And I expect these 'alien' grammars and technological setups to inform my writing, redo it in both senses of the French version of this word: *refaire* as rewire and undo, undermine until a resistance, a *pharmakon* of sorts is invented . . . (Game 2018: 136)

Engagement with the other arts does not lead to the writing of prose poem objects that act as a response to visual art. Instead, the writer looks beyond the page to find ways of reinventing and undermining the format of words on the page: contact with what is outside linguistic or poetic techniques and norms reinvigorates textual practice. The prose poem may, in this particular instance, be the most suitable vehicle for Game, but that does not mean that he or other poets accord it privileged status as a form. They are more interested in disrupting than in defining form.

Alessandro De Francesco, whose parallel prose poems were discussed above, mounts augmented reality visual, text, and sound installations. He is not so much interested in the power of virtual reality technology for its own sake, but rather in the ways in which such affordances enable fresh engagement with texts and images, focusing in particular on placing the visitor/participant in immersive poetic-artistic environments. Visual-verbal form is once again at the service of effects and affects rather than an end in its own right (De Francesco 2019).

This essay has argued, first, that in the early-to-mid-twentieth century, writing in the form of the prose poem by French poets is associated with an interest in the visual arts, but that that interest, with the exception of texts such as those by René Char on Giacometti, is not generally expressed via the prose poem; rather, essays or poetic prose are the means for reflection on art or the championing of new art movements. Writers' prose poems instead imply an understanding of the text as object that might suggest the influence of Cubism. Second, in the latter part of the twentieth century, those poets influenced by the transatlantic focus on the object and writing the quotidian are different from those who pursue reflection on modernist art and on poetry. Writing the everyday in French texts departs from the dense style of the prose poem, which has a more comfortable relationship with visual art that invites reflection on artistic and poetic creativity. That does not mean that writers of prose poetry are uninterested in what poetry can do, but that syntax, rather than any sense of poetic inspiration, constitutes their impetus. Syntax is brought into contact with other nonverbal arts in the twenty-first century: innovative writers are interested in art to the extent that they engage in intermedial poetic practice rather than responding specifically to the visual arts.

The French prose poem in its relation with visual art has, therefore, not followed a single clear trajectory from its nineteenth-century origins, nor is it isolated from other languages: connections with American poetry include the importance of the Objectivists to subsequent French writers. The association between writers of prose poetry and visual art was striking at the time when art focused on objects (Cubism) and poetry did so too. Work by Francis Ponge involves a subjective reflection on the creative process through the medium of the prose poem that is subsequently employed by experimental writers as well as by those who continue to respond to visual art and think through the power and purpose of poetic language in ways that would seem suspicious to those who insist on prosaic prose. The prose poem comes to serve two distinct purposes: as poetic object, and as suitably neutral verbal format for work that rejects the poetic. The prose poem has moved far from an enclosed vessel of "stylistic sophistication" (Delville 1998: 4). It remains to be seen whether the engagement of the creative arts with new technologies will lead also to new forms and purposes of the prose poem.

Notes

1. An early exception would be Aloysius Bertand's *Gaspard de la Nuit* (1842), whose preface refers to the artists Paul Rembrandt and Jacques Callot.
2. Translations are mine unless otherwise indicated.
3. Mary Ann Caws, in her discussion of Cubism and prose poetry in this volume, asks whether a long poem with line breaks but no punctuation might be called a prose poem.
4. Stout refers to Pierre Laszlo's article "*La Leçon de choses*, or Lessons from Things" (Laszlo 1993).
5. Fauchereau also published the critical volume *Lectures de la poésie américaine* (1968) and edited a special issue of *Europe* on American poetry with Jacques Roubaud and Charles Dobzynsky (1977).

Works Cited

Alferi, Pierre, and Rodolphe Burger (2004), *Cinépoèmes et films parlants*, Aubervilliers: Les Laboratoires d'Aubervilliers.
Baudelaire, Charles (1992), *Salon de 1846* in C. Baudelaire *Critique d'art*, ed. Claude Pichois, Paris: Gallimard, pp. 75–156.
Bonhomme, Béatrice (1998), *L'Embellie*, ill. with photographs by H. Maccheroni, Cannes: Tipaza.
Bonhomme, Béatrice (2004), *Photographies, Journal 1992–1995*, Colomars: Mélis.
Bonhomme, Béatrice (2013), *Variations du visage et de la rose*, Jégun: L'arrière pays.
Botha, Marc (2016), "Microfiction," in *The Cambridge Companion to the English Short Story*, ed. A.-M. Einhaus, Cambridge: Cambridge University Press, pp. 201–20, <https://www.cambridge.org/core/books/cambridge-companion-to-the-english-short-story/microfiction/7677423B4FE542D4CCFDCE62EF7A6C8D/core-reader#> (last accessed December 19, 2019).
Char, René (1983), *Œuvres complètes*, Paris: Gallimard.
De Francesco, Alessandro (2015), *La Vision à distance*, Paris: Éditions Mix.
De Francesco, Alessandro (2019) "Portfolio," <http://www.alessandrodefrancesco.net/text/portfolio_defrancesco_en.pdf> (last accessed December 19, 2019).
Diepeveen, Leonard (2018), "Introduction," in G. Stein, *Tender Buttons*, ed. L. Diepeveen, Peterborough, Canada, Broadview Editions.
Dupin, Jacques (1961), *Miró*, Paris: Flammarion.
Dupin, Jacques (1962), *Alberto Giacometti: Textes pour une approche*, Paris: Maeght.
Dupin, Jacques (1999), *Le corps clairvoyant, 1963–1982*, Paris: Gallimard.
Dupin, Jacques (2009), *Par quelque biais vers quelque bord*, Paris: P. O. L.
Eichbauer, M. E. (1989), "The Surrealist Muse and the sister arts: René Char's 'Artine,'" *Paragraph*, 12, 2, 124–38.
Fauchereau, Serge (1968), *Lecture de la poésie américaine*, Paris: Minuit.
Fauchereau, Serge (ed. and trans.) (1971), *41 poètes américains d'aujourd'hui*, Paris: Denoël.
Fauchereau, S., Roubaud, J. and Dobzynsky, C. (eds) (1977), "Une littérature méconnue aux USA," in *Europe*, Nos 578–9, pp. 78–91.
Game, Jérôme (2007), *Flip-Book*, Bordeaux: Editions de l'Attente.

Game, Jérôme (2016) from *Flip-Book*, trans. Barbara Beck, repr. in *Writing the Real: A Bilingual Anthology of Contemporary French Poetry*, ed. N. Parish and E. Wagstaff, London: Enitharmon, pp. 72–81.
Gleize, Jean-Marie (1992), *A noir. Poésie et littéralité*, Paris: Seuil.
Greene, R. W. (1994), "On Ponge and Char Writing About Art," in *Figuring Things: Char, Ponge and Poetry in the Twentieth Century*, ed. C. D. Minahen, Lexington, Kentucky: French Forum, pp. 161–73.
Hocquard, Emmanuel (2001), *ma haie*, Paris: P. O. L.
Hocquard, Emmanuel and Claude Royet-Journoud (eds) (1986), *21 + 1 American Poets Today*, Paris, Delta.
Java (1990), *Les Objectivistes américains*, Vol. 4.
Krieger, Murray (1998), "The Problem of *Ekphrasis*: Image and Words, Space and Time—and the Literary Work," in *Pictures into Words: Theoretical and Descriptive Approaches to Ekphrasis*, ed. V. Robillard and E. Jongeneel, Amsterdam: VU University Press, pp. 3–20.
Lang, Abigail (2018), "La réception française des objectivistes: politique de la traduction," in *Poetry's Forms and Transformations*, ed. N. Parish and E. Wagstaff, special issue of *L'Esprit Créateur*, vol. 58, no. 3, pp. 114–30.
Laszlo, Pierre (1993), "'*La Leçon de choses*', or Lessons from Things," *Sub-Stance* 71/72, pp. 274–88.
Lloze, Evelyne (1993), *Approches de Jacques Dupin*, Amsterdam: Rodopi.
Maulpoix, Jean-Michel (1989), *La voix d'orphée. Essai sur le lyrisme*, Paris: J. Corti.
O'Connor, Clemence (2013), "Étoilement du poème: légèreté et *punctum* d'une écriture," in *Béatrice Bonhomme. Le mot, l'amour, la mort*, ed. P. Collier and I. Thomas, Bern: Peter Lang, pp. 127–41.
Ponge, Francis (1962), *Pièces*, Paris: Gallimard.
Ponge, Francis (1967a), *Le parti pris des choses* suivi de *Proêmes*, Paris: Gallimard.
Ponge, Francis (1967b), *Le Savon*, Paris: Gallimard.
Ponge, Francis (1977a), *L'Atelier contemporain*, Paris: Gallimard.
Ponge, Francis (1977b), *Comment une figue de paroles et pourquoi*, Paris: Flammarion.
Portugal, Anne (2002), *définitif bob*, Paris: P. O. L.
Portugal, Anne (2010a), *absolute bob*, trans. Jennifer Moxley, Anyart, Providence: Burning Deck.
Portugal, Anne (2010b), "Entretien avec Anne Portugal," in *Entretiens avec 21 poètes françaises* by J. C. Stout, Amsterdam and New York: Rodopi, pp. 192–207.
Quintane, Nathalie (1997), *Chaussure*, Paris: P. O. L.
Quintane, Nathalie (2016), from *Chaussure*, trans. Macgregor Card, *The Germ #5*, repr. in *Writing the Real: A Bilingual Anthology of Contemporary French Poetry*, ed. N. Parish and E. Wagstaff, London: Enitharmon, pp. 28–35.
Reverdy, Pierre (1973), *Note éternelle du présent: Ecrits sur l'art (1923–1960)*, Paris: Flammarion.
Reverdy, Pierre (1975), *Nord–Sud, Self defence et autres écrits sur la poésie 1917–26*, Paris: Flammarion.
Reverdy, Pierre (1981), *Roof Slates and Other Poems of Pierre Reverdy* trans. with prefaces by M. A. Caws and P. Terry, Boston: Northeastern University Press.
Reverdy, Pierre (2004), *Plupart du temps. Poèmes 1915–22*, Paris: Gallimard.
Reznikoff, Charles (1934), *Testimony*, New York: Objectivist Press.
Rimbaud, Arthur (1957), *Illuminations and other prose poems*, trans. L. Varèse, rev. edn, New York: New Directions.
Rimbaud, Arthur (1984), *Poésies, Une saison en enfer, Illuminations*, Paris: Gallimard.
Rothwell, Andrew (1989), *Textual Spaces: The Poetry of Pierre Reverdy*, Amsterdam and Atlanta, GA: Rodopi.

Scroggins, Mark (2013), "From the Late Modernism of the 'Objectivists' to the Protopostmodernism of 'Projective Verse,'" in *The Cambridge Companion to American Poetry since 1945*, ed. J. Ashton, Cambridge: Cambridge University Press, pp. 16–30.

Stein, Gertrude (1909), *Three Lives*, New York: Grafton.

Stein, Gertrude (1973), "A Transatlantic Interview 1946," cited in *A Primer for the Gradual Understanding of Gertrude Stein*, ed. R. Bartlett Haas, Los Angeles: Black Sparrow.

Stout, J. C. (2018), *Objects Observed: The Poetry of Things in Twentieth-Century France and America*, Toronto: University of Toronto Press.

Zukofsky, Louis (2000), *Prepositions+: The Collected Critical Essays*, ed. M. Scroggins, Hanover, NH: Wesleyan University Press.

8

The Homeless Heart: Abstraction and the Prose Poem

Richard Deming

A NEARLY DEFINITIVE ASPECT OF THE PROSE poem is its literalized formal ambivalence. The most evident characteristic of a prose poem is, of course, that it is poetry that is not broken into lines of verse, let alone formed along the grouping of recurring syllabic and rhythmic patterns that so characterizes traditional lyric poetry. At the same time, it is a literary form that is not simply prose in that very often it can avoid strict narrative structure and plot so necessary to fiction by means of the oblique logic of poetry. By the same token, prose poetry is not guided by the conventional rhetorical strategies of argument and persuasion upon which nonfiction prose depends in order to be persuasive of its points. Prose poems can, however, have a degree of high lyricism not often so characteristic of prose, and often the compression and condensed nature of a prose poem serve to establish and support a powerful, moving trope, of the sort that is so often a characteristic feature of a lyric poem. They also tend toward compression and specificity of detail, as does so much poetry. Such compression is not marshalled for the sake of brevity alone, but rather because it focuses its force toward those particular and particularizing insights that arise from prolonged engagement with a specific detail or image. More importantly, many prose poems seem to bear in mind the dictate from William Carlos Williams, "no ideas but in things," a principle that is central to the poetics of numerous modern and contemporary poets and that is often the catalyst that keeps an arresting, provocative image the *sine qua non* of lyric poems.

Already one can see the problems with such a thumbnail sketch of the prose poem, undoubtedly. The hesitant, tentative language employed in the description I offer in the above paragraph signals just how unstable any definition of the form must be. The fact that the form resists definition explains why there are many more anthologies devoted to collecting and presenting prose poems than there are monographs on the topic. Every assertion about the prose poem as a genre or form immediately calls to mind convincing counterexamples that do not prove the rule so much as suggest how it has no strict rules. For instance, although I have gestured toward the difference between a piece of flash fiction and a prose poem, a prose poem can—and very often does—tell a story or move toward some kind of conclusion of an argument or point.

Consider, for instance, one of the most canonical of prose poems, Robert Hass's "A Story about the Body." The piece clearly offers a narrative with a beginning, middle, and end. Indeed, the very opening of the poem sets up the narrative structure: "The young composer, working that summer at an artist's colony, had watched her for a week. She was Japanese, a painter, almost sixty, and he thought he was in love with her." Hass's use of "thought" invokes a hesitation about the protagonist that foreshadows the conflict that occurs later when the composer changes his mind about his feelings upon learning that the painter has had a mastectomy. It is clear that what the composer felt was not actually love and was at best physical attraction, which is why he leaves when he learns of her operation. The next morning the composer learns that the painter provided a response to his callous and shallow behavior: "He walked back to his own cabin through the pines, and in the morning he found a small blue bowl on the porch outside his door. It looked to be full of rose petals, but he found when he picked it up that the rose petals were on top; the rest of the bowl—she must have swept them from the corners of her studio—was full of dead bees" (2011: 158). The bowl of flower-covered dead bees that the painter leaves behind at the composer's door at the writer's residency is the *coup de grâce* that gives the piece its intensity. It is an image for the composer—on the surface he is lovely, but beneath he is cruel—but the poem does not explain the feelings other than to let the image of the bowl serve as a vehicle for the complex of emotions. In that way, we can see it as having something in common with a lyric poem. Yet, is there a way to draw a clear line of demarcation between Hass's prose poem and a short parable by Franz Kafka, perhaps, given that there is a moral resonance to that final image?[1] Is there some intrinsic aspect that makes it a poem other than the fact that Hass is himself primarily known as a poet and that the piece appears in a collection of poems? The very title of Hass's prose poem highlights that it is a narrative, after all. Is there a way to state conclusively that this is not a piece of flash fiction? The trope of the bowl of bees is a resonant and poignant image, naturally, one that calls out for interpretation, but is that enough to pull it into the realm of poetry?

In the ways that prose poetry can and often does rely on familiar narrative and rhetorical conventions, a skeptic of prose poetry would argue, a prose poem never actually distinguishes itself from prose. A prose poem, so runs the argument, simply is not a poem; it is actually just a form of prose that is limited in length and that does concern itself with the musicality of language and pays attention to detail. The great prose stylists can all be said to be writing prose poetry, if not poetic prose. Is what we have said about prose poetry so different from the lyricism of Virginia Woolf's sentences in her novel *The Waves*, or from the final paragraph of James Baldwin's short story "Sonny's Blues" and its poignant, transcendental final image?

Of course, what we call a thing matters in terms of what readers bring to bear in the act of weighing the text against conventions and expectations. Such labels activate interpretive categories. If a particular text is called "prose poetry," then we hold it to some of the aspects of poetry that have already been mentioned. This still would not silence the protests of skeptics, who might, one imagines, insist that in light of such flexibility the word "poetry" is susceptible to being reduced to an ornamental descriptor. "This coffeecake is pure poetry" does nothing for our understanding of poetry or coffeecakes—it merely suggests that the coffeecake is carefully and perhaps exquisitely made.

Such a concern is based on some specious arguments about "slippery slopes," of course. If someone says that the graceful speed of an athlete is "poetry in motion" or that a "coffeecake is pure poetry," the context is not a literary one and so it leaves the formal, textual signification alone, as it is. Why even mention such remonstrances, then? Because they still persist despite the decades of examples of prose poems, and because we can see that the extremes of the argument do not diminish the concerns that the term "prose poetry" does more harm than good in the minds of some readers, those who feel a certain anxiety about the very "neither fish nor fowl" nature of the form. In back of these issues, one can suspect a desire for a verifiable authenticity or even for a purity of poetic form. Although, historically speaking, prose poetry begins appearing before the widespread dominance of open form (or free verse) poetry, it still is marked by a concern about the formal authenticity of free verse, the concern that open form might in reality be merely prose chopped into lines. If there is such concern that open form poetry might not actually be poetry, then prose poetry, a fortiori, represents the next step—that *vers libre* inevitably becomes text that is instead "*libéré du verset*," as if prose poetry were the final dismantling of what makes poetry poetry.

It is not my intention solely to rehearse the arguments against considering the legitimacy of prose poetry as a form, though these still linger, which accounts for what the poet Karen Volkman once described in her short essay "Mutable Boundaries" as prose poetry's "continued status as shady and suspect to the mainstream poetry world" (2005, unpag.). Even a more contemporary practitioner of the form such as Mark Strand neglected to include any examples of prose poetry in *The Making of a Poem: A Norton Anthology of Poetic Forms*, a collection with a pedagogical, if not definitive, intent that he edited with Eavan Boland. Such an omission underlines the suspicion surrounding the prose poem, a suspicion apparently held even by some poets who have been known to write whole volumes of them, as Strand himself has done. Nevertheless, I do want to invoke in broad strokes the opposition that holds the form as "shady and suspect" because such fears about the legitimacy or authenticity or purity often fuel what is most interesting about the form—its tendency to raise the issue of what actually constitutes a text's claims to being poetry, if being written cannot offer the final constitutive characteristic. The problem might ultimately be that the prose poem is not actually a form at all (at least not in a technical sense), though that does not mean it is not therefore poetry.

Let us step back for a moment to Hass's "A Story of the Body." To categorize it as "flash fiction" would be to underline its fictive nature, and the result would be that the major image of the bowl containing the flowers and the dead bees—not to mention the rejection and humiliation of the painter by the composer—would be framed as having been invented. Such framing might undercut to some extent the force of the painter's gesture, if we indeed see that gesture as coming from a fictional character. In other words, it might feel symbolic. A poem, however, does not necessarily indicate that its content is fictive and invented as fiction by its categorical definition must do. Instead, a poem, centered on the image as it is, suggests that things, gestures, are actual objects worthy of sustained attention and from that sustained attention comes the realization that aspects of the world can become vehicles of meaningfulness beyond intention. Such was T. S. Eliot's argument about the centrality of an objective correlative. This claim ultimately valorizes poetry at the expense of fiction by suggesting that poetry rewards such attention in ways that fiction does not. The images in a novel by William Faulkner or Leslie Marmon Silko or Caryl Phillips can be resonant, of course, but they become nodes of affect within the horizontal, sequential flow of the narrative events in which the images are located. Poems, on the other hand, do not necessarily insist on their fictive, constructed nature, and suggest that their images, their insights arise not through imagination but through apprehension of a thing in its phenomenological context. Thus, within the structure of "A Story of the Body" that creation of a poignant metaphor comes not from the poet, Hass, but from the painter; it is part of the narrative itself rather than a comment on the actions of the composer. In reading the poem, we are meant, it is supposed, to read not only the image as significant but the action as well. The poignancy of the poem gains in the fact that although it is certainly a story, it may be a real one after all. What we cannot know is to what extent the text can be wholly subsumed within an idea or category of fiction, and this impacts a reader's stance toward the elements of the story. It matters, for instance, when we think of a story in which someone dies whether or not that is a real person or not. Fiction, being fiction, allows some ontological distance between the reader and his/her/their "real world" and the fictional world. As for a prose poem, it may or may not be a true representation of the world. In a moment, I would like to come back to the idea that prose poems, either French or American, are predominantly small surrealist fables.

That "may" so intrinsic to a prose poem is an important aspect to continue to bear in mind as we consider the genre, because since its very categorization is unstable it is, at some level, always utilizing that formal ambivalence rather than ignoring or denying it. The prose poem, no matter which mode it employs, always challenges which analytical tools, which assumptions a reader brings to it. Michel Delville usefully observes that one way of approaching the prose poem "consists in speaking of genre not as a 'given thing' but as the expression of the relationship between a reader and a text" (1998: 10). If we place this comment alongside Tzvetan Todorov's argument that locates genre, in part, as "the *point of intersection* of general poetics and literary history," we can see how the relationship continues to evolve even as different forms and possibilities become part of the overall literary economy (1976: 164). As more forms enter into the cultural understating of literary texts, as large and small historical events unfold, those relationships continue to change. Prose poetry does not develop along the same axes as prose or poetry, which respectively have longer histories, and their respective developments are always weighed against such long traditions as prose poetry does not quite have.

Because the recognizable features of a prose poem are themselves so open to question, its unsettledness is part of its identity, and that unsettled relationship exists between reader and text. Inevitably, then, the prose poem is always to some extent involved in enacting and manifesting that instability. It provides an oblique comment on its own being. Ironically, if it did not enact that ambivalence, it would risk a form of resolution that would change its status. If a prose poem veers too much into the realm of prose or is too identifiable as a poem, it is no longer prose poetry, and by that it nullifies its own openness.

If we can, however provisionally, accept this literal and categorical ambivalence as a fundamental aspect of the prose poem, then what becomes a compelling issue is the way a prose poem often finds itself needing to teach the reader how to navigate it as a text, especially when there is no guide provided by narrative. The reason there might be an ongoing sense that a compressed narrative—such as we see from poets from Robert Bly to Russell Edson to Robert Hass—so often gives shape to prose poetry is that narrative, story (no matter how compressed), allows the reader to follow a sequence of events. Narrative structure provides some assurance that the poem is directed forward, provides a stable point for understanding, even if that reliance on narrative creates its own series of difficulties.

It is at this point that it becomes evident that we might not be able to reliably describe a prose poem as a poetic form, other than in the sense that we can see that it is not lines, which is too vague a criterion to be of much use. Perhaps this is why Strand left the prose poem out of the anthology of poetic forms he edited with Boland, since it is not actually a form that can be identified regardless of context, in contrast to sonnets, say, or villanelles, which are readily identifiable forms, no matter the context.[2] We are in a better situation if we see the prose poem as a genre rather than a literary form, which foregrounds the fact that it is a text always in the act of establishing its relationship, its interpretive context, with its readers. Form suggests a replicable, iterable pattern: genre indicates an acknowledgment of a text's engagement with a horizon of negotiated expectations. Steven Monte, in *Invisible Fences*, his extensive historical study of prose poetry as it moves from France to the US, makes a succinct and cogent statement that I wish to echo: "formal considerations may provide an interpretive framework for reading; generic considerations always will" (2000: 115). As a genre, prose poetry perpetually asks for those considerations to unsettle what we most assume about the very genre of genre and how we differentiate it from form.[3]

This confusion, this blurring, between fictional narrative and poetic narrative that I noted in thinking about a prose poem such as Hass's "A Story of The Body" is itself ever a cloudy distinction, for the reason that any fictional narrative may have veiled biographical references and a poetic narrative can be completely fictive. While on balance we take a narrative to be either real or invented, the prose poem often leaves open the possibility that it is an essay. Rather than addressing the impurity of narrative, it embraces its ambivalence.

Take, for example, the opening sentences of James Tate's prose poem "Lists of Famous Hats," which does sound like the beginning of an essay and employs a title that leans a reader toward reading the poem in such a manner, that of an engaged meditation. The poem begins, "Napoleon's hat is an obvious choice I guess to list as a famous hat, but that's not the hat I have in mind. That was his hat for show. I am thinking of his private bathing cap, which in all honesty wasn't much different than the one any jerk might buy at a corner drugstore now, except for two minor eccentricities" (2013: 225). The poem ends with the facetious but surprisingly insightful observation: "My theory is simple-minded to be sure: that beneath his public head there was another head and it was a pyramid or something." Witty as it is, the poem asks us to think about the distinction between the public existence of Napoleon and the possibility of a secret, private self—one that was nonetheless unique, strange, different from everyone else. Yet, within the poem lies the possibility of asking another question besides what it might be saying about Napoleon's subjectivity: who is the "I" in this poem? It does not seem apt to refer to the "speaker" of the poem since this text does not present itself, as John Stuart Mills defined the lyric poem, as "utterance overheard." Is the "I" then meant to be Tate himself? Or is there a distinction between Tate, the living person, and the authorial voice of Tate? As the poem considers the comically exaggerated difference between the public and the personal selves of an actual historical figure, one cannot help but think about this "I" that appears in the poem, since the poem is a result of his or her "thinking" ("I am thinking . . .," the poem states). Given what Delville says about genre being a relationship between reader and text—or rather a relationship between a reader's experiences and literary history—it matters after all that it is not clear if this is a compressed comic essay told by Tate or a piece of fiction. If the poem is essayistic, it serves thus as a form of Tate's own subjectivity rendered by way of the prose poem. If we take it as such, the "voice" of the poem is Tate's, is his perspective, no matter how skewed or idiosyncratic. Or perhaps the essayistic mode is part of the narrative of a fictive essay written by whoever is the "I" in the poem, a figure whose subjectivity only exists in and as the prose poem. The Napoleon in "The List of Famous Hats" is both real and imagined, and so possibly is the voice of the poem.

While this tension between real and imagined exists with any lyric poem, the effect is increased with a prose poem because prose itself always navigates whether or not it is fiction or nonfiction. That is a foundational question whenever we encounter a piece of prose and the answer shapes how we experience the text and its claims. Thus, with a prose poem, we need to determine not only to what extent it is poetry but to what extent it is fiction or nonfiction. In the case of Tate's "The List of Famous Hats," it may very well be imagined as a fragmented essay by some fictive writer.

There are whole collections of prose poetry in which the tension between fictive and non-fictive is much more fraught. Take for example Lyn Hejinian's influential *My Life*. This is a book-length series of prose pieces with a set number of sentences or sentence fragments. First published in 1980 by Hejinian, a key figure in a loose confederation of writers arising in the 1970s and 1980s known as Language Poets, the book contained thirty-seven prose blocks, each comprising thirty-seven sentences paratactically juxtaposed from sentence to sentence, and from prose block to prose block. Each block has an italicized sentence fragment floating at the edge that suggests it could be a title, but its odd placement could just be a typographical gesture of poetic intent. There is no clear linear sequencing and one can read back to front, front to back, bottom to top, without disrupting any textual grain. Hejinian would subsequently publish a revised version, extending each prose block to forty-five sentences each with the book containing forty-five blocks in all. Many sentences are repeated and reused from block to block across the collection. Each new context creates a new inflection and a new meaning for a given sentence. Moreover, the language moves from the lyrical to the theoretical:

> I am urged out rummaging into the sunshine, and the depths increase of blue above. A paper hat afloat on a cone of water. The orange and gray bugs were linked from their mating but faced in opposite directions, and their scrambling amounted to nothing. This simply means that the imagination is more restless than the body. But, already, words. Can there be laughter without comparisons. (2013: 9)

The title *My Life* encourages the reader to regard the work as autobiographical, and yet due to the density of the language as well as the fact that many sentences that seem autobiographical are redeployed in different contexts, one cannot take the work to be representing the life as a clear narrative. Indeed, there is little within the work that necessarily marks that the "life" of the title is in fact Hejinian's, yet there is an "I." Again the prose might suggest we need to determine if it hews closer to fiction or nonfiction. As with Tate's poem, the "I" comes into question because of the ways prose tends to be categorized. The prose poem allows for the challenging of that binary so laden by history and expectations, without also providing a resolution.

I want to move back to Tate's "The List of Famous Hats," however, but only because its less explicitly experimental mode indicates how subtle the complexities of any prose poetry can be in terms of how it raises thorny hermeneutical questions. I said earlier that a prose poem often is self-reflexive because it needs to offer ways of determining how to read it. In Tate's poem, we can see the ways in which the work does thematize thinking about conventions and the limitations of familiar forms:

> The first one isn't even funny: Simply it was a white rubber bathing cap, but too small. Napoleon led such a hectic life ever since his childhood, even farther back than that, that he never had a chance to buy a new bathing cap and still as a grown-up—well, he didn't really grow that much, but his head did: He was a pinhead at birth, and he used, until his death really, the same little tiny bathing cap that he was born in, and this meant that later it was very painful to him and gave him many headaches, as if he needed more. So, he had to vaseline his skull like crazy to even get the thing on. (2013: 225)

While the text does turn on a single trope—Napoleon's bathing cap—its style is decidedly prosaic rather than lyrical. The language is informal, loose. Narrative elements are to be found, but its primary mode is essayistic. If we try to fit this into literary categories with long and clearly defined histories, a poem like this does not quite fit, and to force it into those labels would be to do it damage and to give the reader, well, headaches. Moreover, such labels, if at all necessary, seem to be held on to out of habit, despite the damage they might do, the pain they might inflict. At a certain level, the poem thematizes the problems one encounters in having to submit to limited choices, choices limited by convention, which is a recurring facet of prose poems in general insofar as they create a separate, non-binary possibility. Because the prose poem is a genre that avoids narrowed differences prescribed by fixed categories and because the prose poem necessitates consideration of elusive criteria for its own definition, the prose poem is by its nature given to abstraction. It is ever a genre thinking about itself and what it can accommodate. Indeed, the reason some poets insist on narrative as being part of a prose poem may be a guard against its intrinsic openness. Earlier, I suggested that the narrative might be a guard against or a guide through the unavoidable abstraction of a literary genre that often is defined by what it is not.

This is not to suggest that narrative in a prose poem is simply a crutch or a spell against indeterminacy. In essence, genre itself is a form of narrative, one that tells a story of acts or reading and that seeks to establish a tie of a text and its reader across history to conventions, expectations, and traditions of reading that inhere so as to form an understanding of how we respond to the text at hand and so that we can detect to what degree such a text violates or diverges from conventions only to later fulfill expectations in a satisfying way. It tells the story of reading. For this reason, I wish to work against the claims of prose poetry as being necessarily hybrid in nature, as that prevents us from reading it as a genre unto itself, one that by now has established its own history and has a characteristic set of practices—readerly, writerly—surrounding it.

With an understanding of the prose poem as a genre rather than a form firmly in place, we can return again to thinking about the possibilities of a tradition of the prose poem in order to see how we might trace out abstraction and the prose poem. As has been well explored in a number of key studies of the genre of the prose poem, Aloysius Bertrand and his collection of short fantastical pieces published in 1842 as *Gaspard de la Nuit* provide a starting point for what might constitute a tradition. In many ways,

Bertrand's work established a particular template for an oneiric set of compressed narratives of actions and profiles of characters standing outside what we might call reality in an uncanny and quite literary space. Indeed, the subtitle of the book is "Fantasies in the Manner of Rembrandt and Callot," which also indicates the influence of the short tales of the German Romantic E. T. A. Hoffmann on Bertrand's work with its clear allusion to Hoffmann's 1814 *Fantasiestücke in Callots Manier*, a collection of the author's previously published stories.[4] Within the preface of Bertrand's book, we are given the metanarrative that Gaspard is a shadowy, mysterious figure who joins Bertrand, who is sitting on a bench in the *Jardin de l'Arquebuse* in Dijon. Soon the two begin a discussion about the imagination, with Bertrand asking his new acquaintance about the essential nature of art. Gaspard claims that within the manuscript that he is holding is to be found evidence of the "many processes" he has tried in order to discover "the note pure and expressive" that renders "the Absolute in Art" (1994: 11), which is an admixture of both the scared and the profane. Gaspard gives to Bertrand the text of *Gaspard de la Nuit*. The book's overarching trope positions Bertrand as not the author of *Gaspard de la Nuit*, but merely the agent who brings it into print. In that way, Bertrand, in true Romantic fashion, is not the true source but rather the vehicle for "the Absolute in Art."

It is from Bertrand that Charles Baudelaire discovers the possibilities of a way of thinking about form that is attuned to the lyricism of language but does not adhere to the rigid dictates of traditional form available to French writers. Seeking to move Bertrand's formal experiments from a fantastical past to a modern, urban and cosmopolitan reality of contemporary life, Baudelaire writes in the dedication to *Paris Spleen*, the collection of *"petits poèmes en prose"* published posthumously in 1869: "Which one of us, in his moments of ambition, has not dreamed of the miracle of a poetic prose, musical, without rhythm and without rhyme, supple enough and rugged enough to adapt itself to the lyrical impulses of the soul, the undulations of reverie, and the jibes of conscience? It was above all, out of my exploration of huge cities, out of the medley of their innumerable interrelations, that this haunting ideal was born" (1970: ix–x). What Baudelaire suggests here is that the openness of the genre of the prose poem could be more responsive to a given writer's interiority. One can sense in the freedom Baudelaire sees in Bertrand's prose poems an analog to the long sweeping lines of Walt Whitman's *Leaves of Grass*, which sought to enact a wideness and wildness of imagination uncontainable by the dictates of the neoclassical verse forms that virtually defined French poetry of the nineteenth century. To change the imagination, such writers as Baudelaire and Whitman contend, one has to change the discourse through which it is expressed.

That oft-cited passage from the opening of *Paris Spleen* describes the impetus to move away from received forms which, by their very nature, are neither personally nor privately determined in order to bring into language a writer's individual interiority. The mark of authorial subjectivity appears in the types of variations that appear within the given frame and in terms of the expertise by which the formal requirements can be navigated to make a claim or set the terms of a poem's argument. Such forms do not, however, spring from the imagination of the poet. They become the constraints for that imagination, and as such they predetermine the direction of that thought and, more importantly, how the very activity of thought itself is represented. In the passage from Baudelaire's dedication to *Paris Spleen*, we see that he places form as that which ideally should "adapt itself the lyrical impulses of the soul" rather than the other way around.

Decades later, the American modernist William Carlos Williams would write, in a seminal statement on poetics that appears as his introduction to the 1944 collection *The Wedge*: "It isn't what [the poet] *says* that counts as a work of art, it's what [the poet] makes, with such intensity of perception that it lives with an intrinsic movement of its own to verify its authenticity. Your attention is called now and then to some beautiful line or sonnet-sequence because of what is said there. So be it. To me all sonnets say the same thing of no importance" (1954: 255). One particular element worth emphasizing in this passage is that expression of Williams' belief that the poem of modern life needs to constitute and verify its own authenticity rather than be granted legitimacy by the past or history. Moreover, the poem, according to Williams, is a measure of the "intensity of perception" that "lives with an intrinsic movement of its own" rather than an extrinsic movement delineated by an adherence or even fealty to prior cultural authority. This resonates with the poetics Baudelaire articulates in the dedication to *Paris Spleen* and suggests that the prose poem is bound up with poets seeking a means by which a reader cannot rely on a priori rules and mores for literary texts in order to understand them. The reader's own experiences become much more actively a part of the interpretive process if there is no place for an ideal form against which a poem can be judged in terms of excellence of artistic execution.

It is no surprise, then, that Williams' own breakthrough book was 1923's *Spring & All*, a collection which combines poetry and prose, poems and poetics. Arguably, the poet directs the perceptions guided by the imagination, channels them, and so it becomes necessary to have as many modes, genres, and possibilities of form available in order to be receptive to those perceptions as they occur. The imagination is "an actual force," Williams insists, and writing, then, is the attempt "to perfect the ability to record at the moment when the consciousness is enlarged by the sympathies and the uniting of understanding which the imagination gives, to practice skill in recording the force moving, then to know it, in the largeness of its proportions" (1970: 51). These lines themselves sound like poetic theory, and indeed they articulate Williams' poetics, yet they appear in a collection that interweaves such discourse with poems written in open form. Rather than citing scholars or the work of other poets, the theoretical prose moves back and forth between and among some of Williams' most important verse poems—"By the Road to the Contagious Hospital," "A Red Wheelbarrow," and "To Elsie"—as if to suggest that in estimating value there is no difference between the two, that we cannot differentiate the prose from the poetry, the theory from the practice, especially as both come from the imagination, the understanding, of one writer.[5] Even today, this combination of theoretical prose and lyric, image-driven poetry within the covers of a single volume by a single author, seems a radical rethinking of what a book of poetry must look like. Indeed, even many advocates of prose poetry would be hesitant in describing the discursive, philosophical prose of *Spring & All* as prose poetry, yet it may fit within Williams' own definitions of what poetry must do in the modern age for it to be relevant and even to be authentic poetry.

Michael Benedikt, in his foreword to *The Prose Poem: An International Anthology*, reads Baudelaire's statement about poetry as being the justification for arguing that prose poems necessarily are characterized by surrealist, oneiric impulses. Benedikt writes somewhat moralistically about the "need to attend to the priorities of the unconscious," a position that Robert Bly, a devotee of Jungian psychology, also held. Benedikt goes on to state that this "attention to the unconscious, and to its particular logic, unfettered by the relatively formalistic interruptions of the line break, remains the most readily apparent property of the prose poem," and, more polemically, he insists that this is the prose poem's "most basic principle—one shared by virtually every prose poet of importance" (1976: 48). This grand claim does explain why figures such as Gertrude Stein, William Carlos Williams, H. D., Elizabeth Bishop, or John Ashbery do not appear in Benedikt's collection. These poets do not share the same points of reference in terms of surrealism or a commitment to the dreamlike, irrational realm of the "deep unconscious." Thus Benedikt's anthology, being influential, as it continues to be despite having gone out of print long ago, has perpetuated a particular aspect of prose poetry that embraces narrative and avoids discursivity.

Perhaps the issue is not that Benedikt is altogether wrong, however, so much as that he is too limited in his sense of how one investigates consciousness. Baudelaire's statement of prose poetics is not necessarily axiomatic, but even so consciousness itself is not able to be discussed let alone represented in a monolithic way. There is in fact room for abstraction since consciousness exists in the mind rather than in the external world. We see in Bertrand's preface to *Gaspard de Nuit* that it is a discussion about the nature of art that generates the book itself. Read in allegorical terms, it is the author's conversation—however spiritual in nature—with his own imagination that gives rise to the text. Such a conversation is not wholly irrational, and indeed, the Gaspard figure indicates that it is not purity but rather the yoking together of various tendencies and impulses that creates powerful art: the sacred and the profane, the discursive and the spiritual. Moreover, Williams' statement, which I have already cited, also serves as discussion of the connection of poetry to consciousness through the capability of the former "to perfect the ability to record at the moment when the consciousness is enlarged by the sympathies and the uniting of understanding which the imagination gives, to practice skill in recording the force moving, then to know it, in the largeness of its proportions." The prose poem a fortiori is not the *representation* of an inner world, but is the expression of the attempt to record the movement of consciousness or the "the lyrical impulses of the soul." Again, Gaspard says that in his book are "the many processes" to articulate the Absolute, which resonates with Williams. By extension, the prose poem is, at its core, a form of abstraction, which is why it evades reifying into a specific, replicable form with a set of stable characteristics.

Thus, abstraction here is not meant to be placed against "concrete," nor is it meant to imply some givenness to generalizing. Rather, I have in mind something akin to the abstraction of the New York painters of the mid-twentieth century in which every stroke on the canvas was not a mimetic representation of a specific thing to be found in nature, but rather was itself the expression of interiority meeting with the materiality of paint, brush, canvas, even the painter's own body. As the critic Harold Rosenberg would describe things in his landmark essay, "The American Action Painters": "At a certain moment the canvas began to appear to one American painter after another as an arena in which to act—rather than as a space in which to reproduce, re-design, analyze or 'express' an object, actual or imagined. What was to go on the canvas was not a picture but an event." (1959: 25). With this in mind, the event in prose poetry is the poet articulating interiority, the warp and woof of consciousness as it encounters experience by way of language, discourse, and the expectations surrounding the use of words. In other words, abstraction is predicated on the principle that everything is in the process of becoming. Like the best art, the abstraction sloughs off the a priori, to reveal the present moment in all its vital and complex intensities, latent in every gesture. The prose poem is an arena insofar as it is a genre that is perpetually discovering itself, and in that way it mirrors a poet's attempts to discover consciousness or what we might call the "experience of experience."

In many ways, what I have been arguing about prose poems—that they are often self-reflexive, that they are intrinsically invested in abstraction, that they are in the process of determining their own tradition—is illustrated in a late prose poem by John Ashbery titled "Homeless Heart":

> When I think of finishing the work, when I think of the finished work, a great sadness overtakes me, a sadness paradoxically like joy. The circumstances of doing put away, the being of it takes possession, like a tenant in a rented house. Where are you now, homeless heart? Caught in a hinge, or secreted behind drywall, like your nameless predecessors now that they have been given names? Best not to dwell on our situation, but to dwell in it is deeply refreshing. Like a sideboard covered with decanters and fruit. As a box kite is to a kite. The inside of stumbling. The way to breath. The caricature on the blackboard. (2012: 42)

While clearly this poem can be read as an older poet contemplating his own mortality, we can also see it as the creative process reflexively commenting on itself.[6] The work is the writing of the poem and the poem is the evidence of the processes. To be finished with the process of self-discovery creates joy, but the sadness means that the processes are complete—whatever is to be expressed is no longer out in front. If the work is by its nature an activity, an action, then the poem is fixed, and the consciousness becomes reified, "the being of it takes possession" and once that happens, it becomes "secreted behind drywall." The homeless heart is trapped, like its predecessors, which seems to be a comment on the mercurial nature of prose poems. To be trapped, to be secreted behind drywall, is not to be at home, however. In this poem, the heart has no home, and remains homeless. At best, the house is rented, not owned, which is why no one poem fully expresses consciousness. None can, because the mind, and the heart—within the realm of aesthetic abstraction there is no difference—needs to be in motion, needs to be alive.

Traced back to its roots, then, the prose poem is a genre that always reveals its unsettledness, always demonstrates how its every instance and example adds to an understanding of what the genre is coming to be. Ultimately, this must be the case, if it is to enact the restless conversation with itself, the ongoing conversation between literary history and poetic maker, between text and reader, between a genre with itself that moves toward discovering *"the note pure and expressive."* While this is perhaps true of any work of literature, the very fact that the prose poem actively, intrinsically, resists a settled definition, its "circumstances of doing," can never be put away, and if we can never satisfyingly resolve what is poetic about prose poetry, that only means we have not yet come to the end of what poetry might prove to be.

Notes

1. In his important and influential *The Prose Poem: An International Anthology*, editor/poet/translator Michael Benedikt does include short prose pieces by Kafka, so it is clearly possible to consider Kafka's short work as prose poems, despite the fact that for others, these prose pieces are short fiction. It would have been useful if Benedikt had made a case for their inclusion,

especially as that would defend against any arguments that its purpose was to include as many highly visible names as possible.
2. Ron Padgett, another well-known practitioner of the prose poem, does include an entry on the prose poem in the reference book he edited titled *The Teachers & Writers Handbook of Poetic Forms*.
3. Delville and Monte in their respective monographs, offer long and insightful discussions about the role of genre in thinking about the prose poem. Monte, especially, offers a comprehensive overview of genre to such an extent that that the prose poem tells us more about genre than genre does about the prose poem. What I offer is thus not a disagreement with either, but I do show how in terms of thinking of internal structure we are led away from considering the prose poem as a form per se. Nevertheless, this is not a settled question. Not only does Padgett position the prose poem as a form in his handbook, but we see that David Lehman—in his succinct and perceptive history of the prose poem offered as the introduction to *Great American Prose Poems: From Poe to the Present*—indicates that even for him the final verdict is still undecided, and refers in one sentence to the prose poem being either "a form (if it is a form) or genre (if that's what it is)" (2003: 24). Ultimately, it may be an academic question—Lehman, a deft cultural critic as well as a gifted poet, indicates it may be—but again, since there is still such much wariness about prose poetry, getting at the fundamental uncertainties that attached to it is warranted.
4. Valentina Gosetti acknowledges Bertrand's clear debt to Hoffmann, but she also expands the network of influences in order to show how Betrand's description of the various pieces of Gaspard as being *fantaisies* refers not only to the nature of the content, but to the liberated form of the work itself as well. In that light, the term calls to mind the musical term "fantasia," which refers to work that is free and improvisatory in regard to form (2016: 68–87). Ultimately Gosetti seeks to position the term in its fullest historical context so as to illuminate how Bertrand's contemporaries would have understood what the author intended to communicate in using that particular word.
5. Titles for Williams' poems were added later when they were pulled from *Spring & All* for inclusion in his *Collected Poems*.
6. I read this poem in different but related terms in *Art of the Ordinary* (2018: 85–91).

Works Cited

Ashbery, John (2013), *Quick Question*, New York: Ecco Press.
Baudelaire, Charles (1970), *Paris Spleen*, trans. Louise Varese, New York: New Directions.
Benedikt, Michael (1976), *The Prose Poem: An International Anthology*, New York: Dell.
Bertrand, Aloysius (1994), *Gaspard de la Nuit*, trans. John T. Wright, Lanham, MD: University Press of America.
Delville, Michel (1998), *The American Prose Poem: Poetic Form and the Boundaries of Genre*, Gainesville, FL: University of Press of Florida.
Deming, Richard (2018), *Art of the Ordinary: The Everyday Domain in Art, Film, Philosophy, and Poetry*, Ithaca, NY: Cornell University Press.
Gosetti, Valentina (2016), *Aloysius Bertrand's Gaspard de la Nuit: Beyond the Prose Poem*, Cambridge, UK: Legenda and Routledge.
Hass, Robert (2011), *The Apple Trees at Olema: New and Selected Poems*, New York: Ecco Press.
Hejinian, Lyn (2013), *My Life and My Life in the Nineties*, Middletown, CT: Wesleyan University Press.
Lehman, David (2003), *Great American Prose Poems: From Poe to the Present*, New York, Scribner's.

Monte, Steven (2000), *Invisible Fences: Prose Poetry as Genre in French and American Literature*, Lincoln, NB: University of Nebraska Press.

Rosenberg, Harold (1959), "The American Action Painters," *The Tradition of the New*, New York: Horizon Press pp. 23–39.

Tate, James (2013), *Selected Poems*, Middletown, CT: Wesleyan University Press.

Todorov, Tzvetan (1976), "The Origin of Genres," *New Literary History*, vol. 8, no. 1, pp. 159–70.

Volkman, Karen (2005) "Mutable Boundaries: On Prose Poems," <https://poets.org/text/mutable-boundaries-prose-poetry> (last accessed August 6, 2020).

Williams, William Carlos (1954), "The Author's Introduction to *The Wedge*," *Selected Essays*, New York: Random House, pp. 255–7.

Williams, William Carlos (1970), *Spring & All*, Buffalo, NY: Frontier Press.

Part III

Genres and Discourses

9

THE PROSE POEM, FLASH FICTION, LYRICAL ESSAYS AND OTHER MICROGENRES

Michel Delville

CRITICS OF THE PROSE POEM, AND I include myself in the category, have described the form as a genre which emerged as a reaction against dominant poetic forms, "a critical, self-critical, utopian genre, a genre that tests the limits of genre" (Monroe 1987: 16), a genre which is representative of "how literary forms conceal traces of their own underlying aesthetic contradictions, including the fact that such meta-genres as 'poetry,' 'narrative' and the 'lyric' are always already contaminated by the traces of other generic categories they tend to subscribe to or exclude" (Delville 1998: 9).[1] In France, the growing popularity of the French prose poem in the second half of the nineteenth century—since Baudelaire's *Paris Spleen*—is in direct proportion to its capacity to break through the metrical and rhythmic constraints of the alexandrine. If one had to account for the prose poem "revival" which took place in the United States from the 1970s (Russell Edson, Michael Benedikt, David Ignatow, Charles Simic, Rosmarie Waldrop, Language and post-Language poetry . . .), something similar could be argued about the potential of the genre not only to enact a continuation and reevaluation of familiar French Symbolist and Surrealist paradigms but also to respond to, pastiche or subvert genres other than traditional, versified poetry, genres which, like fiction or the essay, are more or less exclusively associated with prose literature. Perhaps this is why Edgar Allan Poe described his 1848 cosmo-philosophical treatise *Eureka* as a "prose poem," a term he used to convey the singular hybridity of a "Book of Truths" offered to the reader, "not in its character of Truth-Teller, but for the Beauty that abounds in its Truth; constituting it true" (Poe 1997: 3). His insistence on the necessity to consider his poem-essay "on the Material and Spiritual Universe" as "an Art-Product alone:—let us say as a Romance; or, if I be not urging too lofty a claim, as a Poem" (3) reflects the struggle between poetic ambiguity and the objective value of the essay that is still typical of many recent prose poetry works combining critical, philosophical, and lyric material pointing in the direction of a work suspended between an ideal of self-sufficient, self-directed poeticity and the syllogistic imperatives and contextual discursiveness of the essay.

It has been argued that some readers may be attracted to the prose poem format, whether of the speculative or narrative kind, because they have no patience or time for longer forms (at least if one assumes that brevity is, by and large, one of the genre's dominant features). What happens when they start to read prose poetry, however, is a rather different experience which is likely to prompt as much questioning as answering, the prose poem being, by definition and by necessity, a mongrel genre combining lyric and analytical, private and public content in varying measures and combinations and thus torn between the utilitarian and the autotelic vocation' of its own discourse. In the best of cases, these hybrid textual creatures, far from closing the reader's mind, are likely to encourage a different, more associational, para-critical reading which some see at work in "microessay" writing.

Despite the increasing popularity of such labels as the microessay or the "proem," the proximity of the prose poem to neighboring speculative prose genres has been the subject of very little attention or reflection outside creative nonfiction writing programs over the last, say, thirty or forty years. The essays devoted to the "personal" or "lyric" essay contained in the Spring 2017 issue of *TEXT* prepare the ground for a (re)consideration of the relationship between prose poetry and expository prose. In their Introduction, the editors, Rachel Robertson and Kylie Cardell, begin by quoting Robert Manne:

> I had thought of an essay as any brief piece of non-fiction prose. I no longer do . . . For me at least, an essay is a reasonably short piece of prose in which we hear a distinctive voice attempting to recollect or illuminate or explain one or another aspect of the world. It follows from this that no essay could be jointly authored. It also follows, that, with an essay, we trust that the distinctive voice we hear is truthful or authentic, even when perhaps it is not. (ix)

The emphasis here is as much on the personal, distinctive voice of the essayist as on (vague) considerations of required length. To say that an essay should be "reasonably short" rather than "brief" does not mean much and bears echoes of similar controversies surrounding the generic status of the "short short" vis-à-vis the short story, or, for that matter, the narrative, "fabulist" prose poem à la Russell Edson, of which more will be said later. To be honest, for many of us, the only intrinsic quality which distinguishes a discursive prose poem from an essay is precisely its limited length, just as what ultimately distinguishes sudden fiction from a short story is its narrative scope and, ultimately, its sheer word count (a couple of pages for some, 2,500 words according to Irving Howe), which is well below the usual length of a short story. Further in the issue, the dissolution of boundaries between creative and essayistic writing promoted by writers of "lyric" essays is explored by Michelle Dicinoski's chapter on Rebecca Solnit and Maggie Nelson, which argues that their book-length works can be regarded as long lyric essays insofar as they "construct an essaying 'I' whose associative approach presents not just a view of the world but a method for viewing the world" (Dicinoski 2017: 1). Dicinoski proceeds to examine different uses of juxtaposition, association, and citation (in the manner of Barthes' *A Lover's Discourse*) in these works, and concurs with Brenda Miller that many writers "have tried to pin down the lyric essay, defining it as a collage, a montage, a mosaic," an aspect of their work which "recognize[s] in the lyric essay a tendency towards fragmentation that invites the reader into those gaps, that emphasizes what is unknown rather than the already articulated known" (Miller cited in Dicinoski 2017: 2). She also argues that Solnit's and Nelson's respective uses of characterization are "found in the character of thought itself: in how it leans, and with whom, and how it leaps and connects, and how it makes its wild associations" (11), a definition which is entirely in tune with Baudelaire's dream of "a poetic prose, musical, without rhythm and without rhyme, supple enough and rugged enough to adapt itself to the lyrical impulses of the soul, the undulations of reverie, the jibes of conscience" (Baudelaire 1947: ix).

Whereas Judith Kitchen emphasizes what she identifies as the "musicality of devices such as alliteration and assonance, and other devices of poetry, such as metaphor and repetition" (Kitchen cited in Dicinoski 2017: 2) as key features of essayistic writing, Leslie Jamison notes that as "a genre grounded in productive uncertainty—collage rather than argument, exploration rather than assertion"—the "lyrical" essay can stand accused of "maintain[ing] a tenuous grasp on rigor and momentum": "When does associative thinking feel productive—establishing important connections, peeling away layers, dissolving boundaries between registers—and when does it feel evasive, gliding over one idea too quickly in order to tackle the next?" (Jamison 2013: unpag.).

One way of answering this question is to look at Rosmarie Waldrop's *Lawn of Excluded Middle* (1993), a poetic extension of Wittgenstein's project to "make language with its ambiguities the ground of philosophy" (Waldrop 1993: unpag.). Waldrop's collection emerges both as an illustration and a *mise en abyme* of the prose poem's capacity to bypass the epistemic gaps allegedly separating science, philosophy and poetry by incorporating them in an alternative form of knowledge—one that combines the heuristic pedestrianism of the Baudelairian *flâneur* (as well as of its more recent exemplars, such as the Situationist drifter and Laura Elkin's *flâneuse*), the speculative mind of the scientist, and what Habermas has termed the "problem-solving" aspirations of philosophy:

> I knew that true or false is irrelevant in the pursuit of knowledge which must find its own ways to avoid falling as it moves toward horizons of light. We can't hope to prove gravity from the fact that it tallies with the fall of an apple when the nature of tallying is what Eve's bite called into question. My progress was slowed down by your hand brushing against my breast, just as travel along the optic nerve brakes the rush of light. But then light does not take place, not even in bed. It is the kind of language that vanished into communication, as you might into my desire for you. It takes attention focused on the fullness of a shadow to give light a body that weighs on the horizon, though without denting its indifference. (Waldrop 1993: 73)

One of the most remarkable features of Waldrop's *Lawn* is its willingness to integrate many different discourses from areas such as philosophy, science, narrative, and the lyric. But is this polygeneric quality what makes Waldrop's paragraphs "prose poems"? As we know, the mixing of different genres and styles per se is by no means the privilege of poetry written in prose: Pound's *Cantos* and Zukofsky's "A" come to mind, not to mention many recent poetry collections made up of interwoven lyrics, stories, newspaper cuts or even drawings and photographs. What makes Waldrop's work so interesting is precisely that it does not confine itself to mixing or juxtaposing antipodal modes and registers. One of the main strengths of *Lawn of Excluded Middle* indeed lies in its playful and critical *appropriation* of Wittgenstein's philosophical formulations. Waldrop does not resort to the asyntactic and disjunctive strategies encountered in many experimental works of the "language-oriented" variety. Rather, she proceeds to undermine the logical, syllogistic authority of expository prose from within by confronting it with the changing psychic terrain displayed by a consciousness that is using all its rhetorical vigor to keep up with the "accelerating frame" of a world that is "edging away and out of reach" (Waldrop 1993: 67).

As is apparent in the paragraph I've just quoted, Waldrop's prose poems account for the particulars of subjective experience in a way that accounts for the geometries of language, body and self and combines them in "an alternate, less linear logic" (unpag.). The constant shifts from the general to the particular, the abstract to the sensuous, the metaphorical to the literal ("logic is no help when you have no premises. And more and more people lacking the most modest form of them are wandering through the streets" [74]) need to be understood in the context of the author's proposition that "we have to pass from explanation to description in the heroic hope that it will reach right into experience" (74). It is a tribute to Waldrop's extraordinary stylistic talents that the transitions always remain fluid, achieved by almost unnoticeable shifts of tone, register, and grammatical structure. The result of the poet's meditations on the principle of ambiguity encompassed by "the gravity of love" reads like Barthes' *A Lover's Discourse* translated by Wittgenstein into a Poundian "dance of the intellect," one that allows the self to struggle with the "uncertainty of fact" (60) indicated, in various ways, by a post-Newtonian model of the universe. Waldrop's investigation of the contradictions and paradoxes that undermine the consistency and authority of logical thinking invalidates what Charles Bernstein has described as the anachronistic assumption that "philosophy is involved with system building and consistency and poetry with the beauty of language and emotion" (Bernstein 1986: 218). In this sense, her work is in keeping with the ongoing project shared by modern poetry and philosophy: that of "*investigating the possibilities (nature) and structures of phenomena*" (220).

These various attempts at defining and practicing the "lyrical essay" have the refreshing, albeit slightly disquieting effect of reminding us that Baudelaire's prose poems were equally informed by the need to convey the mechanics of the mind itself and that they were inextricably linked with the development of journalistic prose (and its "dispersed" layout and design on the page), at a time when the circulation of French newspapers had increased dramatically and constituted a valuable source of revenue (forty out of the fifty pieces which compose the volume were published in journals and magazines, some of them in such popular daily venues as *Le Figaro* or *La Presse*, which published the first twenty poems of the collection). In his study of symbolic resistance in nineteenth-century France, which includes extensive chapters and sections about the rise of the newspaper culture, Richard Terdiman insists on the resemblances between the fragmented, disjunctive structure of Baudelaire's collection and the principle of "ordered disorganization" (122) which prevails in the newspaper format. More than a century before the birth of attention span and cognitive development theories, Baudelaire—commenting on the work's lack of fixed linear telos and describing the book as having "neither head nor tail, both head and tail, alternately and reciprocally"—writes in his Preface to *Paris Spleen*, "how admirably convenient this combination is for all of us, for you, for me, and for the reader. We can cut wherever we please, I my dreaming, you your manuscript, the reader his reading; for I do not keep the reader's restive mind hanging in suspense on the threads of an interminable and superfluous plot" (Baudelaire 1947: ix).

In doing so, Baudelaire is not merely attempting a desperate career move (he was hoping to turn his collection into a financial success, which he badly needed at this stage in his career): more importantly, at least in the context of this essay, the prose poem's rejection of the continuity of "plot" extends the author's critique of lyric self-containedness to a critique of the linear, teleological transparency of essayistic prose as well as of accepted institutional divides between high and low genres and discourses. As Jonathan Monroe (1987: 102) aptly puts it, the prose poem effects a "broadening of the dialogical [struggles enacted in Novalis and Schlegel] from a virtually exclusive focus on struggles *within* high culture to include a concern with struggles *between* high and low culture" ("including the languages of poetry, prose, salesmanship, private ownership, the artist's milieu, religion, social unrest, history, philosophy, myth, philanthropy, social theory, and political confrontation; the languages as well of adults and children, men and women, rich and poor" [124])—which is "crucial to the social reinscription of the lyric that the prose poem advances." Addressing the paradoxical dialectics of closed and open form within the collection, Monroe concludes that "as resolutely cohesive in its individual texts as it is fragmented as a collection, *Le spleen de Paris* marks the persistence of organicist notions of form even as it begins to effect the break with such notions later manifest in the more radically *anti*-organic texts of a Rimbaud or a Mallarmé" (102).

It was that same Stéphane Mallarmé who as early as in the 1870s prolonged Baudelairian prose poetic revolution and began to experiment with the possibilities of poetic reportage. The proximity of French Symbolist prose poems to articles and "faits divers" and the possibility of converting "poetic" blocks of prose into sellable commodities liable to "please" and "amuse" the reader (Baudelaire 1947: ix) is also underlined by both Terdiman and Monroe as a symptom of modern poetry's gradual departure from art for art's sake in favor of "a means for acquiring both an audience and an income" (Monroe 1987: 97).

As Baudelaire's foundational example shows, the shifting destinies of the prose poem and essayistic writing were inextricably linked from the genre's very first inception. Baudelaire's (at least in part) financially motivated obsession with author/publisher/reader relationships already signals a departure from the traditional essayistic writing, one which places the emphasis on the potential of volume and page space to reinvent and reach a new readership which, in Baudelaire's time, largely reflected the rise to hegemony of prose in a world dominated by bourgeois interests and ideology (which arguably included a demand for brief nonfiction textual units which were easy to consume at one sitting between meals and working hours).

Short Shorts

To distinguish a discursive or analytical prose poem from a poetic or paracritical essay is a rather complex and uncertain task. An attempt to distinguish between the prose poem and such generic neologisms as the "short short story," "sudden" or "flash" fiction, or "Twitterature" would amount to skating on even thinner ice. Like the so-called "narrative" prose poem, the "short short story" generally appears as a further reduction of the thematic and narrative scope of the traditional short story, either in the form of an "internal" narrative or of a "plot" restricted to a single anecdote or incident (Howe 1983: x). For some, such a reduction would seem to respond to "the need for simultaneous intensification and acceleration marked by new media," when it is not associated with "an erosion of deep reading" in the age of Facebook, Twitter and Instagram (Botha 2016: 216). In his anthology of "short shorts," Irving Howe differentiates the "ordinary short story" (whose length he gauges as ranging between three and eight thousand words) from the short short (whose outer length limit he sets at twenty-five hundred words) on the ground of their respective formal and thematic development. While the short story, says Howe, still admits *some* development of action, theme and character, the short short is based on "the barest, briefest incident" and presents "human figures in a momentary flash" and "in archetypal climaxes which define their mode of existence." "Situation," Howe argues, "tends to replace character, representative condition to replace individuality" (Howe 1983: x). While emphasizing the opposition between lyrico-epiphanic immediacy and epic extension, Howe also insists on the aborted realization of individuality and "character" which results from the extreme shortness of the story:

> Consider Ernest Hemingway's 'A Clean, Well-Lighted Place.' What do we know, or need to know, about the man who sits in the café piling up saucers? Next to nothing about his past, very little about his future. What we do know, unforgettably, is the wracking loneliness and lostness of his life in the present.
>
> Or consider Octavio Paz's 'The Blue Bouquet.' We know almost nothing about the man threatened with the loss of his eyes, since the crux of the story is not biography but confrontation—that moment of danger in which the man finds himself, a moment such as any of us could experience. Faced with that danger, he loses whatever fragment of individuality he may have for us, and all that matters is the color of his eyes.
>
> In both Hemingway's and Paz's miniature masterpieces, circumstance eclipses character, fate crowds out individuality, an extreme condition serves as emblem of the universal. (x)

Howe's insistence on transindividual "situations" and "archetypal climaxes" definitely draws the short short story toward the impersonality of allegorical narratives. As a result of its universal quality, Howe's short short indeed "often approaches the condition of a fable," projecting "not the sort of impression of life we expect in most fiction, but something else: an impression of an *idea* of life" (xi–xii). In addition to this "universalizing" tendency, one of the main features which emerge from Howe's description of the short short is the disappearance of the protagonist of the story, at least in the traditional sense. What remains is a semi-allegorical content or, sometimes, a voice, as happens in many of Russell Edson's "fabulist" prose poems such as this one, entitled "The Terrible Angel":

> In a nursery a mother can't get her baby out of its cradle. The baby, it has turned to wood, it has become part of its own cradle.
>
> The mother, she cries, tilting, one foot raised, as if in flight for the front door, just hearing her husband's car in the driveway; but can't, the carpet holds her . . .
>
> Her husband, he hears her, he wants to rush to her, but can't, the door of the car won't open . . .
>
> The wife, she no longer calls, she has been taken into the carpet, and is part of it; a piece of carpet in the shape of a woman tilted, one foot raised as if to flight.

The husband, he no longer struggles towards his wife. As if he sleeps he has been drawn into the seat of his car; a man sculptured in upholstery.

In the nursery the wooden baby stares with wooden eyes into the last red of the setting sun, even as the darkness that forms in the east begins to join the shadows of the house; the darkness that rises out of the cellar, seeping out from under furniture, oozing from the cracks in the floor . . . The shadow that suddenly collects in the corner of the nursery like the presence of something that was always there . . .
(Edson 1976: 5)

One of the typical "recipes" for this particular kind of prose poem involves a contemporary everyman who suddenly tumbles into an alternative reality in which he loses control over himself, sometimes to the point of being irremediably absorbed—both figuratively and literally—by his immediate and, most often, domestic everyday environment. Often, the "turning point" at which something "goes wrong" or "just does not seem right" propels the protagonist into a logic-of-the-absurd sequence whose stages are depicted, one after the other, with painstaking, almost hallucinatory precision. Constantly fusing and confusing the banal and the bizarre, Edson delights in having a seemingly innocuous situation undergo the most unlikely and uncanny metamorphoses; a method reminiscent not only of Kafka's parables but also of Edward Gorey's domestic gothicism. Edson's personae usually appear at the mercy of an environment which does violence to human subjectivity. "The Terrible Angel" is also an example of how these basic conceptual premises of Edson's prose poems often lead him to dwell on the unsavory, the macabre and the monstrous—a tendency generally attenuated by the lightheartedness of the author's absurdist rhetoric.

Characteristically, the concluding paragraph of Edson's prose poem is built on a single imagistic motif—that of the "creeping darkness"—which adds a touch of "poeticalness" to an otherwise most prosaic narrative. This albeit tentative move away from the narrative drive toward the more meditative tones of the last sentence is further reinforced by the recurrence of suspension points. An important typographical hallmark of Edson's prose poems, they have the effect of constantly slowing down the action, while making room for moments of verticality and non-narrative presence between the different metonymic "leaps" which make up the story.

In her Introduction to the 1964 collection *The Very Thing That Happens*, Denise Levertov comments on the microcosmic quality of Edson's narratives: "Seen as through the wrong end of a spyglass, minuscule but singularly clear, this world within a world of his is one in which 'things'—chairs, cups, stones or houses—may be immobile but are not inanimate, and therefore experience solitude and suffering; where animals are unlikely to be dumb; and where man is often essentially immobilized by the failure to communicate. There is interaction but no interrelation. The inanimate before the animate, a child before his parents, man before woman, the eye before the world of appearance, each is alone" (Edson 1964: v).

This overwhelming sense of utter solitude and helplessness is indeed an essential aspect of Edson's imaginary worlds. In them, anonymous people or things get "mislaid" and fall apart, abandoned by the traditional roles and functions which have so far conditioned the cosy, reassuring atmosphere of their everyday existence. The point at which "things start to go wrong" therefore often constitutes the dynamic crux of the poem. In a more general sense, the objects and concrete surroundings described in Edson's fables seem to prevail over the poem's "personae." When Edson's characters are not simply referred to as "a man" or "a woman" (the author's favorite grotesques also include the "old woman," the "fat man" and the "large woman"), they are systematically deprived of physical or psychological complexity. In fact, Edson's "types" are actually no types at all, as their "personalities" or even their dominant characterological feature are hardly ever described. This radical anonymity of Edson's prosaic personae reflects the author's desire to write "a poetry of miracles—minus the 'I' of ecstasy . . . [and] not caught and strangled on particular personalities" (Edson 1995a: 297). This uncompromising rejection of the latent solipsism of lyric poetry would seem to invalidate Levertov's point about the "pervasive desperation" (Edson 1964: vi) of Edson's writing. Even though one cannot overlook the overall "feeling" of frustration and helplessness pervading "The Terrible Angel" and countless other poems in the same vein, one could still object that Edson's personae, despite the atrocious treatment they are frequently submitted to, seem incapable of expressing, or even experiencing, "solitude and suffering." Like Kafka, Edson deals precisely with the loss of affect in a mummified world in which human beings are always on the verge of shrinking into negligible quantities of impersonal matter. More often than not, Edson's characters are merely used as starting points for Edson's absurdist rhetoric. In the absence of a temporal, emotional or contextual frame of reference, they seem to exist in a quasi-allegorical and profoundly untragic (and un-lyrical) vacuum.

At the level of the story itself, the rambling patterns resulting from Edson's "involuted nonsense" owe a lot to the kind of logic of the absurd which generates the multiple narrative ramifications of Lewis Carroll's *Alice's Adventures in Wonderland*. Edson's plots often involve a familiar situation either "logically" extended to absurdist extremes or simply turned upside down, as in "The Pattern," in which a woman gives birth to an old man, or "Piano Lessons," which tells the story of a piano given to a young girl as a birthday present and which becomes the greatest girl-player in the world. More generally, some of Edson's favorite motifs, like the spiral staircase or the tunnel, suggest the complex, labyrinthine dynamics of his prose poems. To resort to one of the author's own favorite metaphors (see, for instance, "The Bride of Dream Man" in *The Intuitive Journey and Other Works*), reading a prose poem by Russell Edson often amounts to peeling an onion: there seems to be always a yet-to-be-discovered layer of meaning (or nonsense) beneath the latest image or "turn of events," one which is always likely to snowball into further sequential and perspectival immoderations.

Edson's prose poems have often been compared with newspaper cartoons (Edson's father created the famous "Andy Gump" series in the 1940s), as both genres indeed largely rely on a number of common formal and thematic constants. These recurrent features include an interest in burlesque situations and grotesques (in more than one respect, Edson's collections can also be seen as a literary equivalent of the freak show), an apparent "economy of effort" and the use of a very short narrative format. In many of them, however, the sequential arrangement of the different images or scenes which compose the "plot"—far from subscribing to the relatively conventional linearity of cartoon narratives—seems to follow the logic of a dream or, more precisely, that of a nightmare. To quote Edson himself, this particular kind of prose poem resembles "a kind of mental pantomime that arises from the part of the mind that is mute" (Edson 1995b: unpag.). This oneiric quality, which lends itself to every kind of syntactic or imagistic "idiosyncracy," has now become something of an unmistakable trademark for the particular kind of formal exoticism commonly associated with "the" American neo-Surrealist prose poem.

In this respect, the most likely putative influence pervading a poem such as "The Terrible Angel" is to be found not so much in the free-wheeling, associational imaginings of automatic writing associated with French Surrealism as in the more controlled and self-conscious fantasies of Max Jacob and the early Henri Michaux. The prose poems of Max Jacob were recently rediscovered and revalued by the American public: a relatively minor figure in the French canon, Jacob headlined the March/April 1994 issue of the *American Poetry Review*. They have exerted a tremendous influence on a whole generation of American prose poets who, in the last fifty years, have tried to emulate, more or less successfully, the surreal and playful miniatures collected in *The Dice Cup* and other collections (1917). Many of Edson's prose poems also read very much like Bertolt Brecht's *Kalendergeschichten* or like Kafka's short short stories/parables. In Edson's fables, however, the underlying didactic-satirical impulse still present in Brecht's and Kafka's fables is smothered by the grotesque quality of Edson's rhetoric. Edson's prose poems are indeed utterly deprived of any allegorical content and often tend to refer to nothing outside their own logic-of-the-absurd conventions. Despite the vividness of the images and the dramatic burlesque, one can easily see how such "nonsensical" synopses can feel a bit strained and turn into a predictable ploy, especially as they are used quite often in Edson's collections. In this respect, Edson's prose poems do not seem quite to live up to his utopia of a poetry without artifice, "a prose free of the self-consciousness of poetry; a prose more compact than the story teller's; a prose removed from the formalities of literature" (Edson 1995b: 296). Indeed, one could argue that Edson's "anti-narrative" and "anti-lyric" prose poems display their own particular kind of formality and self-consciousness by resorting to a number of recipes which are themselves arguably as "artificial" and, most certainly, as predictable as the conventions Edson denounces as being the unhappy privilege of "traditional" poetry, as well as longer narratives like the novel. Some of Edson's through-the-looking-glass and down-the-rabbit-hole stories fail to produce anything more than an occasional forced smile, particularly when they are read one after another in a collection. Somehow, Edson's volumes of prose poems indeed gain by an infrequent, sporadic reading.

The Fabulist School

The poetic fables and parables of Russell Edson, Lawrence Fixel, Morton Marcus, Peter Johnson, Maxine Chernoff and many other American prose poets break with a number of famous precedents within the tradition of the prose poem in English, including the English Decadent tradition of parable-like prose poems and even American precursors like Sherwood Anderson and Arturo Giovannitti. While Wilde and Anderson were still trying to pastiche the laconic limpidity of style and sober didacticism of the King James Bible and tinge it with *fin-de-siècle* pastel ornamentalism, Edson's parables/prose poems depart from the Decadent and modernist tradition at the level of both style and content. The prevailing influences and affinities here (conscious or not) are the writings of Henri Michaux, Julio Cortázar, Peter Altenberg, Jorge Luis Borges and, above all, Franz Kafka, in which ambiguity and playfulness constantly undermine the story's didactic potential:

> In it were the things a man kept, otherwise they were not in the box: a toy person with an arm missing; also a leg.
> Actually, both arms were missing. And, as one leg was missing, so was the other; even the torso and the head.
> But, no matter, because in it was another toy person. This one was also missing an arm and one of its legs.
> Actually, it had no arms at all; same with the legs, the torso and head.
> But, no matter, the box was full of armless and legless toys without torsos or heads. But again, no matter, because even the box was missing . . . And then even the man . . .
> In the end there was only an arrangement of words; and still, no matter . . .
> (Edson 1985: 15)

"The Matter" summarizes Edson's poetics of fabulation. As the "toy-person" is gradually dismembered into nothingness and as the "story" gradually turns into a snake eating its own tail, both reveal themselves to be only a pretext or a springboard for the author's whimsical verve. They thereby make the "matter" into a mere pretext for the creation of a poem eventually reduced to an "arrangement of words." This foregrounding of discourse, which is further enhanced by the poem's tendency to self-referentiality, is what distinguishes Edson's prose poems not only from the traditional parable or fable, but also from some of their modern avatars, many of which (one thinks, for example, of T. F. Powys and James Thurber) are still basically faithful to the genre's original didactic impulse, albeit in a updated fashion.

This increased, overt self-consciousness about the process of composition indirectly reminds us that Edson began to publish prose poems in the mid-1960s, at a time when the so-called "fabulators" had begun to establish themselves as a major influence on the American literary world. Like Robert Scholes' "fabulators," Edson deliberately foregrounds and violates a number of conventions ruling traditional narrative genres, and often does his best to remind the reader that the text before him is merely an artificial and fictional artefact. Like many of his fellow fabulist novelists (such as John Barth, Robert Coover and Thomas Pynchon or their common "precursor," Jorge Luis Borges), Edson also likes to blur boundaries between fiction and reality, the everyday and the nightmarish, tragedy and comedy. He shares with them a strong interest in black humor and the literature of the absurd. By defining himself as a poet, Edson also violates standard expectations concerning the alleged lyric content of poetry: ironically, the art of fabulation is here applied to a genre usually relying more than any other on a set of assumptions of "direct," unmediated naturalness and authenticity.

Robert Scholes has described the kind of "satiric" black humor exploited by a fabulator like Kurt Vonnegut as "qualified by the modern fabulator's tendency to be more playful and more artful in construction than his predecessors: his tendency to fabulate." "Fabulative satire," Scholes goes on to say, "is less certain ethically but more certain esthetically than traditional satire," as fabulators "have some faith in art but reject all ethical absolutes." Rejecting "the traditional satirist's faith in the efficacy of satire as a reforming instrument," they have "a more subtle faith in the humanizing value of laughter" (Scholes 1967: 41). Scholes' distinction between traditional and modern fabulists is also valid within the context of the postmodern parable-fable-prose poem, in which the original didactic or satirical aim of the genre is irremediably drowned in an amoral turmoil of rhetoric and textual games. In Edson's prose poems, the satiric impulse is directed solely at the very conventions ruling both the lyric and the narrative modes. As suggested above, the self-referential, sometimes self-parodying quality of Edson's prose poems questions our conception of what a (prose) poem should be made of. The myth of the self-present, transcendental lyric self is here deconstructed by means of a foregrounding of the methods determining its coming into being. The fabulists' parodic subversion of poetico-lyric material also affects the treatment of the didactic sub-genres parodied by the prose poem, whose heuristic potential is now problematized. As in Scholes' "amoral" fables (37), the final "truth" of the story is also ultimately textual (and, more often than not, intertextual) as opposed to transcendental.

Despite these important distinctions, the difference between the classical fable and the "fabulist" one is, once again, more of degree than of kind. As Scholes has pointed out, even the traditional fable displays "an extraordinary delight in design." "With its wheels within wheels," Scholes continues, "rhythms and counterpoints, this shape is partly to be admired for its own sake" (10). One of the features of Scholes' "traditional" fable the postmodern prose poem has so far preserved and developed is precisely its distinct quality of self-conscious craftsmanship. Edson himself has commented on the tendency of even the arguably "classical" fables of Marie de France to take a life of their own and "reach beyond the lesson to tell a strange tale for its own sake" (Edson 1990: 92). As is particularly clear from Edson's "The Matter," the telescopic strategies of the narrator's absurdist rhetoric tend to become ends in themselves, as they cease to merely filter reality and become the creators of their own private fictional realms, the "poetic" content of the fabulist prose poem therefore resulting primarily from its exploration of the movements of consciousness itself.

In this respect, what the fabulist prose poem and the poetic essay share, in different but related ways, is what Steven Fredman has described as "a fascination with language (through puns, rhyme, repetition, elision, disjunction, excessive troping, and subtle foregrounding of diction) that interferes with the progression of story or idea, while at the same time inviting and examining the 'prose' realms of fact and reclaiming for poetry the domain of truth" (Fredman 1990: 80). Besides emphasizing the double (and bilateral) contamination of poetry by prose and of prose by poetry which characterizes the whole history of the contemporary prose poem, Fredman's argument suggests that sometimes the focus in prose poems is on the very hermeneutic process which leads to the epiphanic moment we associate with the lyric, and, therefore, on the "telling of the tale" rather than the tale itself.

As Donald Wesling reminds us, the prose poem has long been a preferred form for the "narrative of grammar," in which the movements of consciousness and sensibility take the place of epic progression, so that action becomes "a cognitive and linguistic sequence, where the events are thoughts, words" (Wesling 1985: 176). This "tendency" characterizes the whole history of the contemporary prose poem from Baudelaire's "flexible prose" to the "New Sentence" of the Language poets, to use Ron Silliman's terminology. Echoing Mallarmé's definition of the "critical poem" as one that reproduces "the immediate thought rhythms which organize a prosody," Wesling's narrative of grammar (or "narrative of consciousness") is one in which "every sentence of the poem is a narrative, insofar as it puts into an order the reader's acts of attention and habits of response to language; and the sequence of sentences make up another, larger narrative" (176), a description not unlike Baudelaire's foundational definition in the above-quoted Preface to *Paris Spleen*. As Richard Deming suggests elsewhere in this volume, "[w]hile on balance we take a narrative to be either real or invented, the prose poem often leaves open the possibility that it is an essay" (<Add page number.>). For Deming, it is less a matter of addressing "the impurity of narrative" than embracing its constitutive ambivalence. Rather than trying to answer the idle question of whether, say, Montaigne and Cioran were prose poets, or that of whether Charles Simic and Rosmarie Waldrop write "sudden" essays, one can only hope that future studies of the prose poem and other affiliated short forms will take these considerations as a starting point for a discussion of the specific cultural and institutional practices which govern established or ephemeral generic labels or designations alongside considerations of intrinsic originality or aesthetic value.

Notes

1. This chapter is an expanded revision of an article which appeared in the a special prose poetry issue of *TEXT: Journal of Writing and Writing Courses* (vol. 46, October 2017) reproduced with kind permission from the journal. Elements of this essay also appear in Delville 1998.

Works Cited

Baudelaire, Charles (1947), *Paris Spleen*, trans. Louise Varèse, New York: New Directions.
Bernstein, Charles (1986), *Content's Dream: Essays 1975–1984*, Los Angeles: Sun & Moon.
Botha, Marc (2016), "Microfiction," in Ann-Marie Einhaus (ed.), *The Cambridge Companion to the English Short Story*, Cambridge: Cambridge University Press, pp. 201–20.
Cardell, Kylie, and Rachel Roberts (2017), "Essay Now: The Contemporary Essay in Australia and Beyond," *TEXT: Journal of Writing and Writing Courses*, vol. 21, no. 1.
Delville, Michel (1998), *The American Prose Poem: Poetic Form and the Boundaries of Genre*, Gainesville: University Press of Florida.
Dicinoski, Michelle (2017), "Wild Associations: Rebecca Solnit, Maggie Nelson and the Lyric Essay," *TEXT: Journal of Writing and Writing Courses*, vol. 21, no. 1.
Edson, Russell (1964), *The Very Thing that Happens: Fables and Drawings*, New York: New Directions: 1964.
Edson, Russell (1976), *The Intuitive Journey and Other Works*, New York: Harper & Row.
Edson, Russell (1985), *The Wounded Breakfast*, Middletown: Wesleyan University Press.
Edson, Russell (1990), "The Soul of Tales," *Parnassus*, vol. 16, no. 1, pp. 87–92.
Edson, Russell (1995a), "Portrait of the Writer as a Fat Man," in Stuart Friebert and David Young (eds), *Models of the Universe: An Anthology of the Prose Poem*, Oberlin: Field Editions, pp. 293–302.
Edson, Russell (1995b), Letter to the author, December 4.
Fredman, Stephen (1990), *Poet's Prose: The Crisis in American Verse*, 2nd edn, Cambridge: Cambridge University Press.
Howe, Irving, and Ilana Wiener Howe (eds) (1983), *Short Shorts: An Anthology of the Shortest Stories*, New York: Bantam.

Jamison, Leslie (2013), "What Should an Essay Do?," *New Republic*, July 8, <https://newrepublic.com/article/113737/solnit-faraway-nearby-and-orange-running-your-life> (last accessed January 16, 2020).

Kitchen, Judith (2011), "Grounding the Lyric Essay," *Fourth Genre: Explorations in Nonfiction*, vol. 13, no. 2, pp. 115–21.

Monroe, Jonathan (1987), *A Poverty of Objects: The Prose Poem and the Politics of Genre*, Ithaca: Cornell University Press.

Poe, Edgar Allan (1997), *Eureka: A Prose Poem*, New York: Prometheus.

Scholes, Robert (1967), *The Fabulators*, New York: Oxford University Press.

Terdiman, Richard (1985) *Discourse/Counter-Discourse: Theory and Practice of Symbolic Resistance in Nineteenth-Century France*, Ithaca: Cornell University Press.

Waldrop, Rosmarie (1993), *Lawn of Excluded Middle*, Providence: Tender Buttons.

Wesling, Donald (1985), *The New Poetries: Poetic Form since Coleridge and Wordsworth*, London and Toronto: Associated University Presses.

10

The Prose Poem and the Antinovel: Unsettling Form in Nathalie Sarraute's *Tropismes*

Jane Monson

Twentieth-century literary criticism and more general debates about the prose poem have predominantly focused on the form in relation to poetry rather than prose, and where comparisons are drawn the points of view tend toward short prose, from journalism to anecdote and six-word story to sudden prose or flash fiction. Understanding the prose poem from the point of view of poetry is logical, and it is often described as poetry without the line break, or a text that looks like prose but otherwise reads as poetry; read aloud you would not know the difference. Either way, we commonly start from poetry rather than prose to understand a text that minuses how we immediately identify and recognize poetry and puts in its place key aspects of what we have always associated with prose: sentence, paragraph, justified margin. Approaching a block of prose on the page, which then reveals itself silently and experientially as poetry, can be rewarding, but also unsettling. The text has a seemingly duplicitous relationship with the reader, giving with one hand and taking away with the other—leaving us in limbo, while we try to reconfigure not just the form or genre we're dealing with, but the content in relation to that form. All too often, this seeming incongruity distracts the reader from entering the piece itself while they try to work out where they are, or how they are supposed to get there. In a recent insightful essay, "The Prose Poem as Igel," Cassandra Atherton and Paul Hetherington eloquently summarize this unsettling dichotomy or tension in the prose poem:

> the prose poem's containment within one or more paragraphs—something readers immediately register as a visual cue—promises a contained, reasonably complete and narrative-driven rendering of experience, yet delivers instead a fragmented narrative replete with (in metaphorical terms) gaps and spaces. The prose poem's brevity is at odds with the usual, or conventional, expectations attached to the reading of prose and, as a result, the reader is left wondering: 'What happens next?', 'Where is the rest of this narrative', and 'What comes after the final line?' The visual attributes of the block of text—from its borders to its rectangular shape—encourage readers to anticipate a complete story and they receive something very different indeed. (Atherton and Hetherington 2016: unpag.)

Arguably, today, there are increasing numbers of exceptions to completely new readers of prose poetry, and these aesthetic and ingrained literary expectations are shifting all the time as the prose poem is more settled than ever creatively, and by turns, critically. But change is slow, and so in parallel with each shift, the "poetry or prose?" question continues to be asked as part of re-framing and readjusting our views on what a text is and what its function and place are in our lives. Rather than answer this here, I want to offer the possibility that we have reached a kind of cul-de-sac in terms of the either/or angle. The "is it poetry or prose?" question has been an essential part of understanding the prose poem, but at length risks perpetuating the idea that poetry and prose are opposites, that the form is complacently dogged by paradox and will forever be labeled an oxymoron in negative terms. If, however, we approach the form less via the usual critical framework of poetry versus prose, and more via the avenue of prose versus prose, there is a convincing wealth of material and evidence showing that the prose poem emerged as much through writers rebelling against established rules within poetry as from divisions and divergences within prose itself. The most pertinent of these divisions is the antinovel, subsequently known to mid-twentieth-century authors, readers and theorists as the Nouveau Roman. The antinovelists of the Nouveau Roman—Alain Robbe-Grillet, Nathalie Sarraute, Claude Simon and Michel Butor eminent writers among them—set in motion a useful breakdown and reassembling of rules around the traditional (outmoded, as they saw it) apparatus of the novel, that continues to be pertinent to the nature, formation and development of the prose poem today. While each antinovel has its own style and interpretation of what going against tradition means, common ground shared within the group was formed by a dissatisfaction with and distrust of the novel's central focus on character, recognizable situations, plots, predictable use of linear or progressive time and identifiable dialogue. In lieu of the novel's key ingredients and underlying formula, the antinovelists essentially played a variety of tricks on the novel, placing value on the inner world of characters rather than their outer description and actions. By reconfiguring the novel's structure, they drew attention away from pure content and the reassuring invisibility of form, to form itself and the machine, if you like, of fiction. They deemed it no longer fit for purpose and held that "reality" as presented by Stendhal, Flaubert or Balzac, for example, was no longer relevant to postwar culture and life. To this end, the antinovelist authors replaced central characters with objects, thought patterns and memories and unsettled the reader's expectations of context, time and space by focusing intently on the inner world of the self, rather than an imposed plot that motivated identifiable characters toward action. In the words of Susan Sontag when discussing the objection to fictional reality shared by Sarraute and her contemporaries:

> Reality is not that unequivocal; life is not that lifelike. The immediate cozy recognition that the lifelike in most novels induces is, and should be, suspect . . . Not only must the novelist not tell a story; he must not distract the reader with gross events like murder or a great love. The more minute, the less sensational the event the better. (Sontag 2009: 105–6)

As well as twisting and upsetting the reader's expectations of conventionally handled and classically delivered plots and themes, the antinovelist in turn toyed with the logical relationship between speech, dialogue and action. Where in the classic novel the reader could enjoy predictable actions following on from what someone had said, this balance or sense of reason was instead eradicated altogether. Spoken word became thought conveyed as a stream of consciousness and used to explore a lack of sense rather than lucidly progressing the novel forward. For the reader this created a disorienting, rather than a reliable, experience where narrative seemed either under threat or in a state of disorder and chaos.

The term "antinovel" was introduced most emphatically into literary modern currency by Jean Paul Sartre in his 1948 and 1956 Preface to Nathalie Sarraute's *Portrait d'un inconnu* [*Portrait of a Man Unknown*], in which he states: "les anti-romans conservent l'apparence et les contours du roman . . . Mais c'est pour mieux décevoir: il s'agit de contester le roman par lui-même, de le détruire sous nos yeux dans le temps qu'on semble l'édifier' (Sartre 1956: 7) ["Anti-novels retain the appearance and the outlines of the novel . . . But they do so only the better to deceive: the aim is to use the novel to contest the novel; to destroy it before our eyes as it is apparently being constructed" (Sartre 2009: 3–4)]. Sartre goes on to compare Sarraute's antinovel to the detective story; "a 'parody' of the quest novel" (4) and, notably, "anti-novel" was used over three centuries earlier in France, also in relation to satire, by the French novelist Charles Sorel, who published *Le Berger Extravagant, ou l'Anti-Roman* in 1633, a parody of the Romance novel, which destroyed its conventions whilst mimicking them. Earlier still (1605 and 1615), Cervantes' *Don Quixote* is considered, predominantly by the poet, critic and historian Aron Kibédi Varga, to be the first example, not so much of the founding novel of modern literature as is widely considered, but of the original antinovel, which leaves room for the possibility that the novel followed on from what it was not. French literature, whether through play, satire, or revolt, has a long history of unsettled forms and genres, with many examples through the eighteenth century of genres mixing "irreverence towards established boundaries" (Moore 2017: 13) and the Establishment's hierarchical system of dividing high art from low, poetry from prose. Fabienne Moore's study of the pre-history, as she sees it, of the French prose poem during the Enlightenment notes how the authors of prose poems "worked on shifting ground" and "absorbed as well as participated in the displacement of not only the lyric and the novel, but also pastoral, epic and dramatic genres" (15). She goes on to say, in the wake of Fénelon's *Les Adventures de Télémaque*, "the first fiction to be interpreted as a prose poem" was a parody of it: Marivaux's *The Télémaque Travesti* (1775) mocked "the salient components of prose poems, which many authors had reverently tried to imitate" (16). She then posits something that resonates with the early stages of the French prose poem as much as it does with the birth of the antinovel:

> One of the laws of a new genre's formation seems to be that parody accompanies its birth, a parody often adopting the new genre's form. Therefore it is of no surprise that a few authors penned self-reflexive prose poems poking fun at the instability and hybridity of this newcomer, the prose poem. (16)

While early examples of antinovels were associated with parody and a subversion of the novels before them, simply by undermining the narrative even as it was being written, the more recent antinovel of the twentieth century focused less on mocking the novel's past or current form, and more on taking apart what was considered a stale or outmoded formula in order to bring out what was being hidden, quashed or subverted by the traditional novelist's upholding of conventional narrative and narration.

In the 1940s through to the 1960s, when the antinovel moved into the sphere of the Nouveau Roman, Sartre and Robbe-Grillet hailed Sarraute as their founder and inspiration. Sartre and his contemporaries more widely deemed her the pioneer of the antinovel, which by mid-century was more or less synonymous with the Nouveau Roman. Although Sarraute's earliest published text, *Tropismes* (1939), was referred to as the founding text of their theories and practices as writers, Sarraute in fact strongly disagreed with antinovelist terms applied to her work and asserted that she simply wrote "romans modernes" (Sarraute 1981: 34–9). It is characteristically rare of Sarraute to agree with terms and labels placed upon her, as she moves far more fluidly among them in steady pursuit of her own vision, but she was undoubtedly working within the parameters of the antinovel in the way she creatively and critically wrote against the traditional novel's conventional use of plot, time and character development and adopted a more anti-mimetic approach to the novel.

In terms of influence, she is commonly discussed in relation to Sartre and his contemporaries, many of whom took Sarraute's destruction of the novel as they saw it and creatively and theoretically took the genre to task, quite brutally exposing its apparatus and make-up, devolving in order to evolve the form in other ways. They displaced the novel's use of overheard dialogue, recognizable time progressions and identifiable settings with hidden, less graspable things, feelings, moments and tiny overlooked objects, insisting on revealing what the novel was not doing, rather than what it was hailed for. All antinovelists recognized how the novel's structure and formula—Realist or Romantic—was stifling and overlooked everyday objects, feelings and subtexts in favor of a more macro and discussable view of the world. Within the formula or system of what made a novel a novel, the novelist made the reader feel held and gave its faithful audience a place to escape, with their sense of reality more or less intact. Sarraute, in particular, took away this all-seeing view of the world to focus on what was being denied or suppressed in both Romantic and Realistic renditions of truth or reality, moving from the surface to what was hidden or submerged and placing it center-stage, under spotlight and microscope. During this critical process of exposing what historically had made the novel and novelist, and publishing the creative results that arose in the wake of this unsettling, she not only delivered a new novel to readers, critics and writers alike, but subtly helped to shape and make sense of the perpetually unsettled prose poem. What was questioned and discarded via the anti- and the new novel were the very things unnecessary for the prose poem as well, and what was needed to form the antinovel were the same ingredients as those used to make prose poetry.

Nowhere is the symbiotic meeting between the prose poem and the antinovel more marked than in Nathalie Sarraute's *Tropismes*, viewed from several angles: as prose poetry, as small novel or as novel fragmented into twenty-four pieces. It is at once an antinovel, a foreshadowing of the Nouveau Roman, and an early example of French prose poetry that was not of the Baudelarian, Mallarméan or Rimbaldian tradition and not as object-focused as Francis Ponge or Gertrude Stein, but something else entirely, while drawing on many of their values and questions about traditional approaches to language, subject matter and form. Akin to the prose poem, these brief texts are compressed stories of moments, where both form and content work together implicitly to produce dense, highly focused forms of narrative that never develop "beyond a stressed moment" (Sarraute 2019: unpag.).

Tropismes was Sarraute's first published work, begun in 1932, released in France in 1939, then republished in 1957. In 1963, the English edition appeared, published by Calder and translated by Maria Jolas, a celebrated translator and founder of *Transition*, a literary quarterly in Paris that she set up with her husband, featuring articles by key modernists, including James Joyce, Gertrude Stein, Samuel Beckett and Franz Kafka. The Calder edition, unlike the French, contains in a single volume key creative and critical works: *Tropismes* and Sarraute's pivotal essays on the novel, *The Age of Suspicion* (1956). The book maps out Sarraute's symbiotic creative and critical breakdown and understanding of the novel and paints a detailed picture of the relationship between the prose poem and the antinovel, equipping the reader for a critical view of language that is equally applicable to both forms. In the same way the prose poem is discussed in terms of being an oxymoron and fitting neither poetry nor prose, the antinovel is seen in the same terms, as being incongruent with the novel itself, and any other genre in prose. But belonging nowhere, ultimately it becomes its own thing. In turn, Sarraute's opening acknowledgment of the apparent incongruous nature of the English edition of *Tropisms*, with prose poems and essays on the novel bound together, represents the very polarity she used to discern their inextricability and indebtedness to one another:

> The publication in one volume of a work like *Tropisms*—which some considered a collection of prose poems—with what, quite obviously, is furthest removed from it: a series of essays on the novel, may cause legitimate surprise. And yet, this proximity is justifiable . . . the present volume, to which two such dissimilar works as *Tropisms* and the *Age of Suspicion* may give an appearance of incongruity, by virtue of this very juxtaposition, gives a fair account of my endeavours, as they progressed from my first *Tropisms* to the theoretical viewpoints that derived from them. (Sarraute 1963: 9, 11)

In this sense, both the prose poem and the antinovel share a similar parodic nature, where in order to become what they are they are viewed in terms of what they are not, exposing all the while their affinity to each other. What the prose poem did to poetry and the antinovel to prose was the same, in that each form or genre reorganized or reconfigured definitions around poetry and prose and their respective forms, not by denying or abolishing their characteristics completely, but by exposing the machine and apparatus behind the finished products and using them in other ways. Superficially, they appeared to go against tradition, but on a much deeper level they simply distilled their differences down to a sameness and shared ground. In this sense, the antinovel and the prose poem become "texts" again: things woven, joined, fabricated and built together.

While, creatively, *Tropismes* works as prose poems that have come about through Sarraute's reworking of the novel, critically it is another story, and again, this is typical of both prose poetry and the antinovel. Creatively they are settled, where critically they are inconsistently unsettled. *Tropismes*, even today, is far from "still" in terms of where it belongs in any given form or genre. The long list of labels includes twenty-four sketches, vignettes, a novella, a slim novel, texts, short passages of prose, a series of miniatures, pieces, an antinovel, the foundational text of the Nouveau Roman, and, occasionally, prose poetry. This unsure labeling is also typical of many prose poems that have come before and after *Tropismes*. Incongruity and unsettled categorizations are an essential part of the antinovel's and the prose poem's history, but in the hands of Sarraute, for example, open up far more discussions around where prose and poetry are deeply embedded in each other, rather than distinctly separate. Sarraute herself welcomes the notion of unsettledness, in that she does not set up hard and fast fences between categories to dismantle in the first place. Her consistent approach to *Tropismes* as a text to which the usual rules do not apply is summed up in an interview she gave in her ninetieth year in the *Paris Review*:

INTERVIEWER

With the tropisms, did you feel that it was fiction, did you wonder what to call it?

SARRAUTE

I didn't pose myself such questions, really. I knew it seemed impossible to me to write in the traditional forms. They seemed to have no access to what we experienced. If we en-closed that in characters, personalities, a plot, we were overlooking everything that our senses were perceiving, which is what interested me. One had to take hold of the instant, by enlarging it, developing it. That's what I tried to do in *Tropisms*. (Sarraute 1990: unpag.)

Although considered an early exponent of ideas pertinent to boundary fluidity and a move away from tradition, Sarraute was of course writing in a time and environment which at the very least nurtured as much as challenged what she was doing. During the first half of the twentieth century, key texts in France, Europe more widely, the UK, Russia and America were emerging that were deemed neither poetry nor prose. Instead they were labeled pieces, texts, short texts, brief narratives, little essays, prose poems, antinovels or similar, and they all challenged, subverted or played with literary rules and conventions around form and genre. Creatively and critically, the text was being increasingly scrutinized as an object, made up of components that were unfixed, that did not need to follow a formula provided by the writer and expected by the reader. Among these texts were James Joyce's *Giacomo Joyce* (written 1914, published 1968), Virginia Woolf's *Street Haunting and Other Essays* (1930), Jean Paul Sartre's *Nausea* (1938), Sarraute's *Tropismes* (1939), Daniil Kharms' *Incidences* (1939) and Francis Ponge's *Le Parti Pris Des Choses* (1942), all following on from Samuel Beckett's short prose of 1920, and Borges' "difficult to classify" stories or essays from the 1920s onwards. Further back still, in 1882, but relevant to Sarraute's study of Russian novelists, especially the "psychological novel" of Dostoyevsky, the merging of the antinovel and the prose poem that she refined in *Tropismes* and future works was firmly established in Russia. Turgenev's 1882 "Poems in Prose" marked the birth of the Russian prose poem at the same time as offering a prime example of the antinovel. The new genre is backlit with controversy, and conflated with the antinovel, as the editor assumed Turgenev was writing another novel; he not only passionately denied this, but claimed he "would never write one again," proving this by waving about what he referred to as "a collection of sketches that an artist would draw before completing a large painting" and declaring that "he was not writing anything now or in the future" (Wanner 2003: 13). As Adrian Wanner points out in his seminal text on the Russian prose poem and the antistory:

> Turgenev defines his new genre negatively. Not only is the prose poem not a novel, but the author uses it as justification for his refusal to write any more novels. We could almost call it an anti-novel . . . the new genre suggests the breakdown of the novelistic form. (13–14)

So, in France and further afield, at the end of the nineteenth century and turn of the twentieth, Sarraute's literary environment and heritage were marked by flux and shift and proved to be fertile ground for the prose poem and related forms. Sarraute herself acknowledged some of these influences, and was aware of key changes in literature around her:

> I had received the shock of Proust in 1924, the revelation of a whole mental universe, and I thought that after Proust one could not go back to the Balzacian novel. Then I read Joyce, Virginia Woolf, etcetera . . . I thought *Mrs. Dalloway* was a masterpiece; Joyce's interior monologue was a revelation. In fact, there was a whole literature that I thought changed all that was done before. (Sarraute 1990: unpag.)

Along with Proust, Joyce, Gide and Sartre, Sarraute also hailed Dostoyevsky's and Kafka's undoing of convention as instrumental in the changes she made to established expectations of narrative, plot and character, moving from more objective portraits of people and places toward their unseen movements, and turning inside out all that readers do not see in characters behind the façade of society's and literature's accepted behaviors. The unsettling of form is inextricable from the unsettling content in *Tropismes* and the general atmosphere of disorientation and alienation in French literature and culture at the time.

Reminiscent of Baudelaire's infamous recognition of the possibilities of a marriage between poetry and prose that he had wanted to emulate after reading Bertrand's *Gaspard*, and the need to find a form to suit fundamental changes in approach to content and environment, Sarraute was more convinced by where poetry and prose met than by where they divided. In fact, she saw no distinction between them, and, like Baudelaire, looked to writers who were merging the forms rather than keeping them separate:

> I've always thought that there is no border, no separation, between poetry and prose. Michaux, is he prose or poetry? Or Francis Ponge? It's written in prose, and yet it's poetry, because it's the sensation that is carried across by way of the language. (unpag.)

Sarraute in her attitude toward the antinovel—that it is an evolution rather than outright rejection of the form—helps also to offset the view that the prose poem was a result of anti-poetry. In the case of both the antinovel and the prose poem, the past is not wrong, it is just not right in its current form for that time. Robbe-Grillet concurred:

The New Novel is "is merely pursuing a constant evolution of the genre" in the face of those who hold that the "true novel" was set once and for all in the Balzacian period, with strict and definitive rules. (Robbe-Grillet 1989: 135–6)

Sarraute enabled the evolution of the antinovel by refusing to engage with polarities or imposed boundaries, of any kind, preferring instead to use the concept of inner movements provoked by external stimuli, otherwise understood as imperceptible invisible moments which occur in people that are prompted by external changes in the environment that happen throughout the day, no matter what situation they might find themselves in. In *Tropismes* 1, IV and VI, for example, these hidden movements caused by external demands or prompts are realized in everyday situations, but conveyed in such a way that solid characters are at the mercy of invisible strings and puppeted about: one minute completely docile, the next utterly frantic. Sarraute's agile traversing of time, space and emotion is enabled by her use of compression, density and juxtaposition of imagery, well-timed sentence and paragraph rhythms and brevity, all typical of prose poetry. In *Tropisme* I, adults and children are out shopping. This is Sarraute's tropistic rendition:

Ils s'étiraient en longues grappes sombre entre les façade mortes des maisons. De loin en loin, devant les devantures des magasins, ils formaient des noyaux plus compacts, immobiles, occasionnant quelques remous, comme de légers engorgements.

[They stretched out in long, dark clusters between the dead house-fronts. Now and then, before the shop-windows, they formed more compact, motionless little knots, giving rise to occasional eddies, slight cloggings.] (Sarraute 1957: 15)

In IV, the Sarrautian "Ils" [they] move from the state of a slow-moving trance, toward a kind of mania, purely in response to external demands, here in the shape of a nameless "lui" [him]:

Quel épuisement que cette dépense, ce sautillement perpétuel devant lui: en arrière, en avant, en avant, en avant, et en arrière encore, maintenant mouvement tournant autour de lui, et puis encore sur la pointe des pieds, sans le quitter des yeux, et de côté et en avant et en arrière, pour lui procurer cette jouissance. (Sarraute 1957: 29)

[How exhausting all this effort, this perpetual hopping and skipping about in his presence: backwards and forwards, forwards, forwards and backwards again, now circling about him, then again on one's toes, with eyes glued to him, and sidewise and forwards and backwards, to give him his voluptuous pleasure.] (Sarraute 1963: 21)

In each *Tropisme*, people (in loose musical terms) are either slack-stringed, out of tune and redundant until fixed and played, or so tightly tuned that they are one turn away from snapping.

During the course of all twenty-four prose poems, these rhythms (and in turn "characters") play out, overall within an unpredictable organization, but up until *Tropisme* VI they seem to alternate between being passive and disturbingly active. By VI, "they" and "elle" [she] are completely at the mercy of others and other things:

Le matin elle sautait de son lit très tôt, courait dans l'appartement, âcre, serrée, toute chargée de cris, de gestes . . .

Même quand ils étaient cachés, enfermés dans leur chamber, elle les faisait bondir: 'On vous appelle. Vous n'entendez donc pas? Le téléphone. La porte . . . .' Il fallait de précipiter, vite, vite, houspillé, bousculé, anxieux, tout laisser là et se précipiter, prêt à servir. (Sarraute 1957: 39, 41)

[In the morning she leapt from her bed early, dashed about the flat, tart, tense, bursting with shouts and gestures . . .

Even when they were hidden, shut up in their rooms, she made them leap up: 'Somebody called you. Didn't you hear them? The telephone. The door. . . .' You had to rush, quick, quick, berated, browbeaten, apprehensive, drop everything and rush forward, ready to serve.] (Sarraute 1963: 24–5)

The term "tropism" itself is from the Greek word *tropos*, 'a turning', and "refers to the involuntary tendency of an organism to react to an external stimulus, as a sunflower, for example, turns towards light" (*Encyclopedia*: 156). Creatively, Sarraute's use of this concept is perfectly apt for these new, brief distillations of narrative and narration. The idea for exploring these hidden movements in people initially came from what she had touched on when reading Dostoevsky and Proust. In *Tropismes* she takes her predecessors' focus on moments much further, probing inwardness, hidden gestures and pre-speech to the farthest point possible; where prose, poetry and the antinovel coalesce seamlessly by virtue of doing the same thing: absolving themselves of the rules that make a poem a poem, prose prose, and a novel a novel. For Sarraute, the process of adhering to the fundamental rules neither of the poem nor of the novel means she treats their characteristics, or technicalities if you like, as concepts, rather than as a set of more physical and set rules to be broken or changed. So rather than consciously creating prose poetry by taking typical elements of prose and poetry and combining them, she goes underneath both of their superficial attributes and fuses them via these hidden sensations. Her search for what she calls the "sous-conversation" in content is therefore also inseparable from discovering this in form, and less about her use of imagery, rhythm and juxtaposition than about addressing a far more conceptual and abstract notion of how poetry is useful for her tropistic approach to form and content. In her friendly but irascible tone when questioned about the place of poetry in her work, she says:

For me, the poetry in a work is that which makes visible the invisible . . . You ask me whether I think my own works are poetic. Given what my view of poetry is, how could I possibly be expected not to think so? (Minogue 1981: 28)

Sarraute wasted little time on challenging generic distinctions and instead redefined "the concepts and assumptions contained within those divisions" (Jefferson 2000: 119). The development, as she sees it, in the novel "has its counterparts in other arts and other literary genres" (121):

Thus music has got rid of feeling and melody in order to allow pure sound to emerge.

Thus so-called 'abstract' painting endeavours to fix the viewer's attention on the painterly element alone.
Thus poetry is getting rid of rhetoric and rhyme. (121)

At this subterranean and more experiential level of literature, poetry and prose have everything in common, down to their pure essence. As Ann Jefferson points out in her astute study of Sarraute's fiction and theory, "Sarraute is not just condemning an outworn fictional convention. She is shifting the centre of gravity of the novel's concerns" (79). Sarraute's a-physical treatment of character, if you like, is an equivalent of "pure sound." Jefferson again notes that Sarraute rejects

> physical manifestations of human existence in favour of . . . the universal sameness of the tropism . . . At the level of the tropism it does not matter whether a character has a lump on the end of his nose . . . is fair or dark, tall or short . . . even male or female . . . because the focus of attention is so inward. (79–80)

Sarraute's use of the tropism, critically as much as creatively, is useful in terms of reassessing the prose poem and edging it toward working on its own terms, rather than as something at odds with itself. Sarraute applies these inner movements that respond to external stimuli to the unseen interior changes that occur in people: their conversations, gestures, thoughts and behaviors. These moments occur before speech, in the space between thought and what we say or do. In Sarraute's words:

> These movements, of which we are hardly cognizant, slip through us on the frontiers of consciousness in the form of undefinable, extremely rapid sensations. They hide behind our gestures, beneath the words we speak and the feelings we manifest . . . They . . . seem to be to constitute the secret source of our existence, in what might be called its nascent state. (Sarraute 1963: 8)

Sarraute's sensations and movements not only recall Baudelaire's "lyrical impulses of the soul," but touch on his "desire to transmute the Glazier's strident street-cry into a song, and to express in lyrical prose all the saddening implications that such an utterance throws up to garret and attic through the mist-bound streets" (Baudelaire 1989: 25). This perspective, again, on what we cannot see with the naked eye, but wish to translate or transmute in language and form, foreshadows not only key approaches to subject matter in Sarraute and the antinovel, but also writers a century away from Baudelaire in Britain and America. In focusing away from the realistic aspects of the traditional novel and burrowing deeply into the interior, psychological and more abstract notions of truth and reality, there is a tangible route between the prose poem and the antinovel via the stream of consciousness novel, exemplified by pivotal modernists, namely Woolf, Joyce and Stein. As Delville neatly puts it in his introduction to the American prose poem:

> At a time when British and American novelists became increasingly interested in registering the full spectrum of mental life (what William James had described in his *Principles of Psychology* (1890) as "the stream of thought, of consciousness, or of subjective life" [Bradbury and McFarlane 1991: 197]), it is hardly surprising that the first genuinely modern experiments with the short prose lyric were carried out

by two major representatives of the stream-of-consciousness novel: James Joyce and Gertrude Stein. [...] Joyce's early 'dream epiphanies' (1900–1904) constitute the first modern attempt to use the prose poem as a vehicle for approaching the capricious 'flow' of consciousness and the process of subjective experience from the side of the lyric. (Delville 1998: 7)

In Woolf, Joyce, Beckett, Stein and Baudelaire, we find different, but supporting variations on Sarraute's use of the tropism. According to his brother, Joyce said of his "epiphanies"—the bridging texts between his early poetry and early fiction—that they were like "little errors and gestures—mere straws in the wind—by which people betray the very things they were most careful to conceal" (Joyce 2001: 157). In Stein's "Portraits and Repetition" she elaborates on her quest for the unseen behaviors of people, their inner movements: "I had to find out inside every one what was in them that was intrinsically exciting . . . by the intensity of movement that there was inside in any one of them . . . that makes them them" (Stein 1957: 183). Sarraute, with her contemporaries and predecessors, among them Baudelaire, offered something fundamentally important for the development of the prose poem, not only because of the limitations they saw in preceding traditional formalities repeated in both poetry and the novel during the nineteenth century in France, but because they wanted a form that best suited the content of a changing reality, rather than to impose and fix that reality within a set form. To convey reality as it apparently was, as with the realist novel, did not appeal to Sarraute and merely provided readers with a superficial representation of so-called real life. For Baudelaire too, there was a jarring disparity between the strict French meter of the alexandrine and traditional verse, and what he saw and heard in urban modern life. A critical interpretation of this is put well by Michael Butor and applies to both of these aims in Sarraute and Baudelaire:

Now it is clear that the world in which we live is being transformed with great rapidity. Traditional narrative techniques are incapable of integrating all the new relations thus created. There results a perpetual uneasiness; it is impossible for our consciousness to organize all the information that assails it. (Babcock 1997: 75)

At the turn of the century this resulted in what Malcolm Bradbury called the "introverted novel" whereby "it seemed this sophisticated medium had no more territory to develop, for it turned in upon itself" and by degrees "became markedly more 'poetic', in the sense that it become more concerned with precision of texture and form, more disturbed by the looseness of prose as popular usage" (Bradbury and McFarlane 1991: 394). The unsettling of form is increasingly inseparable from the unsettling of content, and Sarraute finds almost suffocating ways of having the components of what she is doing mirror each other or simply switch places. What is deemed socially solid and conventional becomes air and what is empty becomes full, oppressive and tangible, like a substance or matter. In *Tropisme* X, matter that fills a void is manifest in what Sarraute would call "equivalent images" (Sarraute 1963: 8). Here the stuff of "life" is distilled, in repeated conversations, meaningless platitudes, "roulant sans cesse entre leurs doigts cette matière ingrate et pauvre qu'elles avaient extraite de leur vie . . . jusqu'à ce qu'elle ne forme plus . . . qu'un petit tas, une petite boulette grise" (Sarraute 1957: 65) ["continually rolling between their fingers, this unsatisfactory mean substance that they had extracted from their lives ... until it ceased to form anything ... but a little pile, a little grey pellet" (Sarraute 1963: 33)]. *Tropismes* is rich with these images of nothingness, her texts full of intense non-states of physical being; oppressive ghosts, where definition and outline of character, incident and physical space are traced so lightly as not to interfere with the more present significance of sensations that we cannot see, hold, touch or identify with, but are permeated by constantly. The characters are not just devoid of name, stripped back to their pronouns, he, she and they, but are so palely drawn that they are barely there and yet they are intoxicating to read, and get into the reader's imagination as securely as any character more soundly rendered. In the following passage, from *Tropisme* III, place and people alike are described more in terms of what they are not. Place, synonymous with existence, is "semblable à une salle d'attente dans une gare de banlieue déserte, une salle nue, grise et tiède, avec un poêle noir" (Sarraute 1957: 22) ["like a waiting room in a deserted suburban railway station, a bare, grey, lukewarm room, with a black stove" (Sarraute 1963: 18)]. People bear an uncanny resemblance to clones or aliens:

> Ils avaient tous les trois de longues têtes aux yeux pales, luisantes et lisses comme de grandes œufs d'ivoire. La porte de leur apartement s'entr'ouvrait un instant pour les laisser passer. On les voyait poser leurs pieds sur des petits carrée—et s'éloigner silencieusement, glissant vers le fond sombre du couloir. (Sarraute 1957: 23)

> [All three had pale eyes set in long heads as shiny and smooth as large ivory eggs. The door of their apartment opened narrowly for a second to allow them to pass. They were seen to put their feet on little felt squares laid out on the entrance floor—and move silently away, gliding towards the end of the corridor.] (Sarraute 1963: 19)

Sarraute's peculiar minimalist approach results in a chilling distillation of people, places, homes, things, speech and society, rendered down to everything they are before speech, bricks, clothing, decoration, furnishing and rhetoric are imposed and put in place to direct the reader toward knowing who they are, where they are and what they are about. The reader's perceptions of people and place or preconceptions of everyday reality are undone before them. This disconcerting act on the part of author and reader in turn is supported by the form, the brevity of the pieces and the almost stifling concision of the sentences and their juxtapositions. It is what Wanner, discussing minimalism in the Russian prose poem and the anti-story, calls the development from miniaturism to minimalism, the prose poem and the anti-story being natural progressions of each other, much in the way Sarraute's prose poem is a progression (as much as a forerunner) of the antinovel. As Wanner points out in defense of the prose poem:

> Once the form is allowed to follow its own internal logic, the prose poem realizes what we could call its Aristotelian entelechy. Poetic prose lyricism is replaced by an ascetic starkness, as the prose poem mutates into the minimalist anti-story. (Wanner 2003: xi)

Simply by stripping away superfluous content, tradition, and style, the author is not so much depriving the reader of meaningful and convincing ways of transcending "reality," as exposing them more to hidden treasures inside sub-narratives and sub-speech. The author's efficient decision to divest from erstwhile forms, therefore, becomes a new economy within literature—one that gives way to what is not seen or has otherwise become lost. Jefferson's account below of Sarraute's trademark unsettling style is also applicable to the most effective ways in which the prose poem functions through its singular and intensely concentrated approach to its content and subject matter:

> Reading Sarraute is often a deeply disorientating experience. Characteristically, the opening page of a Sarraute novel pitches one into a situation in which nothing is immediately explained, and where the unnamed and unidentified participants exacerbate the reader's sense of disorientation by expressing themselves in the form of questions . . . Who is "il"? Whom or what can he hear? Does "elle" refer to a person or an object? (Jefferson 2000: 17)

Questions around structure and form become synonymous with questions about society, manners, habits, habitual situations, and the material content of life. That which we do not see and say, but hide in conventional responses and manners, is turned inside out for all to see. Each *Tropisme*, in no more than a page or so, lays bare the stuff that sits between thought and speech; in the very space where we edit according to situation and context, Sarraute burrows and brings the buried out into the light, unflinchingly and without mercy. We face ourselves naked in Sarraute's texts, and characters, place and time serve as triggers and means to reveal, rather than support a place in which the reader is held and safe. Sarraute does not need to guide us, nor settle us in any way, or convince the reader to believe in the made-up reality of her narratives; she just asks us not to turn away from our own existence.

Without exception, all of Sarraute's tropisms unnerve the reader through a series of uncertainties that the nameless characters go through. The clues are in the psychological details and the way objects and everyday situations as banal as window-shopping or going to bed become inseparable. What we see becomes intoxicated with everything we do not see, that is hidden in our nightmares, our fears, our deepest thoughts and our suppressed responses to things we do, say and think daily. Objects and ordinary automatic situations which make up our lives are there to serve everything we try to hide, rather than being props of scenes that are described for their own sakes and for the sake of a more widely understood fictional reality. Nowhere in Sarraute's world is there a place where we feel comfortable, where the plot leads us from setting to drama to conclusion. The prose poem's box-like shape is fitting, but also double-edged in terms of its support of unsettling content. On the one hand, it gives the impression through its shape that it is capable of containment and holding, offering an element of security, but once inside you are more aware of not knowing how you got in and therefore not knowing how you can get out. Sarraute frames a situation as simple as shopping or crossing the road and turns it inside out until it is something else entirely. Each decision, each kerb, wall and margin, constantly borders what we know and do not know, life and death and meaning and non-meaning. These borders are where we try to connect, but never succeed, and this is nightmarishly portrayed in the isolated hinterlands between people and people and people and place. Significantly, Sarraute ends *Tropismes* on this note, leaving the reader without any sense of comfort and security, as framed in the first, middle and last sentences of the final *Tropisme*, XXIV:

Ils se montraient rarement, ils se tenaient tapis dans leurs appartements, au fond de leurs pièces sombres et ils guettaient.

Ils se souvenaient de tout, ils veillaient jalousement; se tenant par les mains en un rond bien tendu, ils l'entouraient.

Et quand ils le voyaient qui rampait honteusement pour essayer de glisser entre eux, ils abaissaient vivement leurs mains entrelacées et, tous s'accroupissant ensemble autour de lui, ils le fixaient de leur regard vide et obstiné, avec leur sourire légèrement infantile. (Sarraute 1957: 139–40)

[They were rarely to be seen, they remained buried in their apartments, shut up in their dark rooms, watching and waiting.

They remembered everything, they kept jealous watch; holding hands in a tight ring, they surrounded him.

And when they saw him crawling shamefacedly to try and slip in among them, they quickly lowered their entwined hands, and crouching down all together around him, they fixed upon him their empty, dogged eyes, they smiled their slightly childish smile.] (Sarraute 1963: 56)

This particular prose poem is also disturbing because of the way it undercuts at every turn the connections that people have amongst one another, whether adults or children, and the piece purposely swims nebulously between ages. The hand-holding only shows physical connection, but it is chillingly set against an utter disconnect between these humans as they look at their victim through "empty, dogged eyes" and keep him in closed isolation. Lonely, trapped and surrounded, the critical equivalent of this *Tropisme*, as well as many others, can be found in a passage from Sarraute's essay "From Dostoievski to Kafka" in *The Age of Suspicion*. Where Sarraute focuses on Kafka, she recalls the world he evokes for his characters as "the world without exit, enlarged to the dimensions of an endless nightmare, in which Kafka's characters were to flounder" (Sarraute 1963: 78). Using an analogous image of the children's game Blindman's Buff, Sarraute elaborates on a key focus in her work, which is the absurd and damaging ways in which humans try to establish connections with each other. Sarraute recalls, in the same essay, Katherine Mansfield's famous line "this terrible desire to establish contact," in which humankind either grapples with an inability to reach out to others effectively or—as demonstrated in XXIV—becomes intentionally hostile. Either way, such futile and damaging actions toward seeking contact create a disorienting, ungraspable and unknowable reality:

We all know this world, in which a sinister game of blindman's buff is in constant progress, in which people always advance in the wrong direction, in which outstretched hands 'claw the void,' in which everything we touch eludes us ... in which questions are left unanswered ... in which 'others' are half-human creatures with identical faces ... who observe you from a distance with sly, childish curiosity, who look at you 'without speaking to one another, each man for himself, with no other tie than the target they are looking at ...' (78–9)

The prose poem in this sense, being critical fertile ground for unsettling, is one of the most congenial forms in which to explore this disorientation and disconnect with what we know, assume or would like to have in place. In *Tropismes*, fittingly, the shape of the prose poem, with its block-like walls, floors and ceiling, is consistently explored or demonstrated in the architecture and restricted movements of the characters. People always seem to be trapped in the margins of places, in rooms or outside in Parisian squares, by window frames, neither inside nor outside and often pressed up against walls, sliding along them anxiously and finding it hard to move between spaces. Children are often in a liminal place between life and death, safety and danger in the care of adults, whether they are being ignored or "taught" by them. In *Tropisme* VIII a grandfather teaches his child to cross the road. The child in turn experiences a weight, "une masse molle et étouffante... qu'on lui expliquait comme il fallait toujours avancer avec précaution... et faire bien attention, très attention, de peur d'un accident, en traversant le passage clouté" (Sarraute 1957: 53) ["a soft choking mass... while it was explained to him that he should always proceed cautiously... and be careful, very careful, for fear of an accident, when he crossed between the lines" (Sarraute 1963: 29)]. In V, a figure remains "sans bouger sur le bord de son lit, occupant le plus petit espace possible, tendue, comme attendant que quelque chose éclate, s'abatte sur elle dans ce silence menaçant" (Sarraute 1957: 33) ["motionless on the edge of her bed, occupying the least possible space, tense, as though waiting for something to burst, to crash down upon her in the threatening silence" (Sarraute 1963: 22)]. She leaves the tight frames of bed, room and house to find herself no more settled in the street, and proceeds "modestement le long des trottoirs, le long des murs, juste pour respirer un peu... et puis revenir chez soi, s'asseoir au bord du lit et de nouveau attendre, replié, immobile" (Sarraute 1957: 36) ["unobtrusively along the pavements, along the walls, just to get a breath... and then come back home, sit down on the edge of the bed and, once more, wait, curled up, motionless" (Sarraute 1963: 23)]. On the page, there is very little white space in Sarraute's *Tropismes*, and the black type does not denote sharpness or definition. Instead a grey merging of the two sits underneath, behind or between words and is explored with a Beckettian fervour and single-mindedness. In both authors, what could simply border on bleak and remain there yields some of the most promising examples of synergy between form, content and subject matter, to produce, in equal proportions, the antinovel from one angle and the prose poem from the other, depending on where the reader, rather than the writer, is coming from.

Although Sarraute's content is unequivocally disturbing and unsettling and the form of the prose poem and antinovel an intrinsic part of this unsettling material, it is interesting to note that historically the forms themselves have shared a long and relatively settled and consistent narrative. We have seen this across Europe, but of course it is also prevalent in the history of the English-language prose poem. John Taylor, in "Two Cultures of the Prose Poem," provides a useful list of the English prose poem's roots in prose and anti-prose:

> As precursors of the English-language prose poem, Lehman cites the King James Bible, Shakespeare's prose (in *Hamlet*), John Donne's sermons, Blake's "Marriage of Heaven and Hell," and other pertinent examples ... similar prose-poem antecedents in French literature can be identified as far back as *Aucassin et Nicolette* (late twelfth or early thirteenth century), a love story alternating verse and poetic prose, and perhaps even in the metrically cadenced prose sermons of Saint Bernard (1091–1153). As to more recent (pre-Baudelairean) periods, prototypes of the prose

poem emerge in certain prose passages of the plays of Molière (1622–73), in various "pensées" by Pascal (1623–62), in sermons by Bossuet (1627–1704), in *Télémaque* by Fénelon (1651–1715), in sundry descriptions of nature by Rousseau (1712–78) or Chateaubriand (1768–1848), not to forget in some of Montesquieu's *Persian Letters* (1721). (Taylor 2005: unpag.)

But while we can appreciate the historical and cultural affinity between prose, antinovels and prose poetry, Sarraute continues to help the reader, posthumously, ascertain how their ongoing relationship is still relevant and shaping other texts today. Contemporary evolutions of the antinovel toward the prose poem can be found in Meghan Hunter's *The End We Start From*, Jenny Offill's *Department of Education*, Maggie Nelson's *Bluets*, Cynan Jones' *Stillicide*, Sarah Manguso's *Ongoingness*, Liz Rosenberg's *17: A Novel in Prose Poems*, Lucy Ives' *The Hermit*, a book-length "poem about trying to write a novel" (Ives 2017: unpag.) and Derek Owusu's *That Reminds Me*. In a 1984 interview with Anne Jefferson, Sarraute remained emphatic about the evidence, and need, for a fluidity between forms, and although it is interesting that before her death she noticed a natural shift in the novel toward poetry, what she is witnessing is less of a progression from an anti- or fractured novel to prose poetry than simply boundaries between the novel and poetry shifting:

> For me, the novel is moving closer, or trying to move closer to poetry; like poetry, it seeks to grasp sensations, something felt, as close as possible to its source. Novels should become large poems. And in the same way, a number of poetic works are being created in forms which until now were considered to belong to prose. (Jefferson 2000: 71)

That Sarraute was framed as an antinovelist and her work read accordingly is of course fitting, and *The Age of Suspicion* is rife with negative terms toward the state of the novel: "waning," "fall apart," "devoid," "looking for a way out," "suspicious," "destroying" (Sarraute 1963: 83, 95) among them. However, she used these terms as part of her quest to discover the new; to look back in order "to go farther forward" (120). So how does Sarraute's optimism sit today with public assertions of the death or breakdown of the novel, alongside clear examples of the novel simply changing via connections with poetry and prose poetry? Jorge Luis Borges, Philip Roth and Jonathan Safran Foer have all proclaimed that the novel is a dying form. In 2009 Roth asserted that the novel would be a minority cult within twenty five years and simply cannot compete with the screen (Roth 2009: unpag.), If, as they suggest, the antinovel has potentially sown the seeds for the breakdown or death of the novel, and the prose poem is very much tied up with the antinovel's history and make-up, is the current rise of prose poetry part of that death? Or is it more that the novel's current life is made more possible because of the use of prose poetry? These writers cannot settle between these questions either. Safran Foer says that "novels can't compete with little bursts and fragments" (Foer 2016: unpag.) but can learn from poetry. Borges in *This Craft of Verse* begins by saying that

> the novel is breaking down ... that all those very daring and interesting experiments with the novel—for example, the idea of shifting time, the idea of the story being told by different characters—all those are leading to the moment where we shall feel the novel is no longer with us. (Borges 2000: 54–5)

But like Foer, Borges swiftly follows despair with a more hopeful note; that perhaps the death of the novelist is also the birth of the poet, or rather the essential conflation of the two: "I believe that the poet shall once again be the maker. . . he will tell a story and he will also sing it. And we will not think of those two things as different" (Borges 2000: 55). The antinovelist's underlying mantra, that destruction is a natural part of creation, is as relevant today as it ever was and can be used to focus new ambitions across forms, where the "prose poem" and "antinovel" will be seen less and less as incongruous in themselves, as unsettled oxymorons in search of negation and rebellion, and far more as consistently unified, justified and efficiently settled.

Works Cited

Atherton, Cassandra and Paul Hetherington (2016), "The Prose Poem as Igel: A Reading of Fragmentation and Closure in Prose Poetry," *Axon Journal*, Special Issue, unpag., <https://www.axonjournal.com.au/issue-c1/prose-poem-igel> (last accessed January 29, 2020).

Babcock, Arthur E. (1997), *The New Novel in France: Theory and Practice of the Nouveau Roman*, New York: Twayne.

Baudelaire, Charles (1989), "Letter to Arsène Houssaye," in *Baudelaire, Volume II, The Poems in Prose and La Fanfarlo*, trans. Francis Scarfe, London: Anvil.

Borges, Jorge Luis (2000), *This Craft of Verse*, ed. Călin-Andrei Mihăilescu, Cambridge, MA and London, England: Harvard University Press.

Bradbury, Malcolm and James McFarlane (1991), *Modernism: A Guide to European Literature*, London: Penguin.

Delville, Michel (1998), *The American Prose Poem: Poetic Form and the Boundaries of Genre*, Gainesville, FL: Florida University Press.

Encyclopedia Americana (1966), definition of "Tropism," New York: Americana Corp., Vol. 27, p. 156.

Foer, Jonathan Safran (2016), "Novels Can Learn From Poetry," *Louisiana Channel*, December 6, 2012, Web, March 9, 2016, <https://channel.louisiana.dk/video/jonathan-safran-foer-novels-can-learn-poetry> (last accessed October 26, 2019).

Ives, Lucy (2017), *The Hermit* [review], <https://theculturetrip.com/north-america/usa/articles/lucy-ives-the-hermit-new-book-poem/> (last accessed November 12, 2019).

Jefferson, Ann (2000), *Nathalie Sarraute, Fiction and Theory: Questions of Difference*, Cambridge: Cambridge University Press.

Joyce, James (2001), *Poems and Shorter Writings*, ed. Richard Ellmann and A. Walton Litz, London: Faber.

Minogue, Valerie (1981), *Nathalie Sarraute and the War of the Words: A Study of Five Novels*, Edinburgh: Edinburgh University Press.

Moore, Fabienne (2017), "Genre Trouble," in *Prose Poems of the French Enlightenment: Delimiting Genre*, Surrey: Ashgate, p. 13.

Robbe-Grillet, Alain (1989), *For a New Novel: Essays on Fiction*, trans. Richard Howard, Evanston IL: Northwestern University Press.

Roth, Philip (2009), "Philip Roth Predicts Novel Will Become Minority Cult Within 25 Years," *The Guardian*, October 26, <https://www.theguardian.com/books/2009/oct/26/philip-roth-novel-minority-cult> (last accessed November 2, 2019).

Sarraute, Nathalie (1957), *Tropismes*, Paris: Éditions de Minuit.

Sarraute, Nathalie (1963), *Tropisms and The Age of Suspicion*, trans. Maria Jolas, London: John Calder.

Sarraute, Nathalie (1981), "Nathalie Sarraute" [interview], Jean-Louis Ézine in *Les Écrivains sur la sellette*, Paris: Éditions du Seuil, pp. 34–9.

Sarraute, Nathalie (1990), "Nathalie Sarraute, The Art of Fiction" [interview], Shusha Guppy and Jason Weiss, *Paris Review*, Issue 114, Spring, <https://www.theparisreview.org/interviews/2341/nathalie-sarraute-the-art-of-fiction-no-115-nathalie-sarraute> (last accessed October 20, 2019).

Sarraute, Nathalie (2019), *Tropisms*, New Directions website, <https://www.ndbooks.com/author/nathalie-sarraute> (last accessed November 6, 2019).

Sartre, Jean-Paul (1956), "Préface," in Nathalie Sarraute, *Portrait d'un Inconnu*, Paris: Gallimard.

Sontag, Susan (2009), "Nathalie Sarraute and the Novel," *Against Interpretation and Other Essays*, London: Penguin, pp. 105–6.

Stein, Gertrude (1957), "Portraits and Repetition," in *Lectures in America*, Boston: Beacon Press, p. 183.

Taylor, John (2005), "Two Cultures of the Prose Poem," *Michigan Quarterly Review*, vol. 44, no. 2, Spring, <http://hdl.handle.net/2027/spo.act2080.0044.223> (last accessed January 29, 2020).

Wanner, Adrian (2003), *Russian Minimalism: From the Prose Poem to the Anti-Story*, Illinois: Northwestern University Press.

11

Bishop, Lowell, and the Confessional Prose Poem

Lizzy LeRud

What happened to the American prose poem at mid-century?[1] After Gertrude Stein's *Tender Buttons* (1914), Williams' *Kora in Hell* (1920), and Eugene Jolas' journal *transition* (1927–38), those things we call prose poems stopped interesting writers until the revival of the 1960s, or so the story goes. So much is implied by the major studies: books by Stephen Fredman, Margueritte Murphy, and Steven Monte all move from chapters on Stein and Williams to chapters on Ashbery, Bly, and Creeley, and Jonathan Monroe turns to Europeans Ernst Bloch and Francis Ponge to discuss the World War II era (Monroe 1987; Fredman 1990; Murphy 1992; Monte 2000). Only Michel Delville finds continuity via Kenneth Patchen's writing, but even he admits that the prose poem "vanishes almost completely from the Anglo-American literary scene" between the 1930s and 1960 (Delville 1998: 16).

Were mid-century American poets simply uninterested in formal innovations, in pushing against generic norms like their modernist forebears? Some think so: critics from Stephanie Burt to Bob Perelman argue that the major breakthroughs of mid-century poets were in poetic content, not craft.[2] But those who argue against such thinking often end up pointing to formal innovations long associated with the prose poem. Take, for example, the case of Robert Lowell, whose *Life Studies* (1959) epitomizes the mid-century aesthetics associated with "confessional" poetry.[3] Steven Axelrod points out that Lowell conceived of his contribution to American poetry as a "technical" one, the poet's own term (Axelrod 2015: 329). Axelrod reads Lowell's project as resulting in "a new permutation of free verse," which Deborah Nelson calls "a relaxation of iambic pentameter or the loosening of the rhyme scheme (without its abandonment)" to create "an impression of casual and intimate conversation" (Nelson 2013: 34). To Marjorie Perloff, technical innovations like this one are the direct result of Lowell's "highly original conjunction of verse and prose"—to her, Lowell's greatest achievement (Perloff 1973: xi). When Perloff describes the formal interplay in Lowell's writing, it sounds very much as if she's talking about a prose poem.

In fact, Lowell was not the only mid-century confessional poet whose writing probed the distinction between poetry and prose. It is well-known that these poets were prolific in traditional prose genres. In addition to their prose criticism, Lowell, Elizabeth Bishop, Karl Shapiro, Delmore Schwartz, Randall Jarrell, Sylvia Plath, and John Berryman all wrote autobiographies, short stories, or novels. A case hardly needs to be made for the importance of this group's letters; Langdon Hammer and Siobhan Phillips both read confessional poets' letter writing as a hybrid mode, one where poetic discourses intersects with prosaic ones (Hammer 1997; Phillips 2012).[4] With all this work in prose, it is no surprise to see these writers mixing prose and poetry conventions on the pages of their books. Schwartz's break-out volume, *In Dreams Begin Responsibilities* (1938), combines short stories, verse, and a verse-drama. Shapiro's *Essay on Rime* is conventional literary criticism composed in blank verse rather than the usual prose paragraphs (1945). Lowell's *Life Studies* includes "91 Revere Street," a prose memoir. And Bishop wrote several pieces that she classed as prose poems: shorter works, like "12 O'Clock News," "Rainy Season; Sub-Tropics," and "Santarém," as well as longer ones, like "In the Village," which she published at the center of her poetry collection *Questions of Travel* (1965).[5]

But too often, scholars of confessional writing have siloed traditional prose genres from poetry ones, despite these writers' distinct attempts to avoid such divisions. Consider the example of Bishop's prose poem "In the Village." After *Questions of Travel* went out of print, Farrar, Straus & Giroux reproduced that volume in *The Complete Poems, 1927–1979* (1983) and later in *Poems* (2011), still in print today. But both of these collections give us *Questions of Travel* without its prose poem; "In the Village" was moved first to *The Collected Prose* (1984) and then to *Prose* (2011). The full text of Bishop's volume—with "In the Village"—was not available again until the 2008 publication of Bishop's Library of America volume *Poems, Prose, and Letters*. As a result, this hybrid text that Bishop herself called a prose poem has been read as strictly prose.[6]

If the prose poem does seem to vanish at mid-century, it is not because these poets were not writing them. In fact, this generation's dedication to poetry, prose and their intermixture is fertile ground for thinking about prose poetry—for them and for us. That these writers didn't always use the generic term "prose poem" to describe their projects makes their work all the more significant to the history of the genre. Of course, this is a genre that has long facilitated resistance to conventional notions of genre, so it should come as no surprise that poets responsive to the prose poetry tradition might navigate around its terminology. Thus, at times these poets gravitated toward other terms of description even as they deployed techniques associated with the prose poem. But, at other times, avoiding the term "prose poem" was strategic, a way around publication norms anchored in fixed genre expectations. Attending to the circumstances that prompt avoidance teaches us about the reception of the prose poem and other hybrid genres at mid-century, and it likewise makes any usage of the term all the more remarkable.

Thus, this essay follows the development of "In the Village," that text Bishop continuously labeled a prose poem, first because it is a distinct example of confessional prose poetry but secondly because it was a guiding force for many of this era's major publications, publications not always associated with the prose poem genre. Before it was excised from *The Complete Poems* version of *Questions of Travel*, "In the Village" was the source of a dynamic exchange between Bishop and Lowell about poetry and prose. The exchange ushered Lowell through the difficult development of *Life Studies*, his own breakthrough poetry volume with a prose core, and it prompted Bishop to create the hybrid structure of *Questions of Travel*. Ultimately, to trace the path of "In the Village" is to look anew at the technical innovations of confessional poetics, shaped indelibly by prose poetry.

From early in her career, Bishop was interested in perceived differences between poetry and prose, and her writing vacillated between the two modes. During high school and college, Bishop worked intermittently on a collection of short prose pieces based on her childhood, telling the story of her mother, Gertrude May Bishop, who had been hospitalized for mental illness throughout most of Bishop's life.[7] Bishop's father, William Thomas Bishop, had died shortly after Bishop was born. When the poet Marianne Moore became Bishop's mentor after college, Bishop put away her stories and focused on verse forms for a time. But after publishing her first poetry volume, *North and South* (1946), she returned to the stories, sharing them with Lowell, who noticed their congruity with her poems. By 1951, Lowell was already pushing Bishop to merge poems with prose, at least by publishing them together: "I think your poems and stories explain and light each other up, and that anyone will or should be dazzled by their combination" (Bishop and Lowell 2008: 126).

At first, Bishop resisted Lowell's encouragement to blend poems and prose. When, in 1952, she decided to start publishing her prose, she turned to *The New Yorker*, a venue that maintained sharp distinctions between the two modes. Then, as now, what *The New Yorker* deems "prose" is printed in orderly, evenly spaced journalistic columns, and "poetry" is inset in spaces that interrupt two columns of prose together.[8] As Bishop would soon find out, the *New Yorker* of her day also expected certain conventions in prose stories and memoirs, like dialogue attributions, paragraphs, distinct characters and a sense of setting.

The first story Bishop sent in fitted easily into *The New Yorker*'s expectations for a prose story. Small-town Nova Scotia is warmly evoked in "Gwendolyn," named for its focal character, who Bishop describes as a childhood playmate. The text depicts the last days of young Gwendolyn's life, but this sadness is eased by the narrator's own ease with her subject and its retelling. Who says what is clear: every piece of dialogue is accounted for with "he said," "she said," and "I said." This is a confident narrator calling up a story that is easy enough to recall and costs no emotional pain to retell: that phrase, "I remember," recurs frequently, and "If I care to, I can bring back the exact sensation of that moment today," she tells us once (Bishop 1953a: 30). She enjoys storytelling so much that she even gets caught up in her own descriptive details, pulling herself back with a reluctant "Anyway," after a lengthy account of a favorite set of marbles (Bishop 1953a: 30). Past-tense narration places the events of "Gwendolyn" comfortably in the past, and the chatty, first-person storyteller counteracts the story's troubling imagery. Gwendolyn's casket, her soiled underwear and an insect crushed in a matchbox are all rendered harmless in scenes generously enriched with Bishop's wry reportage—like when, after getting in trouble with her cousin for re-enacting Gwendolyn's funeral, Bishop deadpans, "Billy was sent straight home and I don't remember now what awful thing happened to me" (Bishop 1953a: 31).

"Gwendolyn" was a light, even funny, conventional prose memoir; Bishop called it just a "little story" (Bishop and Lowell 2008: 141). The next piece Bishop sent to the *New Yorker*, "In the Village," was none of these things. Like "Gwendolyn," "In the Village" centers on death and loss, but its sadness recalls Bishop's greatest childhood tragedy: the loss of both mother and father. When "Village" begins, the father character has already passed, and Bishop's text depicts a series of events that center loosely around efforts to convince the mother to shift from wearing strictly black mourning clothes to wearing transitional purple ones. The efforts prove only to deepen the mother's mourning and emotional instability, and by story's end she has been moved to a sanitarium for intensive care. Representing such an agonizing experience called for something more than the conventional storytelling of "Gwendolyn."

From the beginning, Bishop described the text she sent to *The New Yorker* as "poetic," "poetic-prose" and "a prose-poem" (Bishop 2011: 90, 95, 113, 291, 431). But the hybrid text didn't suit the inflexible *New Yorker*. When editor Katherine White responded to Bishop's letter submitting the piece for publication, she explained that the editorial staff were enthusiastic about the "poetic quality" of "In the Village" but concerned that the story did not have a strong "thread of narrative": "In one or two places this thread is so thin that it seems to break entirely," she wrote (Bishop 2011: 95). White assured Bishop: "We do not mean by this that you need to turn your lovely prose poem into a conventional short story," yet she went on to request changes that would indeed conventionalize Bishop's poetic prose, such as supplying quotation marks and pronouns to indicate characters' speeches, restructuring single lines into paragraphs, and adding exposition. Bishop's letters in response defend her unconventional choices: "I'm not sure that I'll feel able to change as much as you may want changed—the paragraphing, for example, and the quotations. I've worked over them for a long time to try to get a certain tempo that I *think* I've got" (Bishop 2011: 98). The disagreement led to an impasse: Bishop set the story aside for several months and did not return to it until the next summer, 1953, when she once again revised it extensively. In July, she tried the story on White again, meanwhile venting to Kit and Ilse Barker, "I'm so sick of re-typing my best story—I gave up after long correspondence with the N Yer last January. Now I've redone it a little, but will not concede another comma for clarities sake [. . .] But one tires of typing even a masterpiece I find" (Bishop 1994: 268). Certainly Bishop, self-effacing to a fault, is poking fun at her own righteous indignation; "masterpiece" is used lightly here. But Bishop's resistance to *New Yorker* strictures and commitment to the formal irregularities of her text suggest that "Village" mattered as much for its representation of Bishop's staggering childhood loss as for its unusual hybrid aesthetic, painfully wrought and forcefully defended.

Bishop's perseverance won an unusual concession from *The New Yorker*. After reviewing Bishop's summer edits, White joyfully reported that she had "simply canceled out all the millions of conventional punctuation and style-rule and clarity queries," and she rejoiced that "In the Village" would be "a breath of fresh air in the magazine" (Bishop 2011: 120). According to White, *The New Yorker* tolerated these ambiguities because the editors ultimately came to read the piece as a poem: "Our argument about not getting it further corrected in the normal way was that the story was really like a poem and therefore had every right to be unconventional in matters of punctuation, usage, repetitions, etc." Thus, labeling this prose poem simply "poem" facilitated its publication, pushing it past the literary gatekeepers who would otherwise balk at its unconventional technique.

But what *The New Yorker* ultimately published on December 19, 1953, is much more than either a poem or a story. Instead, the text evokes conventions traditionally associated with poetry or prose stories and fuses them, subverting certain conventions in order to redeploy them in new ways. By drawing our attention to its own unusual construction, "In the Village" becomes as much a depiction of traumatic events as it is about the task of representing emotional disruptions in art.

Unlike a typical short story, "In the Village" resists a sense of plot, avoids dialogue attributions, incorporates unusual paragraph structures, and toggles between more than one narrator's voice. Where "Gwendolyn" began each new scene with expository sentences establishing time and place—"Some time after this, Gwendolyn was brought to visit me again"—the scenes in "Village" shift abruptly and rarely give a clear sense of time (Bishop 1953a: 28). Even the narrator seems unsure which time period she's describing: "Perhaps it is all the same summer," she wonders as she tries to piece together the days after the mother's departure for the sanitarium (Bishop 1953b: 33). Instead of progressing linearly through time, the events of the text circulate around the mother's emotional distress, represented by her scream, which is prompted by that new purple dress meant to replace her black mourning clothes. A more conventional story might have narrated the events leading up to the scream, but "In the Village" begins and ends with it: in the opening frame, it resounds in the village like an enduring painful feeling, hanging "over that Nova Scotian village [. . .] unheard, in memory—in the past, in the present, and those years between" (Bishop 1953b: 26). By the end, the scream is "almost-lost" but still lingering, a tenuous through-line that hardly satisfies a sense of narrative progression (Bishop 1953b: 34).

If the text thwarts expectations of forward progress typically associated with traditional stories, it also fails to satisfy characteristic expectations for a poem. Like many poems, sound effects and repetition are crucial to the text, but "In the Village" does not employ figures of sound like traditional poetic rhythm or rhyme schemes. Instead, sound becomes a feature of the narrative, transforming and evolving over the course of the text. The scream itself is a foremost example: in the text's opening paragraph, the scream settles into the sonic landscape of the village, becoming "the pitch of my village" rather than a mother's unique grief, and then the source of the scream is relocated to the spire of the village church: "Flick the lightning rod on top of the church steeple with your fingernail and you will hear it" (Bishop 1953b: 26). The church becomes fancifully scaled to a hand, a hand with the power to call up the sound of the scream and to control the sad memories. Thus, instead of deploying sound through patterns of phonemes, like a villanelle or a sonnet, "In the Village" does it through a story.

The fusion of verse and prose forms is most evident in the typography of "In the Village." On the pages of *The New Yorker*, the columns of prose are frequently interspersed with sentences forming a jagged right-hand margin, short sentences printed on a single line that are more reminiscent of lines of poetry than the journal prose. These typographic disturbances on the page are also some of the most traumatic moments for the mother and, in turn, the child. Tellingly, the first such instance highlights the scream, paired here with another recurring sound, a "clang" resounding from the neighboring smithy:

> *Clang.*
> The pure note: pure and angelic.
> The dress was all wrong. She screamed.
> The child vanishes. (Bishop 1953b: 26)

It is easy to imagine *The New Yorker* editors' opposition: gone is the connective tissue guiding readers between the blacksmith's shop and the dress-fitting room or pointing out which "she" is screaming. Instead, the logic of line breaks only hints at a story, turning instead to flashes of imagery to compound clang, scream, and the silence of a suddenly erased child. When Bishop mentioned the "tempo" of the piece, she may have been referencing moments like this one, where line breaks unsettle the progress of paragraphs. These verse interruptions change the pace of the narrative in order to draw out an important moment, one of extreme grief for the mother and traumatic confusion for the child. Bishop draws in verse strategies—here, the parataxis of lineation—embedding lines amid prose paragraphs to represent these disorienting feelings.

When the scream resurfaces in the closing frame of the text, the text once again shifts from paragraphs to lines suggesting a stanza, and the scream is paired again with the "beautiful, pure" sound of the blacksmith at work. At first, the "clang" seems to overpower everything, including the mother's voice:

> Clang.
> *Clang.*
> Nate is shaping a horseshoe.
> Oh, beautiful pure sound!
> It turns everything else to silence. (Bishop 1953b: 34)

Critics have noticed that the role of the blacksmith in the story parallels that of a poet: the blacksmith adroitly wields fire and metal to shape valuable and even beautiful things, like horseshoes and a ring for the girl, much as a poet might transform difficult, dangerous life circumstances to create poems.[9] Fire is useful in the blacksmith's control but dangerous when it destroys a neighbor's barn in the night, for example, an event that is portrayed as the catalyst for the mother's final breakdown and removal from her daughter. Likewise, "In the Village" suggests the risks of transforming life experiences into stories or poems: lovely sounds or a cohesive, compelling plot might well make good art, but aestheticizing the significant moments of our lives carries risks of its own. Thus, "In the Village" ends ambivalently: Nate's beautiful sound seems at first to cancel the scream, turning "everything else to silence"; still, the mother's wail is never fully silenced but ultimately "almost-lost" in the closing lines of the story (Bishop 1953b: 34).

By exposing its own gaps and fissures in its atypical, poem-prose construction, "In the Village" gestures toward what's almost lost, what art fails to capture. Can a text ever represent a mother's bereavement, not to mention an orphaned child's profound unease? It can be disorienting and frightening when life and texts fail to meet our expectations, and perhaps emotional stability depends on rules and regularity like those we associate with literary conventions. But for Bishop, the concept of a prose poem—its creative unsettling of genre—invites constructive reflection on moments of extreme duress that a more predictable form of storytelling might foreclose.

Did such questions about deep sadness and its appropriate representation register for Lowell when he read Bishop's poetic prose in *The New Yorker*? Brief but fervent, his initial approbation narrowed in on the story's poignant tragedy: "Your *New Yorker* story is wonderful. A great ruminating Dutch landscape of goneness" (Bishop and Lowell 2008: 151). As if sparked by "In the Village," it was after its publication that Lowell began to follow Bishop's lead, incorporating prose into his own writing practice. First, he planned a prose autobiography, even signing a publishing contract for one in April 1955, and he worked up several chapters over the next two years (Lowell 1987: ix). But by 1957, Lowell had transitioned into a new project; he began to blend the autobiographical prose with his poetry, specifically, the poems that would eventually become *Life Studies*. Critics would later mark this shift in style as the "confessional" turn; to Lowell then, the texts were simply more "personal" (Bishop and Lowell 2008: 235). This was the word he used to explain his breakthrough to Bishop, adding appreciatively, "really I've just broken through to where you've always been" (Bishop and Lowell 2008: 239).

That Lowell's "breakthrough" was facilitated by the process of breaking prose sentences into verse forms is epitomized by a poem like "My Last Afternoon with Uncle Devereux Winslow," which was drawn from a chapter originally intended for the autobiography, entitled "Near the Unbalanced Aquarium." The prose chapter splices various scenes from Lowell's life with scenes from the Payne Whitney Clinic, where he received treatment for bipolar disorder. It reads as if, from inside the locked ward of the clinic, Lowell's mind is ranging back over important periods of his life: the death of both of his parents, especially, as well as a summer spent at Chardesa, his grandfather's country home in Rock, Massachusetts. "My Last Afternoon with Uncle Devereux Winslow" takes as its source the description of a summer spent at the country home. This scene, too, is marked with death: Uncle Devereux is sick with Hodgkin's disease, which would eventually take his life.

Creating a poem out of the prose chapter meant more than adjusting the typography of paragraphs or puzzling out end-stops and enjambment. Lowell revisited every detail of the story, rewriting sentences devised for the autobiography even as he aligned them into verse stanzas. He added a depiction of the summer house's interior at the poem's start, fleshed out the character of his Aunt Sarah with a story of the "jilted Astor" that she had refused to marry, and added a description of a "last honeymoon" that Uncle Devereux would take with his wife (Lowell 2003a: 163–7).[10] He changed a foreboding detail, the death of a "silly gun-shy setter" to that of "Cinder, our Scottie puppy / paralyzed from gobbling toads" (Lowell 2003a: lines 49–50). In a poem where the agony of death stays just below the surface, Cinder becomes the only creature to fully embody this pain. Most importantly, Lowell adds a reoccurring image of himself as a young boy sitting in the background of each scene, mixing up two small piles of color-contrast garden supplies, black soil and white lime. It's only through these substances that the poem tells us about Uncle Devereux's eventual death. In the original chapter, the section on Chardesa ended by explaining only that Devereux "was dying of the incurable Hodgkin's disease" (Lowell 1987: 361). The poem ends instead, "Come winter, / Uncle Devereux would blend to the one color," the lifeless gray (Lowell 2003a: lines 151–2).

"My Last Afternoon with Uncle Devereux Winslow" opens the book's eponymous "Life Studies" sequence; it has held that spot in the volume since Lowell's first *Life Studies*, the British Faber & Faber edition of 1959. When Lowell published *Life Studies* in the United States a few months later, he placed an additional life study earlier in the volume, "91 Revere Street," which, like "Near the Unbalanced Aquarium," was originally intended for his autobiography, and remains in prose paragraphs rather than lines of verse. With prose anticipating the poems, Lowell invites readers to experience the transition he himself had undergone in writing *Life Studies*: from sets of paragraphs to stanzas, sentences to lines and line-breaks, those typographical shifts that signal a much more complicated revision process.

And yet, when Lowell spoke of the poetry and prose of *Life Studies*, he glossed over the complications of his adaptation process and described something much easier. In fact, when asked to describe what he had learned about the difference between poetry and prose, he points first to a simple typographic distinction: "I mean I've never thought it out but it seems to me poetry differs from prose, if you want a sort of definition, that it's written in lines not paragraphs" (Lowell 1961: 43). Lowell concedes that typography itself "tells you nothing about the content," suggesting that the same or similar content could be handled in any typographical arrangement (Lowell 1961: 43). Then, he attempts to draw a line between the rhythm of a free verse line and that of prose paragraphs: "if you write free verse, you're very conscious of some line unit; you feel that rhythm and a sense of rhythm stops and you have another line, something you don't feel in prose" (Lowell 1961: 43). Of course, Lowell's own composition process suggests a much more complicated story: "My Last Afternoon with Uncle Devereux Winslow" is not simply a passage from "Near the Unbalanced Aquarium" rendered in rhythmic lines. But Lowell was determined to draw a clear boundary line between poetry and prose, scrupulously avoiding the compound phrases Bishop adopted, like "prose poem" and "poetic prose."

After arriving at such an oppositional definition of poetry and prose, Lowell began to suggest more traditionally generic modes of publication for Bishop's own stories. He suggested "a Nova Scotia growing-up novel," and when "In the Village" was reprinted in a 1962 *New Yorker* short story anthology, Lowell once again commended Bishop on her work, this time by speaking of prose and poetry as her two distinct métiers: "You are a prose classic to ever so many people, as well as a poet classic" (Bishop and Lowell 2008: 141, 383). Around this time, Bishop did indeed entertain the idea of a prose volume, planning out a table of contents for a volume to be called *In the Village & Other Stories* or *In the Village: Stories and Essays*. But the book didn't cohere. So, she put off Lowell again, writing: "I've been going over the stories and don't think they're good enough" (Bishop and Lowell 2008: 386). This time, Lowell stopped pressing for a volume of prose and decided to show his friend that "In the Village" was "good enough" through a different method: rewriting "In the Village" as a conventional poem. He revised it into eight cinquains, gave the narrator two new lines of dialogue, and titled his creation "The Scream." "I send it with misgivings," he explained in the letter enclosing the poem, worried that he was taking liberties with Bishop's work (Bishop and Lowell 2008: 390). He urged her to take his draft as a starting point for something new: "Maybe you could use it for raw material for a really great poem," he wrote.

Certainly, Lowell meant well. But once again, "In the Village" would face an editor bent on untangling the interwoven threads of this poetic prose creation—this time, to pull out the makings of a poem. Perhaps recalling that painful season back in 1952 when White and the *New Yorker* editors had pressed her to make "In the Village" into only prose, Bishop responds to Lowell ambivalently: "'The Scream' really works well, doesn't it," she begins, "But I was very surprised" (Bishop and Lowell 2008: 402).

Indeed, considering that all but two lines of Lowell's poem "The Scream" come from Bishop's original text, the stark difference between the two pieces is surprising. Lowell selected the words for his poem from just one section of "Village": seven of the eight "Scream" stanzas are sourced from the first page of the *New Yorker* piece. In this section of the story, its most radical, hybrid elements are well displayed: inconsistent narratorial voice, fluid transitions between scenes and settings and atypical paragraph structures all feature prominently. But Lowell's poem offers none of these. Instead, "The Scream" gives a version of Bishop's concept now rigidly contained within cookie-cutter stanza shapes, a simple story arch and the purview of a reminiscing, first-person narrator.

Unlike Bishop's original, where scenes and events are so closely juxtaposed on the page as to run into each other semantically and formally, each of the five-line stanzas in "Scream" depicts a distinct scene extracted from Bishop's text, and each correspondingly comprises separate syntactic units, removed from each other on the page by stanza breaks. Compare, for example, the moment on *New Yorker* page twenty-six when the mother screams and the child disappears, discussed above. In Bishop's original, these verse-like lines are couched amid a bird's-eye view of the whole village that carries the reader from the dress-fitting room, into the blacksmith's shop, back to the dress-fitting room, then out to the back porch where the child's mother sits in the shade with her mother and sisters. On the pages of the *New Yorker*, the narratorial perspective doesn't follow any single character's point of view: the child, who is only sometimes an "I," is in the dress-fitting room before she vanishes, and she resurfaces in the blacksmith's shop, not the back porch with her mother, aunts, and grandmother. In "The Scream," though, the perspective is strictly the child's, recounted as reminiscence: "As a child in Nova Scotia, / I used to watch the sky," the poem begins (Lowell 2003b: 326).[11] Then too, in "The Scream," each location the text describes is contained within a single five-line stanza. Stanza three, for example, describes the blacksmith's shop, and two stanzas later, the dress-fitting scene appears, taking place in the main house. Each stanza concludes with the end of a sentence, the syntactic separation reinforcing the overall sense of clearly delineated space and time, a sense Bishop's original had repeatedly pressed against. Finally, gone are those lines from "In the Village" that were practically already verse, linking "clang," scream, and the vanishing child through the parataxis of line breaks rather than the linkages of expository prose. Ironically, by rearranging Bishop's "prose poem" into just a poem, Lowell has edited out what was typographically the most conventional poetic element of "In the Village": its moments of lineated verse, which Bishop had interposed between the prose paragraphs.

Ultimately, in the process of editing out those typographic irregularities that made Bishop's version both poem and prose according to his own definition, Lowell unwittingly underscores the value of the hybrid form to the original. Indeed, it is the irregularities of "In the Village" themselves that matter: by drawing attention to what is unconventional about Bishop's text, they help us ask how literary conventions themselves might in turn conventionalize human pain. By reintroducing the formal guidelines typical of traditional poems, Lowell devises a far more orderly Nova Scotia landscape and a far more manageable tragedy than Bishop's original had portrayed. Just as it invites little consideration of the capacity of poetic techniques to relate a personal tragedy, "The Scream" ends with no lingering questions about the scream itself and the ache it signifies. Where "In the Village" ended ambivalently—"no scream" quickly reverted to an "almost-lost scream"—the scream in Lowell's poem is "all gone": "they are all gone, / those aunts and aunts, a grandfather, / a grandmother, my mother— / even her scream—too frail / for us to hear their voices long" (Lowell 2003b: lines 40–5).

Bishop never did write that "really great poem" that Lowell had advised. But while he went on to publish "The Scream" in his own collection, *For the Union Dead* (1964), she finally decided to put out a book of poems and stories by making "In the Village" part of her 1965 poetry collection, *Questions of Travel*. Unsurprisingly, the decision to put her hybrid text in a book of poems found Bishop defending and explaining the prose poem all over again. When she first broached her plans to Randall Jarrell, for example, she defensively played up the prose poem's hybridity and association with other poems: "There are three or four poems that go with it, and it is more a prose-poem than a story, anyway" (Bishop 1994: 431).

To say that the poems of *Questions of Travel* merely go *with* "In the Village" is an understatement. Together, the pieces within this volume accrete to a picture of a life—loosely, Bishop's life. Indeed, the two subsections of the volume correspond to Bishop's life at the time of writing: the "Brazil" section contains poems inspired by her experiences living in Rio, and the poems of "Elsewhere" mostly comprise her earlier memories of life in Nova Scotia or the surrounding New England area. "Brazil" opens with Bishop's arrival to the continent, and together the first three poems explore the idea of traveling to a new place and making a home there. The remaining eight poems of the "Brazil" section illustrate life in the new home, and these poems can be loosely divided into the poems of everyday Brazil life—"Squatter's Children," "Manuelzinho," "Electrical Storm," "Song for the Rainy Season" and "Armadillo"—followed by three poems that describe local and historical Brazilian life beyond Bishop's immediate purview—"The Riverman," "Twelfth Morning; or What You Will" and "The Burglar of Babylon." These poems illustrate other lives in Brazilian "villages," anticipating the village of Bishop's childhood in "In the Village." Thus, "In the Village" now links the book's two sections, appearing just after the final poem of "Brazil" and at the beginning of "Elsewhere." Following "Village," the poems of "Elsewhere" start by moving chronologically through Bishop's childhood in Nova Scotia in "Manners," "Sestina" and "First Death in Nova Scotia." Then "Filling Station," "Sunday, 4 a.m.," "Sandpiper," "From Trollope's Journal" and "Visits to St. Elizabeths" are loosely North American, sometimes pertaining directly to Bishop's New England life.

Together, poems and prose poem glaringly evoke a life narrative, yet the book debates the idea of such a story, questioning especially what counts as "story," what form it should take and who should tell it. Underscoring that theme in her table of contents, Bishop lists "Village" as "In the Village (a story)," but the distinction rings hollow: "Village" is flanked by poems that are as narrative as the others. Preceding "Village" in the "Brazil" section is "The Burglar of Babylon," a ballad—a traditional poetry storytelling form—that depicts the tragic capture and death of Micuçú, a thief who lives in Rio de Janeiro. On the other side of "Village" is "Manners," another ballad, this one set in Nova Scotia; it depicts a child and her grandfather on an afternoon wagon drive and describes the people they meet along the way in sequence.

Even to say that all the poems share an autobiographical perspective would be too simple. When the poems in *Questions of Travel* seem most autobiographical, their poetic speakers resist easy equivalence to the poet. The speaking personae change considerably from poem to poem, with multiple speakers who we might call "autobiographical." For example, "Manners," "Sestina," and "First Death in Nova Scotia" all include a child speaker, yet even in this trio the perspective changes, moving from the first-person narration of a child's perspective in "Manners," to omniscient narration in "Sestina," and back to the first-person child speaker in "First Death." Though each text clearly represents Bishop's childhood memories, to read the personae of these poems as renditions of Bishop may cause us to overlook how the perspective fluctuates.

Of course, a shifting narratorial perspective had long been a hallmark of "In the Village," a key feature of its unconventional, poetry-prose storytelling mode. Placing it amid the poems of *Questions of Travel* serves to highlight how they, too, work narratively, inviting us to read for plot and perspective—those attributes long associated with prose novels and short stories—as much as for the traditionally poetic features of Bishop's verse, like figures of sound, linguistic patterns, and juxtaposition of images. If the poems of *Questions of Travel* tell a story together, it is one where many of the expository linkages that typically shape a plot are noticeably absent. Instead, this type of autobiography situates its life story amid a landscape of the people and places, both past and present, that support that life and give it meaning. Thus, *Questions of Travel* doubles the storytelling mode at its core, that of "In the Village," leaning on fusion for coherence rather than linearity.

As a genre, the confessional prose poem is similarly poised: although it is at the core of these poets' driving questions—about narrative versus the poetic and life versus the representation of life—its ties to the story we tell about confessional writing are loose. Indeed, the term itself surfaces often enough in Bishop's poetics, but it is ignored outright by Lowell. Yet, to overlook the role of multi-genre, poetry-prose writing among these poets is to elide a key conversation, one sustaining the highpoints of their careers. Ultimately, the fact that the notion of the prose poem was perpetually peripheral to these writers suggests that this genre works by decentering our conversations about prose and poems, unsettling the expectations we too readily ascribe to one or the other. "In the Village" served just such a purpose for both Bishop and Lowell.

For indeed, in the end, Lowell stopped seeing "In the Village" as only prose. After rereading it for the umpteenth time but now in its new context, *Questions of Travel*, Lowell wrote to Bishop, admitting, "You were very right to put your story in, it's one of your finest poems" (Bishop and Lowell 2008: 591). Of course, after its long journey from the pages of *The New Yorker*, to "The Scream," to *Questions of Travel*, the fact that "In the Village" is no simple poem was also abundantly clear. As Bishop knew all along, it is both: a prose poem.

Notes

1. My thanks to Karen Jackson Ford and Geri Doran for incisive comments on earlier versions of this essay.
2. Critics reading mid-century poets as formally conservative remain divided over whether or not the poetry was ultimately politically conservative. Bob Perelman epitomizes the critique that the group known as "confessional" writers were formally uninventive and anti-intellectual and disengaged politically, the source of contemporary mainstream poetry that is equally uninterested in social or aesthetic subversion (Perelman 1996: 12). By contrast, Stephanie Burt argues that mid-century poets aimed to "preserve" traditional forms, but that they took a radical stance on postwar America. As a result, Burt says, "literary history has viewed them (sometimes quite misleadingly) as 'conservative'" (Burt 2013: 128).
3. I use the term "confessional" with hesitation owing to the label's pitfalls, exposed almost as soon as M. L. Rosenthal coined the term in his 1959 review of *Life Studies*—and quickly acknowledged by Rosenthal himself. Indeed, to call poetry "confessional" is to invite readings that stall out on too-easy equivalences between a poet's life and poetic representations of a life. Proponents of the poets classed this way have been right to push back against such limited readings, which often preclude full consideration of technical complexities in the

poems themselves. Yet the label has long served to corral a community of poets who shared influences, traded drafts, sat in on each other's workshops, and, indeed, pursued similar questions about the ethics and techniques of self-writing in their work. Thus, I invoke the term in order to extend our understanding of the tendencies and traditions associated with it, which this essay does by focusing on the intersection between self-writing and the technical complexities of confessional poems, prose, and prose poems.

4. This essay's analysis of the relationship between Bishop's "In the Village" and Lowell's poem "The Scream" was inspired by Phillips' analysis of the letters and writings between Bishop and May Swenson. Like Lowell, Swenson, too, made her own poem out of Bishop's writing: "Dear Elizabeth" is derived from the language of their letters.
5. See Vidyan Ravinthiran for an assessment of these shorter prose poems by Bishop (Ravinthiran 2015: 155–77).
6. Even Ravinthiran, in his extensive assessment of the intersection between Bishop's prose and poetry styles, classes "In the Village" as strictly "literary prose," and he does not discuss the piece in his chapter on Bishop's prose poetry (Ravinthiran 2015: 125–42). Interestingly, other critics who class "In the Village" as prose still often describe the story as poetic. For example, Thomas Travisano observes, "This prose is of stunning poetic intensity" (Travisano 1988: 169).
7. Bret Millier describes Bishop's early prose writing, then centered on a semi-autobiographical character named "Lucius," and she assesses the connections between the Lucius stories and "In the Village" (Millier 1993: 6–9).
8. Further, the placement of "Village" after two other humorous prose pieces signaled its gravity as a literary short story or memoir. Former mid-century *New Yorker* employee Francis Kiernan recalls that the organization of each issue of the magazine followed a pattern: "the first piece of fiction was light or humorous, but because humor was hard to come by, they sometimes had to put two stories together. The third piece, which ran in back, was usually but not always reminiscence. At the *New Yorker*, memoirs had always been handled as fiction" (Kiernan 1998: 85).
9. David Kalstone credits James Merrill with first noticing the parallels between the blacksmith character and the artist (Kalstone 1989: 164). Thomas Travisano points to an earlier passage on the blacksmith and calls the clang "symbolic of the consoling power of art," a force that "stands against the eternal sound of the mother's scream" (Travisano 1988: 171).
10. Hereafter, this poem will be cited by line number; the lines cited here are 83 and 138.
11. Hereafter, this poem will be cited by line number; the lines cited here are 3–4.

Works Cited

Axelrod, Steven Gould (2015), "The Three Voices of Robert Lowell," in Mark Richardson (ed.), *Cambridge Companion to American Poets*, Cambridge: Cambridge University Press, pp. 327–39.
Bishop, Elizabeth (1953a), "Gwendolyn," *The New Yorker*, June 27, pp. 26–31.
Bishop, Elizabeth (1953b), "In the Village," *The New Yorker*, December 19, pp. 26–34.
Bishop, Elizabeth (1965), *Questions of Travel*, New York: Farrar, Straus & Giroux.
Bishop, Elizabeth (1994), *One Art: Letters*, ed. Robert Giroux, New York: Farrar, Straus & Giroux.
Bishop, Elizabeth (2011), *Elizabeth Bishop and* The New Yorker, ed. Joelle Biele, New York: Farrar, Straus & Giroux.
Bishop, Elizabeth and Robert Lowell (2008), *Words in Air: The Complete Correspondence Between Elizabeth Bishop and Robert Lowell*, ed. Thomas J. Travisano and Saskia Hamilton, New York: Farrar, Straus & Giroux.

Burt, Stephanie (2013), "Mid-Century Modernism," in Jennifer Ashton (ed.), *The Cambridge Companion to American Poetry Since 1945*, Cambridge: Cambridge University Press, pp. 128–42.
Delville, Michel (1998), *The American Prose Poem: Poetic Form and the Boundaries of Genre*, Gainesville: University Press of Florida, 1998.
Fredman, Stephen (1990), *Poet's Prose: The Crisis in American Verse*, 2nd edn, Cambridge: Cambridge University Press.
Hammer, Langdon (1997), "Useless Concentration: Life and Work in Elizabeth Bishop's Letters and Poems," *American Literary History*, vol. 9, no. 1, Spring, pp. 162–80.
Kalstone, David (1989), *Becoming a Poet: Elizabeth Bishop with Marianne Moore and Robert Lowell*, New York: Farrar, Straus & Giroux.
Kiernan, Francis (1998), "Fiction at The New Yorker," *The American Scholar*, vol. 67, no. 4, Autumn, pp. 81–92.
Lowell, Robert (1961), Interview with Cleanth Brooks and Robert Penn Warren, *Conversations on the Craft of Poetry*, New York: Holt, Rinehart & Winston.
Lowell, Robert (1987), *Collected Prose*, ed. Robert Giroux, New York: Farrar, Straus & Giroux.
Lowell, Robert (2003a), "My Last Afternoon with Uncle Devereux Winslow," *Collected Poems*, ed. Frank Bidart and David Gewanter, New York: Farrar, Straus, & Giroux, pp. 163–7.
Lowell, Robert (2003b), "The Scream," *Collected Poems*, ed. Frank Bidart and David Gewanter, New York: Farrar, Straus & Giroux, p. 326.
Millier, Brett C. (1993), *Elizabeth Bishop: Life and the Memory of It*, Berkeley, CA: University of California Press.
Monroe, Jonathan (1987), *A Poverty of Objects: The Prose Poem and the Politics of Genre*, Ithaca, NY: Cornell University Press.
Monte, Steven (2000), *Invisible Fences: Prose Poetry as a Genre in French and American Literature*, Lincoln: University of Nebraska Press.
Murphy, Margueritte (1992), *A Tradition of Subversion: The Prose Poem in English from Wilde to Ashbery*, Amherst: University of Massachusetts Press.
Nelson, Deborah (2013), "Confessional Poetry," in Jennifer Ashton (ed.), *The Cambridge Companion to American Poetry Since 1945*, Cambridge: Cambridge University Press, pp. 31–46.
Perelman, Bob (1996), *The Marginalization of Poetry: Language Writing and Literary History*, Princeton, NJ: Princeton University Press.
Perloff, Marjorie (1973), *The Poetic Art of Robert Lowell*, Ithaca, NY: Cornell University Press.
Phillips, Siobhan (2012), "Elizabeth Bishop and the Ethics of Correspondence," *Modernism/Modernity*, vol. 19, no. 2, April, pp. 343–63.
Ravinthiran, Vidyan (2015), *Elizabeth Bishop's Prosaic*, Lewisburg, PA: Bucknell University Press.
Travisano, Thomas (1988), *Elizabeth Bishop: Her Artistic Development*, Charlottesville, PA: University Press of Virginia.

12

Trans-verse: Prose Poetry, Translation and Border Crossing in Baudelaire and Emerson

Adam R. Rosenthal

Vous-même, mon cher ami, n'avez-vous pas tenté de traduire en une *chanson* le cri strident du *Vitrier*, et d'exprimer dans une prose lyrique toutes les désolantes suggestions que ce cri envoie jusqu'aux mansardes, à travers les plus hautes brumes de la rue? (Baudelaire 1975: 276)

[You yourself, dear friend, have you not tried to translate in a *song* the *Glazier's* strident cry, and to express in lyric prose all the dismal suggestions this cry sends up through the fog of the street to the highest garrets?] (Baudelaire 1970: x)

I

THE CONCEPT OF TRANSLATION REMAINS TODAY both extremely important and extremely contested. One speaks of both interlinguistic and intralinguistic translation. One translates from one code to another, whether it is those represented by "English" and "French," or the semi-private vernacular of a rarefied elite and the "common speech" of the masses. One continues to argue about the legitimate focus of translations, whether it is the vehicle or the tenor, the word or the line, the gap between languages or the fragmented nature of language as such. "Google translate" shapes, more and more, the everyday experience of translation, while focus on "untranslatables" reminds us of the limits of any translative project.[1] Globalization is perhaps only the most recent—and high-pitched—name for the experience of this Babelian confusion, the sources of which may ultimately lie internally, within the concept itself. For as soon as translation is envisioned as bridging the divide between two separate domains—and "translate," like its French and German counterparts, "traduire" and "übersetzen," bears the etymological sense of carrying or leading across—it cannot but struggle with itself and the impossibility of its task. This is either because, *in bridging* the one and the other, they are revealed not to be two after all, or because, *in failing to bridge*, the very project of translation is itself brought into question.[2]

In the passage cited above, taken from Baudelaire's oft-quoted dedication to *Le Spleen de Paris*, the poet asks, in semi-rhetorical fashion, whether his friend has not also attempted to translate the strident cry of the *Glazier* into a *song*. He asks whether he too has not wished to make music from the sounds of the street, and then—what may amount to the same thing, indeed, what may very well be a translation of the first question, in the second, and thus already a translation of "translation" by way of the figure of "expression"—whether he hasn't wished to express in lyrical prose all the depressing suggestions that this cry sends up to the rooftops, through the pavement-level fog. Baudelaire asks Houssaye, in sum, whether a similar prose-poetry project has not also occurred to him and, in doing so, suggests that the writing of "prose poetry" should itself be understood, somehow, *to be* translative. In what sense of the word, whether literal or figurative, of course remains to be seen.

That this is all part of an elaborate ruse to situate his "little work" against Bertrand's *Gaspard de la Nuit*, the "brilliant model" that Baudelaire ironically admits to having failed to emulate in the following paragraph, goes without saying. Nevertheless, by first alluding to Houssaye's own "song"—the prose poem "Chanson du vitrier" that the editor of *La Presse* had published a few years earlier—Baudelaire here points to the first indications of a modern symptom. Houssaye is one more man subject to modern life, and thus, one who is also possibly sensitive to the same temptations to which Baudelaire here attests. "Which one of us, in his moments of ambition, has not dreamed of the miracle of a poetic prose?" (1970: ix) ["Quel est celui de nous qui n'a pas, dans ses jours d'ambition, rêvé le miracle d'une prose poétique?" (1975: 275)]. And, as he here makes abundantly clear, those temptations have their source *in* the modern city. The "dream" of "the miracle of a poetic prose" is one "musical, without rhythm and without rhyme, supple enough and rugged enough to adapt itself to the lyrical impulses of the soul, the undulations of reverie, the jibes of conscience" (1970: ix–x) ["musicale sans rythme et sans rime, assez souple et assez heurtée pour s'adapter aux mouvements lyriques de l'âme, aux ondulations de la rêverie, aux soubresauts de la conscience" (1975: 275–6)]. It is a dream whose temptation is, for Baudelaire, nothing short of a "haunting ideal [idéal obsédant]," but most importantly, it is one that is itself born—or at least mostly or probably born, born *above all (surtout)*—of the "exploration of huge cities" ["la fréquentation des villes énormes], and "the medley of their innumerable interrelations" (1970: x) ["croisement de leurs innombrables rapports" (1975: 276)]. The modern city begets the dream of poetic prose. And poetic prose—insofar as it takes the matter of these streets and puts them into language—may therefore itself be understood, somehow, someway, to be essentially translative.

Though posited at the most front-facing portion of the text, this is not the version of *Spleen de Paris* to which one is by now accustomed. Certainly, when it comes to considering the text as a translation, it has been much more common to think of it as transposing the poetic substance of the *Fleurs du mal* into fresh prose compositions.[3] Yet what Baudelaire proposes here is not a process of *dérimage*, whereby a source text in verse is unrhymed, or prosaicized, such as was common among thirteenth-century writers. Instead, what Baudelaire suggests, what he gives to think, is that *prose poetry as such* would be translative, or even a genre of translation, insofar as it takes up the ephemera of *modernité* and transmutes it into something more memorable. "Prose lyrique," as he puts it here, would not simply de-versify lyric, nor lyricize prose, but would correspond, in all the monstrosity of its form, to something otherwise unattainable by either. Like the yet-unknown but longed-for class of expressions, specially adapted to the movements of the soul, of which Edgar Allan Poe lamented the lack, or the novel mnemonic art of Constantin Guys, singularly attuned to the *actualités* of his day, prose poetry would translate the agitation of the modern city along with its "dreadful intimations" (*désolantes suggestions*) in a way that neither traditional lyric nor prose would be adequate to.[4] It alone could attain to this agitation's attic-height, because it alone is intermediate through and through.

Such would be the suggestion, anyway. Rather than taking this cry up and idealizing it in a *poésie pure*, prose poetry, this troublesome hybrid, would refuse to let one forget the materiality of that cry, just as it refuses to let one forget the materiality of the letter, as many critics have keenly observed.[5] If Baudelaire calls on the figure of "translation" at this moment of his dedication, it is because translation names neither an act of transposition modeled on pure prosaic mimeticism—whereby one ends up with a perfect representation of the source text—nor one of seamless lyrical transposition—whereby the resulting text effectively effaces its model.[6] Like the theory of translation put forward by his most famous and most insightful reader, Walter Benjamin, the text of the prose poem would remain uneasily caught between source and destination, origin and artifact, or *cry* and *song*, because it troubles the ontological distinctions that ought to separate each pair.

It is certainly no accident, then, that the Glazier's cry, the figure Baudelaire selects as being paradigmatic of such "huge towns" and, as a result, the supreme fascination and *idée fixe* of prose-poetry composition, is itself one caught between genres, if not genuses. For this cry, as readers of Herder or Rousseau might recognize, is itself strangely situated between animal and man, or the pre-linguistic howl of the beast and signifying phrase of the language-bearer.[7] It is an utterance, in other words, at the edge of articulation, be it understood as the first indication of the phoneticization to come, or the last wail of the mere animal within "man." What grates, but also entices, in the Glazier's call is not simply its unmusicality, or "discordant" tone, but the possibility of hearing within it the vestigial traces of something not quite human, just as some laughter, we learn in "On the Essence of Laughter," betrays a purely "animal contentment" or "vegetal joy," rather than the satanic fallenness proper to man and his hideous rictus (1976: 534–5).[8] Once turned toward the Glazier's cry, what lyrical prose *translates*, or expresses, is not merely a linguistic content, then, but the very indeterminacy of the linguistic, in all the shock of its indetermination:

> La première personne que j'aperçus dans la rue, ce fut un vitrier dont le cri perçant, discordant, monta jusqu'à moi à travers la lourde et sale atmosphère parisienne. Il me sera d'ailleurs impossible de dire pourquoi je fus pris à l'égard de ce pauvre homme d'une haine aussi soudaine que despotique. (1975: 286)[9]

> [The first person I noticed in the street was a glazier whose piercing and discordant cry floated up to me through the heavy, filthy Paris air. It would be impossible for me to say why I was suddenly seized by an arbitrary loathing for this poor man.] (1970: 13)

This is perhaps reading a bit much into a single, possibly metaphorical, appeal to the task of the translator. Yet the suggestion that "prose poetry," as a genre, might somehow be translative, or speak to a problem of translation, is not exclusive to Baudelaire, even among its earliest adopters. In the space that remains, I would like to explore some of the directions that other nineteenth-century authors saw fit to follow, in conceiving of the conjunction between these forms. I would like to ask how we might conceive of "prose poetry," not merely as a point of contradiction between established genres, whose tensions were mobilized for political and artistic ends, but perhaps also as an imperfect, impossible, yet no less *necessary* hybrid form, whose inherent failure would in no way alleviate its incessant indispensability.[10] What if one only ever spoke in prose poems, even if no single prose poem ever lived up to this name? What if the prose poem, as translation, named the truth of its genres—their originary fractured and incomplete nature—rather than a mere contradiction in terms? I would like to suggest that to understand prose poetry as translation would be to understand it as an intermediary form uniquely suited to capture what is itself already incomplete and unfinished in its model(s), be it the cry of the Glazier, the sanctity of metrical composition, or the uncertain borders of language as such.

II

According to the annals of literary history, Ralph Waldo Emerson will have made one contribution to the genre of the prose poem. In September of 1839, writing in his journal, Emerson penned the short text "Woods: A Prose Sonnet."[11] In it, he draws, in prose, upon the fourteen-line form of the sonnet, in order to make his plea to "ancient woods." Though he never saw fit to publish his experiment, it would eventually find its way to print in 1969 as part of the publication of his complete journals. For this reason, the list of critical treatments of "Woods" is short.[12] It is, generically speaking, something of a *hapax legomenon* within his writings, and even without them, the tradition of the "prose sonnet" is itself not much greater.[13] This means that the impact of "Woods: A Prose Sonnet" on the history of nineteenth-century literary forms is probably close to nil.[14]

Naturally, then, the primary interest of this text cannot lie either in its immediate influence or its late reception. Unlike Baudelaire's dedication, which has nearly come to define the genre of prose poetry in France over the last hundred and fifty years, Emerson's attempt would go wholly unnoticed in nineteenth-century America. If, however, this short, forgotten sonnet is of interest to us, it is because it too, like Baudelaire's *dédicace*, takes up the problem of the relationship between disparate linguistic—and possibly non-linguistic—realms. Like Baudelaire's dedication, "Woods" asks about the possibility of translating from one "language" to another, and poses the hybrid form of the prose poem as a potential answer to this difficulty.

"Woods: A Prose Sonnet" thus takes up the very problem outlined above: "lyrical prose" as a necessary, even if impossible (or miraculous) possibility of translating something otherwise unable to be captured either by prose or poetry. "Lyrical prose" as the name for a particular form of mediation of something at the edge of language, and perhaps even as the name for the linguistic repetition of that very edge. "Woods" takes this problem up. It does so explicitly, in the content of its apostrophe, but is doubly notable for offering itself as an example of such a mediation, in its form. The question, however, in "Woods," is no longer one of bridging the gap between "cry" and "song," or the countless interconnections of the modern city (such as the inhumanity of the masses) and artistic expression, but one of the possibility of mediating (or translating) between the "language of men" and that of nature, or what Emerson here calls "woods." "Woods" poses itself within the (apparently) unbridgeable divide that it articulates, as though the gap between these two irreconcilable "languages" were also, nevertheless, modeled *within* human language, as the gap between poetry and prose, whose void the prose sonnet fills, or fails to fill, in exemplary fashion.

While, then, the term "translation" is nowhere named by Emerson, the entire text of "Woods" remains mired in the difference between languages and the bridgeability of the one by the other, all while offering itself, the "prose sonnet," as the space in which this gap can at least be articulated. Though "Woods" lacks the distinct focus on "modernity" that would come to define the prose poem for Baudelaire, its function, for Emerson, is already one of traversal, and part of the task of tracing the progress of prose poetry in the nineteenth century should consist in accounting for how Emerson's still apparently Romantic apostrophe to Nature could metamorphose into Baudelaire's apprehension of the modern city's innumerable, inhuman cries. It should consist, in other words, in showing how the project of the prose poem could go from testifying to the evident untranslatability of Nature's wisdom, to embodying what of modern life would be lost, if not for its inscription within this paradoxical form.

As was noted above, however, the text of "Woods" itself lies at the edge of legibility. Never published during his lifetime and left as one entry among others within the space of his journals, Emerson's naming of the "poem" is all that stands between it and the surrounding series of notes, citations, and anecdotes. For this reason, before proceeding with a more thorough discussion of the prose sonnet, I will present the text as it appears in his journals, along with its immediately preceding and succeeding contexts. As will become clear, "Woods" appears in September of 1839 as part of a series of reflections, collectively focused on probing the nature of poetry and poetic inspiration:

[364]
'These applications of the wit & mind are tender things; they do not fancy the sun & the crowd, but delight in shade & retirement. Like noble & delicate maidens, they must rather be kept safe at home, than brought forth into engagements & perils'.
Milton to Cromwell.

 Se mai continga che'l poema sacro
 Al quale ha posto mano e cielo e terra
 Sì che m'ha fatto per più anni macro
Dante; Il Paradiso, Canto 25[15]

In common hours we have the same thoughts the same facts as in the uncommon & inspired, but they do not sit for their portraits, they are not detached but lie in a web.

 'Tis not every day that I
 Fitted am to prophesy'
  [Herrick, 'Not Every Day Fit for Verse', ll. 1–2]

[365] *Woods*   A Prose sonnet.
Wise are ye, O ancient woods! wiser than man. Whoso goeth in your paths or into your thickets where no paths are, readeth the same cheerful lesson whether he be a young child or a hundred years old. <I cannot> <In> Comes he in good fortune or

bad, ye say the same things, & from age to age. Ever the needles of the pine grow & fall, the acorns on the oak, the maples redden in autumn, & at all times of the year the ground pine & the pyrola bud & root under foot. What is called fortune & what is called Time by men—ye know them not. Men have not language to describe one moment of your eternal life. This I would ask of you, o sacred Woods, when ye shall next give me somewhat to say, give me also the tune wherein to say it. Give me a tune of your own like your winds or rain or brooks or birds; for the <tunes>songs of men grow old when they have been often repeated, but yours, though a man have heard them for seventy years, are never the same, but always new, like time itself, or like love.

  The bishop of Cavaillon[,] Petrarch's friend[,] in a playful experiment locked up the poet's library intending to exclude him from it for three days but the poet's misery caused him to restore the key on the first evening. 'And I verily believe I should have become insane', says Petrarch, 'if my mind had longer been deprived of its necessary nourishment'. (Emerson 1969: 247–8)

Emerson's investment in prose poetry, though short-lived, does not stand alone. Framed by the words of others, "Woods" emerges as an exhortation caught between the epic of Dante and the lyric of Petrarch, the specter of Milton and the verse of Herrick. Amidst ponderings on the heights of inspired thought and the lows of common hours, it offers a generically distinct commentary on such heightened composition, a composition, nevertheless, in which it (evidently) does not itself participate. As we shall see, the reference to Dante in this context is particularly suggestive, but before returning to the latter's sacred poem we must first delve deeper into "Woods" itself, and how it imagines its own space of intervention.

Emerson's prose sonnet opens with an apostrophe. The subject of this apostrophe, "ancient woods," is wise and eternal, and its wisdom and eternity are explicitly opposed to the foolishness and mortality of men, in which latter group the speaker, we are led to believe, himself participates. Though ancient woods do not employ the language of men, in the language of the poem they are said to "say," and what they say is ever "the same things, & from age to age." Despite the purported repetitiveness of their speech, however, we eventually learn, at the conclusion of the sonnet, that their sayings "are never the same, but always new, like time itself, or like love." Their sayings, which are there to be read by men ("Whoso goeth in your paths or into your thickets where no paths are, *readeth* the same cheerful lesson whether he be a young child or a hundred years old"), are none other than the life and death of the forest, the "incommunicable"—as Emerson puts it in "Nature" (1844)—blossoming and decay of the natural world as it gives itself (1950: 407).[16] As if to reflect formally the independent, inhuman nature of the sayings of Nature, "Woods" gives the singular example of its "tune" in the least mediated sentence of the sonnet. In what would be the fifth and sixth lines of the poem, were we to follow Monte's breakdown, we find the only sentence not to possess any reference to *man*, or a speaker whatsoever. The wisdom of ancient woods is spoken, if spoken it must be, in the third person: "Ever the needles of the pine grow & fall, the acorns on the oak, the maples redden in autumn, & at all times of the year the ground pine & the pyrola bud & root under foot."

Given the difficulty, propounded by the poem, of giving voice to the "voice" of Nature, one can clarify the apparent contradiction of the ancient woods' wisdom by way of the necessity of translating this wisdom into a language not adequate to it: that of man. As Kant might put it of Emerson's antinomy, the fact that woods appear to say the same things, yet what they say is in fact never the same, is only a problem *for us*. Yet this problem, native to the legibility of their wisdom, is only the first, but certainly not the last, evidence of the linguistic disparity at work in the poem. For, as is made abundantly clear in what would be the concluding tercets, the necessity of and motivation for opening the apostrophe had always been the plea—now explicit—to be given not simply "somewhat to say," but also "the tune wherein to say it." To speak, or sing, the eternal song of nature, and to do so in a fashion that remains true to its eternity—what is certainly beyond the power of any man—motivates the opening of the prose sonnet.

So far, in spite of the generic novelty of Emerson's short text, the story it tells remains an extremely unexceptional one. Not only unexceptional in the sense of having been told and retold, over and over again, from one age to another—like the initially repetitive sound of the ancient woods' unchanging song—but perhaps also unexceptional at the level of structure—like the eternal, but ever-novel story that ancient woods tell in truth. This is because the story told by the prose sonnet is itself the very one already implicit in the concept of "poetry," so soon as it appeals to its own linguistic difference in order to differentiate itself among the arts or from lesser, non-art forms. "Woods: A Prose Sonnet" tells the endlessly common, but always novel, story of "language" attempting to differentiate itself from itself. This story takes many forms: one is that of the difference between "poetry" and "prose," another, that between a speech called "eternal" or "divine," and one called "vulgar" or "mundane." Yet another, between the pre-linguistic, immediate, yet for all that incommunicable text of nature, and the linguistic, mediate, and evidently communicable language of man. Or, again, this story might emerge as the difference between the inspired and uninspired, or the prophetic and unprophetic, or what, in the language of Herrick, would come down to the presence and absence of the Godhead:

> 'Tis not ev'ry day that I
> Fitted am to prophesy:
> No, but when the spirit fills
> The fantastic pannicles,
> Full of fire, then I write
> As the Godhead doth indite.
> Thus enrag'd, my lines are hurl'd,
> Like the Sybil's, through the world:
> Look how next the holy fire
> Either slakes, or doth retire;
> So the fancy cools:—till when
> That brave spirit comes again. (1877: 5–6)

The above are not simply *some* stories, but *the* story of "poetry," and its infinitely varied attempts to differentiate itself from some other, be it prose, the profane or the uninspired. And, within this context—which is, let us recall, the very context within which Emerson situates his "prose sonnet," between Milton and Dante, Herrick and Petrarch—"Woods" emerges as one more expression of the desire to bridge this gap, between poetry and prose, divinity and humanity, inspiration and calculation. "Woods" is one more expression of the desire to bridge this gap, but it is also, at the very same time, one more affirmation of the gap thereby to be bridged.

All of which is to say that, in spite of being a "prose sonnet," "Woods" appears to reaffirm, rather than to deconstruct, the difference between languages. Rather than inscribing the undecidability of the language of Nature within that of Man, it appears to set the former outside the purview of the latter. One does not translate the untranslatability of nature, as one does that of the cry of the Glazier, but instead sits in awe before it, as before the wholly other. Which situation, of course, raises the following question: Why write "Woods" as a *prose sonnet*, if only to repeat the same story of nature's, or poetry's, untranslatability? Given what we know about Emerson's difficulties with verse composition, one could always assimilate a poem such as "Woods" within his personal struggles, as Monte does: the speaker of "Woods," who writes in prose, wishes to be given the gift of verse. Yet this interpretation, while perhaps autobiographically accurate, would be inadequate to account for a difference that Emerson clearly gives between *the language of man as such* and the *sayings of woods*, rather than between *poet* and *non-poet*. Even if each of these binaries, structurally speaking, models the other, what is here opposed are two kinds of "tunes": the songs of men (including those of poets) and the sounds of nature. One must therefore look to the woods themselves for clarification on how to hear their air.

I mentioned above that of all the co-texts that Emerson's journal of September 1839 offers, it was perhaps that of Dante's *Paradiso* that was most significant for the penning of his lone prose sonnet. According to the work of Joseph Chesley Mathews, Emerson had been familiar with the *Divine Comedy* at least as early as 1825 (1942: 172). And yet, it was only a few months before he wrote "Woods," in January 1839, that he first received and read a copy of the medieval poet's *Vita Nuova*.[17] Dante's first major work, his semi-autobiographical love story, famously written in prosimetrum, so moved Emerson that he completed a translation of it "into English, the ruggedest grammar English that can be," only four years later, in 1843 (Emerson, 1939b: 183). Ellery Channing, in turn, helped Emerson to set his "prose sonnets & canzoni into verse," and though he never published them, Emerson tried for many years to do just that (1939b: 183). Not only, then, is the form of the "prose sonnet" explicitly linked by Emerson only a few years later to his translations of Dante's "lyrical prose"—a fact that perhaps ought to draw into question whether, indeed, "Woods" is the former's *only* prose poem— but there is also some reason to think that the very reference to "woods," in the 1839 text, might also, already, be an allusion to the Italian poet's oeuvre. That is, anyway, if one follows the trail laid out by Ugo Foscolo's review essay of two then-recent Dante publications, published in the February 1818 issue of the *Edinburgh Review*. Foscolo's piece—which Emerson evidently knew quite well and which, according to Igor Candido, must have been influential for the transcendentalist's early study of Dante—offers the following description of Dante's work:[18]

> The poem of Dante is like an immense forest, venerable for its antiquity, and astonishing by the growth of trees which seem to have sprung up at once to their gigantic height by the force of nature, aided *by some unknown art*. It is a forest, curious from the extensive regions which it hides, but frightful from its darkness and its labyrinths. The first travelers who attempted to cross it have opened a road. Those

who followed have enlarged and enlightened it; but the road is still the same; and the greater part of this immense forest remains, after the labours of five centuries, involved in its primitive darkness. (Foscolo 1818: 454)

Foscolo's description begins in simile and ends in metaphor. Declaring the poem of Dante, at first, to be *like* an immense forest, it ends by effacing this gap and presenting the poem, as though by virtue of its antiquity, *as* a natural growth. Such is the effect of "primitive darkness," attainable evidently only by "unknown art," and thus explainable—if at all—only by recourse to its originary, and eventually fully naturalized, status. Were one to take Emerson's evident interest in Foscolo's piece seriously, it would at least suggest the possibility that his own "ancient woods" were themselves a transposition, adaptation or translation of the "antique," "immense forest" of Dante's primitive works, as set forth by Foscolo. Where, for Foscolo, the road opened upon the labyrinth of Dante's poem remains, after five centuries, "still the same," one would find, in Emerson, the repetition of the "same lesson" of these woods, from age to age. The primitive darkness that makes of Dante's antique text something always and ever to be discovered would in Emerson be transposed upon the wisdom and eternal life of woods, winds, rain, brooks and birds. And the travelers, who in Foscolo "have opened a road" *in the text*, in Emerson would become the *readers* who, in entering ancient woods, now "goeth in your paths or into your thickets where no paths are." From leaves to leaves, one passes from the "sacred poem" of *Paradiso* to the "sacred woods" of pine and pyrola. That is, if in passing from the one to the other, one ever truly "passes" at all.

The possibilities of interpretation, of going back and forth not only between the text of Foscolo and that of Emerson, but also, between the *dark paths* of the immense forest of Dante's poem and the *readable lessons* of ancient woods, are endless. Indeed, my interest, in proposing that we draw from Foscolo in reading Emerson's journal entry, is less to establish a source text for the latter's prose sonnet than to show how the very determination of the referent of "woods," or by extension "nature," itself remains in suspense. Although such suspense is not of the same order as that which was previously found to be at work in Baudelaire, it nevertheless bears comparison with it. For, just as one would be hard pressed to establish *what*, exactly, Baudelaire's prose poetry *translates*, in translating the strident cry of modernity, so too would one encounter difficulties, were one seriously to try to establish the referent of the "tune" of "woods." Is this tune the sound of poetry become natural (or divine), or nature (or the sacred) become poetry? Are "ancient woods" a cipher for the primitive text of Dante, once granted its proper antiquity, or do they refer to some other text of Nature? The prose sonnet records this uncertainty. With or without Foscolo, with or without Dante, it speaks to the difficulty of discerning in what the sound of the truest form of poetry would any longer consist.

And is this not the very sense of its impossibly ironic, titular term? Of the "straightforward sound" of "Woods," once conceived as a "prose sonnet"? "O ancient woods!" Once, these words might have presented a clear attempt to articulate the gap between the enflamed spirit of the inspired poet and the cold embers of the prosaist in composition. Now, however, once pronounced *in lyrical prose*, it is no longer clear in what language this tune is finally meant to be heard, or uttered. "This I would ask of you," demands the prose sonneteer, "when ye shall next give me somewhat to say, give me also the tune wherein to say it." Though the effort to perform the difference between languages persists in "Woods," it is no longer evident that such effort any longer has *a* language in which to express itself, nor that the poem itself knows at what it truly takes aim. Through all the bramble of the wood and the immense confusion of the forest, whose innumerable branches intersect without end, "Woods: A Prose Sonnet" allows us hear this discordant tone.

Notes

1. See, in particular, Barbara Cassin's *Dictionary of Untranslatables*.
2. On the impossibility of translation, see Jacques Derrida, "Des tours de Babel."
3. On the relationship between the *Fleurs du mal* and *Spleen de Paris*, see especially Barbara Johnson's *Défigurations du langage poétique*.
4. On the links between Baudelaire's prose-poetry project and Poe's vision for a new linguistic form, especially suited to the "fancies," see Jean-François Delesalle, who points to Poe's *Marginalia* as a possible source. In his *Marginalia*, Poe describes the yet-unknown form in the following way: "How very commonly we hear it remarked, that such and such thoughts are beyond the compass of words! I do not believe that any thought, properly so called, is out of the reach of language. I fancy, rather, that where difficulty in expression is experienced, there is, in the intellect which experiences it, a want either of deliberateness or of method . . . There is, however, a class of fancies, of exquisite delicacy, which are *not* thoughts, and to which, *as yet*, I have found it absolutely impossible to adapt language. I use the word *fancies* at random, and merely because I must use *some* word; but the idea commonly attached to the term is not even remotely applicable to the shadows of shadows in question. They seem to me rather psychal [*sic*] than intellectual. They arise in the soul (alas, how rarely!) only at its epochs of most intense tranquility—when the bodily and mental health are in perfection—and at those mere points of time where the confines of the waking world blend with those of the world of dreams . . . Now, so entire is my faith in the *power of words*, that, at times, I have believed it possible to embody even the evanescence of fancies such as I have attempted to describe . . . For these reasons—that is to say, because I have been enabled to accomplish thus much—I do not altogether despair of embodying in words at least enough of the fancies in question to convey, to certain classes of intellect, a shadowy conception of their character" (1846: 117).
5. On Baudelaire's prose poetry and materiality, see especially Johnson and Bajorek.
6. Baudelaire's use of the figure of translation in "Le Peintre de la vie moderne," where the spectator becomes the "translator of clear and intoxicating translations," confirms this interpretation. See especially the section on "Mnemonic Art," where Baudelaire explains: "Ce mot *barbarie*, qui est venu peut-être trop souvent sous ma plume, pourrait induire quelques personnes à croire qu'il s'agit ici de quelques dessins informes que l'imagination seule du spectateur sait transformer en choses parfaites. Ce serait mal me comprendre. Je veux parler d'une barbarie inévitable, synthétique, enfantine, qui reste souvent visible dans un art parfait (mexicaine, égyptienne ou ninivite), et qui dérive du besoin de voir les choses grandement, de les considérer surtout dans l'effet de leur ensemble. Il n'est pas superflu d'observer ici que beaucoup de gens ont accusé de barbarie tous les peintres dont le regard est synthétique et abréviateur, par exemple M. Corot, qui s'applique tout d'abord à tracer les lignes principales d'un paysage, son ossature et sa physionomie. Ainsi, M. G., traduisant fidèlement ses propres impressions, marque avec une énergie instinctive les points culminants ou lumineux d'un objet (ils peuvent être culminants ou lumineux au point de vue dramatique), ou ses principales caractéristiques, quelquefois même avec une exagération utile pour la mémoire humaine; et l'imagination du spectateur, subissant à son

tour cette mnémonique si despotique, voit avec netteté l'impression produite par les choses sur l'esprit de M. G. Le spectateur est ici le traducteur d'une traduction toujours claire et enivrante. Il est une condition qui ajoute beaucoup à la force vitale de cette traduction *légendaire* de la vie extérieure. Je veux parler de la méthode de dessiner de M. G. Il dessine de mémoire, et non d'après le modèle, sauf dans les cas (la guerre de Crimée, par exemple) où il y a nécessité urgente de prendre des notes immédiates, précipitées, et d'arrêter les lignes principales d'un sujet. En fait, tous les bons et vrais dessinateurs dessinent d'après l'image écrite dans leur cerveau, et non d'après la nature" (Baudelaire 1976: 697–8) ["The word 'barbarousness,' which may seem to have slipped rather too often from my pen, might perhaps lead some few people to suppose that we are here concerned with defective drawings, only to be transformed into perfect things with the aid of the spectator's imagination. This would be to misunderstand me. What I mean is an inevitable, synthetic, childlike barbarousness, which is often still to be discerned in a perfected art, such as that of Mexico, Egypt or Nineveh, and which comes from a need to see things broadly and to consider them above all in their total effect. It is by no means out of place here to remind my readers that all those painters whose vision is synthesizing and abbreviative have been accused of barbarousness—M. Corot, for example, whose initial concern is always to trace the principal lines of a landscape—its bony structure, its physiognomy, so to speak. Likewise Monsieur G. brings an instinctive emphasis to his marking of the salient or luminous points of an object (which may be salient or luminous from the *dramatic* point of view) or of its principal characteristics, sometimes even with a degree of exaggeration which aids the human memory; and thus, under the spur of so forceful a prompting, the spectator's imagination receives a clear-cut image of the impression produced by the external world upon the mind of Monsieur G. The spectator becomes the translator, so to speak, of a translation which is always clear and thrilling" (Baudelaire 1995: 15–16)].

7. For both Herder and Rousseau, the "cry" is the first language of man, and insofar as it is the first, it is also one shared with animals. See, for example, Herder's *Essay on the Origin of Language*, which begins: "While still an animal, man already has language. All violent sensations of his body, and among the violent the most violent, those which cause him pain, and all strong passions of his soul express themselves directly in screams (*in Geschrei*), in sounds, in wild inarticulate tones" (1966: 87). In the *Second Discourse*, Rousseau explains that "Man's first language, the most universal, the most energetic and the only language he needed before it was necessary to persuade assembled men, is the cry of Nature" (1997: 146), and then later associates this cry with the animal as such: "Regarding the inferences that might be drawn in a number of animal species from the fights between the Males that bloody our poultry yards at all seasons or make our forests resound in Springtime with their cries as they feud over a female" (1997: 156). Again, in his *Essay on the Origin of Languages*, Rousseau makes a similar point: "It is neither hunger nor thirst but love, hatred, pity, anger, which drew from them the first words (*leurs premiers voix*). Fruit does not disappear from our hands. One can take nourishment without speaking. One stalks in silence the prey on which one would feast. But for moving a young heart, or repelling an unjust aggressor, nature dictates accents, cries, lamentations. There we have the invention of the most ancient words; and that is why the first languages were singable and passionate before they became simple and methodical" (1966: 12).

8. What distinguishes the human in "On the Essence of Language" is its divided, fallen, satanic character. For Baudelaire, the laughter of an infant expresses joy to the precise extent that it remains animal in nature: "Le rire des enfants est comme un épanouissement de fleur. C'est la joie de recevoir, la joie de respirer, la joie de s'ouvrir, la joie de contempler, de vivre, de grandir. C'est une joie de plante. Aussi, généralement, est-ce plutôt le sourire, quelque chose d'analogue au balancement de queue des chiens ou au ronron des chats. Et pourtant, remarquez bien que si le rire des enfants diffère encore des expressions du contentement animal,

c'est que ce rire n'est pas tout à fait exempt d'ambition, ainsi qu'il convient à des bouts d'hommes, c'est-à-dire à des Satans en herbe" (Baudelaire 1976: 534–5) ["For the laughter of children is like the blossoming of a flower. It is the joy of receiving, the joy of breathing, the joy of contemplating, of living, of growing. It is a vegetable joy. And so, in general, it is more like a smile—something analogous to the wagging of a dog's tail, or the purring of a cat. And if there still remains some distinction between the laughter of children and such expressions of animal contentment, I think that we should hold that this is because their laughter is not entirely exempt from ambition, as is only proper to little scraps of men—that is, to budding Satans" (Baudelaire 1995: 156)].

9. Compare this interpretation to Elissa Marder's gloss of the Glazier's cry as at once too poetic and too unpoetic: "In the brief second it takes for him to do so, in one fell swoop, he catches sight of the *vitrier* and is stunned and assaulted by the shattering sound of his shrieking, piercing, discordant voice. The sound of that voice that fills the public space, penetrates the filthy Parisian atmosphere, and enters the narrator's private room so that he can no longer hear the sound of his own voice—that voice is the very antithesis of poetry. However, to the extent that it is a public song that fills the public space, it also has something of poetry in it. The sounds of its prosaic false notes—at once too close and too far from poetry—are certainly the narrative trigger that pitches the narrator into his annihilating fury" (2014: 82).

10. For a now-classic study of the prose poem as an exercise in the politics of genre, see Monroe 1987.

11. See David Lehman's collection on the *Great American Prose Poem: From Poe to the Present*, where it is, by chronology, the second entry in the genre, following Poe's "Shadow—A Parable," which is dated to 1835. Jeffrey C. Robinson also includes it as an early Romantic example of "prose/poetry mixing" (2012: 1024), and Elizabeth J. LeRud notes that it was, evidently, Emerson's only venture in the genre (2017: 3).

12. See, above all, Steven Monte's *Invisible Fences*, where he breaks down Emerson's prose poem into a 14-line partitioned text (2000: 128–9). Monte, however, argues that Emerson's choice of the prose poem genre is made from "the author's inability to write in verse," which he contrasts to "the bolder claim, explicit or implicit in the work of many nineteenth-century French poets and some British and American poets of the modernist period, that the prose poem enables the writer to express aspects of modern experience that traditional verse poems cannot" (2000: 129). While there have been very few critical treatments of this poem, in 2006 Julie Dolphin was commissioned by the Foundation for Universal Sacred Music, of Katonah, NY, to compose a nine-minute musical piece based on Emerson's prose sonnet.

13. One of the most notable references to the form is found some years later in Oscar Wilde. In order to defend himself in court, Wilde contends that a letter penned to Lord Alfred Douglas should be read as a "prose sonnet," written "in the manner of Shakespeare." On Wilde's use of this term and its Shakespearian origins, see Laroche.

14. For an excellent study of Emerson's influence on nineteenth-century American verse, see Stephen Fredman, *Poet's Prose*. Unfortunately, however, though Fredman treats Emerson's use of the term "prose-poetry" to refer both to his essays and his notion of "panharmonicon," nowhere does he mention "Woods: A Prose Sonnet" or address its place within this broader context.

15. "If it ever happens that the sacred poem / To which both heaven and earth have set their hands, / So that it has made me thin for many a year" (Canto 25. 1–3, 1993: 459).

16. Compare to the following passage from "Nature": "The tempered light of the woods is like a perpetual morning, and is stimulating and heroic. The anciently-reported spells of these places creep on us. The stems of pines, hemlocks and oaks almost gleam like iron on the excited eye. The incommunicable trees begin to persuade us to live with them, and quit our life of solemn trifles" (1950: 407).

17. On January 18, 1839, Emerson writes to Margaret Fuller: "I have read for the first time in the Nuova Vita a few pages the other day & will try it again" (1939a: 178–80).
18. On Emerson's relationship with Dante, see Candido, "'The Bible of Love': Emerson's and Rossetti's Early Translations of the *Vita Nuova*."

Works Cited

Bajorek, Jennifer (2008), *Counterfeit Capital: Poetic Labor and Revolutionary Irony*, Stanford, CA: Stanford University Press.
Baudelaire, Charles (1970) *Paris Spleen*, trans. Louise Varèse, New York, NY: New Directions.
Baudelaire, Charles (1975), *Œuvres complètes*, Vol. 1, ed. Claude Pichois, Paris: Gallimard.
Baudelaire, Charles (1976), *Œuvres complètes*, Vol. 2, ed. Claude Pichois, Paris: Gallimard.
Baudelaire, Charles (1995), *The Painter of Modern Life and Other Essays*, trans. Jonathan Mayne, New York: Phaidon Press.
Candido, Igor (2018), "'The Bible of Love': Emerson's and Rossetti's Early Translations of the *Vita Nuova*," *Studj romanza. Nuova serie. XIV. Vita nuova. Archeologie di un testo*, pp. 125–48.
Cassin, Barbara and Emily Apter, Jacques Lezra, and Michael Wood (eds) (2014) *Dictionary of Untranslatables*, Princeton, NJ: Princeton University Press.
Dante, Alighieri (1993), *The Divine Comedy*, trans. C. H. Sisson, ed. David H. Higgins, Oxford, UK: Oxford University Press.
Delesalle, Jean-François (1973), "Edgar Poe et Les Petits Poemes en Prose," *Bulletin Baudelairien*, Vol. 8, No. 2, pp. 19–21.
Derrida, Jacques (2007), "Des Tours de Babel," in *Psyche: Inventions of the Other*, Vol. 1, trans. Joseph F. Graham, Stanford, CA: Stanford University Press, pp. 191–225.
Emerson, Ralph Waldo (1939a), *The Letters of Ralph Waldo Emerson, Volume Two*, ed. Ralph L. Rusk, New York, NY: Columbia University Press.
Emerson, Ralph Waldo (1939b), *The Letters of Ralph Waldo Emerson, Volume Three*, ed. Ralph L. Rusk, New York, NY: Columbia University Press.
Emerson, Ralph Waldo (1950), "Nature," in *The Complete Essays and Other Writings of Ralph Waldo Emerson*, ed. Brooks Atkinson, New York, NY: Random House, 406–21.
Emerson, Ralph Waldo (1969), *The Journals and Miscellaneous Notebooks of Ralph Waldo Emerson, Volume VII: 1838–1842*, ed. A. W. Plumstead and Harrison Hayford, Cambridge, MA: Harvard University Press.
Foscolo, Ugo (1818), "Art. IX. *Dante: with a new Italian Commentary*. By G. Baglioli. Paris, 1818. *The Vision of Dante*. Translated by the Reverend H. F. Cary, A. M. 3 vol. 18mo. London, 1818," *The Edinburgh Review, or Critical Journal: for Nov 1817. . . Feb. 1818. Vol. XXIX*, London, UK: Printed by David Wilson, pp. 453–74.
Fredman, Stephen (1990), *Poet's Prose: The Crisis in American Verse*, Cambridge, UK: Cambridge University Press.
Herder, Johann Gottfried and Jean-Jacques Rousseau (1966), *On the Origin of Language*, trans. John H. Moran and Alexander Gode, Chicago, IL: Chicago University Press.
Herrick, Robert (1877), *Chrysomela: A Selection from the Lyrical Poems of Robert Herrick*, ed. Francis Turner Palgrave, London, UK: Macmillan.
Johnson, Barbara (1979), *Défigurations du langage poétique: La seconde révolution Baudelairienne*, Paris: Flammarion.
Laroche, Rebecca (1999), "The Sonnets on Trial: Reconsidering *The Portrait of Mr. W.H.*," in *Shakespeare's Sonnets: Critical Essays*, ed. James Schiffer, New York, NY: Garland, pp. 391–410.
Lehman, David (2003), *Great American Prose Poem: From Poe to the Present*, New York, NY: Scribner.

LeRud, Elizabeth J. (2017), *Antagonistic Cooperation: Prose in American Poetry*, University of Oregon, PhD dissertation, <https://scholarsbank.uoregon.edu/xmlui/bitstream/handle/1794/22646/LeRud_oregon_0171A_11837.pdf?sequence=1&isAllowed=y> (last accessed August 3, 2020).

Marder, Elissa (2014), "From Poetic Justice to Criminal *Jouissance*: Poetry by Other Means in Baudelaire," in *Time for Baudelaire (Poetry, Theory, History)*, ed. E. S. Burt, Elissa Marder and Kevin Newmark, New Haven, CT: Yale University Press, pp. 67–84.

Mathews, Joseph Chesley (1942), "Emerson's Knowledge of Dante," *Studies in English* 22, pp. 171–98.

Monroe, Jonathan (1987), *A Poverty of Objects: The Prose Poem and the Politics of Genre*, Ithaca, NY: Cornell University Press.

Monte, Steven (2000), *Invisible Fences: Prose Poetry as a Genre in French and American Literature*, Lincoln, NE: Nebraska University Press.

Poe, Edgar Allan (1846), "Marginalia [part V]," in *Graham's Magazine*, vol. 28, no. 2, pp. 116–18.

Robinson, Jeffrey C. (2012), "Poetic Prose and Prose Poetry," in *The Encyclopedia of Romantic Literature*, Hoboken, NJ: Wiley, pp. 1018–25.

Rousseau, Jean-Jacques (1997), *The Discourses and Other Early Political Writings*, ed. and trans. Victor Gourevitch, Cambridge, UK: Cambridge University Press.

Part IV

Issues and Contexts

13

An Interruption of Boundaries: On Gender and the Prose Poem

Alyson Miller

A "Third" Genre: The Subversive Prose Poem

THE PROSE POEM HAS LONG BEEN UNDERSTOOD in terms of its "protean tendencies" (Hetherington and Atherton 2015: 276), a "borderline genre" (Hecq 2009) that has been a source of anxiety since its nineteenth-century inception. It is a form frequently designated in terms of disruption: as "amorphous and anarchic" (Murphy 1992: 63), "revolutionary" in its potential (Monte 2000: 8), an "extraordinary beast" (Barker 1985: 1), and even as "shady and suspect" (Volkman qu. Bar-Nadav 2011: 44). Defined by its often-troubling polymorphism, the genre is undoubtedly a "disturbing and elusive oddity" (Delville 1998b), yet in its occupation of both the center and the margins it offers a provocative engagement with the politics not only of literature but also of identity. The ambiguous—if not shifting—spaces of prose poetry have been utilized by a range of female poets, including Gertrude Stein, Ania Walwicz, Nin Andrews, and Harryette Mullen, in order to manipulate and subvert the intersections of genre, gender, and power. As a form, prose poetry evokes a complex dialectic that is inherently preoccupied with doubling, particularly via parody and mimicry, to create signifying gaps through which the constituting performances of subjectivity might be revealed. Indeed, the tension provoked between prose and poetry is frequently recognized for its ability to disorder conventional practices and traditions, producing a destabilizing effect which is both cultural and literary, and thus well-suited to capturing the shifting dynamics of the gendered subject. Examining how the prose poem functions as a means of what David Caddy describes as "counter-discourse" (2010: 106), this chapter explores how the genre troubles the delineation of self and other, and provides a medium through which gender might be understood in terms that are plural, mutable, and resistant.

As Paul Hetherington and Cassandra Atherton argue, "prose poetry turns on an anxiety of space," relating not only to formalist questions of aesthetics and composition, but also to extraliterary concerns through which "the familiar is made strange" (2015: 275). Indeed, Margueritte Murphy suggests that the apprehension so clearly associated with the form is connected to its postmodern unknowability, a result of the tension "between the desire of the text or the word to be autonomous and self-empowered and the impossibility of abandoning reference and representation absolutely" (1992: 89). As a heterogeneous genre, one which persistently seeks, Jonathan Monroe contends, to undermine and transform "dominant narratives as well as lyric modes" (1987: 11), the prose poem is intrinsically resistant to traditional hierarchies and resolutions, a characteristic which effects an alignment with ambiguity, fragmentation, and fluidity. In its indeterminacy, it is, moreover, a medium that might be configured as abject; Monroe observes that "both prose and poetry, but neither prose nor poetry exclusively, the prose poem is, as Barbara Johnson has pointed out, the place of confrontation between inside and outside where the distinction between these threatens to collapse" (20). The potential of the form is thus radical: as Hetherington and Atherton assert, in "its creation of a new genre that is at least two other genres at once," the prose poem "emphasises that instability of what may otherwise look fixed and known, also emphasising what is fluid and coming-into-being" (2015: 276). Monroe views such transitional possibilities in terms of an explicit, metamorphic engagement with the strictures of gender and class, highlighting the imbrication of the prose poem with the politics of marginality:

> The prose poem has functioned throughout its history as a self-reflexively inclusive but highly charged, intensely concentrated yet hybrid form for the mingling and confrontation of various literary and extraliterary speech types. In the condensed heteroglot texts of collections of prose poems from Baudelaire or Novak, the genre has consistently served as a reminder, by means of its self-thematizations and its foregrounding of the relationship between form and content, of ongoing antagonistic social relations and of the socio-political impasses and exclusionary literary . . . practices that remain to be overcome. (11–12)

Importantly, as Monroe suggests, the history of the "self-consciously deviant" (Delville: 8) prose poem is entangled within a series of anxieties about expressions of gender and sexuality, positioning the genre as transgressive not only in aesthetic terms but also in relation to stigmatized behaviors and identities. Rachel Blau DuPlessis describes, for example, how the emergence of the "counter-hegemonic" prose poem during early modernism offers an alternative "sex-gender narrative" working against rigid and masculinist poetic traditions: "in its origins and many of its manifestations, the prose poem is variously anti-normative, ethically errant and at times erotically effervescent to the point of being anti-masculinist or anti-virile (as well as anti-bourgeois and sardonic, framing socially suspect gestures)" (2014: 31). Perhaps ironically, such a history of (sexual) deviance neatly positions the genre in terms of its later use by a series of female prose poets, who mobilize its "effete" and epicene tendencies to critique the (il)logic of binary strictures. While the form has been regarded an "apt vehicle for transcriptions of the experience of modernity" (Murphy 1992: 11), suspicions of the mode—at least in Britain—arose in part owing to its evocation in the trials of Oscar Wilde, at which letters to Alfred Douglas, presented as evidence of Wilde's criminality, were defended as "prose poems," an attempt to "excuse their sexual overtones and seductive panache" (DuPlessis: 31). As a result, Murphy contends, prose poetry "gained notoriety as the genre par excellence of homosexual decadence, hiding abominations behind its already damning veneer of 'art for art's sake'" (1992: 47). Irving Babbitt, for instance, of whom T. S. Eliot was a student at Harvard, condemned the prose poem as "unmasculine" for blurring "firm distinctions" in *The New Laokoon: An Essay on the Confusion of the Arts* (1910) (Murphy 2018: 30), associating the form with the "stigma of effeminacy, of a lack of strength and virility" (Murphy 1992: 48). Correlated with taboo sexuality and anomaly, the genre signifies a loss of defined cultural and social norms, a dissolution of propriety that unsettles fixed borders and corrupts the clear distinction between appropriate and degenerate selves. Such a perception is compounded by an understanding that prose poetry was also "hopelessly 'French' at a time of growing English nationalism" (Murphy 1992: 48)—emphasized so eloquently through the "exotic evocations, narcotic obsession, and masturbatory frissons" populating Charles Baudelaire's scandalously perverse *Spleen de Paris* (DuPlessis, 31).

Aligned with "French posturing and effeminate sexuality" (Brophy 2002), the prose poem marks an intersection of socio-sexual and literary angst, a convolution of genre and the fraught politics of identity. Defined by "disorder, anarchy of poetic form, and immorality in art," the mode suggests a "threat of moral and sexual debilitation" and thus, for much of its history, has been "censured as Other ... relegated to the experiments of the marginal avant-garde" (Murphy 1992: 60). In addition to its framing within the polarizing attributes of Decadent transgression, the prose poem, as both Murphy and Monroe observe, is a form "invested in a genre binary (prose/poetry) mapped on a gender binary (male/female)" (DuPlessis: 31). DuPlessis notes that the "nineteenth-century stylization of realistic prose as masculine and picturesque, and of poetry as beauty-seeking and femininizing" (31), reveals a further tension in a genre already defined by its restless and provocative conflicts. As Nikki Santilli states, the prose poem "designates the literary space of battle" (2002: 13), yet it is also profoundly cultural in its confrontations, illuminating those politics and structures which delineate both public and private spheres. Fabienne Moore thus explicitly links the ambiguities of gender and genre to suggest a kind of synthesis: "sexual ambivalence, tellingly detected by Baudelaire, symbolizes the generic indeterminacy of prose poems" (2009: 247). The radical blurring of gender binaries via the rule-breaking prose poem highlights the "androgynous" nature of the genre, which as "epicene," contests totalizing frames and discourses. As Stuart Merrill lyrically states: "To my mind, the prose poem, freer than lyric verse, less enslaved than logical discourse, would be disturbing through a certain epicene charm, wavering ceaselessly between order and freedom" (quoted in Murphy 1992: 51).

In its disturbance of those parameters which define the expectations of both gendered and genre-d behaviors, the prose poem is doubly threatening. Delville observes T. S. Eliot's (somewhat ironic) disquiet concerning the ability of prose poetry to "hesitate between two media" (qu. Deville: 5), an uneasiness that seems premised on a failure to commit. Such an anxiety is expressed in the critical framing of the genre in terms of its otherness, central to its deviations from convention and therefore its capacity to perform difference and change. Yet in the context of ideas about the prose poem as an "odd, androgynous mixture" (DuPlessis: 31), the process of othering is inherently, or at least historically, connected to the abjuring of "marginal" subjectivities, evoking a distinctly heteronormative fear of the unknown: "the prose poem, possessing formal affinities with prose, but claiming a poetic nature, is unknowable, 'other', hard to read, thus suspect—eschewing the 'firm and masculine' distinction that appeals to the common-sense reader and guards against the femininizing of prose, or of poetry, for that matter. A 'third' genre, like a 'third' sex, may well be suspect" (Murphy 1992: 51). In these terms, the prose poem also seems to operate within a complex process of usage and disavowal, a return to Kristevan notions of abjection in which the mode both relies upon and expels its constitutive elements: "the prose poem is ... a genre that does not want to be itself. Although on the one hand the name 'prose poem' suggests a synthetic utopian third term, it also implies the continued irresolution of the two opposing terms that constitute it" (Monroe: 20). The result is an endless sense of agitation, a pushing against borderlines as the prose poem resists completion (despite its neat, block-like image), remaining a "fragment of discourse" (Murphy 1992: 66), or an indeterminate space.

If the prose poem is understood as both a hybrid and resistant form, it lends itself to the expression of a politics in which continuity and closure are contested; to representations that are deconstructive; and, as Linda Hutcheon asserts, to contexts in which "the centre no longer completely holds" (1988: 12). Mary Ann Caws' vision of the prose poem as composed of "floating borders and shifting contours" (1983, 180) is thus an apt image for a genre which relies upon performance and propensity to metamorphosis in order to assert its difference. Andrew Zawacki goes so far as to describe its functions as "schizophrenic," desiring a position "within both the context of literary discourses and the context of antagonistic collective discourses" (2000: 303). In these terms, the prose poem is an uneasy medium, prone to disjuncture and conflict, promising cohesion yet delivering only a part of an unknown whole. Indeed, as Hetherington and Atherton note in an analysis of the prose poem as akin to the Romantic fragment, the result of such incompleteness is a form of epistemological tension or anxiety: "Fragments may not present wholes, but in suggesting them—in presenting a part that metonymically stands in for the absent, completed work—they imply a whole. Further, it asserts the sufficiency of knowing less rather than more. As fragments affirm the possibility of addressing the 'more' they simultaneously characterize this 'more' as unavailable and not fully knowable" (2016: 28). Moreover, Murphy's attention to the contradiction between prose poetry as a form—or a genre, medium, or mode, another point of contestation—which appears total or complete, and its content, which is only ever a splinter, highlights the possibilities it provides in the representation of "marginal" voices and perspectives: the prose poem attends to the potential of the liminal. As Gertrude Stein writes in *Tender Buttons*: "A whole is inside a part, a part does go away" ([1914] 1997: 39). This sense of disconnect quite radically facilitates a "rethinking and putting into question of the bases of ... Western modes of thinking" (Hutcheon: 8), in preference to complication, contradiction, and change. In this way, prose poetry not only "celebrates dichotomies" but also dissembles "existing distinctions" to challenge whether they are really very meaningful at all (Hetherington and Atherton 2015: 279).

"re letter and read her": Gender and Prose Poetics

The prose poem is, then, a powerful cultural agent. In understanding it as a form of disruption, it is clear, as Delville observes, that the genre functions as "the locus of convergence or conflict of various discourses which in turn reflect a variety of extra-discursive realities, including a number of specific social, political and ideological agendas" (8). As noted, a number of female writers have thus utilized prose poetry as a means with which to contest hierarchies of power, specifically those relating to gender and sexual identity. A form already imbricated with anxieties relating to binary distinctions, and with its affinity for fragmentation and ambiguity, the prose poem proves apposite for transgressing extra-literary as well as literary norms. It is particularly useful in terms of resistance to fixity and resolution, essential to challenging patriarchal discourses of gender, and to positing renewed visions of self that are capable of disturbing "absolute" correlations between signifier and signified. Such a function or usage is vividly evidenced by Gertrude Stein's radical experimental poetics in *Tender Buttons* (1914), a "poetry of inclusion," Monte argues, that is "especially concerned with displacing the centre" (2000: 160, 171). Indeed, Stein's attention to "eccentric syntax and unexpected juxtapositions" (Monroe: 180) results in a series of language strategies or games that force readers to reconsider not only the (political) construction of meaning, but also the place of the subject within a complex cultural matrix that both defines and disrupts self and other. Monroe notes that, in "composing many passages of virtually impenetrable density, the fundamental elements (words)" of Stein's texts "cannot entirely detach themselves from the everyday sociohistorical contexts and uses in which they are embedded" (180–1). The three sections of *Tender Buttons*, titled "Objects," "Food" and "Rooms," transform sequences of domestic objects, routines, and discourses into new patterns and rhythms, stripping away usual meanings, structures, and connotations so that a new language emerges, one which subverts a patriarchal ontology by parodying its preoccupations and insistences. In "Food," for example, poems imitate, in fragmented form, "the diction of cookbooks, of guides to etiquette, and other 'authorities' for women, besides the overtones of philosophical definition and description taken from a more male-centered tradition" (Murphy 1992: 95). The result is the appearance of nonsense, a mimicry of the rites and rituals which define domesticity and femininity, but received only as a sense of these things, an approximation of meaning via suggestion, pattern, and sound. In the poem "Breakfast," for instance, Stein plays upon the role of women as caretakers, confined to the margins of the private sphere to cook and soothe as a form of feminine magic, and yet biting back against such relegation:

> A hurt mended sick, a hurt mended cup, a hurt mended article of exceptional relaxation and annoyance, a hurt mended, hurt and mended is so necessary that no mistake is intended.
>
> What is more likely than a roast, nothing really and yet it is never disappointed singularly.
>
> [...]
>
> Burden the cracked wet soaked sack heavily, burden it so that it is an institution in fright and in climate and in the best plan that can be. (27)

Through the use of repetition, the confusion of verbs and nouns, and the dislocation of object and subject, Stein corrupts standard grammatical configurations in order to emphasize the importance of phonic play, thereby refusing ordinary meaning and creating a series of associative, emotive links. Murphy suggests that as a result, "while the syntactic status of words remains ambivalent and pivoting, all words are ... reduced ... to a common denominator, and are nearly free-floating" (81). Similarly, in "Apple," the rapid-fire concatenation implies the sexual as well as the mundane, an alliterative puzzle of pleasure and practicality that is also wistful, pleading, and instructive: "Apple plum, carpet steak, seed clam, coloured wine, calm seen, cold cream, best shake, potato, potato and no no gold work with pet, a green seen is called bake and change sweet is bready, a little piece a little piece please" (30). The four entries titled "Chicken" form a consecutive rhyming sequence, which, when read chronologically, reveal a provocative image of the colloquial slippage that objectifies women as birds, evoking the discursive transitions made between the human, the animal, and food: "Pheasant and chicken, chicken is a peculiar bird. / Alas a dirty word, alas a dirty bird, alas a dirty bird. / Alas a doubt in case of more go to say what it is cress. What is it. Mean. Potato. Loaves" (35). Indeed, "what is it mean" is a frequent anxiety within Stein scholarship, particularly given the frequent accusation that her avant-garde prose poems are fundamentally unreadable: "Is Stein playing a trick on her readers, giving them patent *non*sense, even silliness, in the name of literature, or does *Tender Buttons* engage in a complex semantic game that allows 'reading between the lines' for subtexts, other 'stories' embedded in the text?" (Murphy 1992: 138). By attending to in-between spaces, and playing up the associative and the fragmentary in hyperbolic terms, Stein not only "undercuts" the conventional "referential functions" of language (81), but also calls into question those systems and signs that delineate other cultural processes by which identity, particularly of women, is written and circumscribed. Crafting an "inherently polysemous" style (141), Stein thus utilizes the polymorphous ability of the prose poem to defamiliarize those objects and spaces whose meanings have become invisible, and in doing so, subverts both literary and extraliterary contracts. As Murphy observes:

> This subversion takes place on a number of levels: [the poems] are subversive of a prose genre (description), of prose syntax, of ordinary meaning in discourse (semantics), and finally, of decorum for women's prose. In other words, Stein gives us 'descriptions' in which the object eludes us, sentences that tax the capabilities of syntactic English, language that consequently gestures toward nonmeaning, and parodies or scramblings of conventional feminine discourse that leave room for the imitation of lesbian love, the essence of her domestic situation. (140)

Such unsettling and transgressive tactics—which reveal the epicenity of the genre—are also observed in the prose poetry of Ania Walwicz, whose work has most often been received in terms of its complex experiments that question, as Sneja Gunew argues, "when one speaks (history) and how (enunciation), from where (positionality) and partially (subjects-in-process)" (1991: 13). Lyn McCredden has similarly noted how Walwicz's "taking up of marginality" offers a position from which to "investigate and rewrite the contours of the self" (1996: 235), an endeavor that is located in an exploration of the self as migrant and the self as a series of gendered inscriptions. These identity deconstructions are, further, connected to notions of authorship, and how the limits of language might be contested. McCredden suggests that "such ideas are redolent of a desire for traditional authorial lineage and control . . . a contradictory desire, both for self-birth, and for acknowledgement of a formal tradition from which the poet emerges" (235). Indeed, these conflicting impulses are also recognized by Walwicz, conveyed as a struggle between definition and belonging, and rejection and resistance:

> My own work has been identified with the positions of marginality, multiculturalism, ethnicity, migration, abjection, experimentation, feminist literary theory, postmodernism, the avant-garde. Do I have to provide a definition, an affiliation, a sense of belonging to a group? Will I still be an author if I do not write or publish? One can call oneself an author. One can name oneself. One can call oneself, 'author'. (Walwicz 1995: 162)

As the prose poem dissembles clear boundaries of genre, so too does Walwicz problematize essentialist notions of identity, especially those associated with gender and sexuality. McCredden has noted that the "impulse to return to origins, to childhood and new beginnings, is a recurrent one in Walwicz's work" (235); it is significant, for example, that the first poem of *Boat* (1989) should be about a girl who re-makes herself outside of the narratives told by others: "They brought me up to be ugly and ugly. To be clever and useful. To be a drone. I'm queen. I've got the beauty on me and in me...They were keeping me under. They were not letting me be as I really...Then I let it come out. Let her come out. I was beautiful" (1). Similarly, Walwicz's more recent *Palace of Culture* (2014), with its attention to the predatory and sexualized tropes and motifs of fairy tales, opens with "begin," an affirmation of identity focused on the liberating effects of self-construction: "i begin i begin to i begin to dream i dream what i begin say say what you see now i dream about what i dream i have a dream now what i see now" (1). The repeated "i," a characteristic feature of Walwicz's poetry, is fluid yet controlling, assertive and defiant in claiming a sense of freedom, including its risks, which are neatly but fiercely captured in an extended metaphor about lighting fires: "now i light me" (1). The insistence on identity as something that is ceaselessly evolving is central to Walwicz's conceptualization of subjectivity and, as McCredden posits, often emerges from images of birth and childhood, with what Sue Gillett describes as an "emphatic insistence" (1991: 239). This attention to nascent selves makes sense in the context of ideas concerning the relationship between language and "the possibility of renewal" (McCredden: 235), hence an experimental approach which repeatedly demands the performance of the poet and endless interpretations, many of which are made problematic by Walwicz's linguistic slipperiness. In incanting a new self, for instance, Walwicz's distinctive lack of punctuation, use of repetition, neologisms, and colloquial phrases slip between the post-structural gaps in ideas about fixed meaning and fixed selfhood. Indeed, as Gillett contends:

> Through the variety of her permutations of language—wayward, untutored, childish, foreign, hysterical, extravagant, depleted, mechanical, freewheeling—Walwicz dramatizes the tension between the personal desire for expression and the public demands of language ... This gap between "how it should be" and "how it is" written is the gap between the institution and the individual: it enacts the struggle to express oneself as special, new, different, the attempt to make one's own personal place within the impositions of the already encoded signs, the already limiting, standard Language. (248)

As Monroe argues, in "bringing together the socio-ideological struggle of a wide variety of 'languages' into a highly compact space where these languages may both fuse with and clash against one another, the prose poem at its best presents an explosive tension" (42). The complex permutations of language observed in Walwicz's work highlight the capacity of the prose poem to function as a kind of crucible for dissent, yet also suggest the potential of liminality, for a reinvention of the subject within the complex negotiations between meaning and meaninglessness. Such a dynamic reflects Murphy's observation of the ways in which the mode is "curiously allied with the tendency toward dissolution" (8), framing the prose poem as existing in perpetual tension both with itself and with those outside forces that demand comprehension and totality. In such a mystified space, the uncanny nature of the prose poem (Hetherington and Atherton 2015: 275), in which the familiar becomes unknown and strange, offers a key tactic through which to challenge normative structures of both meaning and power.

Certainly, the linguistic tactics employed by Stein and Walwicz echo Hélène Cixous' theorization of *écriture feminine*, a new language through which women might escape the symbolism of phallogocentric discourses and take patriarchy apart, both in theory and in practice. Murphy notes that Stein, for instance, "wanted to revitalise verbal representation, to move beyond descriptive mimesis to recreation of the medium, language, just as Picasso sought to transform visual representation" (141), while Gillett observes the deconstructive effects of Walwicz's "re-languaging": "Walwicz gets inside language ... cracks its codes ... Identity becomes destabilized, unfixed, but not nonexistent or meaningless: it becomes a game of creativity, a place of shifting boundaries, shifting moods, a light, skipping thing, a sliding from image to image, a release from the pre-established picture" (243). Yet as suggested by Stein and Walwicz's deliberate evocation of those cultural and domestic objects used to confine women within marginal spaces, the function of repetition with difference, of irony and parody, is also central to the capacity of the prose poem—a genre recognized for its many mockeries (Murphy 1992: 85)—to transgress delineating structures. Zawacki notes that the prose poem "engages in a discourse that is not simply course, but course and re-course" (297), a means of defying conventional linearity in order to present existing systems as tenuous, open to the possibilities of change. In *Why God Is a Woman* (2015), for example, Nin Andrews utilizes a series of complex reversals and inversions in order to challenge gender hierarchies, reflecting Lee Upton's vision of the prose poem, which is described in the context of Russell Edson's work as a form of culture-jamming that resists purely aesthetic characterizations: "They are not aesthetically boxed curiosities or a minimalist's freak show; instead, as rather remarkable mirrors, they reflect the psychic effects of social and cultural behaviours" (1993: 102). Andrews' prose poems imagine an elaborate female utopia, an island on which women, all called Angelina (because they "all look like Angelina Jolie"), "rule. They run the country, control the wealth, and decide who will do what, why, and when" (11), are so "fertile ... a single woman can populate an entire town" (29), and possess the remarkable talents of "sexual aficionados" who can "make love until every pore on their bodies opens and sends bliss into the horizon like an Island sunrise" (28). Alternatively, men are regarded as "incomplete souls," dependents who like "their children, their dogs," respond only to simple instructions and occupations (11). Such inequality, "of course, was not the men's fault. Men, my mother said, can't be blamed for their genetic defects and limited work ethic or abilities" (14).

Andrews' mirroring arguably plays upon Judith Butler's theorization of gendered identity as something which "ought not be construed as a stable identity or locus of agency from which various acts follow; rather, gender is an identity tenuously constituted in time, instituted in an exterior space through a *stylized repetition of acts*" (1990: 139). The inversions of *Why God Is a Woman* expose gender as a performance that is both fluid and changeable, albeit not within the logic of the narrative itself. Extratextually, however, the effect works powerfully in sync with the mechanics of the prose poem, the "radical unpredictability" of which, Murphy argues, "empowers the text vis-à-vis its readers, by leading them intimately into its subversive discourse if they are to 'make sense' of it all, making them 'writers' in Barthes' sense" (89). Importantly, such unpredictability comes from the "instability" or "problematisation of reference" which emerges in the prose poem owing to a "sometimes adversarial dynamic between the text and reader" (Murphy: 89). In a world in which "biology is destiny" (Andrews 2015: 18)—a self-consciously parodic challenge to performance—the powerful women of the island entrench their control via systematic acts of othering, reducing men to sex slaves, assistants, housemaids, and stay-at-home fathers: "When bored or frustrated, the men quit their jobs without notice, and stay at home to watch soap operas and preen in front of bathroom mirrors. Even the best working men quit their jobs as soon as they have children of their own. Who better to raise the children...?" (19). The reversals and conflicts presented are further reflected in the tensions of the prose poem, highlighted by Derrida, who claims that genres are dependent in order to function within recognized parameters but also to gain definition; similarly, within the paradigms of gender, the dominant is dependent upon the less powerful "other" to attain identity, whilst the "other" relies on its difference from the dominant so as to achieve identification. The dialectic is thus revealed as a matter of law and counter-law: identity and difference "are intertwined at their most fundamental; neither may appear without beforehand summoning the other" (Crimmins 2009: 50). The centrality of opposites in maintaining unequal power relations is a recurrent trope in Andrews' prose poems, utilized as a strategic emphasis on the ways in which simple inversions merely replicate the patterns and norms of existing social structures: "created everything and its opposite in a single week...day and night, earth and sky, woman and man. While woman was light, always carrying a glow in her belly like a small sun, man was cold like the moon, his only light a dim reflection of her own" (82).

Indeed, the politics of inversion might suggest that such a strategy risks merely reproducing a structure in which power is always divided upon gendered lines, exchanging a castrated object for a castrating subject. Inverting paradigms, however, is arguably essentially pragmatic, a means through which to observe how inequality is manifested in order to debunk its seeming naturalness and provoke transformation. Angela Carter argues that such tactics function to calculate "what certain configurations of imagery in our society, in our culture, really stand for, what they mean, underneath the kind of semi-religious coating that makes people not particularly want to interfere with them" (1994: 11). The danger of reiterating prescriptive systems in *Why God is a Woman* is mitigated via textual codes which signal parody, and what Lucy Atkins describes as a "self-referential play on notions of fact and fiction, authorship, genre and gender" which destabilizes assumptions and forces readers to question the function of ostensibly "simple" power reversals (2016: 39). As Hutcheon might argue, it is a process through which Andrews "uses and abuses, installs and then subverts, the very concepts" being challenged (1988: 1) in order to make "real" those machinations which seek to determine the gendered subject. Further, it is a strategy which once more engages with the impetus of the prose poem to "make strange"; as Caddy notes, "the prose poem—often associated with the modern world, unofficial language and thought—can, through its hybrid nature, present unsettling and unfamiliar aspects of that world" (2018: 21).

Importantly, the use of the prose poem as a medium through which to agitate against cultural proscriptions repeatedly returns to the material or the concrete as evidence of ideological realities, even within imagined worlds. Monroe observes that in "accordance with the objectlike density and compactness of its form, the prose poem has evidenced over the course of its relatively brief history an extraordinary preoccupation with the prosaic world of everyday material objects" (11). As discussed in relation to Stein, such attention works to confuse the ordinary patriarchal dicta of good housekeeping and etiquette, as objects are wrenched from ordinary uses and contexts in order to destabilize their traditional associations. Murphy contends that "instead of bowing to conventional wisdom," Stein "explains and fortifies with the tones of maxims her own unconventional arrangement," disrupting "semantics and syntax" to reveal a new world of "domestic interiors" (153). In "Oranges In," for example, a punning play on "Arranging," Stein mimics the language of recipes in characteristically paratactic style: "Cocoa and clear soup and oranges and oat-meal / whist bottom whist close, whist clothes, wooling" (38). Alternatively, Walwicz recalls the fetishized items of fairy tales in highlighting the reduction of women to empty and doll-like selves, a performance of a master-narrative in which their identities are horrifyingly curtailed, trapped in stasis: "mister zeezee gives me a slipper to fit it's made of jell and jelly it fits my foot easy say cindy cinderella and barbie doll no say barbie i slip in easy i slip in oily i put my right foot and left foot and all fits me my skin fits me now" (90). By emphasizing the centrality of objects in the construction not only of gendered roles but also identities per se, both Stein and Walwicz expose the sexual and economic subjugation of women; perhaps ironically, the "radical semantic 'openness'" (Monroe: 179) which defines the prose poem, as well as the political strategies of each poet, functions to stress the effects of limitation and control.

Similarly, Harryette Mullen's *Recyclopedia* (2006), a compilation of the prose poetry collections *Trimmings*, *S*PeRM**K*T* and *Muse & Drudge*, draws upon the discursive patternings of Stein in order to further challenge the stereotypical tropes associated with female subjectivities. Indeed, Mullen explicitly acknowledges a profound engagement with Stein as a means of responding to the possibilities of the language technicalities at play, as well as testing their potential for resistance and the critical exploration of difference:

> The language is elusive and there is a secretive quality about Stein's work . . . The language seems to create an alternate subjectivity [. . .] I was analyzing what Stein was doing to figure out what I could use and I found that on a lot of levels, I could use what she was doing: the structure of the book itself, in terms of using a prose-poetry form, and a paratactic sentence that is compressed, that is not really a grammatical sentence but that makes sense in an agrammatical way, in a poetic way. (Mullen in Hogue 1999)

Also using parataxis to create a vivid series of associative images and sounds, Mullen, as Elisabeth Frost observes, attends to both "adornments and things discarded," employing "linguistic play to hint at the relations between . . . physical sensations . . . and the experience of using language" to suggest that "the female body and the word need not be divorced" (1995). In doing so, Mullen transforms Stein's insistence on a "hermetically sealed locale" in order to underline the "conjunctions between racial identity and gender in a semiotics of American culture" (Frost 1995). By asserting the centrality of difference, Mullen critically evokes "cultural and racial specificity into her word games" (Frost 1995), including anxieties about the female body in terms of its positioning in relation to cleanliness, whiteness, and consumption: "It must be white, a picture of health . . . Dainty paper soaks up leaks that steaks splayed on trays are oozing. Lights replace the blush red flesh is losing. Cutlets leak. Tenderloins bleed pink light" (71). Throughout *Trimmings* (fittingly first published by a small press called Tender Buttons) there are repeated references to "girls in white" (34)—brides and wedding dresses, a blushing virgin with "starched petticoat besmirched" (31)—alongside skin that is often "pinked" (31), "pink in the flesh," or "flush tight," a telling counterpoint to blackness and a means of insisting upon the intersections of power. The materiality of race, for example, is envisioned through a re-coding of a commercial for detergent, in which "clothing-become-laundry" (Frost 1995) signifies an obsession with light, white bodies, bleached sterile and therefore "pure": "Heartsleeve's dart bleeds whiter white, softened with wear...O most immaculate bleached blahs, bless any starched, loosening blossom" (27). The privilege of whiteness is made visible by way of a packet of nylon stockings, "the colour 'nude', a flesh tone" (12) exposing how "neutral" is a myth that contributes to the silencing of black and colored bodies, part of a hegemonic discourse in which white is always the default norm. Via what Frost describes as a "semiotics of clothing" (1995), Mullen thus reveals the ways in which "whiteness is produced through the operation of marginalizing blackness" (Mullen 1994: 74), emphasizing how the politics of gender and power are inherently racialized:

> The black woman remains in last place within the colour/economic hierarchy, her disadvantaged status reinforcing the already existing prejudice against her. She is always the fly in the buttermilk ... It is this woman furthest from whiteness who is therefore imagined as being also furthest from all the advantages that whiteness has to offer in a racist-sexist hierarchy of privilege and oppression, in which the privilege of whites and males is based upon and unattainable without the exploitation and oppression of blacks and females. To be white in melting pot America is to be allowed to operate without a limiting ethnic identity—which is precisely what has never yet been granted to African-Americans as a group, although the mulatto figure is a way of imagining in microcosm what this kind of social mobility might be like, at the level of the individual. (73)

The economics of the material are also embedded in the sexual, as subject–object distinctions are blurred alongside verb–noun confusions in order to present charged and complex erotic imagery. In a prose poem about washing a car, for example, Mullen's alliterative sequences slip between the body of the vehicle and the female driver, creating fluid transitions between metal and flesh to suggest arousal, gratification, and power: "Champagne dreams wet shammy softly. Hands-on carwash, a pampering ... Pearl diver's paradise. All sparkling steel and spritzed crystal rubbed down clean to the squeak" (87). Further, by stressing "the erotic charge of feminine objects," Mullen not only blurs the distinction between public and private selves, but also echoes the Steinian "fetishization of language" that "exalts it to the status" of materiality (Frost 1995). Putting on a dress is likened to a double form of consumption—"holes breathe, and swallow. Openings, hem, sleeve" (29)—while a description of a "good old girl" who "got hipped" utilizes the language of architecture, of buildings and structures, to equate the body of a woman to a space that might be breached, entered, or inhabited: "Most worthy girth, providing firm. Foundations in midriff. Across (between) girdled loins, tender girders. Gartered, perhaps, struts. Stretching, a snap crotch" (22). The physical self is further divided into a series of articles that both define and contain, as women are repeatedly connected to the fear of unruliness, of growing beyond the spaces to which they have been allotted: a belt, for instance, adds "waist to any figure, subtract, divide," but more importantly, "sucks her in" (3), while a suffocating, albeit playful, image of adornment suggests strangulation and devourment: "Starving to muffler moans, boa scarfs her up" (6). As in Walwicz's portrayals of the female body as a series of prescribed functions and desires, women are depicted as "warm stitched-together soft" toys, curios trapped in a dangerous, ambiguous space between childhood innocence and adult sexuality: "voluptuous imaginary mammal made of lovely lumps . . . plump-cheeked plaything taken to bed and hugged in the dark" (16). The tension between knowing and unknowing evokes the transgressive binaries of the prose poem (a mode so well suited to complex interstices), revealing a series of cultural contradictions about the gendered performances demanded by patriarchy.

Significantly, and in line with the characteristic fragmentation of the prose poem, the representation of sexual identity occurs via instances of synecdoche, ensuring that the female body in particular is never presented as whole. In Cassandra Atherton's "Luna" (2020b), for instance, the lovers are riven into parts—shoulders and spine, hands and chest—and linger as "silhouettes," whilst in "Volcano" (2018), the protagonist is an elemental force, transformed from fire and lava occupying "the spaces between your ribs" and the "thick absences between embraces" to "glassy rock" in the "cooling aftermath." Attending to liminal gaps and locations, the effect is nonetheless of freedom and domination, suggesting the constitution or expression of self via a violent process of difference, possession, and change: "I am subtle as a volcano." Importantly, Atherton's prose poems are inherently subversive, presenting, in line with Stein's relocation of domestic objects in order to dismantle authoritative voices, women who overturn discourses traditionally associated with marginality to reclaim the male gaze as their own: "You try to squeeze me into your glass slippers, but I'm soaring towards the ceiling." There is also an emphasis on pleasure and playfulness, articulated via often humorous stream-of-consciousness linkages that weave between things and beings to suggest transition, movement, and desire. In "Tinker," for example: "As you tinkered with my scapula, I told you if I was a pan, I'd be a cocotte—so you pulled me on top of you until I boiled over" (2019: 17). Alternatively, Mullen, echoing Stein's proclivity for nouns that might be static objects or active, acting parts, dissects both bodies and gendered performances by way of routines that are strikingly conscious of audience, and the stylization of the (sexualized) self: "Cuts curls, frail frounce . . . Frilled up to here, she starts sleeking. Flat, flatter, flatterer" (52). In line with the aesthetic of dislocation celebrated by the prose poem, the expression of sexuality via its parts—of bodies, objects, and actions—offers a counter-discourse, one in which the "riven" subject is not disappeared into gaps and silences, but, perhaps ironically, embodied and potently self-aware: "In feathers, in bananas, in her own skin, intelligent body attached to a gaze" (43).

While an emphasis on the material is most frequently employed in relation to the subjugating effects of gender hierarchies, it is also crucial to note the ways in which such a strategy is utilized to challenge power structures via incisive humor. Indeed, if the prose poem is an object that appears complete yet delivers only the partial, then much of its subversive potential arises in relation to its ability to elide expectations, to mirror convention and yet present as something other. As Monroe argues, "illegitimate literary genre par excellence, the prose poem typically seeks its legitimacy not by trying to get around reification but by meeting it head on" (207). The double-play of the mode, enabled by its its "Janus-faced" behavior (Hetherington and Atherton 2015: 279), often results in a mischievous engagement with politics that is as much liberating as it is a critical examination of oppressive norms and systems. As many critics have noted, for instance, it is in many ways impossible not to regard Stein's word-games as a form of teasing or mockery, a challenge to read sense into the semantic and syntactical confusion that embraces slipperiness, punning, and the absurd: "SALAD: It is a winning cake" (37). In *The Six Senses* (2019), Atherton's "touch" sequence depicts a series of eccentric lovers, including "Poor Man," a miser who "ended it by saying I wasn't cheap enough to be a really good deal" (22), and "Professional Netflix Watcher," whose aptitude for television far eclipses any sexual prowess: "On Netflix the credits only go for fifteen seconds but you still finished before they ended" (14). In *S*PeRM**K*T*, as suggested by the satirical title, Mullen parodies the commoditization of self via the growth of the supermarket, a behemoth of commodity culture—"Bigger better spermkit grins down family of four. Scratch and sniff your luck number. You may already be a wiener" (94)—whilst inasmuch as Andrews' *Why God Is a Woman* presents a confronting vision of the logic of gender hierarchies, it does so by emphasizing the ridicule associated with expecting men to experience the strictures endured by women: "The salons, the hubs of male social activity, were where my father and uncle caught up on the latest gossip and clothing styles. As a boy I watched them leave the house, hairy and grizzled, only to return hours later, as soft and smooth as nectarines" (54). Such instances reveal what Russell Edson has described as the "humour of the deep, uncomfortable metaphor" (1975: 102), which defines the ability of "a good prose poem" to confront the manifestations of culture via a "darkly comic" approach (Upton: 102).

These female prose poets thus create a new vernacular through which to contest structures of power, one based in a materialism which attends to the symbolism of objects and spaces, but is also realized via the physical realities of the body, and its intersection with the complex economics of gender, race, and sexuality. In the context of Stein, Murphy notes how an alternative language is created, one which exploits the "vocabulary, syntax, rhythms, and cadences of conventional women's prose and talk, the ordinary discourse of domesticity" in order to subvert traditional discourses and suggest a different way of seeing (149). Indeed, by playing both with and upon existing significations, it is possible to also reinvent, to contest the limits of language as well as the strictures of identity constructions. As Walwicz so vividly demonstrates in "author" (2014), in which the poet proudly declares authorship as both an occupation and a process of selfhood, the effects of these transgressions might well be emancipating: "i made this i am author of who writer the one that does that does this that does to me i am author autor the one who writes" (107). Importantly, such subversions remain located in material terms: in "Overwritten" (2019), for example, Atherton imagines the body as a "palimpsest," constantly superimposed by new experiences and desires, whilst in "Letter" (2020a), there is an insistence on the ways in which language is fluid and shifting; the protagonist is not "a silent object of love," a letter fixed to "the ruckles of your bed," but a vehicle through which change might be provoked. Invoking the transgressive spirit of Veronica Franco, she writes: "Together, our words overwrite the roar of accusations and the lapping silence of inequality." Similarly, Mullen breaks associative codes to evoke "aspects of a shared, social identity" rather than an "idiosyncratic, private language" (Frost 1995). In the final poem of *Trimmings*, that which is relegated to the margins, made invisible and silent, creates a space of its own: "Thinking thought to be a body wearing language as clothing or language a body of thought which is a soul or body the clothing of a soul, she is veiled in silence. A veiled, unavailable body makes an available space" (62).

"A form of being content": Conclusion

In the dedication of *The Parisian Prowler*, to the editor of *La Presse*, Arsène Houssaye, Baudelaire described the prose poem in anatomical terms as a genre that would freely submit to dissection: "Remove one vertebra, and the two pieces of that tortuous fantasy will reunite without difficulty. Chop it up into many fragments, and you will find that each one can exist separately. In the hope that some of these segments will be lively enough to please and divert you, I dedicate to you the entire serpent" ([1869] 1997). As a reptilian beast, Zawacki argues, the prose poem is "resilient to all sorts of transmogrifications," a creature that is fundamentally malleable, open to change (292). Indeed, with its "multiple negotiations with literary and utilitarian discourses" (Delville 1998a: 250), and its resistance toward reduction, the prose poem is a form that revels in the possibilities of interstitial spaces. As Hetherington and Atherton lyrically suggest, prose poetry is multi-faceted, "looking forwards and backwards, understanding transitions, providing passageways and doorways. Space opens before and behind it, sometimes like closed rooms, sometimes like expanding fields" (2015: 279). In its liminality and "deviant" proclivities, the prose poem is a mode that powerfully connects with a politics of subversion, creating a "third place"—or as Monroe describes it, a "utopian third term" (22) beyond binaries—in which to imagine new languages and ways of being whilst critically engaging with present realities. By taking up marginality and offering a complex position from which to trouble the contours of self and other, the prose poem thus challenges the borderlines of language and meaning, suggesting the potential for plural, shifting and dynamic selves that can be undone and remade:

> i want to start all over said i don't like what i have start all over said clean slate table cloth undo dress unpluck undo what i did me i want to do me all over said unclothe said undo undone. (Walwicz 2014: 51)

Works Cited

Andrews, Nin (2015), *Why God is a Woman*, Rochester, New York: Versa Press.
Atherton, Cassandra, Paul Hetherington, Paul Munden, Jen Webb and Jordan Williams (2019), *The Six Senses*, Canberra: Recent Work Press.
Atherton, Cassandra (2018), "Volcano," in *Metre*, Canberra: Recent Work Press.
Atherton, Cassandra (2019), "Overwritten," *Venetian Blind*, European Cultural Centre: Personal Structures exhibition, Venice Biennale.
Atherton, Cassandra (2020a), "Letter," in *Leftovers*, Sydney: Life Before Man Press.
Atherton, Cassandra (2020b), "Luna," in *Leftovers*, Sydney: Life Before Man Press.
Atkins, Lucy (2016), "Girl Power: Women Dominate the World in a Darkly Witty Play on Gender Roles," *Sunday Times*, October 23.

Barker, George (1985), "The Jubjub Bird, or Some Remarks on the Prose Poem," in *The Jubjub Bird, or Some Remarks on the Prose Poem & A Little Honouring of Lionel Johnson*: Warwick: Greville Press.

Bar-Nadav, Hadara (2011), "Who is Flying This Plane? The Prose Poem and the Life of the Line," in E. Rosko and A. Vander Zee (eds), *A Broken Thing: Poets on the Line*, Iowa: University of Iowa Press.

Baudelaire, Charles (1997), *The Parisian Prowler: Le Spleen de Paris, Petits Poemes en Prose* [1869], Georgia: University of Georgia Press.

Brophy, Kevin (2002) "The Prose Poem: A Short History, A Brief Reflection and A Dose of the Real Thing," *TEXT: Journal of Writing and Writing Courses*, vol. 6, no. 1, n.p.

Caddy, David (2010), "Hidden Form: The Prose Poem in English Poetry," in T. Chivers (ed.), *Stress Fractures: Essays on Poetry*, London: Penned in the Margins, pp. 103–14.

Caddy, David (2018), "'Hidden' Form: The Prose Poem in English Poetry," in J. Monson (ed.), *British Prose Poetry: The Poems Without Lines*, London: Palgrave, pp. 19–28.

Carter, Angela and Anna Katsavos (1994), "An Interview with Angela Carter," *Review of Contemporary Fiction*, vol. 14, no. 3, pp. 11–17.

Caws, Mary Ann and Hermine Riffaterre (eds) (1983), *The Prose Poem in France: Theory and Practice*, New York: Columbia University Press.

Crimmins, Jonathan (2011), "Gender, Genre, and the Near Future in Derrida's 'The Law of Genre,'" *diacritics*, vol. 39, no. 1, pp. 45–60.

Delville, Michel (1998a), *The American Prose Poem: Poetic Form and the Boundaries of Genre*, Gainesville: University Press of Florida.

Delville, Michel (1998b), "Stephen Fredman's *Poet's Prose: The Crisis in American Verse*," *The Prose Poem: An International Journal*, 7, n.p.

DuPlessis, Rachel Blau (2014), "'Virile Thought': Modernist Maleness, Poetic Forms and Practices," in N. Lusty and J. Murphet (eds), *Modernism and Masculinity*, Cambridge, New York: Cambridge University Press, pp. 19–37.

Edson, Russell (1975), "Portrait of the Writer as a Fat Man: Some Subjective Ideas or Notions on the Care and Feeding of Prose Poems," in D. Hall (ed.), *Claims for Poetry*, Ann Arbor: University of Michigan Press, pp. 95–103.

Frost, Elisabeth A. (1995), "Signifyin(g) on Stein: The Revisionist Poetics of Harryette Mullen and Leslie Scalapino," *Postmodern Culture*, vol. 5, no. 3, n.p.

Gillett, Sue (1991), "At the Beginning: Ania Walwicz's Writing," *Southerly*, vol. 5, no. 2, pp. 239–52.

Gunew, Sneja (1991), "Authentic Self-Representation and the Temptations of Irony in Recent Australian Migrant (non Anglo-Celtic) Women's Writing," *Review of Japanese Culture and Society*, 4, pp. 11–17.

Hecq, Dominique (2009), "The Borderlines of Poetry," Margins and Mainstreams: Refereed Conference Papers of the 14th Annual AAWP Conference.

Hetherington, Paul, and Cassandra Atherton (2015), "'Unconscionable Mystification'?: Rooms, Spaces and the Prose Poem," *New Writing*, vol. 12, no. 3, pp. 265–81.

Hetherington, Paul, and Cassandra Atherton (2016), "Like a Porcupine or Hedgehog? The Prose Poem as Post-Romantic Fragment," *Creative Approaches to Research*, vol. 9, no. 1, pp. 19–38.

Hogue, Cynthia and Harryette Romell Mullen (1999), "Interview with Harryette Mullen," *Postmodern Culture*, vol. 9, no. 2, n.p.

Hutcheon, Linda (1988), *A Poetics of Postmodernism*, London: Routledge.

McCredden, Lyn (1996), "Transgressing Language? The Poetry of Ania Walwicz," *Australian Literary Studies*, vol. 17, no. 3, pp. 235–44.

Monroe, Jonathan (1987), *A Poverty of Objects: The Prose Poem and the Politics of Genre*, Ithaca and London: Cornell University Press.

Monte, Steven (2000), *Invisible Fences: Prose Poetry as a Genre in French and American Literature*, Lincoln: University of Nebraska Press.

Mullen, Harryette (1994), "Optic White: Blackness and the Production of Whiteness," *Diacritics*, vol. 24, nos 2/3, pp. 71–89.

Mullen, Harryette (2006), *Recyclopedia: Trimmings, S*PeRM**K*T and Muse & Drudge*, Minneapolis: Graywolf Press.

Murphy, Margueritte (1992), *A Tradition of Subversion: The Prose Poem in English from Wilde to Ashbery*, Amherst: University of Massachusetts Press.

Murphy, Margueritte (2018), "The British Prose Poem and 'Poetry' in Early Modernism," in J. Monson (ed.), *British Prose Poetry: The Poems Without Lines*, London: Palgrave, pp. 29–46.

Stein, Gertrude (1997), *Tender Buttons* [1914], Dover, New York: Mineola.

Upton, Lee (1993), "Structural Politics: The Prose Poetry of Russell Edson," *South Atlantic Modern Language Association*, vol. 58, no. 4, pp. 101–15.

Walwicz, Ania (1989) *Boat*, Sydney: Angus & Robertson.

Walwicz, Ania (1996), "Look at Me, Ma—I'm Going to Be a Marginal Writer!," *Southerly*, vol. 56, no. 1, pp. 58–61.

Walwicz, Ania (2014), *Palace of Culture*, Glebe: Puncher & Wattman.

Zawacki, Andrew (2000), "Accommodating Commodity: The Prose Poem," *The Antioch Review*, vol. 58, no. 5, pp. 286–303.

14

Pastoral and Ecocritical Voices in Modern Prose Poetry

Lynn Domina

"We didn't know what we were seeing, and so, saw less" (Kwasny 2015: 2). So begins Melissa Kwasny's prose poem "Pictograph: Avalanche Mouth". Such a statement could serve as a summary of much nature writing over the past two centuries, at least from an ecocritical perspective. Degrees of knowledge provide degrees of context such that seeing isn't so much believing as understanding. A speaker who sees without understanding often seems to see only an extension of him- or herself. A speaker's character is often informed by personal knowledge, and it is this perspective of the speaker that often distinguishes traditional pastoral poetry from its more recent ecocritical descendants. In more conventional pastoral poetry, whether in lineated verse or prose paragraphs, nature (or "nature") is often approached with longing, entered or observed by a speaker in order to provide solace or reveal some new truth about the speaker. Nature is the means through which the poem creates meaning, but that meaning often reverberates back to the speaker and humanity in general. Ironically, while pastoral speakers often long for a prelapsarian past, their own naïveté suggests that they themselves haven't yet fallen into a world marked by ecological disaster. When poems engage in the more recent ecocritical project, however, the voice is more activist, and the speaker is not simply in but of nature. More is at stake than the speaker's loneliness or melancholy; ecocritical poetry is instead a form of witness, testifying to humanity's willful destruction of the earth and all that lives upon it. Ecocritical poetry seeks to be a competing voice to challenge the more historically dominant pastoral voice, and it often arises with or through social engagement (Thompson 2002: 34).

The poets I will consider in this essay—Mary Oliver, James Wright, Joy Harjo, and Melissa Kwasny—all write traditionally lineated verse as well as prose poems. As the prose poem has become more popular in American writing during the second half of the twentieth century, many poets have published at least a couple of prose poems, even if the vast majority of their work is structured as verse. More recently, however, the prose poem seems to have issued an invitation for poets seeking to explore explicitly ecocritical concerns. As prose poetry opened up possibilities for American writers interested in surrealism during the 1960s and 1970s, prose poetry seems to offer a congenial container for ecological exploration and protest. One reason for this might be that the prose poem, as a genre that is often perceived as an oxymoron, a genre that isn't one, is more susceptible to political exploration, or that poets exploring these generic boundaries might also be interested in exploring, or violating, other boundaries (Zawacki 2000: 297). Another and softer way of saying this is that a genre like "prose poem" doesn't arouse the number or depth of expectations that lineated verse does and so can say what has heretofore remained unsaid (Horvath 1992: 12). By its very nature, the prose poem draws attention to form, forcing readers to consider their own assumptions, formed by tradition, convention, or the desire to subvert those expectations (Delville 1998: x). For the purposes of this essay, I am less interested in why prose poetry has often become aligned with ecological writing than I am in exploring the effects of this shift and the opportunities the prose poem provides for ecocritical poets as well as for some more traditional pastoral poets.

That said, though, a critic could reasonably assume that a writer chooses a form—or a form chooses a writer—in part for its ultimate effects. A block of prose, even a short block, offers a different kind of invitation to a reader than does a lineated poem, even a poem with particularly long lines. If prose doesn't inevitably suggest narrative, most readers do affiliate story with prose. The contemporary prose poem draws attention to form, simultaneously daring the reader to classify it and frustrating any attempts at classification. Such frustration makes an appropriate entry point particularly for ecocritical poems, those challenging the characteristic tone of more traditional pastoral poetry.

Obviously, in prose poetry, writers cannot direct readers' pauses or amplify meaning through strategic enjambment as they can do with lineated poetry, especially free verse. However, neither do readers ingest a prose poem, or even a single sentence, as a complete unit. Discussing Harjo's work, Robert Johnson emphasizes the prose poem's frequent organization by association rather than primarily by plot—and in this the prose poem retains more of the characteristics of poetry rather than adopting organizational features of prose (Johnson 1999: 14). Still, the reader likely receives the text, not line by line but by grammatical unit, often the phrase. Regardless of the prose poem's organization, then, the reader reads it similarly to other prose. This juxtaposition—a chunk of text whose content is organized similarly to the lyric poem's but whose interpretation is achieved logically, through grammatical units uninterrupted by line breaks—permits contemporary writers to explore material that depends on the image for its effect. Ecocritical poetry especially often suggests a story—a story of an ecological future—without actually telling a story. The reader is expected to translate the imagery into the future, thereby creating a story, to be disturbed by that translation, and to therefore understand the ecocritical theme.

None of the poets I will discuss, I want to be clear, should be positioned entirely in one category or the other. The appreciation for nature found in pastoral poetry also informs and even motivates much ecocritical poetry, and environmental concerns arise in much poetry characterized by a more pastoral voice. Neither of these styles is responding to nature as nature, for "nature" by definition is a term responding to culture and cultural shifts (Elder 1996: 26). Shifts in culture, especially over the last fifty years or so, have significantly influenced poets' responses to nature. These two terms—pastoral and ecocritical—are not binary opposites; they are not even necessarily truly opposed; instead they exist as two points along the spectrum of nature poetry. In the words of Glen A. Love, even those two points need not be that far apart: "Pastoral, rightly understood, has always been a serious criticism of life. Ecocriticism, I think can give us a serious criticism of pastoral. It is time for pastoral theory and ecocriticism to meet" (Love 1992: 198).

The Penguin Dictionary of Literary Terms and Literary Theory includes a comparatively lengthy entry for "pastoral," focusing on its idealized view of nature. Pastoral poetry, it says, "creates an image of a peaceful and uncorrupted existence; a kind of prelapsarian world" (Cuddon and Habib 2014: 517). Later, the definition elaborates on this view:

> pastoral displays a nostalgia for the past, for some hypothetical state of love and peace which has somehow been lost. The dominating idea and theme of most pastoral is the search for the simple life away from the court and town, away from corruption, war, strife, the love of gain, away from "getting and spending." In a way it reveals a yearning for a lost innocence, for a pre-Fall paradisal life in which man existed in harmony with nature. (Cuddon and Habib 2014: 518)

Nature itself is often perceived sentimentally, less "red in tooth and claw" than a "tender blossom flutter[ing] down" (Tennyson 2004: 41, 75). Although not all details of this definition will fit every pastoral poem, the emphasis on nostalgia, innocence, and harmony with nature certainly characterizes the pastoral voice of poems I will discuss.

Terry Gifford delineates the pastoral in similar terms, elaborating especially on the idealized and nostalgic tendencies within much pastoral poetry. He also includes another telling feature: the "unproblematic" view of nature exhibited in much pastoral writing (Gifford 2013: 50). Writers and others can feel nostalgic about their imagined pasts, during which individuals were not compelled to flee to nature for respite from their crowded, unsanitary, noisy cities because nature was all there was. According to this view, nature is comforting and abundant. One needn't worry about food or shelter because ripe pears are always bursting with juice, and the sun is always shining, and a refreshing breeze always wafts over hill and through dale. Gifford contrasts this pastoral style with the anti-pastoral, in which nature is presented as dangerous and threatening, the place where one freezes or starves. Yet, Gifford argues, categories of pastoral and anti-pastoral are insufficient and fail to acknowledge the complexity of the pastoral or of nature itself. Not all pastoral poetry, for example, concludes with the speaker still reclining against soft grass and warm soil. Most speakers return to the social world, committed to communicating the value of the natural world and to challenging anthropocentric hubris. These speakers understand humanity as a small component of creation, rather than as its center or peak, and their tone is not nostalgic but often awed. This writing Gifford calls "post-pastoral," and it overlaps in many ways with writing I am calling ecocritical (Gifford 2013: 55–60).

As an interdisciplinary and theoretical movement still in its early development (at least compared to the pastoral, which can be traced back a couple of millennia), an agreed-upon definition of ecocriticism is harder to achieve. On the one hand, it is

> a term used for the observation and study of the relationship between the literature and the earth's environment. It takes an interdisciplinary point of view by analysing the works of authors, researchers, and poets in the context of environmental issues and nature. (*A Simple Guide* 2019: unpag.)

Yet ecocriticism is also more than "observation and study," for ecocritics nearly always subscribe to a specifically activist agenda. In contrast to much contemporary literary theory which focuses on language, identity, or political context, "eco-critics take nature as a dominant factor as they believe that our evolution as a society is largely dependent on the forces of nature" (*A Simple Guide* 2019: unpag.). More pointedly, ecocritics acknowledge that the human perspective or human priorities are not the only ones worth considering, and specifically, "The nonhuman environment is present not merely as a framing device but as a presence that begins to suggest that human history is implicated in natural history" (Buell 1995: 7). This final statement is consistent with Gifford's emphasis on a post-pastoral writer's necessary humility when confronted with nature's vast dimensions.

Given those definitions, much of Mary Oliver's work falls clearly within the pastoral tradition, via Romanticism. James Wright's poems also often adopt strategies of the pastoral.[1] Joy Harjo's and Melissa Kwasny's poems, on the other hand, choose an ecocritical stance. This is not to say that Oliver or Wright didn't or wouldn't support an environmentalist agenda but that their work is characterized by the more nostalgic and idealized voice of the pastoral, the desire to receive comfort in and from nature (Love 1992: 202). It might be tempting to assume a generational correlation with these practices (and, in the case of Harjo, to also assume stereotypic ethnic values), but both of these assumptions are problematic. It is certainly true that environmental concerns and controversies have increased in significance since the turn of the twenty-first century as global climate change has approached the catastrophic. James Wright died in 1980 and Mary Oliver in early 2019, while both Joy Harjo and Melissa Kwasny were born closer to the mid-twentieth century and are still living and writing. However, many poets of earlier generations wrote fiercely environmentalist poems, Denise Levertov being one example. J. Scott Bryson's influential *Ecopoetry: A Critical Introduction* (Bryon 2002a) opens with a section called "Forerunners of Ecopoetry" and includes essays on Emerson, Robinson Jeffers, and others. While "forerunners" are not exactly ecopoets themselves, neither can these figures be accurately classified as pastoral writers—as I state above, pastoral and ecocritical are two points on the continuum of nature writing. These forerunners might not have predicted our precise environmental crisis, but they certainly understood the potential consequences of human behavior. Despite these literary interventions into cultural approaches to the environment, however, the pastoral voice remained and to some extent remains prominent and popular. The ecocritical voice, while gaining more prominence recently, still inserts itself into literary discussions as a minority perspective. The pastoral voice seldom challenges and sometimes even reinforces the dominant narrative. It is safe. While readers might or might not share the speaker's longing for life away from the metropolis, few readers would find the pastoral offensive or describe it as political. Its attitude toward nature is, ironically, naturalized. The ecocritical voice, however, expressly attempts to intervene in the dominant story, the asserted consensus of a nation's history and values. The imaginations of these two voices differ in their directions—the pastoral reaches toward the past for what might have been but never was; the ecocritical turns toward a threatened future.

Mary Oliver's poems "Tiger Lillies" and "Goldfinches" can serve as two examples of poems that center the speaker and utilize nature as a means to understanding human life, rather than, for example, as an entity with value in itself. Here is "Tiger Lillies":

They blew in the wind softly, this way, that way. They were not disappointed when they saw the scissors, rather they braced themselves sweetly and shone with willingness. They were on tall and tender poles, with wheels of leaves. They were soft as the ears of kittens. They felt warm in recognition of the summer day. A dozen was plenty. I held them in my arms. They were silent the way the deepest water is silent. If they wondered where they were going they didn't show it, as they sprinkled freely over my shirt and my hands their precious gold dust. (Oliver 2005: 31)

Although this poem doesn't overtly long for the past, it presents the present almost as if nostalgia has been fulfilled in the speaker's own time. The speaker at times describes the lilies more or less objectively: "They blew in the wind"—though even the word that follows, "softly," seems intended to evoke a conspicuously tender response from the reader. By the second sentence, however, as well as later in the poem, Oliver conveys her attitude toward these flowers through the pathetic fallacy.[2] The flowers' purpose here is not only to create human happiness but to do so via human-like responses and decisions. Cut from their stems, they are "not disappointed." Indeed, they "shone with willingness"; they offered themselves, it seems, as sacrificial victims, pre-emptively absolving the speaker of guilt. One generally permits one's own sacrifice only for a greater good; here, only one action follows the sacrifice and so only it can possibly be defined that way—the speaker gathering the flowers in her arms. Oliver purports to speak for the flowers, who can only remain silent, who must remain silent in order to be available for representation by the speaker (Nielsen 1993: 695).

Laird Christensen argues that Oliver invites the reader into ecological awareness in an attempt to reduce human alienation from the non-human, an alienation that occurs when humans assume that their place in the universe is dominant and central (Christensen 2002: 137). Similarly, Jeffrey Thomson suggests that readers will be changed through her work because of its elegiac tone, mourning the disappearance of so much of the natural world (Thomson 2002: 155). Oliver's work, Christensen suggests, encourages connections among human beings and other elements of nature, as different life forms exchange elements via mortality: "Traditional distinctions between mortality and immortality quickly break down in Oliver's poems as the material elements of each being are transformed into the elements of other bodies. This is the dynamic process that Oliver finds so redemptive" (Christensen 2002: 137). Although I do not disagree with either Christensen or Thomson here, and although Christensen explicitly and Thomson implicitly position Oliver within the Romantic tradition, I find Romanticism less compatible with ecocritical work than they seem to. Romantic writers often do present an appreciative view of nature, and their worldview is closer to an ecocritical view than a dominionist theology permits—the theology that not only insists on the centrality of human beings within creation but explicitly understands every other created thing as available to fulfill human needs and desires—but appreciation is not activist. As a thought experiment, remove the human from Oliver's work—does a world remain? If a world without humans is inconceivable within, or at least unavailable via, these poems, then they share more with a pastoral than with an ecocritical perspective.

Oliver could have described the sacrificial moment in many ways, with or without attributing emotion to the lilies. That she chooses, though, not only to assign emotion to them but to interpret that emotion as so specifically consistent with the speaker's own desire is telling. Although the poem doesn't overtly allude to "I Wandered Lonely as a Cloud," it does adopt some similar strategies, as Wordsworth too interprets the flowers that overwhelm his vision via human emotion. Although at several individual points the lilies are described metaphorically, "soft as the ears of kittens," the poem as a whole also functions metaphorically. The lilies satisfy some unnamed human need—for connection, for warmth, even perhaps for transcendence as they "sprinkled freely over my shirt and my hands their precious gold dust". These flowers to this speaker are more significant than Wordsworth's iconic daffodils, which he possesses in memory only. Oliver's speaker possesses the lilies literally, for although "A dozen was plenty", those dozen must remain materially present rather than arise exclusively through memory.

The modifiers in this poem—"softly", "sweetly", "tender", "freely", "precious"—do most to confirm Oliver's sentimental and pastoral agenda. Since modifiers are never grammatically necessary, their inclusion must be particularly intentional. If such adverbs and adjectives were struck from the poem, the tone would become slightly more neutral and the speaker's projection of herself somewhat less overt. The speaker's stance is an effect of more than just the modifiers, of course, and this poem could never be other than pastoral. Closely attending to the modifiers, however, reveals how these choices reinforce the speaker's assumptions regarding her relationships to wind, flowers, pollen, and likely other flora.[3]

"Goldfinches" also reveals how the speaker identifies elements of nature according to their human purpose. The poem describes several birds splashing near a puddle and then flying off, though it includes an apparent tangent in the middle, between the birds' two acts. It opens with this sentence: "Some goldfinches were having a melodious argument at the edge of a puddle" (Oliver 2005: 103). "Melodious" is the operative word here, for it contributes to the poem's associative structure. Initially, the speaker seems simply to be an observer (although her observations are inevitably tinged with interpretation, hence "melodious"), but soon she reveals herself as a thinker:

> I stood in the distance, listening. Perhaps in Tibet, in the old holy places, they also have such fragile bells. Or are these birds really just that, bells come to us—come to this road in America—let us bow our heads and remember now how we used to do it, say a prayer. (Oliver 2005: 103)

Why Tibet? Certainly there are houses of prayer in America, perhaps not far from where the speaker was standing, churches and cathedrals that also ring bells. Why are Tibetan bells specifically "fragile"? Tibetan tingsha bells are small cymbal-like instruments used during meditation; their sounds are certainly more delicate than gongs echoing from a cathedral bell tower, but bells rung inside churches, during some Roman Catholic masses, for instance, are also softer and higher-pitched.

Perhaps the goldfinches' "melodious argument" sounded specifically like those Tibetan bells, but the reference to Tibet here accomplishes an additional purpose—it appeals to the exotic. Tibet is about as far culturally from Oliver's New England as a national reference could be, and this particular proper noun evokes specific connotations: the Dalai Lama, oppression by the Chinese, short brownish people layered in colorful woolen clothing. Tibet functions here not simply as a metaphor, for it is the bells, not the region, which are positioned as the vehicle to the "melodious" tenor.

In the poem, Tibet becomes part of nature, aligned with the birds, from whom the speaker feels estranged. Tibet, one of the "old holy places", and implicitly Tibetans, remember how to "bow our heads ... and say a prayer". Ringing their bells, Tibetans resemble the birds more closely than they remember the "we" of Oliver's society. Again, though the reference to bells invokes sound, it is sound that must be interpreted by the speaker; neither Tibet nor Tibetans speak for themselves. Oliver's willingness to metaphorize an ethnic minority in order to extend her other figurative language, to enhance her description of a moment in nature, is explicitly pastoral, rather than post-pastoral or ecocritical (Gifford 2013: 59). An ecocritical poem relying on similar material would more likely draw attention to European or Chinese exploitation of Tibetan people as part of an exploration of the relationships among humans or between humans and other elements of nature. Here, the poem most tellingly reveals Oliver's pastoral impulse, for here is where she most explicitly expresses a longing for a past that never, at least for westerners, existed, a past that for some people, people unlike the speaker, enviably exists within the present.

In this section, the pronouns shift from singular to plural.[4] Before the speaker mentions Tibet, she is standing alone, an "I". Then the "bells come to us" and the subsequent invitation is also to "us": "let us bow our heads and remember how we used to do it, say a prayer". The "us" includes only people in the speaker's geographic or perhaps psychological vicinity, that is, Americans, for the bells come from Tibet "to us". The "us" is likely intended to include the readers as first person plural references often do. In shifting from singular to plural, the speaker assumes a similar longing and lack in her readers, who must also somehow have abandoned the sacred, found as it is in nature and those people perceived to be closer to nature, that is, primitive. The shift seems almost unconscious, as if the speaker assumes not simply a similarity but an identification between herself and others. Some readers will find this assumption off-putting, for it reveals the speaker's privilege—only members of dominant cultures can assume that differences don't matter. Following this interlude, the speaker returns to observing the goldfinches, who "fly off, their dark wings opening from their bright, yellow bodies; their tiny feet, all washed, clasping the air" (Oliver 2005: 103). The birds are "washed", cleansed, perhaps as spiritually clean as they are physically, but the speaker remains where she was, perhaps having said the prayer she instructs her readers to remember, perhaps not. She never reveals what the prayer consists of, unless it is simply an acknowledgment of the sacred. The birds have come, functioned as symbols, and gone. The speaker believes she has received a message that she herself created. If the speaker is changed, that change is limited to her individual psyche.

"Tiger Lillies" and "Goldfinches" are representative of the tone and style of Oliver's prose poems. Although they consistently seem oriented toward nature, it is a nature created and described to soothe humanity, without apparent value in itself. In these poems, nature's value resides exclusively in a human being's interpretation of it. Within the pastoral imagination, such interpretation is invariably aligned with human longing to escape the human condition, to recover a past in which plant and animal life, the earth, the sea, and the sky did in fact provide sufficient comfort and reassurance to their human counterparts, who nevertheless identified themselves as distinct from nature. Such a longed-for situation is not paradoxical, for in paradox two mutually exclusive situations do exist simultaneously. Here, the exclusive situations of a human being being comfortably part of yet distinct from nature never did exist. Because the pastoral voice cannot recognize this impossibility, its only possible conclusion is frustration.

Although James Wright was less than a decade older than Oliver, his work gained significant national attention many years before hers did. He won the Yale Series of Younger Poets Award in 1954, and all of his books thereafter were attentively reviewed and eagerly read. His last book, *This Journey*, was published posthumously in 1982. Several of the pieces in this collection are prose poems, as are others in his late collections, including *To a Blossoming Pear Tree*, though not in his collected poems published in 1971. During his last decade, Wright published a few dozen prose poems, enough to suggest that he was committed to the form as well as to his lineated free verse.

Wright's poems remain in the Romantic tradition, similarly to Oliver's, and Wright's are also more pastoral than ecocritical, but they rely less on the intense personification that we often find in Oliver's work. In "The Turtle Overnight", the turtle functions metaphorically and permits the speaker to attempt a reconciliation with his past. That is, though the poem is somewhat less sentimental than the ones I discussed by Oliver, the poem's attention to nature nevertheless serves primarily to grant access to the speaker's interior life. The first paragraph describes the turtle physically, and it is the turtle's appearance that permits the speaker to relax into tenderness:

> I remember him last twilight in his comeliness. When it began to rain, he appeared in his accustomed place and emerged from his accustomed place and emerged from his shell as far as he could reach—feet, legs, tail, head. He seemed to enjoy the rain, the sweet-tasting rain that blew all the way across lake water to him from the mountains, the Alto Adige. It was as near as I've ever come to seeing a turtle take a pleasant bath in his natural altogether. All the legendary faces of broken old age disappeared from my mind, the thickened muscles under the chins, the nostrils brutal with hatred, the murdering eyes. He filled my mind with a sweet-tasting mountain rain, his youthfulness, his modesty as he washed himself all alone, his religious face. (Wright 1982: 7)

The opening description, with the turtle's double emergence, emphasizes its reptile form and its ability to entirely close itself off from the rest of the world. Here, the speaker interprets the animal's mood without asserting omniscience—the turtle "seemed to enjoy the rain". The most interesting shift in this paragraph occurs three sentences later, when the speaker reverts to memory, of faces that could resemble the turtle's but don't, the "legendary faces of broken old age". The details Wright provides, of "thickened muscles", "nostrils brutal with hatred", and "murdering eyes", could seem to describe a reptile, but they don't; they describe human faces he remembers, while the turtle's face is "religious". The human faces here are most savage, though Wright classifies them as "broken", not evil. The speaker projects "religious" onto the face of the turtle, though the speaker too, in his attitude toward other men, demonstrates mercy.

The speaker continues watching the turtle and interpreting its movements. Then, in the last two paragraphs, the vision of the turtle provides the speaker with access to another memory, this one more gentle:

Along his throat there are small folds, dark yellow as pollen shaken across a field of camomila. The lines on his face suggest only a relaxation, a delicacy in the understanding of the grass, like the careful tenderness I saw once on the face of a hobo in Ohio as he waved greeting to an empty wheat field from the flatcar of a freight train.

But now the train is gone, and the turtle has left his circle of empty grass. I look a long time where he was, and I can't find a footprint in the empty grass. So much air left, so much sunlight, and still he is gone. (Wright 1982: 7)

Again, the turtle's face evokes an image of a human face. The "hobo" the speaker recalls might have been described as the earlier men were, characterized by implicit violence, but instead it's as if the longer the speaker watches the turtle, the easier it becomes to interpret humanity hospitably. In this section, too, Wright's interpretation of the turtle's state is self-aware, for "the lines on his face suggest", rather than determine, "a relaxation". Through verbs like "seemed" and "suggest", the speaker conveys his own carefulness not to assume more than he can know.

Whereas much of the poem is nostalgic, the concluding paragraph becomes nearly mystical. Despite the early hour, the turtle has departed, as has, the poem implies, so much else. The speaker can find no evidence of the turtle's presence, and this paragraph hints at the mortality of us all, speaker, turtle, and reader alike. The speaker understands that he will one day be but a memory himself, like all of the faces he has recalled in this poem. The poem doesn't reveal a longing for an unrealized past so much as a longing for an eternal present. Yet, without time and the passing of time, without mortality, there would be no need for the mysticism Wright approaches here, no desire to transcend this world and yet remain in it, for mystical experiences by their nature exceed time. The speaker's close observation of the nature around him, particularly of one individual animal and its habits, releases him from any weighty self-consciousness.

"Camomila", another prose poem in the same collection, releases the speaker even further, as it thrusts him not only into his own history but into an evolutionary past. Here, foliage is compared not to the faces of hobos or old men but to people traumatized by war. After describing these people in some detail, Wright concludes the poem by superimposing his vision of the camomila upon these imagined faces:

Just like such brutally ransacked people, the camomila leaves turn their faces away. If I could look toward them long enough in this field, I think I would find them trying to hide their birthmarks and scars from me, pretending they had no beards or ribbons or long braids or half-legible letters from home hidden uselessly beneath their clothes. The faces of camomila leaves would wish me away again, wish me back into the sea again, wish me to leave them alone in peace. (Wright 1982: 78)

The only way peace can be achieved, it seems, is if evolution reverses itself and humanity utterly disappears. Humanity isn't the center or purpose of creation here but the inevitable means of its destruction. Unlike in "The Turtle Overnight" and some of Wright's other poems, "Camomila" does not gesture toward or long for mysticism. Wright's use of personification here also serves a different purpose from the personification in the other poems I've discussed. In "Camomila", the personification does not reveal thoughts or emotions of the plants in order to excuse human behavior. Instead, the personification creates ambiguity—is it the plant or the human faces of the "ransacked people" who are "trying to hide their birthmarks and scars"? Which form of life is "pretending they had no beards or ribbons or long braids"? Grammatically, the description refers to the plants, but the detail is so consistent and accumulative that the difference between the literal plants and the figurative humans becomes indistinct. This slippage reveals how the personification is critiquing, not celebrating, human life and its relation to other life forms. While this poem might remain within the Romantic tradition, centering the ordinary person and elevating emotion, its tone is much less overtly pastoral. It acknowledges a more complex understanding of "nature", as something that can provide comfort to human beings but whose purpose exceeds that act. Yet the poem is still characterized by an implicit longing, if not for an idyllic pastoral past, then for an idyllic geologic past, a time before humans arrived to rule through violence and destruction. This geologic past did in fact exist, unlike the pastoral past, but suggesting that only before mammals developed could humans (or plants) achieve peace is paradoxical at best.

To its end, though, the poem retains the first person singular. The speaker doesn't interpret the flowers/faces as suggesting "we" should disappear but only that the speaker should. Here is how the personification becomes complicated. For it is the flowers metaphorized as other war-weary people who want the speaker to leave, to devolve into a sea creature, not simply the flowers as flowers. If Wright had simply personified the flowers as thinking flora, the poem could have been interpreted to support universal human disappearance, but that's not what he has done. It is the image of other pained faces as much as the flowers themselves that evokes the speaker's longing for another place and time, another way of being. Readers, too, absorbing Wright's metaphor, position themselves with the speaker and understand their own place within a field of flowers as individuals adrift with longing (Woods 2009: 13). The speaker's longing for a resolution of his own individual loneliness or guilt keeps this poem in the Romantic tradition, for despite the concluding reference to pre-human eras, he is not suggesting that environmental catastrophe can be averted only by human extinction. Neither of those ideas—environmental catastrophe or human extinction—is even a part of this poem, and it is only in the context of subsequent ecocritical work that we even ask these post-Romantic questions of a poem like "Camomila".

Joy Harjo's "Invisible Fish" seems almost a response to Wright's "Camomila", at least to his interpretation of the flowers' final instruction. This poem, too, explores geologic time and the environmental effects of human choices. It concludes, though, not with a gesture toward recovery of that past but with a suggestion that human desire, once transcendent and mystical, has restrained itself, opting for the more limited material world. The poem itself is short, entire millennia collapsed into single sentences:

Invisible fish swim this ghost ocean now described by waves of sand, by water-worn rock. Soon the fish will learn to walk. Then humans will come ashore and paint dreams on the drying stone. Then later, much later, the ocean floor will be punctuated by pickup trucks, carrying the dreamers' descendants, who are going to the store. (Harjo 2002: 60)

The tone of this poem is initially much more neutral than the tone in Oliver's or Wright's work. The structure of the first sentence is interesting, in that the initial clause provokes the reader's curiosity, while the phrases that follow provide the context indirectly. The speaker is standing among evidence of the distant past, as many of us often do, but this speaker both notices the evidence and makes an intellectual leap into that past, that leap providing the content for her opening words. She notices the "waves of sand", perhaps fossilized rock but more likely a windswept landscape that includes the "water-worn rock". Neither of those features provides absolute evidence that a desert was formerly an ocean, but the speaker doesn't feel obligated to explain this fact; instead, she trusts her readers to follow her associative leaps, even when evidence for the leap has already occurred earlier in the sentence. The fish that swam in this space are invisible because they are no longer alive. They haunt the landscape just as the "ghost ocean" does. Despite the intervening millennia, their presence remains palpable to this speaker. The neutral tone, informative without being pedagogical, is particularly effective here, as the speaker seems to have experiential, rather than simply intellectual, knowledge of this past.

After marine life migrates to land, humans appear with their longings, their creative impulses, their need for self-expression and desire for connection. They discover how to convert crushed rocks or dissolved plants into a medium for communication and art, and they begin painting images on stones. These images last, longer than most of their corpses or personal effects. All these years later, Harjo's readers witness their paintings and etchings, unable to know exactly what they meant but able to understand, nevertheless, that these figures held symbolic value for their makers, just as much of the human creative impulse still originates with a desire to express emotions or responses that can never be fully expressed. Harjo suggests that the dreams and the paintings reveal some quality about these early humans, some more holistic link to the land from which they came and the spirits of which they are a part.

With the next sentence, however, the tone shifts dramatically. This last sentence is easily the longest in the poem, comprising nearly half of the poem's total length. "Then later, much later", Harjo says, though the actual passage of time between the previous sentence and the final one might be less than the amount of time that passed during the first half of the poem. She returns to the "ocean floor", though readers will recall that this ocean floor is the current sandy desert, and the future the poem gestures toward is the reader's present: "the ocean floor will be punctuated by pickup trucks, carrying the dreamers' descendants, who are going to the store." So many of us are always and everywhere "going to the store". Harjo's readers, her contemporaries, are no longer dreamers but only their descendants, alive because of dreams perhaps but lacking dreams themselves. Or if these current humans hold fast to dreams, they are the dreams of things that can be purchased at the store. Humans are no longer connected to the land or to their evolutionary ancestry. Instead, they are connected to consumerism, to planned obsolescence, to material products that all too often do end up at the bottom of the ocean or swirling within the Great Pacific Garbage Patch.

The tonal shift that occurs between the early material and the final sentence reveals how the prose poem can sometimes accomplish more than either a lineated poem or a short story or longer prose piece. The beginning of "Invisible Fish" relies on many of the elements of poetic craft—the imagery and figurative language of "ghost ocean" and "waves of sand", for example. Harjo's description of humans as creatures who "paint dreams on the drying stone" is particularly evocative, suggesting that human enterprises are more poetic than utilitarian. If the poem had ended here, readers might rightfully wonder how this form works to the material's advantage, rather than an arrangement of it into lines. The final sentence, however, is much less lyrical. The action is straightforward and ordinary, contrasting significantly with earlier humans' dreams. It sounds like prose. Harjo's choice to convey this material in a prose poem illustrates the flexibility of prose poetry, its ability to absorb and expand content that would be much more difficult to accomplish in either traditionally lineated poetry or in essays or fiction, the two most literary of prose genres.

The tone of this last sentence is debatable, hovering somewhere among irony, flippancy, and judgment. Any critique in this sentence, however, is directed not toward big business or big oil or any other capitalistic empire, at least not exclusively. The critique is most directly addressed toward ordinary Americans who have forsaken their heritage for trinkets. While corporations market their products to people such that people become consumers, the poem nevertheless implicates these people/consumers in their own susceptibility to manipulation. The identification of people as consumers replicates the identification of the environment as commodity, which "empties human life of the significance it had derived from living in and with nature and alienates individuals and communities from their rootedness in place" (Heise 2006: 507). Commitment to place has been especially significant to Native American nations and has been a continuous source of conflict since European contact. Harjo doesn't identify the individuals in the pick-up trucks as Native American. Regardless of their ethnicity, they have surrendered to this store-bought gratification; if they are Native American, they have also surrendered some of their national traditions, even if unintentionally or unconsciously, for Western values. Human dedication to consumerism, begun by Western cultures and exported via colonialism, is the primary contributive factor to our current ecological disaster and has been critiqued frequently by ethicists and theologians, if not always directly by literary critics (though such a critique might motivate much ecocriticism). John Linstrom, however, calls attention to religious narratives that could offer some alternatives to the identity of human as consumer:

> Christian theology certainly provides precedence for the humble servant model of life, as do many other rich mythologies. It may be that the proper counter to contemporary overconsumption and arrogant human disconnection and speciesism is a revival of such literatures of humility and frugality and a charge for writers to take up such themes ... Ultimately, however, it is hard to say whether or not postmodern consumerist secularism is a force adequately susceptible to the transformative potential of such literary efforts.[5] (Linstrom 2011: unpag.)

Some of the "other rich mythologies" Lindstrom refers to are certainly Native American, though a challenge for most westerners reading indigenous mythologies is to learn deeply from them rather than simply appropriate them.

An even shorter example of Harjo's prose poems, "If You Look with the Mind of the Swirling Earth," offers the reader a means toward ecological wisdom:

If you look with the mind of the swirling earth near Shiprock you become the land, beautiful. And understand how three crows at the edge of the highway, laughing, become three crows at the edge of the world, laughing. (Harjo 2002: 56)

Harjo states that the earth has a mind, implicitly a consciousness, without speculating about what that mind is thinking. Rather, access to the mind provides an embodied experience. A person becomes beautiful by becoming absorbed into the earth. The next sentence, in turning toward crows as avenues to wisdom, challenges stereotypic notions of the sublime, those grand landscapes or even grander mountains. The grammar of the sentence, the verb choice of "become," suggests that the crows change, until we realize how the object of "become" is identical with the subject. This sentence is actually a sentence fragment, with the subject, "you," implied from the previous sentence. The attentive reader is charged with understanding. What changes is an understanding of the boundary of the earth, the distinction between local and global. These locations, too, are identical, as "the edge of the highway" becomes "the edge of the world". This poem describes for readers, offers readers, a mystical experience, through immanence rather than transcendence. Here, it is as if a desire for transcendence is a mistaken urge. One must become the earth to know the boundaries of the earth and to understand that these boundaries are illusory.

Melissa Kwasny's poems also explore boundaries, of time and place and states of being. *Pictograph*, published in 2015, consists entirely of prose poems, all of which are informed by ecocritical concerns. Several of them are inspired by literal pictographs and petroglyphs while many others are set in environments where such markings, such dreams of the ancestors, as Harjo might say, could be found. In addition to birds, flowers, small and large mammals, and constellations, landscape is crucial to these poems. Caves, rocks, stalactites, ordinary dirt all suggest a life available to humans but different from the lives humans most often lead. Caves especially offer a journey into the earth as well as into the self, and the book often refers to these spaces as sacred.

In composing an entire collection of prose poems, Kwasny highlights the possibilities of the prose poem. The individual pieces are most often lyrical, and they take advantage of every poetic device excepting the line. In keeping with the lyric tradition, most of these prose poems attempt to capture a moment, examining one crystalized segment of space and time from multiple angles, rather than telling a full story that requires an expansion of time and likely also of space. Yet taken together, the sixty-one prose poems in this collection do imply a story, one that includes humans, a speaker, occasionally a "we", often also a "you". The story occurs both over millennia, as Harjo's "Invisible Fish" also does, and within discrete moments. Human experience, explored here through ancient traces, the pictographs and petroglyphs, forms part of this story, but the story itself exceeds the human. Because she considers such vast swaths of time, Kawsny challenges several aspects of the pastoral, which nearly always looks to a more recent past, a past that can be easily imagined. The ancestors Kwasny evokes in *Pictograph*, however, are virtually unknown and even unknowable to contemporary humans—we know about them only through tool shards or bones left in their fire pits and through the images they left on rocks and cave walls. The story Kwasny tells begins in the nearly unimaginable past and proceeds teleologically toward another unimaginable future, for as the book's last line describes the speaker, she is "being moved to some end" (Kwasny 2015: 65). The lyric aspects of this collection hint toward human purpose, while its narrative aspects suggest that such a purpose shall remain unknowable. Part of *Pictograph*'s accomplishment is its ability to explore this story that moves ever onward without centering any developed or even individual character, relying instead on geologic and geographic revelation.

The opening poem, "Outside the Little Cave Spot", illustrates one way an ecocritical voice can examine the relationships among humans and other elements of nature, here by producing the speaker's examination of conscience:

> The opening to the world is lopsided, irregular, dipping down like a lock of hair over someone's eye. Outside the cave: liquid gold, silver. Inside: as if flesh had been scraped off. Of the many ancient virtues, hope is the one you almost forgot. Limestone so dry and jagged, so pockmarked, it could cut your skin. It stops you. Like a clock stops: you are here. From inside, you see that you are often unkind to others. You shake hands without taking off your gloves. There is a motor of living water outside your ear. Little socket, the earth is frozen, cold and skinny and breaking down. You could lean out and lend your warmth to it. You sit here and the cries are muffled. You worry how, in the matter of a single letter reversed, a bit of food during a fast, a shade too dark for the sky-paint, sacred can turn scared and cause harm. This is how large you are. A thumbprint in a cliff. How much you are asked to keep in mind. (Kwasny 2015: 1)

Much of the effectiveness of this poem depends on its use of inside/outside metaphors, with each use functioning on multiple levels. The first phrase, "The opening to the world", could indicate either an entrance into the cave or an exit from the cave and into the world we generally think of as "the world". The first option seems more likely here, and more mysterious, for in entering a cave, one often becomes disoriented, unable to see. A few lines later we read, "From inside, you see . . ." Here the speaker, or the "you" who is a stand-in for both the speaker and the reader, is both inside the cave and inside herself. From inside the depths of the earth, that is, away from outer distractions, the speaker sees inside herself, and from that multiply-leveled inside, she witnesses her own imperfections. She recognizes a broad failure, first, that she is "often unkind to others", aligned with the fact that she shakes hands with her gloves on. That second statement could be interpreted simply as a breach of etiquette, but following the first failure, it serves as an example of unkindness. The speaker refuses to touch another skin to skin; she keeps her distance, separates herself from others. This separation, this viewing of oneself as a discrete entity rather than a nodule within a web of being, is the same separation that permits exploitation of other people and of the environment.

As long as the speaker remains inside and apart from others, she can feel safe, deaf to the world's cries. She realizes her presence is necessary, though, that the world needs the warmth inside her. She is part of the world's sacredness, but that sacredness can be realized only if she enters into the world. So why doesn't she do it? Fear. "You worry how, in the matter of a single letter reversed, a bit of food during a fast, a shade too dark for the sky-paint, sacred can turn scared and cause harm" (Kwasny 2015: 1). Many ecocritical poems demonstrate how the sacred has turned scared, Joy Harjo's "Invisible Fish" above, for example, wherein people become consumers, an identity wherein possession attempts to smother the fear that being isn't enough.

In Kawsny's poem, the speaker's fear isn't connected to consumerism but to the idea that she is necessary to the world and connected to other beings in the world. Her awe of the sacred threatens to slide into the awful recognition of her responsibility as a human being, a "large" human being, "A thumbprint in a cliff." Ordinarily, a thumbprint might seem trite, but here, in the opening poem of a collection about the permanence of pictographs, this metaphor reveals the long-term consequences of her being and her decisions. Time seems almost to lose its meaning in this poem, which depends less on sequence than on a potential eternity. Although human beings exist within time, time has become so vast that the speaker isn't concerned with measuring it in the usual way. She is not relating to nature as a conduit to an idyllic past; instead, past, present, and future seem to exist nearly simultaneously. Her recognition of the earth and of herself as sacred is authentic, readers realize, because rather than romanticize what might have been, she is frightened by the wholeness of all that is.

Another poem, "Cave System", more directly explores the human tendency to trivialize earth's majesty. The speaker is participating in a cave tour, where rocks, stalactites, and stalagmites are named for fairy tale figures. The tour's purpose is entertainment, and the guide's patter intended for participant consumption. The speaker refers briefly to geological time, the transition of Montana from ocean floor to land marked by water-carved caves. But then humans arrived, with their worries and needs and noise. What if this group of people had approached the cave differently, the speaker asks. "What if we had moved through it, instead, as a silence? No, slower, as if we were its blood? If we had acknowledged what a rare thing it is to be here? That the weather held for generations, hospitable to us" (Kwasny 2015: 11). That last line is crucial, the assertion that the earth extends hospitality to humans. The earlier details imply that these humans make poor guests, disregarding the value of what has been offered.

Kwasny's poems call their readers to conscience, as do some of Harjo's. Both poets call their readers to attention. In the work of these and other ecocritical poets, the earth and all that is in it is real, and that material reality motivates the poetry. Environmental details might provide imagery for figurative language, but their primary value, unlike in more pastoral poetry, is in material reality. Prose poetry, in merging lyric with story, and hence acknowledging time differently from how a lyric can alone, gestures toward the future as well as the past. For an ecocritical poet, that future is activist. The role of the poet is not simply to guide the reader in turning to nature for comfort, but to challenge the reader to recognize sites of true value.

Notes

1. Wright's friend and contemporary Robert Bly was one of the more influential American poets to experiment with prose poetry during the mid-twentieth century. His work in this genre, though, is most influenced by French and Spanish surrealists, even given his simultaneous attraction to the rural life. In a comprehensive survey of American prose poetry, Bly would be a prominent figure. Aside from perhaps Wright, his direct influence on the specific poets I consider here is less significant.
2. It is interesting to note that J. Scott Bryson points out that many twentieth-century poets moved away from the pathetic fallacy as an approach to nature, rejecting that common nineteenth-century mode (Bryson "Introduction" 2002: 2–3). Oliver's poetry, however, is rife with it, though she composed most of her work in the last quarter of the twentieth century and the beginning of the twenty-first. Her work is also particularly popular with

people who don't otherwise read much poetry. I am not interested in criticizing Oliver for her popularity—would that more poets could be so widely read—but it might be worth exploring how or why (or if) this otherwise rejected technique contributes to her popularity in an age of climate disaster.
3. Here and throughout this essay, my readings illustrate Michel Delville's comment that referring to a piece as a prose poem, rather than, for example, a short story, invites readers to read "leisurely", spending more time mulling over individual words, phrases, metaphors, and other figurative language (Delville 1998: 109). Foregrounding the word "poem" encourages readers not to read primarily for narrative, wherein the narrative hook hurries readers along, the eye tumbling past rather than settling upon the specific language.
4. Discussing some other of Oliver's poems, Janet McNew suggests that Oliver's address to the reader is a result of her attention to the material world, rather than the symbolic world of language: "Oliver gives primary emphasis not to the symbolic order of poetic language but to the more literal power of poetry to invoke inarticulate, intuitive experience itself. The frequent imperatives of her poems . . . insist on moving outside art, into the lives of trees, damselflies, owls, and ponds" (McNew 1989: 74). The shift from singular to plural in this poem is more invitational than imperative, but what she is doing in this poem in gesturing toward Tibet within a poem focused on nature is not so much "moving outside art" as it is redefining the boundaries of nature.
5. Bryson also describes humility as a component of contemporary ecopoetry, in contrast to some other varieties of nature poetry (Bryson 2002b: 6). See also Gilchrist for a discussion of the relationship of ethics to ecocriticism (Gilchrist 2002: 26).

Works Cited

Buell, Lawrence (1991), *The Environmental Imagination: Thoreau, Nature Writing, and the Formation of American Culture.* Cambridge, MA: Harvard University Press.
Bryson, J. Scott (ed.) (2002a), *Ecopoetry: A Critical Introduction.* Salt Lake City: University of Utah Press.
Bryson, J. Scott (2002b) "Introduction," in Bryson (2002a), 1–13.
Christensen, Laird (2002), "The Pragmatic Mysticism of Mary Oliver," in Bryson (2002a), 135–52.
Cuddon, J. A. and M. A. R. Habib (eds) (2014), *The Penguin Dictionary of Literary Terms and Literary Theory*, New York: Penguin.
Delville, Michel (1998), *The American Prose Poem: Poetic Form and the Boundaries of Genre*, Gainsville, FL: University of Florida Press.
Elder, John (1996), *Imagining the Earth: Poetry and the Vision of Nature*, Athens, GA: University of Georgia Press.
Gifford, Terry (2013), "Pastoral, Anti-Pastoral, and Post-Pastoral as Reading Strategies," in *Critical Insights: Nature and the Environment*, ed. Scott Slovic. Ipswich, MA: Salem Press, 42–61.
Gilchrist, David (2002), "Regarding Silence: Cross-Cultural Roots of Ecopoetic Meditation," in Bryson (2002a), 17–28.
Harjo, Joy (2002), *How We Became Human: New and Selected Poems: 1975–2001*, New York: Norton.
Heise, Ursula K. (2006), "The Hitchhiker's Guide to Ecocriticism," *PMLA*, vol. 121, no. 2, pp. 503–16, <https://www.jstor.org/stable/25486328> (last accessed April 3, 2019).
Horvath, Brooke (1992), "The Prose Poem and the Secret Life of Poetry," *The American Poetry Review*, vol. 21, no. 5, pp. 11–14, <https://www.jstor.org/stable/27780821> (last accessed April 3, 2019).

Johnson, Robert (1999). "Inspired Lines: Reading Joy Harjo's Prose Poems," *American Indian Quarterly*, vol. 23, nos 3/4, <https://www.jstor.org/stable/11858326> (last accessed November 12, 2019).

Kwasny, Melissa (2015), *Pictograph*. Minneapolis: Milkweed Editions.

Linstrom, John (2011), "Seeking a Center for Ecopoetics," *Valparaiso Poetry Review*, vol. 12, no. 2, <https://www.valpo.edu/vpr/v12n2/v12n2prose/linstromseeking.php> (last accessed January 8, 2016).

Love, Glen A. (1992), "Et in Arcadia Ego: Pastoral Theory Meets Ecocriticism," *Western American Literature*, vol. 27, no. 3, pp. 195–207, <https://www.jstor.org/stable/43024440> (last accessed April 3, 2019).

McNew, Janet (1989), "Mary Oliver and the Tradition of Romantic Nature Poetry," *Contemporary Literature*, vol. 30, no. 1, pp. 59–77, <http://www.jstor.org/stable/1208424> (last accessed August 19, 2015).

Nielsen, Dorothy M. (1993), "Prosopopoeia and the Ethics of Ecological Advocacy in the Poetry of Denise Levertov and Gary Snyder," *Contemporary Literature*, vol. 34, no. 4, pp. 691–713, <http://www.jstor.org/stable/1208806> (last accessed August 19, 2015).

Oliver, Mary (2005), *New and Selected Poems, Volume Two*, Boston: Beacon Press.

"A Simple Guide into Ecocriticism," *A Research Guide for Students*, <https://www.aresearchguide.com/ecocriticism.html> (last accessed November 8, 2019).

Tennyson, Alfred Lord (2004), *In Memoriam*, ed. Erik Gray, New York: Norton.

Thomson, Jeffrey (2002) "'Everything Blooming Bows Down in the Rain': Nature and the Work of Mourning in the Contemporary Elegy," in Bryson (2002a), 153–61.

Thompson, Roger (2002), "Emerson, Divinity, and Rhetoric in Transcendentalist Nature Writing and Twentieth-Century Ecopoetry," in Bryson (2002a), 29–38.

Woods, Gioia (2009), "A Fairer House Than Prose: Poetry, Science, and the Metaphors That Blind," *Interdisciplinary Literary Studies*, vol. 10, no. 2, pp. 5–16, <https://www.jstor.org/stable/41210015> (last accessed April 3, 2019).

Wright, James (1982) *This Journey*, New York: Vintage.

Zawacki, Andrew (2000), "Accommodating Commodity: The Prose Poem." *The Antioch Review* vol. 58, no. 3, 286–303, <https://www.jstor.org/stable/4614021> (last accessed April 3, 2019).

15

Grzegorz Wróblewski's *Kopenhaga* and the Process of Inscription

Piotr Gwiazda

In this essay I discuss several issues that arose when I was translating Grzegorz Wróblewski's book of prose poems *Kopenhaga* from Polish into English. I hope these reflections will offer new insights into the prose poem genre, especially its movement across national and linguistic borders. My essay also places the genre in relation to the concept of world literature, defined for my purposes as "a mode of circulation and of reading" (Damrosch 2003: 3).

I should state at the outset that I view translation as a practice that requires a great deal of craft and expertise, but also some deliberation and strategizing. As much as it entails a pursuit of formal and semantic correspondence, translation calls for a reflection on what it means to introduce a foreign text into a new cultural context—what Lawrence Venuti calls the "process of inscription":

> This process of inscription operates at every stage in the production, circulation, and reception of the translation. It is initiated by the very choice of a foreign text to translate, always an exclusion of other foreign texts and literatures, which answers to particular domestic interests. It continues most forcefully in the development of a translation strategy that rewrites the foreign text in domestic dialects and discourses, always a choice of certain domestic values to the exclusion of others. And it is further complicated by the diverse forms in which the translation is published, reviewed, read, and taught, producing cultural and political effects that vary with different institutional contexts and social positions. (Venuti 1998: 67)

The "process of inscription" became salient to me as I began translating Wróblewski's *Kopenhaga* in the autumn of 2009. Specifically, I found myself confronting the following issues: (1) the problem of translating hybrid genres; (2) the movement of hybrid genres across national borders, with the related question of transnational literary influence; (3) the challenge of annotating translations in the age of the internet; (4) the status of English as a global language and its implications for the concept of world literature.

I

Born in Gdańsk and raised in Warsaw, Wróblewski moved to Copenhagen in 1985 at the age of twenty-three, just as he was getting noticed as one of Poland's most promising younger poets. Although he still lives in Copenhagen, and is now a naturalized

Danish citizen, he writes almost exclusively in Polish. A playwright and essayist as well as poet, he publishes frequently in the country of his birth, releasing approximately one volume per year. His work has been translated into several languages, among them Danish, Russian, Czech, Spanish, and English.[1] Wróblewski is also a talented visual artist who has exhibited his paintings in galleries in Denmark, Germany, England, and Poland.

Kopenhaga, Wróblewski's sixth book, first appeared as a collection of 103 texts from a small press, Kartki, in Białystok, Poland, in 2000. It was reprinted by Wydawnictwa Uniwersytetu Warszawskiego (University of Warsaw Press) in 2010 as the opening section of *Pomyłka Marcina Lutra: proza i szkice kopenhaskie* (Martin Luther's Error: Prose and Sketches from Copenhagen). The prose poem has never been a popular genre in Poland, at least compared with other European countries or the United States—a reminder that while some genres migrate easily across national and linguistic borders, others do not.[2] So it is not surprising that reviewers in Poland tended to identify *Pomyłka Marcina Lutra* as a collection of "poetic prose", "experimental prose", or "essays", "sketches", and "journals" as a way of distinguishing it from Wróblewski's numerous books of verse. In the prominent Polish literary journal *Twórczość*, Krzysztof Gryko referred to it as "a series of well-thought-out notations, accounts of reality, not lacking in strong ironic punchlines" (Gryko 2011: 99 [my translation]). In light of this terminological ambiguity, my first practical consideration had to do with determining the text's genre. I needed to find the most suitable way of introducing it to anglophone editors, publishers, and eventually readers.

Unlike the Polish reviewers, I chose to call *Kopenhaga* a collection of "prose poems". Why? It seemed clear to me that Wróblewski's text exhibits the major characteristics of the prose poem genre, especially its classic French variety best exemplified by Charles Baudelaire's *Paris Spleen* (first published as *Le Spleen de Paris* in 1869): thematic cohesion (with a focus on the self's uneasy interaction with the world), serial construction, brevity, musicality. Like *Paris Spleen*, *Kopenhaga* is a cumulative work, written over the course of a decade while the author was also writing and publishing poems in verse. The individual pieces range between one and several paragraphs in length, with some as brief as one sentence (unlike Baudelaire, however, Wróblewski prefers no titles). While the basic unit of composition is the sentence, the author often introduces the kind of patterning that is typical of verse, especially repetition, as well as paratactic structures and linguistic density that are characteristic of modern poetry. All these features assist Wróblewski in conveying the tragicomic sensibility of his narrator, the "lyrical movements of the soul, undulations of reverie, the flip flops of consciousness", as Baudelaire described his own experiments with the prose poem (in Keith Waldrop's translation) (Baudelaire 2009: 3).

My designation of *Kopenhaga* as a collection of prose poems created an unexpected—though not necessarily unwelcome—generic instability when it came to journal and book publication. The online magazines *AGNI Online* and *Poetry at Sangam* featured excerpts under the heading "poetry", as did the print-based journals *Colorado Review* and *The Nation*. The editors of *Denver Quarterly*, which features no genre categories in its table of contents, published three texts on three separate pages, thereby treating them as stand-alone poems. The editors of *Seneca Review*, while also not designating the genre, fitted as many as nine texts into three pages, clearly treating them as prose rather than poetry. In 2013, *Kopenhaga* was published in book form by the US-based Zephyr Press, which specializes in contemporary poetry translations from Eastern Europe and Asia. Reviewers by and large accepted my designation, though in *Three Percent* Vincent Francone was partial to the term "fragments", while in *The Antioch Review* John Taylor commented: "it is no less useful to think as well of Wróblewski's pieces, which include many personal reflections, on-the-spot notes, and diary-like jottings, as *prose* that is neither specifically poetic nor experimental, but rather concise, pithy, and provocative" (Francone 2014; Taylor 2015: 573). What I learned from the experience is that although since Suzanne Bernard's pioneering study the prose poem has had its own history, theory, and canon, categories like "prose poem" and "prose poetry" are still used unsystematically by editors, publishers, and reviewers. But my point is (going back to Venuti's concept of "inscription") that the translator's strategy sometimes entails the need to identify the right *form* for the translation as much as the right *word*.

Interestingly, Wróblewski himself does not have strong feelings on this topic. In the 1990s he published two pieces from *Kopenhaga* as verse rather than prose, just like Baudelaire had done with some poems from *Paris Spleen*. During our book tour in the United States in April 2014, when I asked him directly whether I was justified in describing the book as a collection of prose poems, he responded: "Yes, because it's partly poetry and partly prose. Some texts are closer to poetry, others to prose. I myself have used the term 'essays' [*szkice*] to emphasize the mixture of these two elements. But there is no reason to worry about definitions. You can choose any definition you want, as long as you can defend it" (Wróblewski 2014). However, there was another formal aspect of the volume in which the author's input was critical. Translators occasionally alter the texts they translate; they expand or abridge them on the basis of artistic or practical considerations. At Wróblewski's urging, I translated the entirety of the 2000 edition as well as several texts he composed in the following decade and included in other parts of *Pomyłka Marcina Lutra*—specifically those that in my view complemented the earlier sequence stylistically and thematically. At that point, he and I worked together to incorporate those additional parts into the 2000 edition. This means that in terms of structure my translation of *Kopenhaga* published by Zephyr Press differs substantially from the Polish original. In fact, strictly speaking it has no Polish original but is an independent, collaboratively produced text.

II

As my earlier quotation from Baudelaire indicates, the prose poem often features an autobiographical component. It conveys the self's interaction with the world, exemplifying what Tzvetan Todorov calls "a thematics of duality, contrast, opposition" (Todorov 1983: 64). Deeply emotional if not expressionistic, *Kopenhaga* is suffused with the hypersensitivity of its narrator, who functions as the author's fictional representation (and is even identified as "Grzegorz Wróblewski" on two occasions). Like *Paris Spleen*, the book offers a picture of the horrors of contemporary society as seen by the self-described "neurotic stranger from nowhere" (Wróblewski 2013: 87). It also contains enough allusions to and parallels with Baudelaire's volume of "little poems in prose" to convince me that Wróblewski enters into an imagined dialogue with the French poet—and so with the entire prose poem tradition as well.

I borrow the term "imagined dialogue" from Gordana P. Crnković's study of Eastern European literature in conversation with its American and English counterparts. What she means by the term are the unexpected ways in which literary works respond to one another outside of the context of their respective national traditions. As she argues, such dialogues "make connections among literary works of various national origins, connections that do not have to have confirmation in 'facts' outside of the particular act of reading" (Crnković 1999: 12). In my introduction to *Kopenhaga* I mention affinities between Wróblewski and the key figures of American modernism like William Carlos Williams and Charles Reznikoff, as well as some later US poets like Charles Bukowski, Bob Kaufman, and Ron Padgett. But it is the influence of the nineteenth-century French poet that seems particularly noteworthy in this context, since it is the only literary relationship that rises to the level of "imagined dialogue" by Crnković's definition.

This dialogue takes many forms. Both *Paris Spleen* and *Kopenhaga* include texts that are primarily lyrical (capturing moments of reverie or powerful emotion), discursive (incorporating quoted speech and borrowed material), and narrative (based on the author's observations or experiences). Both have private and public aspects, with depictions of intense psychological states frequently overlapping with strident social critique. They feature various tropes and genres, such as the address, the advice, the anecdote, the aphorism, the dialogue, the diary, the reportage, the essay, and even something that approaches the short story. They express a range of attitudes and moods, some of which do not portray the author in the most positive light. Each volume describes a metropolis, the symbol of the new social, political, and economic order (Copenhagen literally means "merchant's port"). Each is populated by scores of characters, many of them real-life individuals or friends and acquaintances of the author.

Then there are the thematic parallels. The stranger who, in the opening poem of *Paris Spleen*, professes his love for the clouds becomes, in Wróblewski's book, the mentally ill Clausen who excitedly points to the clouds while repeating "There! There!" "What did Clausen see in the sky? Probably no one will ever know," the narrator concludes. The "old woman" whose withered appearance frightens a newborn baby is reinvented as "the elderly" on the Children's Radio in Denmark: "Children [are] talking about old people: *old people stink, they dress funny, they have unfashionable hairdos.*" The artist who associates the immensity of the sky and sea with delight and dismay returns in the form of the ebullient "Marcus" in *Kopenhaga*: "It's wonderful to live by the sea!" The drunk who gives New Year greetings to a donkey and by doing so exemplifies, in Baudelaire's view, the stupidity of the French corresponds to precautionary articles published in Copenhagen newspapers: "In Scandinavia everything is well-researched and prearranged. Even the cure for New Year's Day hangover" (Wróblewski 2013: 41, 93, 105, 149).

So far I have mentioned the first four poems in *Paris Spleen* and found what I believe to be their analogs in *Kopenhaga*. Of course, not every poem has a counterpart, but similarities continue, especially if we read the two volumes in terms of thematic clusters. Baudelaire often describes his apartment as a place of solitude, a refuge from what he calls "the tyranny of the human face" (Baudelaire 2009: 18). So does Wróblewski, especially when he depicts a prolonged period of isolation—"zero contact with the outside world"—in the only titled poem in the collection "Seventeen

Days" (Wróblewski 2013: 151). Baudelaire often juxtaposes crowds with outsiders and loners, stating famously: "those who cannot people their solitude can never be alone in a busy crowd" (Baudelaire 2009: 22). Wróblewski too contemplates the human multitude, but his alienation is heightened by his position as an immigrant confronting what appear to him comfortable, well-ordered lives of the Danish middle class. Baudelaire's exhortation to "be drunk" resurfaces in Wróblewski's numerous references to alcohol and drug use; like his Romantic-era predecessor, he writes about the pursuit of altered states, the allure of sleep, the temptation of suicide. Both volumes feature the male gaze: Baudelaire's observations of women, especially widows and mothers, have an equivalent in Wróblewski's meditation on "a young, beautiful woman at the bus stop [. . .] Watching her, I imagine how she will look in thirty or forty years" (Wróblewski 2013: 23). The beautiful Parisian coquette Dorothea taking a stroll on a sunny afternoon is transformed into nameless prostitutes often mentioned in *Kopenhaga*. Indeed, both poets seem to be fascinated by the figure of the prostitute, "seller and sold in one", as Walter Benjamin put it in one of his essays on Baudelaire (Benjamin 2009: 41).

Another shared element between the two volumes is the rejection of public morality, often under the guise of satire. The acquaintance in *Paris Spleen* who intentionally gives a false coin to a beggar is not unlike the character in *Kopenhaga* identified simply as "R" who daily rearranges the "coffers" in his apartment out of fear of thieves (Wróblewski 2013: 61). Two destitute Parisians who engage in "fratricidal war" over a piece of bread anticipate the ethnic conflicts and civil wars of the late twentieth century—Cambodia, Congo, Kosovo—which Wróblewski references (Baudelaire 2009: 30). Baudelaire has only contempt for politics, at one point invoking Pascal's dictum that identifies the world's problems with our inability to stay alone in our room. Compare with Wróblewski: "Again, life goes on without me. . . Their little shitty revolutions—outside my well-insulated window!" (Wróblewski 2013: 141). These instances of human deprivation are contrasted with images of artistic fulfillment. Baudelaire's celebration of artistic genius, embodied by Franz Liszt in "The Thyrsus", finds its equivalent in Wróblewski's tributes to his fellow artists Robert Frank, Aleksandras Vozbinas, Henrik Nordbrandt, Tom Palazzolo, among others. Lastly, the two poets write about animals with greater sympathy than they reserve for humans. Baudelaire's admiration for an aging, ugly thoroughbred parallels Wróblewski's eccentric love of ponies: "Nothing moves me as much as these small, frisky, thick-maned creatures. (Their perverse tails and yellow teeth!)" (Wróblewski 2013: 63).

The existential melancholy to which Baudelaire gives the English word "spleen" becomes Wróblewski's "samotność kosmiczna" ["cosmic loneliness"] (Wróblewski 2013: 25). Baudelaire converses with his soul about his desire to travel to Lisbon, Rotterdam or Batavia (Djakarta): "Anywhere! anywhere! out of this world" (Baudelaire 2009: 93). Wróblewski too entertains fantasies of escape, for instance to Barcelona, where one poem is actually set. But even then "you always return to the starting point. The Master Plan: your-hard-wired appetites; people you are going to meet; death" (Wróblewski 2013: 117). In another poem Baudelaire finds himself onboard a passenger ship; unlike other passengers, he appears to be in no hurry to reach the land while he praises the "incomparable beauty" of the sea (Baudelaire 2009: 72). Early in *Kopenhaga* Wróblewski recalls his stay on the ship *Norrøna*, which in the mid-1980s was designated by the Danish Red Cross as a temporary refugee camp: "A thousand crazy, anxious people from practically all over the world! Muslims, Christians, extremists, housewives. Bearded politicians and loud, mustached provocateurs from countries in the former Bloc. Owners of ice cream stands (eastern Poland), Palestinian kamikazes, Tamil Tigers, thieves, hookers, smugglers ... Among them Grzegorz Wróblewski and his wife Beata" (Wróblewski 2013: 7). Quite a contrast to Baudelaire's fellow passengers impatiently awaiting their return home.

I could go on ... but I think my point is made. *Kopenhaga* echoes some of the most disturbing findings of *Paris Spleen*. Reality seems as puzzling to Wróblewski as it does to Baudelaire; here as in the rest of his *oeuvre* the Polish poet "notes a world of widening disjunctions between nature and civilization in which humans are diminished by larger mechanizing forces", according to Kacper Bartczak (Bartczak 2005: 88). At the same time, Wróblewski demonstrates a genuine interest in other human beings, however diminished or deformed they may have become; the impulse behind his report is scientific curiosity (perhaps as an antithesis to "cosmic loneliness") rather than artistic estrangement. In this respect he significantly differs from Baudelaire. In *Paris Spleen* Baudelaire depicts himself as a "true Parisian" (Baudelaire 2009: 27) rubbing shoulders with his fellow city-dwellers. But his overall disdain for them creates a sense of moral superiority that in effect produces, as Peter Nicholls argues, "an essentially closed model of the self" (Nicholls 1995: 4). Wróblewski comes across as less indignant and less antisocial than Baudelaire. A newcomer from behind the Iron Curtain, he is estranged from but also fascinated by his new surroundings. He is not a "solitary walker" (one of Baudelaire's alternative titles for his collection) but, again in Bartczak's words, "a patient, detached and inquisitive collector" (Bartczak 2005: 88) of the manners and morals of his adopted country.

When I asked Wróblewski about possible connections between *Paris Spleen* and *Kopenhaga*, he responded similarly to how he would later respond to my question about the book's genre. He accepted my interpretation as long as it made sense to me: "Such traces—they appear and disappear. All in all, it's hard to say WHO has been my most inspiring model" (Wróblewski 2011 [my translation]). Of course he may have easily come across a Polish translation of *Paris Spleen* during his formative years in Poland; at least two such translations existed in the late 1970s and early 1980s. Influence is always a vague and mysterious phenomenon, but when it takes place outside the same national or linguistic framework what matters more than particular intertextual gestures is the adoption of certain forms and genres, and even themes and attitudes. Moreover, as Crnković argues, the concept of "imagined dialogue" depends less on identifying the proof of deliberate borrowing or rewriting than on the reader's interpretive choices, what she calls a "freedom" to bring together two writers who seem to have, at least at first, little in common. Such an affinity is "created by a reader who simultaneously reads these writers' books coming from different cultural contexts and who sees how these books are interconnected and implicated in each other, and how they—without knowing it—indeed talk to each other" (Crnković 1999: 13).

There are multiple structural and thematic parallels between *Paris Spleen* and *Kopenhaga*, as I have tried to demonstrate; Baudelaire's volume clearly provided Wróblewski with a formula for creating a kind of self-portrait while also creating a portrait of his age. But the main story here is the durability and flexibility of the prose poem genre.

As Franco Moretti argues, "the morphology of hybrid texts is an invaluable vantage point from which to observe the endless spiral of hegemony and resistance created by world literature" (Moretti 2013: 134). Viewed from the standpoint of world literature, the relationship between *Paris Spleen* and *Kopenhaga* presents an example of the prose poem genre traveling from center to periphery, or at least semi-periphery. The movement assumes a dynamic interaction, perhaps even tension, between the foreign form perfected by Baudelaire and the local content supplied by Wróblewski's personal experiences and inimitable literary style. It is already a complex movement, occurring across space (Paris to Copenhagen via Warsaw) and time (mid-nineteenth to late twentieth and even early twenty-first century). But it does not end here.

III

Another issue that arose while I was translating Wróblewski's *Kopenhaga* had to do with the amount of explanatory material to be included in the published volume. Translation always involves a transfer of cultural knowledge. Shoshana Blum-Kulka has written about "shifts of coherence" that take place during the process:

> Whether real world or literary, allusions to persons, places or other texts may play a central role in building up the coherence of a given story. Writers themselves may be aware of the fact that their reference network is not shared by their readers and take pains to explain it in footnotes or otherwise. In translation the translator becomes the judge as to the extent to which he or she finds it necessary to explain the source text's reference network to the target-language audience. (Blum-Kulka 2000: 306)

Such judgments, however, are never easy. On the one hand, the translator may be tempted to explicate every single potentially unclear reference in order to maintain the coherence of the text. On the other hand, the translator may run the risk of becoming overzealous, especially if he or she underestimates the audience's ability to reconstruct "the reference network" on their own.

After weighing several options, I decided to take a minimalistic approach to annotation (three footnotes, to be exact: one glossing the name of the Warsaw neighborhood in which Wróblewski grew up, one clarifying wordplay specific to the Polish language, one indicating a dedication). A highly allusive text, *Kopenhaga* features dozens of references to Denmark (Assistens Cemetery, Damhus Tivoli, Christianshavn, Prime Minister Poul Nyrup Rasmussen, Queen Margrethe II, among others) and Poland (Dolny Mokotów, Świnoujście, Kraków, Tadeusz Brzozowski, Stanisław Wyspiański, among others). All these serve as contexts for the author's comparison of places and people. But the volume also includes many references that have nothing to do with either Denmark or Poland. As Wróblewski and I realized, in order to make the translation fully transparent to anglophone readers we would have to equip most of the poems with explanatory notes. Here is a representative excerpt:

> Genialny Ignacy Wieniewski! Oto rodzynek z jego wstępu do *Iliady:Np. znamiennym epitetem, jakim Homer stale obdarza piękną boginię Herę, a czasem i urodziwe śmiertelniczki, jest 'wolooka'. Nam wydaje się to wątpliwym komplementem i budzi w nas asocjacje i reakcje wyobrażeniowe inne, niż w owej odległej starożytności. Podobnie

zadziwia nas porównanie Menelaja, który na początku XVII księgi Iliady *staje nad trupem Patrokla, by go bronić, do krowy stojącej nad cielęciem. Wrażenie na poły komiczne tego porównania, użytego notabene w scenie szczególnie tragicznej, jest miarą zmienności smaku i upodobań w różnych epokach.*

Czy ktoś jeszcze chodzi w skórzanych kurtkach 'ramoneskach'? (Coraz mniejsze odległości!) Nawet Johnny Rotten (wywiad) uważa, że to była tylko zmowa producentów odzieży. A starcy w przedpotopowych kapeluszach? Ben Webster grający w bilarda? Polski poeta Julian Tuwim (w wierszu *Spacer fantastyczny w lesie Fontainebleau*):*Jedno wiem: trzeba iść, trzeba iść / Naprzód w leśnym zielonym obłędzie.*Na to nikt już nie da się nabrać! Nasze dziewczyny muszą być teraz chore na anoreksję ('wolookie' są znowu mile widziane!), moda na duże piersi skończyła się, gdy zaczynałem pić wódkę (obecnie zaleca się ponownie wino, seks i marihuanę).

[The brilliant Ignacy Wieniewski! A nugget from his preface to the *Iliad*: *For instance, Homer consistently bestows on the beautiful goddess Hera, and occasionally also on comely mortal women, the distinctive epithet 'ox-eyed.' This seems a dubious compliment to us, producing associations and imaginative reactions that are different from those found in remote antiquity. Likewise we are surprised by the comparison of Menelaus, who at the beginning of Book XVII of the* Iliad *stands protectively over the dead body of Patroclus, to a cow standing over her calf. The simile, which produces an almost comical effect despite being used in a particularly tragic scene, is a measure of the changing tastes and predilections across different eras.*

Does anyone still wear the Ramones-style leather jackets? (Distances are collapsing!) Even Johnny Rotten (in an interview) says they were just a marketing ploy of the clothing industry. What about the old-timers in antediluvian hats? Ben Webster at the pool table? The Polish poet Julian Tuwim (in his poem 'An Extraordinary Walk through the Forest of Fontainebleau'): *One thing I know: I must go, I must go / Forward through the forest's green madness.* No one is fooled by that anymore. Our young women suffer from anorexia (the 'ox-eyed' would be welcome once more!). The vogue for large breasts was over when I started to drink vodka. (Wine, sex, and marijuana are again being recommended.)] (Wróblewski 2013: 52–3)

As Wróblewski told me, when a version of *Kopenhaga* in Danish translation appeared in 2001 it included only sixty-three poems because of the obscurity of certain references and allusions. The above poem became one of the casualties of that domesticating strategy, even though it perfectly exemplifies the book's citational technique and even one of its major themes. The rapid succession of temporal and spatial frames is almost vertigo-inducing. Wróblewski follows a scholarly commentary on Homer with a paraphrase of an interview with a British punk rocker. He links an African American saxophonist's game of pool with a Polish poet's imaginary stroll through a Parisian suburb. With a typical sense of urgency (note the frequency of exclamatory and interrogative sentences, quite common in *Kopenhaga*) he brings together epic and song, elite and mass culture, and a whole gamut of attitudes toward sex, death, the body, even fashion. As the "nugget" from Wieniewski teaches, every historical age has its own systems of beliefs and behaviors. But the slogan of globalization suggests otherwise: in the postmodern era of fluidity and fragmentation, everything *au courant* is already *passé*. Distances are collapsing indeed!

Which of the above references should be annotated? It is perhaps worth mentioning that Wróblewski alludes to the 1967 documentary film *Big Ben: Ben Webster in Europe*, which features the musician playing pool in Amsterdam, or the fact that Julian Tuwim was a popular twentieth-century poet who, like Wróblewski, often wrote about cities. But ultimately those would be examples of hyperannotation, because they would do little in terms of maintaining the text's coherence (I should mention that the Polish version carries no footnotes whatsoever). Even if certain references in this or other poems in *Kopenhaga* require contextualization, the difficulty this poses is merely contingent. It is the most common and most easily resolved kind of difficulty according to George Steiner, which simply entails looking things up in a dictionary or encyclopedia.

And the practice of looking things up has changed considerably since the year Steiner published his essay on difficulty (1978). As David Bellos observes, the expertise and skills of individual translators and the basic design of online tools like Google Translate—a widely used statistical machine translation system—can be regarded as "parallel reflections of our common humanity" (Bellos 2011: 257). The same can be said about Google Search and Wikipedia—again widely used if unavoidably imperfect reference tools in the digital age. The World Wide Web has not only revolutionized the way people communicate with one another but also the way they access, process, and share information. Again, in many respects *Kopenhaga*, most of which was composed throughout the 1990s, portrays the advent of the digital age—its new structures of knowledge, its new concepts of what it means to be in the world. (A couple of poems actually include links to popular websites.) Precisely because of their indiscriminate, always self-revising character, Google Search and Wikipedia seemed appropriate reference tools for my translation. This should not mean, of course, that Wróblewski's references and allusions are superficial or merely ornamental. Rather, they function as vectors, directing readers to specific persons, places, and cultural artifacts, and thus enabling more dialogic, interactive encounters with the text.

My goal was also to underscore the transnational character of *Kopenhaga*. The above excerpt is a discreet tribute to Ignacy Wieniewski, a Polish literary historian, essayist, and translator of Greek and Latin classics who settled in London after World War II. But the fact is that Wróblewski's book features numerous references to émigré or at least transnational writers, artists, and musicians. These include Stefan Themerson, a Polish intellectual who spent most of his creative life in London; Jonas Mekas, a Lithuanian-born American filmmaker; Dexter Gordon, an American jazz musician who lived for several years in the Copenhagen district Valby; Karen Blixen (Isak Dinesen), a Danish author who spent over a decade of her life in Kenya. But I felt that it would be more effective to have the readers make this discovery on their own; I did not want them always to rely on the safety net of a footnote, however judiciously chosen. This strategy of eschewing notes seems to go against Vladimir Nabokov's famous ideal of scholarly translation, "footnotes reaching up like skyscrapers to the top of this or that page so as to leave only the gleam of one textual line between commentary and eternity" (Nabokov 2000: 83). But my argument is that Nabokov's ideal can be attained as long as translators are flexible about their control over the text and its reception.

IV

Yet another issue I faced when translating Wróblewski's *Kopenhaga* concerned the primary material from which poems are made: language. As Marjorie Perloff argues, "the materiality of the poem [. . .] is always central, even in translation" (Perloff 2010: 105). One sure way of enhancing the poem's materiality (linguistic, formal, typographical) is to print the source text and the translation on opposing pages. This was in fact the format in which Zephyr Press published *Kopenhaga*, following its own decades-old precedent. Regardless of the availability of this option, translators themselves often do their best to refashion the material aspects of the source text. Even when translating extensive works of fiction, they strive, as Edith Grossman puts it, to "recreate as far as possible within the alien system of a second language all the characteristics, vagaries, quirks, and stylistic peculiarities of the work we are translating" (Grossman 2011: 10). While translating *Kopenhaga*, I also tried to produce the closest equivalent of the material features of the source text. Owing to differences between Polish and English linguistic conventions, on several occasions I adjusted punctuation and typography, sentence and paragraph length, but in doing so I attempted to highlight rather than obscure the tonal and rhythmic effects found in the Polish version. However, like most translators, I sometimes confronted aspects of the text that presented more than usual difficulty. I mean interjections (which Roman Jakobson called the "purely emotive stratum in language" [Jakobson 1960: 354]), idiomatic and onomatopoeic expressions, clichés, puns.

One challenge was of an entirely different order. *Kopenhaga* is a linguistically heterogeneous text; in addition to Polish, it includes numerous words and sentences from Danish, German, Spanish, Italian, and especially English. This excerpt immediately follows the poem I quoted earlier:

Czasy się zmieniają—szepczą mi z lękiem podstarzali rówieśnicy. *As we get older we do not get any younger*—stwierdził kiedyś Henry Reed. Im dłużej się nad tym zastanawiam, tym częściej przyznaję im wszystkim rację. Naszego starego listonosza zastąpił nagle młodziak z wytatuowanym na czole napisem: *Garbage—Version 2.0*.
   Dziwne.

['Things are different now,' my aging contemporaries whisper anxiously. *As we get older we do not get any younger*—Henry Reed once said. The longer I think about it, the more I'm convinced they are right. Our mail carrier has been replaced by a teenager with a tattoo on his forehead that says *Garbage—Version 2.0*.
   Weird.] (Wróblewski 2013: 54–5)

As Antoine Berman states in his 1985 "analytic of translation", the effacement of the superimposition of languages "demands maximum reflection from the translator" (Berman 2000: 296). After much reflection, the only sensible solution seemed to me to follow the standard practice of changing the typeface (using italics, capitals or quotations marks as needed) or, as in the above example, keeping the text essentially unchanged. However, even this noninterventionist approach failed to "recreate" the deliberately self-foreignizing effect in the source text. Something was clearly lost in my translation. And that loss had to do with the status of English as a global language.

Since the fall of Communism English has made inroads in Polish society, so much so as to begin to transform the Polish language itself. This of course worries the purists, though is hardly at odds with the way languages usually evolve by assimilating words and expressions from other languages. *Kopenhaga* certainly gains artistically from the interaction between Polish and English (and it is worth remembering that the setting here is Denmark). Yet despite the dominance of English as the language of popular culture and communication technologies, and by now the most frequently-studied foreign language in Polish primary and secondary schools, any passage in that language—like the above quotation from Henry Reed—still looks different on the page. At the *textural* as well as the textual level it still carries that unmistakable aura of the foreign. The effect disappears in my English translation; or to put it in Berman's terms, my translation is also a deformation. Paradoxically, the passages in English proved to be its most difficult "characteristics, vagaries, quirks, and stylistic peculiarities" to translate. It was perhaps too blunt a reminder of the unintended consequences of translation: the violence that inheres in it even when it attempts to be, in Pascale Casanova's phrase, "an act of consecration" of literary work within the international literary space (Casanova 2003: 135).

But again let's note how the linguistic and stylistic dilemmas are tied to the process of inscription. It is actually not easy to place Wróblewski within the international literary space. First, because of his self-exile to Denmark in 1985, he has a complicated relationship with the Polish literary scene. While he often publishes in Poland and has received his share of critical recognition, he is, as Casanova would say, "structurally" disconnected from Poland, especially in terms of access to government-funded support (stipends, awards, promotional efforts abroad). Secondly, Wróblewski's work does not easily fit with the idea of Polish poetry as it has existed in the past half century in English-speaking countries, especially the United States—not an insignificant segment of the international literary space into which I was after all bringing *Kopenhaga*. Associated with poets like Czesław Miłosz, Zbigniew Herbert, Tadeusz Różewicz and, to a lesser extent, Wisława Szymborska, this idea assumes poetry to be a vehicle of historical and moral exploration. Harking back to the Romantic era, but mainly growing out of Poland's tragic experience during World War II followed by almost half a century of Communist rule, it elevates poets as the conscience of the nation. Wróblewski also has little in common with the generation of poets shaped by the political upheavals of 1968 and 1970—Stanisław Barańczak, Adam Zagajewski, Ewa Lipska, Julian Kornhauser, Ryszard Krynicki, among others—who likewise grapple with political and ethical questions by way of existential or metaphysical lyricism. And he firmly dissociates himself from poets who came of age after the fall of Communism but who still capitalize on the legacy of the so-called "Polish school". During our 2014 conversation Wróblewski was disarmingly honest about his unease with the concept of the poet as a figure of moral authority: "sometimes I feel like I'm just here for the ride; you know, the passenger syndrome. Ultimately I have no idea what my role is as a poet" (Wróblewski 2014). And although he expressed admiration of Różewicz's formal experimentalism, he listed Andrzej Bursa and Miron Białoszewski as his main influences. Both were innovative poets of the second half of the twentieth century drawn to urban spaces and portrayals of "existential boredom" (rather like Baudelaire). Both remain little-known to anglophone readers.

To put it differently: Wróblewski's work seems at odds with the paradigm of "world poetry" which, as Stephen Owen argued in 1990 and then again in 2003, too often depends on the erasure of "the foreign" in the name of false universality, a literary equivalent of the shopping mall food court, with offerings "neither too common nor too exotic; [world poetry] has to be on some comfortable margin of difference for the target audience" (Owen 2003: 537). However exotic the poetry of, say, Miłosz may have seemed to its first readers in the English-speaking world, there was clearly something in it that proved equally palatable or even worth imitating. Among other things, that meant a philosophical approach to writing poetry of protest that made Miłosz ask abstractly, in one of his most famous poems: "What is poetry which does not save / Nations or people?" (Miłosz 2003: 77).[3] The impact of Polish poets was so powerful that it was responsible for "polonizing" American poetry of the 1970s and 1980s, as Charles Altieri has argued, offering US poets "an aesthetic of witnessing that made addressing political situations a fundamental part of poetry" but at the same time "a general perspective on the self"s embeddedness in the world" (Altieri 2004: 81).

But *Kopenhaga* clearly does not meet so defined expectations of civic poetry. Aspiring to objectivity yet emotionally charged, it is a sequence of prose poems with a distinctly Baudelairean provenance. Bleak yet prone to self-deflating humor, it is a foreigner's account of Denmark, but also a meditation on the rapidly globalizing planet. Written predominantly in Polish, it is a bricolage of languages and references to other literary and cultural artifacts. In fact, what is most striking about Wróblewski's book is how far it departs from the Western idea of Polish poetry in terms of its formal, stylistic, linguistic, and thematic conception.

V

Once *Kopenhaga* began to appear in English translation, it entered the sphere of circulation and of reading that David Damrosch identifies as world literature. "[W]orks of world literature", he argues, "take on a new life as they move into the world at large, and to understand this new life we need to look closely at the ways the work becomes reframed in its translations and in its new cultural contexts" (Damrosch 2003: 24). As we look closely at this particular example of reframing, we should note that the process was hardly one-dimensional or even one-directional. It did not always involve a simple conversion from Polish into English, given the heteroglossia of the source text and the fact that I was working with just one variety of English, namely the American English. It did not entail a straightforward reproduction of the source text into its translated version. In fact, there is a limit to which the term "source text" can even be applied to the Polish version. Not only is my translation a unique, collaboratively produced text, but Wróblewski, as I have tried to demonstrate, relies significantly on Baudelaire in terms of form, tone, and subject matter. Even before *Kopenhaga* took on a new life in my translation, it was subjected to the process of inscription. That process had to do with a variety of stylistic and structural decisions I made as the translator and even with more mundane activities like annotating and marketing.

In recent years Venuti has expanded the meaning of the term "inscription" beyond a set of deliberative choices and strategies adopted by the translator to achieve specific effects. His current understanding of the concept focuses on the importance of interpretation, consistent with his promotion of the hermeneutic notion of translation:

> Far from reproducing the source text, a translation rather transforms it by inscribing an interpretation that reflects what is intelligible and interesting to receptors. The transformation occurs even when the translator tries to maintain a fairly strict formal and semantic correspondence. The complex of meanings, values, and functions that the source text comes to support in its original culture insures that any translation will at once fall short of and exceed whatever correspondence a translator hopes to establish by supporting different meanings, values, and functions for its receptors. This ratio of loss and gain allows a translation to be constructed as an object of study that is relatively autonomous from the source text but always tied indissolubly to the receiving situation. (Venuti 2013: 193)[4]

Even as I tried to maintain "a fairly strict formal and semantic correspondence" between the Polish and the English versions of *Kopenhaga*, I was aware that through the process of translation I was also providing an interpretation. This interpretation was undoubtedly shaped by personal considerations, not least of them being my own experience as an immigrant to the United States and the challenge of translating from my native into my adopted language (my version of *Kopenhaga* is what linguists call L2 translation). These considerations subsequently guided my attention to the book's two main motifs, as I outline them in the introduction: the migrant's double identity and the ethnographer's search for patterns. Parts of the book read like an autobiographical transcript, with lyrical elements accommodated by the self-expanding, self-propelling Baudelairean prose poem. Wróblewski candidly documents the indignities of émigré life: ignorance of the new language (at least initially), economic insecurity, loneliness intensified by a sense of uprootedness. Though tempted by self-pity, he often turns to self-irony (the "untranslatable" quotation from Henry Reed comes from his poem "Chard Whitlow", a hilarious parody of T. S. Eliot). And yet it would be a mistake to read *Kopenhaga* solely along personal lines; as Wróblewski himself insists: "if I had wanted it to be an autobiography, I would have used the form of a journal" (Wróblewski 2014).[5] As an outsider, he is in an optimal position to study his adopted country, not only what it is but how it represents itself (which is why he also obsessively follows its media—newspapers, radio, television, occasionally the internet). His poems become repositories of observations, situations, and reflections. In addition to lyricism, he employs description and narration, for which the prose poem has also traditionally been a perfect vessel.

The personal and the cultural motifs in *Kopenhaga* are not mutually exclusive, even within individual poems. Indeed, they can even be gleaned from the book's paratexts. The front cover features a black-and-white photo of a haunted-looking building on Amagerbrodage in Copenhagen, a street not far from Wróblewski's apartment (Figure 15.1). Taken in 1999 by the Polish photographer and writer (and the author's close friend) Wojciech Wilczyk, it produces anxiety that is part of any immigrant's experience but also helps to place the book in its local setting.

The three blurbs on the back cover also highlight the dual focus of *Kopenhaga*, though with different emphases. Joshua Clover detects Wróblewski's affinity with

Figure 15.1 The cover of *Kopenhaga*. Photo by Wojciech Wilczyk

Joyce's notions of silence, exile, and cunning. Gabriel Gudding describes the book as an intimate study of cosmopolitanism. In Marjorie Perloff's view, *Kopenhaga* offers "a relentless, sardonic, and hilarious picture of a culture (at once highly particular and yet any culture) as insane as it is public-spirited and kindly". Generously provided by influential US writers and scholars, of course these endorsements serve mainly promotional purposes. But they are also small-scale interpretations—and as such they function as key elements of the process of inscription.

The process of inscription loomed large in my mind while I was translating *Kopenhaga* and preparing it for publication in the United States. During that period, I often asked myself the following questions: (1) How does the instability of genres, especially hybrid genres, impact the production, circulation, and reception of translations?; (2) What is the nature of poetic influence when it crosses national borders?; (3) What effect does the ubiquity of the internet have on Nabokov's conception of translator-as-scholar?; and (4) How much of "the foreign" does one deliberately leave out when one translates, especially from a minor into a major language? As the English translator of *Kopenhaga*, I wanted to find a way to acknowledge its former existence in its "original culture", to signal its cultural and linguistic alterity, especially in light of Wróblewski's own exploration of the concept. By leaving numerous allusions and references largely unglossed but keeping certain syntactical and verbal effects (including the Polish title), I tried to draw attention to the element of "the foreign" in my translation. At the same time, like most translators, I also found myself pulled in the opposite direction. Keeping in mind my version's intended audience, I made all kinds of strategic decisions that were meant to help me situate the translation in its new context. By casting *Kopenhaga* as a volume of prose poems, and so linking it with the prose poem tradition, I tried to make it legible to a literary culture that historically has been exceptionally hospitable to the genre. Whether *Kopenhaga* is now tied "indissolubly" (Venuti's word) to that culture is perhaps for others to say, though the issue does raise questions about the degree to which translations of foreign works challenge the concept of an autonomous national tradition. At the very least, the case of *Kopenhaga* seems noteworthy for what it reveals about translation, world literature, and the evolution of the prose poem.

Notes

1. Additional English translations of Wróblewski's poetry appear in *Our Flying Objects*, translated by Joel Leonard Katz, Rod Mengham, Malcolm Sinclair, and Adam Zdrodowski (2007); *A Marzipan Factory*, translated by Adam Zdrodowski (2010); *Let's Go Back to the Mainland*, translated by Agnieszka Pokojska (2014); and *Zero Visibility*, translated by Piotr Gwiazda (2017).
2. As Agnieszka Kluba observes in her study of the prose poem in Poland: "The prose poem has so far led a secret life in Poland. It was the form recognized and practiced by an initiated few, usually connoisseurs of French poetry. [. . .] For others it was something invisible, not quite discernible, and not quite legible as a genre" (Kluba 2014: 9 [my translation]).
3. Miłosz, of course, lived and taught for many years in California and played a major role in creating the notion of the "Polish school" as the editor and translator of the influential 1965 anthology *Postwar Polish Poetry* (Rosenthal 2011: 221–8).
4. Venuti elaborates on this notion in his most recent book *Contra Instrumentalism*: "A hermeneutic model conceives of translation as an interpretive act that inevitably varies source-text form, meaning, and effect according to intelligibilities and interests in the receiving

culture. [. . .] In my view, all translation, whether the genre of the source text is humanistic, pragmatic, or technical, is an interpretive act that necessarily entails ethical responsibilities and political commitments" (Venuti 2019: 1, 6).
5. Wróblewski also told me in person that his book owes much in its conception to Bernal Diaz del Castillo's *The Discovery and Conquest of Mexico* and Claude Lévi-Strauss' *Tristes Tropiques*.

Works Cited

Altieri, Charles (2004), "Polish Envy: American Poetry's Polonising in the 1970s and '80s" *Metre* 15, Spring 2004.
Bartczak, Kacper (2005), "The Hazards and Hopes of New Polish Poetry," *lyric* 8, 2005.
Baudelaire, Charles (2009), *Paris Spleen: Little Poems in Prose*, trans. Keith Waldrop, Middletown, CT: Wesleyan University Press.
Bellos, David (2011), *Is That a Fish in Your Ear? Translation and the Meaning of Everything*, New York: Penguin Books.
Benjamin, Walter (2009), *The Writer of Modern Life: Essays on Charles Baudelaire*, trans. Howard Eiland, Edmund Jephcott, Rodney Livingstone, and Harry Zohn, Cambridge, MA: Belknap.
Berman, Antoine (2000), "Translation and the Trials of the Foreign," trans. Lawrence Venuti, in *The Translation Studies Reader*, ed. Lawrence Venuti, London and New York: Routledge.
Blum-Kulka, Shoshana (2000), "Shifts of Coherence and Cohesion in Translation," in *The Translation Studies Reader*, ed. Lawrence Venuti, London and New York: Routledge.
Casanova, Pascale (2003), *The World Republic of Letters*, trans. M. B. DeBevoise, Cambridge, MA: Harvard University Press.
Crnković, Gordana P. (1999), *Imagined Dialogues: Eastern European Literature in Conversation with American and English Literature*, Evanston, IL: Northwestern University Press.
Damrosch, David (2003), *What Is World Literature?* Princeton and Oxford: Princeton University Press.
Francone, Vincent (2014), review of Grzegorz Wróblewski's *Kopenhaga*, Three Percent, 2014, <http://www.rochester.edu/College/translation/threepercent/2014/02/03/latest-review-kopenhaga-by-grzegorz-wroblewski/> (last accessed July 30, 2019).
Grossman, Edith (2011), *Why Translation Matters*, New Haven, CT: Yale University Press.
Gryko, Krzysztof (2011), "Pozory małomówności," *Twórczość*, April.
Jakobson, Roman (1960), "Closing Statement: Linguistics and Poetics," in *Style in Language*, ed. Thomas Sebeok, New York: Wiley.
Kluba, Agnieszka (2014), *Poemat Prozą w Polsce*, Warszawa and Toruń: Wydawnictwo Naukowe Uniwersytetu Mikołaja Kopernika.
Miłosz, Czesław (2003), *New and Collected Poems 1931–2001*, trans. Czesław Miłosz and Robert Hass, New York: Ecco.
Moretti, Franco (2013), *Distant Reading*, London and New York: Verso.
Nabokov, Vladimir (2000), "Problems of Translation: 'Onegin' in English," in *The Translation Studies Reader*, ed. Lawrence Venuti, London and New York: Routledge.
Nicholls, Peter (1995), *Modernisms: A Literary Guide*, Berkeley and Los Angeles: University of California Press.
Owen, Stephen (2003), "Stepping Forward and Back: Issues and Possibilities for 'World' Poetry," *Modern Philology*, vol. 100, no. 4, May 2003.
Perloff, Marjorie (2010), "Teaching Poetry in Translation: The Case for Bilingualism," *Profession*.
Rosenthal, Mira (2011). "Czesław Miłosz's Polish School of Poetry in English Translation," *Przekładaniec* 25, 2011.

Taylor, John (2015), "Homelands, Adopted Homelands: Four New Polish Poets at Our Door," *Antioch Review*, vol. 73, no. 3, Summer.

Todorov, Tzvetan (1983), "Poetry Without Verse," in *The Prose Poem in France: Theory and Practice*, ed. Mary Ann Caws and Hermine Riffaterre, New York: Columbia University Press.

Venuti, Lawrence (1998), *The Scandals of Translation: Towards an Ethics of Difference*, New York: Routledge.

Venuti, Lawrence (2013), *Translation Changes Everything*, New York: Routledge.

Venuti, Lawrence (2019), *Contra Instrumentalism: A Translation Polemic*, Lincoln: University of Nebraska Press.

Wróblewski, Grzegorz (2011), email message to author, April 30.

Wróblewski, Grzegorz (2013), *Kopenhaga*, trans. Piotr Gwiazda, Brookline, MA: Zephyr Press.

Wróblewski, Grzegorz (2014), "The Passenger Syndrome," interview conducted and translated by Piotr Gwiazda, *Jacket2*, August 28, <https://jacket2.org/interviews/passenger-syndrome> (last accessed September 28, 2019).

16

THE CHINESE PROSE POEM: GENERIC METAPHOR AND THE MULTIPLE ORIGINS OF CHINESE SANWENSHI

Nick Admussen[1]

SOME CRITICS WRITING ON CHINESE PROSE poetry identify the 1917 poem "Moonlit Night," by Shen Yinmo 沈尹默, as the first original prose poem written in Chinese.[2] Other arguments abound, but this piece is identified early and often as the initiator of the genre in China. To those who study prose poetry from other times or places, it may seem a strange choice:

月夜

霜风呼呼的吹着，
月光朗朗的照着。
我和一株顶高的树并排立着，
却没有靠着。

[Moonlit Night

A frosty wind whistles as it's blowing,
the moonlight shining so brightly.
A towering tree and I stand side by side,
but without touching.] (Zhang 1998: 77)[3]

This essay intends to demonstrate the mutability of prose poetry as an appellation and a genre in China, as a way of arguing that what coheres around genres is not an ideology, a lineage of influence, or even a set of formal restrictions, but a web of hermeneutic methods, a habit of grouping similar works that allows readers to understand the texts they read.[4] Chinese prose poetry, or *sanwenshi* (散文诗), has, from this reader's perspective, two major origins, each arising from separate groups of people reacting to drastically different historical and literary contexts. These contexts train communities to read and group texts, and it is these shifts in hermeneutic practice that give the genre its layered, diverse quality.

"Moonlit Night" represents the earlier of these origins, during the revolutionary New Culture Movement (*c*.1915–20), a period typified by popular disillusionment with China's Republican government, broad opposition to Western and Japanese imperialism, radical intellectual critique of Confucian values, and a wave of new writing and translation in the Chinese vernacular. What initially astonishes about this poem as a progenitor of the genre of prose poetry is that it is *lineated*: even assuming that each sentence is a paragraph, which seems unlikely, there is a break after the commas in lines one and three, something that would clearly never happen in prose. This lineation, further, is not a mistake or an artifact of a prose sentence fitted into a particular column width; each line in the original Chinese ends in the particle 着 *zhe/zhao*, which provides a kind of sonic and visual return familiar from rhyme.[5]

It makes little sense to read this poem in relationship to contemporary Chinese prose poetry, think about its relationship to early twentieth-century prose, or examine it through its foreign influences. It is only interpretable in relationship to the classical tradition: it is named after a Du Fu (杜甫, CE 712–70) poem of the same title, which ends, "When will we lean at the empty window, / both shone upon, the tracks of our tears dried?"[6] Shen Yinmo's "Moonlit Night" both belongs to and intentionally counters its lyric tradition, not least by rewriting the unanswerable question at the end of Du Fu's poem with a strong, cold declaration of independence. This opposition is both conceptual and formal, but the poem's lack of enjambment, its use of some traditional heptasyllabic meter and a strong but idiosyncratic identical rhyme make the piece seem uninterested in, or disengaged from, the qualities and limitations of the free-verse line.[7] The concept of free verse is necessary for many contemporary definitions of prose poetry, both in China and abroad. During the New Culture Movement, though, few writers had it, and even those who did could not depend on a community of readers who were familiar with the distinctions between metrical poetry, free verse, and prose. Reading this era of the genre without respect to the community of writers and readers that produced it prevents an understanding of the distinctions and oppositions that *did* matter to early Chinese prose poets: the dismantling of the metrical and rhythmic traditions of imperial-era poetry.

Influential New Culture writers Zheng Zhenduo 郑振铎 and Guo Moruo 郭沫若 both wrote critical essays about *sanwenshi*, and both advocated for what they considered to be prose poetry. In "On Prose Poetry," Zheng consistently opposes prose poetry with rhymed poetry, for example by writing "The works of many prose poets have already shattered the article of faith that is 'no poetry without rhyme'" (Wang 2008: 1197). He goes on to argue, "If an expression must have rhyme to be considered a poem, then can the works of poets Whitman, Carpenter, Henley, Turgenev, Wilde, and Amy Lowell[8] be considered poems?" Wilde and Turgenev wrote works that could very strictly be considered prose poems; Lowell wrote what she called "polyphonic prose," which is very similar to what we consider prose poems; Carpenter called his works prose poems, but they feature some lineation; Henley seems to be a metrical poet with strong free verse tendencies, and Whitman has mostly been considered a free verse poet. Guo Moruo applied the term *sanwenshi* even more broadly to works originally intended as prose: he advocated for prose poetry and against the stricture of end-rhyme in the Introduction to his translation of *The Sorrows of Young Werther*, which he considered to be a prose poem. "Recently some of my countrymen have been discussing poetry; what is surprising is that the debate over rhyme has been especially fierce and that prose poems have been slandered as somehow unsound" (Denton 1996: 204–5). Prose poetry in his formulation is the poetic nature of all exceptional prose, as set against rhymed verse: it is identical to the term *wuyun shi* 无韵诗, rhymeless verse.[9]

That Zheng and Guo's definitions of poetry are not based on the presence or absence of lineation makes perfect sense in their milieu. Classical Chinese poems were often written or printed continuously, and it was instead rhyme and rhythm that indicated the end of one poetic phrase and the start of another. The difference between free verse and prose poetry, highly visible to readers habituated to modern lineation practices in poetry, was not relevant to writers or audiences who were in the initial stages of adapting to typeset, negative space as it is used in twentieth-century Western-style newspapers and magazines. Where some critics used *ziyou shi* 自由诗, free verse, or *xinshi* 新诗, new verse, to indicate modern poetry unfettered by traditional rules, Zheng used *sanwenshi*; where others used generic titles for short prose like *zawen* 杂文, *meiwen* 美文, or *xiaopinwen* 小品文, Guo called the introduction to *Young Werther* "prose poetry." Underneath the new generic titles lay an old, well-understood distinction: Chinese writing has long been divided into *yunwen* (韵文, with rhyme) and *wuyunwen* or *sanwen* (without rhyme) categories, and it is reasonable to think that both Zheng and Guo meant the term *sanwenshi* as "poetry without rhyme" or "fine writing without meter."[10] In fact, in this context, prose poetry seems to be defined against *yunwen*, to be the polar opposite of *yunwen*, and to have few if any positively defined qualities that are not terms in an argument that denies the necessity of *yunwen*. Their particular sense of what did or did not count as a prose poem was substantially different from each other's because neither of them was engaged in the establishment of a cohesive and distinctive genre; they were using the term as a tool to critique those who insist on traditional formal rules for poetry, and to typify traditional poetics as anti-international and anti-modern.

The focus of the genre against traditional poetics is clear in the self-descriptions of New Culture poets who were reading prose poetry from abroad. Liu Bannong 刘半农, to whom is ascribed the first recorded use of the term *sanwenshi* and who had intimately encountered Turgenev's work by at least 1920 (Hockx 2000: 105),[11] wrote: "In regards to the form of poetry, I am one who is most capable of playing fresh tricks. The rhymeless poetry of the time, the prose poetry, and the use of dialect to imitate folk songs that came later ... all these were things I attempted first" (Liu 1926: unpag.). Xu Zhimo 徐志摩, who had studied in England and produced some of the most elegant verse of the New Culture movement, grouped a quartet of prose pieces in his seminal book *Zhimo's Poems*; describing one of them, he later wrote "I have a poem called 'Poison'—a formless, cursing poem, that vented all my pent-up feelings" (Xu 1987: 139). Zhou Zuoren 周作人, in discussing his poem "Rivulet," pointed out that such a thing exists as prose poetry, that his own lineated composition was probably not prose poetry, and then threw his hands up at the entire question: "perhaps it doesn't count as poetry, we'll never know; but this is irrelevant" (Jia 1986: 443). Zhou's tone is representative of many of those who wrote poetry at the boundary between the empire and the republic: they have a system of lyric traditions to dismantle, and if there is any interpretively useful cohesion to *sanwenshi* in the period, it can best be understood in the way that many different "tricks" and "formless" shapes can participate in similarly negative poetics.

Understanding the prose poetry of the New Culture movement as a practice pointed against past poetry helps us read and understand poems. Looking again at "Moonlit Night," above, we can see the repetition at line's end not just as an identical rhyme, but as an almost ludic violation of traditional couplet rhyme. Adding insult to injury, the repeated character 着 is a vernacular grammatical particle that indicates continuous action (in English terms it marks a verb as a gerund). In traditional poetics, this kind of particle would be called an empty word (虚词, *xuci*) and considered a compositional defect. Lines are broken at punctuation marks in a way that emphasizes their role as caesura, and shows readers that the semantic power of traditional poetic rhythms—their ability to help readers predict where a phrase ends—is easily replaced by modern typography. Accordingly, although the first couplet is in a classical heptasyllabic meter, the second couplet breaks that form. To see the piece's genre as oppositional and its form as critical reinforces and extends the poem's rejection of Du Fu's dream ("When will we lean at the empty window, / both shone upon . . .?"). Reunion, cohesion, music, and closure—the promise of regimes from the poetic to the imperial—are replaced in Shen's poem by an insistent realism, an acceptance of fracture.

Poems from the New Culture Movement that look and even sometimes feel like contemporary prose poetry are also meaningfully interpretable through an understanding of the form as anti-traditional. Liu Bannong, who as we saw above was an initiator and innovator of the form in China, has a prose composition called "Rain" that starts like this:

Rain

This is all in Xiaohui's words, I just took it down for her and linked it together, that's all.

Ma! Today I want to sleep—snuggle close to my mother and go to bed early. Listen! On the lawn behind you, there's not even a whisper; it's my friends, all snuggled up with their mothers and gone to bed early. (Wang 2008: 20)

The poem continues with the sleepy, plaintive musings of Xiaohui, which become increasingly surreal as she drifts off, until the poem ends so:

Ma! I want to sleep! Close the window, don't let the rain in and make the bed wet. Give my rain jacket to the rain, don't let the rain get the rain's clothes wet. (Wang 2008: 20)

Were one reading this piece as a contemporary prose poem, one might focus on the way in which it expressed some poetic quality in prose; this might involve examining the position of the speaker, the persona of Xiaohui, and the aesthetic arrangement of their speech. Were one reading it as a New Culture prose poem, on the other hand, one would examine the way this composition was pitched against classical writing, the documentary flatness of it, the lack of design and pattern, and the way it feels like art *despite* the unintentionality of its arrangement. There is a great deal of evidence for the latter interpretation—Liu Bannong really did have a daughter named Xiaohui, and rather than intentional generic participation, the poem is legible as a "fresh trick" in which speech reported verbatim generates a surreal music usually associated with high art. The ease of this trick would call the fetishization of writerly craft into question; Liu Bannong did so explicitly in the preface to the collection in which "Rain" appears, writing: "I am not a poet. This word 'poet,' originally it just meant a person who makes poems. But ever since it became a name, it hasn't been able to avoid acquiring the stench of 'professionalism'" (Liu 1926: unpag.). The overlapping, multiple quality of generic metaphor—a situation in which each concept of genre reveals different facets of a text—has led to a situation in which contemporary prose poetry anthologists list "Rain" as a prose poem, but literary historians and specialists in Liu Bannong list it as a "penetrating sketch."[12] In a less historicized context, it can serve as an early example of contemporary prose poetry; for scholars engaged in the period of its composition, it performs work that is pitched against the associations that have accumulated around the practice of poetry.

Seeing early Chinese prose poetry as a genre pitched against the classical poetic tradition does not provide a universal and unmitigated key to every poem written under the name of prose poetry: as Rosmarin points out, the metaphor of genre is a "strange loop . . . not simply a suggestively incomplete series but one that explicitly turns back on itself" (1986: 44). One work from the period that stands out as ill-served by the genre categorization outlined above is Lu Xun's 1927 collection *Weeds* (野草, also translated as *Wild Grass*), a book comprising dream sketches, stories, parables, a satiric rhyme, and a short one-act play.[13] Lu Xun, a giant of the New Culture Movement and the author of deeply influential vernacular modern fiction, once introduced the collection by saying "I had some little emotional impressions, so I wrote short pieces, to exaggerate a bit they were *sanwen shi*, and later they were printed into a book which I called *Weeds*." The lack of interest in categorization common to New Culture prose poets is fully audible; as the critic Michelle Yeh writes, Lu's "choice of prose poetry was haphazard rather than conscious; it was more a matter of convenience than a conscious formal experiment" (Yeh 2000: 120). There are poems in the collection, like "My Lost Love" and the anti-Baudelaire poem "The Dog's Retort," that have substantively negative poetics, in each case imitating the form of another poem in a way that destabilizes the original.[14] And yet, inside the capacious, disorganized generic envelope of *Weeds*, positive constructions emerge. Sun Yushi, as well as a substantial group of prose poetry scholars in Mainland China, sees it as the real spiritual origin of the genre of prose poetry: "Because of the appearance of *Wild Grass*, modern and contemporary Chinese prose poetry began its march towards the summit of mature independence" (2006: 22). Charles Laughlin points out the way it shares generic characteristics with the magazine for which the pieces were originally written, *Yusi* (语丝) or *Threads of Talk* (2014: 59). And I have written about the way that the collection codifies a prosodic music for vernacular poetry that retains and adapts rhythmic structures from classical literature (Admussen 2009). By 1927, after some elements of the New Culture Movement had passed, and others had become more or less institutionalized, the cohesive opposition of early twentieth-century prose poetry is less useful as an interpretive lens than it was for earlier poetry. Eileen Chang, for example, sees *Weeds* refusing to mourn the loss of the past as a way of keeping that past open, lingering over the moment of its death in order to serve a radical and even revolutionary focus on the deaths of the present and future (2013: 219–33).

If *Weeds* is a liminal text, written on the temporal boundary of a movement by one of its major participants, then the prose poetry that came after it is a strong indication that our hermeneutic metaphors of genre need constant refreshing, looping and twisting to suit diverse literary practices. After the Anti-Japanese War, the foundation of the People's Republic, and the codification of Maoist principles of literature, new kinds of people with new audiences and new habits began writing *sanwenshi* with different generic origins and different rules from those of the writers of the New Culture Movement. It is to those poems, and their influence on contemporary literature, that we now turn.

*

The following appears on the first page, before the preface or the table of contents, of a 1981 reprint of a 1957 prose poetry collection by the arts cadre Ke Lan 柯蓝 that is titled *Short Flute of Morning Mist*:

> This book is a collection of prose poetry. The author has selected meaningful scenes from life, expressed his own emotion, and with deep feeling sung the praises of the party's leaders, the socialist system, the magnificence of labor, sincere friendship and pure love, etc. Its language is elegant, and the poems' meanings are quite significant. (Ke 1981: unpag.)

Besides the shrill and politically protective claim of Communist orthodoxy, which appropriately reflects the tone of much of the work's content and ideology, what is interesting about this brief publisher's note is its unequivocal categorization of the work: this practice of foregrounding the formal distinction between prose poetry and other literary art is one that remains exceptionally popular today, when we have magazines called *Prose Poetry* and *The World of Prose Poetry*, as well as a proliferation of prose poetry anthologies and organizations that are specifically identified as such.[15] From the perspective of Ke Lan and his publishers, this categorization may serve a purpose similar to the political claims also made in the note, a disclaimer that this is aestheticized language and not, as Liu Bannong's poem seems to argue for itself, a direct report of real-life events. Contradictorily, however, the note indicates that the scenes of the book are drawn from life, "selected" rather than created: the overall effect is a kind of tightrope-walk between a poet who intends to write realistically, but worries about making claims concerning the nature of reality. This tipping point, between the documentary nature of prose and the individual, invented quality of poetry,[16] is one that the book encounters again and again, as in this poem, which almost serves as a title piece:

朝霞

　　春天的早晨，草地上出现了朝霞。这闪亮的水珠，有人说他是先烈的眼泪，是那圣洁的心灵的泉水......
　　看着看着，这亮晶晶的朝霞，又象那会说话的眼珠，它却又有无尽的说不完的话.......
　　朝霞呵，不要再沉默了！太阳出来了。草地上的朝霞马上成了千万个发光的太阳。太阳进到了水珠里......
　　于是先烈的眼泪被揩干了。草地上跑来一群玩耍的小孩，踏破了草地上千万个发光的太阳，现在孩子们就是朝霞，孩子们就是太阳......
　　　　　　　　　　　　　　　—— 写于虹桥保育院

[Dawn Mist

Spring mornings, a rainbow mist appears over the lawn. These brilliant pearls, some say they are the tears of martyrs, are the pure source of spirit . . .

Look look, the glittering morning mist, it looks like eyes that can speak, and have inexhaustible, unending words . . .

Ah, early mist, you should stop being silent! The sun has come out. The lawn's morning colors immediately become a million shining suns. The sun dives into the dewdrops . . .

And so the tears of the martyrs are wiped dry. A mass of cavorting children gallops across the lawn, trampling the million shining suns, and now the children are the morning dew, they are the sun . . .

—Written at the Hongqiao Nursery School] (Ke 1981: 209)

The fundamental formal character of this piece is its emphatically prose structure: a straightforward temporal narrative about the sun burning off the dew and the beginning of a school day, it goes so far as to specify, in a kind of aside or byline after the poem that is common in Ke Lan's work, the position of the writer. Paragraphs are the dominant division of the piece: its shape would be appropriate for a personal letter. Ke Lan's writer watches the nursery school lawn, and interacts with it, speaks to it, assesses it, names it. The prose assumption, the prose form—a short description of children coming out to the lawn to play—is invested with what Ke Lan's foreword calls "his own emotion." The Chinese term for "lyric," as in "lyric poetry," is *shuqing* 抒情, "pouring out emotion," and while one might struggle to find how Liu Bannong feels about the content of his poem "Rain," there is no question as to what Ke Lan feels. His feelings, which appear in every poem in this three-hundred-page collection, highlighted by liberal use of the ecstatic exclamation point, are the *shi*, the poem of these works: their form is *sanwen*, prose.

This is not a New Culture-era understanding of these terms. To readers trained in classical literature, *sanwen*, "scattered writing," indicates many types of writing that do not follow regular rules. Accordingly, for early twentieth-century authors, it does not indicate any kind of codified idea of prose; it is a blanket term to be opposed to *yunwen*, "rhymed writing." By the early Communist period, however, the classical term *sanwen* had long been used to refer to prose, the official form in which reports, newspaper articles, political position papers, communications among the masses, and the stories of socialist realism are all written. *Sanwen* is the literary form most strongly assumed to directly represent reality, and to imbue it with the lyric voice is particularly fraught. Huang Yongjian writes that the subjective position in this literary form opens all prose poets of the Mao period to political criticism: punishment came first to Xu Chengmiao 徐成淼, a student of Ke Lan's, and then to Ke Lan himself, when he was criticized by Yao Wenyuan 姚文元 in the late 1950s (Huang 2006: 99–100), beginning a period of political trouble and punishment that plagued Ke until the regime change of the late 1970s. This context helps make more sense of the choice to define prose poetry at the start of *Short Flute*, as well as the absolutely fervent political orthodoxy the book strives for: the underlying organization of the form was to filter an objectivity often supplied by the state through a subjective, individual author, and the safest way to attempt that filtering was to ensure that the subjectivity in question was a strong proponent of the Party line.

In criticism, as well, authors since the 1950s and 1960s have reached a kind of consensus on definitions of prose poetry. This is Ke Lan, published in 1981:

> To use simple language, [prose poetry] is poetry written through the use of prose, and not poetry created through the use of rhymed writing. Unrhymed poetry is called free verse, prose poetry is a variant of free verse. First, they don't use verses that are lineated and made into stanzas according to the length of their phrases, but are instead verse compositions that use prose in order to link together their parts, and please remember, no matter what the form, in the final analysis they should be poems, it's only in a formal way that they are different from poems. So you can say that it is an artistic form born from the school of poetry. (Wang 2008: 1221)

And here is the opening of the poet-critic Wang Guangming's encyclopedia entry on prose poetry:

> PROSE POETRY. A lyrical literary style possessing special qualities of poetry and of prose. It joins the expressiveness of poetry to the various qualities of prose narrativity. With regards to its basic nature, it belongs to poetry, and has the emotion and fantasy of poetry, it gives readers a sense of beauty and imagination, but its content remains prosaic detail with poetic intent; where form is concerned, it has the exterior appearance of prose, and does not resemble poetry in regards to lineation and rhyme, although it does not lack the beauty of internal music and the feeling of rhythm. (Wang 1987: 82)

These writings are definitional rather than polemic, a far cry from the most common New Culture practices. One of the technical particularities that can be seen in these definitions is the attention to the importance and impact of lineation: after decades of newsprint typesetting and free verse poetry, the definition of prose poetry is now highly sensitive to the distinction between line length designed by poets (free verse poetry) and lines determined by editors, or the size and shape of publications (prose poetry).

The abstract language in the definitions above, in which texts have the inner "expressiveness" of poetry with an outer layer of "prosaic detail," is in part a reaction to their Mao-era roots. In the 1942 "Yan'an Talks on Literature and Art," Mao Zedong sets up an aesthetic system in which artists are personally responsible for transmuting or transforming daily life into art products. Bonnie McDougall interprets:

> It may be argued that in Mao's view, the mind of the writer (consciousness) is in any case determined by the social environment (being), but by discussing the whole issue in terms of 'mind' rather than environment, Mao seems automatically to imply and encourage the personal response to life (the raw material of literature), and to allow considerable room for the play of individual imagination and technique. (McDougall 1980: 19)

This is visible throughout the "Talks," although perhaps not in an internally consistent, ideologically pure way. Mao is explicit about the individual author's responsibility not just for art's politics, but for its effects on the reader (McDougall 1980: 82); in matters of form, because feudal forms are improper for socialist art, the artist is responsible for "restructuring them and filling them with new content" (McDougall 1980: 28–9). This is very different from the attitudes of the early twentieth-century artists outlined above, who set themselves against classical forms; writers in Mao's view internalize the deterministic, materialist environment around them (an environment often most directly described by prose) and use technique to work it into "processed forms of art" (McDougall 1980: 69). The poetic transformation of prose forms, as well as the transformation of objective life through individual poetic subjectivity, are methods of conceptualizing art that are common both to Communist literary criticism and to much contemporary Chinese prose poetry. Communist literary theory also reflects one important difference between contemporary prose poetry and May Fourth or earlier works that are highly subjective: in the contemporary period, the subjectivity of prose poetry is expressed through "processing," the technical work of the artist. Generic and formal distinctions and methods become, therefore, increasingly central as an individual and shared means of self-expression.

With these genre habits and contexts in mind, it is possible to return to "Dawn Mist" and read it more thoroughly. The tears of the martyrs are necessarily those of the Communist martyrs, whether from the civil war, the war against Japan, or the Korean War. The children wipe them from the land like dew off grass, and then supplant them as shining suns. The emotion that Ke Lan brings to the nursery school scene is joy—because the romping children announce the end of the losses from revolution, the end of the age of the martyr. Those feelings are a political position, an expectation that the rewards of revolution have arrived: they suited, broadly, the Party's mood during the more freewheeling and utopian "Hundred Flowers" Campaign of 1957, but then made an easy target for the Anti-Rightist Campaign of 1959, when intellectuals and others who were insufficiently revolutionary, and indeed the genre of prose poetry as a whole, came under concerted attack. To understand the way prose poetry, in the 1950s, rested on the fulcrum between individual expression and objectively correct assessment is to understand the drama and appeal of the poems, what they risk. It is also to understand that the genre was responding to an official directive for writers and other artists to insert the power and pathos of their subjectivities into the prosaic, daily truth of socialism. Writers in the genre had no intent to subvert the dominant ideology or the state: they were part of a state-mandated project in which artists apply technique to refine experience into usefully processed forms.[17] Their political trouble was a result not of their imperfect desire to succeed at their task, but of the danger and risk implicit in speaking Chinese socialism in an individual voice. After they were punished, Ke Lan and poets like him did not abandon their affiliation with the state: once the more open Deng government took shape, they were welcomed back into official literary and cultural work as befitted their identities as state writers and cultural bureaucrats. Indeed, the codification of the identity of prose poetry in contemporary China has much to do with their post-1976 leadership, as well as their ability to secure state resources for the publication and circulation of new prose poetry.

The prose poetry that Ke Lan and people like him promoted, edited and circulated after 1976—the majority, by volume, of all prose poetry ever published in the People's Republic of China—is best read through the generic cohesion forged in the defensive postures of 1950s poets and codified in the early 1980s. It most often takes the shape of an intervention from the world of poetry into the world of prose, the investment of prose with the spirit, emotion, or individual voice of poetry. A 2004 poem by Fang Wenzhu makes a good example:

象拔掉一颗钉子那样

象拔掉一颗钉子那样，拨掉稗草，镜中花，爱情的暗斑，夜行者的灯，黎明的梦和雾，湖中的网，雨中的哭泣......
象拔掉一颗钉子那样，拨掉纸张，笔墨和余的词语。
我和白银汉字一起向前，滚动。
象拔掉一颗钉子那样，拨掉眼中的沙子，肉中的刺，骨头的痛心的疤......
象拔掉一颗钉子那样，拨掉自己。

[Kind of Like Pulling Out a Nail
  Kind of like pulling out a nail, pulling out crabgrass, a flower in a mirror, the dark specks in love, the nightwalker's lamp, brilliant dreams and fog, the net in the lake, tears in rain . . .
  Kind of like pulling out a nail, getting rid of a sheet of paper, ink and excess words.
  Me and silvery Mandarin push forward together, we roll along.
  Kind of like pulling out a nail, pulling a piece of grit from your eye, a thorn from flesh, the scars of grief in your bones . . .
  Kind of like pulling out a nail, wrenching yourself loose.] (Wang 2008: 867)

This is clearly a modern poem, challenging, variable, and wide-ranging; setting it next to "Moonlit Night" or "Rain" only increases a reader's feeling of dissociation and disorientation. Reading it, however, alongside Ke Lan's work as a reaction to prose, as a piece of prose which has passed through an individual, subjective process, makes the poem considerably more interpretable. Most importantly, the idea that this prose poem is focused toward or against prose leads readers to consider *what prose* the poem answers or reacts to. The refrain of this poem is almost exclusively used in one specific educational parable: although versions vary widely, the basic story is that a father tells a young boy with uncontrollable anger that from now on, he can only get into a fight after he pounds a nail into a tree in the front yard. The boy discovers that after he pounds in a nail, he no longer feels the need to fight, at which point the father tells him he can pull out a nail every time he overcomes the urge to lash out at the people around him. Once all the nails are gone, the father shows the boy the holes that are left, and says that what he's done to his friends will never go away.[18] In this case, the poem seems to have been written in tandem with a definition of prose poetry much like Wang Guangming's dictionary entry: the connection between the originary prose, the parable intended to morally educate children and parents, and the prose poem, the "emotion and fantasy" of a speaker trying to describe what it would be like for an individual to undergo the process that the parable simply reports, is the key to understanding the piece in full—much like the process of understanding how Ke Lan takes a completely prosaic moment and, in passing it through his own mind and own language, activates its expressive power and its political potential.

Encountering genre as a set of methods through which communities read and understand literary texts encourages substantial attention to extratextual structures and lived poetics. The circulation of hermeneutic methods happens inside texts, of course, but equally, or more importantly, it happens in critical paratexts, the education system, and through the work of editors. New Culture poets specialized in the critical broadside, like Guo Moruo's preface to *Werther*, but prose poets from the 1950s onward established hermeneutics through educational and editorial structures. Ke Lan, after his return to modest power as a literary cadre in the late 1970s, became an important, powerful editor, founding the *Prose Poetry Newspaper*, where he trained the generation of writers and educators to come, at one point even offering a mail-order masterclass in prose poetic composition (Admussen 2016a: 97). The way in which prose poetry today is deeply engaged in education is visible not only in Fang Wenzhu's interest in children's parables, but in the intentional marketing of *Prose Poetry Magazine* to secondary and even pre-secondary students.[19] This manner of circulating hermeneutic methods relies upon formal Party support, both in the funding of publications (major prose poetry journals often receive substantial public funding) and in interactions with the public school system. We would predict, then, that a writer like Fang Wenzhu might be both a Party member and a member of the Party-organized Writer's Association; he is, in fact, so.[20] Networks of hermeneutic education are a mechanism by which forms and genres grow into affiliations with ideologies, social classes, regions and moments. They are one reason why transregional genres seem meaningful—when different communities have rich interconnections or share generic associations—but global genres collapse into subcategory once they are placed or otherwise situated.

Like any metaphor, though, hermeneutic metaphors are partial, evolving, and imbricated: the present and future of mainland Chinese prose poetry is also one of eruptions-in-progress, situations in which the core cohesion of the genre is colored or threatened by the appearance of competing methods of interpretation. Alternative habits of reading prose poems come from several sources, all of which are accessible to contemporary prose poets in mainland China and any of which might one day supplant them.[21] First, there is the storied tradition of Taiwanese prose poetry, whose writers transformed the New Culture tradition in consistent contact with the Japanese and Euro-American tradition: writers like Ya Hsien 瘂弦 and Shang Qin 商禽 have likely influenced at least some of contemporary mainland prose poets' interest in surrealism, even though Taiwanese poetry and criticism do not now make up a visible part of their hermeneutic network.[22] Second, there is the influence of translation; poets in the People's Republic are eminently well-read in translation, and have the propensity to take a variety of translingual or imported hermeneutic methods into their own practice.[23] Third, there is the mainland avant-garde, in which poets like Xi Chuan 西川 and Yu Jian 于坚 have written complex, experimental work in prose forms that escape classification as orthodox prose poetry and demand new methods of reading.[24] The vitality of genre lies in the fact that it is only meaningful, if it does feel meaningful, for participants in its hermeneutic discourse—the equivalent of deciding that a metaphor feels apt or insightful, the process of coming to see a text through its similarities to other texts. This essay, then, cannot simply be the record of an existing generic boundary, but must also be a request to group certain works in certain ways, an argument about the meanings of poems, and a link in the "strange loop" Rosmarin describes that will necessarily be exceeded, abandoned and twisted as genre's metaphoric mutability protects the anti-hierarchical futurity of its discourse.

Notes

1. This essay is a condensation and revision of Admussen 2010, reproduced with permission from *Modern Chinese Literature and Culture*. The original essay extends this argument to discuss periodization—specifically the line between modern and contemporary Chinese literature—as a type of hermeneutic metaphor comparable to genre. It also goes into more detail about the drawbacks and limitations of the generic metaphors that appear in this chapter. I am grateful to Kirk Denton and everyone at *MCLC* for permission to adapt this essay, and for their invaluable contributions to its content. Elements of this essay also appear in Admussen 2016a, a monograph-length study of contemporary Chinese prose poetry.
2. For instance, Zou Yuehan identifies this poem by name as the earliest attempt at the form in Wang 2008: 12, and so does Huang 2006: 10. After putting Lu Xun at the beginning of his anthology, likely owing to his stature as a writer, Wang Fuming (2008: 13) starts his mostly chronological procession of works with "Moonlit Night." Du (1993: 85) traces the critical position that this poem is the first true Chinese prose poem, a position with which he disagrees, back to a 1922 essay by Kang Baiqing in that year's *Yearbook of New Poetry*.
3. My translation. For an alternate translation, see Hockx 1994: 31.
4. Genre as metaphor is discussed in Rosmarin 1986; I also follow Stephen Monte, who writes that "genre is much more an interpretive framework than a category of classification" (2000: 24).
5. Viewing the poem in its original publication, *Xin Qingnian* (New Youth or La Jeunesse) magazine, *juan* 4, no. 1 (1918), also makes this clear; the negative space feels highly intentional and designed.
6. Du Fu 2016: 247.
7. See for example his poem "Naked" (*Chiluoluo*) in *Xin Qingnian*, *juan* 6, no. 4 (1918). Its first line is short and ends in a comma, and the second is extremely long, including two sentences, stretching down to one character's space from the bottom margin, and then breaking on another comma. Line three is just four characters long and seems almost to be the overflow from line two; both it and the final line end on rhetorical questions. None of the techniques from Chinese free verse appears—enjambment, use of the line break as a kind of unstated punctuation, dramatic control over the impressions that can be made by long and short lines—but the poems cannot be called prose, in letter or spirit. They seem instead to be classical poems rendered in punctuated, vernacular written Chinese, with an attendant rejection of some of classical poetry's rhythmic expectations.
8. "Carpenter" possibly refers to Edward Carpenter (1844–1929), and "Henley" is most likely William Ernest Henley (1849–1903).
9. Michel Hockx makes this argument as well in Hockx 1994: 66, and Huang Yongjian in Huang 2006: 43.
10. Parts of the *Dao de Jing*, for example, are written in rhyme; in the *Literary Mind and the Carving of Dragons* (c. fifth century CE), Liu Xie divides literature into seventeen rhyming types (which he calls *wen*, literature) and seventeen non-rhyming types (which he calls *bi*, writings). While not all the rhyming types are obviously poems, most of those types which are considered poems or songs do rhyme—this is a version of the traditional stricture against which Zheng and Guo are pitting their energy.
11. It is notable that this is not the same period as that in which he begins to use the term: Hockx 2000 points out that his first use of the term in *Vanity Fair* is mistaken in several ways, and that his first translations of Turgenev's prose poems are published in a fiction magazine.

12. It appears in the prose poetry anthologies Wang 2008: 20 and Luo 1986: 15, but is collected under the category "penetrating sketch" 精到小品 in Liu 1995: 9.
13. *Weeds* has been translated in Lu 2003 and Lu 2019. For a condensation of the debate over the translation of the title, see Admussen 2014. For an English study that emphasizes poem-by-poem interpretation, see Kaldis 2014.
14. "My Lost Love" (Lu 2003: 20) satirizes the empty formality of early twentieth-century Chinese love poetry; "The Dog's Retort" (ibid.: 75) is a response to Baudelaire's poem "Le chien et le flacon," in which a dog responds to Baudelaire's comparison between the public's love for dreck and the dog's love of sniffing excrement. Lu Xun's dog says, "I could never measure up to man . . . I still don't know how to distinguish between copper and silver . . . between officials and common citizens, between masters and their slaves," and the narrator flees from him, ashamed.
15. *Prose Poetry* (*Sanwenshi*) magazine has been published in Yiyang, Henan since 1985, and *World of Prose Poetry* (*Sanwenshi de Shijie*) is an online and print magazine active since 2006, but many other prose-poetry-only publications have started and stopped in the last thirty years. Anthologies are too numerous to mention: some examples are the eleven-volume *Great Collection of Chinese Prose Poetry* (*Zhongguo Sanwenshi Da Xi*) published in 1992 and the yearly series of *Selected Chinese Prose Poetry* (*Zhongguo Sanwenshi Xuan*) published by the Changjiang Wenyi Chubanshe since 2005. Prose poetry societies (*xuehui*) are scattered across many of China's cities, and there exists an all-China society as well as a China-Foreign Prose Poetry Society (*zhongwai sanwenshi xuehui*).
16. I find an early model for this particular kind of interplay between mimesis and identity, object and subject in what I call the sacralization of prose visible in the writer Bing Xin's 1955 translations of Rabindranath Tagore. See Admussen 2016b.
17. For more on mid-century Chinese prose poetry's unsubversive spirit, see Admussen 2016a: 57–9.
18. This story appears repeatedly on blogs, in school textbooks, and in self-help manuals, like Zhao and Tang 2006: 255. Versions differ in a manner reminiscent of oral tales: sometimes the protagonist is an American boy, sometimes Chinese; sometimes the nailing takes place in a tree in the courtyard, sometimes in the family's wooden doorstep. The story changes, as well: sometimes the boy is allowed to remove a nail every time he helps a classmate, but more often simply when he is successful in controlling his anger.
19. *Prose Poetry Magazine* prints two editions a month: the early edition, which has adult work, and the late-month "campus" edition, which runs poetry by students and teachers, and which sells institutional subscriptions to schools.
20. His official biography appears at <http://www.chinawriter.com.cn/zxhy/member/1226.shtml> (last accessed November 7, 2019).
21. The vitality of these alternative networks is reinforced by a sense that since around 2005, the orthodox center of the genre in China feels moribund. Lashed to a state literary apparatus that has little interest in it, dominated by men to the near-complete exclusion of women and queer voices, lately it has seemed that the future of the genre exists on its margins.
22. For poems by these two poets in translation, see Shang 2006 and Ya 2016. For an English-language introduction to modern Taiwanese poetry, see Yeh and Malmqvist 2001.
23. This translation orientation has its roots in the New Culture Movement and was a crucial element in the transition to post-Mao poetry. See Bei 1993.
24. For translated poems by Xi Chuan, see Xi 2012. Translations and discussions of Yu Jian and Xi Chuan are available via open access in Crevel 2008, Chapter 6. I discuss Xi Chuan in Admussen 2016a: 150–62.

Works Cited

Admussen, Nick (2009) "A Music for Baihua: Lu Xun, *Wild Grass*, and 'A Good Story,'" in *Chinese Literature: Essays, Articles, Reviews* 31, pp. 1–22.

Admussen, Nick (2014), "Foreword: The Title of *Yecao*." *Journal of Modern Literature in Chinese*, vol. 11 no. 2, Spring, pp. 8–12.

Admussen, Nick (2016a), *Recite and Refuse: Contemporary Chinese Prose Poetry*, Honolulu: University of Hawaii Press.

Admussen, Nick (2016b), "Genre Occludes the Creation of Genre: Bing Xin, Tagore, and Prose Poetry," in *The Oxford Handbook of Modern Chinese Literatures*, ed. Andrea Bachner and Carlos Rojas, Oxford: Oxford University Press, pp. 578–96.

Bei Dao 北岛 (trans. Wei Deng) (1993), "Translation Style: A Quiet Revolution," in Wendy Larson and Anne Wedell-Wedellborg (eds), *Inside Out: Modernism and Postmodernism in China*, Aarhus: Aarhus University Press.

Chang, Eileen (2013), *Literary Remains: Death, Trauma, and Lu Xun's Refusal to Mourn*, Honolulu: University of Hawaii Press.

Crevel, Maghiel van (2008), *Chinese Poetry in Times of Mind, Mayhem and Money*, Leiden: Brill.

Denton, Kirk (ed. and trans.) (1996), *Modern Chinese Literary Thought: Writings on Literature, 1893–1945*, Stanford: Stanford University Press, Ch. 18.

Du Fu 杜甫 (trans. Stephen Owen) (2015), *The Poetry of Du Fu*, Berlin: De Gruyter.

Du Ronggen 杜荣根 (1993), *Xunqiu Yu Chaoyue—Zhongguo Xinshi Xingshi Piping* 寻求与超越——中国新诗形式批评 [Search and Transcendence—Criticism of the Forms of Chinese New Poetry], Shanghai: Fudan Daxue Chubanshe.

Hockx, Michel (1994), *A Snowy Morning: Eight Chinese Poets on the Road to Modernity*, Leiden: CNWS.

Hockx, Michel (2000), "Liu Bannong and the Forms of New Poetry," *Journal of Modern Literature in Chinese*, vol. 3, no. 2, pp. 83–118.

Huang Yongjian 黄永健 (2006) *Sanwenshi Yanjiu* 散文诗研究 [Prose Poetry Research], Beijing: Zhongguo Shehui Kexue Chubanshe.

Jia Zhifang 贾植芳 (ed.) (1986), *Zhongguo Xiandai Wenxue Zuopin Xuan* 中国现代文学作品选 [Selected Works of Modern Chinese Literature], Fudan: Fudan Daxue Chubanshe, Vol. 1.

Kaldis, Nicholas (2014), *The Chinese Prose Poem: a Study of Lu Xun's Wild Grass (Yecao)*, Amherst: Cambria Press.

Ke Lan 柯蓝 (1981), *Zaoxia Duandi* 早霞短笛 [Short Flute of Morning Mist], Shanghai: Shanghai Wenyi Chubanshe.

Laughlin, Charles (2014), "Intractable Paradox: Revisionism in the Chinese Reception of *Wild Grass*," *Journal of Modern Literature in Chinese*, vol. 11, no. 2, Spring, pp. 40–63.

Liu Bannong 刘半农 (1926) 扬鞭集自序 [Preface to the *Whip Collection*], 《语丝》 [*Threads of Talk*], 70, March 15.

Liu Bannong 刘半农 (1995), *Liu Bannong Zuopin Jingxuan* 刘半农作品精选 [Best Selections from the Works of Liu Bannong], ed. Zhang Jun 章军, Guilin: Guangxi Shifan Daxue Chubanshe.

Lu Xun 鲁迅 (2000), *Wild Grass*, trans. Yang Xianyi and Gladys Yang, Beijing: Waiwen Chubanshe.

Lu Xun 鲁迅 (2019), *Weeds*, trans. Matt Turner, Shanghai: Seaweed Salad Editions.

Luo Kuang 珞旷 (ed.) (1986), *Xiandai Sanwenshi Xuan* 现代散文诗选 [Selected Modern Prose Poems], Changsha: Hunan Wenyi Chubanshe.

McDougall, Bonnie (trans.) (1980), *Mao Zedong's 'Talks at the Yan'an Conference on Literature and Art': A Translation of the 1943 Text with Commentary*, Ann Arbor: Michigan Papers in Chinese Studies.

Monte, Stephen (2000), *Invisible Fences: Prose Poetry as a Genre in French and American Literature*, Lincoln: University of Nebraska Press.
Rosmarin, Adena (1986), *The Power of Genre*, Minneapolis: University of Minnesota Press.
Shang Qin (trans. Steve Bradbury) (2006), *Feelings Above Sea Level*, Brookline: Zephyr Press.
Sun Yushi 孙玉石 (2006), *Ye Cao Yanjiu* 《野草》研究 [Research into *Wild Grass*], Beijing: Beijing Daxue Chubanshe.
Wang Fuming 王幅明 (ed.) (2008), *Zhongguo Sanwenshi 90 Nian* 中国散文诗90年 [90 Years of Chinese Prose Poetry], Zhengzhou: Henan Wenyi Chubanshe, Vols 1–2.
Wang Guangming 王光明 (1987), *Sanwenshi de Shijie* 散文诗的世界 [The World of Prose Poetry], Wuhan: Sichuan Wenyi Chubanshe.
Xi Chuan (2012), *Notes on the Mosquito*, trans. Lucas Klein, New York: New Directions.
Xu Zhimo 徐志摩 (1987), *Xu Zhimo Shi Quanbian* 徐志摩诗全编 [A Complete Edition of Xu Zhimo's Poems], Hangzhou: Zhezhang Wenyi Chubanshe.
Ya Hsien (2016), *Abyss*, trans. John Balcom, Brookline: Zephyr Press, 2016.
Yeh, Michelle (2000), "From Surrealism to Nature Poetics: A Study of Prose Poetry from Taiwan," *Journal of Modern Literature in Chinese*, vol 3, no. 2, pp. 119–53.
Yeh, Michelle, and N. G. D. Malmqvist (eds) (2001), *Frontier Taiwan: An Anthology of Modern Chinese Poetry*. New York: Columbia University Press.
Zhang Baoming 张宝明 (1998), *Huimou <Xin Qingnian> Yuyuan Wenxue Juan* 回眸《新青年》语言文学卷 [A *New Youth* Retrospective: Language and Literature], Zhengzhou: Henan Wenyi Chubanshe.
Zhao Donghai 赵东海 and Tang Xiaolan 唐晓岚 (2006), *Tiaozhan Zhongguoren de Chuantong Siwei* 挑战中国人的传统思维 [Challenging the Traditional Thinking of the Chinese People], Harbin: Harbin Chubanshe.

17

THE *SANBUNSHI* (PROSE POEM) IN JAPAN

Scott Mehl

Introduction: The Uncertain Outlines of Japanese Prose Poetry

AMONG SCHOLARS OF JAPANESE POETRY THERE is disagreement as to who the historically important Japanese prose poets are, as well as disagreement over whether prose poetry in Japan is an exclusively modern phenomenon or is one that can be traced back very nearly to the beginnings of Japanese literature.

On encountering the above statement, some readers will react dismissively—dissensus is an inevitable feature of academic discourse, such readers might say. But I am going to claim that there are reasons for the dispute over Japanese prose poetry: the history of the concept of prose poetry in Japanese has made competing theories inevitable—or, if that is too strong a claim, then at least it made dissensus highly likely. An examination of the disparate paths followed by Japanese critical discourse about prose poetry, on the one hand, and the composition of prose poems in Japanese, on the other, will go far toward explaining why there have been sharply divergent views on fundamentals at virtually every turn.

As an example of the critical disagreement over the canon of Japanese prose poetry, take the two monographs on the subject in English: Dennis Keene's *The Modern Japanese Prose Poem* and Yasuko Claremont's *Japanese Prose Poetry*. Both works mention a few poets in common (Tanikawa Shuntarō, Inoue Yasushi, Tamura Ryūichi, and others), but generally Keene and Claremont delineate canons of prose poetry that are more different than similar. As a point of consensus between the two critics, however, both Keene and Claremont assert that one's definition of prose poetry determines where one will locate the beginning of Japanese poetry on a timeline: both contend that even in Japanese writings from centuries ago there are passages that seem like prose poetry. For example, Claremont and Keene both identify the writer Sei Shōnagon's (CE 966–1017) *Makura no sōshi* [Pillow Book] as a forerunner of poetic prose (Keene 1980: 3; Claremont 2006: 11). Both scholars also imply that prose poetry in the modern acceptation of that term has its beginnings in Japan in the 1930s, or in the late 1920s at the earliest—disagreeing, however, as to the details.[1]

Japanese scholars likewise offer divergent views as to when prose poetry in modern Japanese was first written. Nakaji Yoshikazu, a scholar of French literature, has dated the beginnings of Japanese prose poetry to around 1925, with the Baudelaire-inspired works of the poets Fukunaga Tarō and Ōte Takuji (Nakaji 2002: 82). The comparatist Kenmochi Takehiko treats prose poetry as central to the Japanese literary tradition and in fact describes modern Japanese literature as "beginning from the rediscovery of the prose-poetic qualities of the Japanese language" [*masa ni nihongo no sanbunshisei no saihakken kara hajimatta no de aru*], suggesting that Japanese literature's ancient sources lay in prose poetry;[2] for Kenmochi the earliest Japanese prose poetry in the modern period dates to an 1888 text by Kunikida Doppo (Kenmochi 2004: 43–4). Takeda Kiko claims that the first Japanese prose poem is a 1908 text by Kinoshita Mokutarō (Takeda 1985: 155). The critic Hattori Yoshika, writing in the 1960s about events he had participated in half a century earlier, asserted that the first prose poem in Japanese was actually a different 1908 text, one by the poet and critic Iwano Hōmei (Hattori 1963: 83). Satō Nobuhiro, a scholar of Japanese Symbolist poetry, examines at length the work of Kanbara Ariake—whose first prose poem was published in 1907—but then concludes that the earliest Japanese works in the genre did not have an "awareness about the distinctive qualities of the prose poem," an awareness that was, however, on full display only seven years later, in mid-1910s works by poets such as Yamamura Bochō and Mitomi Kyūyō (Satō 1993: 71). I will observe that the scholars I have just quoted here tend to announce their conclusions in a discursive vacuum: they do not refer to one another's works, seemingly unaware that other scholars had arrived at different conclusions. In a sense, then, there is actually next to no open disagreement over modern Japanese prose poetry, just diverse claims made by scholars working, it would seem, independently.

One might hope that the central question—What is a Japanese prose poem?—would be clarified by recourse to the original language, by investigating the term(s) used to refer to what we are calling "prose poetry" in English. When one looks at the Japanese terminology, however, one uncovers only greater complication, for reasons of translation and history. The history of the prose poem in Japan offers a textbook problem in *Begriffsgeschichte* or conceptual history.

In one influential model of conceptual history, there are two ways of approaching the relation between concepts and language: onomasiologically and semasiologically.[3] The onomasiological approach starts with a category—say, prose poetry—and asks what terms historically were used to name instances of that category. Conversely, the semasiological approach starts with a term—say, "prose poetry"—and asks to what kinds of thing that term referred. This binary is not intended to be exhaustive, but it is a useful distinction for sorting through discourses about disputed concepts, especially considering that the various users of any language are seldom in perfect agreement about either meanings or usages.

As regards prose poetry in Japanese, both approaches should be pursued with caution. From the onomasiological angle, one must decide which basic definition of prose poetry to adopt at the outset. I will not recapitulate here all the debate that has swirled around the meanings of prose poetry in English or other languages, but let us acknowledge that the investigator's principle of selection will tend to exclude any text that does not confirm the very premises from which the investigation began. The problem is compounded when we consider the synthetic nature of prose poetry: it presumes a fusion, however arranged, of the prosaic and the poetic. But what if either of those categories is absent from, or is radically different in, the literary field under investigation—in this case, Japanese literature? To assume in advance that Japanese literature must include what the investigator will recognize as "prose" and "poetry" would be to overlook important questions about the comparability of literary phenomena in different languages.

From the semasiological angle, one is confronted with intractable questions of translation. It so happens that there is in modern Japanese a calque on the term "prose poetry," namely "*sanbunshi*," which was created after Japanese literati had encountered prose poetry in European languages. However, taking *sanbunshi* as one's terminological through-line runs the risk of treating some European-language version of prose poetry as the standard. It also runs the risk of overlooking the possibility that in this case perhaps the best semasiological investigation would follow the careers not of one term alone but of several.

Having made these observations on methodology, I should state here that the present essay will combine elements of both approaches. In this essay I treat the term *sanbunshi* as the crucial ingredient in the creation of modern Japanese prose poetry. But when that term first appeared, it held demonstrably different meanings for different Japanese poets and critics. The variety of meanings ascribed to the *sanbunshi* must be seen in the context of the paradigm shifts then being observed in the very concepts of poetry and prose in Japan.

The Longer Japanese Lyric in the Last Decades of the Nineteenth Century

To help set the scene, it will be useful to introduce readers to the wrenching copiousness of available genres in Japanese literature just over a century ago. A recent scholarly study lists the following varieties of brief prose written in Japanese around the year 1910:

> *bibun*: beautiful text ('belles-lettres'), in an elevated style of literary Japanese
> *hagakibun*: 'postcard text'
> *haibun*: text to accompany a haiku; haiku-like prose
> *hyakujibun*: 'hundred-character text'
> *jojibun*: sketch of an event (cf. *jojishi*, 'epic poetry')
> *jojōbun*: lyric prose (cf. *jojōshi*, 'lyric poetry')
> *jokeibun*: impression of a landscape (cf. *jokeishi*, 'landscape poetry')
> *kansatsuki*: a record of one's observations
> *kansōbun*: one's reflections
> *kikōbun*: travel account
> *konto*: (Fr. *conte*) story
> *sanbunshi*: prose poem
> *setsuwa*: didactic tale
> *shaseibun*: prose sketch
> *shōhin(bun)*: short prose piece
> *shōto sutōrii*: 'short story'
> *shokanbun*: letter, epistle
> *shōwa*: tale
> *suketchi*: sketch
> *tanbun*: short text
> *tanpen shōsetsu*: a short *shōsetsu*, short story
> *zuihitsu*: 'following the brush', essay

This list is based on one provided in Agnes Fink-von Hoff's study of the *shōhinbun* (Fink-von Hoff 2006: 26–7).[4] Not even so long a catalog is exhaustive: such other early twentieth-century forms as the *tokai sanbunshi* or "urban prose poem" could also be added. The above list quickly exposes something fundamental about the milieu in which the Japanese *sanbunshi* appeared: the span of years from 1890 to 1910 saw sweeping transformations in Japanese literature, transformations that destabilized the vocabulary for naming literary forms and genres. It also reveals something about these short prose forms: since their form was indeterminate—brevity alone was their defining trait—the designator for any given form frequently reflected the text's content. A *kikōbun*, for example, would briefly recount an episode of travel; the content of a *jojōbun* would resemble that of a lyric poem. But other designators left content unspecified: the *konto* or the *hyakujibun* could, in principle, be about anything whatsoever.

Today many of the forms listed above are no longer productive. One is unlikely to find a *jokeibun* section, for example, in a contemporary bookstore or periodical: brief descriptions of moving scenery may indeed be published, but under some more neutrally capacious designation, such as nonfiction. However, the *sanbunshi*, along with the *tanpen shōsetsu* and the *zuihitsu*, remains among the productive forms of literary Japanese. There is nothing surprising about finding *sanbunshi* in poetry journals. The October 1993 issue of *Gendaishi techō* (Modern Poetry Notebook), a poetry monthly, ran a special feature titled "Ima, sanbunshi no jidai": "it is now the era of the *sanbunshi*." In a similarly triumphalist vein, Yasuko Claremont proclaimed that "Japanese prose poetry [. . .] has now flourished into independence and achieved international standing, so that it now occupies a place beside *tanka* and *haiku* as part of the poetic tradition of Japan" (Claremont 2006: 158). By all accounts, the *sanbunshi* is a survivor: it continues to be viable, and has even thrived, in the century and more since 1910.

But in 1890, a mere twenty years earlier, there were no *sanbunshi* in Japanese. To be more precise, the term did not yet exist. Nor did many of the other terms that appear in the list above. The *konto*, the *shōto sutōrii*, the *suketchi*, all loanwords that had attained as yet no broad currency, played little role in the Japanese literary ecology at the time.[5] Other terms, though, named forms that had been present for centuries: for instance, the *zuihitsu*, a term that originated in China, dated as far back as the early fifteenth century in Japan; the *haibun* dated to the seventeenth century.[6] For some readers, then, the question arises—as it arose, too, for some of those Japanese who encountered the first *sanbunshi* so designated—whether it was the case that, for the *sanbunshi*, as Francis Bacon said of his essays, "The word is late, but the thing is auncient."

The present essay will not be taking a position on whether the Japanese prose poem was ancient, but there is no question that the word *sanbunshi* was late: being a calque on the English "prose poem," it was the fusion of *sanbun*, "prose broadly conceived," and *shi*, "poetry broadly conceived," which were two terms that had begun acquiring those senses only in the last two decades of the nineteenth century. (I will devote most of my attention here to the meaning of *shi*; the meaning of *sanbun* is examined briefly below.) The word *shi* had for many centuries had a much narrower scope: it had designated poetry written in literary Chinese, as opposed to other forms of poetry written in Japanese, such as the *haikai*, the *waka*, and others. In the last decades of the nineteenth century, following the so-called reopening of Japan after some two and a half centuries of *sakoku* or isolationism, the literary culture of Europe became a new source for study and inspiration on the part of Japanese writers, and in 1882 a self-proclaimed new poetic form was invented as a medium for translating longer lyrics from European languages: the *shintaishi* or "new-style *shi.*" The creators of this term thus consciously repurposed the word *shi*: to borrow vocabulary used by David Bellos in a recent study, the compilers of the *Shintaishi shō* proposed to transform the word *shi* from a hyponym (naming only one form of poetry) into a hypernym, a term for all kinds of poetry (Bellos 2011: 26–7).

The reception of the *shintaishi* shaped the subsequent course of Japanese poetry, including the creation of the *sanbunshi*. The *shintaishi* was originally a poem of any number of lines, with each line generally being twelve morae (either 7–5 or 5–7). The matter of poetic diction was vexed from the beginning, with the creators of the *shintaishi* expressly advocating an update of the vocabulary admissible in poetry, even though in their actual poems they recycled many phrases from ancient *waka* poetry anthologies. And while some commentators regarded the *shintaishi* as a blight on Japanese poetry—one writer described the public's reaction to the *shintaishi* as "laughter coming from all four directions" (Yamada [1897] 1972: 120)—there was sufficient interest in the new poetry to sustain the publication of several collections throughout the 1880s into the 1890s, and the *shintaishi* became, for a time, the established form of longer lyric poetry in Japanese.

When readers derided this new kind of poetry, they frequently alleged that it was prose-like. In a sense, those readers got it exactly right: the *shintaishi*, as later critics have observed, set in motion a prosification of Japanese poetry.[7] While some contemporaries regarded the *shintaishi* as a sign of decline and of capitulation to foreign norms, others regarded it as a vast improvement, promising to bring Japanese verse in line with European standards. It should be said, however, that prose style, too, was a moving target: in the 1880s writers such as Futabatei Shimei and Yamada Bimyō wrote the earliest works in the so-called *genbun itchi* style, or "unification of speech and writing," a style which was proclaimed to be a better approximation of vernacular speech than earlier prose styles had been. The subject matter of the fictions written in this new *genbun itchi* style was informed by Japanese authors' newly acquired knowledge of fiction in European languages. While writers who worked in Japanese prose fiction, however, were venturing into new areas and experimenting with a new prose style, Japanese *shintaishi* poets were retaining many elements of ancient poetic diction and prosody. From the mid-1880s onward, the rapidly widening disparity between ever more "modern" literary prose and the still-classicizing *shintaishi*, combined with the new prestige that accrued to novels in the modern period, created a situation in which it seemed inevitable that Japanese poetry would need to undergo even further reforms.

Debates over the Difference between Poetry and Prose

In 1890, a young writer named Yamada Bimyō (1868–1910) published an essay that would precipitate one of the most consequential debates over metrics in modern Japanese literary history. More significantly for our purposes, his essay is an early statement about—or, to put it in a way that reflects his tone, an early warning against—the possibility of a prose-like poetry in Japanese. Bimyō's "Nihon inbun ron" ["On Japanese verse"], serialized in October 1890–January 1891, asserted that the defining feature of poetic language was the presence of a regular, recurring *sessō* or rhythm. The very title of Bimyō's essay, by designating its subject matter as *inbun*, cast a vote against the *shi*, by suggesting that *inbun* was a better hypernym for designating all poetry—the word *shi* still connoted, for many Japanese readers, poetry in literary Chinese, and therefore (as Bimyō reasoned) a different term was necessary. For Bimyō, *inbun* was the better term; he opposed it to *sanbun*, "prose."[8]

Bimyō's "Nihon inbun ron" began with a section on "The Distinction between Prose [*sanbun*] and Verse [*inbun*]," laying out two related but distinct binary oppositions: the distinction between prose and verse, on the one hand; and the distinction between content and form, on the other. For Bimyō, the fundamental difference between prose and verse was, as just noted, the absence or presence of *sessō* or (recurring) "rhythm": verse has *sessō*, prose does not. From that signal fact the other characteristics of verse could be derived: for example, if verse tends to be brief and prose long, the reason is that prose, although lacking in *sessō*, has for that very reason a greater freedom to modulate its rhythms and thereby avoid repetitiveness (Yamada [1890–1] 2014: 84). The two binary oppositions (prose/verse, content/form) were related inasmuch as *sessō* was, for Bimyō, a question of form, not content.

One consequence of Bimyō's attention to questions of form was his insistence that the various genres should be held distinct, and that is why he is relevant to a study of prose poetry in Japan: he was creating a theory to explain why prose poetry should not exist. The stress is on the word *should*, in part because Bimyō conceded that prose-like poetry had been written in Japanese—even more, that Japanese poetry had always been prose-like. He arrived at this belief through his study of English prosody, uncritically accepting that poetic meter should be organized around iambs, trochees, anapests, and the like.

The solution to this problem was, as Bimyō believed, that Japanese poets should learn from, and employ, English prosody. In Bimyō's account, Japanese syllables are of uniform length and stress but differ in pitch, which is either high or low, and he demonstrated that the feet of English-language verse could be adapted to Japanese, too, by arrangements of high- and low-pitched syllables (Yamada [1890–1] 2014: 120). Bimyō observed, rightly, that Japanese poets working in the *haikai* and the *waka* had historically never given much thought to the distribution of high and low pitches in their poems, which implied (for Bimyō) that "putting it in the strongest terms, [such poems] were prose-like verse [*sanbunteki inbun*]," which was, it almost went without saying, "in no way a satisfactory means of writing verse [*jūbun no inbun to wa kesshite iezu*]" (Yamada [1890–1] 2014: 123). What Bimyō was implying was extraordinary: Japanese poets in the *haikai* and *waka* forms had been writing prose all along. The purpose of Bimyō's study was to point Japanese poets in a better direction, one in line with English standards—which would bring about the eradication of what Bimyō deemed the prose-like qualities of Japanese verse.

Bimyō's project of transferring English-language prosody into Japanese did not bear any lasting fruit—not even Bimyō himself composed a body of poetry of the kind he advocated—but that is not to say that his essay had no influence. Quite the contrary. Bimyō's emphasis on form, in particular, came under attack; some critics maintained that one need not equate prosodic regularity (however defined) with poetry.

Poetry could assume any form, some argued; which implied, for Bimyō's opponents in this debate, that the distinguishing trait of poetry resided in content.

But Bimyō's essay provided powerful support for critics who insisted on metrical regularity as a defining trait of verse. In many cases when a poem deviated from *shintaishi* prosodic norms, that deviation would call up renewed discussion of the difference between poetry and prose. One of the most salient examples was the work of Kitamura Tōkoku, who was an early practitioner of free verse in modern Japanese. In May 1891, Tōkoku published a long dramatic text, *Hōraikyoku* ("Song of Mt Hōrai"), which combined metrically irregular verse with unlineated prose and occasional passages in regular meters.[9] Within a few days of *Hōraikyoku*'s publication, Tōkoku arranged to destroy as many copies of it as he could, probably fearing the incomprehension of critics. His concern was justified; he could not prevent a few reviews of the text from being published, and those reviews expressed little appreciation. In June 1891 the journalist and critic Nagasawa Betten (1868–99) reviewed *Hōraikyoku*, describing it as a *sanbunteki shihen*, a phrase to which he provided the pronunciation gloss "prose poem" (*purōzu poimu* [sic]): in Nagasawa's view, *Hōraikyoku* was not poetic enough to be poetry but was too poetic to be prose (quoted at Hiraoka 1967: 143). For these reasons Nagasawa concluded that Tōkoku's text was a "failure" [*shippai*] (quoted at Hiraoka 1967: 144).[10]

Other texts that attempted non-standard prosodies—and such texts were not numerous—suffered similar fates, derided as being prose-like and unpoetic. In September 1895, one of the originators of the *shintaishi*, Toyama Masakazu (1848–1900), published the anthology *Shintai shiika shū*, which contained a poem perceived as diverging so far from *shintaishi* norms that it was said to resemble prose. That poem, "Ryojun no hirō Kani tai'i" (Captain Kani, Hero of Port Arthur), had been published in the journal *Waseda bungaku* in February 1895; the Japanese had declared war against China in August 1894, and war poems such as Toyama's generally found appreciative audiences. But soon after the first appearance of Toyama's poem, a few writers—who did not mention Toyama by name or his poem—insisted that the Japanese *shintaishi* must have regular prosody, lest it lapse into non-poetry. In an article published in March 1895, an unnamed writer for the journal *Teikoku bungaku* (Empire Literature) went so far as to insist that the sole valid meter for the *shintaishi* was the 7–5 meter; without such a formal feature to mark the text, the "distinction between poetry and prose" would become meaningless ("Shintaishi no keishiki o ika subeki" 1895: 44). In the following month (April 1895), a writer for *Waseda bungaku* reiterated those sentiments (Kaneko 1895).

Even those reviewers who suspended judgment as to the quality of Toyama's *shintaishi* noted that the text blurred the distinction between poetry and prose. In an October 1895 article in *Teikoku bungaku*, "The Future of Our Nation's Poetic Form and Professor Toyama's *shintaishi*" (Waga kuni shōrai no shikei to Toyama hakase no shintaishi), Takayama Chogyū proclaimed that "[w]hat we call prose [*sanbun*] and what we call poetry [*shi*] are necessarily distinguished with respect to *form* [*keishiki-jō*, emphasis in original]. If the *differentia specifica* [*sabetsuteki genri*] of poetry is not in form but rather in content, then the distinction [between prose and poetry] becomes altogether meaningless" (Takayama [1895] 1972: 86). Chogyū here insisted that form was the distinguishing trait of poetry, but he seemed also to assume that a multiplicity of poetic forms would not be admissible. Poetic form required meter, and familiar meter at that.

Another reaction to Toyama's *shintaishi* was Shimamura Hōgetsu's multipart essay published in the journal *Waseda bungaku* in November and December 1895, "On the Form of the *shintaishi*" (Shintaishi no katachi ni tsuite). (This essay includes the earliest appearance that I have found of the term *sanbunshi* in print.) Hōgetsu began his long article by noting that much of the criticism of Toyama's *shintaishi* had stressed its divergence from recognized prosodies. He then attempted to contextualize the whole issue by enunciating four different ways of categorizing poems in Japanese. The first was whether the poem was a *jojishi* (an epic), a *jojōshi* (lyric), or a *gekishi* (dramatic poem). The second was whether the poem was subjective (*shukanshi*) or objective (*kyakkanshi*). The third was whether it was a poem in meter (*ritsugoshi*) or a prose poem (*sanbunshi*). The fourth related to whether the poem had a formal designation, that is, whether it had been designated a narrative (*shōsetsu*), a dramatic poem (*gekishi*), a *shintaishi*, and so on (Shimamura [1895] 1972: 91). His discussion then examined cases, considering well-known non-Japanese poems and poets (such as Milton, Byron, Shelley) to clarify the meanings of his terms. Hōgetsu, too, ultimately advocated a sharp formal distinction between poetry and prose, and had no patience for those who held that form could be made to align with content.

Born Translated: Japanese Versions of Prose Poems from European Languages

We have been wading through Japanese critical discourse because it is important to know the categories with which poets were working. Another reason for dwelling on the statements of critics (about whether such a thing as poetic prose was even possible) is that critical writings about prose poetry arose before prose poems did, whether in translation or as original prose poems.[11]

On the subject of contemporary English-language novels, Rebecca L. Walkowitz has written that many of them are "born translated"—the presumptively ordinary sequence of textual production and dissemination (first original, then translation) is disrupted, as seen in recent novels that are published simultaneously with, or even later than, their translations (Walkowitz 2015). Adapting Walkowitz's natalist analogy, one might say that the Japanese *sanbunshi* was conceived in criticism, then born through translation: the earliest Japanese texts to be denominated *sanbunshi* were the translated prose poems of Ivan Turgenev (1818–83), ten of which appeared in Ueda Bin's 1901 anthology *Miotsukushi* (Channel Markings).

Ueda Bin (1874–1916) was a significant post-horse of enlightenment in Meiji Japan, publishing numerous important translations of poetry and summaries of current theories from many European languages. Bin had no Russian, however; his versions of Turgenev were based, actually, on the English versions of Constance Garnett, published in 1897. As was common at the time, Bin gave no indication that his versions were *jūyaku* 重訳, translations of translations.[12]

In terms that are evocative of how Bin first presented these prose poems, the translation theorist Gideon Toury has described the situation of what he calls "indirect translation" during the Hebrew Enlightenment, a period of modernization comparable in many points with the Meiji years in Japan:

Often, the fact of the translation, or the name of the source-text author, was mentioned only in passing: in short formulas, in very fine print, in parentheses or a footnote, or in the table of contents alone. Not infrequently, even if the name of the original *author* was given, the *text* which had actually been translated was often not specified. (Toury 1995: 133; emphasis in the original)

In Bin's text, Turgenev's name appeared only after the last of the ten translated prose poems, followed by a three-sentence, small-font summary of Turgenev's life. Turgenev was, it is relevant to note, not an unknown figure in Japanese letters: translations of his prose works (by Futabatei Shimei, who was introduced above) were published as early as 1888. Turgenev's stature as a European writer whose works had been acclaimed in Japanese translation may have smoothed the way for the translation of his *sanbunshi*, a form that critics were otherwise primed, as we have seen, to disparage.

The *genbun itchi* style has already been mentioned as an important new feature of literary prose in the last decade of the nineteenth century, but Bin's versions of Turgenev were pointedly written in a more classical style. Bin favored the older verb endings and omitted certain grammatical particles and other connectives, thereby evoking the diction of ancient Japanese poetry. In some respects Bin's translations were utterly modern—they included proper nouns such as "Russia" and "Poland" and such contemporary nouns as "religion," "science," "art"—yet such modernity-signifying novelties were juxtaposed with words from ancient Japanese poetry anthologies. The first words of the prose poem "Waga teki" ("My Enemy") demonstrate many of these qualities:

昔、人を識りぬ、これわが敵。業に、好に、心たえて合はず。遭ふ度ごとに盡きせぬ論争は起りぬ。すべてにつきて争ひぬ、芸術、宗教、科学、地上の生、墓のあなたの生につきて、特に墓のあなたの生につきて。(Ueda 1901: 125)

mukashi, hito o shirinu, kore waga teki. waza ni, konomi ni, kokoro taete awazu. au tabigoto ni tsukisenu ronsō wa okorinu. subete ni tsukite arasoinu, geijutsu, shūkyō, kagaku, chijō no shō, haka no anata no shō ni tsukite, toku ni haka no anata no shō ni tsukite.

I translate the above passage, retaining the punctuation:

[Long ago, I knew someone, he [was] my enemy. In our enterprises, [and] in our preferences, our minds did not at all align. Every time we met there arose inexhaustible debate. We fought about everything, art, religion, science, life on this earth, and about life beyond the grave, especially about life beyond the grave.]

For comparison, Garnett's English version of the poem, titled "My Adversary," began as follows:

[I had a comrade who was my adversary; not in pursuits, nor in service, nor in love, but our views were never alike on any subject, and whenever we met, endless argument arose between us.

We argued about everything: about art, and religion, and science, about life on earth and beyond the grave, especially about life beyond the grave.] (Turgenev 1897: 248)

Bin's Japanese combined two paragraphs in one, and it misrepresented the first line of Garnett's Turgenev by transposing the enmity, which exists on the plane of opinion alone in the English, onto a plane that includes "enterprises" (*waza*) and "preferences" (*konomi*)—both of which are excluded by negation in the English ("*not* in pursuits, *nor* in service"). (Bin also omits the reference to love.)[13] But by treating the disagreement as extending to those other realms of life, the speaker in Bin's prose poem has, one might claim, an even greater score to settle with his enemy than does the speaker in Garnett's version. As for the style, the iteration of diction and syntactic structures that characterizes Garnett's English—"not in pursuits, nor in service, nor in love"; "about life on earth and beyond the grave, especially about life beyond the grave"—reappears forcefully in Bin's Japanese: "*waza ni, konomi ni*"; "*chijō no shō, haka no anata no shō ni tsukite, toku ni haka no anata no shō ni tsukite.*" In Bin's version the phrase "about life beyond the grave" is given a full repetition, with an intensifying *toku ni* added before the second iteration. The speaker of the prose poem expresses his punctilious correctness by airing his thoughts and repeating his key terms as many times as necessary. His disagreement with his enemy continues even after death, as one learns toward the end of the text.

As a whole, the anthology *Miotsukushi* garnered few notices in the press, but a handful of notable readers—notable because they were (or would later become) writers themselves—drew inspiration from Bin's collection.[14] One of these readers was Kanbara Ariake (1875–1952). Ariake, as he is familiarly known, played the pivotal role—one that has gone largely unacknowledged—in introducing French prose poetry to Japan. He was the first to present in Japanese the prose poems of Baudelaire, for instance, and was an early explicator of Baudelaire's works (Takeda 1985: 156). Ariake was also among the first Japanese writers to compose original *sanbunshi*. Ariake came into his role of pioneer prose poet somewhat reluctantly; as modern poetry scholar Satō Nobuhiro has argued, Ariake began writing his own prose poems not only because he was emulous of the French practitioners of the prose poem, but also because he was dissatisfied with the *sanbunshi* as it had hitherto been composed in Japanese (Satō 1993: 59).

But here we must look closely at what Ariake would have understood by the term *sanbunshi*. In the span of a few years he uses the term *sanbunshi* to refer to textual objects that we now might treat as being distinct. In a 1905 text (the preface to his third poetry collection, *Shunchōshū* [Spring Birds]), Ariake made disparaging observations about the *sanbunshi* of Baudelaire and Mallarmé, claiming that they were not much more than *bibun* (belles-lettres); Ariake also claimed that the haiku poet Yamaguchi Sodō's (1642–1716) *haibun* text "Minomushi no setsu" (A commentary on the bagworm moth) was just as good as the prose poems of those vaunted French poets (Kanbara 1905: 8–9). Here was a statement of the thesis that the prose poem, in its European manifestation, was little different from, and had arisen considerably later than, allegedly comparable but historically earlier forms of Japanese writing such as *bibun* and *haibun*.[15]

When Ariake published an article on "Our Country's Prose Poetry" (Wagakuni no sanbunshi) in July 1908, his understanding of the meaning of *sanbunshi* had changed. In late 1907, free-verse poems in a *genbun itchi* style had begun to be written in Japanese; in Ariake's short article, *sanbunshi* was the term he applied to such free-verse poems, giving recent examples by the poets Sōma Gyofū, Hiraki Hakusei, and Iwano Hōmei. He mentioned, too, Toyama's poem about Captain Kani as being "a true *sanbunshi*"

(Kanbara [1908] 1972: 346). But Ariake maintained that other kinds of texts should also be deemed *sanbunshi*, too, such as certain short prose pieces by Kitamura Tōkoku; short works by the poet Shimazaki Tōson and the playwright Osanai Kaoru; and the works of Mizuno Yōshū (1883–1947), whom Japanese literary historians today regard as the representative writer of *shōhinbun*. (We will return to Mizuno below.) Ariake's understanding of the *sanbunshi* exemplifies a key phase in the term's semasiology: for him at the time, the *sanbunshi* included what we might designate as "prose poetry," but it also included "free-verse poetry." Hence the dissatisfaction he felt about the Japanese *sanbunshi* might in part have been dissatisfaction with the trend toward meter-free verse composition in general.

But this did not mean that Ariake attempted to reinsert familiar prosodies into his compositions. In his own verses, he experimented with an ever-expanding number of meters of his own invention, and he maintained a steady output of prose poems. At the end of his July 1908 article on Japanese prose poetry, Ariake observed that "it would certainly be worthwhile [for Japanese poets] to study the most recent Western works [of prose poetry]" (Kanbara [1908] 1972: 347). But it was still the case that relatively few prose poems from Western languages were available in Japanese translation. Ueda Bin's versions of Turgenev from 1901 have already been mentioned; in a 1905 anthology (*Binkashū*) the writer Nakazawa Rinsen had made new versions available of three of the Turgenev prose poems that Bin had already translated (Nakazawa 1905: 100–3, 145–50, 173–7). Ariake himself had only recently begun publishing his translations of prose poems by prominent French writers, beginning in May 1908 with his versions of Baudelaire's "Le galant tireur" and "Le désir de peindre." Over the next five years Ariake continued publishing his versions of prose poems by important French writers: Baudelaire (11 prose poems in all), Mallarmé (2), Huysmans (1), and Rimbaud (1). Ariake's Japanese versions were based on various English translations—some by Arthur Symons, some by F. P. Sturm, some by Stuart Merrill (Satō 1993: 55, 71–2, n. 4).

In a turn that probably astonished some of his contemporaries, Ariake wrote his translations in a style that was clear and easy to read. His contemporaries would have been astonished, I suggest, because Ariake, known mainly as a poet, was renowned (and sometimes reviled) for his difficult Symbolist verse, with its mystifying syntax and hyper-allusive diction. His prose poetry, whether in translation or original, hewed closely to the implicit stylistic norms of contemporary literary prose. Take the first sentence of Ariake's translation of Baudelaire's "Le désir de peindre" ("The Desire to Paint"), titled "Egakan to hossuru kibō":

この希望を抱きながら心を苦しめるのは、人間としては不幸でもあらうが、芸術家としては幸福である。(Kanbara 1957: 275)

kono kibō o dakinagara kokoro o kurushimeru no wa, ningen toshite wa fukō demo arō ga, geijutsuka toshite wa kōfuku de aru.

[Having this desire and suffering from mental affliction, though it be unhappiness for a human being, is happiness for an artist.]

The verb endings are all recognizably modern, and the style-marking clause endings—such as *de arō* and *de aru*—locate this prose squarely in the contemporary era.

In the opening phrases, at least, nothing about the poem's diction or orthography would have been unusual or difficult for 1908 readers. It is true that the poem does have difficulties in store for its reader: just for two examples, later in the poem, the word *seien* 凄婉 (bewitchingly beautiful) is a bewitchingly uncommon way of writing 凄艷; and the utterly common word *kankei* 関係 (relation, connection) is written as the unusual (but homophonous and synonymous) 干繋 (Kanbara 1957: 276). These and other difficulties, however, appear only later in the text, which has been written in a manner calculated to draw readers in, beginning immediately with a demonstrative pronoun ("*kono* kibō," "*this* desire") and thereby making the reader complicit in crossing back again over the border between text (poem) and paratext (title) to find the referent. The first sentence draws a surprising distinction, between human beings (unhappy) and artists (happy), pointedly disrupting a cliché about suffering creators. Here, clearly, was an invitation to a voyage.

Early Japanese *sanbunshi* and *shōhinbun*

Ariake published eleven of his own prose poems between January 1907 and October 1913. For reasons of space I cannot sample extensively from these varied texts. I here include a complete translation of his third prose poem, published in September 1910:

Footprints

A cold drizzle of rain was falling in the yard. As soon as I turned my attention to it, though, the rain stopped.
 At that time, when I lost all interest in things, when I had nothing to keep me occupied, I would think of a dream I had had one night. It was the same as the dream I always dreamt.
 Regardless of whether I was then conscious of reality or dreaming, not a single ray of sunlight illuminated the place where I was. Yet the rain-shrouded garden in the yard had a harmonious balance of silvery grays and dark greens. The deep reds of the cotton-roses were echoed in the begonias. In spite of all this, I was drawn in, overcome by the magical power of the illusion, like a little boat overwhelmed by a great wave.

You may be surprised to learn I am a realist. It is hardly with eyes of longing that I look upon black dahlias. I want to paralyse my dulled senses by indulging in melancholy fantasies. I never think of so much as wetting my tongue in strong drink. When the bouquet of a wine has called forth from me an unexpected, a rare sensation, it has been because the smell made me shudder.
 I would bury my senses in a dream of etiolation. And I wanted to gaze blankly, with eyes clotted with buried sensations.
 That dream of etiolation would not hold the inherent interest of transformation, such as Romantic dreams have. It would unfurl itself monotonously. It would be but one scene, after which the curtain would fall.

In that scene, it neither rains nor snows. One must of course never expect so much as a glimmer of sunlight. The dull hours pass dully away; a halfhearted breeze stirs up a bit of pale dust. That dust is the powdery remnant, perhaps, of the skeletons of tens of thousands of human beings; and it was the most commonplace dust you could hope to find anywhere.

"Unbearably average dust," I murmured to myself, hardly aware I was speaking. After uttering those words, though, I realised, looking around me, that, other than a pale spectre, hovering in the dust that had been called up by the languid breeze, there was no one there to take issue with what I had said.

To one side of where I was now walking there was a moat-like depression in which the water was stagnating; to the other side there was what appeared to be a row of run-down tradesmen's houses. These houses extended seemingly endlessly, low and gray and unvarying. This being a dream, I was not so foolish as to try to make a minute inspection of each shop one by one. Since there was no sunlight to enliven this dead town, I could hardly be expected to have come upon any vista worth remembering.

Again I said, in spite of myself, "Unbearably average," for the amusement, as it were, of the pale spectre; turning around, I saw before me a desolate little shop, yawning darkly.

In front of it there was a mass of useless, overstock books.

O mediocrity of mediocrities.

I could not but think I was finally experiencing the entombment of my senses.

Steeling myself, I went into the shop. The books on the shelves were nothing but one black graveyard. The faded traces of gold lettering reminded one of nothing more than headstones. A thick layer of dust covered the books. I took one; it appeared to be a Bible in very fine print and I quickly put it down again. The next book I picked up was filled with column after column of meaningless hieroglyphs. My eyes made nothing of the writing, but I lingered over the lovely arabesques left in the pages by the bookworms as they had passed through. I reached to take up yet another book but was frightened when I saw that, in the dust that had accumulated on its cover, there were the footprints as of a tiny animal, as clearly as if they had been printed there.

The shock of making such an unexpected discovery in my dream of etiolation almost brought me completely back to consciousness.

I looked further inside the shop. There I could faintly make out the profile of an old woman in the black shadows. She was dozing. On her lap there were two shining, unwinking stars of gold.

I was going to proclaim yet again how common it all was, but no voice came out. I now wished to escape the confines of the realm of mediocrity.

For a moment I thought the two golden stars were the eyes of a black cat, but those golden eyes wrested me from my dream, summarily establishing their reign over my soul—a reign eternal.

I woke from my dream.

In the yard, as before, a fine rain was falling.

But within the dream, that book, never to be opened, upon which those animal footprints had been traced, contained intimations of mysterious gratifications. I sighed, quietly, to myself, wondering whether this book were not a collection of songs written in a most wonderful meter.

In the rain the insects, shrill, droned on. (Kanbara 1957: 192–4)

As one commentator has observed of Ariake's prose poems, his contemporaries "ignored them to death" (*mokusatsu*) (Hinatsu [1948–9] 1975: 531), but the bleakness of Ariake's work surely would have struck his neophilic contemporaries as distasteful. The speaker of this text intentionally dulls his senses in a vision of pervasive blandness—the word *heibon*, which I have translated variously as "average," "common," "mediocre," recurs like a hypnotist's suggestion. The shock of finding footprints in the dust that has accumulated on an untouched book very nearly dispels the illusion; later, when the speaker has returned to consciousness, he wonders whether that book might have contained poems (*uta*, "songs," sometimes refers to poems in traditional Japanese forms) written in a *mezurashii inritsu*, a rare or wonderful poetic meter. Ariake himself had in mind, quite possibly, the fate of his own books of poems, written in meters that had never been attempted before in Japanese (and many of which have never, as of this writing, been attempted since): the swell of criticism against formal poetry had found, in Ariake's 1908 *Ariake shū* (Ariake Collection), an easy target, as free-verse poetry came into greater prominence. Ariake wrote less and less, soon abandoning poetry altogether. His prose output, as well, shrank to almost nothing.

Above, I mentioned the semasiology of *sanbunshi* in connection with Ariake's understanding of the term: Ariake applied the term *sanbunshi* to either prose poetry or free-verse poetry (for a time, at least). There is also a contrasting observation to be made about the onomasiology of the *sanbunshi* at this time: some of Ariake's contemporaries seem to have conflated the *sanbunshi* with another kind of text, the *shōhinbun*. The two terms appeared together in print, often in immediate proximity: take, for example, the first issue (March 1910) of the journal *Sōsaku* (Creation), in which the editors stated "We will always set aside half [of all subsequent issues of this journal] for *sanbunshi* and *shōhinbun* because we hope for their speedy development" ("Kisha tsūshin" 1910).[16] Not quite synonymous in this passage, the two terms nevertheless were treated as equally deserving of promotion, and by equivalent editorial means.

The writer whose name is now most associated with the *shōhinbun* in the Meiji period was Mizuno Yōshū (mentioned above). But that association has arisen after the fact; Mizuno himself wondered whether his texts should be designated *sanbunshi* or *shōhinbun*. In the preface to *Hibiki* ("Resonance," December 1908), his second collection, Mizuno wrote of how he had been walking along the bank of a river one night, thinking over the difficulties he was having with his prose compositions, when he thought to himself:

> What I am trying to write, now, is prose [*sanbun*]. But prose has a tendency to lapse into exposition. At times I have feelings, however, that arise like a flash, feelings that cannot be explained. I believe such things are poetry [*shi*] . . . Then suddenly the thought of the *sanbunshi* came to mind.
>
> But this thing called *sanbunshi* was not something for someone like me to try their hand at [*jibun nado no gotoki mono no te ni wa kesshite noru mono de wa nai*]. How I wished I could take my flashing emotions and write in a fine high rhythm such as appears in poems, in simple style, condensing [*kondensu shite*] to the fullest possible extent.
>
> What I wrote at that time in such a frame of mind was the poem 'Inu' (The dog) in [my collection] *Araragi* (Yew Tree), and the works 'Yami' (Darkness) and 'Sōsō' (Funeral Procession) in the present collection. . . . I wanted to call these pieces *sanbunshi*, but I felt embarrassed at the thought of using such a name for pieces as unpolished as my own, and thus I regarded them as *shōhin*. (Mizuno 1909: 5–6)

This statement, explaining Mizuno's understanding of the difference between *sanbunshi* and *shōhinbun*, contains elements that are difficult to contextualize. The implied judgment—favoring the *sanbunshi*, pooh-poohing the *shōhinbun*—was not a widely-held position, so far as I have been able to determine, except insofar as the *sanbunshi* was, perhaps, perceived at the time as a novelty item while the *shōhinbun* had gone somewhat stale. (There had been regular *shōhinbun* columns in periodicals as early as 1902, beginning with the magazine *Myōjō* [Morning Star] [Kimata 2006: 225].) In any case, Mizuno's statement may simply be standard authorial humility—and it may be tongue-in-cheek. The suggestion that composing *sanbunshi* would be more difficult than composing *shōhinbun* is intriguing, as well. Whatever else we may assert about Mizuno's self-characterization here, it clearly implies that the term *sanbunshi* had, for some readers at least, a patina of sophistication.

The distinction between *shōhinbun* and *sanbunshi* was not clear enough, at the time, to dispel disagreement over attributions. Take Mizuno's collection *Hibiki* again. An advertisement for that collection proclaimed that Mizuno had written "the first *sanbunshi* that have been attempted in our [Japanese] literature" (quoted at Kimata 2006: 185). Another advertisement for *Hibiki* qualified Mizuno's work rather as "*sanbunshi*-like *shōhinbun*."[17] But in a short article published a month before Mizuno's collection, the poet and critic Kawai Suimei wrote, "There are those who regard Mizuno Yōshū's *shōhin* as *sanbunshi*, but I am of the opinion they are not *sanbunshi*. Of course there are passages here and there that are like poetry [*shi*]; in places, the rhythm of feelings [*kanjō no rizumu*] stands out" (Kawai 1909: 149). For Kawai, the presence of rhythmical passages alone did not suffice, clearly, to raise a *shōhinbun* to (what he regarded as being) the level of a *sanbunshi*.

Kawai himself would come to be a highly regarded practitioner of *sanbunshi*. Like Mizuno's 1908 collection *Hibiki*, Kawai's 1910 *Kiri* [Mist] too was advertised as "the first voice [*dai issei*] of a *sanbunshi* collection"—implying that no earlier collections could claim priority as collections of *sanbunshi*.[18]

Here we have a real-time, contemporary version of the dissensus that would characterize later scholarly studies of the prose poem in Japanese, as mentioned at the beginning of this essay, and it is with this that I would like to conclude. It seems to me that the very amorphousness of the prose poem contributes to disagreement over generic attribution. The fact that the *sanbunshi* was being introduced at the same time as numerous other literary innovations gave rise—and still gives rise—to difficulties that some critics will perhaps want to see resolved neatly. But these questions of categorization have no easy resolution, in my view: the many facets of the *sanbunshi* should rather be held in the mind all at once, like the panels of a polyptych. The polyptych under consideration here contains more panels than any commentator can introduce in a single essay; and more are added with each passing season.

Notes

1. Keene traces modern Japanese prose poetry to the work of Hagiwara Sakutarō, in particular the texts available in Hagiwara's 1935 collection *Shukumei* (Keene 1980: 41). Claremont, rather, recognizes the poets associated with the journal *Shi to shiron* (1928–31) as being the originators of "prose poetry, as a discrete genre in Japanese poetry" (Claremont 2006: 16). As a point about Japanese poetry history, I will note that the poets at *Shi to shiron* opposed

Hagiwara's poetics and formulated their aesthetics in opposition to Hagiwara's; so it is interesting that Keene and Claremont arrived at such different origin stories for Japanese prose poetry. For more in English about the *Shi to shiron* poets and the "New prose-poetry movement" (*Shin sanbunshi undō*) of the 1930s, see Ellis 2004.

2. The topic of Kenmochi's sentence is not "modern literature" but "Meiji bungaku," Meiji literature. That does not significantly alter my claim.
3. The classic account of the semasiological–onomasiological distinction is given by Reinhart Koselleck: see, in German, Brunner et al. 1972: xxii–xxiii; in English, Koselleck 2011: 18–19.
4. Fink-von Hoff specifies that not all the forms listed were necessarily always short; merely that the commonality linking all the listed forms was their potential for brevity. For a concise explanation in English of the *shōhinbun* in particular, see Marcus 1996: 246–8.
5. The entries in the *Nihon kokugo daijiten* provide the following information: *konto* dates to as early as 1919, in a fiction by Satomi Ton ("Kotoshidake"); *shōto sutōrii* is not given a date; *suketchi* dates to as early as 1898, in a text by Kunikida Doppo ("Wasureenu hitobito").
6. For work in English on *zuihitsu*, see for example Groemer 2019: 1–39 on the *zuihitsu* during the Edo period; and see Chance 1997: 46–76 on Yoshida Kenkō's *Tsurezuregusa* and its critical and historical contexts. Chance's work lucidly clarifies the difference between semasiological and onomasiological approaches to historicizing the *zuihitsu* in Japanese: in the case of the *zuihitsu*, the term does not arise as a referent to (vernacular) works in Japanese until the early 1400s, but the *zuihitsu* genre tag was retroactively applied to works written as early as the 1300s. For work in English on *haibun*, see for example Rogers 1979 and Millett 1997.
7. Hinatsu [1948–9] 1975: 28 asserts that a process of *sanbunka* (a "making prose") began in Japanese poetry as early as the Tokugawa period (*c*.1600–1868), treating that development as a consequence of a loosening of prosodic strictures.
8. Which is not to suggest that Bimyō was the only writer who opposed *inbun* to *sanbun*. A nearly contemporaneous text, the *Nihon bungakushi* (History of Japanese Literature) of Mikami Sanji and Takatsu Kuwasaburō, began by asserting: "The literature of every country can be divided into two broad kinds: prose [*sanbun*] and verse [*inbun*]" (Mikami and Takatsu [1890] 1982: 38). The terminology for referring to prose in Japanese was likewise undergoing a transformation, the upshot of which was that *sanbun* became the (mostly uncontested) hypernym.
9. For a longer examination of Kitamura Tōkoku's work in light of Yamada Bimyō and the *inbun ronsō*, see Mehl 2016.
10. This 1891 citation is the earliest mention I have found in Japanese of the English term "prose poem." I have not been able to determine where Nagasawa might have encountered it.
11. That is, no *sanbunshi* appeared if we except Nagasawa Betten's calling Kitamura Tōkoku's *Hōraikyoku* a "purōzu poimu," as mentioned above.
12. I am not aware of any thorough study of Japanese *jūyaku* (translations of translations) in the Meiji period. A few mentions of the phenomenon of *jūyaku* have been made in English scholarship: see, for example, Wakabayashi 2009: 177 n. 5, and Emmerich 2013: 46.
13. Garnett's English is an accurate reflection of Turgenev's original in this paragraph: У меня был товарищ – соперник; *не* по занятиям, *не* по службе или любви; но наши воззрения ни в чем не сходились, и всякий раз, когда мы встречались, между нами возникали нескончаемые споры (Turgenev 1967: 150; emphasis added). I should point out that, on the whole, Bin's translations were accurate; such outright slips as the one I have quoted here are rare in his published work as a translator.
14. Shimada 1981: 615 presents what appears to be an exhaustive list of contemporary responses to *Miotsukushi*.

15. Similarly, in his 1892 *Bungaku ippan* (An Outline of Literature), Uchida Roan mentioned that, in addition to *inbuntai jojōshi* (glossing the latter word as *ririkku*—"lyric"), there was also *sanbuntai jojōshi* or "prose-style lyric" in Japanese: his examples included passages from Yoshida Kenkō's *Tsurezuregusa* (Essays in Idleness), Kamo no Chōmei's *Hōjōki* (An Account of My Hut), and a short text by Matsuo Bashō (Uchida 1892: 191–200).
16. On the basis of this statement by the editors of *Sōsaku*, the scholar Satō Nobuhiro has suggested that, for the contemporary Japanese readership, "there was no distinction between *sanbunshi* and *shōhinbun*" (Satō 1993: 72 note 9). For more about the journal *Sōsaku*, see Kimata 2006: 192–3.
17. Advertisement printed at the end of Mayama 1909.
18. The journal *Sōsaku*, being a consistent advocate for *sanbunshi*, ran several advertisements for *Kiri*. The advertisement I am quoting here appeared at the end of *Sōsaku*, vol. 1, no. 3 (May 1910).

Works Cited

Bellos, David (2011), *Is That a Fish in Your Ear? Translation and the Meaning of Everything*, New York: Faber & Faber.

Brunner, Otto, Werner Conze, and Reinhart Koselleck (eds) (1972), *Geschichtliche Grundbegriffe: Historisches Lexikon zur politisch-sozialen Sprache in Deutschland. Band 1: A–D*, Stuttgart: Ernst Klett Verlag.

Chance, Linda (1997), *Formless in Form: Kenkō,* Tsurezuregusa, *and the Rhetoric of Japanese Fragmentary Prose*, Stanford, CA: Stanford University Press.

Claremont, Yasuko (2006), *Japanese Prose Poetry*, Sydney: Wild Peony.

Ellis, Toshiko (2004), "The Topography of Dalian and the Cartography of Fantastic Asia in Anzai Fuyue's Poetry," *Comparative Literature Studies* vol. 41, no. 4, pp. 482–500.

Emmerich, Michael (2013), "Beyond, Between: Translation, Ghosts, Metaphors," in Esther Allen and Susan Bernofsky (eds), *In Translation: Translators on Their Work and What It Means* (New York: Columbia University Press), pp. 44–57.

Fink-von Hoff, Agnes (2006), *Petitessen, Pretiosen: die Prosaminiatur in Japan um 1910*, München: Iudicium.

Groemer, Gerald (2019), *The Land We Saw, the Times We Knew: An Anthology of* Zuihitsu *Writing from Early Modern Japan*, Honolulu: University of Hawai'i Press.

Hinatsu Kōnosuke ([1948–9] 1975), *Meiji Taishō shishi*, Vol. 3 of *Hinatsu Kōnosuke zenshū*, Tokyo: Kawade Shobō.

Hiraoka Toshio (1967), *Kitamura Tōkoku kenkyū*, Tokyo: Yūseidō.

Kanbara Ariake (1905), *Shunchōshū*, Tokyo: Hongō Shoin, <http://www.wul.waseda.ac.jp/kotenseki/html/bunko03a/bunko03a_00268/index.html> (last accessed November 3, 2019).

Kanbara Ariake (1957), *Teihon Kanbara Ariake zenshishū*, Tokyo: Kawade Shobō.

Kanbara Ariake ([1908] 1972), "Wagakuni no sanbunshi," in Hitomi Enkichi (ed.), *Nihon kindai shiron no kenkyū: sono shiryō to kaisetsu* (Tokyo: Kadokawa Shoten), pp. 345–7.

Kaneko Chikusui (1895), "Muritsu no shintaishi," *Waseda bungaku* no. 85, April, pp. 104–5.

Kawai Suimei (1909), "Sanbunshi no honshitsu," *Bunshō hyakuwa: Bunshō sekai*, vol. 3, no. 14, pp. 147–9.

Keene, Dennis (1980), *The Modern Japanese Prose Poem: An Anthology of Six Poets—Miyoshi Tatsuji, Anzai Fuyue, Tamura Ryūichi, Yoshioka Minoru, Tanikawa Shuntarō, Inoue Yasushi*, Princeton: Princeton University Press.

Kenmochi Takehiko (2004), "Nihon bungaku: sanbunshi ron," *Seisen joshi daigaku Jinbun kagaku kenkyūjo kiyō* 25, pp. 35–58.

Kimata Satoshi (2006), *Meiji Taishō shōhinsen*, Tokyo: Ōfū.

"Kisha tsūshin" (1910), *Sōsaku* 1.1, March, p. 58.
Koselleck, Reinhart (2011), "Introduction and Prefaces to the *Geschichtliche Grundbegriffe*," trans. Michaela Richter, *Contributions to the History of Concepts*, vol. 6, no. 1, Summer, pp. 1–37.
Marcus, Marvin (1996), "The Writer Speaks: Late-Meiji Reflections on Literature and Life," in Thomas Hare, Robert Borgen, and Sharalyn Orbaugh (eds), *The Distant Isle: Studies and Translations of Japanese Literature in Honor of Robert H. Brower*, Ann Arbor: Center for Japanese Studies, University of Michigan, pp. 231–79.
Mayama Seika (1909), *Yume*, 2nd edn, Tokyo: Shinchōsha, <http://dl.ndl.go.jp/info:ndljp/pid/889299> (last accessed November 3, 2019).
Mehl, Scott (2016), "Kitamura Tōkoku and the Versification Debate in Japan, 1890–1891," *SERAS (Southeast Review of Asian Studies)*, vol. 38, pp. 38–56.
Mikami Sanji and Takatsu Kuwasaburō [1890] (1982), *Nihon bungakushi*, ed. Hiraoka Toshio, Tokyo: Nihon Tosho Sentaa.
Millett, Christine Murasaki (1997), "'Bush Clover and Moon': A Relational Reading of *Oku no hosomichi*," *Monumenta Nipponica* vol. 52, no. 3, Autumn, pp. 327–56.
Mizuno Yōshū (1909), *Hibiki*, 5th printing, Tokyo: Shinchōsha, <http://dl.ndl.go.jp/info:ndljp/pid/887987> (last accessed November 3, 2019).
Nakaji Yoshikazu (2002), "Sanbunshi no tanjō," in Komori Yōichi, Tomiyama Takao, Numano Mitsuyoshi, Hyōdō Hiromi, and Matsuura Hisaki (eds), *Iwanami kōza Bungaku 4: Shiika no kyōen*, Tokyo: Iwanami Shoten, pp. 61–93.
Nakazawa Rinsen (1905), *Binkashū*, Tokyo: Shichinin Hakkōjo, <http://www.wul.waseda.ac.jp/kotenseki/html/bunko14/bunko14_d0018/index.html> (last accessed November 3, 2019).
Rogers, Lawrence (1979), "Rags and Tatters: The *Uzuragoromo* of Yokoi Yayū," *Monumenta Nipponica* vol. 34, no. 3, Autumn, pp. 279–91.
Satō Nobuhiro (1993), "Nihon kindai sanbunshi no seiritsu: Kanbara Ariake o chūshin toshite," *Tōhoku daigaku nihon bunka kenkyūjo kenkyū hōkoku* 29, pp. 49–73.
Shimada Kinji (1981), "Kaisetsu," in Yano Hōjin (ed.), *Ueda Bin zenshū* Vol. 2, Tokyo: Kyōiku Shuppan Sentaa, pp. 601–27.
Shimamura Hōgetsu [writing as Hōgetsushi] ([1895] 1972), "Shintaishi no katachi ni tsuite," in Hitomi Enkichi (ed.), *Nihon kindai shiron no kenkyū: sono shiryō to kaisetsu*, Tokyo: Kadokawa Shoten, pp. 88–103.
"Shintaishi no keishiki o ika subeki" (1895), *Teikoku bungaku* 1.3, March, pp. 44–6, <https://babel.hathitrust.org/cgi/pt?id=uc1.$b441566&view=1up&seq=18> (last accessed November 3, 2019).
Takayama Chogyū [writing as Hayashi Onota] ([1895] 1972), "Waga kuni shōrai no shikei to Toyama hakase no shintaishi," in Hitomi Enkichi (ed.), *Nihon kindai shiron no kenkyū: sono shiryō to kaisetsu*, Tokyo: Kadokawa Shoten, pp. 79–88.
Takeda Kiko (1985), "Nihon sanbunshi no kindaisei: janru seiritsu no ikisatsu/keii/tatenuki/tateyoko to shoki sakuhin no kaishaku o chūshin toshite," *Hikaku bungaku kenkyū* 48, October, pp. 152–62.
Toury, Gideon (1995), *Descriptive Translation Studies and Beyond*, Amsterdam and Philadelphia: John Benjamins.
Toyama Masakazu (1895), *Shintai shiika shū*, Tokyo: Dai Nihon Tosho, <http://dl.ndl.go.jp/info:ndljp/pid/876368> (last accessed November 3, 2019).
Turgenev, Ivan (1897), *Dream Tales, and Prose Poems*, trans. Constance Garnett, London: Heinemann, <https://babel.hathitrust.org/cgi/pt?id=uc1.b3962145&view=1up&seq=9> (last accessed November 3, 2019).
Turgenev, Ivan (1967), *Polnoye sobraniye sochinenii i pisem v dvadtsati vos'mi tomakh*, Moscow—Leningrad: Nauka.

Uchida Roan [writing as Fuchian Shujin] (1892), *Bungaku ippan*, Tokyo: Hakubunkan, <http://dl.ndl.go.jp/info:ndljp/pid/992902> (last accessed November 3, 2019).

Ueda Bin (1901), *Miotsukushi*, Tokyo: Bun'yūkan, <http://www.wul.waseda.ac.jp/kotenseki/html/bunko03a/bunko03a_00087/index.html> (last accessed November 3, 2019).

Wakabayashi, Judy (2009), "An Etymological Exploration of 'Translation' in Japan," in Judy Wakabayashi and Rita Kothari (eds), *Decentering Translation Studies: India and Beyond* (Amsterdam and Philadelphia: John Benjamins), pp. 175–94.

Walkowitz, Rebecca L. (2015), *Born Translated: The Contemporary Novel in an Age of World Literature*, New York: Columbia University Press.

Yamada Bimyō ([1897] 1972), "Doppo gin: jo," in Hitomi Enkichi (ed.), *Nihon kindai shiron no kenkyū: sono shiryō to kaisetsu* (Tokyo: Kadokawa Shoten), pp. 119–21.

Yamada Bimyō ([1890–1] 2014), "Nihon inbun ron," in *Yamada Bimyō shū*, Vol. 9, Tokyo: Rinsen Shoten, pp. 82–137.

18

THE ARABIC PROSE POEM IN IRAQ

Sinan Antoon

THE EMERGENCE OF THE ARABIC PROSE poem in the twentieth century constituted the most radical break with an established poetic tradition going back to the sixth century CE. Some poets posited an indigenous cultural genealogy for the Arabic prose poem by referring to pre-modern texts in which rigid generic boundaries separating poetry and prose were blurred. Nevertheless, the prose poem was predominantly viewed as a product of engagements with and translations from foreign, primarily European, poetic traditions. This aura of foreignness and the hybridity of prose poetry itself overdetermined the range of responses and attitudes, both negative and positive. The discourse about the prose poem became a space for polemics about authenticity. The two major "schools" of the Arabic prose poem emerged in Lebanon and Iraq. The most influential figures of the Lebanese school are the Syrian-Lebanese poet and critic Adūnīs (1928–) and Unsī al-Ḥajj (1937–2014). Adūnīs's poems and translations from French, as well as his literary criticism, were very impactful in expanding literary horizons and shaping the contentious debate about the Arabic prose poem. *Shi`r* [Poetry] the literary journal he co-founded in Beirut with another pioneering figure, the Lebanese poet, Yūsuf al-Khāl (1916–87), was the primary and most influential platform for the Arabic prose poem from 1957 to 1970. The Iraqi School was more influenced by Anglophone, and particularly American, poetry. Its most influential figure was Sargūn Būluṣ (1944–2008). In addition to his transcendent poetry, his early translations from English and American poetry which started in the 1960s, and his later translations via English of world poetry until his death, were transformative in Iraq and elsewhere in the Arab world and influenced generations of poets.

Būluṣ and the Iraqi School from which he emerged are both grossly under-researched outside the Arab world. This essay gives an overview of the evolution of the Arabic prose poem in Iraq and concludes with a brief section on Būluṣ and his literary genealogy.

Beginnings

The first attempts to break from tradition and write a new style of poetry in Iraq in the modern era can be traced back to the first few decades of the twentieth century. Such attempts were made against the backdrop of decolonization and a growing desire for political and cultural independence. Britain had invaded Iraq during World War I and occupied Baghdad in 1917, wresting the country away from Ottoman rule. The League of Nations approved a British mandate in Iraq in 1920. That same year, Iraqis rose up in a national revolt against the British. Just as the nation itself was struggling against British colonialism and searching for a new form for national becoming, some of its literary figures were beginning to experiment with new literary forms. Increased access to translation as well as interaction with other parts of the Arab world and the world at large had already started in the late Ottoman period. This opened new horizons and inspired the desire for change. Poetry had long been the most potent and privileged space in which to construct new individual and collective selves and to deconstruct old ones. The *qaṣīda*, the Arabic ode, was the iconic and classical form par excellence. Its symbolic capital as an aesthetic reservoir of a glorious history was unparalleled and undisputed. It represented a long and deeply-rooted tradition dating back to pre-Islamic times. While neoclassical poets had injected it with new themes and concerns in the early twentieth century, its form had remained the same, dictating adherence to meter and symmetrical hemistiches and monorhyme.

The wide range of experimentation and innovation in the twentieth century can be generally measured and marked by the degree and extent to which poets defied the two strictures of meter and rhyme. What later came to be known as *qaṣīdat al-nathr* (the prose poem) called for a total liberation from both.

Unfettered Poetry

The 1920s witnessed the first attempts of formal experimentation and innovation in Iraq. Jamīl Ṣidqī al-Zahāwī (1863–1936), a major Iraqi poet and intellectual, believed that rhyme was a relic of the past and that poets would and should do away with it in time. He published examples of poems without rhyme, but they still retained meter. Al-Zahāwī termed this type of poetry, that he was writing and advocating for, *al-shi'r al-mursal* [unfettered poetry]. This sparked a debate in newspapers and journals in Iraq. One of those who responded to al-Zahawī was Rūfā'īl Buṭṭī (1901–56), a fellow poet, critic, and journalist. Buṭṭī called on al-Zahāwī to liberate himself even further and do away with meter as well in order to be truly unfettered. "We think," Buṭṭī wrote, "that modern selves dislike imitation and abhor chains, therefore they welcome such new and simple ways [of writing]" (al-Ṣigar 1995: 97). Buṭṭī played a pioneering role through his critical contributions on the subject and by providing space for literary experimentation on the pages of *al-Ḥurriyya* [Freedom], the journal he founded and edited. Its first double issue, published July 15, 1924, included translations from contemporary world literature. It also featured poems by Maʿrūf al-Ruṣāfī (1875–1945), one of Iraq's major poets and intellectuals (L`aybī 2013: 10–12). Although a neoclassical poet, al-Ruṣāfī was enthusiastic about writing poetry without either meter or rhyme. He himself tried his hand at it and praised other poets who had published such attempts.

Buṭṭī and other Iraqi poets were inspired by the Lebanese-American émigré poet Najīb al-Rīḥanī (1876–1940), who played an instrumental role in the rise of prose poetry in Arabic through his poetry, discussions, and correspondence (Moreh 1976: 297). Al-Rīḥānī had already published samples of Whitmanesque prose poetry, that was termed *shi'r manthūr*. He visited Iraq in 1922. Both he and Gibrān Khalīl Gibrān (1883–1931) were in search of alternatives to metric rhythm[1] (Moreh 1976: 296).

Buṭṭī collected the poems he wrote between 1920 and 1925 in his first collection, *al-Rabī'iyyāt* [Spring Poems (1925)]. This was the only collection of *shi'r al-nathr* to be published in the first half of the century in Iraq. Many individual poems written in the genre were published in Iraq and elsewhere. While Buṭṭī's poems were not that striking and did not stand the test of time, his role was crucial and pioneering in initiating the critical debate about new forms of poetry (and prose poetry in particular), providing a space for that in his journal, and writing the first prose poems in Iraq.

These initial experimentations with forms that approximated prose poetry did not grow in the following two decades and seem to have subsided. Buṭṭī became more involved in politics and journalism in Iraq. Al-Ruṣāfi, who was mercurial in his politics and positions, withdrew his initial support for this new type of poetry. The cultural climate was still resistant and traditional poetry was not to be dislodged from its throne just yet.

More than two decades later, Buṭṭi wrote the introduction to the first poetry collection, *Azhār Dhābila* (Withered Flowers), of a young poet named Badr Shakir al-Sayyāb (1926–64) (al-Ṣigar 1995: 93–4). Al-Sayyāb, together with another Iraqi poet and critic, Nazik al-Malā'ika (1923–2007), pioneered the so-called Free Verse Movement in modern Arabic poetry. Their poems broke with the symmetrical, two-hemistich, monorhyme form and mixed and matched meters and used lines of varying feet.

While often described as a revolutionary break with the Arabic poetic tradition, this movement was a compromise of sorts, when we take into consideration the more radical formal experiments of Buṭṭī and others in the Arab world a few decades earlier.

The Prose Poem *Avant la Lettre*: Ḥusayn Mardān (1927–1972)

In Iraq there was a person who carried [within himself] all the contradictions ... and [carried out] individual battles with the history of Arabic poetry. Moreover, he had a bohemian, rebellious, fierce, and aggressive personality. His name is Ḥusayn Mardān. The seeds for the future prose poem as a philosophical state instigating the total confrontation in our era were in his writings. Perhaps his revolution was shared by other poets in the world, especially in the 1960s in their revolution against society through a life style that is reflected in writing as if in a convex mirror ... Mardān tries to take us to the abyss, which, in the end, is our own. Other voices emerged from this foundation Mardān built. Our voices, we the generation of the 1960s, who were not content with offering a poem for the reader to look at, but we strove to have the reader collide with a shocking reality. We wrote the poem in a world brimming with contradictions, madness, horror, humiliation, and destruction. This is the phoenix egg laid by anger in Iraq. (Būluṣ 2016: 418–19)

Sargūn Būluṣ' lengthy statement illustrates the significance of Ḥusayn Mardān's work and his persona and how he cleared the ground for other poets to follow. Mardān was an iconoclast who rebelled against bourgeois social and literary norms. He was put on trial in 1950 for what were deemed obscene poems in his first collection, *Qaṣā'id `Āriyya* ("Naked Poems"). The sociopolitical climate in post-World War II Iraq was one of rising oppositional energies. The country had gained nominal independence in 1936, but the British still had military bases and the pro-British monarchy and the elite supporting it were becoming increasingly unpopular. In the 1940s and 1950s, leftist nationalist politics attracted wide sectors of society. This culminated in the 1958 revolution which overthrew the monarchy. Mardān, and many writers and artists, were supportive of the left-leaning republican regime of Abdilkarīm Qāsim (1914–63) and its progressive social and economic programs.

While Mardān's subject matter and themes were Baudelairean in his early poetry, his forms were still traditional. But he soon expressed his dissatisfaction with the "free verse" written by al-Sayyāb and al-Malā'ika. He did not think that they went far enough in their quest to innovate. In the Introduction to one of his collections he wrote:

> Shattering the mono-rhyme in modern poetry did not save poetry from the pool of glue it was drowning in. Mixing and cutting up feet was a great leap forward, but it couldn't sever or uproot the thorns from green branches. In my view, the only hurdle standing in the way of Arabic poetry reaching its peak is meter. That monotonous ring that disrupts the purity of imagination and muffles the pulse and motion of the spirit. It disfigures the novelty of imagination and its colors which cannot be held back by any stress or limitation. It is high time for us to abolish meter and lift that heavy sandbag from the neck of the contemporary poet. (Mardān 1958: 5)

Mardān never used the term *qaṣīdat al-nathr* ["prose poetry"] to designate his new style. He called it *nathr murakkaz* ["concentrated prose"] and went on to publish five collections in that style. Mardān's bold and innovative attempts to write what for all intents and purposes amounts to prose poetry is elided in the dominant narrative of Arabic literary history.[2] The "birth" of the prose poem is often associated, as mentioned previously, with the figures of Adūnīs and Unsī al-Ḥājj. The former claimed to have written the first Arabic prose poem in 1958 after translating a poem by Saint-John Perse (Moreh 1976: 305). Al-Ḥājj's collection *Lann* ("Never"), published in 1960, with its fiery introduction, is considered a foundational moment for the Arabic prose poem. In its preface, "considered a manifesto" (Moreh 1976: 307), Al-Ḥājj declared that "poetry can be without meter provided it has the emotional tension and evocative and suggestive images." Both Adūnīs and al-Ḥājj were directly influenced by Suzanne Bernard's 1959 book *Le poème en prose, de Baudelaire jusqu'à nos jours*. Unlike them, Mardān had no access to French or English. His appropriation and articulation of Baudelairean poetics was through translations he read. His formal innovation was not the product of reading sophisticated scholarship or access to theory, but was rather an organic result, a testament to a precocious and revolutionary spirit. Even after the term *qaṣīdat al-nathr* ["prose poem"] was circulating in the 1960s, Mardān never adopted it and continued to label his writings "concentrated prose." His essays and literary criticism discussed poetics, but never engaged with the term. Compared to earlier attempts, Mardān's poems are more mature and nuanced, and the search for rhythm beyond any traditional structure is rewarding. Here is a short example from 1971 entitled "The Nightmare":

> You are here on top of the rocks
> Go then:
> There is still a cave yet to be discovered
> In the heart of dark forests
> There you may take off your mask
> Understand the language of silence
> Under the light of a green crescent
> The sound of her footsteps will approach
> Quivering on a breeze (L`aybī 2013: 77)

The Kirkuk Group

A significant number of poets who wrote prose poetry in the second half of the twentieth century in Iraq, and who became important figures in modern Iraqi and Arab cultures, were members of what came to be known as the Kirkuk Group, named after the city in northern Iraq. There are several factors that contributed to the distinctive cultural climate the influenced the formative years of group members. The multiethnic culture of the city and diverse composition of the population fused the oral cultures and traditions of the region: Turkish, Persian, Kurdish, Assyrian, Armenian, and Arabic. The presence of the employees of the British Iraqi Petroleum Company (IPC) in the oil-rich city created a demand for English-language journals, magazines, and books in local bookshops. *The Paris Review*, *Poetry* and the *New Yorker*, among other journals, became accessible to aspiring young writers eager to stay abreast of a dynamic world culture. Most important, however, was the collective synergy and the gathering of a group of talented poets and writers.[3] One of them, Sargūn Būluṣ, described it as "a small miracle." This was instrumental in enriching the horizons of the group members in their formative years before they came to Baghdad to participate in its cultural life and work as journalists and editors. Most of them had already published in journals in Iraq and the Arab world before moving to the capital, which was enjoying an intensely rich and productive period in visual arts, theater and literary culture. The productive spirit of the 1960s in Iraqi culture was captured by Fāḍil al-`Azzāwī, one of the members of the Kirkuk Group, in a book appropriately entitled *The Living Spirit: The 1960s Generation in Iraq*.[4]

The first Ba'thist coup in 1963, which overthrew Abd al-Karīm Qāsim (1914–63), was a setback for Iraq's burgeoning civil society and the period of openness stretching from the end of World War I through the wake of the 1958 overthrow of the pro-British monarchy. Nevertheless, the first Ba'th regime was not able to completely crush the spirit of cultural experimentation; Iraqi culture of the 1960s was quite vibrant, and many of its figures went on to become some of the pillars of contemporary Arab culture.

The Prose Poem and the Ba'th

The Iraqi prose poem had to travel a more treacherous road inside Iraq after the so-called Ba'thification of culture and society in the late 1970s. It was even banned officially for a while by the regime. When it was not officially banned, it had to struggle against a semi-blockade from the state's cultural institutions and the regime's intellectuals, which, in turn, led a total academic blackout and cautious avoidance by the great majority of Iraqi critics inside Iraq throughout the 1970s and 1980s.

The Ba'th returned again in 1968, but its social base and popularity were very weak. It did, however, forge a compromise of sorts with the Iraqi Communist Party, which was the most popular and potent political force and whose ranks boasted most of Iraq's writers and intellectuals.[5] This compromise allowed communists and non-Ba'thists to still be active in Iraqi cultural life, but not for long.

The nationalization of Iraq's oil in 1972 and the sharp rise in oil prices provided the Iraqi state with unprecedented revenue. An equally unprecedented process of the commodification of cultural production followed and reached its peak just before and during the eight-year war with Iran (1980–8). Another event which stifled cultural creativity after 1973 was the precarious alliance between the Ba`th Party and the Iraqi Communist Party (ICP) in 1973. The National Front, which was formed in July 1973, had a cultural program which reinstated party guardianship over cultural production and restricted it to the framework of the agreement between the two parties. Throughout the 1970s, there was a process of gradual Ba`athification of all facets of Iraqi society, especially the cultural sphere. Important and influential cultural and media posts were reserved for Ba`thists or those who were seduced by the rewards, while non-Ba`thists were intimidated and terrorized. Radio and television establishments were declared military sites where political activity was banned. Tariq Aziz (1936–2015), the erstwhile minister of culture and editor of the influential *Āfāq`Arabiyya* (Arab Horizons), justified these measures by saying "our cultural and information agencies are not hotels that are open for guests of different political forces." Many intellectuals were forced to emigrate and many others started smuggling their writings for publication abroad. In 1977, the then vice-president, Saddam Hussein, gave an important speech at the Information Bureau of the ruling Ba`th Party about the Ba`thification of cultural discourse in Iraq and the rewriting of history from a Ba`thist perspective. In the meantime, numerous articles expounding Ba`thist art, literature and even ethics were being published in the regime's newspapers. The Ba`th's cultural program was by no means a recognizable theory, but rather an amorphous group of restrictions and signposts on the path of total subservience of Iraqi culture to Ba`thist politics.

In 1979 the regime struck violently against all opposing forces. More than two hundred poets and writers were arrested for refusing to join the Ba`th. Many were executed or disappeared. There was also an attack on the premises housing the ICP's publications. These events resulted in an exodus of tens of writers and artists, who ended in various exiles.

With the July 1979 assumption of full power by Saddam Hussein and the beginning of the eight-year war against Iran in 1980, the personality cult and the aestheticization of violence became the predominant norm in internal Iraqi culture. While already moving in that direction, literary and cultural production, in all of its forms, was now to be fully at the service of the battle being waged against the evil enemy. Dissent, criticism, or hints thereof, were unpatriotic and treasonous. All writing was to be mobilizational. Saddam Hussein's famous slogan, "The gun and the pen have one and the same barrel," which was usually printed on publications and written on the walls of cultural institutions, put it succinctly and ominously. The 1980s also witnessed the regime's success in coopting many Arab and even foreign journalists and intellectuals through handsome financial rewards and invitations to various annual cultural festivals, as well as through the financing of many pan-Arab Arabic-language journals and magazines that were published in Europe.

There was a return, of sorts, in poetry to traditional forms more in line with the Ba`th's version of Arab nationalist ideology and its attempt to cast the war against Iran as an Arab–Persian confrontation, with Iraq as the defender of the eastern flank of the Arab nation. Older, more traditional and classical forms, such as the *rajaz* (classical war poetry), were encouraged. The prose poem, perceived as a genre whose symbolic capital was a revolt against the values the Ba`th embodied, was frowned upon. Nevertheless, the ambiguity and difficulty of the prose poem, meanwhile, allowed many poets to use it as a vehicle of protest and an expression of the absurdity and nihilism of war and life under war.⁶

In the era of war, mobilizational literature and the glorification of the father-leader, the prose poem's symbolic capital and function was a liability at best. It suffered from an institutional blockade. The only venue that would consider the publication of prose poems was *al-Ṭalīʿa al-Adabiyya*, a bimonthly journal published under the auspices of the regime, but with a limited audience of young poets and writers. The two main dailies, *al-Jumhūriyya* and *al-Thawra*, had two regime poets at the helm, Sāmī Mahdī (1940–) and Ḥamīd Saʿīd (1941–). Both were suspicious of and dismissed prose poetry. Mahdī even wrote an entire book delegitimizing and attacking the prose poem, especially in its Iraqi iterations. The genre would continue to suffer from general critical and academic neglect inside Iraq. Arabic departments rejected the prose poem or its main poets as subjects for MA or PhD theses. Those who wrote prose poetry had to try their luck and publish abroad in *Kalimāt* (Bahrain), *Shu'ūn Adabiyya* (UAE), *Mawāqif* (Paris), *al-Nāqid* (London) and *al-Yawm al-Sābi'* (Paris). The rejectionist and radical ideals and perceived foreignness and hybridity of the prose poem were totally at odds with the Ba'th's cultural program, especially in the 1980s, when classical and traditional forms were revived and encouraged.

The Prose Poem as a Prism of the Nightmare

Despite the blockade and the difficulty of interacting with and benefiting from those writers in exile, the prose poem managed to develop in Iraq. Works were smuggled from abroad, and there were glimpses here and there, especially in the second half of the 1980s which witnessed a marked increase in the number of poets writing prose poetry in Iraq and elsewhere. Beyond the usual labels of nihilism and intentional vagueness (which should itself be read as a political act) affixed to such writings by critics, it is in prose poetry that one could read a subtle rejection of the Ba'th's cultural program and an attempt at jamming the totalitarian cultural machine. In many of the poems, the narrative is one of an endless nightmare and/or a compulsory daily enactment of life as a tragicomedy. Many of the poems could also be read as a parody of dominant poems used for mobilizational effects on a daily basis. The following example by Nṣayyif al-Nāṣirī (1960–) stands in contrast to hundreds of poems celebrating the heroism of the Iraqi soldier on the battlefront:

> In 1979 I dreamt of plastic animals, walls of feathers and pineapple
> In 1979 I dreamt of Bacchic feasts and sunny mornings
> longer than the Wall of China
> I am thinking of getting books from Nicosia now
> But how do I get there? My hat falls off just by seeing the waves
> I saw flying balloons carrying blue tombs last night
> Stop the screaming – Oh lightning I hear new calls
> between two rocks
> On a mountain
> I gaze at enchanting motions – the ghosts crowding before me

> They are smuggled families singing and three dead [people] proud of human suffering, but beware, Blood in the caves. Tonight, the divers will bring mythical mummies
> The actors left their makeup and razors in a building
> There is a woman on a wall, perhaps an acrobat
> Smiling unwisely
> There is also a long valley like a tiger's skin
> The strange grass embraces masks and dead actors
> Where have the mountain goats disappeared?
> Were the mountain bears grazing here? Sometime we bring chestnuts and make great fires. We cause avalanches
> Big rocks fall, we hum old songs
> At night in the guard posts we like to talk
> about imaginary blond women
> And when the ground freezes under a snowstorm, we leave the posts
> We take a corner covered with towels
> and stand in line, motionless
> In front of a toilet

Al-Nāṣirī, one of the most playful and surrealist of the poets of that era, represents the daily life of a soldier as a maddening nightmare. The date in the first section, 1979, is the last year of peace before the long war with Iran (1980–8). The soldier's colorful dreams of imagined travel and freedom of movement turn into screams and ghosts as the poem progresses. The glorification of the valiant defender of the nation is nowhere to be found. We find, instead, the mundane existence and the daily spectacle in which one is forced to perform a prescribed role. The culmination of the narrative is waiting in line to go to the toilet.

From from the battlefield, an equally nightmarish reality can be read in the works of Kamāl Sabtī (1954–2006), who fled Iraq in 1989 and died in exile in Spain. The following is an excerpt from a long poem entitled "Debris":

> Avoid screaming about your fate and celebrate your cursed drums until your blood dries near the rain of the wreckage. Go back all you animals. I will not be castrated and no one will blindfold me. The actors came wearing their tribal costumes. Fine. You are happy brothers. What do you have in store for me? The actors were cursing their soles, delighted with their roles. I am not exactly alive. I am not exactly alive. So, avoid screaming about your fate. I was seen in the shape of an outcast from Plato's Republic. Half-standing statues, one of them said: I am the memory of Caligula. He told me about his campaign and the imprisoned sea-shells. Then he asked me to delete this last sentence, but I will be malicious and put it right here: Oh, if I could live again! (Sabtī 1993: 26)

The narrator is not exactly alive, but the performance must go on. Even Caligula's statue, while yearning to return to life to take part in the totalitarian feast, is afraid of having its thoughts recorded and reported.

For the very few critics inside Iraq who dared to accord these kinds of poems any attention, it would have been dangerous to read them as attempts to subvert the official narrative. It was customary to complain of the nihilism, intentional vagueness, and disregard for life and the function of poetry in prose poetry.

A highly eloquent response to the critics of prose poetry is a short poem by Zāhir al-Jīzānī (1948–), one of the important poets of the 1970s and 1980s, published in the first year of the war in 1981:

> You called what I write a nightmare
> and called my madness a luxury
> O horse of the cart
> Whenever crossing paths bring us together
> But then we never meet, nor do we find each other
> Each takes his different destiny
> The poet reads a nightmare and the people do not understand him
> The poet is carried like the dead
> from the bar to the house
> And people do not understand him
> All that the poet has built is a kingdom
> for a coming tomorrow
> is a nightmare sung by drunkards
> and the lost poet
> sings parts of the nightmare (al-Jīzānī 1981: 23)

The legacy of the prose poem in Iraq has been more controversial, especially in the last two decades of the twentieth century. The symbolic capital of the genre, and its association with a rejection of the Ba'th's ideology and its cultural policies, made it a prime target for the regime, especially during the war with Iran. Despite the institutional marginalization and the blackout, two young Iraqi poets (Bāsim al-Mar'ibī and Khālid Jābir) who wrote prose poetry won the then prestigious Yūsif al-Khāl Prize for Poetry awarded by the London-based monthly journal *al-Nāqid* in 1988.

The 1991 Gulf War (when the US "bombed Iraq back to the pre-Industrial age," as then-Secretary of State James Baker put it) and the ensuing economic embargo (1990–2003) destroyed the infrastructure, the economy and the social fabric of Iraq.[7] Three million Iraqis left Iraq for the diaspora during the 1990s, including the majority of writers, poets, and artists.[8] The lack of essentials, including paper, degraded the lives and the output of those who remained inside, including poets.

The desired end of dictatorship in Iraq did not end the woes of its people. It compounded them. The 2003 Anglo-American invasion and occupation of Iraq, the dismantling of Iraqi state institutions and the installation of a sectarian political system plunged the country into chaos and civil war. Amid all the destruction, debris, terrorism, the prose poem rises yet again with a new generation of younger poets,[9] many of whom consider Sargūn Būluṣ (1944–2007) their poetic ancestor.

Sargūn Būluṣ

While a poetic tradition or a generation cannot be reduced to one poet, there are always poets whose work and life accrue immense cultural capital. Sargon Būluṣ (1944–2007) is one of those poets. He is widely acclaimed as one of the pioneers of modern Arabic poetry. He was also a prolific translator of poetry from English into Arabic. His output from the 1960s until his death in Berlin in 2007 exceeded 1000 pages of translation. In addition to book-length selections of W. H. Auden, W. S. Merwin, Ted Hughes, and Allen Ginsberg, among others, he translated (via English) hundreds of poems ranging from Mesopotamian, Chinese, and Japanese poetry to modern Greek, Russian, Polish, Swedish, Italian, German, French, and Spanish poetry (Būluṣ 2016b). These translations were intimately related to his practice as a poet and shaped his own work.

Sargon Būluṣ was born in 1944 in al-Ḥabbāniyah, a town in western Iraq.[10] Būluṣ grew up bilingual: his father spoke Assyrian, and his mother, who was a Chaldean from Mosul, spoke Arabic. In 1956, the family moved to Kirkuk. Būluṣ grew up memorizing the songs sung at night by drunken workers and shop owners in Kurdish, Turkish, Persian and Assyrian. He later described the city as a "divine sponge" soaked with different languages, ethnicities and cultures.

As a teenager, Būluṣ published poems and short stories in various Iraqi journals and magazines, and started to translate American and British poetry into Arabic. In 1967, Yūsuf al-Khāl (1917–87), the co-founder of the influential Lebanese journal *Shiʿr*, encouraged him while visiting Baghdad to move to Beirut, which was, back then, a laboratory for political and cultural modernity. He went to a friend's hometown on the border and, having no passport and very little money, had himself smuggled by night into Syria. He spent three weeks in Damascus before making his way to Beirut, where he worked at *Shiʿr*, enjoyed al-Khāl's mentorship, translated more poetry from English, and continued to write. He edited a special issue of *Shiʿr* on the Beatniks, who had long fascinated him. In 1969, he left for San Francisco, where he would be based for the rest of his life. Once there, he finally visited all the places he had read about, and met all the great poets he had translated: Ginsberg, Snyder, Ferlinghetti and others. California was a reservoir of new cultural treasures, vast libraries and experiences waiting to be enjoyed.

Būluṣ visited Europe often, and especially loved Berlin, but San Francisco remained his base. The first Gulf War (1991), however, marked the beginning of a bitter disenchantment with America. "Everything was exposed in the Gulf War," he said. "It was a bloodied mirror. America had nothing more to offer, as far as I was concerned" (al-Shawwaf 2006: 60). The political aftermath of September 11 in America left him further alienated. In "A Conversation with a Painter in New York After the Towers Fell," he wrote: "I see Rodin's fingers in all this / I see him standing at the gates of hell / pointing to an abyss / From which the beasts of the future will charge / There/where two towers fell /and America went mad" (Būluṣ 2008: 170). He was further alienated and angered by the 2003 US invasion of Iraq, considering it "the biggest blunder in modern history" (al-Shawwaf 2006: 61). The war on Iraq had a profound influence on his late writings. He corrected the proofs of his fifth and last collection, *Another Bone for the Tribe's Dogs*, on the hospital bed in Berlin where he died in 2007. His disappointment with the America that he had been enamored of in the 1960s and 1970s was evident in its pages: "Where is it? / Where is the America for which I, the dreamer crossed the sea / Will Whitman's America remain ink on paper?" (Būluṣ 2008: 220).

When Būluṣ died, eulogies poured in from major poets across the Arab world and its diaspora. Although he had only published four collections, Būluṣ was a poet's poet and had established himself since the 1960s. His poetic voice was unique. In addition to his transcendent poetry, Būluṣ's own unusual trajectory, his background, his exilic existence and his attitude toward poetry all made him stand out and above the rest.

Poetry was a calling, and he genuinely dedicated his life to it. Publishing was never an end in and of itself. His publisher had to hound him for years to get a manuscript. Each of his books was an event when it appeared. Living far away from the cultural centers of the Arab world in the pre-digital age gave him critical and crucial distance from institutional culture and literary networks. He could have exploited his friendships with major American poets in San Francisco and his unique background to gain attention and fame as an Iraqi poet in the United States. But he was focused on writing in Arabic and mining the rich history of the language and its poetic tradition. Arabic was "the umbilical cord" linking him to his language and homeland.

Although he never joined a political party or espoused an ideology, Būlus̩ was intensely political. I have argued elsewhere that a careful reading of his work shows that his engagement was subtler and more consequential (Antoon 2015). Many Arab poets of Būlus̩' generation and later generations initially espoused radical leftist politics, but disavowed their leftism and became neoliberal, especially in the 1990s and afterwards. Būlus̩' trajectory is unusual in this respect as well. The longer he lived in the United States the more disenchanted he became with liberal values and politics and more critical of empire. US wars and sanctions against Iraq deeply wounded him. The ghosts of dead Iraqis populate his posthumous collection.

Būlus̩' impact on his peers, as well as on later generations, was huge. On his death, the Lebanese poet and critic ʿAbdu Wāzin wrote the following:

> Every collection he published was a poetic surprise. Although prolific in writing, he rarely published. He preferred to stay away from the limelight. The poem, in his view, is a moment in life as it is a moment etched in the heart of language. Poetry was a lived experience as well as an experience of writing, contemplation, vision, and encounter . . . His immense knowledge, especially in world poetry, established his singularity as a poet and a pioneer, for he founded a new poem and a climate that did not exist before him . . . He had a great impact on subsequent generations. Young poets were eager to read and emulate him. They found in him the father who refused to practice his paternal authority and a poet who always renewed himself in his rebellion against rhetoric, his openness to the ephemeral and quotidian, and in being seduced by imagination and the unconscious. (Būlus̩ 2009: 134–5)

ʿAbbās Bayḍūn (1945–) described [Būlus̩] as being "one of the most mature and experienced poets, who came closest to the ideal poet . . . [He] was struck by poetry in his life as well as in his writing, was led by it on life's paths into distant territories to which we could not follow him" (Būlus̩ 2009: 135).

Journeying to distant lands was an existential and mental state Būlus̩ inhabited and narrated. His first collection, published in 1985, was entitled *Al-Wus̩ūl ila Madīnat Ayn* [Arriving at the City of Where]. *Ayn* [where] also means "fatigue." For Būlus̩, every arrival was another departure and the start of a new journey. This is the first poem in the collection:

There Are Journeys

I reach my homeland after crossing
a river into which astrologers descend

with rusty instruments
searching for stars
Or I don't reach my homeland
after crossing a river into which no one descends
There are journeys
after which I return pale
thin as a needle's shadow
I meet morning face to face
as if I'd just left a tunnel behind me just a moment before
Steam rises below my hand
from a beautiful cup of coffee
Its one long crack
Is like a wall in an orphanage
I meet a peasant who went mad in famine
begging in the evening of big cities
a woman walking in the light of her white hair
among ruins
I unfetter my eye and journey
I let obscure epiphanies take me
with affection
knowing my goals better than I do
They give me their terrifying gifts
with hands dripping absolute care
like the one carrying
a single drop of water across a desert
Touch is my . . .
It led and guided me
like a train of heartbeats
It travels far to meet me:
at the end of every cave
There is a candle inviting me to sit at a table
upon which my ancestors cried, swore, and fasted
Each cry emitted from any distant window
rouses me from my deepest dreams so I follow it
like a blind man invading the air with his hands
heading to enemy countries
To which his eyes were smuggled and he was asked to pay a tax
I hear the wind with my fingernails
and I know where my bride is hiding (Būluṣ 2003: 5–7)

Notes

1. For more on Gibrān and al-Rīḥānī's influence on Arabic prose poetry, see Būluṣ 2016: 415.
2. Būlus criticized the dominant narrative of the evolution of the Arabic prose poem, its elisions and the exaggeration of the role played by *Shi`r* (Adūnīs and al-Ḥājj). See Būlūṣ 2016: 294–6, 416.

3. Some of the figures include Mu'ayyad al-Rāwī (1939–2015), Faḍil al-'Azzāwī (1940–), Jān Dammū (1942–2003), Anwar al-Ghassānī (1937–2009), Ṣalāḥ Fā'iq (1945–) and Jalīl al-Qaysī (1937–2006). All, except for al-Qaysī, left Iraq in the 1960s and 1970s and spent the rest of their lives in exile.
4. On the Kirkuk Group, see al-'Azzāwī 1997: 279–318.
5. On the second Ba'th, see Batatu 1976: 1073–112. On the formation of the National Patriotic Front, see Sluglett 1987: 156–8.
6. For an overview of the political and cultural context and major themes of the 1980s generation of poets in Iraq, see Maẓlūm 2007.
7. See Gordon 2010.
8. Three of the poets mentioned in this section all ended in exile: Sabtī in Spain, al-Nāṣirī in Sweden, and al-Jīzānī in the US.
9. An overview of the prose poem in Iraq post-2003 is beyond the scope of this essay and my brief remarks do not do justice to an emerging group of poets.
10. For more in English on Būluṣ' life, see al-Shawwaf. The most comprehensive account of Būluṣ' life and his views on writing and translation is the interview (in Arabic) conducted by Khālid al-Maāly in Būluṣ 2016: 5–114.

Works Cited

al-'Azzāwī, Fāḍil (1997), *Al-Rūḥ al-Ḥayya: Jīl al-Sittīnāt fī al-'Irāq*, Damascus: Dār al-Madā.
al-Jīzānī, Zāhir (1981), *Min Ajl Tawḍīḥ Iltibās al-Qaṣd*, Baghdad: Dar al-Rashīd.
al-Shawwaf, Rayyan (2006), "An Interview with Sargon Būluṣ," *Parnassus*, vol. 29, nos 1/2, pp. 31–6.
al-Ṣigar, Ḥātim (1995), *Rūfā'īl Buṭṭī wa Riyādat al-Naqd al-Shi'rī fī al-'Irāq: Muqaddima wa Mukhtārāt* [Rūfā'īl Buṭṭī and Pioneering Poetry Criticism in Iraq: Introduction and Selections], Cologne: Manshūrāt al-Jamal.
al-Tami, Ahmed (1993), "Arabic 'Free Verse': The Problem of Terminology," *Journal of Arabic Literature*, vol. 24, no. 2, pp. 185–98.
Antoon, Sinan (2010) "Debris and Diaspora: Iraqi Culture Now," in *Uncovering Iraq: Trajectories of Disintegration and Transformation*, ed. Chris Toensing and Mimi Kirk, Washington, DC: Georgetown University Press.
Antoon, Sinan (2015), "Sargon Būluṣ's Commitment," in *Commitment and Beyond: Reflections on/of the Political in Arabic Literature since the 1940's*, ed. Friederike Pannewick and Georges Khalil, Wiesbaden: Reichert Verlag.
Antoon, Sinan (2017), "Sargon Būluṣ and Tu Fu's Ghosts," in *Journal of World Literature* (special issue, What is World Literature in Arabic?), vol. 2, no. 3, August.
Bahoora, Haytham (2013), "Baudelaire in Baghdad: Modernism, the Body, and Husayn Mardan's Poetics of the Self," *International Journal of Middle Eastern Studies* 45, special issue 2, May, pp. 313–29.
Batatu, Hanna (1979), *The Old Social Classes and the Revolutionary Movements of Iraq: A Study of Iraq's Old Landed and Commercial Classes and of its Communists, Ba'thists, and Free Officers*, Princeton: Princeton University Press.
Būluṣ, Sargūn (1992), *Al-Awwal wal-Tālī*, Cologne: Manshūrāt al-Jamal.
Būluṣ, Sargūn (1998), *Idhā Kunta Nā'iman fī Markab Nūḥ*, Cologne: Manshūrāt al-Jamal.
Būluṣ, Sargūn (2003), *Al-Wuṣūl ilā Madīnat Ayn*, Cologne: Manshūrāt al-Jamal.
Būluṣ, Sargūn (2008), *'Azma ukhrā li-kalb al-qabīla*, Baghdad/Beirut: Dar al-Jamal.
Būluṣ, Sargūn (2010), *Knife Sharpener: Selected Poems*. London: Banipal Books.
Būluṣ, Sargūn (2016a), *Sāfartu Mulāḥiqan Khayālātī: Ḥiwārāt* [I Traveled Pursuing My Imagination: Conversations], Baghdad/Beirut: Manshūrāt al-Jamal.

Būluṣ, Sargūn (2016b), *Raqā'im li-ruh al-kawn: tarjamāt shi'riyya mukhtāra* [Tablets of the World's Soul: Selected Poetry Translations], Baghdad/Beirut: Dar al-Jamal.

Deeb, Muhammad (2010) "The Conception of the Poem en Prose in Modern Arabic Poetry: Native tradition and French Influence," *Canadian Review of Comparative Literature*, vol. 37, nos 1–2, pp. 174–87.

Gordon, Joy (2010), *Invisible War: The United States and the Iraq Sanctions*, Cambridge: Harvard University Press.

L`aybī, Shākir (2013), *Ruwwād Qaidat al-Nathr ī al-`Irāq* [The Pioneers of the Prose Poem in Iraq], Baghdad: Mizūbūtamyā.

Mardān, Ḥusayn (1958), *al-Urjuha Hadi'at al-Hibal* [A Swing with Calm Ropes], Baghdad: Manshūrāt Maktabat al-Naṣr.

Maẓlūm, Muḥammad (2007), *Ḥaṭab Ibrāhīm aw al-Jīl al-Badawī: Shi'r al-Thamānīnāt wa Ajyāl al-Dawla al-`Irāqiyya* [Abraham's Logs, or The Bedouin Generation: 1980s Poetry and the Generations of the Iraqi State], Damascus: Dar al-Takwin.

Moreh, Shmuel (1976), *Modern Arabic Poetry: 1800–1970: The Development of Its Forms and Themes Under the Influence of Western Literature*, Leiden: E. J. Brill.

Sluglett, Marion Farouk, and Sluglett, Peter (1987), *Iraq Since 1958: From Revolution to Dictatorship*, London: Routledge.

19

AFTER POET'S PROSE: POSTGENERIC WRITING IN THE ONGOING CRISIS OF VERSE

Stephen Fredman

IN THE MID-1970S, AMERICAN POETS began creating book-length works of prose that were proposed as poetry. To many, this was a surprising and even shocking development. Although informed readers could recall the French tradition of the individual prose poem and point to books of prose poems by initial masters Bertrand, Baudelaire, Rimbaud, and Mallarmé, the idea of a book of prose as a single work of poetry was resisted in many quarters as falling outside the domain of the poetic. One might attempt to explain this innovation by imagining it as an equivalent to the long poem, whose reach is often across historical time, but such initially confounding books as John Ashbery's *Three Poems* (1975), Robert Creeley's *Presences: A Text for Marisol* (1976), David Antin's *talking at the boundaries* (1976), and Ron Silliman's *Ketjak* (1978) ask to be viewed in other terms. Although distinct from each other in many ways, these works share a linguistic density, often a hallmark of poetry, which is marshalled in the service not of history but of philosophical inquiry. These poets investigate the texture of everyday life by interrogating the language interwoven into it. Take Creeley's *Presences*, for example. The book consists of fifteen sections of varying lengths, written in a conjectural prose that meditates on aspects of Marisol's sculptural work, especially her autobiographical focus, while simultaneously engaging with words as multiphasic building blocks of being:[1]

> Big firemen. Little firemen. In the flames they are dancing. *Fire delights in its form.* Firemen delight in their form? Inform us, policemen. We call upon them to inform us. Hence all the beatings and shootings and the putting into closed places behind doors. Firemen and snowmen share other fates, the one burning, the one melting. Snow delights in its form, being mutable. It is the immutable that despairs. At least for a time, for any other time, for all time, for bygone times, for times past, for time enough, for in time. Time will tell. (Creeley 1976: 65)

This paragraph is from a three-and-a-half-page section of *Presences*, which begins with waking up to a wailing siren. Although the poet wants to find out what is happening in the present, to himself and others, he does so by engaging with issues in Marisol's sculpture pertaining to scale and to the representation of people as actors or typical characters. In a further twist, some of the features in Marisol's sculpture also refer to herself, since they are cast from the artist's own anatomy, just as Creeley consistently places his own sense of self at risk within his linguistic experiments. And as with Marisol's Pop imagery, Creeley works with stock material (language) whose ability to predicate, to make sense of experience, and to act in the world he constantly questions. In this passage, no word or image or quotation can pretend to be self-explanatory. Whether in the italicized quotation from William Blake (in which Creeley also seems to hear echoes of Heraclitus, for whom the world is an ever-living fire) or in the interconnected statements about firemen, snowmen, and policemen, every term and image is subjected to a conjectural prose of constant interrogation. This is especially true for the words "fire," "delight," "form," and "time." The ordinary word "time," for example, is not allowed to rest easily within clichéd usages ("at least for a time," "for all time," "time enough," or "time will tell"), for like the other terms it bears the force of existential and social concerns thrown into motion by the inventive syntactical play of Creeley's sentences. By the time he finishes playing language games with "time," the word has acquired a perspectival density that renders it equivalent to one of the block-like personages in a Marisol assemblage. The grammatical density of the modes of predication within his sentences allows Creeley to simultaneously cast the words in them as subjects (as though they themselves were actors) and objects (of his conjectures).

In *Poet's Prose: The Crisis in American Verse* (1983, 1990), I call *Presences* and the other lengthy and inquisitive works of the 1970s "poet's prose," which defines a poetic enterprise employing prose conventions to make truth claims for poetry, giving it a new kind of philosophical heft. I argue, too, that there is always a "crisis of verse" in the fundamentally ungrounded culture of the United States, and that poet's prose, with its existentially freighted linguistic investigations, addresses this poetic crisis by means other than verse. Formally, poet's prose is noticeably distinct from any of the familiar prose modes, such as fiction, history, autobiography, or the essay. In poet's prose of the 1970s, the poetic techniques employed are a means of grammatical expansion or renovation of poetic form. In keeping with this grammatical focus, the poets of this time bring renewed attention to two sui generis and mainly overlooked works from earlier in the twentieth century, Gertrude Stein's *Tender Buttons* (1914) and William Carlos Williams' *Kora in Hell: Improvisations* (1920). Silliman's famous 1979 lecture, "The New Sentence," for instance, begins (in the printed version) with an epigraph from Stein and a first sentence that parodies Williams' opening to *Kora in Hell*: "The sole precedent I can find for the new sentence is *Kora in Hell: Improvisations* and that one far-fetched" (Silliman 1989: 63). (Or as Williams had it: "The sole precedent I can find for the broken style of my prologue is *Longinus on the Sublime* and that one far-fetched" [Williams 1970: 6]].) Silliman contends that the "new" sentence can be energized poetically to the same extent as the line, if we mine all of its syntactic possibilities, and that, like the line with respect to the stanza, the sentence achieves maximum suggestiveness within a paragraph (89). *Poet's Prose* ends by observing that the Language poetry practiced by Silliman and others comes to take for granted the once-surprising notion that prose can be made to infiltrate and ultimately to supplant poetry in the service of producing new poetic forms.

In the 1980s and after, book-length prose works written under the sign of poetry increase exponentially in number and to a certain extent change character. The work that follows on the experiments of the 1970s may be as self-reflexive and theoretically aware as Language poetry, but the burning deconstructive questions about language as the ground of reality are joined by other compulsions. In the work cited previously by

Ashbery, Creeley, Antin, and Silliman, inquiries into the relationship between language and truth or between poetry and philosophy are so insistent that I found it necessary to invoke philosophers such as Nietzsche, Wittgenstein, Heidegger, and Gadamer to help explain the aims and stakes of poet's prose. As the relationship between poetry and philosophy came to seem less encompassing for later poets, two new motives for occupying the meeting ground of poetry and prose presented themselves in the 1980s and afterwards: first, the transgression of social boundaries through inquiries into identity; and second, the reassertion of literary writing in a world enraptured by multimedia storytelling. As new interests in identity, personhood, gender, class, and ethnicity supplemented the grammatical investigations, poets began to compose ambitious works of prose that stage a wide-ranging dialogue between poetry and narrative. Adhering to the norm of lengthy works of poetry written in prose, poets of the last four decades have ventured into the modes of fiction, autobiography, and documentary, into mixed genres and performance art, as well as into electronic media. The present essay looks at work written in the wake of 1970s poet's prose, in which the encounter between prose and poetry comes to inhabit a capacious transgeneric or postgeneric terrain. This work not only draws upon a variety of modes of poetry, prose, and performance, but part of its specifically poetic achievement inheres in the very juxtaposition of genres and modes.

Since first publication in 1980, Lyn Hejinian's *My Life* has acquired legendary status as an experimental poetic autobiography, recounting the life of a mid-century, middle-class girl growing into a woman. In fact, *My Life* provides an early instance of the entry of poet's prose into a postgeneric narrative landscape, in which, in this case, the poetic form of the New Sentence interpenetrates the mode of autobiography. In composing this text with a chapter for each year of her life, and with each chapter containing the same number of sentences as there are chapters, Hejinian explores a modal issue that we could call the shift between figure and ground. The largest figure–ground shift appears when the apotheosis of language (the defining quality of poet's prose) metamorphoses into concerns with perception, memory, and identity—concerns that had been taken in the 1970s as illustrative material for investigations of language. This conceptual shift can be seen at work locally in the figure–ground flips that sentences undergo within a chapter. On first impression, Hejinian's prose partakes of the Emersonian style of presenting each succeeding sentence as an entity unto itself, so that the language and ideas within it speak solely to its own occasion. Often lacking hypotactic syntax, these separate sentences resist a ready discursive continuity from one to the next. However, within the context of the chapter (which ostensibly corresponds to a year in Hejinian's life), something new happens to the sentences: each one appears to contain things, language, phenomenological reflections, and theoretical statements that thread through the interests of the chapter as a whole, as if all of the sentences joined in conversation with one another. Ultimately, figure–ground shifts can be found in *My Life* at a number of levels: in the grammatical relationships of words within sentences (for example, how words flicker grammatically between the states of verb and noun); in the surprising shifts in meaning that occur as individual sentences are read in the context of sentences just preceding or succeeding them; in the mutating conversations among individual sentences within the chapters in which they are placed (as mentioned above); and in recurring phrases that migrate and alter meaning across chapters of the book.

Figure–ground shifts have always been an inherent part of poetic artifice and the pleasure it affords. Most commonly, such shifts take place when the reader notices how formal operations encode important aspects of the meaning of a poem. In *My Life*, figure–ground shifts contribute to the interweaving of poet's prose as a writing style with autobiography as a literary mode. As an extended example, consider how Hejinian draws attention to this interweaving through the permutations she works across the chapters on the phrase "a person on paper." It first appears in the chapter for age six as "a pause, a rose, something on paper" (Hejinian 1987: 21), which in context seems to present writing ("something on paper") as a primary means for creating identity as a shared condition. This is hinted at by the next sentence, which reads: "It is a way of saying, I want you, too, to have this experience, so that we are more alike, so that we are closer, bound together, sharing a point of view—so that we are 'coming from the same place'" (21–2)—as though the paper were physically an inhabitable space. In the next chapter, Hejinian continues the shared activity of constructing an identity: "I was eventually to become one person, gathered up maybe, during a pause, at a comma" (25). Here, the word "pause" ties back to the earlier phrase "a pause, a rose, something on paper," and the gathering up into personhood occurs not only temporally at a moment of stasis but also spatially at a comma, a spot of grammatical inscription (a Wordsworthian "spot of time"?). Marjorie Perloff (1985: 225) and Craig Dworkin (1995: 64–5) have noted how, in contrast to fetishizing uniqueness, Hejinian conjures up in *My Life* something closer to what Stein calls *Everybody's Autobiography*. She creates a work in which individual life is interwoven with language, perception, and social constructs, so that it is impossible to say where "Lyn Hejinian" leaves off and the world begins. Perloff finds the concept of identity in the book "less a property of a given character than a fluid state . . . that hence engages the reader to participate in its formation and deformation" (Perloff 1991: 166).[2]

The textual quality of identity returns as an issue in the chapter for age seventeen, where Hejinian tries to understand her relationship to lives that are led in books: "The lives of which I read seemed more real than my own, but I still seemed more real than the persons who had led them" (51). The actions, thoughts, emotions, and insights of novelistic characters seem so much more vivid than those of most literate teenagers, and yet the sense of emerging into personhood felt by a young woman or man bears a stubborn pragmatic reality and has consequences that override the seductive identification with an action in a fictional world. By age twenty-nine Hejinian has come to view her life as much more closely involved with the act of writing: "And if I feel like a book, a person on paper, I will continue" (76). In this sentence, "something on paper," which earlier referred to writing, has metamorphosed into "a person on paper," and Hejinian presents her recognition of being such a person as the condition for continuing to write. To "feel like a book" is to approach what Whitman meant when he proclaimed of *Leaves of Grass*, "Who touches this touches a man" (Whitman 1970: 505), imagining, as he did, the unity of the text and the person fully accomplished.

As adult poet Hejinian no longer seems seduced by fiction, for language, writing, and identity have become so entwined that creating or living through fictional characters does not compel her. By age forty-one, for example, she is so confident in her ability to construct a person in writing that she feels unconstrained by gender inequities, which had plagued her earlier, able to construct sentences that fully encapsulate possible identities: "A sentence is a metaphor since when. I see it continually before me, it impatiently asks for my work. As such, a person on paper, I am androgynous" (105). The three sentences are not necessarily continuous, since the referents for "it" and "as such" are still ambiguous. But if we assign "sentence" as the referent for "it" and working as a writer as the referent for "as such," then the sentences speak of Hejinian's discovery that the work of inhabiting writing can enable the transgression of gender binaries. Over the course of *My Life*, Hejinian employs the phrase "a person on paper" and its cognates to toggle between writing and life to the extent that the attentive reader sees the author's task as the undertaking of a life of writing as much as the writing of a life. This fractured bildungsroman shares several salient features with poet's prose by Creeley, Ashbery, Antin, and Silliman: a phenomenological impulse to "put it all in" (in Ashbery's words [Ashbery 1972: 3]); an engaging sense of playfulness, of trying things out; an attempt to grasp in language the emergence of cognition and the undergoing of experience; and a reliance on the linguistic experiments of Stein, whose pragmatist search for a radical language of experience inspires them all.

Another woman writer who emerges from the context of poetry to construct "a person on paper" in unconventional prose is Kathy Acker. More intent than Hejinian on exploding gender binaries, she writes a propulsive prose characterized by collage, pastiche, and impersonation. Although many critics paint her as a consummate metafictionist, focusing on her delirious appropriations from other texts, Kathryn Hume, for one, disagrees with this as a complete assessment. Across all of the constantly shifting narrative personae in Acker's work, Hume argues, "Centripetally, they pull every experience in and recompose it in the idiom of" a single narrative voice, a voice that "projects itself through lyric lamentation, cries, the vocabularies of sex, pain, and oppression" (Hume 2001: 509). The consistent voice that Hume hears is not hard to locate, appearing on every page of Acker's writing as "a person on paper" constructed less autobiographically than as a kind of emotional filter for the times in which she lives and the experiences she undergoes. This paper person is not a conventional sort of narrator (not strictly first-person, third-person, or implied) but a lyric voice that suffuses the prose, whose origins Acker traces back ultimately to the rebellious urban passions of Baudelaire and Rimbaud. The more proximate sources for this voice, as she attests often in interviews, can be found in first and second generation Black Mountain poetry, which she associates with Charles Olson, Robert Kelly, David Antin, and Jerome Rothenberg (Zurbrugg 2004: 2–3). Of Olson as model she says, "Olson's main thesis was that one sentence comes after another sentence so you might have the movement of meaning, but also a movement where language leads to language. Olson also had his way of seeing the world and putting it down in a certain kind of rhythm, usually a very jagged rhythm, like writing from scat" (Acker 1991: 4). Acker's own prose has a restless, projective quality that, impelled by the imagery and language of sex and pain, follows a jagged rhythm of incipient and deferred meaning in motion.

Even more than Olson, though, Antin provides a determinative model for Acker's poetically charged voice. He figures centrally in every discussion of her becoming a writer, as in the following: "When I met David it was love at first sight. Not sexual at all—I just followed him around" for two years (Zurbrugg 2004: 3). Acker credits

Antin with introducing her to conceptual art and with setting her free to create the voice of her fiction, a voice that bears the imprint of ferocious intention:

> Most poets in those days didn't think why did they write the way they wrote. There was still, and still is, the lingering idea of good poetry as the perfect word in the perfect line. And what David really taught me is, the hell with all that. Just think what do you want to do and do it. Form is determined not by arbitrary rules, but by intention. And intentionality is all. (Acker 1991: 3)

Acker began her writing career in the 1970s by associating with poetry scenes in San Diego, San Francisco, and New York. By the 1980s, in *Great Expectations* (1982) and *Don Quixote* (1986), she developed a mode of writing that bears a strong similarity to Antin's talk poems in its use of the vernacular voice to create an ongoing thrust of speech. A signal feature of the talk poems is the way Antin translates technical material—from the fields of science, engineering, and linguistics, for instance—into the colloquial speech of a mouthy kid from Brooklyn. This voice is certainly not lyrical in a musical sense; it is an intentional form of speech—thinking aloud, asking questions, and testing hypotheses by applying whatever conceptual model comes to mind. The rhythm of Antin's voice, like Olson's, illustrates what Acker calls "the movement of meaning." His talk poems share with her fiction the poetic goal of creating not a persona but a particular voice that consistently interrogates the world, exposing buried social and political cruxes. Acker transfers Antin's conceptual poetic project from the realms of science, politics, and philosophy into the modes of fiction, autobiography, pornography, and poetry—all filtered through the alternately outraged and needy voice of a woman bent on critiquing power relations in the contemporary world. Like Antin, she both appropriates and undermines the authority of the texts on which she draws, re-voicing them in a colloquial manner and keying them to the fluctuations of unquenchable desire.

In *Great Expectations*, Acker tries on Dickens' narrative like a moth-eaten dress from a thrift store—projecting her voice into different characters, delineating in particular the endlessly fraught relationship with her/a mother and with the mother's suicide. In one paragraph she sets up an inescapably co-dependent relationship between mother and daughter: 'Mother didn't want me to leave her. I think she could have loved me or shown that she loved me if she had more time or fewer obsessions . . . She craved my love as she craved her friends' and the public's love only so she could do what she wanted and evade the responsibility' (Acker 1982: 58). This sounds at first like a plausible attempt to parse a painful, complex relationship, but the next paragraph offers a statement of poetic method that is anything but confirmatory of those pop-psychological insights:

> There is just moving and there are different ways of moving. Or: there is moving all over at the same time and there is moving linearly. If everything is moving-all-over-the-place-no-time, anything is everything. If this is so, how can I differentiate? How can there be stories? Consciousness just is: no time. But any emotion presupposes differentiation. Differentiation presumes time, at least BEFORE and NOW. A narrative is an emotional moving. (58)

This paragraph could almost occur in Creeley's *Presences*, especially with Acker's conjectures about the interplay of time and emotion and about the conventional and unconventional ways in which time organizes cognition. From another angle, though, this is a meditation on the possibilities of narrative and whether it can be true to phenomenological reality. Often, we feel situated in the midst of a bewildering array, with forces coming and going—each imposing its own sense of measure or time and offering no determinative direction. At other times, an emotional response to a situation arises and seems to give experience a narrative form, in which one thing leads to another. Can phenomenological reality be congruent with narrative? Silliman points out that Stein tries to solve this opposition by "captur[ing] the balance between the unemotional sentence and the emotional paragraph." He quotes from her lecture "Poetry and Grammar": "We do know a little now what prose is. Prose is the balance the emotional balance that makes the reality of paragraphs and the unemotional balance that makes the reality of sentences" (Silliman 1989: 87). In other words, sentences are structuring devices while paragraphs contain narrative.

Acker undertakes a compulsive search for whether narrative is essential to consciousness, and this obsession drives her poetic voice as much as the raw emotions that govern the previous paragraph about the mother. Antin too worried the question of narrative like a bone over the course of his career, exploring every theoretical account of it he could find, and arriving in his essays and talk poems at the need to differentiate between story and narrative. In *what it means to be avant-garde* (1993), for instance, he views a story simply as a series of events that lead to a transformation, while a narrative is a more complex and motivated activity that submits the possibility of transformation to the pressure of desire. In other words, narrative goes beyond story by placing a previously arrived-at sense of self at risk to an impending change. The self at risk is at the crux of Acker's prose, too, in which the pressure of desire is constant. Consciousness, especially in the throes of sex, threatens to flood narrative by "moving all over at the same time." Acker's reflex is then to reach for narrative—usually that of a pre-existent text from world literature—and to fill it out with her voice as if she were blowing up a balloon. Her work oscillates between the positions of "Consciousness just is: no time" and "A narrative is an emotional moving," so that the unending agon of her prose sets off poetry's intransitive isness against the transitive emotional logic of narrative.

There is a performative quality to the voice in Acker's prose, through which she sets in motion multiple points of view that yet remain tethered to what Roland Barthes calls "the grain of the voice," which signifies through the body. Voice as performance is at the heart of another postgeneric prose work of the 1980s, Theresa Hak Kyung Cha's *Dictée* (1982). *Dictée* grows out of Cha's multilingual background, a situation Stein might well have appreciated, since she, like Cha, lived simultaneously in French and English. And Stein's inscription of (1) a verbal performance in which (2) the grain of the voice creates an embodied language that (3) persists within all of the figure–ground shifts of brilliantly fractal texts makes her not surprisingly "the mother of us all" with respect to the poetic inventions of the writers we have been considering. Like Hejinian, Acker, and Cha in the 1980s, Stein writes lengthy prose works that can be seen to renovate poetry. The one difference between Stein and more recent writers is her delight in and adherence to genre, even if her generic definitions, in works such as *How to Write* (1931), can be quite eccentric. The postgeneric writers of the 1980s and beyond often draw sustenance from Stein but claim a greater freedom to mix and juxtapose genres, making that interplay a noteworthy part of their poetic undertaking. If prose written after 1980 can tell us something about the fate of poetry, then perhaps it is that women writers have rethought some of the primary poetic concepts, such as form, voice, and performance—using prose to teach us anew what poetry can do.

Cha's multilayered *Dictée* has been viewed from many vantage points. When it is claimed by critics as a poster child for Asian American identity, the focus often rests on passages chronicling the struggles of the Korean martyr Hyung Soon Huo and those of Cha's own Korean mother exiled in China during the Japanese occupation. Another strain of criticism traces the impact on Cha of French film theory and especially of Barthes and his late, Buddhist-derived concept of "the neutral" (Barthes 2005). An exhibition of her work at the Berkeley Art Museum (Lewallen 2001) and a more recent selection of her writing, *Exilée | Temps Morts* (Cha 2009), point out the extent to which Cha—known primarily during her lifetime as a performance artist—wrote *Dictée* as a prose text that implies poetic performance. To begin with, the central conceit of dictation, from which the book takes its title, depicts a performative situation in which a language learner takes down and translates phrases and sentences as part of a rigidly prescribed site of instruction. In many tableau-like scenes, some set in a French class in a Catholic high school, the text is haunted by a voice receiving dictation from the past and rendering it palpable in the present. As in the case of many of Acker's works, the wounded mother is also a central figure in *Dictée*. And like Acker, Cha goes back to classical texts (for Acker, these are usually Latin writers, such as Propertius, Catullus, or Petronius) in search of paradigms to translate into contemporary forms of liberation. Cha divides *Dictée* into sections named for each of the nine Muses, and she begins the book with an epigraph from Sappho that might easily have found a place in Acker's work: "May I write words more naked than flesh, stronger than bone, more resilient than sinew, sensitive than nerve" (Cha 2001: unpag.).

Acting as a kind of prayer, the epigraph in itself has a performative component. Beyond this supplication, though, *Dictée* consists mainly of instructions for actions to perform, some mental and some physical, which implicate the reader or audience as much as the writer. In this sense, Cha's work belongs in the tradition of Happenings, conceptual art, and performance art—much of whose verbal material consists of directives for events. In 1968, Jerome Rothenberg attempted an early summation of this performative tradition in his anthology *Technicians of the Sacred*, which provides an important model for understanding the aims, methods, and materials of *Dictée*. As Jonathan Stalling (2010) demonstrates, *Dictée* is permeated by references to Daoist alchemy and to Korean *kut* shamanism (performed mainly by women)—exactly the sorts of texts included in *Technicians*.[3] Rothenberg's compendium of tribal and archaic works from around the world, with commentaries that marry the translated material to modern poetry and performance, demonstrates an implied thesis that Cha would endorse: truly avant-garde poetry can re-envision the present as though from the perspective of a society distant in time or space, finding new efficacy in ritual language and actions. The commentaries in *Technicians* also report extensively on the conditions in which the poetry is performed, stressing, as Cha does, its roots in incantation, song, chant, prayer, dance, and drama. In all of her pieces, whether in texts, installations, videos, or performances, Cha presents herself as a very quiet but commanding presence, taking the audience with her into a world of dream, memory, nightmare, and potential healing.

Dictée cannot be read correctly without acknowledging the performative quality of the dictation and translation that pervade its prose:

Being broken. Speaking broken. Saying broken. Talk broken. Say broken. Broken speech. Pidgon [sic] tongue. Broken word. Before speak. As being said. As spoken. To be said. To say. Then speak. (Cha 2001: 161)

This performative passage commands and enacts a sacrifice of competence at the site of interlingual strife. Language is broken because in conditions of colonialism (such as Japan's colonizing of Korea) or exile (such as Cha's mother's relocation to China) it cannot establish a direct connection between a speaker and a listener. Each of these (mostly) two-word sentences expresses a barrier or interruption through an inability to speak correctly, to demonstrate competence, to join two languages in a pidgin (itself misspelled as "pidgon"), to express what is "being said." Even at the level of the individual word, Cha shows how languages come together and break apart in uncontrollable ways. For instance, one key word in *Dictée* is "diseuse," which looks like it should mean "disuse," but actually is an Old French word derived from *dire*, to say, that came into English at the turn of the twentieth century as a term for a professional female reciter. This strange, misrecognized word defines Cha's shamanistic vocation as woman performance artist, as if she were rising from the underworld as an avatar of Persephone, goddess of spring: "*Dead words. Dead tongue. From disuse . . . Let the one who is diseuse, one who is daughter restore spring with her each appearance from beneath the earth*" (Cha 2001: 133).

As a language mender, Cha makes *Dictée* the site of an interlingual contest, goading her three languages, Korean, English, and French, into an uneasy conversation. This interchange reveals not only the buried political relations among the languages but also issues of verbal competence, phonetic ability, and listening to pure sound. Contemporary writer Caroline Bergvall carries forward these concerns into the present by staging confrontations between her three languages, Norwegian, French, and English, using mediums employed by Cha—text, installation, and performance—and adding digital installations on her website. In books such as *Meddle English* (2011) and *Drift* (2014), Bergvall rewrites classic works of English poetry, such as Chaucer's *Canterbury Tales* and *The Seafarer*, exploding the language into Anglo-Saxon, French, and Nordic voices that overlap, pun homophonically, fracture into sputtered consonants, and spill out into critiques of contemporary scenes of exile and flight. *Drift*, for example, reads works such as *The Seafarer* and the Icelandic *Vineland Sagas* as if they were narrating the fate of the notorious "Left-to-Die Boat," which received unprecedented electronic surveillance but no assistance as it drifted around the Mediterranean in 2011, while all but nine of its seventy-two African refugees perished. Like Cha, Bergvall combines poetry, documentary, translation, and memoir to create a multivalent prose performance of uneasily intermixed identities.

Alongside invocations of young female martyrs, such as Hyung Soon Huo and Joan of Arc (as represented in Carl Theodor Dreyer's *Passion of Joan of Arc*), Cha considers in detail her namesake, St. Thérèse of Lisieux—a not surprising choice for a young woman learning French in a Catholic school in California. Issues of sainthood and martyrdom link *Dictée* to another book-length work of prose by a California poet, D. J. Waldie's *Holy Land* (1996). Waldie places Catholicism at the heart of a documentary exploration of the rise of suburbia after World War II. *Holy Land* interweaves the history of one of the first communities built at industrial scale, Lakewood, California (near Long Beach), with Waldie's own autobiography. It opens with the ominous statement, "That evening he thought he was becoming his habits, or—even more—he thought he was becoming the grid he knew" (Waldie 1996: 1). A central image in the book, the grid rigidly defines the streets of Lakeland, with its 17,500 houses erected in three years, in one of whose houses Waldie grew up and continues to live and fashion an identity: "He thought of them as middle class even though 1,100-square-foot tract houses on streets meeting at right angles are not middle class at all" (1). As Waldie digs deeper into what it means to live in a grid, he discovers not only its unyielding constraints but also the power structure it manifests through practices of land use, zoning, development, banking, and so forth. Looking at photographs taken when the land was developed in 1950, he sees the gradual imprinting of the grid on "3,500 acres of Southern California farmland" (4):

> The photographs celebrate house frames as precise as cells in a hive and stucco walls fragile as an unearthed bone.
> Seen from above, the grid is beautiful and terrible. (5)

The "stucco walls fragile as an unearthed bone" contrast with the words that are "stronger than bone" invoked in Cha's epigraph from Sappho. Each poet, though, seeks to ground writing about social conditions in the particulars of the felt human body. When he alludes to "A terrible beauty is born," the line that ends three of the four stanzas of Yeats' "Easter 1916" (Yeats 1956: 177–80), Waldie paints the grid as ultimately a tragic pattern, which (like the Easter Rebellion in Ireland) derives from a political as much as a religious conflict. Ultimately, he learns, "The streets of my city are a fraction of a larger grid, anchored to one in Los Angeles . . . laid out in September 1781" (22). The Los Angeles grid was carried north from Mexico City, and it "originally came from a book in the Archive of the Indies in Seville. The book prescribed the exact orientation of the streets, the houses, and the public places for all the colonial settlements in the Spanish Americas." Having traced the grid back to its inception, Waldie makes the leap from politics to religion: "That grid came from God" (22). This may sound ironic, but in context it doesn't seem so. Not only does the grid accomplish the functions of enclosure and control, but it also takes a cruciform shape. In strikingly Catholic terms, Waldie portrays the humble life he has chosen (he continues to live as an adult in the same Lakewood house) as an acceptance of being crucified on the grid: "He believes, however, that each of us is crucified. His own crucifixion is the humiliation of living the life he has made for himself" (3). As he explains later, "His religion and living in this suburb have taught him shame" (51). Across the grid of 316 numbered sections in *Holy Land*, Waldie uses the plain style of the simple declarative sentence as a remarkably subtle instrument for conveying grief, shame, self-abnegation, and a growing sense of wonder that the severely circumscribed life he has accepted in Lakewood anchors him in unanticipated ways to the transpersonal realms of history, geography, government, religion.

Waldie's invocation of Catholicism occurs mainly in reflections on his father, who came from a pious family and even belonged to a religious order. The varied emotional colors of these reflections are framed by grief, as Waldie recounts the death of his mother, his subsequent refusal to speak about her with his father, and then his father's death. The counterbalancing narrative to this melancholy family history is Waldie's investigation of the history of Lakeland, which was developed by three Jewish businessmen—who could not, at the time they bought the land, have lived on it, for "the lots were protected by 'restrictions of an all-inclusive nature.' Written into deed covenants, these restrictions prevented the sale of lots to Negroes, Mexicans, and Jews" (73). Embarking on building the largest planned suburban community in the world, the three developers moved quickly to satisfy the need for housing for young families flooding into Southern California after the end of the war. This meant that the developers, too, subscribed to the metaphysics of the grid, regardless of its associations with industrialized slaughter, such as that practiced during the Holocaust:

> When places to live must be built quickly, cheaply, and profitably, they are built on a grid of right angles.
> The neat rectangles of two-story, red brick barracks for political prisoners at Auschwitz—and the rows of wood sheds at the nearby Birkenau camp for the extermination of Jews—are built on a grid. (99)

Throughout the book, the grid takes on conflicting values as a multivalent symbol. In Waldie's poetic narrative, the grid is woven of strands that intermingle the Catholic with the Jewish, family history with suburban neighborhoods, the Southern California landscape with the industrial production of housing, crucifixion and redemption with confinement and extermination. Like William Carlos Williams in *Paterson* and Charles Olson in *The Maximus Poems*, Waldie conducts a poetic and historical investigation of a locality that, viewed from the outside, seems merely eccentric to the nation, but seen from the inside is situated at the center of the cosmos.

Beginning with poet's prose of the 1970s and continuing in the book-length works of prose we have been examining, poets have mined the resources of the sentence, using syntax to generate poetic effects. As Waldie employs his quiet, discrete, declarative sentences for historical research and investigations of his father's beliefs and behaviors, Laura Mullen, in *Murmur* (2007), devotes her propellant, consistently interrupted sentences to forensic explorations of her mother's status as obsessive reader and unsatisfied artist. Right at the outset, Mullen adds textual frame after frame, to alert the reader that this is a book about reading and writing. Several pages of hors-texte frontload *Murmur* with an epigraph from Wilkie Collins' novel *The Law and the Lady*; a dedication "*for my mothers*"; a two-page chapter, "The Audience," whose collage form mimics chapters to come in *Murmur*; a "Table" (of contents); a list of imaginary "Illustrations"; and then the most striking bit of hors-texte, an entire unpunctuated page of words beginning with the letter "m," separated only by capital letters:

> MemoryMarriageMurderMotherMysteryMuseMarkerMenMereMisplacedMemory MarketMulledMonumentMendacityMisprintMr.Mrs.MeshesMachineMilkMarble . . . (unpag.)

This metonymic chain sets up equivalencies between murmur, mother, murder, and memory, with further "m" words amplifying what Mullen claims is "a call for the mother (that 'mmmm')," which "marks an effort—in part—to deal with this urgently difficult figure: she is danger and she's in danger" (Robbins 2016: 205).

Focusing on the physical sensation of the voiced labial consonant—"(that 'mmmm')"—the "m" words that march down the page are grammatically distinct (they are not all nouns, by any means), but they are not syntactically connected. The contrast between visual joining and syntactic separation is striking. More consistently throughout the book, Mullen introduces radical syntactic disjuncture by refusing to end many of her sentences, breaking them off in order to suggest multiple possible endings or to indicate the cross-talking that regularly occurs in normal conversation. In an interview, she remarks on this stylistic feature: "almost every passage comes to an unpunctuated end in the middle of a sentence: sometimes a voice cuts off because other stories ride over the one being told, or thoughts trail away, or the person we were listening to falls silent, or we become distracted" (Fava 2007: unpag.). If, in narrative, she complains, "We impose neat endings," then cutting off sentences mimics how "essentially every encounter is unfinished and impossible to categorize." She insists that the lack of endings is a virtue: "I let that state of uncertainty be an experience: spending time with questions not answers." If in life "the story is collapsing all the time around us, and mostly on us," then Mullen's goal for her prose is "to make a narrative structure where nothing happens, to imitate that, to enact it—not cover up the pain and the shame" (Robbins 2016: 208). In the reading experience, the truncated sentence allows for predication to remain fluid, in potential, offering multiple ways to proceed. And at another level, the sentence's broken edges alert the reader to the collage nature of the text, to its constant arousal without the fulfilling of generic expectations.

Mullen's focus on the oppressive mother and the "pain and shame" she evokes in her daughter echoes the emphasis we saw in Acker's *Great Expectations*. When asked if Acker is an influence, Mullen replies:

> I didn't read Acker until I was teaching her (1989), but I immediately fell head over heels in love with her work, with the boldness of it, the swagger of transgression, her sense that she could take what had been written and remake it hers, and that in fact, there was no reason to go on telling the story the way the story had been told. (Robbins 2016: 208)[4]

In its new ways of telling the story, *Murmur* is a mashup of the genres of murder mystery, film noir, police procedural, Hitchcock thriller, Nouveau Roman, and memoir—all of which exist across the media of text, film, and television. It is also an investigation of how language allows us to repeat endlessly the story of a woman's body found on the beach, a story that both dismays and delights. If most of these genres typically offer readers a satisfying conclusion, in which we learn "who done it" and why, this book is about the recursive experience of reading and writing a mystery, rather than an attempt to solve a murder—although the detective is repeatedly invoked as a crucial character. The crime occurs as much on the cover of a mystery, in which a body is shown despoiled on a beach, as it does to an actual woman, and the reader (of the mystery and of *Murmur*) is immediately implicated. Just as the corpse seems to rise up bizarrely, as though in reverse action, and to join in the murder investigation, the fact of reading a book collapses over and over into the crimes occurring therein: "The corpse struggles to its knees, what you thought was the corpse, and—muttering to itself—starts scrubbing at the bloodstains. It's too late to offer to help her, clearly. She says, *Well, to tell you the truth*" (Mullen 2007: 58)—and there the paragraph ends.

Inside the generic reader of the generic mystery resides Mullen's own mother (whom we are meant to hear exclaim, "*Well, to tell you the truth*"), an inveterate reader of genre fiction, especially mysteries, for whom they act as both lure to and escape from clinical depression. The chapter "Forensics" appears to contain many memories of Mullen's mother as reader: "She shut the book, stomped into the kitchen, dropped a pan as if to call attention to her activity, her service. I thought she was faking or at least exaggerating that clumsiness to make me, what? Help her? Pity? Identify with?" (57). These are a daughter's questions about her dissatisfied mother and they are a reader's questions about a writer's intentions and responsibilities: how does she make me feel?; how am I implicated in what she says?; do the details of the story she tells add up to an adequate argument for what happened? Speaking of argument, "Forensics" begins with an epigraph that is a sentence from a chapter by that name in Stein's *How to Write*: "Forensics is so true" (Stein 1973: 390; Mullen 2007: 55). But what is the truth of forensics? Forensics is the art or the study of argument, but it also denotes the scientific approach to legal questions, especially the analysis of physical evidence from a crime scene. Mullen weaves these divergent definitions of forensics to construct arguments that forever seem to collapse, concerning her mother's dissatisfaction and her relationship to it, as though she were lifting up and examining the remains of a crime scene that break up and fall away as she holds them. Speaking of the dissatisfaction: "Couldn't we see we were in the way, that we stood between you and happiness, you . . . and your art . . . I invented a past for you I tried to inhabit; you would have been happier without us, I guessed" (67). So what is the crime? The thwarting of the mother's creativity? The daughter's inability to understand or fully identify with her? The constant retreat into reading mysteries? The inevitable murder of the attractive woman? The murdered woman's complicity in her own death and attempt to exonerate the murderer? All of these possibilities are hinted at in the following paragraph:

> Perched on the living room couch (she'd opened a plastic garbage bag to sit on so as not to stain the upholstery), the corpse refuses to remove the bloody dress. I'm helping her clean her nails: she's afraid she might have caught a thread from his suit there, so some skin from his wrists. I've been trying to tell her she reads too many detective novels. She sighs. She doesn't like the tentative way I'm holding her fingers, she doesn't think I'm going deep enough. *Honestly*, she says, *do I have to do* everything. (64)

Or maybe the ultimate crime is the act of writing itself, something that is always invasive, always complicit, constrained by the communal nature of language, often dependent on the experiences of someone else: "*Honestly*," says the subject of the writing, "*do I have to do* everything." Is it a crime to trot out into public view the intimate relationship between a mother and a daughter, between a victim and a perpetrator, between language and experience? In this sense, the word "forensics" is "so true" because it derives from the Latin *forum*, the site of public debate, where personal quarrels are aired in the market place and become political, where arguments are offered that might bring crimes into the light. Mullen portrays writing as a Moebius strip, as inside and outside at the same time. Her sensitivity to language, to genre, to gender, to class, make her a brilliant inheritor of the poet's prose of the 1970s and the narrative experiments that burgeon forth in its wake, extending investigations of language into narrative collage, which intercuts genres and mediums, bringing techniques and concerns of poetry (its ongoing "crisis of verse") into the contemporary media-saturated world.

And maybe forensics is the proper task of recent book-length works of poetry, as in the examples of Hejinian, Acker, Cha, Waldie, and Mullen. In these texts, the investigation of language performed by poet's prose of the 1970s opens out into forensic interrogations of identity through narrative means, such as family history, social inquiry, and the collage of genres. Building on the inspiration of Williams and Stein and the breakthroughs of Ashbery, Creeley, Antin, and Silliman, poets after 1980 have taken the ongoing American crisis of verse—the constant questioning of poetry's purpose and place in American culture—as an occasion to argue for new forms of writing that themselves lay bare crises in the forum of social and political reality.

Notes

1. For a discussion of Creeley's "conjectural prose," see Fredman 1990: 57–100. The collaboration of Creeley, Marisol, and the designer William Katz on *Presences* is discussed in my introduction to Creeley and Marisol 2018: xi–xxvi.
2. More discussion of the concept of personhood in *My Life* can be found in Chapter 12 of my *American Poetry as Transactional Art*.
3. See Chapter 5 in Stalling 2010.
4. Amy Robbins' interview (2016) with Mullen offers many insights into *Murmur*, and her chapter on Mullen in *American Hybrid Poetics* (Robbins 2014: 44–70) mines these insights for a chapter-by-chapter analysis of the text. See also Fleisher 2012.

Works Cited

Acker, Kathy (1982), *Great Expectations*, New York: Grove Weidenfeld.
Acker, Kathy (1986), *Don Quixote*, New York: Grove.
Acker, Kathy (1991), *Hannibal Lector, My Father*, New York: Semiotexte.
Antin, David (1976), *talking at the boundaries*, New York: New Directions.
Antin, David (1993), *what it means to be avant-garde*, New York: New Directions.
Ashbery, John (1975), *Three Poems*. New York: Viking.
Barthes, Roland (1991), *The Grain of the Voice: Interviews 1962–1980*, trans. Linda Coverdale, Berkeley: University of California Press.
Barthes, Roland (2005), *The Neutral: Lecture Course at the Collège de France (1977–1978)*, trans. Rosalind E. Krauss and Denis Hollier, New York: Columbia University Press.
Bergvall, Caroline (2011), *Meddle English: New and Selected Texts*, Callicoon, NY: Nightboat Books.
Bergvall, Caroline (2014), *Drift*, Brooklyn and Callicoon, NY: Nightboat Books.
Cha, Theresa Hak Kyung ([1982] 2001), *Dictée*, Berkeley: University of California Press.
Cha, Theresa Hak Kyung (2009), *Exilée | Temps Morts: Selected Works*, ed. Constance Lewallen, Berkeley: University of California Press.
Creeley, Robert (1976), *Presences: A Text for Marisol*, in *Mabel: A Story and Other Prose*, London: Marion Boyars.

Creeley, Robert and Marisol Escobar (2018), *Presences: A Text for Marisol: A Critical Edition*, ed. Stephen Fredman, Albuquerque: University of New Mexico Press.

Dworkin, Craig Douglas (1995), "Penelope Reworking the Twill: Patchwork, Writing, and Lyn Hejinian's *My Life*," *Contemporary Literature* 36, pp. 58–81.

Fava, Colleen (2007), "Interview with Laura Mullen," http://www.lauramullen.biz/_i_murmur__i__63629.htm> (last accessed November 22, 2019).

Fleisher, Kass (2012), "Laura Mullen: Threatened as Threat," *Eleven More American Women Poets in the 21st Century*, ed. Claudia Rankine, Lisa Sewell, Middletown, CT: Wesleyan University Press.

Fredman, Stephen ([1983] 1990), *Poet's Prose: The Crisis in American Verse*, 2nd edn, Cambridge: Cambridge University Press.

Fredman, Stephen (2020), *American Poetry as Transactional Art*, Tuscaloosa: University of Alabama Press.

Hejinian, Lyn ([1980] 1987), *My Life*, 2nd edn, Los Angeles: Sun and Moon.

Hume, Kathryn (2001), "Voice in Kathy Acker's Fiction," *Contemporary Literature*, vol. 42, no. 3, Autumn, pp. 485–513.

Lewallen, Constance (2001), *The Dream of the Audience: Theresa Hak Kyung Cha (1951–1982)*, Berkeley: University of California Press.

Mullen, Laura (2007), *Murmur*, New York: Futurepoem Books.

Perloff, Marjorie (1985), *Dance of the Intellect: Studies in the Poetry of the Pound Tradition*, Cambridge: Cambridge University Press.

Perloff, Marjorie (1991), *Radical Artifice: Writing Poetry in the Age of Media*, Chicago: University of Chicago Press.

Robbins, Amy Moorman (2014), *American Hybrid Poetics: Gender, Mass Culture, and Form*, New Brunswick, NJ: Rutgers University Press.

Robbins, Amy Moorman (2016), "Interview with Laura Mullen," *Pacific Coast Philology*, vol. 51, no. 2, pp. 199–209.

Rothenberg, Jerome (ed. with commentaries) (1968), *Technicians of the Sacred: A Range of Poetries from Africa, America, Asia, & Oceania*, Garden City, NY: Doubleday.

Silliman, Ron (1978), *Ketjak*, San Francisco: THIS.

Silliman, Ron (1989), *The New Sentence*, New York: Roof.

Stalling, Jonathan (2010), *Poetics of Emptiness: Transformations of Asian Thought in American Poetry*, New York: Fordham University Press.

Stein, Gertrude ([1931] 1973), *How to Write*, West Glover, VT: Something Else Press.

Waldie, D. J. (1996), *Holy Land: A Suburban Memoir*, New York: Norton.

Whitman, Walt (1973), *Leaves of Grass*, ed. Sculley Bradley and Harold Blodgett, New York: Norton.

Williams, William Carlos (1970), *Imaginations*, ed. Webster Schott, New York: New Directions.

Yeats, William Butler (1956), *The Collected Poems of W. B. Yeats*, New York: Macmillan.

Zurbrugg, Nicholas (2004), *Art, Performance, Media: 31 Interviews*, Minneapolis: University of Minnesota Press.

20

"Prose in Prose" in Contemporary French Poetic Practice: Appropriation, Repurposing and Pornography

Jeff Barda

Since its very genesis in nineteenth-century France with Charles Baudelaire's foundational *Spleen de Paris* (1889), the prose poem has veered off in various directions, becoming a transgressive form to the extent that "any attempt at a single monolithic definition of the genre would be doomed to failure" (Delville 1998: 1). A brief survey of the twentieth-century onwards—from Max Jacob's revaluation of Baudelaire's project in *Le Cornet de dés* (1916) to Pascal Quignard's unclassifiable prose of *Petits Traités* (1981), passing through Pierre Reverdy's refashioning of the genre to Jacques Réda's urban prose—reveals a plurality of methodological, stylistic and modal approaches to the genre. While it is true that some poets have either practiced poetry and prose intermittently or advanced poetry at the expense of prose, some others have repudiated this clear-cut divide, holding contradictory, ambivalent and sometimes radical positions. Distancing themselves from the heated debates on whether prose should encompass poetry or whether poetry should find refuge in prose, some poets have decided to bring these terms into play to break with the clichés associated with these forms of writing in order to create new hybrid and amorphous forms.[1] Jude Stéfan has sought to create a "poème de prose" (Stéfan 1967), Jean-Christophe Bailly to create a "prose coupée" (Bailly 2000); or, to cite another example, Michel Deguy posits "prose en poème" (Deguy 2000). Although these practices enshrined in experimentalism lend weight to the fact that poetry and prose can fuse together into something that nonetheless remains of the essence of poetic language, another breed of radical poets overtly deemed such practices and questions outdated, conservative, and no longer relevant, calling instead for an exit from the institutional and historical aura that had accrued around what we usually recognize as "poetry."

Working beyond the formal divide *verse* and *prose*, these poets, who forcefully eschew traditional postures and models associated with "poetry in itself" (notably those of poetic subject, and figural, rhythmic or phonic patterns), consider that the time of poetry is gone once and for all. As Jean-Marie Gleize, one of the most significant poetry theorists in France, notes, "ce qui est pertinent c'est de savoir si l'on tient à faire œuvre de poésie, de poète où si l'on a d'autres projets" (Gleize 2009: 173) [It has to be decided if it is a matter of making a work of poetry, of a poet, or if there are other projects]. These other projects, which Gleize calls "postpoésie," as opposed to identified poetic forms, favor contextual displacement, code shifting, repurposing and remediation. For Gleize, such operations constitute the cardinal functions of what he calls "prose en prose," a regime of writing that is not only removed from decorative and lyric patterns of expression in favor of a sober, clear idiom which endeavors to register the surrounding buzz of the world in an era of hypermediation. Such a regime of writing is defined as "une poésie tapée aplatie en prose ou prose aplatie. Vers un peu de prose froide et plate. Vers un peu de prose *en prose*, tapée sèche aplatie" (Gleize 1999: 37) [A typed poetry flattened into prose or a flattened prose. Toward a little prose cold and flat. Toward a little prose *in prose*, typed dryly flat].[2] Resolutely ambiguous, that expression entails different acceptations. First, it can suggest the idea of a prose without quality, that is to say, a prose that is nothing else than prose, a tautological prose which simply refers to itself.[3] Second, it can also point toward a mode of writing (prose) and a certain conception of language characterized by semantic and symbolic deflations (prosaic). Thirdly, such paradigm can also be understood dialectically and historically as the results of the successive "crises" in French poetics, since as Gleize observes, "après le vers en vers, il y a les vers en prose, après les vers en prose ou la prose en vers, il y a la prose en prose" (Gleize 2007: 172) ["after the verse in verse, there is the verse in prose, after the verse in prose or the prose in verse, there is the prose in prose"].

Gleize's unsettling argument is that Baudelaire prefigures such developments. In what may sound an anachronical claim, Gleize's diagnosis not only provides an original reading of French poetic history as opposed to linear, institutionalized accepted narratives, but also serves as a justification of his own practice. Baudelaire's main literary output—his departure from verse to prose, shift from metaphors to a seemingly nonfigurative use of language joined with a strict rejection of unity, coherence and dismantlement of the poetic edifice—is indeed analyzed by Gleize as a foundational gesture in French poetics dedicated to undermining poetic essentialism and the expressive stance of poetry. And yet, rather than heralding a return to Baudelaire—a move which would seem regressive and anathema to the avant-garde ethos—Gleize suggests it is time to draw all axiological consequences of his project to pursue it by other means. Crucially, Baudelaire's aesthetic development of "une prose poétique musicale, sans rhythme et sans rime, assez souple et heurtée" (Baudelaire 1968: 146) ["a musical poetic prose, without rhythm, without rhyme, rather supple and driven"] chimes for Gleize with the distressful behaviors of "Les Bons Chiens." Rather than construing dogs as allegories of poets, Gleize understands their postures and indistinctive modes of being as inseparable from territorial functions. Like all living creatures, dogs exist in a series of milieus, each possession their own codes and rhythms. And yet, unlike birds, for instance, who shift from one site to another whilst generating new melodic patterns in their engagement with contingent environments, the Baudelairean dogs do not switch milieus but constantly fall back into sterile repetition and single measure. These poor and dirty dogs follow a-melodic patterns as they limp, stay on the floor or descend in the dark:

> . . . il va falloir encore descendre d'un cran, descendre d'une marche, ou d'un étage, et même franchir le niveau rue et continuer vers le premier, le deuxième sous-sol, là peut-être à côté des grands pots verts en plastique, et avec sur la tête tout le poids du béton, du métal, de verre, de feuillage, etc. (Gleize 1999: 15)

[... we have to go down a rung, go down a step, or a floor, and even cross the street level and continue towards the first, the second basement, perhaps there beside the large green plastic pots, and with all the concrete, the metal, the glass, the foliage weighing on our head, and so on.]

These mono-coded dogs who sift through the detritus of the city ("béton," "métal" or "verre") provide a remarkable illustration both for the way in which the production of prose is interwoven with the collection of refuses, and also of the stylistic posture of that prose, which not only conveys a sort of degree-zero writing but also a lack of expressiveness and dynamism.

This investigation in the prose of the world carried out by those who Gleize qualifies as "ultrabaudelairiens, baudelairiens radicaux" (Gleize 2007: 172) ["ultrabaudelairean, radical baudelairians"] came of age in the late 1990s. This period, characterized by the decline of emancipation and critical thought in France, is often regarded by cultural historians as a schizophrenic decade. On the one hand, it signaled the rise of neoliberalism and the triumph of conservatism—what Bernard Noël eloquently termed "la castration mentale" ["mental castration"] (Noël 1994)—but also the increasing development of mass media and modern technological organization to the ends of consumption industry—echoing Deguy's analysis of "le culturel" (Deguy 1986) or what Eric Sadin termed later as "la société de l'"anticipation" ["anticipatory society"] (Sadin 2011). On the other, it indicated the emergence of new movements of resistance and forms of political engagement within French cultural production.[4] Notably, this period saw in poetry the revival of interest in praxis and action after a hiatus of several decades which provides important reconfigurations of poetry's relationship to politics. Striving for effectiveness and impact, Gleize observes that unlike the neo-avant-gardes of the 1960s which upended language conventions through opaque language (a "contre-usage"), an entire generation of poets, including Christophe Hanna, Thibaud Baldacci, Anne-James Chaton, Nathalie Quintane, Daniel Foucard and Stéphane Bérard, but also Jacques Henri-Michot, Franck Leibovici and Manuel Joseph, amongst many others, explore instead a "méta-usage" based on "des languages dominants pour en faire la matière d'une écriture poétique critique qui ... va revendiquer comme lieu d'intervention et d'action, l'espace public—panneaux publicitaires, écrans-vidéos, posters, etc." ["meta-usage based on dominant languages to make them the matter of a critical poetic writing which ... will reclaim public space as a place of intervention and action—advertisements, video-screens, posters, and such"] (Gleize 2011: 39–40) in order to provide new forms of objectification and representation of the political. Investigating new forms of resistance through the recycling of ready-made materials and mainstream mass media (text, images, sounds, ideas, discourses, affects ...) and absorbing the lessons of Lautréamont, William S. Burroughs, Fluxus or Guy Debord, these poets not only attempted to fuse the avant-garde with the advent of new technology but also to short-circuit, through spins and viruses, what mediatized our attention. As Gleize explains, "ils s'approprient la langue de l'ennemi pour mieux s'insinuer dans ses réseaux de communication, pervertir ou détourner ses messages, ses systèmes de figuration" ["they appropriate the tongue of the enemy so as to insinuate themselves in his communications, pervert or misdirect his messages, his systems of figuration"] (39). Such diversity of approach looks more for effects than aesthetic outputs. Like the "neo-conceptualists" or "uncreative writers" (to speak like Kenneth Goldsmith), these poets consider that digital technologies have significantly impacted the way one produces, perceives and processes language, and therefore, "one should exploit them in extreme ways [. . .] to create works that are expressive and meaningful as works constructed in more traditional ways" (Goldsmith 2011: 15). By disrupting the flow of information through a cumulative bricolage, such practice seeks to infiltrate mass media in order to produce new perceptual apparatus, concepts and tools. As Yves Citton observes, such practices sought to produce "de nouveaux moyens d'interagir, de nouveaux milieu d'action [. . .] mais aussi de nouveau 'publics' [. . .] qui se trouvent impliqués, même dans les pratiques, les résonances, les enjeux, les institutions, les problèmes, les débats suscités à l'occasion de l'aventure créatrice" ["new means of interacting, new kinds of actions . . . but also new 'publics' now implicated, even in the practices, the resonances, the wages, the institutions, the problems, the arguments arising during the creative adventure"] (Citton 2017: 366). In this chapter, I shall engage with these models through the examination two books published in 1998—Christophe Hanna's *Petits poëmes en prose* and Jacques Henri-Michot's *Un ABC de la barbarie*. I will analyze the terms and consequences of these new forms of viral prose in order to see how they conceptualize the issue of the real in response to new forms of orderings concerning human existence in a globalized world and offer new perspectives on the relationship between prose, ethics and politics in contemporary French poetic practices.

The Lurid and Sensational Prose of the World

Christophe Hanna's first book, titled *Petits poëmes en prose*, provides a direct link with Baudelaire's seminal project and offers a remarkable illustration of prose in prose. Akin to Mallarmé, who famously associated prose with the "universel reportage" (Mallarmé 2003: 667), and Apollinaire, who equally considered "les journaux [. . .] les livraisons à 25 centimes pleines d'aventures policières"(Apollinaire 1971: 36) as a paradigmatic model of prose, Hanna does so too when he asserts drawing from "prose [. . .] celle des journeaux de faits divers, des avis de décés" ["that of newspaper anecdotes, obituaries"] (42). Effectively, Hanna's book offers an investigation of the numerous sensational and lurid *fait-divers*, ironically also known as "chiens écrasés" [literally "runover dogs"] in French, and yet interesting in reference to earlier canine discussions of the late 1990s in France. Hanna's cutting-and-pasting method consists in drawing from the constant amalgams of experiences, sensations and perceptions of that time: sexual classified ads, newspaper extracts related to the trial of the French spree killer Jean-Claude Romand, but also, amongst other instances, the death of Khaled Kelkal, a French and Algerian terrorist affiliated with the Armed Islamic Group Algeria, who was involved in the 1995 bombings attack in France. Published two years before the new millennium by the iconoclastic and avant-garde publisher Al Dante, this book flaunts its Baudelairean credentials right down from its rhematic title and various paratexts. With its blatant archaic dieresis on "poëmes" which clearly functions as an ironic commentary on the obsolete character of the poem as a genre, Hanna seeks to unmuffle or unclasp what is too often associated with poetry. Rejecting the idea of a poetic and autotelic language as separate and distinct from the everyday, Hanna calls for an heterologic understanding of poetic language, that is to say, a language without hierarchies capable of encompassing a range of symbolic forms, conventions, codes and affects which are not only linked to "use" but also shape our ways of worldmaking and categorizing. Browsing through the book, one may feel familiar with the clearly intertextual thematic titles, such as "Les Foules" or "L'étranger," which function both for Hanna and for readers as a point of reference. Re-actualizing Baudelaire's project with the means of today through the repurposing of ambient discourse is of crucial importance as long as the reader is kept awakened:

> * ici on s'adapte au scenario proposé   ici on devient adapté   on finit par s'adapter   par se sentir en confiance   par se sentir en harmonie maintenant [. . .] laissez-vous aller   à suivre les paroles du scénario   les paroles simples de la scène paisible   vous avez confiance en moi   et vous êtes au centre d'une scène paisible   simplement au centre   allongé tranquillement   maintenant j'ai votre confiance (5)

> [* Here we adapt to the proposed scenario   here one becomes adapted   one eventually becomes adapted   feels confident   feels in harmony now [. . .]   let go   and follow the words of the scenario   the simple words of the peaceful scene   you trust me   and find yourself in the midst of a peaceful scene   simply at the center   lying peacefully   now I have gained your trust]

In what clearly sounds like a transcription of an exercise of meditation or hypnotherapy, this poem, which appears in a bulky footnote, functions as a statement of intent. Deprived of punctuation, this text, which mimics the pace of such exercises, holds two functions. First, it acts as *captatio* which hails at the reader—the illocutory act initiates a situation, a communication; a voice (an "I" appears in the last line) talks to an "on" and a "vous." Second, such a model is quickly undermined by the reader, who identifies the formulaic nature of such process: the saturation of reflexive formulae, repetition of syntagma, draw readers' attention to the formal mechanisms of such exercises, inviting them not only to identify those schemes but also to distance themselves from the auctorial voice too often present in poetic discourses. The idea of using language as a vehicle for imagination, which normally underpinned such exercises, is thus nullified. Such a strategy in fact enables Hanna to get rid of the idea of a "soporific" poetry in favor of what he calls a "poésie action directe" (Hanna 2003), an expression synthesizing both Bernard Heidsieck's conceit of "poésie action" and the far-left terrorist group "Action directe." To trigger this awakening, Hanna not only decontextualizes and recontextualizes textual residues but also creates a temporal shock between the old frame of reference (Baudelaire) and the new (the present). "Chacun sa chimère" starts, indeed, as follows:

> attend vos mots et photos/photocopies plein
> pied + visage pour sélect **homme** moins de 30
> ans TBM + sa photo **homme** la trentaine
> 1m75, 66 kg, 21x 6 et discr + tel je réapprends
> à vivre après un grave accident réapprends

à retrouver une vie normale je cherche à venir
vous rejoindre (1m77, 66kg) à loisir **homme** [. . .]
aimerait vivre dans le respect de chacun et la réalisation
douche cabine shopping violence sauna strings portés extrême
(24–5)

[Awaits your words and pics/xeroxes full
Body + face xeroxes for select **man** under 30
yo VWH + his pic **man** in his thirties
5'7" tall, 145 lbs, 21x 6 and discr + tel am relearning
to live after a serious accident relearning
to find a normal life I try to come and
meet you (5'7", 145 lbs) at leisure **man** [. . .]
would like to live in respect of each other and realization
shower stall shopping violence sauna extreme worn G-strings]

Unlike Baudelaire's poem where men walked with their heads bowed down and bore upon their back an enormous chimera, Hanna reveals that in an age of late capitalism what drives modern men is no longer an irresistible desire to walk despite their crushing chimeras, but an unconquerable desire to have sex. If sexual language rests on certain stereotypical assemblages (acronyms, abbreviations, plain syntax . . .) but also certain criteria, Hanna also shows how these disclose affects and memories ("je réapprends / à vivre après un grave accident réapprends à retrouver une vie normale. . ." ["I am learning again / to live after a serious accident learning again to find a normal life. . ."]). The monotony and homogeneity of the language etched in those "annonces sexuelles" here indexed provide also a collective and anonymous portrait of a generation. The juxtaposition—loop effect—of heterogeneous segments gives rise, at the same time, to a myriad of associations creating through a lack of differentiation a "chimera," an expression of desire beyond representation. Each segment not only seems interchangeable or gives the impression of replacing the others, but also reveals a certain "semiotics" ('clichés') of desire that the following nominal syntagma encapsulates ("douche cabine shopping violence sauna strings portés extrêmes").

As Pierre Bourdieu aptly observed in 1996, "les faits divers, ce sont aussi des faits qui font diversion. Les prestidigitateurs ont un principe élémentaire qui consiste à attirer l'attention sur autre chose que ce qu'ils font" ["Human interest stories, those are also stories that divert. Magicians have an elementary principle consisting in drawing attention to something other than what they are doing"] (Bourdieu 1996: 16). Hanna is indeed less interested in the content of lurid stories or in the way they attempt to set aside main narratives, but he seeks to investigate the mechanisms, conditions of productions and circulations that surround what Citton calls "mediarchie" (Citton 2017). By returning to the way information is broadcast or framed, he seeks to interrogate the conditions of receptions and perceptions embedded in media apparatuses. This is why, as Nathalie Quintane notes, he is more interested in "rédaction" than in "écriture" (Quintane 2008: 139). As "data is anything but raw" (Gitelman 2013), Hanna's work consists in editing or reframing data produced by media to reveal both the ecology of media coverage and its agents. It is therefore a process of "remediation" (Bolter and

Grusin 1999) that is at stake, in the sense that he seeks to redescribe a given material by a way of another medium not so much to see how the superseding medium presents its version as an improvement of the original, but rather to reveal salient elements seen but left unnoticed in the original documents or formal architecture. Heuristic in essence, such process seeks to investigate the way one processes information whilst providing the means to examine the way media conditioned our attention. Close to the epistemology of information theory rather than aesthetics per se, Hanna thus undertakes to make readers aware of the forms of transmission, extraction and utilization of information.

Several strategies are deployed through the book to trigger such reflexive process. Hanna, for instance, explores the architecture of newspapers (headlines, bylines, lead, lead paragraph, explanation) as well as the grid design, but swaps contents through a technique of superposition, as in "Le mauvais vitrier" (Figure 20.1).

Parodying the famous French tabloids (*Gala, Nice Matin, Le Dauphiné*) which focus on sensational crime stories, gossip columns about the life of celebrities, junk food news, Hanna aims to offer a compact digest of the so-called most significant "events" of "la semaine tragique." Although it is a known fact that such a model is used by media to ignite and draw readers' attention to stories to create a shock, Hanna is also aware that such apparatus is also often used to give the impression of truth. Through a montage of heterogeneous data, ranging from Sharon Stone's famous *Basic Instinct* interrogation scene where the actress uncrosses her legs to reveal she is not wearing underwear to a lurid car accident in the north of France, in passing to the "serious" heart operation of Caroline de Monaco, Hanna does not seek to replicate a faithful narrative. Rather, he replicates the editorial gestures to divert these narratives and to suspend them in the flow. Segments are quickly interrupted, mixed with others, to the extent that a narration establishes itself as quite quickly diverted, so that it allows meaning to start being established but not so that a narration starts taking place (discontinuities, breaks, set a reflexive space that make readers aware of flow and conditions of reception of information).

Alternatively, Hanna copies-and-pastes textual residues, reducing them to pure facts. Through a cleansing effect, Hanna indeed seeks to remove all that is flowery or superfluous to maintain the barebones despite a frequent use of ellipses, shortcuts, so much that the simplification of language functions as a key operator of that prose: "il faudra que ça aille vite, qu'on comprenne vite et surtout qu'on conserve en mémoire ce qu'il y a de vraiment utile" ["It has to go quickly, be quickly understood and above all what is really useful must be remembered"] (Hanna 57). "La Chambre double," which alludes to the murder crime that took place in Gournay-sur-Marne in 1997, offers a thought-provoking illustration of such techniques. In December 1995, Véronique Herbert, who was still a student, met Sébastien Paindavoine, a handsome 17-year-old young man, and suggested to him that they commit a murder together. Both of them were passionate about poems and film scripts about murderous fantasies, and about the Oliver Stone movie *Natural Born Killers*, and they both intended to kill Abdeladim Gahbiche, a sixteen-year-old Tunisian who appealed sexually to Véronique. Invited to Sebastien's basement room, Abdeladim, once undressed, was stabbed in the neck and repeatedly in different parts of the body. Instead of going into details, Hanna offers a synthetic

Catherine Tramell, les fans de l'actrice qui joue le rôle de Catherine peuvent croire voir le sexe de cette actrice = **Sharon Stone**

Il n'est plus question du personnage

⇒ ils ne voient plus C. Tramell. [I.e. l'apparition délibérée/dans le scénario de son sexe a, chez certains (nombreux), pour conséquence qu'il n'est plus question du personnage : l'espace de trois secondes, le film est perçu comme un reportage sur **Sharon Stone**.]

12h : C'est donc un second coup de poignard. **Ducruet** devrait perdre en quelques semaines tous les avantages acquis par son mariage : adieu princesse, bonjour tristesse.
Le destin de **Steph** a pris un tournant irrévocable : elle en a trop vu

Elle en a trop vu pour pouvoir encore supporter

bénéficierait plus d'une exonération d'impôts. Elle est abandonnée et
23h10 : confie à une proche qu'elle manque un peu de tendresse...

Fini le temps où le couple descendait fièrement les marches du palais...

Et c'est encore les derniers rayons de soleil
13h : Comme tous les dimanches, les derniers rayons de l'été : **Steph** en profite et redevient la maman courage.
15h05 : Elle expose son visage aux rayons. Pour leur montrer à tous à tous, à eux, qu'elle n'est pas que la femme bafouée : elle fait front. Le temps passe à une vitesse folle et elle commence à s'y faire.
21h15 : Il passe des soirées entières sans elle, il ne

du **Replay Store** la boutique où il lui arrive de tenir parfois elle-même la caisse
ou 23h30 accoudé à la table du **Jimmy's**, la boîte branchée de Monaco, **DD** vide verre sur verre. Il se sait pris au piège.

NB : XXXVI
LE DÉSIR DE PEINDRE

Notule
M. S*** fabrique, avec quelques complices, des *événements réels* (accouplements, guerres, etc.) dans le seul but de les photographier et de les revendre aux revues les plus offrantes, qui pourront, dès lors, publier le mélange photos + texte qu'on connaît.

17h : trop entendu pour pouvoir supporter encore cette estocade.
C'est le moment inéluctable du sacrifice, c'est l'instant incontournable.
Dimanche 15 septembre :

Le piège sur lui se referme chaque seconde compte malgré ses efforts, l'intervention de son frère, de ses proches, l'adultère sera dévoilé dans quelques jours
malgré ses efforts pour empêcher la sortie des photos du scandale, [NDLR : on sait qu'il a fait pression sur M. S***, le paparazzi (et ami de **Fili Houteman**) qui fut l'auteur de cette machination, organisa la rencontre dans le seul but de prendre des photos (voire de faire une vidéo) et de les revendre pour une petite fortune]

M. S*** fabrique des événements réels

l'intervention de son frère et de proches
0h : Ivre mort il réveille **Stéphanie** et avec des mots embrumés d'alcool il avoue, il lui explique la trahison.
Sous le choc : comment crier sa douleur et sa tristesse
elle fuit il la rattrape fou furieux, est sur le point de la maltraiter : il réclame son droit.

terrible ironie du calendrier : il y a tout juste quatorze ans, ce samedi **14 septembre**, **Grace** disparaissait dans un tragique accident de voiture et comme si tout cela ne suffisait pas, le magazine italien Oggi publie une photo de **Caroline**

Laquelle est la vraie ?

surprise dans son jardin de St Rémy totalement chauve. Émoi en principauté.

Plusieurs hypothèses ont été émises : outre celle d'une grave maladie, on suppose que cette calvitie soudaine serait liée à des troubles d'origine psychosomatique dus à un choc plus ou moins ancien. D'aucuns, cependant, prétendent avec optimisme que la princesse suivrait une nouvelle mode [NDLR : on aurait photographié l'actrice **Demi Moore**, le crâne entièrement rasé, elle aussi] **Caroline** est presque méconnaissable dans son refuge de **Saint Rémy**

a démenti la rumeur : une maladie grave
Caroline a caché son crâne rasé sous une casquette le 14 septembre
malade et encore solitaire pour se rendre au palais
nous sommes le 14 septembre, il est 18h 30 passées à **Saint Rémy** (Provence)
fini le temps où le couple descendait fièrement les marches du palais
A minuit, c'est une véritable malédiction qui frappe ce **15 SEPTEMBRE** à Monaco les **Grimaldi** (la famille) [juste avant, **Rainier** se reposait loin de la Principauté, après une grave opération du cœur : NDLR]
fragile du cœur depuis son triple pontage coronarien à l'héliport 17h28 sa démarche est pesante, il sort

L'hologramme photographique porno sera la prochaine étape

de l'hélico on est le jeudi 17 septembre, il est précisément

Figure 20.1 Christophe Hanna, from "Le mauvais vitrier"

form—a sketch—which clarifies the facts of this lurid affair, adopting a simplistic and straightforward vocabulary and grammar:

II] L'exécution

> 1°) Véronique fait monter Abdeladim dans sa chambre sous prétextes érotiques.
> 2°) Ils sont suivis par Sébastien. Abdeladim ne se doute de rien.
> 3°) Véronique et Sébastien poignardent Abdeladim et le tuent. (17)
>
> [1°) Véronique has Abdeladim come up to her room with an erotic pretext.
> 2°) Sebastien follows them. Abdeladim suspects nothing.
> 3°) Véronique and Sebastien stab Abdeladim and kill him.]

Hanna thus removes stylistic emphasis in favor of a simple idiom and basic syntax reducing language to its simplest expression. Such a model can, however, give rise to humoristic effects when external elements (a virus) are embedded in the flow:

> Plusieurs hypothèses ont été émises pour
> expliquer la calvitie soudaine de **Caroline**, nous en retenons deux :
> 1°) une maladie psychosomatique ; 2°) une nouvelle mode suivie aussi par **Demi Moore**. (40)
>
> [Several hypotheses have been suggested to
> explain the sudden baldness of **Caroline**, and we retain two:
> 1) a psychosomatic sickness; 2) a new mode **Demi Moore** also adopts.]

Rather than opacity as an essential quality of avant-garde writing, what is praised here is the vow of literality, an approach to language which consists of rejecting the deciphering of material entities by representing things in their sheer immanence. Lack of ambiguity and stress on a purely denotative function of language provides the means to make the present immediately *readable*. As Gleize notes, "la prose en prose serait littéralement littérale elle voudrait dire ce qu'elle dit en le disant en l'ayant dit et la prose en prose comme poésie si elle existait n'aurait littéralement, proprement, aucun sens que le sens idiot de dire ce qui est" ["Prose in prose would be literally literal meaning to mean what it says in saying it and having said it and prose in prose like poetry if it existed would not have literally, really, any meaning but the idiotic meaning of declaring what is"] (Gleize 1992: 228). Hence, unlike Michel Deguy in *Le Spleen de Paris* (2001) (a short volume recycling Baudelaire's repertoire), who observes how late capitalism transforms culture into a commodity rather than a genuine experience, Hanna seeks to reflect neither on the issue of dwelling in the globalized metropolis nor on what can be done to suspend the passing of time to save something of the past in the present. Rather, he intends to let readers reflect on language processing, news layout, and on the conditions of reception and interpretation embedded in everyday communication.

Lingua Quintae Reipublicae

Published in 1998 but re-edited and revised in 2004, *Un ABC de la barbarie* by Jacques Henri-Michot offers a deafening compilation of the received ideas and hackneyed sentences which inundate newspapers, radio broadcasts, and TV coverage of the last two decades. This contemporary version of Flaubert's *Dictionnaires des idées reçues* can be read as typology of what Eric Hazan aptly termed the "Lingua Quintae Reipublicae" ("the Language of the Fifth Republic") (Hazan 2006), in reference to Victor Klemperer's analysis of "Lingua Tertii Imperii" (The Language of the Third Reich). For several years, Michot wrote down everything he heard or saw, the lunacy accepted as reality and the spitefulness, building a corpus of ready-made expressions. Yet, if that method may be associated with one of a socio-linguist examining the stylistic constructions or variations of a certain expression in a given language, Michot does not intend to analyze the linguistic relativity of the constant use of certain buzzwords, but rather to make them visible in their sheer immanence, decontextualized from their original environment.

The use of an ABC whose main principle is pedagogical and didactic functions as a mnemonic aid, a prosthesis of perception, to observe the lingo of neoliberalism that pervades our language, and conditions our behaviors and habits of action. The choice of an ABC is twofold: on the one hand, it is a "technology of intellect" and of "writing" (Goody 1977: 10), as it consists in classifying and organizing knowledge through new layout and visual arrangements like a "list" or a "memo"; on the other, an ABC is also like a "dictionary," the avant-garde book par excellence. From Max Ernst to Ezra Pound, passing through Man Ray or Kurt Schwitters, the ABC has been construed as a space of experimentation—a poetic of montage—characterized by a logic of heterogeneity. Yet, Michot's project bears much resemblance with Bertolt Brecht's *Kriegsfibel* (1955), translated int French as *ABC de la guerre*. In this anthology of anger and horror written during World War II, which combines photographs from newspapers and popular magazines, as well as poortraits of leading Nazis and short verses which function as captions about the truth of war, Brecht disrupts the narrative chronology in favor of a synthesis of relations between distant elements which altogether unravel aspects about waging war left unnoticed.

What interests Michot here, however, is not the visual but the capture of "noises," of parasitic disturbances that populate our social space in an era of hyper-mediation and globalization. Unlike Christian Prigent, who also has recourse to similar materials turning textual residues into material for performance, Michot does not transform them. He simply lists and assembles them by entries. Using techniques of concrete and visual poetry, Michot produces an inventory of the utterances which orient and control our thought. The entry "I" starts as follows:

   3. *Il en faut pour tous les goûts !*
   4. Illuminations féériques
   5. Illusions de courte durée *Cf.* Répits
   6. Images de marque. *Cf.* **Journée de tous les dangers**
   7. Images du jour *Cf.* Héros
   8. Images insoutenables (*Cf.* Suspenses), images virtuelles.
   9. Imaginations du pouvoir

10. **IMMOBILISMES**
11. Immunités parlementaires
12. Impacts
13. Impasses [. . .]
24. **Impressionnant déploiement des forces de l'ORDRE.**
(Michot 2014: 97)

Tabular systems are often used in contemporary French poetics and serve multiple purposes. Here, it first provides an objectification of discourses, since they are dislodged from their original context and exposed as pure signifieds, stereotypes. Michot shows how decontextualization is not used to re-invigorate instituted forms and norms of language, but to illustrate certain properties of stereotypical assemblage (nominalization, euphemism, superlative, desemantization, semantic subduction, use of general terms, use of definite article, etc.). Secondly, it makes reading interactive, enabling readers to check, compare, relate disparate elements in the reading process as indicated by the various abbreviation and tagging systems. Thirdly, such apparatus enables Michot to make tangible the disorder within the order, the holes within wholes, as in the entry "C":

162/1. **Coups** bas
162/2. **Coups** d'accélérateur
162/3. **Coup** d'aile
162/4. **Coups** de baguette magique
162/5. **Coups** de balai
162/6. **Coups** de barre à droite (vieux ?)
162/7. **Coups** de *blues*
162/8. **Coups** de chapeau, en passant
162/9. **Coups** de cœur
162/10. **Coups** de colère [. . .]
162/15. **Coups** de fouet
162/16. **Coups** de frein (53)

Here, language nearly functions in an automatic mode to the extent that each utterance seems to beget the next one. The use of the anaphora provides an intrinsic rhythmic quality that reminds the reader of the scheme of the epic. The emphasis on the signified "coup" which drills each segment also provides a sort of reflexivity in which language simply has its own end but also never ends. This rotating discourse is like a broken record. The barbarity of language is in fact rooted in automatism, opinions rather than truth. Roland Barthes famously defined it as the *doxa*, "l'opinion publique, l'Esprit majoritaire, le Consensus petit bourgeois, la Voix du Naturel, La Violence du Préjugé" ["public opinion, the Mind of the majority, the petit bourgeois Consensus, the Voice of the Natural, the Violence of Prejudice"] (Barthes 1975: 51). The *doxa* is not only the locus where idea, thought and subject solidify—like "Méduse: elle pétrifie ceux qui la regardent" ["turns those who look at her to stone"] (51)—but also what is assimilated by a given culture under the appearance of nature.

Stereotypes are in fact opaque rather than transparent. Jacques Lacan has remarkably shown how stereotype assemblages that he termed "le disque-ourcourant" (Lacan

1975: 35), as opposed to the analytical discourse between patient and psychoanalyst, refer to the sum of impressions that a given subject has internalized to the extent that this leads to a repression of the unconscious, blocking from the inception the production and expression of desire. To opinions which function as signs rather than as a chain of elements (as in the logic of desire), Michot opposes "une contre-liste" comprising statements from authors, directors or thinkers. The idea, therefore, is to counter *doxa* (opinion) not so much with *episteme* (truth) but with *poesis* (creative thought). This list thus functions as a counterpoint which short-circuits the flow of jabbering by inserting a gust of air, that is to say: "aérer [. . .] 'casser la nausée' en insérant au milieu de gluantes proférations de l'époque, tantôt de simples titres (livres, films, musiques, tableaux . . .), tantôt quelques pincées ou plages d'écriture" ["Aerate . . . 'interrupt nausea' by inserting in its middle some sticky sayings of the moment, sometimes simple titles (books, films, music, paintings . . .), sometimes some pinches or beaches of writing"] (Michot, 12). Such a dialectics, suggested in an elliptic formula ("En-E-é-touff-ras. En K-res-pi-re-ras") (13), is clearly made tangible in entries like "E," full of jabbering, as opposed to "K," full of empty spaces (Figure 20.2).

This tension between inertia and movement, alienation and emancipation, linearity and event is also emphasized by a difference between roman characters and italics, drawing a distinction between everyday and poetic language:

Perplexités des milieux d'affaires Cf. Nervosité, Satisfactions

PERRONS

> *Les hommes sont occupés (Sens militaire.)* (Georges Perros, *Papiers collés 1*)
> **L'enfer, c'est de ne plus pouvoir s'arrêter.** (Georges Perros, *Papiers collés 3*)

Persistances de malaises
Personnages de chair et de sang (149)

[Perplexity of business circles *Cf.* Nervousness, Satisfactions

STEPS

> The men are busy (military sense.) (Georges Perros, *Glued paper 1*)
> **Hell is not being able to stop.** (Georges Perros, *Glued paper 3*)

Persistence of discomfort
Fully-fledged characters]

Here, "noms propres" go against "noms communs." What such apparatus reveals is that creative thought is on the opposite side of repetition. As Barthes suggests, "le stéréotype, c'est cet emplacement du discours *où le corps manque*, où l'on est sûr qu'il n'est pas. Inversement dans ce texte prétendument collectif que je suis en train de lire, le stéréotype (l'écrivance) cède et l'écriture apparaît: je suis sûr que ce bout d'énoncé a été produit par *un corps*" ["The stereootype is this use of discourse *where the body is missing*, where we are sure it isn't. Conversely, in this text claiming to be collective that I am

Dans ce palais où Bahram saisissait son verre,
Une biche met bas, un tigre saisit son sommeil ;
Bahram passa toute sa vie à saisir des Ânes sauvages ;
Regarde ! voici Bahram pris par une tombe sauvage saisi.

(Umar Khayyām)[++]

... *La sagesse de la langue a depuis longtemps mis en évidence la nature lumineuse du monde. Son « Je » coïncide avec la vie de la lumière. Le feu perce à travers les mœurs. L'homme vit sur « notre monde » qui a une vitesse supérieure à celle de la lumière ? La sagesse de la langue a précédé la sagesse des sciences. Voici deux colonnes où la langue parle de la nature lumineuse des mœurs et où l'homme est conçu comme phénomène lumineux.*

« L'AUTRE MONDE »

Telo, tusha *(corps, carcasse)*
Tukhnut' *au sens de décomposition du corps*
Voskresat' *(ressusciter)*
Delo, dusha *(affaire, âme)*
Molodost, molodec *(jeunesse, gaillard)*
Groznyj *(menaçant)*
Sobotka *(réglisse), sladost' (douceur)*
Soj, sernija, syn, semja *(semence, famille, fils, graine)*
Chorty *(diable)* [...]
Kholostoj *(célibataire)*
Zhit' *(vivre)* [...]

« PRINCIPE DE RELATIVITÉ »

Ten' *(ombre)*
Tukhnut' *au sens de disparition du feu*
Kresalo, ognivo *(pierre, briquet)*
Den' *(jour)*
Molnija *(éclair)*
Groza *(orage)*
Solnce (solnija) *(soleil (solaire))*
Sijat', solnce *(briller, soleil)*
Chornyj svet *(lumière noire)* [...]
Kholod *(froid)*
Zhech' *(brûler)* [...]

(Viktor Vladimirovich - dit Vélimir - Khlebnikov)

Où est la maison de mon ami ?

(Abbas Kiarostami)

Klaxons de la victoire

[++] « 'Umar Khayyām est-il le véritable auteur de ce quatrain ? – Il n'a jamais, que je sache, écrit dans notre langue. – Dis-moi, railleur à peu de frais, toi qui connais le persan sur le bout des doigts, pourrais-tu éclairer ma lanterne sur cette autre traduction : "Bahram qui chassait pendant toute sa vie l'onagre / As-tu vu comment l'onagre chassa Bahram ?" – La tombe, je le déplore, manque. Souviens-toi de cet *Enterré vivant* par quoi l'on a traduit *Zende-Be-Gour*. *Gour, donc, la tombe, Gour*, aussi, l'onagre. Chasseur émérite que Bahram-Gour, qui trouva la mort en pourchassant un âne sauvage... Le persan me charme, il est vrai. – Revenons à Khayyām. A-t-il écrit : "Toi sans cesse en flamme à cause du 4 et du 7" ? – Ce sens à peu près, avec d'autres mots, ses mots à lui. – Son apparition sur la terre est-elle postérieure à l'invasion, et au saccage, en 1038, par un Turc seldjoukine dont j'ai oublié le nom, du Khurassān et de sa capitale Nīshāpūr "qui eut longtemps le goût du paradis sur terre" (comme tu quelque part), ville où il fit entendre ses premiers cris de nourrisson ? – Voilà au moins une certitude. – A-t-il vécu 99, 100, 101 ou 102 ans ? – D'où te vient ce savoir ? – D'une *Encyclopédie*. – Changes-en. Il n'a vécu, aux 5ᵉ et 6ᵉ siècles de l'Hégire, que 73 ou 74 ans. – En es-tu bien sûr ? – Presque. – Sa proposition d'ajouter 1 jour tous les 4 ans a-t-elle inauguré l'ère Djalālī, qui commença au printemps ? – Un quidam aurait-il prétendu le contraire ? – Ses divers travaux de mathématiques et d'astronomie ont-ils provoqué en lui une telle déception, une telle amertume qu'il s'est mis, sur le tard, à écrire ses *rubāʿīyāt* (121 ? 132 ? 143 ? 154 ? 165 ? 176 ?) ? – Cette hypothèse est quasi avérée. Quant au nombre, certains s'en tiennent à 143. – Pourquoi, dans son *Histoire des philosophes* parue en 1248, Alī al-Qifṭī a-t-il attaqué Khayyām en ces termes : *Le fond de ses vers se compose de serpents venimeux pour la loi divine et leur enchaînement mène à la perdition ?* – Tu me le demandes ? – Notre poète ne s'appelait-il pas, en réalité, Ghiyāth al-Dīn Abū l-Fat'h Ibn-I Ibrāhīm al-Khayyāmī ? – Si fait. – Khayyām ne signifie-t-il pas "fabricant de tentes" ? – Il l'a écrit lui-même, à plusieurs reprises, en évoquant la figure de son père. – Ce détail me ravit. Restons-en là. »

Figure 20.2 Jacques-Henri Michot, from *ABC de la barbarie*

reading, the stereotype (l'écrivance) gives way and writing appears: I am sure that this statement has been produced by *a body*"] (Barthes: 93). The body is therefore not only the index of the expression of desire but also the singularity as such, that is to say, a pure difference which counters consensus, generality and repetition. Literature is an event.

And if, as Rancière reminds us, literature is the space of dissensus, of multiplicity of bodies, noises and disorders (Rancière 1995), an *ABC* belongs to the realm of literature. From the outset, the reader is led astray by the fact that there is a mismatch between the front cover of the book, which indicates that the author is Jacques-Henri Michot, and the following page, which discloses that the book was written by a certain Bernabé B. As reported in the foreword, the so-called Barnabé, who died "dans la nuit du jeudi 18 au Vendredi 19 Mars 199–" ["on Thursday night the 18th to Friday the 19th of March, 199–"] (Michot: 10), did not complete the writing of that book. Two of his close friends, François B and Jérémie B, decided to complete this enterprise by assembling its sections, adding a very abundant series of footnotes to justify their choices:

> Vu l'inachèvement criant de l'ABC, champ de bataille zébré de ratures, de remarques marginales, de feuilles volantes insérées, etc. François B s'estime, à tort ou à raison, dans l'obligation d'apporter un peu d'ordre dans ce fatras, de donner à l'ouvrage interrompu une forme 'présentable'. En particulier, il complète. Il ne rajoute rien aux bruits, mais il rajoute souvent des citations. (Michot, 2000: 10)

> [Given the obvious unfinished ABC, the battlefield streaked with crossings out, marginal remarks, separate sheets inserted, and so on, François B believes himself, wrongly or rightly, obliged to bring a little order into this mess, to give to the interrupted work a 'presentable' form. In particular, he completes it. He doesn't add anything to the sounds, but he often adds quotes.]

Such apparatus serves, in fact, two purposes. On the one hand, it reveals the conditions of production, revisions, choices, contradictions (the ecology of the project), that is to say, elements that are usually mute or made invisible in the writing of a book. In one of the footnotes can be read, for instance, "à la suite de ce bruit, une longue plage de Johannes de Silentio a été barrée, en oblique au feutre vert" (Michot 2014: 185). Thus, Michot like Hanna not only breaks with the conceit of lack of origin showing how all these elements are linked to a context, but he also shows how the "medium is the message" (McLuhan 1964). On the other hand, the apparatus enables Michot to give a fictional dimension to his work. The abundant peritext enhanced that effect. For instance, the book starts with what Genette termed "une preface auctoriale dénégative" ["an authorial unnegative preface"], which unravels several functions such as "exposer, c"est-à-dire raconteur les circonstances dans lesquelles le pseudo-éditeur est entré en possession de ce texte" ["exposing, that is, telling the circumstances in which the pseudo-editor has acquired this text"] or simply indicates "des corrections apportées" ["corrections made"] (Genette 1987: 283–7). At the same time, the use of heteronyms enables Michot to unravel different voices, styles, postures and speeds, disrupting the transcendental representation of the author or of the authorial voice. In a footnote, for instance, can be read:

> +- Toute forestière, la lettre, avec troncs et branches ? Ou, à l'horizontale, trois traits d'ailes—à moins que deux seulement—mais alors l'autre ? Ou encore ... ?

(pour plus de clarté sur ce questions de Barnabé dont il peut sembler étrange qu'il les ait laissés *telles quelles* dans l'*ABC*, cf. ma note 1 en I—François B).
++- Sans cet entretien avec toi, au matin du 4 mai, aurais-je, cher Hervé F., pensé à ce bruit ? (Je n'ai pu identifier de quelle personne il s'agissait.—François B). (Michot, 65)

[+-All forest-like, the letter with a trunk and branches? Or horizontally, three wing strokes—unless only two—but then the other? Or still. . .? (for more clarity about this question of Barnaby about whom it seems strange that he left them *like that* in the ABC, cf. my note I in I—François B).
++-Without this conversation with you, on the morning of May 4, dear Hervé F., would I have thought about this sound? (I haven't been able to identify who made it.—Francois B).]

An *ABC* can be therefore read as a pharmakon—both poison and remedy—but it breaks binary paradigms, and logocentric oppositions: the book functions as a multiple-choice exercise where one can follow A, B, or C. The tripartite structure constitutes a "collective assemblage" of intertwining and mutual references, calling for an exit of personology and the logic of the signified: it is in effect a practice exercise to learn to read the present. In an era where "l'éther médiatique impose la non-vérité publicitaire, l'imaginarium universel des images" ["the mediatic ether imposes the advertised non-truth, the universal imaginarium of images"] (Deguy 2007: 130), appropriation and repurposing of the prose of the world provide an antidote to contemporary modes of subjectification. Those works invite us to pay attention to the manner in which we are situated with the flow of information that precedes us, and by the way this flow conditions and commodifies our attention. Functioning as war machines, these parasitic practices aim at taking position in the communication flow by disrupting the format, the discursive logic, through spins, viruses and glitches. They provide new forms of classification, objectification—apparatuses—that reveal the mechanisms of production and interpretation in an age of mediocracy.

Such investigations in the prose of the world, however, suggest that pornography is prose and that all prose is pornographic. In *Idea of Prose*, Giorgio Agamben had already made that link clear, showing how pornography constitutes in the period of late capitalism the false promise of happiness: "in pornography, the utopia of a classless society displays itself through gross caricatures of those traits that distinguish classes and their transfiguration in the sexual act" (Agamben 1995: 73). The advent of pornography signifies the peak of the development of what Guy Debord termed "la société du spectacle" (Debord 1967) and what Baudrillard coined "l'hyper-réalité" (Baudrillard 1981). The most intimate had lost its immediacy, since all reality had now been absorbed into a system of exchange and circulation. In pornography, bodies are reduced to pure commodities subject to the law of exchange or exhibition. But pornography does not necessarily need to be sexual: physical violence, representation of suffering as well as the consumption of food, fall into this category as long as it is brought to maximal visibility. Despite intrinsic difference between visual and textual systems, Hanna draws a compelling analogy between these two regimes of representation:

La pornographie moderne proposait comme une synthèse métaphorique du fonctionnement pragmatique de toutes les formes de proses. Devant un film X, on ne lit plus la fiction filmique, on n'interprète plus des figures cinématographiques (photographiques et narratives), on voit, on quête des yeux, une réalité. Le film a réussi quand il a pu devenir l'équivalent de : voici la réalité (de l'action sexuelle des stars fascinantes (de beauté et de capacité sexuelle)). Des représentations porno doivent donc émaner quelques stimuli qui nous touchent en sorte qu'on soit comme aspirés (au moins momentanément) vers une vérité matérielle, phénoménale et qui transcende la représentation, sort d'elle et la dépasse. Le lecteur/ voyeur, l'espace de l'impact pornographique, demeure lié à un régime de réception où il capte, cadrés dans des formes de fictions, certains éléments qu'il prend pour bribes de réalité pure. (Hanna 2003, unpag.)

[Modern pornography proposed something like a metaphoric synthesis of the pragmatic working of all the forms of prose. Faced with a porn flick, we no longer read the filmic fiction, we no longer interpret cinematographic figures (photographic and narrative) we see, we seek with our eyes, a reality. The film has succeeded when it has been able to become the equivalent of: here is reality (of the sexual action of fascinating stars (in beauty and sexual capacity)). Porn representations should then emanate some stimuli which touch us so that we are drawn (at least momentarily) towards a material truth, phenomenal and which transcends representation, leaves it and goes beyond. The reader/voyeur, the space of the pornographic impact, remains linked to a receptive regime where he seizes, framed in fictional forms, certain elements that he takes for fragments of pure reality.]

The apparent difference between textual and visual systems is here nullified when one considers them as signs. The logic of prose has two imperatives. First, it disrupts classical hermeneutics based on the deciphering of entities for an immediate access to the real with its violence and brute facticity. Second, prose is ultra-realist since it rests on a surplus of reality with maximal graphic features, as it is devoid of flowery rhetoric or analogies found in poetic language which often distort reality, hinting at a reality as an indirect object. In *Les Chiens de la prose*, Gleize also equates prose with pornography. Is this to say that radical poetics should now be pliant to the same logic of commodification of late capitalism? Surely not, as Hanna notes "il ne s'agit pas de résister au spectacle par les moyens du spectacle optimisés" ["It is not a matter of resisting spectacle through the use of optimized forms of spectacle"] (Hanna 2003: 28–9). The horizon of prose is not to duplicate pornography. Rather it seeks to create "un modèle pornographique" (Gleize 2009: 338), not to replicate a facsimile of the original, but a miniature or a *doublure* of the original, by following different scales, frames and arrangements. A differential copy. That is to say a prose reduced to its simplest expression, devoid of unnecessary tropes; a prose which seeks to seize the real in its sheer violence but also a prose which upends the flow of images and the commodification of thoughts and ideas. In sum, a prose of investigation which objectifies the real and whose chief preoccupation is the *graph* rather than the *imago*, that is to say the letter which is the foundation of any literal poetics.

Notes

1. For a thorough examination of the historiographical debates and an analysis of such tensions, see M. Collot, *L'hybridation du vers et de la prose dans la poésie française contemporaine*, in *La poésie, entre vers et prose* [online] (Tours: Presses universitaires François-Rabelais, 2016), <http://books.openedition.org/pufr/9521> (last accessed August 10, 2019).
2. All translations are by Mary Ann Caws and Michel Delville, unless otherwise indicated.
3. The recourse to tautology or tautological utterances is very common in French poetics. See J. Barda, *Experimentation and the Lyric in Contemporary French Poetry* (Basingstoke: Palgrave Macmillan, 2019).
4. See François Cusset, *La décennie: le grand cauchemar des années 1980* (Paris: La Découverte, 2006). See also F. Cusset (ed.), *Une histoire (critique) des années 1990: de la fin de tout au début de quelque chose* (Paris: La Découverte, 2014).

Works Cited

Agamben, Giorgio (1995), *Idea of Prose*, New York: SUNY Press.
Apollinaire, Guillaume (1971), *Alcools*, Paris: Larousse.
Bailly, Jean-Christophe (2000), *Basse continue*, Paris: Le Seuil.
Barda, Jeff (2019), *Experimentation and the Lyric in Contemporary French Poetry*, Basingstoke: Palgrave Macmillan.
Barthes, Roland (1975), *Roland Barthes par Roland Barthes*, Paris: Le Seuil.
Baudelaire, Charles (1968), *Œuvres complètes*, ed. Marcel A. Ruff, Paris: Le Seuil.
Baudrillard, Jean (1981), *Simulacres et Simulations*, Paris: Galilée.
Benjamin, Walter (1997), *Charles Baudelaire: A Lyric Poet in the Era of High Capitalism*, London: Verso.
Bolter, Jay David, and Grusin, Richard (1999), *Remediation: Understanding New Media*, Cambridge: MIT Press.
Bourdieu, Pierre (1996), *Sur la télévision, suivi de l'emprise du journalisme*, Paris: Liber.
Citton, Yves (2017), *Médiarchie*, Paris: Le Seuil.
Debord, Guy (1967), *La Société du Spectacle*, Paris: Gallimard.
Deguy, Michel (1986), *Chose de la poésie et affaire culturelle*, Paris: Hachette.
Deguy, Michel (2000a), *L'Impair*, Paris: Farrago.
Deguy, Michel (2000b), *Le Spleen de Paris*, Paris: Galilée.
Deguy, Michel (2007) *Réouverture après travaux*, Paris: Galilée.
Delville, Michel (1998), *The American Prose Poem: Poetic Form and the Boundaries of Genre*, Gainesville, FL: University Press of Florida.
Genette, Gérard (1987), *Seuils*, Paris: Le Seuil.
Gitelman, Lisa (2013), ed. L. Gitelman, *Raw Data is an Oxymoron*, Cambridge: MIT Press.
Gleize, Jean-Marie (1992), *A noir. Poésie et littéralité*, Paris: Le Seuil.
Gleize, Jean-Marie (1999), *Les chiens noirs de la prose*, Paris: Le Seuil.
Gleize, Jean-Marie (2007) "Les chiens s'approchent, et s'éloignent," *Alea: Estudos Neolatinos*, vol. 9, no. 2, pp. 165–75.
Gleize, Jean-Marie (2009), *Sorties*, Paris: Questions Théoriques.
Gleize, Jean-Marie (2011) "Opacité critique," in J.-C Bailly (ed.), *Toi aussi tu as des armes*, Paris: La Fabrique, pp. 27–44.
Goldsmith, Kenneth (2011), *Uncreative Writing: Managing Language in the Digital Age*, New York: Columbia University Press.
Goody, Jack (1977), *Domestication of the Savage Mind*, Cambridge: Cambridge University Press.

Hanna, Christophe (1999), *Petits poëmes en prose*, Romainville: Al Dante.
Hanna, Christophe (2003a), *Poésie action directe*, Romainville: Al Dante.
Hanna, Christophe (2003b) "Entretien avec Christophe Hanna"—propos recueillis par Olivier Halévy, *Musica Falsa*, August 8.
Hazan, Eric (2006), *LQR: La Propagande du quotidien*, Paris: Liber.
Lacan, Jacques (1975), *Le séminaire, Livre XX, Encore*, Paris: Le Seuil.
Mallarmé, Stéphane (2003), *Œuvres complètes*, ed. Bertrand Marchal, vol II, Paris: Gallimard.
McLuhan, Marshall (1964), *Understanding Media: The Extensions of Man*, London: Routledge.
Michot, Jacques-Henri (2010) "De l'entaille (à propos de l'écriture d'*Un ABC de la barbarie*)," <http://horlieu-editions.com/brochures/Michot-de-l-entaille.pdf> (last accessed August 15, 2019).
Michot, Jacques-Henri (2014), *ABC de la barbarie*, Romainvilles: Al Dante.
Noël, Bernard (1994), *La castration mentale*, Paris: P.O.L.
Quintane, Natalie (2008), "Faire de la poésie une Science, politique. Tentatives d'expulsion de la Littérature, du montage ducassien aux cut-up contemporains," in Sylvie Coëllier (ed.), *Le Montage dans les arts au XXe et XXIe siècles*, Aix-en-Provence: PUP, pp. 131–44.
Rancière, Jacques (1995), *La Mésentente*, Paris: Galilée.
Sadin, Eric (2011), *La société de l'anticipation*, Paris: Inculte éditions.
Stéfan, Jude (1967), *Cyprès*, Paris: Gallimard.

Index

Acker, Kathy, 7, 299–301, 302, 308
  Don Quixote, 300
  Great Expectations, 300–1, 306
Adūnīs (Ali Ahmad Said Esber), 281, 284
Agamben, Giorgio, *Idea of Prose*, 324
al-ʿAzzāwī, Fāḍil, *The Living Spirit: The 1960s Generation in Iraq*, 285
al-Ḥajj, Unsiī, 281, 284
al-Ḥurriyya (journal), 282
al-Jīzānī, Zāhir, 289
al-Khāl, Yūsuf, 281, 290
al-Malaʾika, Nazik, 283, 284
al-Nāṣirī, Nṣayyif, 287–8
al-Rīḥanī, Najīb, 282
al-Ruṣāfī, Maʿrūf, 282, 283
al-Sayyab, Badr Shakir, 283, 284
al-Zahāwī, Jamīl Ṣidqī, 282
Alféri, Pierre, 116
Altieri, Charles, 241
Andrews, Nin, 197
  Why God Is a Woman, 204–5, 209
Antin, David, 299–300, 301, 308
  talking at the boundaries, 295, 297
  what it means to be avant-garde, 301
Apollinaire, Guillaume, 35, 92, 101, 313
  Les Mamelles de Tiresias, 91
  Méditations Esthétiques: Les Peintres Cubistes, 91
  'Toujours,' 91
Ashbery, John, 81, 130, 168, 299, 308
  'Homeless Heart,' 131
  Three Poems, 4, 295, 297

Astro, Alan, 56
Athenaeum (literary magazine), 36, 47
Atherton, Cassandra, 150, 197–8, 200, 210
  'Letter,' 209
  'Luna,' 208
  'Overwritten,' 209
  The Six Senses, 209
  'Tinker,' 208
  'Volcano,' 208
Atkins, Lucy, 205
Axelrod, Steven, 168

Babbitt, Irving, 67
  The New Laokoon: An Essay on the Confusion of the Arts, 86, 198
Bailly, Jean-Christophe, 310
Bakhtin, Mikhaïl, 6
Banville, Théodore de, *Petit traité de poésie française*, 33
Barrès, Maurice, 78
Bartczak, Kacper, 235
Barthes, Roland, 5, 204, 301, 302, 320, 321–3
  Fragments d'un discours amoureux, 138, 140
Baudelaire, Charles, 3, 11–18, 20–1, 23–4, 25, 33, 36, 47, 48, 53, 61, 69, 70, 71, 74–5, 103, 128, 129, 130, 138, 140–1, 147, 156, 159, 185, 189, 198, 241, 262, 271, 272, 284, 311
  'De l'Essence du rire,' 183
  Les Fleurs du Mal, 13, 15, 68, 182

'J'aime le souvenir de ces époques nues,' 79
'Tableaux parisiens,' 23
Un mangeur d'opium, 50, 56, 57–8, 63
Les Paradis artificiels, 50–1, 55
'Le Palimpseste,' 59
Le Peintre de la vie moderne, 23
Le Spleen de Paris (Petits poèmes en prose), 1, 3, 4, 6, 11, 12, 13, 15, 24, 35, 50–2, 56–7, 59–60, 62, 68, 77, 128, 129, 137, 141, 148, 181–4, 199, 210, 231, 232–6, 310
 'Assommons les pauvres !,' 15
 'À une heure du matin,' 57
 'Les Bienfaits de la lune,' 74
 'La Chambre double,' 57
 'Le Crépuscule du soir,' 57–8
 'L'Étranger,' 14
 'Le Gâteau,' 14
 'L'Invitation au voyage,' 14
 'Le Mauvais vitrier,' 13–14, 57
 'Perte d'auréole,' 15
 'Le Thyrse,' 14, 60, 234
Baxter, Edmund, 62
Baydūn, Abbās, 291
Beckett, Samuel, 154, 155, 160, 164
Bellos, David, 238, 266
Benedikt, Michael 1–2, 129–30, 137
Benjamin, Walter, 183, 234
Bergvall, Caroline, 303
Berman, Antoine, 239, 240
Bernard, Suzanne, 12, 14, 16, 17, 18, 35, 68, 71, 82, 232, 284
Bernstein, Charles, 140
Bertrand, Aloysius, 1, 47, 71, 75, 295
 Gaspard de la Nuit, 3, 4, 12, 13, 35, 51, 68, 70, 118n, 127–8, 130, 156, 182
Betten, Nagasawa, 268
Bible, the, 1, 85
 King James Bible, 145, 164
Bin, Ueda, 269–70, 272
 Miotsukushi, 271
 'Waga teki,' 270

Bishop, Elizabeth, 5, 130, 168, 169–70, 174
 'Gwendolyn,' 170–1, 172
 North and South, 170
 Questions of Travel, 169, 176–8
 'The Burglar of Babylon,' 177
 'First Death in Nova Scotia,' 177
 'In the Village,' 169, 170–3, 175–7, 178
 'Manners,' 177
 'Sestina,' 177
Blake, William, 1, 296
 The Marriage of Heaven and Hell, 164
Blum-Kulka, Shoshana, 236
Bly, Robert, 4, 124, 129, 168, 227n
Boland, Eavan, 123, 125
Bonhomme, Béatrice, 112
Borges, Jorge Luis, 145, 146, 155, 165
 This Craft of Verse, 165–6
Bourdieu, Pierre, 315
Bradbury, Malcolm, 160
Braque, Georges, 105
Brecht, Bertolt
 Kalendergeschichten, 145
 Kriegsfibel, 319
Breton, André, 35
Breunig, LeRoy, 12, 16, 92
Bryson, J. Scott, 216
Būluṣ, Sargūn, 281, 283, 285, 289–91
 "A Conversation with a Painter in New York After the Towers Fell," 290
 Al-Wuṣūl ila Madīnat Ayn, 291
 Another Bone for the Tribe's Dogs, 290
Burt, Stephanie, 168
Butler, Judith, 204
Butor, Michel, 151, 160
Buṭṭī, Rūfā'īl, 282–3
 al-Rabī'iyyāt, 282–3

Caddy, David, 197, 205
Callot, Jacques, 51, 118n, 128
Candido, Igor, 188

Cardell, Kylie, 138
Carter, Angela, 205
Casanova, Pascale, 240
Caws, Mary Ann, 1, 2, 3, 5, 73, 118n, 200, 326n
Cervantes, Miguel de, *Don Quixote*, 152
Cézanne, Paul, 101, 104
Cha, Theresa Hak Kyung, 7, 302–3, 308
  Dictée, 301, 302–3
  Exilée /Temps Morts, 302
Chang, Eileen, 251
Channing, Ellery, 188
Char, René, 4, 108
  'Alberto Giacometti,' 108–9, 117
  'Célébrer Giacometti,' 108, 117
Charles, Michel, 62
Chateaubriand, François-René de, 1, 11, 165
Chaucer, Geoffrey, 303
Chillida, Eduardo, 111
Christensen, Laird, 217
Citton, Yves, 313, 315
Cixous, Hélène, 204
Claremont, Yasuko, 262, 265
Clifford Barney, Natalie, 85
Clover, Joshua, 242
Coleridge, Samuel Taylor, 1, 52
  'The Wanderings of Cain,' 59
Cortázar, Julio, 1, 2, 145
de Costa, René, 101
Creeley, Robert, 168, 299, 308
  Presences: A Text for Marisol, 295–6, 297
Crnković, Gordana P., 233, 235
Cubism, 4, 82, 91–2, 96–101, 104–6, 109, 117

Damrosch, David, 241
Dante (Alighieri), 188–9
  Divina Commedia, 186, 187, 188
  Vita Nuova, 188
De Quincey, Thomas, 61–3
  Autobiographical Sketches, 52, 54

Confessions of an English Opium-Eater, 3–4, 50–60
'The English Mail-Coach,' 53, 54, 55
Suspiria de Profundis, 50–1, 54, 55, 56, 59, 60, 62, 63
'System of the Heavens as Revealed by Lord Rosse's Telescopes,' 53
Debord, Guy, 312, 324
Decadence, 2, 4, 67, 145, 199
Deguy, Michel, 310, 312, 318
Delville, Michel, 1, 2, 3, 5, 87n, 103, 118, 124, 125, 132n, 159, 160, 168, 197, 198, 199, 200, 210, 214, 228n, 310, 326n
Derrida, Jacques, 37, 39, 205
Dicinoski, Michelle, 138
Diepeveen, Leonard, 104
Dostoyevsky, Fyodor, 155, 156, 158, 163
Dowson, Ernest
  Decorations in Prose, 85
Du Fu, 73, 248, 250
Dupin, Jacques, 110–12
  L'Embrasure, 111
DuPlessis, Rachel Blau, 85, 198
Duranty, Edmond, 29
Dworkin, Craig, 298

Edson, Russell, 124, 137, 138, 143–7, 204, 209
  'The Bride of Dream Man,' 144
  'The Matter,' 146, 147
  'The Pattern,' 144
  'Piano Lessons,' 144
  'The Terrible Angel,' 142–3, 144, 145
Eliot, T. S., 4, 67–8, 70, 81, 85, 86, 123, 198, 199, 242
Emerson, Ralph Waldo, 1, 216, 297
  'Nature,' 186
  'Woods,' 6, 184–9

Fang Wenzhu, 257
  'Kind of Like Pulling Out a Nail,' 256
Faris, Wendy, 62
Fauchereau, Serge, 113, 114

Fautrier, Jean, 109
Fénelon (François de Salignac de La Mothe-Fénelon)
  Les aventures de Télémaque, 1, 152, 165
Fink-von Hoff, Agnes, 265
Flaubert, Gustave, 24, 104, 151, 319
  L'Éducation sentimentale, 32
Foer, Jonathan Safran, 165, 166
Fort, Paul, 78, 81
Foscolo, Ugo, 188–9
De Francesco, Alessandro, 4, 117
  'Espaces habités,' 113–14
Francone, Vincent, 232
Fredman, Stephen, 147, 168, 190n, 296
Fried, Michael, 28, 29
Friedrich, Hugo, 18
Frost, Elisabeth, 206–7
Futabatei Shimei, 266, 270

Game, Jérôme, 116–17
Garnett, Constance, 269, 270–1
Gautier, Judith, 4, 67, 70
  Le Livre de Jade, 71–3
  Le Second rang du collier, 74
Gautier, Théophile, 24, 67, 72, 74, 75
Giacometti, Alberto, 108–9, 111
Gide, André, 78, 81, 85, 156
Gifford, Terry, 215–6
Gleize, Jean-Marie, 310–12, 318
  Les Chiens de la prose, 325
Goethe, Johann Wolfgang, *Die Leiden des jungen Werthers*, 35, 248
Goldsmith, Kenneth, 312–13
Gosetti, Valentina, 132n
Greene, Robert W., 108
Gris, Juan, 4, 93, 97, 100–1
  Still Life with Poem, 101
Grossman, Edith, 239
Gryko, Krzysztof, 231
Gudding, Gabriel, 244
Gunew, Sneja, 202
Guo Moruo, 248, 249, 257

Hagiwara Sakutarō, 276n
Hammer, Langdon, 168–9
Hanna, Christophe, 312, 313–18, 323, 324–5
  Petits poëmes en prose, 313–15
  'Chacun sa chimère,' 315–15
  'Le Mauvais vitrier,' 316
Harjo, Joy, 213, 214, 216, 227
  'If You Look with the Mind of the Swirling Earth,' 224–5
  'Invisible Fish,' 222–4, 225, 226
Hass, Robert, 'A Story about the Body,' 121–2, 123–4, 125
Hattori Yoshika, 263
Haussmann, Georges Eugène, 77, 78
Hegel, Georg Wilhelm Friedrich, 47
Hejinian, Lyn, 308
  My Life, 126, 297–9
Hemingway, Ernest, 'A Clean, Well-Lighted Place,' 142
Henri-Michot, Jacques, 312
  Un ABC de la barbarie, 313, 319–24
Herrick, Robert, 186, 187
Hervey-Saint-Denys, Léon d', 73
  Poésies de l'époque des Thang, 72
Hethcrington, Paul, 150, 197–8, 200, 210
Hocquard, Emmanuel, 114
Houssaye, Arsène, 13, 16, 77, 182, 210
  La Chanson du vitrier, 13–14, 182
Howe, Irving, 138, 141–2
Howells, W. D., 86
Huang Yongjian, 253
Hugo, Victor, 73
  Les Travailleurs de la mer, 18
Hume, Kathryn, 299
Hutcheon, Linda, 200, 205
Huysmans, Joris-Karl, 4, 61, 62, 69, 86, 272
  À rebours, 5, 67, 71, 78, 79
  Croquis parisiens, 71, 74, 75–7, 83
  'Vue des remparts du Nord-Paris,' 75, 77–8
  Le Drageoir aux épices, 71, 74–5
  'Le Hareng Saur,' 75–6
Huyssen, Andreas, 69

Impressionism, 23, 25–8, 30–3
Iwano Hōmei, 263, 271

Jacob, Max, 2, 4, 6, 91, 92, 94, 98, 99, 100, 145
  Le Cornet à dés, 94, 145, 310
    'Erreurs de la miséricorde,' 94–5
    'Kaléidoscope,' 95
    'Mystère du ciel . . .,' 95
    'Un peu de modernisme en manière de conclusion,' 96
    'Poème de la lune,' 94
    'Mauvais caractère,' 93
Jamison, Leslie, 139
Jefferson, Ann, 159, 162, 165
Johnson, Barbara, 1, 67, 68, 70, 198
Johnson, Robert, 214
Jolas, Eugene, 154, 168
Jolas, Maria, 154
Joyce, James, 154, 155, 156, 159–60, 244

Kafka, Franz, 122, 143, 144, 145, 146, 154, 156, 163
Kahn, Gustave, 78, 81
Kanbara Ariake, 263, 271, 272
  Ariake shū, 275
  'Egakan to hossuru kibō,' 272
  'Footprints,' 273–5
  Shunchōshū, 271
Kant, Immanuel, 52–3, 187
Kawai Suimei, 276
  Kiri, 276
Ke Lan, 254, 257
  Short Flute of Morning Mist, 252–3, 256
  'Dawn Mist,' 252–3, 255
Kenmochi Takehiko, 262–3
Kibédi Varga, Aron, 152
Kinoshita Mokutarō, 263
Kirkuk Group, 285
Kitamura Tōkoku, 272
  Hōraikyoku, 268
Kitchen, Judith, 139
Kluba, Agnieszka, 244n

Krieger, Murray, 105
Kunikida Doppo, 263
Kwasny, Melissa, 216, 225
  Pictograph, 225–6
  'Cave System,' 227
  'Outside the Little Cave Spot,' 226–7
  'Pictograph: Avalanche Mouth,' 213

Lacan, Jacques, 320–1
Lacoue-Labarthe, Philippe, 47
Laforgue, Jules, 26
Lang, Abigail, 113, 114
Language poetry, 126, 137, 147, 296
Laughlin, Charles, 251
Lehman, David, 132n, 164
Leroy, Christian, 12, 14, 15
Levertov, Denise, 216
  The Very Thing That Happens, 143, 144
Linstrom, John, 224
Liu Bannong, 249
  'Rain,' 250–1, 252, 253, 256
Lloze, Evelyne, 111
Louÿs, Pierre, 85
  Les Chansons de Bilitis, 83–4
  Vie de Bilitis, 84
Lowell, Robert, 5, 170, 173–5, 178
  For the Union Dead, 176
  'The Scream,' 175–6, 178
  Life Studies, 168, 169, 174
  'My Last Afternoon with Uncle Devereux Winslow,' 174, 175
  'Near the Unbalanced Aquarium,' 174, 175
  '91 Revere Street,' 169, 174
Lu Xun, *Weeds (Wild Grass)*, 251

McCredden, Lyn, 202–3
McDougall, Bonnie, 254–5
McNew, Janet, 228n
Macpherson, James, 1
  Ossian, 35, 71
Magnard, Francis, 78

Mallarmé, Stéphane, 1, 3, 4, 11, 18–20, 24–5, 27, 67, 68, 70, 71, 78, 81, 141, 147, 271, 272, 295, 313
  'La Chevelure vol d'une flamme . . .,' 20
  'Un Coup de dés,' 18, 68
  'La Déclaration foraine,' 19, 20
  Divagations, 19, 67, 71, 78
    'Conflit,' 80
    'Le Démon de l'analogie,' 78, 79
    'Les Fenêtres,' 99
    'La Gloire,' 19, 79–81
  Le Livre, 18
  Pages, 70, 71
  'Un Spectacle interrompu,' 19, 79
  Vers et prose, 68, 70
    'Frisson d'hiver,' 71, 79
    'Plainte d'automne,' 71, 79
Manet, Édouard, 27, 30, 31
Manne, Robert, 138
Mansfield, Katherine, 163
Mao Zedong, 254–5
Mardān, Ḥusayn, 283
  'The Nightmare,' 284
  Qaṣā'id `Āriyya, 283–4
Marie de France, 147
Marivaux, Pierre Carlet,
  Le Télémaque Travesti, 152
Maulpoix, Jean-Michel, 112
Mendès, Catulle, 4, 24, 70
Merrill, James, 179n
Merrill, Stuart, 199, 272
  Pastels in Prose, 67, 70, 71, 86
Michaux, Henri, 145, 156
Mill, John Stuart, 125
Miller, Brenda, 138
Millier, Bret, 179n
Milosz, Czesław, 2, 240, 241
Milton, John, 186, 187, 269
Mizuno Yōshū, 272
  Hibiki, 275–6
Modernism, 23, 103, 110, 154, 233
Monroe, Jonathan 2, 6, 69, 70, 141, 168, 197–8, 199, 201, 203, 205–6, 208, 210

Monte, Steven 2, 125, 132n, 168, 186, 188, 201, 258n
Moore, Fabienne, 152, 199
Moretti, Franco, 235–6
Mullen, Harryette, 197, 206–8
  Recyclopedia, 206
  S*PeRM**K*T, 206, 209
  Trimmings, 207, 210
Mullen, Laura, 7
  Murmur, 305–8
Murphy, Marguerite, 85, 168, 197, 199, 200, 202, 203, 204, 206, 209

Nabokov, Vladimir, 238–9, 244
Nakaji Yoshikazu, 262
Nakazawa Rinsen, 272
Nancy, Jean-Luc, 47
Nelson, Deborah, 168
Nelson, Maggie, 138
  Bluets, 165
New Yorker (magazine), 170–2, 173, 175, 176, 178, 285
Nicholls, Peter, 235
Noel-Tod, Jeremy 1–2
Nord-Sud, 91, 105–6
Nouveau Roman, 5, 151, 153, 155, 157, 306
Novalis (Georg Philipp Friedrich Freiherr), 1, 3, 38, 141
  Christenheit oder Europa, 37
  Hymnen an die Nacht, 35–47

O'Connor, Clémence, 112
Objectivism, 112–13, 114, 117
Oliver, Mary, 213, 216, 220, 223
  'Goldfinches,' 216, 218–19
  'Tiger Lillies,' 216–18, 219
Olson, Charles, 299, 300
  The Maximus Poems, 305
Owen, Stephen, 241

Padgett, Ron, 132n, 233
Paris Review, 155, 285
Parnassianism, 24, 25, 71, 72
Pascal, Blaise, 165, 234

Patchen, Kenneth, 168
Paz, Octavio
   'El ramo azul,' 142
Perelman, Bob, 168
Perloff, Marjorie, 168, 239, 244, 298
Philips, Siobhan, 168–9
Picasso, Pablo, 91, 103, 105, 204
   Three Musicians, 91
Poe, Edgar Allan, 182, 190n
   'Eureka,' 5, 137
Poetry (magazine), 112, 285
Ponge, Francis, 1, 4, 6, 103, 109, 112, 113, 117, 156, 168
   L'Atelier contemporain, 109
   Comment une figue de paroles et pourquoi, 109
   Le Parti pris des choses, 109, 155
     'De l'eau,' 110
     'Le Galet,' 110
   Le Savon, 109
Portugal, Anne, 4, 115
   définitif bob, 115
Pound, Ezra, 81, 319
   The Cantos, 139
La Presse, 70, 140, 182, 210
Proust, Marcel, 27, 156, 158
   À la recherche du temps perdu, 32

Quignard, Pascal
   Petits traités, 310
Quintane, Nathalie, 115, 312, 315

Rancière, Jacques, 70, 83, 323
Rankine, Claudia, 1, 2
Reed, Henry, 239, 240, 242
Rembrandt (Harmenszoon van Rijn), 51, 76, 77, 118n, 128
Reverdy, Pierre, 2, 4, 91, 92, 93, 94, 99, 101, 105–6, 109, 112, 310
   Les Ardoises du toit, 105, 106–7
   'Sortie,' 106
   'Une Aventure méthodique,' 105
   'Belle étoile,' 99
   'Entre deux crépuscules,' 100
   L'Étoile peinte, 107
   'Vieux port,' 107–8
   'Fronts de bataille,' 105
   'Gardiens,' 105
   'La Lampe,' 97
   'Perspective,' 96–7
   'Plus Loin que là,' 100
   'Plus lourd,' 97–8
   Poèmes en prose, 105
   'Les Poètes,' 99
   'Saltimbanques,' 100, 105
   'S'entre-bâille,' 98–9
Revue Contemporaine, 50–1
Revue fantaisiste, 70
Rexroth, Kenneth, 72
Reznikoff, Charles, 233
   Testimony, 113
Rimbaud, Arthur, 3, 11, 16–18, 19, 20, 21, 24, 26, 28–33, 36, 47, 48, 141, 272, 295, 299
   Les Illuminations, 3, 6, 16, 25, 26–7, 29–33, 36, 71, 81, 107
   'Après le déluge,' 16, 29, 32, 82
   'Bottom,' 18
   'Conte,' 32, 82
   'Dévotion,' 82
   'Enfance,' 32
   'Fairy,' 82
   'Fleurs,' 29, 82
   'Génie,' 17
   'H,' 32, 82
   'Jeunesse,' 28
   'Métropolitain,' 29, 83
   'Ornières,' 31–2
   'Ouvriers,' 30–1, 83
   'Parade,' 32
   'Les Ponts,' 31–2, 83, 107
   'Ville,' 16–17, 83
   'La lettre du voyant,' 17
Robbe-Grillet, Alain, 151, 153, 156–7
Robertson, Rachel, 138
Romanticism, 2, 12, 25, 47–8, 153, 185, 200, 216, 217, 220, 222, 234, 240
Rosenberg, Harold, 130
Rosenblum, Robert, 91, 92

Rosenthal, M. L., 178n
Rosmarin, Adena, 251, 257
Rothenberhg, Jerome, 299
   Technicians of the Sacred, 302
Rothwell, Andrew, 106
Rousseau, Jean-Jacques, 11, 165, 183
Rousselot, Jean, 106
Royet-Journoud, Claude, 114

Sabtī, Kamāl, 'Debris,' 288
Santilli, Nikki, 199
Sappho, 84, 304
Sarraute, Nathalie, 151, 156, 158–9, 162, 165
   L'Ère du soupçon, 154, 163–4, 165
   Portrait d'un inconnu, 152
   Tropismes, 5, 153–5, 156, 157–8, 160–3, 164
Sartre, Jean-Paul, 152, 155, 153, 156
Satō Nobuhiro, 263, 271
Schapiro, Meyer, 31
Schelling, Friedrich Wilhelm Joseph (von), 47
Schlegel, Friedrich, 1, 3, 38, 45, 47, 141
   Universalpoesie, 35–7, 46–7
Scholes, Robert, 146, 147
Schultz, Gretchen, 84
Schwartz, Delmore, 168, 169
Scroggins, Mark, 112–13
Sei Shōnagon, *Makura no sōshi*, 262
Shang Qin, 257
Shapiro, Karl, *Essay on Rime*, 169
Shen Yinmo
   'Moonlit Night,' 247–8, 249–50, 256
Shi'r (journal), 281, 290
Shimamura Hōgetsu, 269
Silliman, Ron, 147, 299, 301, 308
   Ketjak, 295, 297
   'The New Sentence,' 296
Simic, Charles, 137, 148
Smith, Barbara, 36
Sontag, Susan, 151
Sorel, Charles, *Le Berger Extravagant, ou l'Anti-Roman*, 152
Sōsaku (journal), 275

Štáfová, Vendula, 84
Stalling, Jonathan, 302
Stäuble-Lipman Wulf, Michèle, 57
Stéfan, Jude, 310
Stein, Gertrude, 2, 6, 92, 98, 103, 112, 130, 154, 159–60, 197, 204, 206, 209, 298, 301–2, 308
   How to Write, 301–2
   Tender Buttons, 1, 4, 104–5, 168, 200, 201–2, 206, 208, 296
   'A Box,' 92–3
   'Apple,' 201
   'Breakfast,' 201
   'Chicken,' 201–2
   'Dirt and not copper,' 104–5
   'A Table,' 93
   'A Time to Eat,' 93
   Three Lives, 103
   'Portraits and Repetition,' 160
Steiner, George, 238
Stout, John C., *Objects Observed*, 104
Strand, Mark, 123, 125
Strong, Rowland, 84
Sun Yushi, 251
Surrealism, 3, 18, 48, 81, 91, 103, 108, 137, 145
Swenson, May, 179n
Symbolism, 4, 68, 72, 81, 137

Takayama Chogyū, 268
Takeda Kiko, 263
Tate, James
   'List of Famous Hats,' 125–7
Taylor, John, 232, 164
Terdiman, Richard, 68–9, 81, 140, 141
Thomson, Jeffrey, 217
Todorov, Tzvetan, 124, 232
Tolstoy, Leo, 78
Toury, Gideon, 269
Toyama Masakazu, 'Ryojun no hirō Kani tai'i,' 268–9, 271
transition (journal), 153, 168
Turgenev, Ivan, 1, 248, 249, 269–71, 272
   'Poems in prose,' 155–6

Upton, Lee, 204

Valéry, Paul, 78, 81
Venuti, Lawrence, 230, 232, 242, 244
Verlaine, Paul, 25, 27, 81
Volkman, Karen, 'Mutable Boundaries,' 123
Vonnegut, Kurt, 146

Waldie, D. J., 7, 308
   Holy Land, 304–6
Waldrop, Rosmarie, 137, 148
   Lawn of Excluded Middle, 5, 139–40
Walkowitz, Rebecca L., 269
Walwicz, Ania, 197, 202–4, 206, 208, 209
   Boat, 203
   Palace of Culture, 203
Wang Guangming, 254, 256
Wanner, Adrian, 156, 161
Waseda bungaku (journal), 268, 269
Wāzin, Abdu, 291
Wesling, Donald, 147–8
Whistler, James Abbott McNeill, 67
White, Katherine, 171, 175
Whitman, Walt, 248, 290
   Leaves of Grass, 36, 128, 298
Wieniewski, Ignacy, 238
Wilczyk, Wojciech, 242
Wilde, Oscar, 85, 103, 145, 248
   Poems in Prose, 85
   Wilde trials, 4, 67, 85–6, 192n, 198
Williams, William Carlos, 121, 130, 233, 308
   Kora in Hell, 168, 296
   Paterson, 305
   Spring & All, 4–5,
Wills, Alfred, 86

Wittgenstein, Ludwig, 139, 140, 297
Woolf, Virginia, 155, 156, 159–60
Wordsworth, William, 52
   'I Wandered Lonely as a Cloud,' 218
Wright, James, 213, 216, 220, 223
   This Journey, 220
   'Camomila,' 221–2
   'The Turtle Overnight,' 220–1
   To a Blossoming Pear Tree, 220
Wróblewski, Grzegorz, 230–1
   Kopenhaga, 6, 230, 231–44
   'Seventeen Days,' 233–4
   Pomyłka Marcina Lutra, 232

Xu Zhimo, *Zhimo's Poems*, 249

Ya Hsien, 257
Yamada Bimyō, 266,
   'Nihon inbun ron,' 266–8
Yamaguchi Sodō, 271
Yeats, William Butler
   'Easter 1916,' 304
Yeh, Michelle, 251
Young, Edward
   Night Thoughts, 35, 71
Yu, Pauline, 72, 73

Zawacki, Andrew, 200, 204, 210
Zheng Zhenduo
   'On Prose Poetry,' 248, 249
Zhou Zuoren, 249
Zola, Emile, 23, 24–5
   'Les Poètes contemporains,' 24–5
   Salon reviews, 23–4
Zukofsky, Louis, 112–13, 114
   'A,' 113, 139
   An Objectivists' Anthology, 112

EU representative:
Easy Access System Europe
Mustamäe tee 50, 10621 Tallinn, Estonia
Gpsr.requests@easproject.com